THE ENCYCLOPEDIA OF PRO BASKETBALL TEAM HISTORIES

THE ENCYCLOPEDIA OF PRO BASKETBALL TEAM HISTORIES

Peter C. Bjarkman

Carroll & Graf Publishers, Inc.
New York

Copyright © 1994 by Peter C. Bjarkman

First Carroll & Graf edition 1994

Carroll & Graf Publishers, Inc.
260 Fifth Avenue
New York, NY 10001

Library of Congress Cataloging-in-Publication Data

Bjarkman, Peter C.
    The encyclopedia of pro-basketball team histories / Peter C.
Bjarkman.
        p.   cm.
    Includes index.
    ISBN 0-7867-0126-9
    1. Basketball teams—United States—History.   2. National
Basketball Association—History.   I. Title.
GV885.515.N37B53   1994
796.323'0973—dc20   94-22306
                                                          CIP

Manufactured in the United States of America

For **Richard Stanley O'Brien** of East Hartford, Connecticut—a friend I lost many years ago, and the one who always played Bill Russell to my Bob Cousy and Tom Heinsohn in the narrow driveway on Tolland Street.

Acknowledgments

The author owes a large debt of gratitude to Dale Ratermann of the Indiana Pacers, without whose help this book never could have come together in quite the shape it did. And there are other debts and thank yous as well: to Herman Graf for his patience and faith in seeing the project through; to Terry Pluto for inspiring me by producing the second and third best books ever written on professional basketball; to Tony "Magic" Formo for friendship and some serious one-on-one action; to Mark Montieth for some wise counsel on hoops and on the book business; to Mike OrRico for intelligent conversations about basketball and life; to Rich Westcott who knows nothing of basketball but was nonetheless willing to play Spike Lee to my Reggie Miller; and most especially to my coach—Ronnie Wilbur—for lovingly paying the bills, sharing the fast breaks, and putting up with all the extended overtime periods.

Contents

Introduction: From Hardwood to Hangtime—Launching America's Game

Part One: Dynasty Teams

Chapter 1:   Boston Celtics   3
               Celtic Mystique and Basketball's Unmatched Legacy

Chapter 2:   Los Angeles Lakers and Minneapolis Lakers   42
               A Very Expensive Bridesmaid Indeed!

Chapter 3:   New York Knicks   80
               Noble Tradition of Losing in the Big Apple

Chapter 4:   Chicago Bulls   98
               Long and Painful Prelude to Air Jordan

Chapter 5:   Golden State Warriors and Philadelphia Warriors   117
               Two Coasts, Two Identities, Two Heroes

Part Two: Traditional Franchises

Chapter 6:   Philadelphia Sixers (76ers) and Syracuse Nats   137
               One Giant, One Magician, and One Magical Season

Chapter 7:   Detroit Pistons and Fort Wayne Pistons   154
               Somehow the Wheels Always Manage to Fall Off

Chapter 8:   Atlanta Hawks and St. Louis (Milwaukee) Hawks   171
               Penthouse to Low Rent District—Basketball's Tale
               of Two Cities

Chapter 9:   Washington (Capital) Bullets and Baltimore Bullets   187
               Finally They Made the Fat Lady Sing

Chapter 10:   Sacramento Kings and Cincinnati (Rochester) Royals   200
               If At First You Don't Succeed, Move and Move and
               Move Again

Chapter 11:   Houston Rockets and San Diego Rockets   218
               Manchild, The Twin Towers, and Mr. T

Chapter 12: Seattle SuperSonics   232
             Slow Train for the Jet Age

Chapter 13: Milwaukee Bucks   244
             Quite Fast at the Gate, Even Faster in the Homestretch

Chapter 14: Phoenix Suns   255
             One Phoenix That Couldn't Rise from the Ashes

Chapter 15: Los Angeles (San Diego) Clippers and Buffalo Braves 269
             Staying Afloat in a Rudderless Ship

Chapter 16: Cleveland Cavaliers   281
             Hardwood Follies in the Topsy-Turvy Land of the Cavaliers

Chapter 17: Portland Trail Blazers   291
             At Least They Always Fill the Arena

Chapter 18: Utah Jazz and New Orleans Jazz   307
             Out of Tune in Salt Lake City

Part Three: Expansion-Era Franchises

Chapter 19: Indiana Pacers   323
             Middle-of-the-Road Franchise in America's Heartland

Chapter 20: New Jersey Nets and New York Nets   345
             Stepchild in Hoopdom's Biggest Market

Chapter 21: San Antonio Spurs   359
             The Case of the Landlocked Admiral

Chapter 22: Denver Nuggets   372
             Mile High and Almost Always Earthbound

Chapter 23: Dallas Mavericks   387
             Some Teams Can't Even Lose Successfully

Chapter 24: Charlotte Hornets   398
             Expansion Blues Turn Teal Green

Chapter 25: Miami Heat   408
             Turning Up the Heat on Basketball's Gold Coast

Chapter 26: Minnesota Timberwolves   417
             A Very Ugly Baby Indeed!

Chapter 27: Orlando Magic   426
             Mixing Hype With Hustle in the Magic Kingdom

Part Four: Other Leagues and Forgotten Cities

Chapter 28: American Basketball Association (1967–1976)   439
             Only the Ball Was Red, White and Blue

Chapter 29: National Basketball League (1946–1949)   455
             Just Where is Sheybogan, Anyway?

Chapter 30: Basketball Association of America (1946–1949)   466
             A Good Idea Whose Time Had Definitely Come

Epilogue: Basketball's Dozen Greatest Heroes
Oscar "Big O" Robertson   484
Wilt "The Stilt" Chamberlain   485
Earvin "Magic" Johnson   487
Bill Russell   489
Michael "Air" Jordan   490
Julius "Dr. J" Erving   493
Larry Bird   494
Jerry West   496
Bob Cousy   497
Kareem Abdul-Jabbar (a.k.a. Lew Alcindor)   499
Elgin Baylor   501
George "Mr. Basketball" Mikan   503
Honorable Mention: A Second (Baker's) Dozen
  Among Basketball's All-Time Greatest Stars   505

Bibliography   510

NBA Statistical Appendix   517

INTRODUCTION

From Hardwood to Hangtime—
Launching America's Native Game

Basketball, especially the professional variety, is not quite yet America's foremost sporting pastime. Despite decades of doomsaying about the summertime game of baseball, it is still the diamond sport, admittedly, which most inflames the passions of America's sports-crazy public and most effectively links generations of fathers with sons and daughters in an ongoing celebration of sports-imitating-life. Yet basketball—with its space-age imagery and highly visible celebrity media stars like Michael "Air" Jordan, Shaquille O'Neal, Magic Johnson and Larry Bird—today also has every legitimate claim as America's upcoming game of the future.

Nor is basketball—basketball NBA style—in any immediate danger of becoming outdated and passé, and thus suddenly finding itself out of synch with the pulse rate of our American temperament. Football, which swung into vogue with the war-plagued decade of the sixties and the parallel boom-era of corporate America, seems now to have lost its grip on a nation less enamored with raw violence, military discipline, male rites of passage, and mindless sacrifice of the individual to a dominant will of the "company team." For awhile it looked like that other wintertime game—basketball—had fallen far behind the times as well.

The NBA game of the '70s indeed sagged in popular interest as parity among teams and a lack of colorful highscoring stars left the pro game altogether bland and predictable. After Wilt and Oscar and Cousy there no longer were dynasty teams like the Celtics and Lakers to love or despise; huge defensive titans like Russell and Chamberlain had disappeared and the magicians of the jump shot—Elgin Baylor, Jerry West and the "Big O"—had faded from the scene as well. But an infusion of exciting new talent, two superstars named Bird and Magic, and a marvelous marketing coup changed all that at the outset of the '80s. Television first learned how to turn the game of high-flying, slam-dunking, rim-rattling, instant gratification into a thrill-a-minute spectacle bound to leave viewers clinging to the edges of their seats. And the dribbling and shooting game has now again taken off with Air Jordan and a new generation of high-flying super athletes seemingly made especially for a celebrity-filled video age.

American sports seem to provide a new generation of heroes attuned to the special needs and imagination of each generation and each epoch. Babe Ruth, Joe DiMaggio and Willie Mays were the appropriate icons for the Roaring Twenties, the pre-war thirties, and the post-war fifties. The Babe's stock rose with a surging economic marketplace as business profits and home runs soared simultaneously. The down-and-dirty Gas House Gang Cardinals touched the pulse of a following depression-scarred decade. DiMaggio was a perfect touchstone for the stoicism of the war-time era. Willie Mays (and also Mickey Mantle, to be sure) provided the glamor and boyish wonder of an optimistic boom-era fifties. And when America became again preoccupied with a war-time culture during the decade consummed by Vietnam, suddenly it was the football player and the gridiron game of televised mock warfare that seemed more in tune with our shared national psyche.

In this sense it has been the NBA athlete who has dominated our attention for much of the 1980s and 1990s. It started with the rivalry of Bird and Magic, force-fed to a nation which was for the first time falling in love with the indoor roundball game on national television. Then Michael "Air" Jordan set new standards for on-court thrills and off-court commercial marketability, to be followed immediately by other superhuman flyers of the MTV video era like Clyde Drexler, Scottie Pippen, and Dominique Wilkins. And now Shaquille O'Neal, Patrick Ewing, "Sir Charles" Barkley and David "The Admiral" Robinson have provided a still younger generation with a fresh new arsenal of basketball culture heroes.

The fact that today's pro basketball has been so exclusively focused on the heroes of the present moment has been both the strength and the Achilles' Heel of the modern NBA game. Where the NBA now suffers a marketing deficit with its fans seems to be in the missing sense of shared history which has always been baseball's surest grip upon its adoring masses. Everyone remembers the most insignificant details of baseball history (the last 30-game winner, the all-time winningest lefty pitcher, the only World Series unassisted triple play, etc.), but almost no one remembers Wilt Chamberlain's 100-point game, Bob Cousy's pace-setting ball-handling style, the Big O's dominance of the '60s which made him arguably (sorry Michael Jordan fans!) the greatest player ever, or even the birth of "slam dunk" two short decades ago with high flyers like Julius Erving, Connie Hawkins and Earl Monroe.

As author and noted play-by-play broadcaster Eric Nadel has recently reminded us on this topic, every passing baseball fan knows reams about Babe Ruth and the Murderers' Row Yankee teams of the '20s, about Jackie Robinson's pact with Branch Rickey that broke baseball's colorline in the 40's, or about the misdeeds and indiscretions which left Shoeless

Joe Jackson waiting on the doorstep outside of Cooperstown. But with basketball almost nothing from the immediate or remote past is even vaguely familiar: it is a rare enthusiast indeed who knows of George Mikan and the Lakers dynasty in the '50s, who recalls that broken NBA backboards began with Gus "Honeycomb" Johnson in the '60s and not Darryl Dawkins in the '80s or Shaq O'Neal in the '90s, who can tell you what role Earl Lloyd and Chuck Cooper played in the integration of professional basketball several winters after Jackie Robinson's more heralded baseball debut in Brooklyn. Baseball glories in its past and is often weighed down and threatened by the meddlings and tinkerings of its electronic present. Pro basketball, by stark contrast, seems to have almost no remembered past at all.

For many baseball diehards and traditionalists—and baseball tends to attract traditionalists more than any other sport—the best of the national pastime may well have come to an end with the introduction of such tinkering as the Designated Hitter Rule, plastic indoor fields, and the realignment of American and National Leagues into first four and then six divisions. For the bulk of hoop fans, by dramatic contrast, basketball began not with Naismith, Mikan, or even Lew Alcindor, but only with those first network post-season head-to-head confrontations of Magic Johnson and Larry Bird. Baseball fans look only backward and are blinded by nostalgia; basketball fans look only forward and are jaded by lack of tradition. Both views are, of course, narrow and largely inaccurate. But basketball seems to have suffered the most from this dual failure of historical appreciation.

Basketball history, however, has now slowly but surely begun to come out of the closet, at least in the printed work of the historians and scholars, if not quite yet in the popular imagination. The aforementioned Eric Nadel (in *The Night Wilt Scored 100*, 1990) has provided literate fans with a delightful recent collection of vignettes which bring to life rare, exhilarating and largely forgotten moments from the hardwood game. Nadel resurrects the memory of such pioneering hoops figures as Ron Boone (basketball's all-time ironman with 1,046 consecutive pro games played), Kevin Porter (the forgotten point guard of the '70s who long held an NBA single-game record for assists), Maurice Stokes (whose brilliant NBA career was struck down in the '50s by a rare and fatal disease), George Yardley (the NBA's first star to be known as "Bird"), and dozens and dozens more among the game's colorful characters and unappreciated pioneers. Black culture historian and jazz critic Nelson George (in *Elevating the Game—Black Men and Basketball*, 1992) has provided crucial understanding of the origins of today's colorful trash-talking style of mano-a-mano NBA play, origins emanating from the ghetto playgrounds of New York as well as from the Julius Erving-dominated courts of the outcast American Basketball Association in the late 1960s. And most recently, veteran sportswriter Terry Pluto has offered a pair of essential oral history tomes (in *Loose Balls*, 1990, and *Tall Tales*, 1992) which revive the glory years of the '60s-era ABA and NBA in the words and personal reminiscences of the game's greatest pioneering players themselves. One can now read Nadel and George and Pluto and rediscover a rich legacy of American sport which has all too long remained unaccountably buried in shadow and lost to public consciousness.

Basketball has always had heroes as talented and legendary as those in any sport—Chamberlain, Robertson, West, Arizin, Cousy, Bradley, Pettit—the list is ongoing if not endless. Their performances and triumphs have simply remained more the province of specialists and "true fanatics" and thus have never quite entered widespread public consciousness. This is not very surprising given the low public profile (especially on television and radio) of pro basketball in the several decades preceding the arrival of Magic Johnson, Larry Bird and Ted Turner's TBS-NBA broadcasts. In the beginning there was only giant George Mikan who established singlehandedly the role of the big man in the roundball gymnasium game. Out of the sport's golden era of the late fifties and early sixties came the first great pure shooters—Baylor, Pettit, Yardley, Arizin and Jerry West, as well as perhaps the two greatest all-around players of all time—Chamberlain and Oscar Robertson. And in the '70s there was Julius Erving, who invented "hangtime" and sold spectators on the magnetism of the dunk shot. One can only imagine the hero-worshipping and hype that might have surrounded Wilt, Oscar and Dr. J had they benefitted from the same television era as Magic and Michael "Air" Jordan.

Why precisely is it that the NBA did not burst upon the American sporting scene until the arrival of Bird versus Magic Johnson in 1980? For one thing the answer lies partially in the fact that basketball as a game was simply not yet fully in tune with the times before then. Much of the raw appeal of today's game turns on the celebrity status of acrobatic stars who control every moment of breathtaking on-floor action. The NBA game now thrives on the close cramped quarters and aggressive physical style of a fast-paced, frenetic, and even dangerous urban survival experience. And it is also a spectacle of instant gratification and high economic gain, both reflected by the continuous scoring and rapid-fire swings in fortune which mark the play of the modern court game. Basketball is so popular today precisely because it mirrors and intensifies our personal and national life, just as baseball did to our betterment in the '50s and football did to our detriment in the '60s and '70s.

Despite its fitful starts and stops in the 1950s, its lost glory years of the 1960s, and its slide into partial obscurity during the 1970s, the NBA does indeed boast a colorful and glorious four-decade history which rivals that of major league baseball or professional football for thrills, excitement and epic performance. Historical evolution in the National Basketball Association can—with only the slightest stretch of the imagination—be seen to mirror those established cycles of history from the larger world of transpiring human affairs. Basketball, like all other endeavors, seems to move naturally through its own pre-ordained yet altogether familiar evolutionary eras.

Basketball's dim *pre-history* is found in the age of towering George Mikan and the dynasty Minneapolis Lakers of the early and mid-fifties. Standing at 6'10" in an era when even six-footers were rare specimens, Mikan was such a force that the style of play in the fledgling pro game had to be drastically altered simply to stop him. Able to camp a stride outside the narrow six-foot-wide foul lane and drop in "baby hooks" against defenders often a full foot shorter, Mikan forced the first double and even triple teams from defenders who often resorted to merciless fouling, despite the big man's deft free throw shooting abilities. At the defensive end of the floor, the Mikan-led Lakers merely set up zone patterns and waited for the towering center to guard the middle like a soccer goalie. The resulting tactics of fouling and slowdowns were so injurious to the game—as well as to Mikan's own performance—that the whole sport had to be quickly recast by the rules makers or face possible extinction of fan interest. The foul line was thus widened in 1951 from six to twelve feet, precisely with Mikan in mind; three seasons later the 24-second shot clock was introduced in response to games like the one in November, 1950, when Fort Wayne's Pistons tested a strategy of simply holding the ball for long stretches against Mikan and his mates. Never before or since has any single player had such impact on the game's rules or its structure. It was is if today's rule makers were suddenly to hike the basket rims to 14 feet and institute a hockey-style "off-side" rule in order to negate Michael Jordan's break-away slam dunks.

Mikan was thus the sport's first true marketable star, one whose scoring (he averaged better than 28 ppg. for the 1949, '50 and '51 seasons) put fans into the seats and whose revolutionary playing style recast the game's very appearance. Such was the appeal of the NBA's first one-man attraction that New York City promoters could advertise Minneapolis Laker visits to Madison Square Garden on the arena marquee as "Tonite, George Mikan Versus the Knicks!"

The game as a whole had not yet evolved very far from its primitive barnstorming era by 1951, however. The oft-times embarrassing signature of the league thus remained its musty gymnasiums and somewhat bizarre playing circumstances. While dance halls (frequent venues for exhibitions by pro teams during the '30s and '40s) had given way to larger arenas for the league's games, numerous regulation games were still being scheduled for off-the-beaten-path non-league cities in the search for much-needed nightly attendance. Wilt Chamberlain's remarkable 100-point game a full decade later in 1962 would occur not in the Philadelphia Spectrum or in Madison Square Garden, for example, but in front of a few thousand wide-eyed fans (4,124 to be exact) crammed into a converted local hockey arena in Hershey, Pennsylvania. Fans had come out that night largely to see a featured preliminary exhibition matchup between two popular NFL teams—the Philadelphia Eagles and Baltimore Colts—and many had headed home already satisfied with an evening's entertainment before the historic NBA half of the card had even begun.

And even the established home courts of Mikan's era were prone to incredible idiosyncrasies befitting the true "dark ages" of a still minor-league sport. Syracuse's State Fair Coliseum (home to the Syracuse Nats until 1963) was not only musty, dimly lit and without ventilation, but also featured basket-supporting guidewires which extended into the stands and could be yanked by the home crowd to rattle the basket while opposing players attempted free throws. Edgerton Park Sports Arena in Rochester (home of the Rochester Royals until 1957) boasted double doors a few feet behind the basket and a player charging in for a layup was occasionally known to careen straight through the portals and into a hidden outside snowbank. And Keil Auditorium in St. Louis (home to the St. Louis Hawks until 1968) featured perhaps the strangest arrangement of all. One half of the auditorium was a convention hall featuring the basketball floor and grandstands; the other half was a theater with its stage backed up against the sports arena and separated from the latter by only a thin portable wall. A concert or ballet was often in progress at the same hour as a league game, and if players emerging from the locker room were not careful to enter the correct auditorium door they could conceivably dribble smack into the midst of an ongoing symphony or operatic aria.

Mikan was a towering hulk whose presence altered the rules by which Naismith's game had long been played; but a decade later came two even more formidable giants who also altered the very ethics and ambiance of the game. Mikan's only advantage was size, but with Wilt Chamberlain (1959) and Bill Russell (1956) we suddenly had monsters who were also marvelous athletes. And with them basketball suddenly became an art form and the closest sporting equivalent to classical ballet.

This was the great **Golden Era** of the sport of basketball and it emerged with a decade of head-to-head Chamberlain-Russell confrontations (more than a dozen each season) which stretched from one end of the '60s all the way to the other. Chamberlain foreshadowed a future when the game would no longer revolve around the tussle between big men who dunked and the little men who simply dribbled, shot and passed. The next generation of skimpy-clad basketballers would bring giant redwoods who could perform both shooting and ball-handling tasks with almost equal proficiency. Chamberlain unleashed scoring and offense at unheard of rates— Wilt across his first seven pro seasons never posted a scoring average below 33.5 ppg. (nor ironically did he ever play on a championship team during that stretch). Before Wilt arrived no NBAer had ever averaged as much as 30 ppg. for an entire season. Chamberlain's constant foil, Bill Russell of the perennial champion Celtics, provided a volley of defensive salvos that guaranteed the greatest head-to-head struggle of giants ever known. Russell brought defense back into the game at the very moment when Wilt was exploding the horizons of unfettered offense; here was the first (and perhaps last) player who could dominate a game at the highest levels without bothering to put the ball in the hoop himself; Russell would never crack the 20 ppg. barrier (he only twice averaged 18 ppg. for a season) and yet led his Boston team to an incredible 11 NBA world championships over a mere 13-year career. Historians still speak and write of the Red Auerbach Boston Celtics of the 1960s as basketball's greatest team ever, yet Auerbach never won a single title without a man named Bill Russell in the lineup. And every big man since—from Nate Thurmond to Abdul-Jabbar (née Lew Alcindor) to Ewing and Olajuwon and finally Shaq have been measured by but one standard—the original matchups of Russell and Chamberlain on Mount Olympus.

Basketball in the '60s had more memorable stars than any other single era and soon featured the game's greatest shooting forwards and guards as well as its two (and perhaps three counting Nate Thurmond) classic centers. Oscar Robertson and Elgin Baylor and Jerry West did the work of true magicians. Robertson never won an individual league scoring title (his seven greatest years overlapped with Chamberlain's) and yet still merits serious consideration as the greatest offensive guard ever to dribble, pass and shoot. Named for James Thurber's "The Wonderful O" of popular literature, basketball's "Big O" made a mockery of what are today considered statistical milestones: his 30.5 ppg. average as a rookie outstripped any backcourt performer before him (and any but Jordan after him) while he also replaced Cousy as the game's leading playmaker and proved a proficient rebounder at one and the same time. Against lineups more stacked with talent than any ever faced in the modern era by Michael Jordan (see Chapter Four) Oscar pulled off perhaps basketball's second most amazing feat ever when he *averaged* a triple-double (31 ppg., 12 rpg., 11 apg.) for an entire season; unfortunately for Robertson's sake the feat was nearly buried by Wilt's unthinkable 50.4 ppg. seasonal scoring average registered during the same campaign (1961–62).

"Mr. Inside" and "Mr. Outside" simultaneously performed for the transplanted Los Angeles Lakers. Baylor was basketball's first true airbourne flyer, the acknowledged original "avatar of aviation" and a pioneer of "hangtime" and incredible above-ground moves which he invented a full decade before Connie Hawkins and Julius Erving came on the scene. West bombed with such proficiency from long range that his career scoring totals would have assuredly exceeded 30,000 career points if registered in an era that included 3-point field goals.

And near the end of the decade, along came Rick Barry, a well-travelled professed "basketball gypsy" who shuttled between the established NBA and rival upstart ABA and burned up the nets whenever he stepped upon the court. Some will today argue that Rick Barry (not Julius Erving) was the greatest offensive forward ever to play the game of basketball, and a 14-year career total of 25,279 points (ABA and NBA combined) and a 24.8 scoring average spread over 1,020 games at least make such arguments somewhat tenable. With larger-than-life legends like Russell, Chamberlain, Robertson, Baylor, West and Barry occupying the floor for a full decade and lighting up the sports pages with their magic, the sport indeed seemed altogether ready to enter the mainstream of American popular culture.

But then came the ruinous "Dark Ages" of Dr. Naismith's original American game. In the '70s basketball almost died on the very doorstep of its widely expected success. The generation of legendary stars was soon followed by less colorful players. As the decade unfolded the rookie glamour of Lew Alcindor in Milwaukee seemed to fade into the methodical veteran efficiency of a west coast Kareem Abdul-Jabbar. George Gervin took over the scoring burdens of Baylor, West and Barry but lacked anything approaching the pizzazz or personality of those earlier net-fillers. Youngsters could hardly be expected to take to the concrete alleys and schoolyards aping every move of a colorless player like "Iceman" Gervin. Phoenix forward Truck Robinson captured a league rebounding title late in the decade and Kevin Porter was at the same time an NBA pacesetter in assists. Such players were neither household names nor the stuff of which playground legends are built.

A change in the American psyche had also undercut the national pastime of baseball, elevating football but not basketball during the years of cold war and post Vietnam calm. Over-expansion and emergence of the ABA had left the NBA without superstars and without any hate-'em or love-'em dynasty teams. Fans could not be excited about champions like the Milwaukee Bucks or Washington Bullets or Seattle SuperSonics. Nor could they warm to the cool efficiency of Jabbar, Cowens, Havlicek and Gervin the way they had once warmed to the raw power of Russell and Chamberlain and the epic grace of Baylor and Robertson. Absence of a national TV contract for basketball, in the face of football's video explosion, only served to widen the gap between a diminishing fan population and a sinking game. Earlier growth of basketball—at least the pro variety—now seemed to be on permanent hold.

It was actually the ill-fated ABA which ironically saved Naismith's sport as it reached middle age and faced such an uncertain future. The rebel league sought its own niche by emphasizing speed—running, jumping, and getting the ball up the court and toward the hoop with the most outrageous possible display of "moves" fashioned in true urban playground style. The ABA was thus a league of free-lancing forwards and not a league for lane-clogging centers and playmaking guards. It was initially in the ABA, therefore, that "hangtime" and the modern age of rim-rattled dunk shots was actually born, along with the reputations of daredevil showmen named Connie Hawkins, Darnell (Dr. Dunk) Hillman, Marvin Barnes, Spencer Haywood, Joe Caldwell, David Thompson, and the marvelous Julius Erving. And this new sky-bourne flair in turn saved the modern game from extinction and brought to it the new audiences it desperately required. Here was a sport now back in tune with the emerging world of cramped urban centers, space flight and instant gratification—the very world that much of America would soon become by the mid-1980s. And here too was an ABA hero named "Dr. J"—a pure embodiment of athletic innovation and excitement whose magnificently huge "Afro" and equally huge hands combined with his tomahawk slams to put dance and flight back into the fast-moving game of pro basketball.

Finally came basketball's "Renaissance Epoch" which arrived with the revival of the NBA under Magic, Bird and Jordan in the 1980s. Every era seems to find its "sports saviors" just when they are most needed. Ruth pulled baseball up by the bootstraps, hoisting it out of the Black Sox scandal and out of the increasingly dull dead-ball era as well. The Bambino singlehandedly saved diamond play from declining interest with his ceaseless barrage of run-producing long balls. So too Magic and Bird brought basketball to a new fever pitch of excitement. And they received a huge boost from several quarters while doing so. First television learned how to present the game properly, exploiting its unfolding ebb and flow of rapidly building and receding drama, and also highlighting magical passes and slams with multiple-angle instant replays. Second, the American public and its sporting tastes once again changed radically. Raw pounding violence and territorial warfare were now out and graceful and soaring rhythms were now in. Thirdly, the league developed marketing strategies under astute and farsighted commissioner David Stern. Basketball had learned to capitalize on its new mega-star personalities (making video stars and omnipresent pitchmen out of its charming new demigods like Magic Johnson, Michael Jordan and Shaquille O'Neal) and to sell the non-stop excitement of the instant-gratification game. It was the new marketing pitch and not the players alone that made basketball front page news and the hot stuff of the emerging video age. (Just imagine for a moment what the present league under David Stern would have done with Wilt, Oscar or Dr. J had they been at their primes in the mid-eighties!) What was born was the marketing of NBA players as TV pitchmen for an endless flood of sporting apparel, soft drinks, and all other trinkets of consummerism. As a result the players (and thus the NBA game itself) became omnipresent video heroes of the 1990s.

Close on the heels of the basketball "renaissance" came the basketball "Space Age." This was the era of Michael "Air" Jordan and a new generation of highflying heroes who elevated a style born with Dr. J (and earlier with Connie Hawkins) to its final artistic heights. And those heights were now literal as well as metaphorical. Today's game is one of "spectacular moves" and shattering one-on-one battles, all carried out at breathless speed and usually several feet above the surface of the playing floor or even above the plane of the suspended hoop itself. It is a thrill-a-minute pagent that mirrors but yet elevates a free-lance playground sport, born of the inner-city fifties and sixties and nurtured by the spirit and rhythms of Afro-American culture. And it is a made-for-television symphony of dramatic motion and instant gratification totally in tune with the modern-day MTV generation of youthful American sports fans. Today's basketball hero is, of course, now king of the sportsworld largely because of the accidental nature of the game itself. No sport lends itself quite so well to the penetrating eye of the video camera. It is the basketball player who is before the camera's view almost consantly: basketball's performers wear no forbidding masks as in football; nor do they sit on a bench or stand helpless in an infield or outfield for 90% of a game's unfolding action.

The basketball star controls his sport from thrilling beginning to dramatic end. Jordan is but the prototype—he lives out through his soaring flights and improvised moves the recurring urban-age fantasy of total liberation and personal freedom from a depersonalizing surrounding universe and social order. It is the NBA player from Barkley to O'Neal to David Robinson to Chris Webber with whom America identifies most fully in the century-closing 1990s.

As Eric Nadel cogently observes, basketball lore and legend indeed has somehow utterly failed to make its way into the consciousness of the huge and growing legion of basketball followers. Stop the average "NBA fanatic" on any street corner in any city—replete with his Chicago Bulls three-peat tee-shirt and pair of Shaq-Attaq Reeboks—and quiz him about Paul Arizin's or George Yardley's team affiliations, about Bob Pettit's scoring milestones, or about Jerry West's or Wilt Chamberlain's famous nicknames. It is a sure bet he will stare blankly and tell you he has never even heard of any of the five names mentioned. Ask for his all-time NBA all-star team and it is almost guaranteed to begin with Magic and Bird and end with Jordan, Shaq and David Robinson. He knows neither who the NBA hall of famers are nor that basketball actually has its own version of Cooperstown.

One mission of this present book, therefore, is to adequately record the essential and evolving history of an exciting brand of NBA professional basketball which, since the 1980s, has rapidly ascended toward the rank of America's (and even the world's) most popular spectator sport. This mission is driven as much by the exciting tales still waiting to be widely told as by the historical injustices of the sport's murky past. Indeed, the saga of no other American sport—the national game of baseball included—overflows with as many colorful personalities, as many action-packed moments of heroic and even incredible athletic performance, as many unmatched tales of adventuresome front-office maneuvering. And it is all made the more fascinating by the freshness of so many of these stories for the mainstream sports fan and sports-fan-turned-reader.

A second mission is to suggest by detailed reference to historical record that the great game of pro basketball was indeed filled by legendary superstars long before the televised images of Magic Johnson, Larry Bird and Michael Jordan soared into the American living room. Perhaps the most dominant half dozen American athletes of all-time once played in the NBA, and their names were Chamberlain, Russell, Robertson, Baylor, West and Cousy—not Magic, Larry, Michael, and Shaq.

Wilt Chamberlain introduced prodigious scoring to Naismith's simple peach-basket game with Herculean feats that have never again been equalled, and likely never will—100 points in a single NBA game; four different season's averages all better than Air Jordan's peak year and one incredible seasonal scoring mark which stood a full 30% higher than the best total ever achieved by Jordan or anyone else; better than 30 games with 60 or more points scored, compared to only five by Jordan. Bill Russell, in turn, was the most intimidating single defensive figure to take the field or court in any major sport; and certainly Russell was the only NBA player in history who could totally dominate a game without ever himself scoring a single point. Robertson, Baylor and West together changed basketball forever with their hard-driving and jumpshooting styles, in precisely the same manner and to the same degree that Babe Ruth saved and redefined baseball with his prodigious home runs.

These five incomparable basketball figures of the '60s carried the entire sport on their substantial shoulders and together provided a true Golden Age so essential to any sport. It was an age when the heroes were bigger and more noble and more god-like than any before or since. Wilt, Oscar, Russell, Baylor and West are the "larger than life" figures of the basketball Pantheon who match—feat-for-prodigious-feat—Mathewson, Ruth, Cobb, Speaker, Walter Johnson, Lou Gehrig and Rogers Hornsby in baseball's similar golden era four decades earlier. It was simply that the hoopologists' "Age of Olympians"—unlike its diamond counterpart—occurred most unfortunately while only a handful of the nation's sports fans were paying much attention to the still-growing (and largely east coast based) indoor sport of basketball.

But the focus of this book is not on the superstars alone. While basketball has always provided the sportsworld with glamorous heroes like Wilt, Oscar or Bob Cousy, it is afterall first and foremost a team game. Past generations of hoop fans (albeit in smaller numbers than their baseball counterparts) have grown up rooting passionately for the Knicks or Celtics or Lakers or Warriors. Modern-era boosters have hitched their allegiances to a couple of dozen franchises now spread widely across the face of the USA (and soon Canada as well) and now providing regional passions and loyalties which did not exist in the '50s and '60s when the pro sport was largely restricted to a handful of cities on the east and west coasts.

Fans can here—for the first time in a single NBA history—now relive (or more likely discover for the first time) the failures and glories of each of these favored hometown teams. While the Celtics, Knicks and Lakers have already generated a small cottage industry of team histories, championship-season tributes, and even biographies or memoirs of star players, many other NBA teams, both new and old, offer absolutely nothing in the way of documented history. Here, then, is the first volume that brings histories and statistical summaries for all these ballclubs together under one cover. And the contrasting and complementing histories of individual teams down through the decades are utilized, in turn, to recreate in considerable detail the evolving history of the league and of the entire sport itself.

Ultimately the goal of this volume, then, has been to add some much needed historical perspective to the living saga of professional basketball. While America's present-day premier sports league, the NBA, nears its fiftieth anniversary (celebrated in 1996) there remains a pressing need for serious historians of American sport to document lost legends of the pro game and to transplant basketball lore firmly in the American consciousness. It is with this goal in mind that these pages aim at bringing back to life the great heroes and great games of the sport's sometimes murky past.

True achievements of basketball's two earliest dynasties—the Minneapolis Lakers and Boston Celtics—are thus articulated, as are the contributions of pro basketball's earliest pioneering stars like George Mikan, Joe Fulks, Bob Cousy and Paul Arizin. The title strings of modern-era teams like Magic's Lakers, Isiah's Pistons, Bird's Celtics and Michael Jordan's Chicago Bulls are measured against achievements of the dim past. The lost histories of the ABA, NBL and BAA are capsulized and the contributions of each of these rival circuits to the growth and health of the NBA is examined. A brief epilogue also brings needed historical perspective to the issue of assessing and ranking the game's greatest players, and an opinion is rendered as to why Jordan—for all his skill, achievement and notoriety—fails to outstrip Oscar Robertson or Wilt Chamberlain as the game's most talented overall player. Modern-day expansion of the NBA is also contrasted with earlier barnstorming exploits and franchise shifting during the game's less stable evolutionary days. Trades and front office moves that often escape daily notice or are lost in the shuffle of passing years are set against the evolving histories of each and every franchise.

Pro basketball (NBA-style) as a major American sport and entertainment spectacle is about to turn a hoary fifty years of age at the midpoint of the present decade. Hopefully this chronicle will work to help set the record straight—on both the game's sometimes fitful growth as well as its awesome achievements. Hopefully these chapters will also add to the unbounded joy of simply watching America's and the world's most glamorous and exciting team sport. Basketball's time has now unquestionably come. And thus so has a time for proper celebration of basketball history.

Suggested Readings on Pro Basketball History

Bjarkman, Peter C. **The History of the NBA**. New York and Avenel, New Jersey: Crescent Books (Outlet Books, Random House), 1992.

Koppett, Leonard. **24 Seconds to Shoot: An Informal History of the National Basketball Association**. Silver Anniversary Special Revised Edition (1945–1970). New York: Macmillan Publishers, 1970.

Lazenby, Roland. **The NBA Finals—The Official Illustrated History**. Dallas, Texas: Taylor Publishing Company, 1990.

Nadel, Eric. **The Night Wilt Scored 100—Tales from Basketball's Past**. Dallas, Texas: Taylor Publishing Company, 1990.

Pluto, Terry. **Loose Balls—The Short Wild Life of the American Basketball Association As Told by the Players, Coaches and Movers and Shakers Who Made It Happen**. New York: Simon and Schuster, 1990.

Pluto, Terry. **Tall Tales—The Glory Years of the NBA in the Words of the Men Who Played, Coached and Built Pro Basketball**. New York: Simon and Schuster, 1992.

Salzberg, Charles. **From Set Shot to Slam Dunk: The Glory Days of Basketball in the Words of Those Who Played It**. New York: Dell Publishing (Bantam Doubleday), 1987.

Wolff, Alexander. **100 Years of Hoops—A Fond Look Back at the Sport of Basketball**. New York: Oxmoor House (in cooperation with *Sports Illustrated*), 1991.

THE ENCYCLOPEDIA
OF PRO BASKETBALL
TEAM HISTORIES

Part I

Dynasty Teams

Chapter 1

BOSTON CELTICS

Celtic Mystique and Basketball's Unmatched Legacy

All-Time Franchise Record: 2358–1365, .633 Pct. (1946–1994)
NBA Championships (16): 1956–57, 1958–59, 1959–60, 1960–61, 1961–62, 1962–63, 1963–64, 1964–65, 1965–66, 1967–68, 1968–69, 1973–74, 1975–76, 1980–81, 1983–84, 1985–86
Greatest Franchise Players: Bill Russell (1956–1969) and Larry Bird (1979–1992)
All-Time Leading Scorer: John Havlicek (26,395 Points, 1962–1978)
Most Successful Coach: Red Auerbach (795–397, .667 Pct., 1950–1968)
All-Time Franchise team: Bill Russell (C), Larry Bird (F), John Havlicek (F), Bob Cousy (G), Sam Jones (G)

"When the great teams of any professional sports league are discussed, none can approach the Celtics' dominance. Not the New York Yankees. Not the Montreal Canadiens. Not the Green Bay Packers."
—Dale Ratermann

To begin a history of baseball, one might start logically with the Cincinnati Reds, the diamond sport's oldest and most storied senior circuit franchise. Or the argument might be easily made to focus, first and foremost, on the New York Yankees, owners of more pennants and World Series flags than any other ballclub by far. And a case could even be made for American League teams in Detroit and Boston, or National League clubs in Chicago or St. Louis—at least when it comes to picking the sport's most storied and legendary franchise. Then again, what baseball club has a more colorful past on both east coast and west than the Ebbets-Rickey-O'Malley Dodgers?

In the sport of basketball no such paradox exists. The story of professional basketball—in the large bulk of its chapters—reduces neatly to the

3

story of the Boston Celtics. Hands down, no contest, no challenge. In the late '50s and throughout the decade of the '60s, here was not only the first great dynasty club of the infant professional roundball sport, but unarguably the greatest dynasty in the history of American sports. Eight straight world championships, eleven titles in but thirteen seasons. It was the era of Bob Cousy, perhaps the greatest "white" player before Larry Bird—certainly the single ballplayer next to George Mikan who had the greatest individual impact on how the game was subsequently played. And it was also the era of Bill Russell, a mysterious and controversial legend who single-handedly turned basketball into a defensive game.

Throughout the '70s the lustrous tradition continued as Tom Heinsohn succeeded Auerbach and Russell at the reins, and the proud Celtics rebounded from a temporary slide to remain a dominant force during pro basketball's true lost decade. Now it was the era of John "Hondo" Havlicek, basketball's greatest "sixth man" now turned into a franchise player in his own right, and of Dave Cowens, the second great redhead of Boston hardwood legend. And finally in the '80s came the return of glory behind the brilliant play and floor leadership of the second greatest white player in the sport's history. The 1980s was the thrill-packed era of Larry Bird.

Yet it is for a single epoch that the Boston Celtics are most memorable. For card-carrying basketball fans, only one dynasty team comes immediately to mind when complete domination of a league or an era is the topic—the '60s-era Celtics of coach Arnold "Red" Auerbach. Nowhere in all of American sport, in fact, is there to be found another dynasty franchise to compare with those Boston teams formed and masterminded by Auerbach, and led into court action over a 13-year stretch by Cousy and Russell.

The collegiate ranks of the roundball sport seems to offer a competitor for the title. Nowhere in the history of college sport is there anything more remarkable than John Wooden's string of NCAA championships with the UCLA Bruins. But the marks established by Wooden and his UCLA titans fall a fraction short of those posted by Auerbach and the Celtics. Seven NCAA titles in a row and 10 in 12 seasons, versus eight straight NBA crowns and 11 in 13 seasons. (But for an injury to Russell in 1958, the Celtics string would likely have been ten in a row.) It seems a close call, and yet the Wooden teams were not a "dynasty" in the same sense as the Auerbach teams. There were really three different teams at UCLA, constantly shifting personal, and a constantly shifting playing field of opponents in each new two or three year span. The Celtics roster during the Auerbach string remained largely intact; the rival Hawks, Sixers and Lakers squads they battled were almost as stable. And certainly what Auerbach's Boston juggernaut accomplished has never been matched (or even closely approximated) anywhere in professional sports competition.

When the period from 1957 to 1969 is conjured up in the collective memory of hoop fans in every corner of the nation, the first great glory era of the pro game is colored by a bright shade of kelly green. The undying and all-pervasive symbol of the era was the shamrock; its undeniable signature was the parquet floor of the nation's most legendary indoor sporting arena. The collage of images is indeed indelible: "The Cooz" dribbling through traffic and passing behind his back; Russell outplaying Wilt in crucial contest after crucial contest; Sudden Sam Jones "stoppin' and poppin' " and Hondo Havlicek stealing the ball in the single most heart-stopping moment of franchise history. Boston teams did more than dominate the post-season play of this period; Celtics ballclubs of the era were indeed arguably the entire story of professional basketball for almost an entire generation of roundball fans.

The Cousy Era

Arnold "Red" Auerbach—a Jewish kid from Brooklyn who maintained a Washington, D. C. address during his entire four-decade tenure on the Celtics bench and in the club's front office—would be eventual author of the world's greatest sports dynasty ever. But Boston's most celebrated redhead certainly did not work his miracle overnight. In fact, the Red Auerbach Era in Boston got off to anything but a blazing start. And even when it hit full stride, the Celtics "mystique" was a phenomenon that never generated the full appreciation it merited until decades after the original triumphs had been etched into the record books. Boston was foremost a baseball town and a hockey town, and the Celtics were rarely front-page news, even when they were writing the most unmatchable sports story in the city's history. Rarely did the hoop club sell out its games during the championship string of the '60s (six or seven thousand was a good crowd; sellouts of 13,909 were a rare event reserved for a few playoff games), despite the fact that the hockey Bruins rarely had a seat available during the same epoch. Bill Russell, for all his prowess, was far too rebellious and controversial a figure to generate widespread fan appeal. And although the Red Sox were at a low point of franchise history, they remained first in the city's heart. Only Bob Cousy seemed to rise above the Celtics' back-page status. From 1951 through 1963—even in the heyday of Ted Williams—Bob Cousy was the most famous and revered athlete Beantown had ever known. From the beginning of his Holy Cross days in 1946, through his tearful Celtics retirement in 1963, Cooz was the one totally popular and beloved sports hero that Boston could call its own.

Auerbach's NBA coaching career began before Boston, and even before the NBA was called the NBA. It all started for Auerbach in Washington, where the former George Washington University backcourt star first enjoyed a bundle of early successes, both as high school mentor at St. Alban's Prep and Roosevelt High, and then in the fledgling professional ranks. The Basketball Association of American had been launched by east coast hockey club owners just as peacetime followed on the heels of World

War II, and in the nation's capital hockey arena owner Mike Uline turned to the 28-year-old Auerbach to take over a first edition of the Washington entry in the new circuit. Auerbach had just returned from his own military stint, and had convinced Uline of his worthiness for the post by boasting that he could deliver talented ex-service ballplayers to fill up the club roster. Auerbach delivered well enough, and his Washington Caps posted the circuit's best first-year record at 49–11. After two additional winning campaigns in Washington (including a title matchup with the Minneapolis Lakers in his final season), Auerbach was next off for a brief tenure with Ben Kerner's Tri-Cities Blackhawks. It was with the Illinois-and-Iowa-based ballclub that Red suffered through the only losing record of his career (28–29) during a first season of the newly reconstituted National Basketball Association. The Auerbach-Kerner relationship was anything but smooth, however, and Red quit by season's end in a spat over a trade made by Kerner and objected to by Auerbach. Later, the flamboyant coach would get his full measure of revenge, both by beating the transplanted St. Louis Hawks on several occasions in the NBA playoffs, and also by fleecing Kerner in the infamous Bill Russell deal.

The arrival of a new coach named Auerbach in Boston in 1950 brought promises of immediate improvement for a lackluster team that had failed to better 25 wins in any of its first four seasons under coaches Honey Russell and Doggie Julian. But when Boston Garden owner Walter Brown gambled on the feisty yet successful Auerbach, he introduced considerable upheaval into the heretofore staid young Boston franchise as well.

For one thing, it was clear from the moment of Red's arrival who the basketball boss in Boston would always be. Red's first clash with the locals came over a hot-shot prospect named Bob Cousy, who had led Holy Cross to the 1947 NCAA title and was now becoming available in the second-ever NBA draft. There was considerable hometown pressure to draft Cousy, but Auerbach had little use for a hotshot dribbler as the type of ballplayer to build a franchise around. There are two accounts of Red's exact words to the press on the occasion of his introduction as Boston's new coach, words uttered when the issue of Boston's draft selection immediately came up. One version has Red snapping: "I'm not interested in drafting someone just because he happens to be a local yokel." The second quotes Auerbach as retorting: "Am I supposed to win ballgames here, or please the local yokels?" But, either way, there is little doubt today about Auerbach's initial assessment of Cousy's limitations. The new Boston coach refused to tab Cousy with Boston's territorial draft selection, and the Celtics opted instead for center Charlie Share of Bowling Green (traded to Fort Wayne for the rights to Bill Sharman) and guard Chuck Cooper of Duquesne (the first black player ever drafted by the league).

It was an ironic move, of course, since Red's key to success would be his installing of the controlled fast-breaking game he had learned as a player under Bill Reinhart at George Washington University. And Cousy was the perfect ballhandler to run just such an offense—one dependent on pinpoint passing, controlled dribbling, and rapid movement of the ball to an open man. It was one case were Auerbach was clearly wrong in his assessment of talent, but in this case the stubborn coach was saved by fate from his own erroneous ways. Cousy was drafted by Auerbach's former employer, Ben Kerner's Tri-Cities Hawks. Almost immediately, the Hawks traded Cousy to the Chicago Stags, and before the season could even open that struggling club was out of business. Cousy's name was next thrown into a hat along with Chicago stars Max Zaslofsky and Andy Phillip, and offered to teams (Boston, Philadelphia and New York) having claims against the insolvent Chicago franchise. The folding of a franchise and the subsequent dispersal draft and coin flip had stuck Auerbach and Boston with Cousy anyway, much to Red's dismay and owner Walter Brown's equal displeasure. Auerbach was already a brilliant basketball mind—keen on judging talent—but on a few occasions he was more lucky than anything else.

But blind luck aside, Auerbach's vault to the top came largely through rare talent. Auerbach had two strong suits above all others. The first was an ability to keep his domineering personality in check and thus allow his extremely talented players free reign to develop and utilize their athletic skills. Boston players of the glory era (1957–1966) universally hated Auerbach's penchant for lighting up a victory cigar on the bench as soon as a ballgame appeared to be well in hand. Cousy later commented often on how this practice fired up opponents and enemy fans alike, and saddled the Boston players with added oncourt pressures they didn't need. But on all other counts Auerbach was a true player's coach, and his teams adored him for it. With his strongest Boston clubs he kept the offense simple (Boston had six or seven plays and rarely ran them all) and relied instead on great physical conditioning and Cousy's abilities to run the fast-break offense which Auerbach had designed. In crucial situations, especially in late moments of a game, the coach also relied on players to suggest the offensive plays. Auerbach thus soon had five talented coaches on the floor at once. And as Tom Heinsohn put it, if a player suggested the play in the huddle then he had that much more pride at stake in making sure that it worked out.

Auerbach's other unmatched strength was as master trader and stellar manipulator of the college player draft. Knowing that Russell was exactly what he needed, and that Rochester was already sold on Sihugo Green with their own first pick in 1956 lottery, Auerbach engineered a huge deal with Kerner and the Hawks to land his coveted centerpiece ballplayer. And it was only the first of many such history-shaping transactions. Red was never afraid to give up something in return, and he gave up plenty in the Russell deal. But he also made the best acquisition in NBA history. Later the Redhead would build another dynasty team by having the foresight to draft Larry Bird early (as an unavailable underclassman, taken with the sixth overall pick) and also to acquire Parish and McHale (both via Golden State) just two drafts later. Red got McHale by fleecing Detroit coach (and later TV personality) Dick Vitale out of a number one 1980 selection (for Bob McAdoo), then trading that pick (along with the 1980 number 13 selection obtained from Washington) to the Warriors for Parish and a Golden State first-round selection (third overall). Golden State used that number one slot to select disappointing Joe Barry Carroll, while Auerbach banked the number three selection for future Hall-of-Famer McHale. And there was yet one more clever Auerbach deal that only the cruel hand of fate expunged from the record. Red arranged a trade (Gerald Henderson for Seattle's first overall 1986 selection) that allowed the acquisition of number one pick Len Bias out of the University of Maryland. Red seemed to have done it again, but this time pure chance intervened to stop him in a way that the league's other executives never seemingly could.

Even before Auerbach's greatest teams arrived on the scene, the Boston Celtics did have one important date with history. That was the team's somewhat muddled role in the integration of the NBA with the drafting of Duquesne forward Chuck Cooper in 1950. Cooper's pioneering role in basketball's destruction of the color line has often been unfortunately misrepresented by historians who simply haven't done their homework, and have thus overanxiously labelled Cooper as basketball's Jackie Robinson. Cooper's role was somewhat less central than Robinson's: the Celtics' first black was indeed also the first player of his race tabbed by the formal NBA drafting procedure; on the other hand, he was not the first black to ink an NBA contract (New York signed Harlem Globetrotter Nate "Sweetwater" Clifton only hours after Boston had drafted, but not yet signed, Chuck Cooper). More importantly, neither Cooper nor Clifton were the first blacks to set foot on an NBA floor for game action. That honor fell to Earl Lloyd, a West Virginia State 6'6" leaper taken a few slots after Cooper in the same 1950 draft. Due to a quirk in the league schedule, Lloyd's Washington Caps ballclub opened play a night earlier than either Cooper's Celtics of Clifton's Knicks, given Lloyd a cherished if overlooked slot in the history books.

Thus Boston was not actually the first NBA team to integrate its roster on the playing floor as is so often reported. On the other hand, it is an unfair distortion to suggest that Boston and Auerbach have made efforts to keep Celtics teams lily white in the '70s and '80s. Boston's role in integrating the sport is, in fact, quite the reverse. A schedule-maker's trick might have kept Boston from being technically the first team to field a black in their gameday lineup, but more importantly, Boston was the league's first team (in 1963–64) to put five black men on the floor at the same time (Heinsohn was the only white starter, but he often gave way to Willie Naulls). And a season later, Boston's Celtics fielded the first all-black starting lineup in NBA history. This was the five made up of Russell, Sanders, Naulls, K.C. Jones and Sam Jones. And it was Boston, of course, that could boast the first black coach (the first in any major U.S. pro sport) when Russell assumed the post in 1966. Unlike Boston's baseball Red Sox a few seasons earlier, the Celtics were anything but a racial foot-dragger.

The first building block of a future dynasty club was put in place almost by accident. That block was Bob Cousy, a player the new coach didn't really want and only acquired by accident and through more than a small dose of outrageous good fortune. But once Cousy was on the scene, his impact on basketball was truly immense, certainly greater than any player of the league's first decade save Mikan. Mikan had actually forced major rule changes and encouraged rule-bending playing tactics. Cousy's revolutionary impact was more subtle but none the less dramatic. Here was the greatest white player of all time until Bird arrived in the 1980s. And here was also the greatest ballhandler and passer the game has ever known, right down to the present moment. As Heinsohn often points out, Cousy's passing was so superb that only the players receiving his "soft assists" could truly appreciate them. Russell was the missing element to round off the plan for Auerbach's fast-breaking offense. But without Cousy there wouldn't even have been a plan.

Before Russell reshaped the notions of big-man play, diminutive Bob Cousy had already "written the book" on the wizardry of backcourt style. And while Russell was destined to be marked as a sure-fire all-time great before ever actually setting foot in the league, Cousy was the greatest of unanticipated surprises—especially for the Boston Celtics, who twice passed up the opportunity to have him on their roster (they didn't want him in the college draft and didn't want him in the dispersal draft several months later) and yet were still fortunate enough to end up with Cousy in spite of themselves. With Cousy and Russell in tow, the Celtics were almost unbeatable. Not quite, of course, but it certainly appears that way in hindsight. The unit that Auerbach molded by the end of the 1950s developed a unique freelancing fast-break style which altered forever the strategies by which basketball was played. It might even be said that it was the Celtics' fast-break offense (Russell rebounding and outletting to Cousy, who found Heinsohn or Ramsey ahead of the pack) more than any other single feature which eventually allowed the professional game to overhaul the rival collegiate version of roundball in fan popularity.

With Cousy at the helm the Boston clubs of the mid-fifties were respectable and competitive. They also had some good supporting players on board, like Arnie Risen and Bill Sharman. Risen was an accomplished point-maker who had already helped other teams in Rochester and Indianapolis. The skinny 6'9" center was a fixture, between 1947 and 1957, in the league's top ten rankings in both rebounding and scoring. And Sharman was the best pure outside shooter of the entire decade. On the freethrow line especially, Sharman was truly invincible. The University of Southern California graduate had once hoped to play baseball as a second baseman, and had advanced to the top minor leagues, but was eventually stuck behind Jackie Robinson in Brooklyn. (Sharman holds the trivial distinction of having once been thrown out of a major league game for heckling from the bench—while on a late-season call-up with the Dodgers in the early '50s—while actually never having played in a big league contest.) But on the basketball court, Sharman's talents were never overshadowed by others. Beginning in 1951 the crack-shooting Texan teamed with Cousy to create a balanced backcourt combo that surpassed Bob Davies and Bobby Wanzer in Rochester as the best outside duo of that early era. While Cousy ran the offense and did the passing, Sharman simply shot the lights out. He regularly lead the club in scoring throughout the first phase of the Celtics dynasty run (1956–1959).

With Cousy and Sharman running the show in the seasons immediately before Russell's arrival, the Boston Celtics were always respectable if not overwhelming. For six straight years the team played over .500 and finished either second or third in the Eastern Division each season (1951–1956). But before Russell, these guard-heavy Boston teams were also always easy victims of more physical ballclubs like Minneapolis, Rochester or Syracuse, in either round one or round two of the league championship series.

And the pre-Russell Celtics were not entirely without a big man either. For several seasons prior to Bill Russell's fortuitous arrival and the resulting dramatic reversal in Celtic fortunes, there was yet another slightly more modest big man who guided the Boston club into annual league warfare. Some would eve date the first emergence of the dynasty-driven Celtics to coincide with the now long-forgotten deal that brought "Easy Ed" Macauley to his new home in Boston Garden. The St. Louis University star played the NBA's first season with the hometown St. Louis Bombers and was acquired by Boston through the dispersal draft, which followed the folding of the St. Louis outfit. Macauley was an exceptional shooter of his period, and his offensive battles with Mikan foreshadowed the Russell-Chamberlain duels that lay waiting just down the road.

Yet clearly the greatest contribution of Boston's first exceptional pivot man to the emerging Celtics dynasty would rest, ironically, in Macauley's departure rather than his arrival on the Boston scene. With Macauley and Risen in the forecourt, and Cousy doing the playmaking, the Celtics were already an offensive whirlwind team that could score quicker and more continuously than any team in the league. But such offensive proficiency didn't seem to pay large post-season dividends in a league that was still based far more on muscle and intimidation than on finesse. There was a large missing piece in Boston, and Auerbach seemed to know precisely what the piece was. "Easy Ed" Macauley would soon serve as the valuable trade bait with which Auerbach could hook the incomparable big man around whom he would construct his greatest Boston championship teams.

Auerbach owned the third pick of the 1956 college draft, and it was no secret that the scheming Boston mentor coveted San Francisco University center Bill Russell as the single component needed to convert his team from also-rans into champions. It was also no secret that penny-pinching Rochester management, owning the league's first pick, would bypass the huge center who would demand an unthinkable salary for his services. St. Louis was willing to deal their number two shot at Russell (since Ben

Kerner had apparently not yet learned to distrust his ex-employee), but the price would be steep. Hawks management required Macauley (who earlier starred at St. Louis University) and promising Cliff Hagan as well, but it was a price Auerbach didn't flinch at paying. The result would not only be Celtic invincibility, but a new national stature for NBA basketball to boot.

Once the Celtics had Russell they had the key to a dynasty that would soon dwarf achievements posted by the then-reigning Minneapolis Lakers. Only Auerbach seemed to know what he was doing at the time. But the impact of his move would quickly transform the league and the sport forever.

The Russell Era

No team has ever so dominated a professional sport for any period that extended beyond a single decade. Over the course of 13 winters—the span of most lengthy careers for individual players—Boston would breeze by the opposition with an incredible 11 world titles. Eight of these championships would come in unbroken succession. In this same 13-year span, the Celtics would average 55 victories a campaign; they would never lose more than seven home contests over this stretch during any single season; and for 12 straight years their winning percentage would remain well above the .600 mark. This was total domination as it has never before or since been experienced in any major league sport in North America.

And if one isn't quite sure where the Celtics stand in regard to the modern-day Bulls or Lakers, or perhaps how they stack up with other sports dynasties like the Yankees of baseball, or Dolphins of football, or Canadiens of hockey, consider one additional fact that speaks necessary volumes. At the end of the 1980s the NBA was 44 years old and had enshrined 47 players and coaches in the Naismith Basketball Hall of Fame. Exactly 8 of those players (plus the coach)—a full 17 percent—were from one team. Not one franchise, but *one team*, which Red Auerbach sent out on the floor during the 1960–'61 NBA campaign. Name another ballclub in the entire realm of professional sports where the complete starting lineup was composed of Hall-of-Famers. Or one where three Hall-of-Famers (Frank Ramsey, Sam Jones, and K. C. Jones) were on the roster and didn't even start! Name, in fact, a team in any sport that has drafted three Hall-of-Famers in a single season—Auerbach's rare feat when he pegged Russell, Heinsohn, and K. C. Jones in 1956. It was like a Yankees roster with Ruth, Mantle, Gehrig, Ted Williams, Ty Cobb, Willie Mays, Cy Young and Walter Johnson all in the same starting lineup and pitching rotation. On personnel factors alone, the early-'60s Celtics were the greatest ballclub ever to share the same locker room of any sporting arena.

And there would be still further domination in the years to come, as

Boston would rebound from the early 1970s doldrums to capture two more titles and five divisional crowns in the next decade. But as storied as the Celtics saga has remained for almost four decades since Red Auerbach first appeared on the Boston scene, still nothing can quite match the glories of those first 10 seasons of Auerbach and Russell-led Boston championship teams. Between the beginning of the 1956–'57 season, and the close of the following decade, one unbeatable Celtics lineup seemed to merge into another (as Heinsohn gave way to Sanders and Havlicek and Cousy-Sharman merged with the Jones Boys). One post-season heroic moment merely set the stage for more dramatic ones to follow. Year after year, it was the same coach, the same stars, the same championship venue, and the same precise result.

Perhaps the only reasonable method of reviewing this period of complete Celtics domination on the hardwood courts of the NBA seems to involve an approach which avoids the chronological continuum in favor of other more distinctive milepost measures of the era. These measures are the images, personalities and magical moments that even today remain indelible—the coaches, superstar performers, largely unheralded role players, legendary rivalries, and titanic post-season clashes which still form the sport's most treasured single era.

The coaches of the period who together define "the Celtic Mystique" were only two—Auerbach, and his pet project and short-term successor, Bill Russell. The Celtics dynasty saga not only begins with Red Auerbach, but it might very well have ended with Auerbach as well. To his lasting credit, Red's vision included not only the drafting of Russell, but also the selection of Russell as his coaching successor (and also the first black man to serve as an NBA mentor) a decade later. It was a bold move that surprised and even shocked almost the entire basketball community. To give Red credit for nothing more than bare expediency, it seems that at the time the resident Celtics genius knew better than anyone that only Bill Russell as coach could adequately handle Bill Russell the player.

Red Auerbach himself would remain the guiding light of the Celtics franchise throughout the seasons and the decades to follow that great glory-span of 1956–'66—first as general manager, later as elder statesman and patriarch, always as spiritual father and visible spirit of the revered Celtic ideal. In future seasons, Auerbach would mold and direct other Celtics dynasty teams from his secure front office post. First came the selection of Russell's rookie teammate Tommy Heinsohn for the plum Boston coaching slot at the outset of the 1970s. Heinsohn would reward his boss with two more world titles and five divisional flags during his own eight seasons at the helm. All of Red's coaches, right down to the end of the 80's (Russell, Heinsohn, Sanders, Cowens, K. C. Jones), would be his former players, with the single notable exception of Bill Fitch, who also earned a world title. Later came the acquisition of frontcourt star Dave Cowens, a brash rookie out of Florida State plucked with the fourth overall pick of the 1970 college draft. And then, of course, the surprise 1978 drafting of Larry Bird (only a college junior at the time, who would not play for another full season) to assure a return to Celtic glory throughout the decade of the 1980s. Finally, the shrewd acquisition of Robert Parish (plus draft rights to Kevin McHale) through yet another bold 1980 trade with the San Francisco Warriors.

If fate had not intervened in the mid-1980s, Auerbach's genius might have built still another team the equal of those of the Russell-Cousy or Cowens-Havlicek-Jo Jo White eras. This time around it would be an unbeatable tandem of Bird and prized rookie Lennie Bias from the the University of Maryland. Bias seemed to have all the tools for immediate stardom when grabbed by Auerbach in the 1986 draft, and was poised to enter the Celtics' starting lineup with all the flare and fury of Tom Heinsohn in 1956, John Havlicek in 1962, and Cowens in 1970. But Len Bias died suddenly of a drug overdose only days after the draft-day festivities, thus stunning the entire sports world. On this single tragic occasion Auerbach's ingenious draft manipulations had come up absolutely empty.

Russell, on the other hand, was arguably the greatest player-coach in all of sports history. Certainly no one else who managed bench strategy, while also taking a full-time role in the game's playing action, ever contributed so heavily in both roles towards winning championship honors—at least not over the stretch of more than a single season. When Auerbach stepped away from the Boston bench, he knew for certain that any replacement would have to make peace with his eccentric center, since Russell was undoubtedly the very heart and soul of the Boston team. It was Red's great genius that he saw the immediate solution and turned directly to Russell himself with the task. And in the three years that followed (1966–'67 through 1968–'69) Russell would surprisingly prove much more like his mentor as a bench strategist than anyone could have ever imagined.

But it was certainly as a player in the previous decade under Auerbach that Bill Russell was absolutely insuperable. Russell's failure to achieve lofty scoring numbers will always bar him from wide support as the greatest NBA player of all time. Never once in his career did the big man average 20 points per game; rarely did he enjoy a 30-point scoring outburst. The huge supporting cast strung around him for so long not only lifted the offensive burden from his shoulders somewhat, but also stole some of the luster from his own often indescribable defensive performances. For those who saw him dominate, time after time, the very man most frequently nominated for all-time best—Wilt Chamberlain—there can be no convincing argument that Chamberlain, or anyone else, was ever any better than Bill Russell. Not if team victory in a team sport is any weighty consideration for canonization. On defense, there has never been another basketball player to challenge Russell's total control over the area of floor and sky around the opponent's basket. Celtics players later referred to it as their ''Hey, Bill'' style of defense—gamble up front and know that if your man got away from you, you could always look over your shoulder and shout ''Hey, Bill'' for a sure defensive stop. Russell would pocket five season MVP awards (1958, 1961–'63, 1965) before he was done, a feat matched in league history only by Kareem Abdul-Jabbar. Fans of slam dunks and miraculous off-balance shots would likely select Air Jordan or Oscar Robertson, or even Magic Johnson, to pace their modern-day dream team; fans or coaches wishing to win the single-money contest would always opt for Bill Russell to key their prized championship lineup.

But there were other larger-than-life Celtics stars of this era, many of whom would have been franchise players for any other ballclub. In Boston, however, these men always lived in the long shadows cast by Russell and Cousy. Tom Heinsohn, for example, was a hard-as-nails force who first defined the NBA prototype of the power forward, and who well-earned his colorful nicknames of "Tommy Gun" and "Ack-Ack" (the sound of a machine gun). Heinsohn loved to shoot, and across nine brilliant seasons (1955–'56 through 1964–'65) he fired up an endless stream of running hook shots and line-drive jumpers that always seemed to find the proper range. While Heinsohn was perpetually shooting, his eventual replacement, John "Hondo" Havlicek, was a man of true perpetual motion. For 16 incredible seasons (1962–'63 through 1977–'78) Hondo piled 20-point year upon 20-point year as he climbed among the NBA's dozen all-time highest scorers with over 26,000 career points. And no other player ever displayed more raw stamina than Havlicek. None ever left a more colorful collage of memorable career moments either. And none ever discovered more ways to beat you than the man who ceaselessly ran circles around the rest of the league for almost two decades.

Bill Sharman, in turn, teamed with Bob Cousy to form the first truly memorable guard combo in league annals. While Cousy was the passing wizard of the duo, Sharman was the premier shooter of the 1950s, flawless at the foul line (.883 over an 11-year career and three seasons above 90% accuracy) and nearly as picture-perfect from the field. So obvious was his offensive prowess to the fans that few understood Sharman's equal reputation among opponents and teammates alike as a matchless defensive back-court man. And there was another, little-known aspect to Sharman's game which elevated him above less talented players of his era. Such was his devotion to scientific conditioning that he was truly decades ahead of his rivals in his approach to preparing himself for the rugged game of professional basketball.

All the important cogs in the Celtics' wheels were not front-line starters, of course. It would be with reliable Frank Ramsey that Red Auerbach would soon build a vital component of his prototype winning team, a component that first became a Celtics trademark, and later a true NBA fixture. For Kentucky University's Frank Ramsey was the first and perhaps the foremost of the league's storied "sixth-man" specialists—the super-sub who charges from the bench in early action to shift a game's momentum with talented and spirited play. Ramsey added the dimensions of speed and intelligence to the Celtics attack, then handed the mantle to John Havlicek, who took sixth-man performance to an even loftier level during his earliest years in the league. Ramsey's lasting signature was also Havli-cek's—an unwavering ability to arrive cold off the bench and immediately hit several long-range shots to break the spirit or momentum of a charging opponent.

Great teams are noted for their uncanny abilities to repeatedly find replacement parts waiting in the wings to sustain a well-tuned winner. By the early 1960s, as Cousy faded and Sharman disappeared completely from the scene, a new pair of backcourt wizards made the dominant perimeter duo of the 1950s almost unnoticed in their absence. Sharman's successor was Sam Jones, a relentless scoring machine out of tiny North Carolina College who patiently played a backup role for half a dozen winters and then burst forth as a prolific scorer of the Bill Russell-coached squads. Here was a player whose trademark was the soft touch, with which his shots kissed the glass, and the lightening first step, with which he left defenders scrambling in his wake. So large was Jones's reputation among peers and opponents that he would be a clear choice in 1971 for the all-time NBA silver anniversary mythic all-star team. And by the mid-1960s, one guard named Jones was found teaming with another, as Russell's former San Francisco teammate K. C. Jones was now more than adequately handling Cousy's former playmaking duties.

Another memorable element in the history of the first great Boston dynasty era was the great Celtics rivalries with a series of worthy league opponents, each featuring marquee players of their own. At the top of the list was the late-1950s matchup between the Celtics paced by Russell, and the high-flying St. Louis Hawks featuring the rare offensive tandem of Bob Pettit and Cliff Hagan. (NBA Finals, 1957, 1958, 1960, 1961). When the Hawks and Pettit quickly faded from the scene and shed their role as legitimate challengers, there quickly arose other rivals most worthy of titanic confrontations with Auerbach's men. First came the Warriors from Philadelphia and their own young tower of power, Wilt Chamberlain (Eastern Division Finals, 1957, 1960, 1962; NBA Finals, 1964). When Chamberlain later took his act back to Philadelphia from his brief west coast tour in San Francisco (new home of the Warriors after 1962), still another Eastern Division challenge arose in the guise of the newly relocated Syracuse Nationals, who now played wearing the logo of the Philadelphia 76ers (Eastern Divisions Finals, 1958, 1959, 1961, 1965, 1966, 1967, 1968). Wilt would challenge Bill Russell and his Boston mates yet a third time under the banner of the Los Angeles Lakers (NBA Finals, 1962, 1963, 1965, 1966, 1968, 1969) during the decade's final two seasons.

The centerpiece—quite literally, of course—of the memorable Celts-Warriors, Celts-76ers, and Celts-Lakers rivalries during the tempestuous 1960s was unquestionably the head-to-head clash of the league's two greatest big men. From his abbreviated rookie season of 1956–'57 (when he reported two months late due to a stint on the US Olympic team), Bill Russell remained a dominant defensive force like basketball had never seen before. A late entry into competition during that first season had cost

"Big Bill" the league's Rookie-of-the-Year honors (won by teammate Tom Heinsohn), and a rebounding title (when his total of 943 caroms placed him fourth among league board sweepers, even though his per-game average of 19.3 was two a game better than official league leader Maurice Stokes). But Russell had served notice from his earliest moments in the league that his defensive presence was every bit as vital as that offered by Wilt on offense. And it was in the semi-final or title rounds of league post-season play that the Russell-Chamberlain clashes would reach their most dramatic moments during seven of the decade's seasons.

Each head-to-head matchup of Russell and Chamberlain during this de-cade-long battle for supremacy was indeed a titanic struggle. Between November, 1959, and May, 1969, the two squared off in league and post-season competition a total of 142 times. The point tally on almost every occasion fell to Wilt, yet the final scoreboard count just as frequently pointed in the favor of Russell and his mates. The measure of Russell's own individual greatness, of course, was that for 10 straight seasons (1957–1966) after his rookie debut, his ballclub outlasted all rivals to race into the league's final championship round. Only twice (1964 and 1969) in this stretch, however, did the two behemoths—Mr. Defense and Mr. Offense—lock horns in the season's final title matchup. On four other occasions Russell's Celtics were able to dominate Chamberlain and com-pany (first the Warriors and then the 76ers) during the hard-fought Eastern Division finals, twice in matchups that stretched the full seven required games.

Chamberlain, for his part, raced to seven consecutive scoring crowns after following Russell into the league in 1959, yet not once in this span did his club walk away with a championship banner. Only after the War-riors had abandoned an east coast home in Philadelphia for a west coast abode in San Francisco did Wilt shake his annual, dreaded, early departures from the playoffs at the hands of the division-rival Celtics and at long last reach a championship-round confrontation with Russell. But the Celtics were at the zenith of their game in the spring of 1964, and although Wilt averaged 34.7 points throughout 12 playoff games that spring to Russell's 13.1 in 10, Wilt's offensive superiority would matter little. The Warriors simply didn't have the manpower to match with Boston at the other four positions, and the Celtics breezed to an easy title in five lopsided contests.

Russell enjoyed his finest outing against Chamberlain in the first game of their first-ever NBA Finals confrontation in 1964. For 21 consecutive minutes throughout the second and third periods of that contest, Russell held the game's greatest offensive force absolutely scoreless. At one point, Russ blocked a Wilt fall-away jumper and when huge Nate Thurmond picked up the loose ball and tried to stuff it back at the hoop, Russ blocked that one too.

Rising from the midst of this memorable series of individual and team rivalries was an almost unbroken chain of unforgettable playoff contests, as well as truly memorable single moments of intense court action still vivid more than three decades later for the generation of fans that witnessed them first-hand. This string of remarkable moments must certainly begin with events which transpired on the Saturday afternoon of April 13, 1957—the scene of Boston's first-ever NBA title celebration. What unfolded that afternoon must still be considered the most exciting and nerve-racking Celtics game ever played.

Boston had just posted their first-ever division title, and had also compiled the best record in the entire league for the very first time in the club's 11-year history. St. Louis, behind third-year frontcourt star Bob Pettit, had finished in a three-way tie for the Western Division crown, then cruised by Fort Wayne and Minneapolis in single-game tie-breakers to earn a first-round playoff bye. While Boston was blanking Syracuse in three straight for the Eastern title, St. Louis was doing the same to the Lakers over in the West. The stage was set for what appeared to the experts as an easy Boston flight to the club's first title flag. But the Hawks were not prepared to be easy victims, and an overtime St. Louis victory (125–123) in the title series opener on the Boston home court provided the momentum that Pettit's club needed to extend Boston to a full seven games. Some additional color was added to the already high-spirited series when Auerbach punched his old boss Ben Kerner in the mouth at courtside preceding game three, the spat resulting from Auerbach's complaints that one of the Kiel Auditorium goals had been intentionally set too low.

Then came the game they still debate and dissect on Congress Street and on the steps of Faneuil Hall. No single NBA contest has been more often relived, its climactic moments more often retold, than that Saturday afternoon finale in which the Celtics, more than a half-dozen times, seemed to take command of the game's ebb and flow, only to have St. Louis roar back on each and every occasion. Pettit sent the contest into overtime with two clutch free throws in the closing seconds. Foul troubles then mounted for St. Louis as Jack McMahon and Cliff Hagan went to the bench, yet Hawks forward Jack Coleman forced a second overtime period with his dramatic jumper moments before the second buzzer sounded. Then it was the hometown Celtics' turn for unprecedented heroics, as Jim Loscutoff sank a pair of clutch free throws to give Boston a final 125–123 advantage, a margin of victory which held up only when Pettit's last-second shot bounced harmlessly off the Boston rim.

If Boston's hitherto lowly Celtics were something of a surprise frontrunner in 1957, the league's championship mantle once more shifted, quite suddenly, to the river city of St. Louis for the following season. Boston again breezed to the Eastern title with a league-best 49 victories. This was the season, as well, when Bill Russell emerged as an undisputed league MVP. The Boston post-man topped the circuit in rebounding with a 22.7 average and directed the Cousy-led fast-break offense with endless pinpoint outlet passes from beneath the defensive goal. Bob Pettit—now also at the very top of his game—was simply too much for the Celtics, and MVP Russell, during the April championship round, however. Slowed by an

ankle injury in game three, Russell was stripped of his mobility and reduced to a token role down the final playoff home stretch. Without Russell
to harass him, Pettit was truly unstoppable during the sixth and final game,
as he poured in a post-season record 50 points and thus single-handedly
dethroned the Celtics after but one season as the league's champions.

The final two seasons of the decade witnessed continuation of the dramatic Boston-St. Louis playoff tap dance. During the campaign which
opened in October, 1958, and folded in April, 1959, both clubs raced to
double-digit final leads in their respective divisions. Boston established a
new league milestone by becoming the first team to amass 50 victories in
a single season since Minneapolis and Syracuse had first turned the trick
10 years earlier. Yet if fans anticipated a titanic Pettit-Russell post-season
rematch, they were to be sorely disappointed. A revived Minneapolis outfit,
behind phenomenal rookie Elgin Baylor, soon shocked the basketball world
by torpedoing the Hawks during a six-game series that turned on a Lakers'
thrilling game-five overtime victory in St. Louis. Elgin Baylor was no
match for the well-balanced Celtics, however, and the Minneapolis Cinderella story ended abruptly in the face of Boston's scoring onslaught led by
Sharman, Cousy and Heinsohn. Boston had already thumped Minneapolis
18 straight leading into the 1959 NBA Finals, and the string included an
embarrassing 173–139 February pasting that had prompted charges of point
tampering. Minneapolis avoided such embarrassment this time around by
keeping all games close (the point spreads were 3, 20, 3 and 5), but the
result was nonetheless a lopsided four-game Boston sweep—the first of
NBA Finals history.

Neither Boston nor St. Louis would lighten up even one iota on their
respective division rivals during the decade-ending 1959–'60 campaign.
Bob Cousy would later inform reporters that throughout his entire tenure
with the club the Celtics were never even once willing to coast during
season's play. They hated to lose two in a row, Cousy observed, and a
single regular-season defeat (whether the victor was the rival Hawks or
the hapless Cincinnati Royals) would cause them to approach the following
contest as though it were playoff sudden-death. And that philosophy was
never more evident than in 1960, when Cousy and his mates rattled off a
then-record 59 wins to bury division-rival Philadelphia by 10 full games.

The Hawks and Pettit had kept pace, however, with 46 victories of their
own and a lengthy 16–game spread over Detroit. And this time out there
would be no upset-minded villain to spoil the anticipated Hawks-Celtics
final showdown. True to season-long form, Boston set out to control the
final series with a 140–122 opening-game romp. St. Louis would not bend
easily, however, and held on to force a seventh-game showdown, one
which only resulted in a Boston 20-point victory waltz. Russell had 22
points and 35 rebounds in the 122–103 laugher; Ramsey added 24 points
and 13 boards; Heinsohn posted 22 points and 8 caroms; Cousy took
advantage of an injury to Hawks playmaker Slater Martin to tally 19 points
alongside his 14 assists. But the biggest number for Boston was the "two"

which stood for repeat. The 1950s would thus end with the first back-to-back champion since the Mikan-led Lakers had accomplished the feat at the outset of the decade. The league's first ten-year span would also bow out with the Boston Celtics holding claim to three titles in four tries, duplicating the very feat with which Minneapolis and Mikan had opened the pioneering league's early seasons.

Beginning with the spring of 1959, the Celtics were off and running to their unmatched string of eight consecutive league championships. That unrivalled string began in 1959 with an altogether easy sweep of the fading Minneapolis Lakers, who were only one season away from their history-making West Coast odyssey. It was punctuated by the victories over St. Louis in both 1960 and 1961—a sufficient measure of revenge for the stunning 1958 title upset in which Bob Pettit had singlehandedly benched the Boston championship machine while Russell sat in limbo with a wounded ankle. The next five seasons saw the "Celtics Express" roll on undaunted past the Lakers, who were now residents of Los Angeles, on four separate occasions, with only a single title-round appearance of Wilt Chamberlain and the San Francisco Warriors sandwiched in between. As these championship years peeled off the calendar one by one, the old Celtics cast of stars departed a single actor at a time. Sharman hung up his black high-top sneakers in 1961 and Cousy took his last dribbles in the NBA Finals of 1963. Ramsey and Loscutoff bowed out at the conclusion of the 1964 championship year; then Heinsohn also decided to retire his battle-weary body a season later. By the time the second half of the decade opened in the fall of 1965, only Auerbach on the bench and Russell in the pivot remained from the original championship club of Russell's rookie season.

But old heroes were relentlessly being replaced with new ones in Boston, and one year's thrills seemed little more than prelude to another's. In an age before television was a household staple and in a sport with comparatively few memorable single moments, one defensive sleight-of-hand by John Havlicek, for example, rates right up there in our sports annals alongside Red Grange's five-touchdown afternoon against Michigan or Babe Ruth's called shot in the 1932 World Series. The moment in question was ironically set upon the stage of one of the more classic Russell-Chamberlain battles, as Philadelphia and Boston entered the waning moments of a seventh and deciding game in the 1965 Eastern Division Finals. Chamberlain had poured in six vital points during the game's final two minutes and sliced a once-safe Boston lead to the narrowest of possible margins. There were but five seconds standing between Philadelphia and an end to Boston's six-year championship string. With the scoreboard reading 110–109 in favor of Boston, Russell had attempted an inbounds pass that had uncharacteristiscally gone astray against a basket support wire. Philadelphia now had the inbounds play and was poised for the clincher; one more Philly basket would mean that the Boston dynasty would at long last—at least temporarily—be at an end. It was at this moment that Havlicek's brilliant career seemed to crystalize into a single reflexive action, as the perpetually moving defender sliced in front of Philly's Chet Walker to steal away an inbounds pass. Hondo's superhuman play had sealed yet another miraculous Boston triumph, and thus clinched yet another Finals opportunity and claimed another Boston championship banner.

Hondo's last-second steal not only fixed the memory of his own career, but also cemented a reputation for the man who dramatically called the moment from the radio broadcast booth for New England's legions of diehard fans. Years of replay on highlight films and audio tapes have now immortalized the call of Celtics long-time announcer Johnny Most, whose raspy voice caught the raw emotion and sudden shock of the moment— "Havlicek stole the ball! Havlicek stole the ball!" Only Russ Hodges's equally dramatic call of Giant Bobby Thomson's 1951 playoff homer remains a more famous moment in the history of American sports broadcasting.

Havlicek's heroics would also allow the Celtics' string of uninterrupted titles to remain intact and stretch to an unprecedented seven straight, once Boston breezed past Los Angeles in a short and anticlimactic 1965 five-game finale. The inevitable fall of the proud and seemingly invincible Celtics would not come until two seasons later, when an aging Boston team was finally overrun by a fresh 1967 Philadelphia Sixers squad, which many still regard as the finest single-season unit of NBA history. The stage was thus set for the most memorable Celtics playoff series of any in the Auerbach-Russell era, the one marked by the amazing comeback of the 1968 season. The flawless Sixers had buried a fine Boston club in both the regular and post-seasons of 1967, and again, in the 1968 campaign, Philadelphia had cruised to regular-season victory with a comfortable eight-game margin over Boston in the season-long divisional race. And March of 1968 would also mark the first season in a decade that Boston did not enter the playoffs as the league's defending champion.

Serious questions were already being raised about Russell's coaching style and leadership effectiveness after the apparent Boston collapse in post-season play a year earlier. Russell did, in fact, seem a strange bench boss when compared to his legendary predecessor. The Boston big man had never been much of a practice player and seemed to possess even less intensity as a practice coach. But Bill Russell had always maintained a "second-season philosophy" concerning the playoffs, and once more his team was primed for a post-season rematch against Philly. The Sixers jumped to a 3–1 lead in the division title pairing (which had begun the day after the assassination of Dr. Martin Luther King) and looked as invincible as they had one winter earlier. But when Boston stormed back to force a seventh game, the momentum had clearly already reversed and the Sixers were now themselves reeling. Before a screaming final-game crowd in Philadelphia's Spectrum, Russell punctuated his head-to-head mastery over Chamberlain with a second half of play in which Wilt managed to attempt but two harmless shots. At the final buzzer Boston was on top by four—100 to 96—and Russell had his team back in the Finals once more. As was so often the case during the Russell-Chamberlain era, the final series with Los Angeles proved largely redundant, as the Lakers simply couldn't handle either an intense-if-aging Russell, or a hot-shooting Havlicek who averaged 25.9 ppg. for post-season play. When the dust had cleared Boston's Celtics now wore their tenth league crown in a span of but 12 short years.

When it comes to sheer drama, the 1969 playoffs which followed twelve months later provided perhaps the most inspired Celtics title series of the entire endless string of post-season derbies. Certainly this final '60s championship fling would remain the most rewarding of all for legions of Boston supporters. The time had finally come when no one in Boston or elsewhere around the NBA actually expected the Celtics to win any longer—Russell was now 35 (and had secretly decided at mid-year that this would be his swansong), Sam Jones was 36 and had announced upcoming retirement, Bailey Howell was 32, and Satch Sanders 30. At 28, Havlicek was the only starter who had not reached his fourth decade. A fourth-place regular-season finish (48–34) was the lowest for the club in 20 years. But Boston followers had long since come to realize that Russell-led teams played at a different level when championships were on the line. They knew, as did the players themselves, that age was no measure of Celtic pride and spirit.

With the post-season fully launched, Boston summoned a last reserve of individual and team strength to glide by Philadelphia in five games and then past the young yet talented New York Knicks in six. What loomed on the horizon, however, was a different matter altogether, a crack Lakers team with Elgin Baylor and Jerry West in the forecourt and which had now added Russell's old nemesis, Chamberlain, to anchor the frontcourt line.

But Russell always found a way to thwart the less defensively minded Wilt, and if Bill had not pushed his aging team during December and January, he certainly lit a fire under them in April. The key game was the fourth, and the decisive moment came when Sam Jones stole victory with a last-second basket that prevented a 3–1 Los Angeles series lead. Game seven was again a classic in which the old warriors from Boston were once more able to work championship magic against a younger and more talented team, while at the same time faced with a hostile enemy crowd. Chamberlain again proved of questionable character as he retired to the bench with a minor injury in the final quarter and saw no further action down the crucial final moments of the disappearing season. (Russell later criticized Wilt for removing himself from the game and the tension be-tween the two over the incident largely ruined their earlier off-court friendship.) Boston would barely hang on to a dwindling lead as the clock shrank and an off-balance jumper by reserve Don Nelson in the final seconds was barely enough to preserve the last and easily the most incredi-ble championship of the incomparable Bill Russell era.

The true extent of the Celtic mystique is perhaps best measured by the mythic status which the team of Russell, Cousy, Havlicek and Heinsohn has now acquired for later generations of NBA Fans. Since those halcyon days when Red Auerbach first acquired Bill Russell off the campus of San Francisco University, and overnight converted the struggling ballclub that Walter Brown had founded a decade earlier into a true titan of the neophyte NBA, the Celtics have remained the most successful and best-loved franchise in all of professional sports. Auerbach's teams have done far more than capture 16 world championship flags in the 43 seasons he has served as coach, general manager and finally franchise president. Boston's Celtics forever remain the benchmark by which the public conception of true dynasty teams will forevermore be measured. Michael Jordan, Kareem Abdul-Jabbar, and Magic Johnson aside, no one has ever again seen basketball—the total team game—as it was once played to perfection by the Boston Celtics of the Bill Russell era.

The Finkel-Havlicek Era

The Celtics were not completely dead after the departure of Bill Russell. It did certainly appear that way, of course, in the immediate wake of Russell's inevitable exit. But the collapse was brief enough, and in fact lasted only a single season.

Without Russell on the bench, and more importantly without the big man stacking the defensive odds their way on the court, the Boston team fell like a lead weight in '69–'70, crashing all the way to sixth spot in the Eastern Division standings, barely ahead of a perennially poor Detroit Pistons outfit. It was a rough beginning for new head coach Tom Heinsohn, whom Auerbach had lured away from a lucrative insurance business back in Worcester, Massachusetts. Heinsohn's inherited lineup of Tom "Satch" Sanders and Don Nelson up front, gentle seven footer "High Henry" Finkel at Russell's center slot, and Havlicek and Larry Siegfried at the guards, could muster only 34 victories. Boston fans who had yawned their way through a decade of taken-for-granted glory now turned their wrath largely on Finkel, a moderately talented giant who had the great misfortune (like millions of other folks around the land) of not being Bill Russell. The iron-fingered and lead-footed Finkel averaged only 9.7 ppg., but easily led the circuit in hometown booing and was cause for sarcastic jabs from the Boston press. Of course, the name didn't help much either, and it wasn't long before some scribes were callously writing about "The Finkel Era" that had now descended on Boston Garden.

But if Henry Finkel was an all-too-easy scapegoat, it was also true that there was now indeed sufficient reason for fan letdown at the Garden. It was Boston's first losing record in 20 years and also the first miss of the playoffs in the same span. And to make matters more embarrassing, the

Cincinnati team that finished a slot ahead of the now ramshackle Celtics was coached by Russell's and Heinsohn's old running mate, Bob Cousy.

The road back for Heinsohn and the Celtics was not much delayed in coming, however, and it began almost immediately with the '70–'71 and '71–'72 rebuilding seasons. In only Heinsohn's second campaign at the helm, the ballclub improved ten full games, climbed above .500, and finished third in the division. This turn-around had been in large part triggered when Auerbach unloaded Larry Siegfried, Bailey Howell and Emment Bryant and installed rookie Dave Cowens in the center slot, moved the versatile Havlicek up front with the improving Nelson, and went with a revamped backcourt featuring youngsters Don Chaney and Jo Jo White. Havlicek responded by upping his game a full notch to superstar status. The former stellar role player enjoyed his best offensive season (28.9 ppg., 2338 points, 730 rebounds—all career highs) and was the league's second best scorer behind Alcindor.

By Year Three of the Heinsohn régime, it hardly seemed that there had been any downturn at all. The 1972 campaign would next bring the first in a run of five straight regular-season first-place finishes. There was already no question that the apparent lull in Boston had been temporary and that the Celtics were back to their old tricks. Havlicek (27.5 ppg.) enjoyed another banner scoring year, this time finishing third behind the renamed Abdul-Jabbar in Milwaukee, and a new little-man sensation named Nate "Tiny" Archibald in Cincinnati. The new Boston lineup of Havlicek, Nelson, Cowens, Chaney and White was suddenly as potent as any in the entire league, although the bench of Sanders, Finkel, Steve Kuberski and others was perhaps too thin for any realistic title hopes. Boston did outdistance runner-up New York by eight games in the new Atlantic Division (the league had shifted to a four-division alignment a season earlier) and did survive one round of the playoffs before tumbling, in five games, to the more experienced Knicks team they had already outdistanced in regular-season combat.

But experience as well as raw talent would once again be residing up in Beantown. While Auerbach's old rivals, the Lakers, were celebrating their first-ever championship out on the west coast at the end of the '71–'72 season, Boston's proud Celtics were now themselves about to re-emerge with a true vengeance. It had been an all-too-short period of rebuilding—at least if you didn't live in or around Boston and rooted for any of the league's 16 other ballclubs.

Renewed Celtic glory was kindled as much as anything by the emerging stardom of undersized pivot-man Dave Cowens, now the league's premier rebounder and shot blocker as well as Boston's unrivalled floor leader. Cowens was a bigger (6–feet–8½ inches) version of Havlicek, who could run all day, outhustle as well as out-maneuver any other NBA center, and was a prized left-handed shooter to boot. With such reinforcements, the 1973 Boston team soared to a franchise-record 68 victories that still stands as the unsurpassed mark for regular-season winning in Boston. Cowens was the league's MVP and Havlicek had another brilliant season as well. But the biggest plus, perhaps, was the rebounding of forward Paul Silas, another Auerbach "steal" who had been obtained from Phoenix in compensation for the signing of original Boston draft choice Charlie Scott.

Yet for all their rapid improvement, the Celtics still couldn't quite handle the veteran New York Knicks contingent of Bill Bradley, Willis Reed, Dave DeBusschere, Earl Monroe and Walt Frazier in post-season action. Boston lost a second-round matchup in seven dramatic games. Perhaps the turning point this time, however, came only when Havlicek was felled by a shoulder injury during the see-saw third game of the series.

The first Boston title under Heinsohn, earned during the following 1974 season, didn't come all that easily either. Milwaukee, in its penultimate year with Alcindor (now known as Kareem Abdul-Jabbar), and its final year with Oscar Robertson (soon to retire), would muster enough brilliant offensive play to extend Heinsohn's men to a full seven final-round championship games. Boston had again climbed into the post-season by outdistancing New York to win the Atlantic Division. And in the Eastern Finals this time around it was the Knicks who were knocked out by injuries—to Willis Reed and Dave DeBusschere—assuring a quick, five-game Boston victory. Thus the title match-up between Boston, with Cowens and Havlicek, and Milwaukee, with Jabbar and Oscar, was precisely the one everyone had expected. And it proved a thrilling tug-of-war right down to the final contest.

Boston held a large advantage against Milwaukee from the start. The Bucks had lost one backcourt star when Lucius Allen was cancelled out by a knee injury, and were suffering at the other guard slot as well. "The Big O" was now at the end of his string and could not be counted on for much firepower in his fourteenth and final campaign. Victories were traded through the first six contests, with Milwaukee gamely forcing a rubber match by eking out a 102–101 double-overtime win in game six. In the finale, Cowens outdueled Jabbar 28–26, and the Celtics cruised 102–87 for NBA title number 12, after only a five-year temporary hiatus.

The Celtics of the seventies had been able to staff their yearly rosters with a whole new contingent of bright superstars. Havlicek was still in high gear for most of the decade, and gloried in his new team-leader and superstar roles. But a new hero figure had also arrived with peerless Dave Cowens. Cowens soon proved one of the greatest Celtics warriors of all— the franchise player of the '70s, and undoubtedly the best center in club history after the immortal Russell. It was soon clear, in fact, that a new Boston Celtics powerhouse had now been reconstructed by Auerbach (from his front-office perch) largely around the most mobile and unconventional center in league history. When Cowens arrived as an unheralded rookie off the campus of Florida State University in the fall of 1970, he immediately revolutionized inside play by moving the conventional pivot position a full 20 feet from the basket. This strategy soon proved infallible as Cowens utilized his rugged style of play to transform the Celtics from a dull and lifeless outfit into the fast-breaking thoroughbred of old, a team suddenly capable of seizing two more championships (1974 and 1976) before the decade of the 1970s rolled into its second half.

And there were other heroes as well. Don Nelson was a mainstay early in the decade and perhaps one of Auerbach's greatest bargains. The future highly successful NBA coach was picked up off waivers (at Tom Heinsohn's suggestion) in 1965 and logged 11 seasons as a steady double-figure scorer and deadly jump-shot artist. Nelson's most outstanding individual campaign was his penultimate year of '74–'75, when he paced the league in field goal percentage at the advanced age of 34, and also proved one of the circuit's most valued sixth-man performers as backup to Havlicek and Silas. High-scoring Charlie Scott (whose 34.6 ppg. ABA mark in 1972 was the highest ever for a guard until Michael Jordan came along) enjoyed three fine Boston years at mid-career, joining the Celtics just in time to contribute heavily to the 1976 championship ballclub. Originally drafted by Auerbach in 1970, Scott opted to star in the ABA; but Boston cleverly traded NBA rights to the North Carolina whirlwind to Phoenix for Paul Silas, then re-acquired Scott for Paul Westphal in May of 1975. Paul Silas himself was a main man in the middle part of the decade, and teamed with Cowens on the 1976 championship club to provide Boston with two of the league's top four rebounders. And finally there was Jo Jo White, a stellar guard out of the University of Kansas who continued the lineage of Cousy and Sam Jones when he manned the controls of the Celts' fast-breaking offensive throughout the entire decade of the '70s. White was a fine defender, pumped in better than 14,000 career points with his patented in-front-of-the-face jumper, and averaged better than 20 ppg. six different times in post-season play. Next to Cowens, Jo Jo White was unquestionably the "glory player" of the Celtics decade between Russell and Bird.

During this period, Tom Heinsohn also carved out a new spot for himself in Celtics history. One of the clubs most successful players now became one of its mastermind coaches. In his eight-plus years on the bench, Heinsohn compiled the second most victories in club history (427), the fifth highest winning percentage (.619), and the third highest total of post-season victories (47) as well. If Heinsohn stands in the top six among all-time Boston playing greats (alongside Russell, Cousy, Bird, Cowens and Havlicek), he certainly rates that distinction among the legendary Boston coaches as well.

Legendary Celtics Coaches (Ranked by Total Victories with Boston)

Name (Years)	Regular Season	Post-Season	Championships
Red Auerbach	795–397 (.667)	90–58 (.608)	9 ('57, '59–'65)
Tom Heinsohn	**427–263 (.619)**	**37–33 (.588)**	**2 (1974, 1976**
K. C. Jones	308–102 (.751)	65–37 (.637)	2 (1984, 1986)
Bill Fitch	242–86 (.738)	26–19 (.578)	1 (1981)
Chris Ford	187–141 (.570)	12–13 (.480)	0
Bill Russell	162–82 (.661)	28–18 (.609)	2 (1968, 1969)

The peak of the 1970s, however, came with the 1975–76 Boston campaign. Regular-season action would find Heinsohn's men posting only 54 victories, something of a slide after the 60-win campaigns of 1973 and 1975, yet still a good enough mark to stand second best overall (Golden State won 59 in the Pacific Division) and to outpace Atlantic Division runners-up Buffalo and Philadelphia by a comfortable 8 games. Boston's backcourt had now taken on a new look as Don Chaney jumped to the ABA, and Auerbach adjusted to this loss by trading Paul Westphal to Phoenix for Charlie Scott. The bench (Nelson, Kevin Stacom, Glenn McDonald, Steve Kuberski, Jim Ard) was now dangerously thin, but the front line was still solid and balanced as Havlicek, Cowens, Scott and White all averaged between 17 and 19 ppg., and Cowens and Silas both cracked the 1,000 rebound plateau.

But if this seemed like just another run-of-the-mill Boston title outfit, there would be nothing at all commonplace about the post-season shootout with Phoenix which soon followed. The Boston-Phoenix Finals would, in fact, be highlighted by one of the greatest individual games in NBA annals. This would be the pivotal fifth game, staged in Boston Garden on June 4th, with fan interest at an all-time high and the two contenders locked up at two games apiece. What transpired was later to be known among hoopologists far and wide as "The Fabulous Fifth"—one of the only two triple-overtime NBA Finals slugfests ever witnessed. It was truly an epic battle of determination and endurance, laced with plenty of raw luck. Fortunately for the Celtics faithful, most of that luck was good for Boston and not quite so good for Phoenix.

It was a game that had something memorable for fans of all tastes— heroic game-saving shots, expected and unexpected last-second heroes, and a near breakdown of law and order to boot. There was also the delightful story line of the rugged, roughhouse, heavily-favored "Goliath" in the form of the Celtics and the slick-shooting and determined underdog "David" in the guise of the Suns. Boston roared to a big 22–point first quarter lead and then faded slightly, yet managed to hold onto a 16-point half-time spread. The pesky Suns cut the margin to 68–64 late in the third quarter and rallied furiously down the stretch behind ex-Celtic Westphal. A foul shot by Havlicek knotted the contest with only seconds remaining, and both teams (Havlicek and Sun's forward Gar Heard) missed final shots to force the first overtime. Curtis Perry then canned four points in the waning seconds to force a second overtime period after Boston again seemed to have a save lead within the final minute of play. Action reached a frenzied peak in the second extra session as Dick Van Arsdale's only score of the night and another bucket by Perry gave the visitors a 110–109 edge with but five seconds remaining. Havlicek (playing with a broken bone in his foot) upped tensions a notch higher, however, by canning an off-balanced jumper for the apparent dramatic game-winner.

But it was not quite over yet. Referee Richie Powers was able to quell the jubilant Boston victory celebration with the news that two seconds remained on the scoreboard clock. But not before near-riot conditions had enveloped the Garden and police had to storm the playing floor to restore order among unruly fans. With play resumed, Suns' coach John MacLeod took advantage of a rules technicality and called a time out which his ballclub no longer had. Jo Jo White's resulting technical foul shot gave Boston a two-point margin, but the ploy also allowed Phoenix a mid-court inbounds pass to Heard, which he promptly sank to force the third extra session. Cowens and Silas had now fouled out for Boston and it was time—in finest Celtics tradition—for the unheralded role players to step forward into their unaccustomed heroes' robes. Jim Ard assumed the center slot and hit 3 of 6 baskets, and both his foul shots, under extreme pressure. And little-used forward-guard Glenn McDonald enjoyed 64 seconds of lasting glory with three key baskets and two clutch free throws of his own. The Suns stormed back one last time with two final clutch baskets by Westphal, but these were split by the two charity tosses of Jim Ard. Ard's tosses represented the final margin (128–126) in one of basketball's most draining games. Two days later, Boston also captured the most anti-climactic finale in NBA championship history, an 87–80 victory in Phoenix. Boston's lucky thirteenth NBA world championship had certainly been one of the hardest earned, and perhaps also the one that turned more on a few lucky bounces than any other.

Just as the Boston club stumbled at the end of the '60s, so would it stumble again at the very end of the '70s (and ironically at the end of the '80s as well). The first decline had coincided with the career swansong of player-coach Bill Russell. The second came when Havlicek and Cowens faded from the scene. John Havlicek would take his final curtain call on the longest and most productive playing career in proud Celtics history during the 1977–'78 campaign (which was also, ironically, Heinsohn's last as a coach). Cowens would perform in Boston Garden for two additional seasons after Havlicek's retirement, then spend one final year in Milwaukee after being traded away for guard Quinn Buckner. A third such collapse would of course come a full decade later, with the demise of Larry Bird.

Two final seasons of the '70s thus witnessed the Celtics once again hit rock bottom with a trip into the league's lower rungs, a place they had not known very often during the first three decades of club history. While Havlicek's and Heinsohn's final campaign saw the team slide no further than third in the Atlantic Division, a ledger 18-games under .500 was the worst Boston finish since the inaugural year of NBA play back in 1950. A year later, the team now coach by Tom Sanders (Heinsohn's replacement 35 games into the 1977–'78 season) logged three victories less and tumbled all the way into the divisional cellar. It was clearly time for another rebuilding campaign, and for Red Auerbach to pull another miracle rabbit (or perhaps this time a Bird) out of his seemingly ceaseless bag of tricks.

The Bird Era

Great teams in any sport seem to find an endless flow of renewed heroes, like the Yankees with Ruth, and Gehrig, and DiMaggio, and Mickey Mantle, each passing the cloak of honor on to the next legend standing in line, an endless inheritance of immortals spread over three and perhaps more decades. For the Celtics, the fifties celebrated Cousy, the sixties Russell, and the seventies Havlicek. And on the horizon in the 1980s was perhaps the brightest one-man team of all—number ''33,'' Larry Joe Bird.

When Larry Bird entered the NBA in the fall of 1979, on the heels of one of the worst Boston seasons ever, he was about to rescue far more than a single once-noble franchise. The league itself had fallen on exceedingly slow times. Dr. J had receded from his prime; Jabbar was piling up milestones, but was too placid a performer to inspire fan passions; David Thompson had flamed out early on his promise to be Jordan before Jordan; Kevin Porter and John Lucas were the premier backcourt aces, but had painfully little of the trappings of legend about them. NBA basketball needed new heroes, and it needed a large dose of new drama as well. Bird would be largely responsible (along with an old collegiate rival now operating out west) for providing the quick fix that basketball sorely needed. And it would be a role he would willingly share. For Larry Bird would always be linked in basketball history with his greatest rival—Earvin ''Magic'' Johnson of the Los Angeles Lakers.

The salvation of the sagging league would be a glamorous rivalry of two new superstars who could now replay, and even upgrade, the earlier tussles of Russell and Chamberlain. The scenario would now be quite different, of course, as the nature and style of the professional game had drastically altered. Russell and Chamberlain were the latter-day towering giants who epitomized a stationary game of shot blocking and board sweeping. Magic and Bird were the mobile shooting and playmaking wizards who captured the flare of the true transition game. And, of course, no small part of the rivalry would be due to the magic of television itself. TV provided a proper forum for the fast-paced and colorful entertainment spectacle of one-on-one fullcourt play. And now the NBA finally possessed precisely the action-packed spectacle that was right for the times.

Larry and Magic brought to the NBA stage and screen a heated rivalry already well established for a hungry audience of college hoops fans. They had both starred for two seasons in the midwestern hotbed of collegiate hoops. Bird had led an unheralded small school to sudden national prominence, while Johnson had shone as a sophomore and paced Michigan State to a rare Big Ten title. And soon the two were on a collision course which took them to one of the most storied Final Four meetings in NCAA history. That game was a vintage head-to-head battle in which Magic had captured round one in storybook fashion: the Spartans cruised to an NCAA title

75–64, and Magic won the individual duel, plus tourney MVP honors, while racking up 31 points.

Both had also entered the NBA under most surprising circumstances at the conclusion of stellar (and in Magic's case, abbreviated) college careers. Bird would be claimed by the Celtics on draft day of 1978, a full season before his collegiate career was over (which would be when his original college class was due to graduate). And Johnson would opt for the NBA as a "hardship case" the same season as Bird would now debut, even though he still had two years of university eligibility remaining.

It was the sort of glamor that seemed to be so long missing from the NBA venues. Clearly there was a lack of the kind of recognizable super-stars that had filled the Celtics epoch of the 1960s, and the "big man" era at the outset of the 1970s. Jabbar was still around, though the rookie luster of Lew Alcindor in Milwaukee had seemed to fade into the methodi-cal veteran efficiency of a West Coast Kareem. George Gervin had now been the league's scoring leader for three seasons, but lacked anything approaching pizzazz or personality. Kids could hardly be expected to take to the alleys and schoolyards aping every move of a colorless player like "Iceman" Gervin. Phoenix forward Truck Robinson had recently captured the league rebounding title. Detroit guard Kevin Porter was the current NBA pacesetter in assists. These were hardly household names either. Bird and Magic brought sorely needed charisma back into the league. Larry Bird displayed the freewheeling flash and flair associated with the street game of urban New York playgrounds, and not the rural Indiana game of the heartlands that had spawned him. And Magic was the most infectious personality ever to hit big-time professional sports.

Bird's arrival in Boston could not help but remind the veteran NBA watcher of Russell's fateful journey into Boston a quarter-century earlier— unprecedented rookie, revived veteran lineup, sudden title surge. The mas-termind was again Auerbach, of course. The Redhead had now more than once manipulated the draft to his advantage to find a franchise player. Magic Johnson would perhaps draw first blood in the new rivalry and win the first team title of the new decade. But Larry Bird would enjoy a bit of magic of his own during a phenomenal rookie season (21.3 ppg., 1745 points, 10.4 rpg., 143 steals, 4.5 apg.). And it would be Bird who would salvage some measure of pride in Boston with coveted Rookie-of-the-Year honors.

The Celtics, for their own part, enjoyed a marvelous resurrection during Bird's rookie campaign. In this year dedicated to revival, it was the Celtics who made the greatest individual turnaround. Embarrassing victory totals of 32 and 29 during two previous campaigns were dramatically supplanted with a league-best 61 in the win column. Veteran guard Nate "Tiny" Archibald, in his second Boston season, was a catalyst as he bounced back with a surprising shooting display (14.1 ppg.) and stellar play as a veteran floor general. Dave Cowens confounded the experts by proving there was still spark and power left in his rugged inside game. Cedric "Cornbread"

Maxwell was a huge offensive force (16.9 ppg.) in the frontcourt, this time with plenty of assistance from the rookie phenom Bird. First-year coach Bill Fitch provided glue to hold it all together as he molded his charges into a winning unit around Bird and the squad of aging veterans. Few were surprised by the choice of Bill Fitch as NBA Coach of the Year. And fewer still could debate Bird's selection as the circuit's stellar rookie.

The message had been sent in 1980 that the Celtics were now back in business. And by the time Bird's sophomore campaign was underway it was clear everywhere in the NBA just how far the team had actually come. The second season of the Bird-Magic era would see the balance shift from Los Angeles to Boston. The key to the Celtics' immediate future had begun on draft day when Auerbach engineered a blockbuster maneuver similar to the one that had earlier brought Bird himself to Boston. First the Celtics sent veteran Bob McAdoo to Detroit for a top first-round pick. The prime draft slot was then peddled to Golden State (who would use it to acquire Purdue seven-footer Joe Barry Carroll) in exchange for established workhorse big man Robert Parish, and another first-round selection who was pencilled in as Minnesota All-American forward Kevin McHale. The front-line pieces were now suddenly in place, ready to be installed around Bird. What had been an excellent team was suddenly a nearly invincible one.

Bird established his future penchant for post-season heroics during the 1981 semi-final rematch with the resurgent Philadelphia Sixers. It was Philadelphia with the ageless Julius Erving that had prevented a Bird-Magic rookie title shootout a season earlier, by thumping Boston in five during the Eastern Conference Finals. Boston would this time scrap back all the way from a seemingly hopeless 3–1 deficit to capture the dramatic series on a last-minute jumper by none other than icewater-veined Larry Joe Bird. After the Philadelphia series laced with Bird's last-second heroics, a championship round with Houston's Rockets was predictably anticlimactic. Bird himself was slowed by a clever and relentless Houston defense anchored by Robert Reid. But Cornbread Maxwell was suddenly white hot at just the right time, and Boston found little enough resistance from an enthusiastic but overmatched Houston team, one that had actually finished under .500 during regular-season play. Bird was still testing the league waters when Boston now had a 14th world title banner already hanging from the rafters of the ancient Boston Garden.

The Celtics and Lakers would continue to own the league for much of the remainder of the decade. The Lakers would enjoy four more titles; Boston would claim another two. Three times they would meet head-to-head in the title round. Through it all, Bird and Magic would time and again renew their battles for supremacy. In the end, Larry Bird would lug away the bulk of the personal honors, at least if one looked at career stats alone. Bird would never win an individual NBA scoring title, yet would consistently rank high among the best point producers. Magic would dominate in the assists category and show great strength of overall play. And they each walked off with three league MVP trophies.

Bird, of course, was not the whole show in Boston in the eighties. Auerbach had constructed another juggernaut from his front office perch, and despite the presence of a budding superstar, this was again a balanced team shaped in the true Celtics mold. McHale continued the great Boston sixth-man tradition of Ramsey and Havlicek before him. Parish was the quintessential team-oriented center, perhaps the best in the league since Cowens. The backcourt was also more than adequate. Dennis Johnson was a championship caliber competitor who had already proved his winning ways in both Seattle and Phoenix. Jerry Sichting and Danny Ainge provided spark and ballhandling under fire. And Bill Walton and M.L. Carr, among others, stepped in as the kind of role players that Loscutoff and Gene Conley and Don Nelson had long ago been.

And on the coaching lines, Auerbach had again followed the formula that had already served him so well in the past. As with Russell, and then Heinsohn, he had again found a bench boss among the stars of his great dynasty team of the '60s. K. C. Jones was now at the Boston helm and he proved a most adequate leader fashioned precisely in the Auerbach image.

The three seasons of 1983–'86 were among the greatest in ballclub history. Three straight winters the team held the best regular-season league won-loss mark. And all three years the win totals (62, 63, 67) equalled or surpassed the best ledger of the '60s Russell era (62—18 in 1965). The true highlight year of the Bird-Magic rivalry, however—at least from the Boston perspective—had to be the campaign of 1983–'84. Bird led the club from wire to wire as rookie coach K. C. Jones enjoyed the best record in the league, a ten-game spread over Eastern runner-up Philadelphia, and convincing victories over Washington, New York, and Milwaukee in the first three post-season rounds.

The 1984 NBA Finals offered a showcase Bird-Magic faceoff, the first long-anticipated matchup of the two rival stars during an NBA finale. Bird and Magic were now in their fifth season in the league and had yet to re-enact their 1979 NCAA duel in front of the nation's TV cameras. Boston had first stumbled against Philly in 1980, blocking the hoped-for celebrity shootout. The following year the Lakers had stumbled out of the gate in the playoff's opening round, and then in 1982, Boston and Bird had again been shot down by Erving and the Sixers in the Eastern Finals. But when it finally did become a reality in 1984, the long-anticipated Boston and Los Angeles championship matchup was a true TV bonanza.

This was not only a personal title rematch of Bird and Johnson, but also the first championship rematch of Boston and LA since the storied days of Bill Russell, a decade and a half earlier. The Lakers won easily in the first and third games, but somehow let both the second and fourth contests gets away from them in overtime. Boston then edged ahead 121–103 in game five, only to have Los Angeles once more reverse the momentum by an almost identical 119–108 count in game six. The deciding battle would provide the setting for a record television audience, as well as for yet another testing ground on which Boston could demonstrate its four-decade rubber match superiority against all comers. This time it was again Boston, 111–102, as the Celtics once more protected their miraculous string of never having lost the seventh game of a title series. Bird finally enjoyed his revenge over Magic—and a championship ring and playoff MVP trophy to boot. In Boston it now all seemed to have been well worth the lengthy wait.

For the next three straight seasons, Bird would lead the ballclub back to the championship round each and every year. First there would be a rematch loss to the Lakers. Then another title earned against Houston. And finally another defeat at the hands of Los Angeles. In the end it was a run almost as glorious as the one once made by Cousy, Russell, Heinsohn, and company.

The 1985 playoff season provided pro hoop fans with the richest of fare—another Boston and Los Angeles classic grudge match. Both juggernauts had cruised to easy defense of their conference titles in divisional playoffs. The Celtics looked unbeatable yet again as they crushed the Lakers 148–114 in historic Boston Garden in the championship series opener. Dating back to Minneapolis days, Laker teams had now faced Boston's green and white for the NBA title eight times, and after each and every encounter yet another banner flew proudly from the rafters of venerable Boston Garden. It looked in the face of the one-sided opener that there was little reason to expect anything different this ninth time around. But a feisty Los Angeles squad soon fought back to carry a three-games-to-two lead back into Boston for the final two deciding contests. Like so many of the championship showdowns between these two proud teams in the past, this one again would hinge upon key injury, as well as an unexpected heroic performance by a wily overlooked veteran.

It was Bird who would go down with an injury this time around, as elbow and finger inflammations would hamper Larry's shooting throughout the round-robin week. And it was Jabbar who would suddenly rise to the occasion with an unanticipated 29 points (backed by James Worthy's 28) in the deciding game six. Magic Johnson again played no small role, with a triple-double in the title-clinching match—14 points, 14 assists, 10 rebounds. At the final buzzer the score stood at Los Angeles 111, Boston 100, and the years of Laker frustration were finally relegated to history. Incredible as it may seem, Los Angeles had become the first team in 16 tries to cop an NBA title against the Celtics while playing on the Celt's charmed parquet floor in ghost-ridden Boston Garden.

The Celtics would bounce back in '85–'86, but not before a serious scare early in the campaign. A back injury would slow Bird in the early going, and although he didn't miss any games the pain reduced his overall effectiveness and seemed to lower his stature from titan to a mere league all-star. Chiropractic treatments were enough to correct the problem in mid-season, however, and a rejuvenated Bird now roared to his third straight season's MVP. The club's 67 victories were also the second best of franchise history.

The toughest post-season challenge for Bird and his mates came in the opening-round matchup with Jordan and the Chicago Bulls. Returning from his own season of knockout injuries (a broken foot which cancelled all but 18 of his games), Air Jordan nearly stole the show with stellar offensive performances of 49 points and then 63 points (an NBA record) during the opening two contests. But Jordan alone was not enough against the veteran Boston club to prevent a three-game Celtics sweep. The Hawks and Bucks also fell easily, and the Celts again entered the NBA Finals against the surprising Houston Rockets (upset winners over the Lakers out West) riding the crest of an 11–1 post-season roll. The roll only continued when the outmanned Rockets fell in a series best remembered for a fifth-game free-for-all featuring towering center Ralph Sampson and Boston's pugnacious Danny Ainge. The 1986 NBA title flight would be Bird's last great moment as a champion, and Larry took full advantage. With a 25.9 post-season scoring onslaught Bird added yet another post-season MVP trophy to his personal stash. And the combined regular and post-season victory total of 82 games now owned by Boston was the highest total in all of NBA history.

The see-saw alternation between NBA titles and bridesmaid losses in the NBA Finals soon continued for a fourth straight year. Again it would be a Magic-Bird and Lakers-Celtics confrontation, the third of the decade. But this time the cards were too heavily stacked against the Beantowners from the outset. McHale was playing on a broken foot, while Parish was reduced to limited effectiveness by a severely sprained ankle. The Lakers ran away from the Celts in each of the first two games, as might have been expected with Boston's lineup so hobbled. Boston would gamely rebound to take two of three on the home floor. But a dramatic last-second game-winning mini-hook by Magic Johnson in game four would prove pivotal. The 1987 Finals provided in the end a last thunderous triumph of sorts for Boston, although perhaps no one would have predicted it at the time. Bird poured in a sparkling 27 points per post-season contest, but couldn't match Johnson for last-minute heroics or overall MVP effectiveness. When the crowd roars had finally died away, the Bird-Magic playoff sideshow had played its last act with Johnson now holding a lasting 2–1 advantage.

Bird would enjoy one more glorious campaign in 1987–'88, and thus appear to be still operating at the very top of his matchless game. Larry would pace the ballclub in scoring for a record ninth straight time, finish third in the league's scoring race, and post his career-high point total. It was enough for Boston to run away with an Atlantic Division title also, the fifth straight (and last under coach K. C. Jones) in a division where no one else broke .500 or stood within 19 games of Bird and company. But in the playoffs the Celts would nonetheless be toppled by Detroit in a six-game Eastern Conference Final. Actually Boston had been lucky to get out of the second round, where only a 20–point fourth quarter rampage by Bird saved a seventh-game showdown with Atlanta. And it all proved to be something of a prophetic final hurrah for both Bird and his Celtic mates. Larry would be struck down by repeated nagging injuries over the course of the next several seasons. Bone spurs in his foot ended Bird's subsequent 1989 campaign after only six games, and Boston slipped to third place and a quick first-round playoff exit (0–3 against eventual champion Detroit) when forced to play without their star forward.

Bird was restored to health for 1990, and again paced the ballclub with a standard Bird season (24.3 ppg., 9.5 rpg., 7.5 apg.). But now another loss hit hard as last year's rookie star Brian Shaw opted (along with Cleveland's Danny Ferry) to escape the NBA for a more lucrative European contract and professional play in Italy. Kevin McHale took up some slack with an excellent year as a stellar sixth-man performer, and second-year coach Jimmy Rodgers guided his forces to a close, second-place finish behind Philadelphia. But age was now becoming a factor as Bird, McHale and Parish all showed considerable wear and tear from their combined 35 winters on the circuit. Again there was a first-round playoff elimination, this time at the hands of New York in five games. Age and physical pain had especially overtaken Bird, a victim of continued bone spur problems, and the '90–'91 season would be his last at anything like full strength. Again Bird paced the team in scoring, and again the Celtics were back atop the Atlantic Division. But a year later Larry Joe Bird was finally done and retirement had seemed to come all too early to one of the game's greatest modern-era superstars.

With Bird gone, and McHale and Parish in the twilight of their own careers, it was not surprising that Boston would again take their predictable end-of-the-decade tumble. This time, however, it would be one of the quickest and deepest falls of all, the kind of collapse that was regular fare in other NBA cities but which Boston fans had almost no clue how to handle. First there would be two more seasons near the top of the Atlantic Division under new coach Chris Ford; and Reggie Lewis would inherit at least a fraction of Bird's stardom as the ballclub's new top scorer and "main man" on offense. But Boston no longer had the firepower to make much noise in post-season play. The 1992 season did bring a lengthy visit to the second round of playoff festivities and a disappointing seventh-game drubbing in the Conference semi-finals by Cleveland. But in 1993 Boston was again quickly and rudely dumped, this time by an expansion team from Charlotte in the opening set of post-season games.

The 1993–'94 season was one of the worst in Boston history. The element of personal tragedy that seem to latch onto the team in the eighties and nineties now struck again with the unexpected death of team captain Reggie Lewis. Lewis had collapsed on the court during the 1993 post-season series with Charlotte, and had been diagnosed with possible heart problems. Then, during a private shooting workout in July, Lewis suffered a fatal heart attack at age 27. The team would dedicate the 1993–'94 season to their fallen comrade, but such a gesture did little to revive sagging ball club fortunes. There would even be a new club record for consecutive home-court defeats. By the end of a dismal campaign, Chris Ford's Celtics were buried in fifth place with an embarrassing 32–50 mark, the fewest wins, lowest standing and first post-season absence since a nearly identical season in 1978–'79. It was, in fact, the first time Boston had sunk below 3rd (there had actually been only one finish below 2nd) in the Atlantic Division in fifteen years. And to put a definitive end to a glorious era, ancient center Robert Parish was not resigned at the close of season's play. (Parish would quickly ink a hefty contract with Charlotte's Hornets for an 18th, and perhaps final campaign.) The only bright spot was a late summer signing of aging superstar Dominique Wilkins to lead a '94–'95 rebuilding campaign.

It would once again be a long climb back. Yet however deep the Boston club might now occasionally stumble, any Boston Celtics fan (and no fans of the hoop sport are more numerous or fanatic, or found in more distant corners of the globe) didn't have to search far for consolations. There were all those championship banners on view in Boston Garden each night. There was the venerable Garden itself—basketball's most hallowed shrine, and still going strong as the only original NBA arena of the 1950s. And there was the uniform itself, and its constant reminder of basketball's noblest tradition. That green and white jersey with the block-lettered ''Celtics'' on the front had remained the same since the primitive days of the league nearly a half-century ago; it was a rare mark of stability in a sport of almost constant chance. The only problem now was a growing concern that if any more numbers were retired, there would hardly be enough numerals left to outfit those expected great Boston teams of the near future.

Suggested Readings on Boston Celtics

Like the Brooklyn Dodgers of baseball, the Boston Celtics are basketball's most literary team, and dozens of books have chronicled the history of the club and the basketball lives of its many legendary players. The fifteen selections below are among the essential volumes for any Boston Celtics fan library.

Auerbach, Red (with Joe Fitzgerald). **Red Auerbach: An Autobiography**. New York: G. P. Putnam's Sons, 1977.

Clary, Jack. **Basketball's Great Dynasties: The Celtics**. New York: Smithmark (W.H. Smith), 1992.

Cousy, Bob (and Bob Ryan). **Cousy on the Celtic Mystique**. New York: McGraw-Hill Publishers, 1988.

Cousy, Bob (as told to Al Hirshberg). **Basketball is My Life**. Englewood Cliffs, New Jersey: Prentice-Hall Publishers, 1957.

Devaney, John. **Bob Cousy**. New York: G.P. Putnam's Sons, 1965. (Juvenile)

Greenfield, Jeff. **The World's Greatest Team—A Portrait of the Boston Celtics, 1957–69**. New York: Random House, 1976.

Havlicek, John (and Bob Ryan). **Hondo: Celtic Man in Motion**. Englewood Cliffs, New Jersey: Prentice-Hall Publishers, 1977.

Hirshberg, Al. **Bill Russell of the Boston Celtics**. New York: Julian Messner, 1963. (Juvenile)

Levine, Lee Daniel. **Bird: The Making of an American Sports Legend**. New York: McGraw-Hill Publishers, 1988.

May, Peter. **The Big Three: The Best Frontcourt in the History of Basketball**. New York and London: Simon and Schuster, 1994.

McCallum, Jack. **Unfinished Business—On and Off the Court with the 1990–91 Boston Celtics**. New York: Summit Books (Simon and Schuster), 1992.

Powers, John. **The Short Season—A Boston Celtics Diary, 1977–1978**. New York: Harper and Row, 1979.

Russell, Bill (as told to William McSweeny). **Go Up for Glory**. New York: Coward-McCann Publishers, 1966.

Ryan, Bob. **The Boston Celtics—The History, Legends, and Images of America's Most Celebrated Team**. Reading, Massachusetts: Addison-Wesley Publishers, 1989.

Shaughnessy, Dan. **Ever Green, The Boston Celtics—A History in the Words of Their Players, Coaches, Fans and Foes, from 1946 to the Present**. New York: St. Martin's Press, 1990.

Boston Celtics Retired Uniform Numbers (20)

Walter Brown (1, Owner)	Jim Loscutoff (18)
Red Auerbach (2, Coach)	Don Nelson (19)
Dennis Johnson (3)	Bill Sharman (21)
Bill Russell (6)	Ed Macauley (22)
Jo Jo White (10)	Frank Ramsey (23)
Bob Cousy (14)	Sam Jones (24)
Tom Heinsohn (15)	K. C. Jones (25)
Tom "Satch" Sanders (16)	Kevin McHale (32)
John Havlicek (17)	Larry Bird (33)
Dave Cowens (18)	Reggie Lewis (35)

Year-by-Year Boston Celtics Summary

Season	Record	Finish	Coach(es)	Scoring Leader(s)	Playoffs (W-L Record)

Key: * =Tied for Position

Basketball Association of America

Season	Record	Finish	Coach(es)	Scoring Leader(s)	Playoffs (W-L Record)
1946–47	22–38	5th*	John Russell	Connie Simmons (10.3)	Did Not Qualify
1947–48	20–28	3rd	John Russell	Ed Sadowski (19.4)	Lost in 1st Round (1–2)
1948–49	25–35	5th	Alvin Julian	George Kaftan (14.5)	Did Not Qualify

National Basketball Association

Season	Record	Finish	Coach(es)	Scoring Leader(s)	Playoffs (W-L Record)
1949–50	22–46	6th	Alvin Julian	Bob Kinney (11.1)	Did Not Qualify
1950–51	39–30	2nd	Red Auerbach	Ed Macauley (20.4)	Lost in 1st Round (0–2)
1951–52	39–27	2nd	Red Auerbach	Bob Cousy (21.7)	Lost in 1st Round (1–2)
1952–53	46–25	3rd	Red Auerbach	Bob Cousy (19.8)	Lost in 2nd Round (3–3)
1953–54	42–30	2nd	Red Auerbach	Bob Cousy (19.2)	Lost in 2nd Round (2–4)
1954–55	36–36	3rd	Red Auerbach	Bob Cousy (21.1)	Lost in 2nd Round (3–4)
1955–56	39–33	2nd	Red Auerbach	Bill Sharman (19.9)	Lost in 1st Round (1–2)
1956–57	44–28	1st	Red Auerbach	Bill Sharman (21.1)	**NBA Champion** (7–3)
1957–58	49–23	1st	Red Auerbach	Bill Sharman (22.3)	Lost in NBA Finals (6–5)
1958–59	52–20	1st	Red Auerbach	Bill Sharman (20.4)	**NBA Champion** (8–3)
1959–60	59–16	1st	Red Auerbach	Tom Heinsohn (21.7)	**NBA Champion** (8–5)
1960–61	57–22	1st	Red Auerbach	Tom Heinsohn (21.3)	**NBA Champion** (8–2)
1961–62	60–20	1st	Red Auerbach	Tom Heinsohn (22.1)	**NBA Champion** (8–6)
1962–63	58–22	1st	Red Auerbach	Sam Jones (19.7)	**NBA Champion** (8–5)
1963–64	59–21	1st	Red Auerbach	John Havlicek (19.9)	**NBA Champion** (8–2)
1964–65	62–18	1st	Red Auerbach	Sam Jones (25.9)	**NBA Champion** (8–4)
1965–66	54–26	2nd	Red Auerbach	Sam Jones (23.5)	**NBA Champion** (8–4)
1966–67	60–21	2nd	Bill Russell	John Havlicek (21.4)	Lost in 2nd Round (4–5)
1967–68	54–28	2nd	Bill Russell	Sam Jones (21.3)	**NBA Champion** (12–7)
1968–69	48–34	4th	Bill Russell	John Havlicek (21.6)	**NBA Champion** (12–6)
1969–70	34–48	6th	Tom Heinsohn	John Havlicek (24.2)	Did Not Qualify
1970–71	44–38	3rd	Tom Heinsohn	John Havlicek (28.9)	Did Not Qualify
1971–72	56–26	1st	Tom Heinsohn	John Havlicek (27.5)	Lost in 2nd Round (5–6)
1972–73	68–14	1st	Tom Heinsohn	John Havlicek (23.8)	Lost in 2nd Round (7–6)
1973–74	56–26	1st	Tom Heinsohn	John Havlicek (22.6)	**NBA Champion** (12–6)
1974–75	60–22	1st	Tom Heinsohn	Dave Cowens (20.4)	Lost in 3rd Round (6–5)
1975–76	54–28	1st	Tom Heinsohn	Dave Cowens (19.0)	**NBA Champion** (12–6)
1976–77	44–38	2nd	Tom Heinsohn	Jo Jo White (19.6)	Lost in 2nd Round (5–4)
1977–78	32–50	3rd	Tom Heinsohn Tom Sanders	Dave Cowens (18.6)	Did Not Qualify
1978–79	29–53	5th	Tom Sanders Dave Cowens	Bob McAdoo (24.8)	Did Not Qualify
1979–80	61–21	1st	Bill Fitch	Larry Bird (21.3)	Lost in 3rd Round (5–4)
1980–81	62–20	1st	Bill Fitch	Larry Bird (21.2)	**NBA Champion** (12–5)
1981–82	63–19	1st	Bill Fitch	Larry Bird (22.9)	Lost in 3rd Round (7–5)
1982–83	56–26	2nd	Bill Fitch	Larry Bird (23.6)	Lost in 2nd Round (2–5)
1983–84	62–20	1st	K. C. Jones	Larry Bird (24.2)	**NBA Champion** (15–8)
1984–85	63–19	1st	K. C. Jones	Larry Bird (28.7)	Lost in NBA Finals (13–6)
1985–86	67–15	1st	K. C. Jones	Larry Bird (25.8)	**NBA Champion** (15–3)
1986–87	59–23	1st	K. C. Jones	Larry Bird (28.1)	Lost in NBA Finals (13–8)
1987–88	57–25	1st	K. C. Jones	Larry Bird (29.9)	Lost in 3rd Round (9–8)

Season	Record	Finish	Coach(es)	Scoring Leader(s)	Playoffs (W-L Record)
1988–89	46–36	3rd	Jimmy Rodgers	Kevin McHale (22.5)	Lost in 1st Round (0–3)
1989–90	52–30	2nd	Jimmy Rodgers	Larry Bird (24.3)	Lost in 1st Round (2–3)
1990–91	56–26	1st	Chris Ford	Larry Bird (19.4)	Lost in 2nd Round (5–6)
1991–92	51–31	1st	Chris Ford	Reggie Lewis (20.8)	Lost in 2nd Round (6–4)
1992–93	48–34	2nd	Chris Ford	Reggie Lewis (20.8)	Lost in 1st Round (1–3)
1993–94	32–50	5th	Chris Ford	Dee Brown (15.5)	Did Not Qualify

Individual Career Leaders and Record Holders (1946–1994)

Scoring Average	Larry Bird (24.3 ppg., 1979–1992)
Points Scored	John Havlicek (26,395)
Games Played	John Havlicek (1,270)
Minutes Played	John Havlicek (46,471)
Field Goal Pct.	Cedric Maxwell (.559)
Free Throws Made	John Havlicek (5,369)
Free-Throw Pct.	Larry Bird (.886)
Rebounds	Bill Russell (21,620)
Rebound Average	Bill Russell (22.5 rpg.)
Assists	Bob Cousy (6,945)
Personal Fouls	John Havlicek (3,281)
Consecutive Games Played	Jo Jo White (488, 1-21-72 to 1-29-78)

Individual Single-Season and Game Records (1946–1994)

Scoring Average	Larry Bird (29.9 ppg., 1987–88)
Points Scored (Season)	John Havlicek (2,338, 1970–71)
Points Scored (Game)	Larry Bird (60, 3–12–85 vs. Atlanta, at New Orleans)
Rebounds (Season)	Bill Russell (1,930, 1963–64)
Rebound Average (Season)	Bill Russell (24.7 rpg., 1963–64)
Rebounds (Game)	Bill Russell (51, 2–5–60 vs. Syracuse Nats)
Assists (Season)	Bob Cousy (715, 1959–60)
Assists (Game)	Bob Cousy (28, 2–27–59 vs. Minneapolis Lakers)
Steals (Season)	Larry Bird (166, 1985–86)
Blocked Shots (Season)	Robert Parish (214, 1980–81)
3-Pt. Field Goals (Season)	Danny Ainge (148, 1987–88)

Best Trade in Franchise History

There is no hesitation here, no room for debate or counterclaim. It was simply the smartest, luckiest, most famous and most lucrative trade in all basketball history. Acquiring the rights to Bill Russell (in the form of a number two draft selection owned by St. Louis) for established scorer "Easy Ed" Macauley, and promising newcomer Cliff Hagan, may have seemed like something of a gamble for Auerbach and the Celtics at the time. The move would give the rival Hawks a potent front line of Macauley, Pettit and Hagan, and make them a championship contender. And not everyone was convinced that a man who specialized in positioning himself for rebounds and in swatting down enemy shots was a true franchise player.

But here was the first sign of Auerbach's budding genius. Choosing first in the draft lottery would be the Rochester Royals, and Auerbach and Boston owner Walter Brown knew that Royals management (they were a small market team living on the edge of financial survival) would avoid getting into a bidding war with the Harlem Globetrotters for Russell's services. It was also obvious to the Celtics braintrust that Russell was precisely the type of ballplayer they needed—Boston had been a high-scoring outfit for several seasons, but had gone nowhere in post-season play without a rebounder to put the ball in Cousy's hands, and without a solid defense to shut down opponents' onslaughts. Russell seemed like the man for the job. Of course no one—not even Auerbach—could envision quite how great Russell's impact on the league would actually be. It was a deal that truly made Auerbach, that made the Celtics, that even made the NBA. It was a deal that put pro basketball squarely on the map.

Worst Trade in Franchise History

On October 16, 1984, Boston traded competent guard Gerald Henderson to Seattle's SuperSonics for a high draft pick (number two overall), the one used to select Len Bias, star forward from the University of Maryland. Tragedy then struck suddenly as Bias was found dead in his university dormitory room only days after the heralded draft pick, a victim of a recreational drug overdose. For once, Auerbach had manipulated the draft day scenario in his favor, made his coveted selection, and then uncharacteristically been left with nothing at all. Of course, it was only unforeseen fate that ruined this latest move by Auerbach. Over four decades as a coach and general manager, the unflappable redhead was never really out-traded by any mere mortals. He had clearly won on his draft-related gambles with Russell, Bird, Parish, McHale, Cedric Maxwell, Brian Shaw, and others. One disaster was probably inevitable somewhere along the line, even for Auerbach.

Boston Celtics Historical Oddity

The true nature of the Boston Celtics' famed "mystique" can be measured by one simple and indelible fact. The Boston franchise now owns sixteen NBA titles and boasts sixteen former players (Larry Bird will soon make it seventeen) enshrined in the James Naismith Memorial Basketball Hall of Fame in Springfield. Eighteen former Celtics players (plus one owner and one coach) have also had their uniform numbers officially retired by the franchise. Yet despite all these trappings of glory, the Boston Celtics have amazingly never had a single player with an individual NBA scoring title. No team has owned a larger collection of truly great players, yet no team has so elevated dedicated and selfless teamwork over the opportunities for personal stardom. It is the Red Auerbach way, and it has been the most successful formula of American sports history.

Celtics All-Time Number One Draft Picks List

Boston Celtics
1947 Eddie Ehlers (Purdue)
1948 George Hauptfuehrer (Harvard)
1949 Tony Lavelli (Yale)
1950 Charlie Share (Bowling Green)
1951 Ernie Barrett (Kansas State)
1952 Bill Stauffer (Missouri)
1953 Frank Ramsey (Kentucky)
1954 Togo Palazzi (Holy Cross)
1955 Jim Loscutoff (Oregon)
1956 Bill Russell (USF)
1957 Sam Jones (North Carolina Central)
1958 Ben Swain (Texas Southern)
1959 John Richter (North Carolina State)
1960 Tom Sanders (NYU)
1961 Gary Phillips (Houston)
1962 John Havlicek (Ohio State)
1963 Bill Green (Colorado State)
1964 Mel Counts (Oregon State)
1965 Ollie Johnson (San Francisco)
1966 Jim Barnett (Oregon)
1967 Mal Graham (NYU)
1968 Don Chaney (Houston)
1969 Jo Jo White (Kansas)
1970 Dave Cowens (Florida State)
1971 Clarence Glover (Western Kentucky)
1972 Paul Westphal (Southern California)
1973 Steve Downing (Indiana)
1974 Glenn McDonald (Long Beach State)
1975 Tom Boswell (South Carolina)
1976 Norm Cook (Kansas)

1977 Cedric Maxwell (UNC-Charlotte)
1978 Larry Bird (Indiana State)
1979 None
1980 Kevin McHale (Minnesota)
1981 Charles Bradley (Wyoming)
1982 Darren Tillis (Cleveland State)
1983 Greg Kite (BYU)
1984 Michael Young (Houston)
1985 Sam Vincent (Michigan State)
1986 Len Bias (Maryland)
1987 Reggie Lewis (Northeastern)
1988 Brian Shaw (UC-Santa Barbara)
1989 Michael Smith (BYU)
1990 Dee Brown (Jacksonville)
1991 Rick Fox (North Carolina)
1992 Jon Barry (Georgia Tech)
1993 Acie Earl (Iowa)

Chapter 2

LOS ANGELES LAKERS AND MINNEAPOLIS LAKERS

A Very Expensive Bridesmaid Indeed!

All-Time Franchise Record: 2191–1422, .606 Pct. (1947–1994)
NBA Championships (11): 1948–49, 1949–50, 1951–52, 1952–53, 1953–54, 1971–72, 1979–80, 1981–82, 1984–85, 1986–1987, 1987–88
Greatest Franchise Player (Los Angeles): Earvin "Magic" Johnson (1979–1991)
Greatest Franchise Player (Minneapolis): George Mikan (1947–1956)
All-time Leading Scorer: Jerry West (25,192 Points, 1960–1974)
Most Successful Coach: Pat Riley (533–194, .733 Pct. 1981–1990)
All-Time Franchise Team: George Mikan (C), Elgin Baylor (F), Jim Pollard (F), Jerry West (G), Magic Johnson (G)

"Basketball should not be permitted in Southern California. It's too warm there. The beaches are too golden ... basketball is an eastern, city game. It is a game of grime and grunt and sweat. Basketball is for screaming fans who come by subway and in dented sedans, who know the strategies as well as they know their birth dates. It is not a game for polite applauders who arrive in sleek convertibles and think of it merely as diversion." —Merv Harris

Save for the Boston Celtics, the Lakers boast the richest tradition and the most storied history in professional basketball annals. What other club can boast individual glory teams like those that have won 12 NBA-BAA-NBL championships, a quarter of the modern-era professional total. Only Auerbach's Celtics stands prouder, with their 16 championship banners dangling from the rafters in Boston Garden. Or consider a record 13 defeats in the NBA Finals. Add together the Lakers' title years with their no-cigar championship-round defeats, and the total reaches 25 visits to the league championship Finals—the World Series of basketball. Boston has only been there 19 times; no one else has reached double figures. It is the Lakers, then, and not the Celtics, who have been most clearly synonymous with NBA championship play.

And there are other boasting points as well. There have only been four (1958, 1975–1976, 1994) of 47 seasons, for starters, in which this team has not been a playoff participant. What team has known more of the drama and frustration of legendary near misses, like four different game-seven losses in the NBA Finals during the same decade (three against the Celtics), or like Frank Selvy's last second shot, which rimmed the bucket in the closing seconds of game seven in 1962, or the game-seven furious rally which fell two points short at Boston Garden in 1966? And what franchise has had a list of glowing stars like Elgin Baylor (inventor of one-on-one moves), Wilt Chamberlain (the game's most dominant offensive force), Jerry West (the purest long-range shooter ever), Kareem Abdul-Jabbar (the paragon of iron men), and Magic Johnson (the only legitimate rival to Oscar Robertson as the sport's greatest all-around, all-time player)?

In terms of franchise stars, at least, the Lakers do not take a back seat to anyone, including the storied Celtics in Boston. No team has had so many true stars spread throughout their history. And no team has featured so many superstars bunched on the same ballclubs—an early '50s roster of Mikan, Pollard, Mikkelsen and Slater Martin; an early '70s starting lineup of Baylor, West, Chamberlain and Happy Hairston; a mid '80s combo of Magic, Kareem, James Worthy and Byron Scott. Such celebrity-heavy rosters might even at times have been part of the Lakers' championship problems. Consider, for example, the Lakers squads of the late '60s and early '70s that could never quite manage to get over the top against first Boston, and then the well-balanced and chemistry-ideal New York Knicks.

And, with the Lakers, there has always been the matter of lots and lots of bad luck. This luck has seemed to culminate recently in the personal tragedy surrounding Magic Johnson. But it has been a thing of destructive force throughout franchise history as well, and it was there to plague Mikan, and Elgin Baylor, and Jerry West and Chamberlain, long before it singled out Earvin "Magic" Johnson. Mikan was a continual victim of shifting strategies and shifting rules (widened foul lanes, revamped fouling rules, shot-clocks) as opposing club owners and coaches adjusted the game to shut off every advantage he had worked so hard to earn. Baylor saw several titles elude his teammates when his own debilitating injuries blocked top-level post-season performances. And then crippling injuries closed out his own playing career exactly one year before the Lakers would finally own their long-sought championship rings. West and Chamberlain also experienced the frustration of post-season injuries and just too much Boston Celtics, both of which continually blocked their championship dreams.

The greatest drama surrounding the Lakers franchise, however, has been the epic struggles and last-minute disasters and frustrations of some of the greatest Lakers teams which made it almost—but not quite—all the way to the top. Usually, of course, it was the Boston Celtics that somehow managed to block the route to glory with their own good fortune, last-minute heroics, and an endless assortment of lucky bounces. The last great Minneapolis team in 1959 pulled off one of the gutsiest Cinderella post-season surges of all-time behind the marvelous Elgin Baylor, yet were nonetheless shot out of the sky by the all-powerful men of Red Auerbach. Baylor's relocated team of the early '60s now had Jerry West—the best clutch player of league post-season history—yet Selvy's famous missed shot cancelled out thunderous post-season scoring performances by both Baylor and West in 1962. There was the seemingly invincible Chamberlain-led team that lost a seventh-game title matchup only because a goldbricking Wilt sulked on the bench with a questionable injury during the crucial final minutes of championship play. And there were even Magic Johnson teams which somehow lost titles in the championship rounds during those very seasons when the Lakers seemed most destined to pile more trophies into the ballclub stash.

In the end, the Lakers have been something like the Brooklyn Dodgers of basketball history. It is an ironically fitting comparison that has nothing to do with parallel migrations into the Eisenhower-era City of Angels. History has often branded the Lakers as the sport's most talented losers, a perfect foil for the victory-saturated Celtics, just as the "Boys of Summer" Brooklyn nine remained a perfect foil to Stengel's Yankees. And yet, like Brooklyn's baseball Bums, the record demonstrates that the Lakers hold the sport's second richest winning tradition. Most of the near-miss Lakers clubs were among the greatest super teams of NBA history. It is perhaps too easy to forget that the league and the sport would have been far, far poorer without them.

The Mikan Years

Pro basketball, as we more or less know it today, began with the heated rivalry between the National Basketball League (NBL) and Basketball Association of America (BAA) during the immediate post-war winter of 1946–'47. For the NBL (see Chapter 29) this season would be dominated by the strange saga of George Mikan and the team which had first signed him, the Chicago American Gears. Mikan joined the Gears too late for regular-season play in 1945–'46 but still in time to carry the club all the way to the semi-finals of a World Professional Tournament staged in Chicago. At the outset of the 1946–'47 NBL campaign, however, Mikan was sitting out action in the midst of a bitter contract dispute. Yet by season's end the 6'11" All-American out of Chicago's DePaul University had returned to uniform and made the Gears again a league force; rearmed with basketball's biggest warrior the Chicago ballclub overpowered Rochester for a championship crown. But a truly bizarre twist to the NBL story transpired next, as Gears' owner Maurice White pulled his club from the circuit and attempted formation of still another rival league. This venture failed immediately, and Chicago players were quickly assigned to new NBL rosters, Mikan going by a stoke of fate to a new Minneapolis franchise (the transplanted Detroit Gems) now sporting the nickname of Lakers.

When George Mikan showed up in Minneapolis in 1947, pro basketball had taken a dramatic turn from which it would soon reap untold benefits. Never again would the league featuring the game's best pro players be quite the same. And never would anyone seriously be able to claim again that all the best cage performers were restricted to the college ranks, while the pro leaguers were nothing but over-the-hill barnstormers of inferior reputation. Mikan and his Lakers raced through the NBL schedule during the winter of 1948 with a 43–17 record that was bested only by a Rochester Royals squad, which finished a single game better. At season's end, and in the first post-season matchup of a promising new rivalry, Minnesota would dispense with the Royals to achieve a second straight league championship for Mikan. Quietly, out in the heartlands, a new sports dynasty was already being born. And all this was occurring only a single year before Casey Stengel, Yogi Berra, and the remainder of the New York Yankees would, in similar fashion, begin dominating America's summer and autumn sporting scene.

By packing his bags for Minneapolis, Mikan had unquestionably set pro basketball off on an entirely new course. Just one year later his full team would join him in a still larger scale vagabond odyssey. The Lakers team that year would skip out altogether on the faltering NBL and seek greener pastures in the now more promising BAA (see Chapter 30). And more devastating yet for the NBL, the Lakers would pull the Rochester Royals, and stellar backcourt ace Bob Davies, along with them in their exodus. There was now a new league as the setting, but the Minneapolis-Rochester dogfight would continue without skipping a single beat. Rochester this time around dominated the regular-season schedule. But Mikan and his Lakers were true money players and were again soaring once the playoffs rolled into clear view. Mikan and company eliminated their Rochester rivals in two quick semi-final contests, then rolled over a Red Auerbach-coached Washington Capitols ballclub in a championship round that lasted six games.

The Lakers first back-to-back championship team was unquestionably led by monster pivot man George Mikan. But the team was powered by 6'5" swingman Jim Pollard as well. Pollard—a native Californian who had led Stanford University to a 1942 NCAA title—had first pursued an amateur career for a series of AAU ballclubs and regularly turned down pro offers in hopes of competing with the 1948 Olympic squad. Once persuaded to don a Minneapolis uniform and forego his Olympic dreams, Pollard discovered that he had come to the right team at the right time, as his play complemented that of Mikan perfectly. And at the helm of this great team was former small-college coach Johnny Kundla. Only 31, the youngest mentor in the league, Kundla had been spirited off the campus of local St. Thomas College in St. Paul, Minnesota. Kundla's first NBL team was to a large extent built around homegrown University of Minnesota talent, most particularly former Gopher stars Don "Swede" Carlson and Tony Jaros, who had primed their talents on Minneapolis high school courts as well. And this fact went no small way toward stirring rabid local following for the championship outfit.

When the landmark 1949–'50 season opened for the brand-new National Basketball Association (a product of NBL-BAA merger), George Mikan and his teammates were competing in a third new league in as many seasons. This was perhaps not so surprising, given the transient career of the early professional circuits and their usually fly-by-night ballclubs. But this was now an almost entirely revamped Lakers team that was taking the court in the equally overhauled league. One significant addition in the forecourt to complement Mikan and Pollard was Minneapolis native Vern Mikkelsen, a 6'7" center out of Hamline University who had recently led the small-college Pipers to three straight NAIB tournaments and a 1949 championship in the tiny-school division. Another backcourt add-on was pepperpot guard Slater Martin, an All-American out of the University of Texas. "Dugie" Martin was not only a standout defensive specialist, but an ace playmaker and long-range bomber as well. Harry (Bud) Grant was another standout newcomer of noteworthy status, who arrived as a three-sport star off the campus of the University of Minnesota and helped out with a backcourt reserve role. Grant would soon enough switch sports and carve out his own larger niche as a player and coach (and eventual Hall of Famer) in the equally young National Football League.

The dramatic lid-lifter of the first season in the new league was a tussle between Minneapolis and Philadelphia matching Mikan against Joe Fulks, the man who owned the only scoring record Mikan himself had not already established—a landmark 63 points poured through the nets in a single game a season earlier. But this particular night the Lakers would ride high with an 81–69 count behind the 30-point offensive show of Jim Pollard (Fulks meanwhile outscoring Mikan 20–17). Then they would settle in for another long league title race against former NBL and BAA rival Rochester, eventually ending glued to the Royals in a flat-footed tie at 51 victories apiece.

Mikan was still invincible in this new circuit and broke hardly a sweat in beating out former Kentucky All-American Alex Groza (now star and part owner of the Indianapolis Olympians) to win yet another scoring title. It wasn't easy, of course, against the fouling tactics regularly employed by opponents of the bulky Lakers center. Mikan's Lakers themselves emerged none the worse for wear from the fierce four-month tussle with

Rochester and Syracuse, and thus won a third-straight league championship banner by besting all comers in a complicated four-tier playoff round.

It was most fitting that the very first NBA championship series would provide such a strong foreshadowing of the great post-season rivalries that lay just a few years down the road. The Syracuse Nats were now led by their own superstar and offensive sideshow, Dolph Schayes, but also featured enough balanced scoring and floor leadership from such veterans as Al Cervi, Alex Hannum and Paul Seymour, to compile the best overall league record at 51–13 (both Minneapolis and Rochester finishing 51–17). And the Nats had proven throughout the long season to be every bit as tough on their home court as the vaunted Lakers, losing but a single game all year on the floor of the ancient State Fair Coliseum. A rather strange league schedule during regular season play had allowed the Nats the bulk of games against a patsy Western Division and handed Syracuse—as owners of the best overall won-lost mark—a distinct advantage during the NBA's first-ever championship round finals. Syracuse would not only draw the extra home game of the championship shootout but also enjoy a bye, while Central and Western Division champs met during a semi-final round. Yet, as the championship series unfolded, this homecourt advantage proved of little leverage for the Nationals. Schayes and company promptly relinquished a home court opener at the buzzer and could not win any of the three road matches held in the Twin Cities.

The final shootout of the hotly contested six-game Minneapolis-Syracuse series turned out to be the wildest pro playoff contest ever seen up to that time. The "battle royal" fittingly epitomized the rough-and-tumble style and spirited competition of that early era of play. Brawls marked much of the on-court action as police even had to take to the floor to break up one punching affair between Pollard and Syracuse reserve Paul Seymour; two additional fights involved guard Billy Gabor, one against Slater Martin and a second with Swede Carlson; Syracuse player-coach Al Cervi was ejected in the third stanza, and four Lakers exited on personal fouls in the fourth frame. But on the scoreboard it was the Nats who received the roughest treatment as the Lakers juggernaut romped to an easy 110–75 title-clinching victory.

In the brief span of three years, George Mikan and his Minneapolis teammates had carried professional basketball to new and unanticipated levels of prestige. While Mikan's performances could certainly never be compared favorably on a statistical basis with those of Wilt Chamberlain a decade later (Mikan never knew a 30 ppg. season, and garnered only a third as many career points), and while his overall skill level did not approach the magical airborne artistry of such modern-day performers as Oscar Robertson, Julius Erving and Michael Jordan—or even that of such agile modern-day big men as Jabbar and Moses Malone—Mikan's superiority, when measured only against players of his own era, was unrivaled.

In reality, no basketball player since has perhaps stood as far above the shoulders of his peers—just as no baseball sluggers after Ty Cobb and

Babe Ruth ever had the field of competition so exclusively to themselves. The evolution of talent and broad-scale popularity of the game simply no longer allows this. And the slimness of talent in Mikan's own era allowed rival teams to marshall all their resources against his performance alone, ignoring an entire lineup of his teammates on the floor. Defenses were so stacked against Mikan that they would be impossible to maintain against today's outside shooting version of the game. And when Mikan overcame such defensive strategies, then the league itself began changing the rules on him—widening foul zones, raising the basket, changing the rules on fouling. There was an open conspiracy throughout the entire league to neutralize Mikan's dominance. This was something that Wilt would never have to face, nor Oscar Robertson and Elgin Baylor, nor Magic Johnson and Michael Jordan. Strategies aimed at Mikan were often as silly and ineffectual as the baseball infield shift used by the American League teams of the late 1940s to offset Ted Williams's unrivaled hitting skills. And just as Williams overpowered those strategic ploys with brute force and superior skills, so too did Mikan on the hardwood. For half a dozen evolutionary years, Mikan and his Lakers teammates seemed to mount every obstacle as if it wasn't even there.

In today's dazzling basketball world of sensational in-your-face slam dunks, original sleight-of-hand moves, spectacular showtime displays of individual self-expression, and racehorse end-to-end, non-stop court action, it has become next to impossible for the modern-day fan to visualize and appreciate the game as it was once played by the NBA's inaugural teams. NBA play of these earliest few seasons was, in fact, more akin to tribal warfare on polished wooden floors. Basketball in the 1940s and 1950s was still largely characterized by physical roughness, and not graceful flight patterns. Once Mikan had revolutionized the sport by demonstrating the tactical advantages of a hulking big man who could reject long-range bombs and muscle everyone else out of rebound range, the bruising under-the-bucket style of contact play was firmly established. The twenty-odd-foot territory that surrounded the offensive basket quickly became the battle zone in which ferocious scrambles for each rebound made it almost impossible for officials to see and thus call even a small percentage of the numerous and quite blatant fouls.

The Lakers and Mikan clearly excelled at this style of game. Mikan, or perhaps Jim Pollard, would snare a rebound over the outstretched grasp of shorter opponents. A lob pass to Slater Martin would be followed by a slow dribble into the frontcourt, as both offense and defense waited for Mikan to lumber downcourt into pivot position. Another lob back to the entrenched giant under the new glass boards would be followed by an easy layup, or perhaps a thundering crash of bodies careening towards a loose rebound.

Much of the game's earliest strategic experimentation—such as it was— was clearly aimed at slowing and hopefully stopping, or at least neutralizing, Mikan and his surrounding mates on the Lakers' front line. One of the most bizarre examples of such acknowledged stop-Mikan legislation was a league game played on March 7, 1954, pitting the Minneapolis team on their home floor against the undermanned Milwaukee Hawks. This particular game was arranged to be played with 12–foot-high baskets—one can hardly even imagine such radical experimentation during a regulation game in the modern era—and would be observed by a host of league officials, on hand to measure its potential successes in neutralizing the presumably unfair "big-man" advantage of the Minnesotans. But the expected results quickly gave way to the opposite outcome—Mikan and giant teammate Clyde Lovellette seemed now to have even greater advantage against smaller opponents, since any outside shooting was much more handicapped by such tampering than were easy layups. The Lakers shot just 28.6 percent from the floor that fateful night, tip-ins and underbasket excitement were neutralized, fans snoozed through a 65–63 Minneapolis win, and players on both teams grumbled that it took them weeks after the disastrous game to approximate their refined shooting touches again, from both inside and outside range.

The 12-foot shooting target would die a quick and predictable death after only one ill-conceived game. Yet there were still other rule tamperings, ones that would generate more lasting shifts in the actual physical appearance of the game. The most noticeable and far-reaching alteration, generated originally by the anti-Mikan forces, was a widening of the foul lanes that accompanied the opening of the 1951–'52 season. Since the three-second rule was already in effect, preventing any oversized offensive player from establishing an advantageous position immediately under the basket's rim, stretching the offending zone from 6 to 12 feet was an effective means of offsetting much of the rebounding advantage of big men—at least at the offensive end of the floor. Most of Mikan's offensive productivity up to this point—to the chagrin of detractors who still felt that basketball should be ruled by setshot specialists of moderate size—had come from simply setting up under the basket and muscling in easy layup shots.

So dismayed was the Lakers management by such plotting aimed against their star player that team general manager Max Winter first protested vehemently, challenging that Minneapolis would not only reject that wider lane on their own home floor, but also would withhold Mikan from play (and thus also drastically harm crucial gate receipts) against road opponents who settled for the expanded foul lane. The severity of Winter's threats should make perfect sense to modern-day NBA fans, who would have no trouble visualizing the riotous uproar of ticket-holding patrons in Indianapolis or Denver at any mere suggestion that Chicago management was withholding Michael Jordan from a game in their town because of some similar protest of a league ruling. But even Jordan's impressive contemporary impact as a league marketing tool can never quite approach the singular marquee stature of Mikan for the fan-starved NBA of the early 1950s. It was not at all unusual for the sign outside Madison Square Garden to contain a single posting—''Tonight, George Mikan vs. Knicks''—whenever Minneapolis was visiting the basketball capital of New York.

But cooler heads prevailed, and even George Mikan adjusted admirably well to this new handicap placed in his path by front office plotters. The big center's scoring average did take a sharp dip that season, however, from 28.4 to 23.8 points per game. For the first time in his six-year pro career George Mikan was not the league's scoring champ under the new floor conditions—that honor now falling to deadeye Philadelphia forward Paul Arizin. Thin and frail compared to Mikan or Lovellette, the undersized Philly ace known as ''Pitch'n Paul'' possessed an awkward arm-flapping style and deadly outside jumpshot that would quickly revolutionize the NBA approach to scoring. The game was suddenly shifting toward the perimeter and only once more would Mikan average 20 points for a full season's play. And while the league's next three scoring champs—Arizin (6'4"), Neil Johnston (6'8"), and Bob Pettit (6'9") were all moderately big men, all three also relied on medium-range jumpers or sweeping hook shots rather than layups for the bulk of their offensive arsenal.

That the pro game was actually becoming more balanced and competitive, and thus also fully coming of age, was first signalled by the arrival of a new league champion at the end of the league's second season. While Mikan was enjoying his last dominant season and Vern Mikkelsen and Pollard were providing a balanced frontcourt attack, Minneapolis was still strong enough to roll to another regular-season league-best record, outpacing Western Division runner-up Rochester by three full games and Eastern Division leader Philadelphia by three as well. But it was now the Rochester Royals who offered the league's most balanced offensive lineup, one with four starters (forward Jack Coleman, center Arnie Risen, and backcourt men Bob Davies and Bobby Wanzer) all scoring at a double-figure clip. The Royals were also every bit as much an experienced veteran ballclub as their Minneapolis rivals, and it was the talented guard play of Davies and Wanzer, in particular, that was able to offset any Laker frontcourt advantage and propel Rochester past the defending champions during the league's second annual title series.

The Rochester Royals would actually unseat the Lakers from their string of three straight titles during the semi-final round of the 1951 playoff series. The fate of the Minneapolis dynasty had actually been largely sealed in the second-to-last regular season contest when Mikan sustained a broken bone in his ankle; the hobbling injury was not enough to end the big man's season outright, but it was certainly enough to slow Mikan's playoff effectiveness to a crawl. George opened post-season play with a miraculous 41 points against Indianapolis, given the condition of his injured limb, then suffered through a career-low two-point game the next night, in which he played for only fifteen minutes. After eking out a 2–1 series triumph over Indianapolis and earning a victory in the opener against Rochester, Mikan and his mates suddenly disintegrated altogether as the backcourt-rich Royals swept to three straight wins and a spot in the Finals against New York.

Rochester's upstart Royals had successfully halted the runaway Lakers express in 1951, but Mikan and crew were far from a state of collapse once the new season opened in the early autumn of that same year. Springtime, 1952, saw the Minneapolis five back in hot pursuit of their upstate New York rivals, once more led by a rejuvenated Mikan, who trailed Arizin by a fraction for the league scoring title but still owned the best rebounding average in the circuit; and Minneapolis still boasted a balanced front line that saw Mikan, Pollard and Mikkelsen all topping 1000 points for the first time. This time around the Lakers finished only a game in arrears of rival Rochester in regular season play, and then gained the needed road victory in game two to scuttled the Royals three games to one during the Western Division final playoff round.

The championship Finals of the 1952 campaign also witnessed the second entry into the title series by a team from the league's largest market—New York. And for the second year in a row the Knickerbockers' very presence in the final playoff round was one of the season's largest surprises. New York started the league's post-season run with a minor upset of the Celtics, taking the deciding match of the three-game set with an 88–87 double overtime thriller. After the Max Zaslofsky-led Knicks outlasted Syracuse as well, and the Lakers had turned the tables on Rochester in the other hard-fought semi-final series, the stage was set for what would prove to be a highly controversial Knicks-Lakers final round shootout. And it didn't take long for the action to heat up to a boil. In the opening contest New York was apparently robbed of victory when officials called an early foul against the Lakers, yet missed seeing Al McGuire's shot drop on the very play that prompted the call. McGuire (brother of teammate "Tricky Dick") missed the first of his charity tosses and thus the officials' miscue proved fatal to the New Yorkers, with the Lakers taking away a questionable 83–79 overtime triumph.

The evenly matched teams then traded wins in the next six contests, necessitating a tie-breaking seventh game at Minneapolis. But now the Lakers would prove anything but gracious hosts, steamrolling the New Yorkers 82–65 in the finale to tuck away their second NBA title in the span of the league's first three seasons. Minneapolis was back on top, and it didn't take great foresight to project that this talented team would probably stay there for at least several seasons to come.

The Lakers had been led into the 1952 title series by what should perhaps still be billed as the most powerful and intimidating front line of the roundball sport's half-century professional history. (Only the recent Boston trio of Bird, McHale and Parish comes close, but that trio never enjoyed the same dominance during their own era as did the Minneapolis contingent.) While Mikan had just lost his first scoring title in four seasons, the big man remained the most intimidating inside force nonetheless, hauling down 36 rebounds in one late-season contest, to establish a new single-game mark. Forecourt mates Vern Mikkelsen and Jim Pollard both joined Mikan in the 1000–point scoring club by each reaching the charmed level in the season's final game. Basketball commentator John Devaney penned the most poetic assessment of the combo when he noted that "standing shoulder to shoulder, Mikan, Mikkelsen and Pollard looked like a ragged row of alpine mountains"—a view certainly shared by the league's defenses that nightly had to take on this trio of imposing hulks. And backing up the front line was a strapping 6'7" forward-center named Howie Schultz, a graduate of local Hamline University (also Mikkelsen's alma mater) who had earlier doubled during the spring season as a reserve first baseman for the Brooklyn Dodgers, until unseated from the Brooklyn major league roster by the 1947 arrival of Jackie Robinson.

The Minneapolis-based juggernaut would open the 1952–'53 season with identical personnel to that of the previous campaign. Mikan and company would also then close the winter's play with the same result as in past years, racing to a four-game divisional margin over Rochester between November and March, and then manhandling the Knicks with little apparent effort during the five-game championship series. In other words, it was business as usual in the Twin Cities during springtime of 1953—especially for the men of coach John Kundla.

When the Lakers took three straight final-round playoff tussles from the outmatched Knickerbockers in New York, they had sealed their second championship in a row and third in only four seasons. Mikan would later call this particular title his "sweetest ever" among the six he and his teammates would eventually win. The title matchup again pitted the expected entrants from Minneapolis against the almost equally regular Knickerbockers contingent, now themselves three-time participants in the league's final series. This time around there would be no surprise in the results; there would, however, emerge a most unexpected hero for the league's showcase year-end playoff fest. New York had celebrated early with a series-opening victory in Minneapolis and had pressed the hometown Lakers throughout the second game as well. When the title round moved into Gotham's 69th Regiment Armory, however, unheralded backcourt reserve Whitey Skoog quickly went on an unexpected tear for the steamrolling Lakers. Handcuffing Knickerbockers' ace Ernie Vandeweghe throughout game three, Skoog next proved an offensive star with two much-needed buckets to preserve victory in crucial game four as well.

If the Lakers had been aging over the course of the past several campaigns, it was quite impossible to tell this by measure of the squad which opened play during the 1953 autumn season. Four future Hall-of-Famers would take the court in Minneapolis silks that season—Mikan, Pollard, Slater Martin, and a newcomer out of Kansas University named Clyde Lovellette. Lovellette was soon being groomed to take the fading-if-not-aging Mikan's slot in the lineup. As a result of the experiment, Mikan's own playing time dropped to less than 33 minutes a game and his scoring average finally slipped below 20 points a contest for the first time. Despite this inevitable decline in the big center's nightly performance, the NBA championship trophy would nonetheless remain firmly lodged in the Twin Cities of Minneapolis-St. Paul for at least one more season. First the Lakers would again maintain their hammerlock grip all winter long on the league's best regular season record. Then during the championship series they would be extended, but not beaten, by an improved Syracuse Nationals squad which had been unfortunately weakened just at playoff time by a crucial wrist injury to scoring wizard Dolph Schayes.

Slowed but not sidelined by his wrist fracture (he simply played with a bulky cast), Schayes was less artistic, but only slightly less effective in the rugged seven-game championship set. The Lakers triumphed in the first and last contests largely due to their distinct height advantage and the heavy scoring of Pollard, who bagged 22 in the rubber-match finale. Syracuse kept the series tight with a pair of thrilling last-second victories, one on Paul Seymour's clutch shot in game two and the other on a Jim Neal bucket with four seconds remaining in game six. When the clock expired on the 87–80 Lakers victory in game seven, the Minneapolis team had earned a three-peat string of titles that would not be surpassed in future eras by anyone save the Red Auerbach Celtics already waiting in the wings. It was, of course, a fitting curtain call for Mikan, who would be announcing his retirement before another season opened. The Lakers star would indeed break that retirement pledge in the fall of 1955 for a brief and unsuccessful comeback attempt, but for all practical purposes the book had now been closed on one of the most brilliant careers of early basketball history.

It was another watershed year for the history of the sport as the 1954–'55 season inaugurated the post-Mikan and post-Laker NBA era. Two bold rule changes drastically streamlined the league when NBA play opened during October, 1954, and soon also turned the circuit standings almost entirely upside down. Ever since stalling tactics by the Pistons against Minneapolis in November, 1950, (a game in which Fort Wayne center Larry Foust held the ball at mid-court for much of regulation "action" and then scored the last-second game-winner in a 19–18 Pistons' victory), scuttlebutt had repeatedly surfaced about official league action to speed the game and prevent such boring ploys by outmanned teams. Finally the league was ready to act and the direct consequence of its bold action would be the most visible signature of professional basketball as we know it today. The brain-child of Syracuse club owner Danny Biasone was a 24-second shooting rule which seemed arbitrary at first blush but clearly had a logical basis for its chosen time clock measure as well as its strategic purpose. Biasone explained to the league's officials that since teams seemed to record about 60 shots a game, this averaged out to one about every 24 seconds over the course of normal play. The rule was merely meant to legislate such a "normal pace" of game action.

And Biasone's rule was not the only change of great impact during that topsy-turvy 1954 season. A second adjustment would be the new dictum which virtually eliminated intentional fouling (a favorite tactic to slow Mikan) by limiting each club to five personal fouls per period. Since any more fouling would give added bonus shots (which were regularly converted in this league of shooting specialists), this rough-style tactic of play was curbed almost immediately in the face of the new foul restrictions.

No single rule change has ever so drastically transformed an established professional sport as did Danny Biasone's 24–second shot clock. What debuted in the NBA with the opening tap of the 1954–'55 season was a vastly different game, one which immediately played to rave reviews and soon generated almost immediate box-office impact. One-hundred-point scores now suddenly became commonplace and the league scoring average soared 14 points above the preceding year. Yet the foremost concern on the sports pages of the day in late autumn 1954 was precisely how this new up-tempo game would curtail the slow-moving Lakers and cramp the style of an aging George Mikan. For his own part, Mikan had already seen the writing on the wall. Though barely 30, the big guy now realized his day in the sun had passed and that the game he had once dominated was no longer designed to accommodate his limited playing style. Having already earned an off-season law degree, George Mikan soon made speculation about his effectiveness under the shot clock a moot point when he announced his retirement just three days prior to the opening of Lakers training camp for the new season.

Mr. Inside and Mr. Outside

If the Lakers had owned the NBA over the first half of the optimistic 1950s, basketball's original dynasty team was back in the headlines once again by decade's closing, yet this time for somewhat different and less glamorous reasons. The once proud franchise had fallen on hard times of late and was now having far more difficulty in maintaining its fair share of the Minneapolis entertainment marketplace than it ever had in overwhelming league foes on the hardwood floor itself.

Of course, a sudden slip in on-court performance had played no small part in the team's rapid fall from favor with Minnesota hoop fans. The club, still coached by John Kundla, had tumbled all the way below .500 in the standings during 1955–'56; this was the team's first losing season in more than a decade of franchise history. And the slide would continue in Kundla's final seasons, with a low ebb being reached during the 1957–'58 campaign when the once-proud Lakers crash-landed in the league cellar, sporting but 19 victories and a dismal .264 winning percentage.

One contributing factor in the Lakers' on-floor and off-floor problems was certainly the inability to find a permanent home arena in which to play league games. While the age of barnstorming was largely over elsewhere in the league, Kundla's club remained something of a vagabond team even in its own home city. The Minneapolis Auditorium served for 12 seasons as the Lakers' primary home court. Yet conflicting dates with more lucrative events now being scheduled for that venue often left the basketball club scrambling for alternative playing sites. Many games were shifted to the Minneapolis Armory, some to the St. Paul Auditorium, and others to Norton Fieldhouse on the Hamline University campus in St. Paul. Local Minneapolis trucking magnate Robert Short, who had taken control of the club in 1957, spend money on renovation of the Minneapolis Armory in 1959 and for the time being the road-weary ballclub indeed had a promising new home. But the situation was far from stabilized, and rookie star Elgin Baylor once arrived late for a game staged in the Armory because he had reported mistakenly to the Auditorium instead. Vern Mikkelsen quipped to local reporters that he was not surprised that fans never knew where the games were when the players had a nearly impossible time keeping it straight themselves.

A single bright spot for the Lakers ballclub was a flashy new star with springs in his legs and radar in his shooting eye who exploded on the league scene during the final two seasons of the decade. Elgin Baylor was, in the minds of all who saw him in those earliest seasons, the most potent single weapon the league—and even the sport as a whole—had so far experienced. The final two seasons of the decade were highlighted, in fact, by curtain-raisers for the two most exciting rookies yet to grace NBA arenas. Wilt Chamberlain was now only a single season away, but the first of these new scoring phenoms was the forward sensation out of Seattle University who would almost single-handedly rescue a post-Mikan Lakers franchise from near extinction. Elgin Baylor made his NBA presence noted immediately by becoming the first rookie ever to shine as the mid-season All-Star Game's MVP performer. And Baylor would also be enough of a one-man team to carry a 33–39 Minneapolis outfit on his broad shoulders throughout the post-season wars as well. With Baylor lighting up the scoreboard for better than 25 points a game, the otherwise hapless Lakers ballclub hung around all the way to the NBA Finals, before finally succumbing in four quick games to Bill Russell and the Boston Celtics.

For a dozen seasons to follow, Baylor would remain the highest scoring forward in the NBA, also displaying his special penchant for championship play by registering the circuit's loftiest post-season scoring average four seasons in a row, beginning with his sophomore campaign of 1960 when he blistered the nets at a 33.5 ppg. playoff pace.

But for the Lakers once-unrivaled franchise, things had taken a decided turn for the worse. Downtown Minneapolis was at that very moment suffering through a long period of urban decline. Arena attendance was dwindling and the constant shifting of playing sites did nothing to attract a stable following. In the face of urban blight and shrinking city resources there was no hope at all for finding or even constructing a much needed new arena in which the Lakers might find permanent residence. But Lakers' boss Bob Short already had his eyes fixed on greener pastures on the western horizon.

Bob Short was not the only sports tycoon to look toward Los Angeles for instant solutions to sagging revenues and limited media outlets. Other basketball men were also on to the promise of promoting the roundball sport in the sunny climes of California. One such competitor was a prominent Los Angeles radio producer, Len Corbosiero, who had worked tirelessly to bring an NBA expansion franchise to the City of Angels. Hoping to get a foot in the door with league officials, Corbosiero had staged a much-ballyhooed October, 1959, exhibition match in the LA Sports Arena between the St. Louis Hawks and Philadelphia Warriors. The game itself—which competed head-to-head with the first-ever West Coast World Series featuring the hometown Dodgers and visiting White Sox—was also the NBA pre-season debut of none other than touted Philadelphia stringbean rookie Wilt Chamberlain.

As the city of Los Angeles moved closer to corralling NBA basketball in 1959, the sagging Minneapolis Lakers outfit was breathing its last desperate gasps out in the Midwest. The club—now without Mikkelsen, who retired immediately after Baylor's rookie campaign—stumbled to its second worst record ever with but 25 victories. Baylor raised his own scoring average during his sophomore campaign by five full points and trailed only Chamberlain and Jack Twyman in the league's scoring derby. And the team with the league's second-worst overall record was given a new life by a playoff system that admitted every one of the league's teams but the two division tailenders. Behind Baylor's 33–plus post-season scoring onslaught, Minneapolis extended the talented St. Louis Hawks to seven games and even held a 3–2 series lead before finally bowing in the action-packed Western Division final showdown.

By the time the Lakers succumbed to St. Louis during post-season play in March, 1960, their fate as a ballclub, a community resource and a revenue-generating entertainment spectacle had already been permanently sealed. The team had already suffered over the previous half-dozen seasons from a series of bad draft choices (Elgin Baylor not withstanding), unwise trades (especially Clyde Lovellette to the Royals for overrated Hot Rod Hundley), and the poorest of coaching selections (first George Mikan in 1957, followed by ineffective John Castellani who lasted but 36 games in 1959). Bob Short had also already been testing the California waters with several league games scheduled into Los Angeles in the late winter of 1960. Thus it came as little surprise when the league approved Short's petition to move his ballclub westward. Only New York Knickerbockers' owner Ned Irish raised his voice in objection to the plan. And it was as plain as punch that Irish's protests were far from selfless. While the crafty Knicks chief professed concern about added expenses coming from travel to West Coast games, few doubted that the true motive of the Knicks braintrust was a hope that the financially wracked Minneapolis club could be forced to unload Baylor to New York if not given a franchise-saving escape route out of the Twin Cities.

Yet if the demise of the Lakers in the Twin Cities was almost as much of a blow to the nation's traditionalist heartstrings as was the hijacking of the Dodgers from Brooklyn during the same era, the regret outside of Minnesota itself was soon buried in an avalanche of euphoria surrounding the inauguration of west coast basketball. And now, for the third year in a row, a sensational rookie was about to enter the league. In fact, this time it would be a sensational *pair* of rookies. Oscar Robertson and Jerry West were still riding a tidal wave of popularity attributed to their spectacular triumphs with the 1960 Olympic team a few months earlier. This had been the most talented and the most hyped national amateur team ever assembled. And at its heart were the two most exciting shooting guards and all-around court wizards ever to play, alongside such additional stalwarts and future NBA greats as Jerry Lucas of Ohio State, Walt "Bells" Bellamy of Indiana University, and Terry Dischinger of Purdue.

With the top sensational draft pick, Oscar Robertson, assured for one new league city, Cincinnati, the erstwhile Minneapolis team—sporting the next worse won-loss marker in 1960—was now in a position to settle for the equally talented Jerry West out of West Virginia University. California's seven-footer Darrall Imhoff was available as a possible franchise-pillar big man. But the clutch-shooting West was the obvious and fortunate Los Angeles choice. Just as Magic Johnson and Larry Bird would give the struggling NBA a needed booster shot exactly two decades later, so in 1960 these two highly heralded Olympic teammates seemed precisely what the circuit needed most to hype its bold West Coast expansion season. And fittingly enough, the two golden rookies would debut on the same court in Cincinnati in October, 1960. Robertson, West and the Los Angeles Lakers—three of the most glorious and magnetic names in league history—thus all arrived on the scene simultaneously.

Yet despite the promise of Baylor (Mr. Inside) and West (Mr. Outside), the newly christened Los Angeles Lakers were anything but a franchise off to a running start. Cincinnati rolled out in the lid-lifter against the Lakers by a 140–123 count, with Robertson outscoring West 21–20. A home opener in Los Angeles days later drew only a disappointing 4,000 patrons. As the opening months of West Coast action unfolded, it became quickly apparent that only Boston with Russell and Philly with Wilt could be counted on to attract sizeable crowds in excess of 5,000. To complicate matters further, the club shared the Los Angeles Sports Arena with other big-gate events and thus had to play a number of "home" contests in shifting, temporary quarters. In one playoff game held later that season in the Shrine Auditorium, for example, gangly center Ray Felix actually rolled off the playing floor and into the adjacent orchestra pit. Even in the glitz of Southern California it seemed as though the league's barnstorming image had not yet been entirely dashed.

The team representing Los Angeles during the first season of NBA West

Coast play had remarkably regrouped by the time late season rolled into view. Fred Schaus, West's coach at West Virginia, had been hired by Bob Short at the season's outset to light a fire under the club's new high-powered offense. When West began finding the range in the season's second half the team suddenly boasted the best inside-outside combo anywhere in the circuit. Even an 11–game improvement in the team's record would still mean that the transplanted Lakers stood deep in the shadow of division-leading St. Louis. But come playoff time there were already signals of things to come as the upstart Lakers again extended St. Louis to seven contests in the West Division Finals. The Hawks seemed invincible on paper, boasting one of the highest scoring front lines in history as Cliff Hagan and ex-Laker Clyde Lovellette averaged 22 ppg. and Pettit registered 28. And yet, for the second straight season, St. Louis required two final game victories (this time by a total of only three points) to dispatch the pesky Lakers and the overcharged Baylor and thus to eke out a spot in the league's championship finale with the Celtics.

Early seasons of the 1960s were also the setting for remarkable individual performances, and the new pair of Lakers hotshots would own a full share of the action. November, 1960, found Elgin Baylor scoring a then unheard-of 71 points against the Knicks in Madison Square Garden. Then during the early 1961–'62 campaign Wilt would top Baylor's mark with an incredible 78, registered during a triple overtime game in which Baylor was also participating and himself scoring 63. And not to be outdone, Baylor's teammate Jerry West pounded home 63 himself later that same year. As though the scoring derby was just heating up, Baylor then returned for another 61 points before that scoring-happy year was out. An of course it was all completely overshadowed on March 2nd, when Wilt Chamberlain netted an even 100 during pro basketball's most outrageous personal scoring onslaught to date.

If the Celtics and Hawks still stood alone as the league's upper echelon, there was now certainly reason for almost limitless optimism in Los Angeles after the first full season of West Coast play. St. Louis had been the single team always shadowing Boston in the late 1950s; now in the early 1960s it would be time for Los Angeles—newly armed with the offensive firepower of Baylor in the forecourt and Jerry West drilling bucket after bucket from long range—to emerge in the dignified trailer's role. One vivid irony of the first Los Angeles NBA season, however, was that club owner Bob Short was suddenly faced with the unexpected embarrassment of having to purchase his own air time in order to provide radio coverage of the ballclub's first round of playoff games. And in the bargain a living legend was unexpectedly born. One of the announcers employed by Short would be a young man named Chick Hearn, still struggling to make his mark on the local broadcasting scene. And over the course of the next three decades Hearn would become the very symbol of the Los Angeles franchise for legions of Lakers fans. As "Voice of the Lakers'' Hearn would become almost as legendary a broadcasting fixture as Johnny Most back east with the Boston Celtics.

The Lakers' precipitous rise to the top of the pack from their new Los Angeles home might have come even more rapidly than it did, had it not been for the untimely and unanticipated interruptions of world politics. Just as the 1961–'62 season opened, the world found itself embroiled in crisis as Cold War powers locked horns over the Soviet Union's erection of the Berlin Wall. President Kennedy had just activated the National Guard Reservists, and one of the many able-bodied young men called to active duty was none other than Elgin Baylor. Since Baylor remained stateside to fulfill his obligation, he was able to play 48 regular-season games on weekend passes, and also to save leave time for the spring playoff season.

With his part-time play the miraculous Baylor soared to a 38.3 scoring average that would have been the highest ever known in league play had not Chamberlain been enjoying his own unfathomable 50–ppg. season. The real challenge to Celtic domination was now clearly coming out of the West, as the Lakers with their devastating frontcourt-backcourt tandem were now ready to romp to back-to-back Western Division titles and two straight playoff shootouts with the perennial champion Celtics. Los Angeles had even more than Baylor and West to provide needed firepower. Rudy LaRusso was averaging high double figures on the front line. And a high-scoring guard named Dick Barnett was now available to team with West out on the perimeter. But without Elgin Baylor full time, the Los Angeles Lakers were doomed to remain only a contender, if a most impressive contender nonetheless.

The "second-season" playoff competitions that followed on the heels of the 1961–'62 season featured additional marvelous individual performances by the upstart Lakers. Wilt may have been the whole show from October through March with his tidal wave of individual scoring records, but the names Baylor and West would grab the lion's share of headlines in the spring season shootouts. Fred Schaus and his Lakers team were bent on making the most of their first-ever West Coast run during the title round, and Los Angeles was indeed off to a rousing start with two victories in the first three championship matchups with the Celtics. West single-handedly won game three with an unparalleled one-man show in the final 30 seconds of the dramatic contest. First the high-scoring guard drilled a patented jumpshot to cut Boston's four-point lead in half; then he converted a pair of charity throws to knot the contest with three seconds left. And if this were not enough, West then stole a Boston inbounds pass and converted a layup to transform what looked like a certain Boston victory into a miraculous Lakers' upset.

Yet even with West pulling off such last-second heroics and a no-longer-rusty Baylor back in the lineup daily, the Lakers simply could not overcome the indefatigable Celtics. Baylor's record-setting 61–point effort in game five did present LA with a golden chance to end Boston's championship streak at three. All that was needed was a single victory over the

course of the final two games. But again Auerbach's Celtics were invincible in the final stretch and roared to a pair of comeback victories of their
own which made them the first four-time back-to-back champions in NBA
history. The true turning point came in the final seconds of the closing
game, a matchup that is rivalled only by the 1957 finale for its final-
second dramatics. As they had in game three, Los Angeles charged from
four points back during the final minute of play on two field goals by
slick-shooting guard Frank Selvy (one-time owner of a 100–point collegiate game for Furman University). Aiming to duplicate West's earlier
effort, Selvy unleashed one final dramatic shot which glanced off the rim
as the regulation buzzer sounded. The overtime period which followed
was all Boston (110–107) and the Celtics had now finally bested the
Lakers' own Minneapolis record for consecutive championship years.

Thus began a full decade of such frustrating near misses and blown
championship opportunities for the Lakers. This incredible run of bad luck
would already be all too clearly visible by the very next season. Jerry
West was lost with a hamstring tear at mid-season, and for the second
year in a row the club was without Baylor and West together, this time
through a crucial 24-game stretch. And the team's run at the division title
was now also transformed from a molehill called the St. Louis Hawks into
a mountain known as Wilt Chamberlain. No other team was as adversely
affected by the Warriors' move to their new West Coast home, which
placed towering Chamberlain and his more-than-adequate surrounding cast
smack in the same division as the front-running Lakers. Yet despite such
adversity the Lakers were nonetheless able to outlast their divisional rivals,
only to be frustrated by the Celtics once more in a rematch six-game
season finale. Baylor's heroic 43–point performance prevented a Boston
wrap-up on their own floor in game five. But then Bob Cousy's Boston
career ended in a blaze of glory back out in LA as the Hall-of-Fame guard
dribbled out the final seconds of a 112–109 title-clinching victory.

The Lakers' persistent string of bad luck continued to run its course in
1965, as now Elgin Baylor took his turn upon the disabling injury list.
Vaulting back over the Warriors who had tumbled all the way to the
league basement, the Lakers had cruised to an easy divisional title, their
third in four years. Then disaster struck as Baylor shattered a kneecap
during the opening playoff round. Stripped of their star forward, the Lakers
battled gamely behind Jerry West's record 40.8 ppg. playoff scoring spree,
yet were no match for the machine-like Celtics. It was now seven league
banners in a row Russell and his mates, and although Cousy was now
gone and four of the Boston starters were now older than 30 (Russell,
Heinsohn, Sam Jones, and K. C. Jones), this determined Boston outfit still
showed no signs of folding anytime soon. The bridesmaid's gown was
starting to fit very snugly out in Los Angeles.

The Chamberlain Years

With the brief interruption caused by a great Philadelphia team in 1967, the entire second half of the 1960s had a familiar ring to it when it came to the story of NBA basketball. Boston's Celtics versus the Los Angeles Lakers in the NBA Finals. And Boston was destined always to be the miraculous eleventh-hour winner. Four times in the decade's final five years this same identical scenario was dramatically played out. Only the details of the action would vary slightly.

The 1966 championship campaign is the one best remembered for the fact that it brought Boston a record and still-unmatched eighth-straight NBA crown. This was also a swansong championship season for Red Auerbach, who had already earlier announced his retirement (in a well-timed psychological move after game one) and his pre-determined replacement the following year by protégé Russell. From the Lakers standpoint it was yet another year in which Baylor, and especially West (34.2 ppg. for the playoffs), were at their post-season most brilliant. A healthy Baylor almost reversed the LA five-game drubbing of the 1965 Finals by keying an opening-game overtime win and also pumping in 41 in a game-five winning effort. Yet the firepower of Mr. Inside and Mr. Outside were again proven insufficient for turning the trick against the clutch play of Bill Russell. Russell netted a rare 25 points and snatched a usual 32 rebounds in the breathtaking 95–93 Boston game-seven triumph.

The 1968 title matchup offered only more of the same. Boston already seemed to be sliding in the East with Auerbach suddenly gone and had slipped quickly behind Wilt and Philadelphia during the regular season. Yet Russell was again able to out-psyche and out-clutch Chamberlain in the championship playoffs, and this set up yet another Boston title matchup with old rivals Baylor and West. Again West was brilliant as a scorer in the Boston series, once more pacing all post-season scorers at 30.8 ppg.— and again it simply wasn't quite enough. John Havlicek exploded for 31 to steal a pivotal game-five overtime victory for the Celtics. The championship matchups now stood six-to-zero in Boston's favor, in what now appeared to be basketball's version of the Casey Stengel Yankees and the Boys of Summer Dodgers. Los Angeles was seemingly doomed to permanent bridesmaid status without some way of neutralizing Russell—even an aging Russell.

Then in 1969 things changed drastically for basketball junkies out in Los Angeles. For one thing there was a brand new venue as Jack Kent Cooke unveiled his Fabulous Forum to replace the weathered LA Sports Arena. And the team sported a daring new look as well, donning purple and gold uniforms (replacing their traditional white and blue) and becoming the first NBA club to sport gold rather than white uniforms on their home floor. Owner Kent Cooke had also finally come to a crucial decision that had far greater bearing on team fortunes than the cosmetic trapping of jerseys and space-age arenas. Beating Boston's Celtics necessitated one thing—Wilt Chamberlain. With Chamberlain in the lineup alongside Baylor and West, the Lakers would finally be unbeatable, even against Boston. Chamberlain was no longer satisfied with his loser's role in Philly, the 76ers ownership was unwilling to meet Wilt's latest salary demands of a $1 million four-year contract, and Kent Cooke had the cash reserves and motivation to buy a championship team whatever the cost. A trade was hastily arranged that provided Wilt to LA in exchange for Archie Clark, Darrall Imhoff and Jerry Chambers. It would be an expensive gamble, but one owner Cooke was finally willing to risk.

But the transformation expected in Los Angeles once Wilt was in the fold did not come as quickly or smoothly as the exasperated fans and skeptical media had anticipated. It took some time for Wilt's talented LA teammates to adjust to the monster center's role in a lineup already packed with deadly shooters, themselves used to owning the ball. And it took Wilt—even a much-mellowed and less offense-minded Wilt—some time to adjust to LA as well. There was tension, for one thing, between Goliath and egocentric coach Butch van Breda Kolff. Kent Cooke had now provided a "dream team" lineup, but he had also stuck himself with a coach who wanted to do everything precisely his own way. Wilt, for his part, later expressed his opinion that an inexperienced van Breda Kolff merely escalated tensions by constantly sniping at his stars (especially Wilt) in both the locker room and the press.

LA did coast through the Western Division schedule and the early rounds of the playoffs with their new all-star lineup of Chamberlain, Baylor, seven-footer Mel Counts (at forward), West, and veteran journeyman point-guard Johnny Egan. Boston, on the other hand, mustered no better than a fourth-place Eastern Division campaign. But in their annual tussle during the NBA Finals Boston still had it all pretty much their own way one final time. Twice it looked like the Lakers would be finally home free against nemesis Boston. First LA shot to a 2–0 series lead by milking the homecourt advantage. Then they again grabbed a 3–2 advantage after a strong Boston comeback. But in the final two games two factors came suddenly to the fore—Boston's invaluable winning attitude, and the lack of harmony between Wilt Chamberlain and his Lakers coach and teammates.

The final moments of the deciding contest are undoubtedly the darkest of Chamberlain's storied career. With 5:45 left on the clock and the Lakers in the midst of a furious comeback charge which had whittled Boston's lead to 103–94 Chamberlain lunged for a rebound and came down wincing on a badly twisted knee. Wilt immediately asked for bench relief and Mel Counts was sent into the fray as Goliath's replacement. Boston and Russell were now completely out of gas and appeared ripe for the plucking as a jumper and pair of free throws from West (along with a surprise bucket from Counts) sliced the lead to a single point. It was apparent at this point that a refreshed Wilt back on the floor would have spelled nothing less than championship for those perennial bridesmaids from LA. And yet Wilt would not again appear as the final seconds ticked off the clock and Boston weathered every final Lakers charge to hang on for a desperate 108–106 victory. Wilt unaccountably sat on the sidelines as another championship slipped through the Lakers' leaky grasp. Some contended in the wake of the unbelievable events that Chamberlain himself refused to re-enter with the game on the line; a more plausible report has Lakers coach Van Breda Kolff choosing to leave his star center on the bench and scolding Wilt that "We're doing well enough without you!" If true, Butch Van Breda Kolff's ill-chosen remarks were perhaps the silliest words in the entire annals of American sports history.

But even the regrettable episode of a malingering Chamberlain in the final post-season moments of 1969 was not quite the darkest page in the long saga of avoidable post-season losses for Los Angeles. There was yet to be one more even more frustrating moment before the Lakers would finally break their transfixing championship jinx. And that final frustration would come in post-season play the following year.

The 1969–70 playoffs were among the half-dozen most memorable in league history. The NBA's biggest market was now gripped by home-team frenzy for the first time ever as the Knicks were extended to seven games by Baltimore in the opening post-season round, then rolled over expansion Milwaukee and their prize rookie Lew Alcindor in a lopsided five-game set. Meanwhile the Lakers, who had limped home behind Atlanta during regular-season Western Division play while Wilt Chamberlain was losing an entire winter to knee surgery, were back at full strength for post-season contests.

Escaping upset at the hands of Phoenix by taking the final three contests of round one, LA had little difficulty sweeping Atlanta's Hawks in four as Wilt made good on his vow to return for playoff action with a vengeance. The Knicks may have just ended two decades of frustration by making their first playoff finals in 17 seasons, yet they hardly seemed to have an exclusive edge in the motivation department. Los Angeles, by sharp contrast to the Knicks, was now venturing upon its seventh title showdown in but 10 seasons of West Coast play, and yet the Lakers' own frustration level seemed now at the breaking point since the proud club was also still without a world championship.

The stage was set for the greatest storybook moment in championship round annals. The series would have plenty of fireworks from the opening tap: both teams won a tightly contested road game and a nip-and-tuck home game as the first four contests unfolded. Games three and four in Los Angeles both extended into overtime play, the third contest reaching the extra session when Jerry West canned a miraculous 55–foot desperation heave at the buzzer ending regulation play. But true dramatics—almost as though the series had been appropriately scripted for Broadway or Hollywood—unfolded suddenly in game five when the pillar of the New York franchise, Willis Reed, crashed to the floor with a debilitating leg injury. Inspired by the loss of their captain, Holzman's men roared back in the second half to hold LA at bay and capture an emotional victory (107–101) that gave the New Yorkers a one-game cushion with but two to play. The Lakers would immediately rebound on their home floor (135–113) and thus set up the fan-pleasing seventh game which this heroic series seemed to demand.

Reed's status was doubtful right up until the moment when he made a dramatic appearance on the Madison Square Garden floor after pre-game warmups had already concluded. Willis Reed's courageous performance on one good leg against the mammoth Wilt Chamberlain would soon leave no doubts, however, about the heart of the New York team and its talented post player and captain. Reed (despite scoring only four points on two early jumpers) outhustled and outmaneuvered Wilt for four complete quarters, and when the time clock expired on a 113–99 Knicks victory, New York at last owned its first NBA title banner of franchise history. For the Lakers, however, it was but another inexplicable title defeat, and for Chamberlain especially there were more doubts than ever about Goliath's ability ever to rise up for championship occasions.

By now the Lakers fans and family had to wonder if Los Angeles could ever find a away to capture a basketball championship. It seemed as though all avenues had been travelled and all had proven to be worthless dead ends. Yet brighter fortune was now finally about to smile at long last on the City of Angels. And that fortune came in the form of a super team comprised of Chamberlain, West, Goodrich, Happy Hairston and Jim McMillan. The Lakers edition of 1971–'72 was indisputably the strongest single-season team in NBA annals. Between November 5th and January 9th the slick LA club would not lose a single contest across 33 outings, upping their midseason record to an unprecedented 39–3 ledger. This would, in fact, be the longest unbeaten string in American professional sports history, and the incredible victory run had far outdistanced the previous league standards set by first New York (18 straight), and then Milwaukee (20 in a row), during the previous three NBA seasons.

It was also a year of raw emotion for both Los Angeles and the league as a whole. Even though Elgin Baylor was tragically forced to retire in late October after two unsuccessful attempts to repair his long-suffering knees, the Lakers nonetheless swept unchallenged through the season and early playoff rounds. During the regular campaign—as if to prove that their consecutive-victory skein was no mere fluke—LA would post a 69–13 win-loss mark to surpass Philadelphia's standard for total victories and winning percentage. The league Finals would now once again match the blue-collar Knicks against the flashy Gold Coast Lakers, and rookie coach and one-time Celtics star Bill Sharman would prove the old adage about being in the right place at the right time. Sharman would miraculously bring a long-sought world title to Los Angeles in his very first try at the coach's end of the bench. Hot shooting by West and Goodrich keyed a crucial 116–111 Lakers overtime victory in game four at New York; game five was the wrap-up match as West, Goodrich and Chamberlain combined for 72 points in the Lakers' 114–100 victory.

The true hero of the Lakers dream season of 1972, of course, was an aging warrior too long saddled with a reputation for post-season failures. While Wilt Chamberlain's scoring average (14.8 ppg.) dipped below 20 for the first time ever, the versatile giant now turned his efforts towards the style of team play he was always widely condemned for shunning. The results saw Chamberlain not only ignite a long-anticipated Lakers' championship drive, but also pace the circuit once more in rebounding (19.2 rpg.) and field goal percentage (.649), and maintain a style of defensive play reminiscent of his career nemesis, Bill Russell.

The Lakers and Knicks would reign supreme for one final year of 1972–'73 and, as was becoming already customary, the New Yorkers would delight in reversing the previous year's results with their own second league title over a four-year span. It was now a battle of two rapidly aging champions, both trying desperately to hold off the ravages of Father Time—Chamberlain was now 36, and West 35; on the New York side of the ledger, backcourt ace Dick Barnett was 36 as well, and all four frontcourt stalwarts (Lucas, Reed, Bradley and DeBusschere) were now well into their 30s. Jerry West was able to muster 24 points and Wilt blocked 7 shots as the Lakers eked out an opening 115–112 nailbiter. But this would be the only time in the series that a stingy New York defense would allow the tired Lakers to crack the century mark. The Knicks surged to four straight wins, paced by a pivotal third game, in which Reed netted 22 and held Wilt to a mere five points. Willis Reed was healthy enough this time around, in fact, to become the first repeat playoff MVP since the inception of the prestigious award in 1969.

For Los Angeles, however, it was at last the long-awaited end of a decade of tantalizing near-glory mixed up with almost unrelieved heart-wrenching near misses. The Los Angeles installment of franchise history had now witnessed nine trips to the basketball equivalent of the World Series—seven over the past nine seasons—and but a single title to show for such relentless effort. The Lakers would now have six years to rest up on such dubious laurels and to experience a taste of what it was like for the remainder of the league's middle-of-the-pack franchises.

The Magic Man

As a business as well as a sport, professional basketball was in definite need of emergency repairs by the closing years of the 1970s. In an age when big-time professional sports was now counting on a lucrative television connection to achieve economic solvency, the league remained the only one of the nation's three major spectator sports spectacles without a major television contract. At the threshold of a new decade, 16 of the league's 23 teams would actually lose money during 1981. There had already been serious talk of abandoning small market franchises like those in Indianapolis, Kansas City, and San Antonio, and shrinking the circuit to a 12–team league. NBA revenue certainly could not compare with that of football or baseball, and yet franchise survival often depended on meeting escalating salary demands of a limited number of superstar players.

As the 1970s closed there was also a significant development on the West Coast, when the Los Angeles Lakers ballclub changed ownership for the third time in its history, coming under the control of land tycoon Jerry Buss. Buss was a self-made entrepreneur who had started out as a Wyoming ditch digger in his youth, and by middle age had built one of the largest real estate empires along California's Gold Coast and on the east coast as well. It was, in fact, real estate empires that actually changed hands with the Lakers' sale, as Buss swapped several of his prime holdings—including the Chrysler Building in New York City—for the Los Angeles pro basketball and hockey franchises owned by Jack Kent Cooke. Cooke sweetened the deal by throwing in the LA Fabulous Forum—home arena of the city's NBA and NHL teams—as part of the total package.

Thus one of the NBA's prime franchises closed the book on a decade which had seen three drastic overhauls of the team's on-court and front office profiles. Ten years earlier, Cooke had transformed his ballclub from yearly bridesmaids into serious title contenders with a deal that had inked Wilt Chamberlain. Five years before relinquishing the team, Cooke had worked yet another blockbuster transaction to again resuscitate his team's sagging fortunes, this time a seven-player swap with Milwaukee's Bucks which landed Kareem Abdul-Jabbar as Chamberlain's successor. And now, as he prepared to hand over control of the club to Buss, Cooke engineered one final front office move that would assure Laker fortunes for the full decade to come. Using the first overall pick of the 1979 draft (acquired from New Orleans as compensation for the 1976 free agent signing of Gail Goodrich) Cooke selected Michigan State sophomore guard-center Earvin "Magic" Johnson. And with that single choice, a new era was about to dawn, both for the Lakers and for the entire NBA as well.

Magic Johnson was perhaps the game's most versatile player ever. He had been a post-man in high school and college, and at the pro level he moved effortlessly to the guard slot. From the backcourt he was equally invincible. Even in a league of towering giants, no others enjoyed the combination of size and speed to match Magic Johnson from his outside post. He passed like a Cousy, rebounded like a small forward cut in the mold of Truck Robinson or Jim Loscutoff, created fast-break action like a Pete Maravich, and shot like a Havlicek or a Dr. J. Never had the league seen quite such a multi-faceted offensive weapon packaged in the body of a single superior player. Elgin Baylor and Oscar Robertson had come close (perhaps Oscar was even the superior player with his shooting edge), but the methodical game of their day had not given free reign to their full athletic potential (Oscar, for example, never dunked because dunking wasn't "cool"). Johnson was unsurpassed in all sports when it came to defining a perfect athlete cut in the desired mold of his unique epoch.

Magic and Boston's Larry Bird both enjoyed sensational rookie seasons. Both found the transition to the professional game to be smooth and almost effortless; each was actually improved under the freewheeling style of NBA play. Larry posted the larger numbers—21.3 scoring average, 10.4 rebounds per contest, a credible 4.5 assists from the frontcourt slot. He also walked away with coveted Rookie-of-the-Year honors. Magic's numbers were nearly equivalent (18.0 ppg. and 7.3 assists, and a surprising 7.2 rebounds nightly at the guard slot) and his value every bit as noteworthy. But most of all, Johnson proved beyond a shadow of a doubt in the early going that his size and flashy style would, almost overnight, revolutionize the league's standard for backcourt play.

If Magic and Bird had a dramatic effect on the league and sport as a whole, this was even outdone by the immediate impact of both on the teams that had acquired them. In Boston, the transition was merely phenomenal, a resurrection from league doormat into fearsome divisional powerhouse. Embarrassing victory totals of 32 and 29 in the previous two campaigns were dramatically supplanted with a league-best number of 61 in the win column. And in Los Angeles, where the immediate pre-Magic years had not been quite so lackluster as those in Boston, the "Magic era" also started with quite a transitional bang—a leap from a respectable 47–35 (third,) to a pace-setting 60–22 (divisional champ).

Thus, out on the West Coast, the improved Lakers were almost matching the rejuvenated Celtics stride for stride, both in the tempo of season's play and in the magnitude of a franchise revival. A total of 60 victories, up by 13 from a season earlier and the most in seven years, was good enough for a first divisional title in three campaigns. Johnson was not the only franchise newcomer, as a flamboyant new owner was also on board. To demonstrate his dedication to rebuilding the sagging ballclub, Buss had shipped Adrian Dantley to Utah for Spencer Haywood. He had next picked up Jim Chones to anchor the front-line attack alongside Haywood and behind Kareem. Things did not start out that well in Los Angeles, however, as coach Jack McKinney suffered a freak bicycle accident at the season's outset. But his sub, Paul Westhead, proved equal to the task of a smooth transition in leadership. By season's end Jabbar had earned his record sixth coveted MVP award with the fifth of eleven eventual seasons as the ballclub's scoring pacesetter. And a potent supporting cast of Johnson, Jamaal "Silk" Wilkes, and Norm Nixon, had recalled glory years of earlier Lakers teams not so long departed.

If Bird would seemingly have the bulk of the trophies in his possession at the end of their joint rookie campaign, it would be Magic who would haul away the truly important prize—an NBA championship. Dreams of an immediate Magic-Bird title showdown were quickly blown out of the water when a surprisingly good Philadelphia team blindsided the Celtics early in post-season play. Thus the first opportunity for a Bird-Magic reunion was lost, and fans would have to settle instead for the romance of Dr. J versus Magic. And such a finale proved to be highly entertaining indeed—at least for everyone except perhaps disappointed Boston boosters. Jabbar would leader the Lakers in the early going before seriously injuring his ankle during a 40–point performance in game five, thus dropping from the fray. In the crucial sixth game coach Westhead would have to turn in desperation to a small lineup featuring the versatile Magic Johnson in his old familiar collegiate post position. And the strategy somehow worked as Magic sizzled for 42 points and 15 rebounds, while Laker teammates were able to hold off the Sixers' final charge to the tune of 123–107. At the end of his very first league season, Magic Johnson was already on center stage, with a league playoff MVP to cap his sensational rookie season.

The drama surrounding Bird and Magic Johnson hardly subsided during the pair's sophomore seasons. Bird would now have his first turn to ring up a championship while Magic suddenly struggled. Johnson was still only a would-be college senior at age 22, yet what should have been a crowning early career year somehow turned into a season of constant highs and lows. Magic quickly went down with a severe knee injury, a blow which buried a fine Lakers team in the Pacific Division race several lengths behind the improved Phoenix Suns. When Magic returned to the lineup, things only went from bad to worse as the struggling newcomer didn't seem to fit in at all with current team chemistry. Johnson would play poorly in post-season as the shaken Lakers were surprise victims of Houston's Rockets in early playoff going. But Lakers owner Jerry Buss was unshaken by such temporary setbacks for his team and his young star, and was even prepared at season's end to offer his true franchise player of the future an astounding $25 million 25-year contract deal, the richest to date to be found anywhere in the insanely lucrative world of professional sports.

The third season of the Magic Johnson and Larry Bird era came down to a post-season rematch between the Lakers and Sixers that was almost an instant replay of the one highlighting Magic's rookie season. Once again the promise of a Bird-Magic showdown would be rudely sidetracked by a determined Philadelphia team with its own post-season agenda. In the NBA Finals, Magic was at his MVP best as his teammates took their second crown in three years, both against Dr. J's Sixers, and both with Magic as the runaway winner of the *Sport* magazine outstanding player trophy. In a deciding sixth game the Lakers star posted a trio of lucky 13's—13 points, assists and rebounds. But it was not all Magic in the Finals, as veteran Bob McAdoo, an early season pick-up, also played a key role with strong scoring (16.7) and board play. Thus McAdoo, one of the greatest big-men shooters of all-time, finally added a championship ring to his own stockpile of league scoring titles and numerous other individual awards.

One negative note surrounding the Lakers' championship campaign was the early-season firing of coach Paul Westhead. Critics of the move charged that Westhead had fallen unfair victim to constant criticism from an unhappy Magic Johnson, who apparently wanted a more freelance offense installed to his own liking. Fans even booed Johnson at the LA Forum, as well as elsewhere around the league, in the aftermath of press speculation about Johnson's role in the Westhead affair. For his own part, Johnson turned in another spectacular all-around season, pacing the NBA in steals and barely losing out to San Antonio's Johnny Moore for the assists crown. Whatever the dissention under Westhead, replacement mentor Pat Riley quickly had the Lakers off and running during post-season under precisely the offensive strategy which Johnson seemingly had mandated.

What had started during Magic's third pro season was a spectacular run for the Lakers which would see Johnson and his teammates make it to the NBA Finals four straight times. But the next two title appearances would not be quite as smooth running for the Magic Man. In '82–'83, the Lakers would provide a full season under Riley that was practically a blue print of their previous partial year under the new mentor. Los Angeles again rolled to a divisional title with a carbon-copy 58–24 record. In the early post-season round they would trample on Portland in five contests and San Antonio in six. Even an injury to James Worthy could not sidetrack Riley's crew or slow his fast-moving and fast-breaking machine. At least not until the Lakers ran headlong once again into Philadelphia's inspired Sixers for the third time in four years. For the tables were now turned completely. Philly had inked power center Moses Malone to complement Erving in the forecourt and Maurice Cheeks on the outside, and the playing field was no longer level. Especially since James Worthy was now sitting out post-season action with a broken leg, and McAdoo and Norm Nixon were slowed by injury as well. The result was only the fourth four-game final series sweep of NBA history, with LA never getting closer than a six-point spread in the opener. The Sixers had indeed reigned supreme with a 12–1 post-season mark that was far and away the best in numerous seasons.

An eventual title matchup between old college rivals Bird and Johnson still seemed about as inevitable as a Kareem Jabbar "sky hook" and finally emerged at the end of the fifth career seasons of these two top superstars. And when it did unfold, it unfolded as one of the most exciting post-season dances in years. Magic had drawn first blood over Larry with two NBA championship rings before the Boston star had even made it all the way to the Finals; but now Bird at last had his measure of revenge. For it was Larry Bird who stood victorious in the first dramatic pro title shootout between the two. The largest TV audience of NBA history sat on the edges of their chairs as Boston earned a hard-fought 111–102 seventh-game victory in which playoff MVP Bird rounded off a stellar series by averaging 27.5 points and 11 rebounds. Los Angeles had once again failed to best the Celtics in a seventh-game title matchup; in fact,

Boston had still never lost a seventh game (despite seven such matchups) in their lustrous NBA championship history.

If Magic was racking up regular appearances in the NBA Finals during his early career years, he was also compiling a rare string of first-place divisional finishes. For the nine straight years that began with his second season, the Johnson-led Lakers would rule as Pacific Division champions. Only the '60s Celtics had made a run of similar proportions, clicking off an identical nine-year string between 1957 and 1965 under Red Auerbach.

Magic, Jabbar, Riley and the rest of the Lakers outfit didn't have to wait very long to even the score with Larry Bird and Boston. The campaign of 1985 witnessed both powerhouse ballclubs storm to defense of their division and conference titles with nearly identical regular-season and post-season ledgers. Boston (63–19) won a single game more, but suffered through a tighter divisional race with Philadelphia. The Lakers came out two games better (11–2 versus 11–4) in post-season games leading up to the rematch Finals. Then, in the title round, the Lakers would gain a sudden unexpected advantage when Bird suffered debilitating elbow and finger injuries. With a boost from Lady Luck in the injury department, the Lakers now had enough of an edge to close out the well-played and high-energy series in six games. And there was an emotional element to this fourth world title for the LA edition of the Lakers. An ancient warrior—balding 38–year-old Kareem Abdul-Jabbar—would average a surprising 26 ppg. and thus experience one of his greatest career moments as the unanimous post-season MVP.

When the Lakers walked off with their tenth overall franchise title and their third in six years (all earned with Magic), they seemed finally to have achieved something of the near-dynasty status long expected of a storied yet snakebit franchise. Yet the Lakers could hardly claim to own the league. While the NBA was anything but a balanced circuit—LA, Boston, or Philadelphia, or even Portland, was light years ahead of lackluster clubs like Indiana or Cleveland or San Diego—there nonetheless remained a steady enough turnover in post-season titleholders. Sixteen full winters had now elapsed since any team had been to the Coronation Ball two seasons in a row. As far as front-running teams went, the Lakers and Celtics had proven a consistent ability to run and hide from the remainder of the league season after season in November, January, or even March; yet neither could paste together championship runs of more than a single season at a time.

The Lakers would come close though. First they would narrowly miss the first repeat in two decades during a wild and wooly 1986 campaign in which Magic and company benefited from the line-up addition of rugged Maurice Lucas, and seemed title-bound before a monumental upset intervened. The fateful stumble came when LA was rudely ambushed in the Western Finals by an overachieving Houston Rockets team which mowed them down by taking four straight after an opening Lakers' victory. LA had duplicated its 62–20 1985 record during the regular season and seemed well on the way to another post-season triumph. But the chemistry never seemed to be quite right in a lineup that now boasted not only Maurice Lucas, but also stellar rookie forward A. C. Green. In the shootout with Houston, the Rockets' Twin Towers combo of Ralph Sampson and Hakeem Olajuwon seemed to play with supreme confidence for just about the only time in their several seasons together. And the timing couldn't have been any worse for the defending champs from LA.

By the middle of the decade, a new force had emerged in the league in terms of a new superstar to join the Magic-Bird reign. Air Jordan was now also flying high in Chicago, piling up scoring titles and dominating highlight films. Jordan was the new unchallenged box-office smash. Yet if Jordan was the unrivaled individual star after 1985, the Los Angeles Lakers, behind Magic Johnson, were still the dominant team as the league's most glorious decade entered its second half.

The Lakers staked their strong claim on the decade with a second title victory over Boston in 1987. This was the series in which Magic would break his deadlock with Larry Bird in the pair's deciding rubber match. A tally of 65 wins during the regular season that year was second highest in team history, surpassed only by the 69 garnered during a first championship campaign in 1971–'72. A battered Boston squad could offer little challenge in the playoff championship round, as Kevin McHale gamely performed on a broken foot and Robert Parish limped through the championship series on a sprained ankle. The Lakers themselves would barely survive several brief scares, including a crucial fourth-game tussle salvaged only by Magic's "junior skyhook" to beat the buzzer and secure a needed 107–106 series-turning victory. Magic with a 26.2 ppg. average and 54 percent shooting from the floor was an easy post-season MVP choice, and his own head-to-head final round battle with Larry Bird now stood two-to-one in Johnson's favor. And in the wake of this exciting last Boston series of the decade, coach Pat Riley chose to put some extra pressure on his championship team. This time around Riley promised a guaranteed repeat.

It was a bold boast, but not one that any team owning Magic and Jabbar (along with an imposing supporting cast) couldn't measure up to. Thus the most dramatic of all Los Angeles NBA titles would be the one earned against the Pistons behind an aging yet still spry Kareem Abdul-Jabbar. It would be neither Magic nor Jabbar, however, who would be the ultimate hero of the first title repeat since the Russell-era Celtics. That role would be saved for James Worthy, who would now enjoy his finest hour in LA purple and gold. A playoff MVP performance by Worthy (23.6 ppg. and a first career triple-double in the game-seven finale) would not only lock up the rare championship defense, but also guarantee a first ever post-season sweep of three straight seven-game series. LA did need a gutsy rally from a 3–2 series deficit in order to preserve Riley's outrageous boast. In game six Detroit had been only one minute from a league title, holding a 102–99 lead before Byron Scott sunk a basket and Jabbar canned two free throws to stave off defeat. And with Isiah Thomas hobbled in the finale, Detroit had little left to counter Worthy's career-best effort of 36 points, 16 rebounds and 10 assists.

Scarcely had the champagne bottles been corked and the championship celebrations died down when the Lakers were destined to meet a new challenge from the East, in the form of these same pesky Detroit Pistons. The following 1988–'89 campaign would again see the Lakers fight their way to the Finals with an eighth divisional title in a row and a seventh Western Conference banner in eight seasons. Only Auerbach's '60s-era Boston team had ever known quite such a quality run. But now the Lakers seemed to be running out of steam, despite 11 straight wins in the first three playoff rounds, and the emotional motive of capping Jabbar's brilliant career with a third consecutive title. Isiah Thomas and Joe Dumars were simply too much for Magic and the long-toothed Jabbar during the rematch test. Series MVP Joe Dumars sparkled in the Detroit backcourt with a 27 ppg. average and paced the Pistons to a shamefully easy four-game sweep. Jabbar would not bow out on top; and more significantly, the Lakers had been swept in the title round for the second time in the decade.

There would still be some measure of revenge, in the form of one more crack at the NBA Finals for Magic and the wilting '80s Lakers. This would come in tandem with Magic Johnson's last great mano-a-mano championship duel—the final glorious episode of the Magic-Larry, Magic-Dr. J, and Magic-Michael sideshow which lent the NBA of the 1980s its special brand of superstar shootout excitement. This time it was not Bird or Dr. J, but rather the game's new resident superstar, Michael Jordan, who would be on hand to provide Magic's personal foil. The Lakers started fast in the 1991 Finals by taking the first game on Chicago's own floor 93–91, thanks only to a last-second three-pointer by Jordan's old college teammate Sam Perkins. But Los Angeles was clearly a shaky contender, and Magic and his surrounding cast could not handle the force of Jordan (31.2 ppg., 11.4 apg., 6.6 rpg.), Scottie Pippen (20.8 ppg., 9.4 rpg., 6.6 apg.) and rebounding and defensive force Horace Grant. As the Lakers celebrated their last title-shot of an era, the Bulls were now launching their own mini-dynasty. Chicago won four straight after the opening loss to start down the road on the way to its own three-peat domination under Air Jordan.

The end of the eighties would be a time of emotional retirements in Los Angeles, the closing of an era that had surpassed even the halcyon days of West, Baylor, and Wilt Chamberlain in the early '70s. First came the much celebrated "last time around the league" for Kareem during the 1988–'89 campaign. Jabbar's retirement was not just the loss of a bright pro star, but the passing of an irreplaceable legend. Perhaps never again in this age of high salaries, comfortable superstars, and lowered personal hunger for victory would basketball again see the likes of an NBA player with nearly 40,000 career points (when 20,000 is now the mark of an immortal), nearly 60,000 minutes, and over 1,500 games logged, and twenty seasons touching three decades. And nostalgic celebrations around the league continued all season to commemorate the historic event.

Next it was Pat Riley's turn to step aside and leave in his wake the most successful coaching skein in ballclub history. Other coaches rank higher on the all-time NBA win list, but only Auerbach has known a nine-year success run like that owned by Pat Riley during the 1980s. Auerbach also copped an identical nine straight division titles. During his decade-long stretch, Auerbach's regular-season ledger stood at 500–190 (.725), his post-season mark was 69–35 (.664), and his NBA championships totaled eight (with a loss in the Finals during the ninth season). Riley's regular-season mark was now 533–194 (.733), his post-season ledger 102–47 (.685), and his NBA title count stood at four (with three additional trips into the Finals). It was a close comparison indeed. Auerbach held the edge in championship rings and Riley in post-season winning percentage (although the Lakers of the '80s benefitted in this department by the increase in less-challenging first-round games). It was also to Riley's credit that his unbroken string of first-place division finishes spanned the entire length of his storybook LA coaching tenure.

Magic's departure from the sport was a much less joyous and pompous occasion. Johnson would in fact shock the entire basketball world with one of the most highly publicized forced retirements in American sports history. If Michael Jordan now occupied a celebrity status never before accorded a basketball player, it was equally true that Magic Johnson had played a unique role in almost single-handedly building a league and a sport to dizzying new heights of popularity. It was thus perhaps the most unsettling news the sporting world had received in decades when Earvin Johnson unexpectedly announced his retirement during the first week of the 1991–'92 season. Johnson had tested positive for the HIV virus and doctors had advised against the further physical strain of pro basketball competition. Magic suddenly grew from the status of sports hero to that of national legend as he handled his painful resignation announcement with the same grace that had marked his entire collegiate and professional athletic career. And as the nation mourned Magic's loss upon the court, it also threw its support behind his post-career efforts to bring education to the nation's youth concerning the threat and treatment of the dreaded AIDS virus.

If Magic Johnson had disappeared from center court action by the time the league's 43rd season unfolded, his name and image nonetheless continued to dominate the NBA scene just as it had for the entire past decade. Speculation continued as to whether Magic would assume his elected spot on the Summer 1992 Olympic "Dream Team," and whether he would also play in the annual mid-season NBA All-Star Classic. The latter event was scheduled in February for the expansion city of Orlando, and Johnson had been the top "vote-earner" despite his official "retired" status. Johnson did perform as both a Dream Team and All-Star Team member, and it was in the All-Star contest especially that Magic etched his final indelible mark on the sport. With his usual flair for the dramatic, the incomparable Johnson even topped the flood of pre-game hype by stagging a remarkable MVP performance (25 points, 29 minutes played, 5 rebounds and 9 assists) as his inspired West squad romped to a 153–113 victory. For perhaps the first time in its nearly four decade history—under the intense national spotlight of Magic's fabulous swansong—the league's mid-season All-Star shootout had proven to be a true high-point moment of another action-packed NBA campaign.

The Lakers have known the roughest of times since Magic Johnson's unexpected departure. Even a brief return of Magic to the coach's bench in 1994 had little about it that was upbeat. Although the ballclub won their first several games under Magic, they soon tumbled to a club-record losing streak. Before the experiment was little more than a month old, Earvin Johnson indicated that he wasn't having much fun and would not return the following season. Magic had other interests now, and life on the road with a dreadful losing basketball team simply wasn't one of them. Under Mike Dunleavy and Randy Pfund and Magic Johnson, the post-Riley Lakers era was nothing more than a steady three-year slide toward an unfamiliar basement lodging. For the first time in franchise history, the Lakers have now been a doormat for more than a single season. And for the first time since their west coast arrival in 1960, the Lakers no longer even owned the pro basketball scene in Los Angeles itself, now being rivaled at the gate and in the headlines by the long-lackluster crosstown Clippers. It is a strange circumstance for California basketball fans and one that seems—given past history—hardly likely to last any noticeable length of time.

Suggested Readings on the Los Angeles (Minneapolis) Lakers

Abdul-Jabbar, Kareem (with Mignon McCarthy). **Kareem**. New York: Random House, 1990.

Clary, Jack. **Basketball's Great Dynasties: The Lakers**. New York: Smithmark (W.H. Smith), 1992.

Harris, Merv. **The Fabulous Lakers**. New York: Lancer Books (Associated Features), 1972.

Johnson, Earvin "Magic" and Richard Levin. **Magic**. New York: Signet Books (Penguin), 1991.

Lazenby, Roland. **The Lakers: A Basketball Journey**. New York: St. Martin's Press, 1993.

Mikan, George (as told to Bill Carlson). **Mr. Basketball: George Mikan's Own Story**. New York: Greenberg Publishers, 1951.

Ostler, Scott and Steve Springer. **Winnin' Times: The Magical Journey of the Los Angeles Lakers**. New York: Macmillan and Company, 1986.

Riley, Pat. **Show Time—The Lakers' Breakthrough Season**. New York: Warner Books, 1988.

Thornley, Stew. **Basketball's Original Dynasty: The History of the Lakers**. Minneapolis: Nodin Press, 1989.

West, Jerry (with Bill Libby). **Mr. Clutch: The Jerry West Story**. New York: Grosset and Dunlap (Tempo Books), 1969.

Los Angeles Lakers Retired Uniform Numbers (4)

Wilt Chamberlain (13)
Elgin Baylor (22)
Kareem Abdul-Jabbar (33)
Jerry West (44)

Year-by-Year Los Angeles Lakers Summary

Season	Record	Finish	Coach(es)	Scoring Leader(s)	Playoffs (W-L Record)

Key: * = Tied for Position; # = League Scoring Leader

Minneapolis Lakers

National Basketball League

Season	Record	Finish	Coach(es)	Scoring Leader(s)	Playoffs (W-L Record)
1947–48	43–17	1st	John Kundla	George Mikan (24.4)#	**NBL Champion** (8–2)

Basketball Association of America

1948–49	44–16	2nd	John Kundla	George Mikan (28.3)#	**BAA Champion** (8–2)

National Basketball Association

1949–50	51–17	1st*	John Kundla	George Mikan (27.4)#	**NBA Champion** (10–2)
1950–51	44–24	1st	John Kundla	George Mikan (28.4)#	Lost in 2nd Round (3–4)
1951–52	40–26	2nd	John Kundla	George Mikan (23.8)	**NBA Champion** (9–4)
1952–53	48–22	1st	John Kundla	George Mikan (20.6)	**NBA Champion** (9–3)
1953–54	46–26	1st	John Kundla	George Mikan (18.1)	**NBA Champion** (9–4)
1954–55	40–32	2nd	John Kundla	Clyde Lovellette (18.7)	Lost in 2nd Round (3–4)
1955–56	33–39	2nd*	John Kundla	Clyde Lovellette (21.5)	Lost in 1st Round (1–2)
1956–57	34–38	1st*	John Kundla	Clyde Lovellette (20.8)	Lost in 2nd Round (2–3)
1957–58	19–53	4th	George Mikan John Kundla	Vern Mikkelsen (17.3)	Did Not Qualify
1958–59	33–39	2nd	John Kundla	Elgin Baylor (24.9)	Lost in NBA Finals (6–7)
1959–60	25–50	3rd	John Castellani Jim Pollard	Elgin Baylor (29.6)	Lost in 2nd Round (5–4)

Los Angeles Lakers

1960–61	36–43	2nd	Fred Schaus	Elgin Baylor (34.8)	Lost in 2nd Round (6–6)
1961–62	54–26	1st	Fred Schaus	Elgin Baylor (38.3)	Lost in NBA Finals (7–6)
1962–63	53–27	1st	Fred Schaus	Elgin Baylor (34.0)	Lost in NBA Finals (6–7)
1963–64	42–38	3rd	Fred Schaus	Jerry West (28.7)	Lost in 1st Round (2–3)
1964–65	49–31	1st	Fred Schaus	Jerry West (31.0)	Lost in NBA Finals (5–6)
1965–66	45–35	1st	Fred Schaus	Jerry West (31.3)	Lost in NBA Finals (7–7)
1966–67	36–45	3rd	Fred Schaus	Jerry West (28.7)	Lost in 1st Round (0–3)
1967–68	52–30	2nd	Bill van Breda Kolff	Elgin Baylor (26.0)	Lost in NBA Finals (10–5)
1968–69	55–27	1st	Bill van Breda Kolff	Elgin Baylor (24.8)	Lost in NBA Finals (11–7)

Season	Record	Finish	Coach(es)	Scoring Leader(s)	Playoffs (W-L Record)
1969–70	46–36	2nd	Joe Mullaney	Jerry West (31.2)#	Lost in NBA Finals (11–7)
1970–71	48–34	1st	Joe Mullaney	Jerry West (26.9)	Lost in 2nd Round (5–7)
1971–72	69–13	1st	Bill Sharman	Gail Goodrich (25.9)	**NBA Champion (12–3)**
1972–73	60–22	1st	Bill Sharman	Gail Goodrich (23.9)	Lost in NBA Finals (9–8)
1973–74	47–35	1st	Bill Sharman	Gail Goodrich (25.3)	Lost in 1st Round (1–4)
1974–75	30–52	5th	Bill Sharman	Gail Goodrich (22.6)	Did Not Qualify
1975–76	40–42	4th	Bill Sharman	Kareem Abdul-Jabbar (27.7)	Did Not Qualify
1976–77	53–29	1st	Jerry West	Kareem Abdul-Jabbar (26.2)	Lost in 3rd Round (4–7)
1977–78	45–37	4th	Jerry West	Kareem Abdul-Jabbar (25.8)	Lost in 1st Round (1–2)
1978–79	47–35	3rd	Jerry West	Kareem Abdul-Jabbar (23.8)	Lost in 2nd Round (3–5)
1979–80	60–22	1st	Jack McKinney Paul Westhead	Kareem Abdul-Jabbar (24.8)	**NBA Champion (12–4)**
1980–81	54–28	2nd	Paul Westhead	Kareem Abdul-Jabbar (26.2)	Lost in 1st Round (1–2)
1981–82	57–25	1st	Paul Westhead Pat Riley	Kareem Abdul-Jabbar (23.9)	**NBA Champion (12–2)**
1982–83	58–24	1st	Pat Riley	Kareem Abdul-Jabbar (21.8)	Lost in NBA Finals (8–7)
1983–84	54–28	1st	Pat Riley	Kareem Abdul-Jabbar (21.5)	Lost in NBA Finals (14–7)
1984–85	62–20	1st	Pat Riley	Kareem Abdul-Jabbar (22.0)	**NBA Champion (15–4)**
1985–86	62–20	1st	Pat Riley	Kareem Abdul-Jabbar (23.4)	Lost in 3rd Round (8–6)
1986–87	65–17	1st	Pat Riley	Magic Johnson (23.9)	**NBA Champion (15–3)**
1987–88	62–20	1st	Pat Riley	Byron Scott (21.7)	**NBA Champion (15–9)**
1988–89	57–25	1st	Pat Riley	Magic Johnson (22.5)	Lost in NBA Finals (11–4)
1989–90	63–19	1st	Pat Riley	Magic Johnson (22.3)	Lost in 2nd Round (4–5)
1990–91	58–24	2nd	Mike Dunleavy	James Worthy (21.4)	Lost in NBA Finals (12–7)
1991–92	43–39	6th	Mike Dunleavy	James Worthy (19.9)	Lost in 1st Round (1–3)
1992–93	39–43	5th	Randy Pfund	Sedale Threatt (15.1)	Lost in 1st Round (2–3)
1993–94	33–49	5th	Randy Pfund Magic Johnson	Vlade Divac (14.2)	Did Not Qualify

Individual Career Leaders and Record Holders (1947–1994)

Scoring Average	Elgin Baylor (27.4 ppg., 1959–72)
Points Scored	Jerry West (25,192)
Games Played	Kareem Abdul-Jabbar (1,093)
Minutes Played	Kareem Abdul-Jabbar (37,492)
Field Goal Pct.	Wilt Chamberlain (.605)
3-Pt. Field Goals	Byron Scott (552)
Free Throws Made	Jerry West (7,160)
Free-Throw Pct.	Cazzie Russell (.877)
Rebounds	Elgin Baylor (11,463)

Rebound Average   Wilt Chamberlain (19.2 rpg.)

Rebound Average	Wilt Chamberlain (19.2 rpg.)
Assists	Earvin "Magic" Johnson (9,921)*
Steals	Earvin "Magic" Johnson (1,698)
Blocked Shots	Kareem Abdul-Jabbar (2,694)
Person Fouls	Kareem Abdul-Jabbar (3,224)

* = NBA Record

Individual Single-Season and Game Records (1947–1994)

Scoring Average (Season)	Elgin Baylor (38.3 ppg., 1961–62)
Points Scored (Season)	Elgin Baylor (2,719, 1962–63)
Points Scored (Game)	Elgin Baylor (71, 11–15–60 vs. New York Knicks)
Field Goal Pct. (Season)	Wilt Chamberlain (.727, 1972–73)
Free-Throw Pct. (Season)	Earvin "Magic" Johnson (.911, 1988–1989)
3-Pt. Field Goals (Season)	Earvin "Magic" Johnson (106, 1989–90)
Rebounds (Season)	Wilt Chamberlain (1,712, 1968–69)
Rebound Average (Season)	Wilt Chamberlain (21.1 rpg., 1968–69)
Rebounds (Game)	Wilt Chamberlain (42, 3–7–69 vs. Boston Celtics)
Assists (Season)	Earvin "Magic" Johnson (989, 1990–91)
Assists (Game)	Earvin "Magic" Johnson (24, 11–17–89 and 1–9–90)
Steals (Season)	Earvin "Magic" Johnson (208, 1981–82)
Steals (Game)	Jerry West (10, 12–7–73 vs. Seattle SuperSonics)
Blocked Shots (Season)	Elmore Smith (393, 1973–74)
Blocked Shots (Game)	Elmore Smith (17, 10–28–73 vs. Portland Trail Blazers)

Best Trade in Franchise History

No team has ever given up so much in a single transaction, and yet come out so far ahead in the bargain. Following the 1975 season the Lakers would make one of the biggest deals in league history by peddling Elmore Smith, Brian Winters, and first-round draft choices Dave Meyers and Junior Bridgeman to the Milwaukee Bucks for reigning superstar Kareem Abdul-Jabbar. This was a deal that almost rivals the one in which Red Auerbach sweetened the pot to the St. Louis Hawks back in 1956 and got Bill Russell, his all-time franchise player. With Jabbar, the Lakers came satisfyingly close to accomplishing every bit as much. One measure of just how fabulous this trade was is the very fact that it still rates as the best the club has ever engineered. Even after the Lakers pulled a deal in 1978 trading Gail Goodrich to New Orleans for the 1979 first round pick that brought them Magic Johnson as the plum of the next year's collegiate draft.

Worst Trade in Franchise History

In 1993, the Magic-less Lakers seemed to be desperate to rebuild their sagging fortunes. They traded Sam Perkins to Seattle for a major league disappointment named Benoit Benjamin. Seven-footer Benjamin was a grand failure everywhere he went and Los Angeles proved to be no exception. Perkins still had good years left, however, and was one of the role players who soon led Seattle to the league's best overall record in 1993–'94.

Los Angeles Lakers Historical Oddity

The best single team in basketball history? It almost has to be the 1971–'72 Los Angeles Lakers outfit. First, the club had the best single-season record in NBA history, winning 69 and losing but 13. The 1967 Philadelphia 76ers and 1973 Celtics would fall a single game short of that standard. Secondly, this team won an incredible professional-sports-record 33 straight games, perhaps the most remarkable winning streak of all time, considering the strain of consecutive victories and the usual evenness of matchups in professional basketball, and especially in the high-powered NBA. And then there was the starting lineup of this once-in-a-lifetime Lakers juggernaut—Chamberlain in the post, Jim McMillan and Happy Hairston on the wings, West and Gail Goodrich at the guards. The bench strength included names like Elgin Baylor (limited to nine games by injury), Leroy Ellis, Flynn Robinson, Jim Cleamons and Pat Riley. Even basketball's greatest spell—seven losses in NBA championship finals play—could not keep this contingent from ultimate glory. It was truly a team for all ages.

Lakers All-Time Number One Draft Picks List

Minneapolis Lakers
1949 Vern Mikkelsen (Hamline)
1950 Kevin O'Shea (Notre Dame)
1951 Whitey Skoog (Minnesota)
1952 Tom Ackerman (West Liberty)
1953 Jim Fritsche (Hamline)
1954 Ed Kalafat (Minnesota)
1955 Bill Banks (Southwest Texas)
1956 Jim Paxson (Dayton)
1957 Jim Krebs (SMU)
1958 Elgin Baylor (Seattle)
1959 Tom Hawkins (Notre Dame)

Los Angeles Lakers

1960 Jerry West (West Virginia)
1961 Wayne Yates (Memphis State)
1962 LeRoy Ellis (St. John's)
1963 Roger Strickland (Jacksonville)
1964 Walt Hazzard (UCLA)
1965 Gail Goodrich (UCLA)
1966 Jerry Chambers (Utah)
1967 None
1968 Bill Hewitt (Southern California)
1969 Willie McCarter (Drake)
1970 Jim McMillan (Columbia)
1971 Jim Cleamons (Ohio State)
1972 Travis Grant (Kentucky State)
1973 Kermit Washington (American)
1974 Brian Winters (South Carolina)
1975 David Meyers (UCLA)
1976 Earl Tatum (Marquette)
1977 Kenny Carr (North Carolina State)
1978 None
1979 Magic Johnson (Michigan State)
1980 None
1981 Mike McGee (Michigan)
1982 James Worthy (North Carolina)
1983 None
1984 Earl Jones (District of Columbia)
1985 A. C. Green (Oregon State)
1986 Ken Barlow (Notre Dame)
1987 None
1988 David Rivers (Notre Dame)
1989 Vlade Divac (Yugoslavia)
1990 Elden Campbell (Clemson)
1991 None
1992 Anthony Peeler (Missouri)
1993 George Lynch (North Carolina)

Chapter 3

NEW YORK KNICKS

Noble Tradition of Losing in the Big Apple

All-Time Franchise Record: 1877–1842, .505 Pct. (1946–1994)
NBA Championships (2): 1969–70, 1972–73
Greatest Franchise Player: Walt Frazier (1967–1977)
All-Time Leading Scorer: Patrick Ewing, (16,191 Points, 1985–1994)
Most Successful Coach: Pat Riley (168–53, .683 Pct., 1991–1994)
All-Time Franchise Team: Patrick Ewing (C), Willis Reed (C-F), Bill Bradley (F), Earl Monroe (G), Walt Frazier (G)

You look at the large picture of New York Knicks history and things seem to be split right down the middle. The oldest and most venerable league franchise had played over 3,600 games across 47 seasons entering the 1993–'94 campaign and had split them almost exactly down the middle. It was also right at the midpoint of team chronological history—the end of the '60s and beginning of the '70s—that the New York Knicks (neé Knickerbockers) enjoyed the single "glory era" of franchise annals. Nothing seems to stray very far from the break-even mark with this venerable ballclub, and neither welcomed championship euphorias or hated cellar-bound ineptitude has visited the Knicks team for any lengthy period of time.

Of course the NBA founding fathers back in the late '40s—and every last league executive since then—could have wished for nothing better than a true showcase franchise in the nation's acknowledged basketball capital of New York City. Basketball as we know it today actually was raised and nurtured on playgrounds and in gyms throughout Manhattan, Brooklyn, and the Bronx. True enough that Dr. Naismith invented the game a few miles northward in Springfield, Massachusetts. And true also that the eventual professional version of Naismith's game got an early jump start with the NBL, a glorified "industrial league" whose franchises were located throughout midwestern towns of Indiana, Illinois, Wisconsin, Iowa and Ohio. But the true post-World-War II boom for the indoor game came with heavily promoted college doubleheaders staged at Madison Square Garden. And it was the Garden's Ned Irish and his cohorts— hockey club owners all—who truly got the pro game off the ground with their successful rival to the National Basketball League, the Basketball Association of America (1946). And once the pro game began to take wings in the '50s and '60s it was also a generation of New York City playground ballplayers like Julius Erving, Billy Cunningham and Connie Hawkins (even Michael Jordan was born in Brooklyn) who redefined the sport as one of altitude and ''hangtime'' and thus gave it its high-flying modern appeal.

And of course, more than simple tradition has argued for a showcase NBA club in New York City. When the game belatedly became a media entertainment spectacle by the early '80s the league's largest potential marketplace was a natural point of gravitation. It is for this reason that NBA and network television bosses breathed a strong sigh of relief in June, 1985, when potential megastar Patrick Ewing was won in the lottery by the New York Knicks and not by their coin-flip opponents, the Indiana Pacers. It is precisely why Ewing and the Knicks have been a most frequent television fixture of recent seasons, even when the ballclub struggled to keep up with the Lakers, and Sixers, and Celtics, and Suns, and even the Johnny-come-lately Chicago Bulls. And it is why a deep groan could be heard in the league offices all the way to the midwest farm belt when the no-name Indiana Pacers almost defeated Ewing and the Knicks, and almost advanced in New York's stead to the league's championship round during the first season after the retirement of Michael Jordan.

But a New York Knicks dynasty team has simply never materialized— for all the fantasizing of NBA mogals and Gotham hoopologists. The stark truth here is that, for all the best laid plans of ballclub officials and even league officials, the dreams of a headline NBA outfit in New York has remained an idle promise. There have been some good Knicks teams in almost every era of NBA history. Early New York clubs featuring forgotten names like Dick McGuire, Max Zaslofsky, Ernie Vandeweghe, Harry Gallatin, Carl Braun and Sweetwater Clifton hung on the coattails of the NBA's first great dynasty outfit, the Minneapolis Lakers with George Mikan. There was one sensational New York team of the early '70s— consisting of Willis Reed, Walt Frazier, Bill Bradley and two-sport star Dave DeBusschere—with whom a whole nation could truly fall in love. And a handful of the game's greatest stars have played in New York across the decades (through two of the best—Julius Erving and Rick Barry—appeared in the ABA, not the NBA, and with the New York Nets and not the New York Knicks). But most of the time the Knicks have been only mediocre and the New York team has thrilled and frustrated only the diehards of the New York City region itself. It is also names like Richie Guerin, Bob McAdoo, Willie Naulls, Jerry Lucas, Kenny Sears,

and Ernie Grunfeld—journeymen all—who provide the truest flavor of the
checkered history owned by the New York NBA ballclub.

Two seasons, more than any others, seem to capture this frustration and
failure of the New York Knicks pro basketball franchise. The first was
the '70–'71 campaign that came on the heels of the Knicks' first NBA
championship, and seemed to hold promise for the blossoming of a long-
running dynasty. The New Yorkers would meet disaster that year in the
second round of post-season play, victims of the upset-minded no-name
Baltimore Bullets, as Bill Bradley missed a vital jumpshot in a race with
the clock and thus earned a spot right next to Ralph Branca in New York
sports infamy. That New York ballclub of Bradley, Reed, Frazier and
DeBusschere would rebound soon enough to win a second title two seasons
later. But the possibility of a dynasty team now seemed lost forever.

A second year of frustration came exactly two decades later. The Bulls
of Chicago (representing both the nation's and sport's "second city") had
just finished a dynasty run of three-peat proportions. And in doing so,
they had several times climbed over the Knicks and star Patrick Ewing in
the closing rounds of post-season play. A 1993 playoff loss to Chicago
had been especially frustrating as the New Yorkers had grabbed a 2–0
lead on the defending champs in the Eastern Conference Finals before
dropping four straight and sending Jordan and company on their way to
a three-peat celebration with Phoenix. But now, a season later, Jordan had
voluntarily walked away from the game. This left Ewing and his mates at
their unchallenged peak and thus an odds-on favorite in the championship
lottery. Pressure was extreme on the New York team to finally take a title
before Ewing was over the hill and those around him had slowed in their
game as well. There could seemingly be no excuse with Jordan gone and
no dynasty ballclubs in sight to take Chicago's place. And the Knicks did
deliver against the Bulls in post-season with a hard-fought seven game
triumph in the eastern semi-finals. But then, an inspired Indiana Pacers
team snuck up on New York as Baltimore had done 20 years earlier. With
Reggie Miller ripping the chords for a record 25 fourth-quarter points, the
upstart Pacers pulled a stunning upset in game five of the eastern finals and
seemed poised to render New York yet another deadly knockout punch.

The Knicks somehow survived Indiana (they roared back for nip-and-
tuck victories in games six and seven) and qualified for the '94 NBA
Finals; yet Pat Riley's team never played with confidence against an
equally erratic Houston Rockets ballclub featuring Ewing's truest nemesis,
Hakeem Olajuwon. The best New York could do was rally to push the
sloppy sleep-inducing series to a full seven games. Fans and critics everywhere responded negatively to the New York rough-and-tumble style of
defense-oriented play—especially in the wake of three years of playoff
showtime with Michael Jordan's stylish Bulls. Knicks jokes now abounded
everywhere (soccer's World Cup performances on US soil a month later
were repeatedly and sarcastically praised as offering better offensive displays than the Knicks-Rockets NBA title series). In the aftermath of Hous-

ton's championship victory over New York, there were even many calls from fans and NBA officials alike for adjustments to the NBA game that would prevent such uninspired displays during future championship rounds.

In the end another expected NBA title run had gone up in flames and another league crown had departed to one of the NBA western outposts, and thus escaped the eastern basketball capital of New York. And this had perhaps been the last shot for the current Knicks team under coach Pat Riley. Other teams in the east (especially Orlando, with Shaq O'Neal, Charlotte with Alonzo Mourning, and much-improved Indiana and Atlanta ballclubs) now seemed on the verge of becoming full-scale powerhouses. Ewing was aging and the players around him (John Starks, Charles Oakley, Charles Smith, Anthony Mason) didn't seem to have what it takes to provide a champion. The June drafting of football's 1993 Heisman Trophy winner Charlie Ward out of Florida State University as a point guard hopeful didn't seem to offer any important reinforcements either.

If two black seasons seem to highlight Knicks basketball history, then it is equally true that two infamous lost post-season games are crammed with all the misery and frustration of the ignoble Knicks tradition. The first was the game that ended the 1971 season.

Despite a continuation of the injuries that had plagued center Willis Reed during the latter stages of the championship 1970 campaign, the Knicks looked for all the world ready to defend their title in the first full season of the '70s. If Milwaukee had shadowed the New Yorkers right down to playoff time during Lew Alcindor's stellar rookie campaign, the addition of veteran superstar Oscar Robertson had made the Bucks even more formidable an opponent. Word everywhere on the street favored a New York versus Milwaukee NBA Final now that the league had realigned into four divisions and Milwaukee sat in the Western Conference as the Midwest Division pacesetter. The Bucks did their part by breezing by the Warriors and Lakers at playoff time; New York looked safe in early outings as well, after disposing of Atlanta and taking a 2–0 lead on Baltimore. But in the end the board strength of Baltimore's Wes Unseld and Gus Johnson (the NBA's first backboard smasher) was too much for a New York team without a healthy Willis Reed. Baltimore took games three, four and six; and when Bradley missed a jumper at the buzzer in game seven, the Knicks were victims of a shocking Eastern Conference upset, to the narrow count of 93–91. Two more trips to the NBA Finals, in '72 and '73, would yet mark the Knicks of the Reed-Frazier-Bradley era as one of the legendary NBA outfits of the early 1970s. But after the infamous upset of April 19, 1971, there would be no talk of dynasties surrounding the basketball team that played its games in the venerable Madison Square Garden.

A second game nearly as disarming to the Madison Square Garden faithful was one played this past spring that will likely be recalled as the game in which often-overshadowed Indiana Pacers star Reggie Miller almost "spiked" the Knicks' dreams and almost silenced a super Knick fan—film director Spike Lee—as well as thousands of other New York faithful already very accustomed to shocking post-season endings. For New York fans this will likely be remembered as "the game that got away" when victory was all but assured. For the Indiana Pacers it was the greatest single moment in ballclub history. For fans everywhere else it was one of the showcase games of NBA post-season history. After two close losses had knotted the Eastern Conference Finals at two games apiece, Ewing and company seemed about to reassert control over a Pacers team that had not won in MSG in more than three seasons (since January 1991). New York enjoyed a comfortable 70–58 margin as the fourth quarter opened. But then the taunting of superfan Spike Lee from a courtside seat seemed to inflame Indiana's streak-shooting Miller, who suddenly burned the nets for a record 25 final-period points. With Miller "on fire" (and gesturing profusely at Lee after every basket) the inspired Pacers surged to a 93–86 victory that sent the heavily favored Knicks reeling. New York would recover in time to edge Indiana in two final contests and earn a championship matchup with Houston. But the stunning MSG loss seemed to have robbed the Knicks of a necessary momentum which never returned to rescue the sliding ballclub against the eventual champion Houston Rockets.

But the story of the New York Knicks has not always been draped in jet-black crepe. For awhile, in fact, as the NBA moved out of its barnstorming first decade and into its growth-spurt second decade, it even looked like the New York franchise (not the one in Boston as it eventually turned out) would be the chosen outfit to supplant the sport's first great dynasty—the George Mikan and Jim Pollard-led Minneapolis Lakers.

Three straight times under coach Joe Lapchick at the start of the '50s, the Knicks appeared as ambitious challengers in the young and still largely unnoticed NBA finals. Yet all three times they lost, and the first two of those defeats were by the narrowest of nerve-wracking margins. The first setback came against the Rochester Royals, a solid and balanced veteran ballclub which had followed the Minneapolis Lakers out of the midwest-based National Basketball League and into the east coast-oriented Basketball Association of America. Rochester had no big-name stars to rely upon, but featured a classy backcourt of Bob Davies and Bobby Wanzer that was the true toast of early NBA seasons.

Once underway, the 1951 NBA Finals seemed like two different series somehow rolled into one. For three straight games it was all Rochester. The Royals romped in an opener at Rochester's Edgerton Park Sports Arena (92–65, with Arnie Risen scoring 24) and took the next two as well by comfortable, if narrower, margins. Then the Knickerbockers rebounded and suddenly took command of a see-saw series with a trio of their own victories. Two of the three New York wins came at the 69th Street Regiment Armory, where the Lapchick club was forced to play post-season games. (The Knicks split home venues between the original MSG—49th

Street and Eighth Avenue—and the musty Armory from 1946 through 1960; the last Armory game was not played until January 16, 1960.) But momentum again shifted at exactly the wrong time and Rochester now regained form to pull out a championship victory back on their home floor when playmaker Bob Davies took control in the final seconds of play. The Knicks had rallied from a 16-point first-half deficit to take a two-point lead into the final minute of play. Then Davies drove to the basket with forty seconds remaining and drew a crucial foul call. Davies's clutch free-throws were enough to ice a 79–75 Royals victory. This was actually as close to a championship as the New Yorkers would ever come in the first quarter-century of franchise exploits.

Lapchick's Knicks failed twice more during the next two straight seasons against the Lakers and towering George Mikan. In the end, in fact, New York contributed heavily to establishing a Lakers' dynasty rather than one of their own. The finals of 1952, for example, were much different than the New York-Rochester series a season earlier. This time the teams neatly traded victories as the pendulum of momentum swung back and forth with precise consistency. Unfortunately for the New Yorkers the pattern continued right down to the bitter end, and thus Minneapolis, who won first (83–79 in overtime), would also win last (82–65). But the final game was not—as the score clearly indicates—at all nip-and-tuck this time around. The final contest in Minneapolis was, in fact, an old-fashioned rout for Mikan and his mates. One irony of this series was that neither team played on its accustomed home floor until game seven transpired in Minneapolis; the Lakers hosted three games in the St. Paul Auditorium, and the Knicks were again forced by April Barnum and Bailey Circus dates at MSG to return to the minor-league environs of the 69th Street Armory.

A second irony was a basket scored by New York's Al McGuire that was mistakenly never counted and subsequently determined the course of game one, and ultimately of the series as a whole. McGuire's bucket on a drive down the lane was somehow missed by the officials after a foul had been whistled. When McGuire subsequently missed one of his two charity tosses, the overlooked basket cost the Knicks at least one and possibly two points. Lapchick protested the contest but to no available. The nip-and-tuck affair ended in a tie, subsequently overcome by the host Lakers in overtime. Had McGuire's basket been properly counted, the Knicks would have owned the opening victory without an overtime session; the one-game turn in results would also suggest a victory for the Knicks who would then have clinched the whole affair with their 76–68 game-six victory back in the Armory.

And a year later, in the 1953 Finals, the pattern of Laker dominance continued. Mikan (19.8 ppg. in post-season action) and Jim Pollard (14.3) were simply too much for the Knickerbockers' front-line defenders, Vince Boryla, Sweetwater Clifton and Connie Simmons. New York did seem to break the Lakers grip with a split in Minneapolis, winning the opener 96–88 and almost pulling out game two (a 73–71 defeat) on the road as well. Sweetwater Clifton enjoyed the finest two games of his career in these openers, teaming with Simmons to at least control, if not silence Mikan. But a return to New York and the 5,000-seat Armory seemed to work reverse magic on the Lakers, who played with even more determination than usual. The defending champs rolled to three straight by counts of 90–75, 71–69, and 91–84. Mikan was again the big scorer (238 playoff points), but backcourt reserve Whitey Skoog played an important role off the bench. Skoog not only threw a defensive blanket over stellar New York sixth man Ernie Vendeweghe, but also canned two game-perserving buckets in the closing seconds of the heated fourth contest.

During their early decades, the New York Knicks took part in two landmark events of early pro basketball history. They would play the first game of BAA history, and thus the "unofficial" first contest of NBA history as well. The locale was Toronto's Maple Leaf Gardens, the opponent the Toronto Huskies, the score 68–66 in New York's favor, and the first points of the new league tossed in by Ossie Schectman.

Also, the Knicks would play a most prominent role in the integration of the NBA scene during the 1950 season. While Boston's Chuck Cooper would be the first black NBA draft choice, and thus receive much of the subsequent tribute as basketball's racial pioneer, it was Sweetwater Clifton who inked the first NBA contract offered to a black man, signing only hours after Walter Brown had tabbed Cooper for Beantown. Clifton, a performer for the Harlem Globetrotters, deserves far more mention than he is usually given as a true black pioneer of the league, though he, like Cooper, missed being the league's first black ballplayer by hours. That honor belongs to another 1950 draftee, Earl Lloyd out of West Virginia State, whose Washington Capitols team took the floor a night earlier than Boston (Cooper) or New York (Clifton) when the fall season officially opened.

Knicks teams, from the mid-'50s to mid-'60s, made the playoffs just once—a first-round drilling by Syracuse (2–0) in 1959. But during these eleven seasons there were some colorful teams and some equally colorful players—Carl Braun, Harry Gallatin, Kenny Sears, Richie Guerin, and Willie Naulls among others. The team had now also settled into Madison Square Garden on a permanent basis by the second half of '59–'60. The following season marked the first in which an entire home schedule would be played at MSG; and the older Garden was itself replaced by its spanking new 33rd Street and Eighth Avenue site on February 14, 1968. The Knicks were indeed established as one of the city's major sports franchises. Only unlike the baseball Yanks, Dodgers and Giants and the football Giants and Jets, the basketball Knicks didn't seem to ever win anything.

In the late '60s there was a definite upswing in talent in Madison Square Garden, inspite of the lack of championship challenges. Much of the new personnel came through effective use of the collegiate draft. The regular string of exceptionally sweet picks would soon read as follows: Willis Reed, Grambling College (1964, second round); Bill Bradley, Princeton

University (1965, territorial choice); Cazzie Russell, Michigan (1966, first overall pick); Mike Riordan, Providence (1967, twelfth round); and Clyde Frazier, Southern Illinois (1967, fifth overall pick in first round). Wise trades also bolstered the talent pool considerably during this period. Dick Barnett came from the Lakers in 1965 for Bob Boozer and immediately posted a 23.1 ppg. scoring season. And in the biggest transaction of all versatile Dave DeBusschere arrived from the Detroit Pistons (where he had served as player-coach) in a hefty 1968 deal for Walt Bellamy and Howard Komives.

Something was now beginning to happen in New York as chemistry clicked and talent amassed. Just when the Celtics were at long last peaking and then finally sliding after Bill Russell's swan-song, New York, after so many fruitless campaigns, seemed ready to make a forceful move. And a final piece of the puzzle was laid in place by 1967. The team got off to a slow start that winter (15–22) and Red Holzman quickly replaced ex-Knick guard Dick McGuire on the coaching sidelines. The team then regrouped strongly and even qualified for the playoffs, as they finished 28–17 down the home stretch under Holzman.

The very next season the Holzman-led ballclub reached a new team record for victories, posting 60 wins and outpacing expansion surprise Milwaukee and rookie Lew Alcindor by four games in the Eastern Division. A lineup second to none in the league found Bradley and De-Busschere under the basket, Willis Reed anchoring the post like an oak tree, and Dick Barnett and Walt Frazier (second in assists that year, behind Seattle's Lenny Wilkens) running the backcourt show. Now expectations were extremely high for the first time in two decades. And in '69–'70 those expectations finally started to be met and then some. The team rolled to a record start, splitting the season's first two matches, and then piling up a new record NBA win-streak of 18 straight. With an insurmountable lead by Christmas, the remainder of the season was truly a dream year in New York—a fantasy joyride like those that come once, and only once, to basketball teams not located in Boston Garden or the Los Angeles Forum.

Post-season, 1970, contained altogether few surprises as the defending champions struggled in an opening-round set with the Baltimore Bullets, but then pulled out a convincing 127–114 victory during the rubber match; New York also had little trouble in a five-game Eastern Conference title matchup with Milwaukee, despite heavy scoring from rookie Lew Alcindor. Out west, the division-winning Atlanta Hawks and runner-up Los Angeles Lakers squared off for the other finals berth. Los Angeles was a team of superstars with Wilt Chamberlain, Elgin Baylor and Jerry West on the roster, but only West (the league's scoring leader at 31.2) had made it through a complete campaign. With Wilt reduced to only 12 games with an early-season knee injury and the often-injured Baylor restricted to only 54 appearances by knee problems as well, the Lakers had limped home only ten games over .500 and two games behind the balanced, but less-talented Hawks. With both Wilt and Baylor now back in playing condition, however, the Joe Mullaney-coached Lakers swept Atlanta in four straight and left little doubt about who was truly strongest in the west.

The NBA Finals at the end of the Knicks' dream season (dubbed "The Miracle on 33rd Street" by more than one over-enthusiastic New York scribe) certainly rank among the two or three most memorable individual championship series in all of NBA history. It was indeed a storybook matchup between the star-rich Lakers and the team-oriented Knicks. One team had three future Hall-of-Famers in Wilt, West and Baylor, and a solid star in forward Happy Hairston (20.2 ppg.) as well. The other was one of the most gritty and confident units ever assembled, with Bradley, DeBusschere, Reed, Barnett and Frazier melding like a well-oiled machine and Mike Riordan, Cazzy Russell and Dave Stallworth providing the best bench-strength in the league. Rookie Lew Alcindor of Milwaukee might now look like a second coming of Bill Russell; the Knicks for their part seemed to be a good imitation of Russell's best Boston Celtics clubs of the past decade.

The dream series didn't disappoint for a moment, either, as the heavy-weights traded blows and star performances in the opening matches. Reed canned 37 to lead New York 124–112 in the MSG opener; Jerry West returned the fire with 34 markers in the Lakers' 105–103 series-evener. Game three at Los Angeles contained the most famous "wasted shot" in basketball history. DeBusschere broke a 100-all tie with a clutch bucket as the clock showed only three seconds remaining. Wilt then inbounded to West who heaved a 55-foot desperation toss that somehow found nothing but net. But West's "miracle shot" was in the end no miracle at all, as the Knicks held on in overtime, 111–108. A second-straight overtime matchup followed as momentum reversed to the Lakers and reserve forward John Tresvant enjoyed a moment in the spotlight by sparking a 121–115 victory in the extra session.

It was back in New York in game five that the memorable series took on its epic proportions and found its waiting storyline. As the Knicks positioned themselves to take command of the game, and perhaps the entire series, in the first half, suddenly unexpected disaster struck for the New Yorkers. Willis Reed went down with a torn thigh muscle and was done for the night and perhaps the year. Coach Holzman was able to find an emergency solution in the second half, however, as his make-shirt "no center defense," with DeBusschere and Dave Stallworth covering Chamberlain, provided the key to an inspired comeback that would eventually prove the pivotal moment of the championship round. The fired-up Knicks rallied from a 13–point half-time deficit to claim an emotional 107–100 victory that positioned them for a possible title-clinching victory back at the Forum. Yet with Reed on the sideline (and Wilt thus pouring in 45 points) the sixth game was no contest at all and fell to the Lakers by an embarrassing 135–113 margin.

The deciding seventh game was a true classic. It was the story of one of the most courageous individual performances ever witnessed on the hardwood. It was also the game New Yorkers will always cite when discussion turns to the basketball version of that city's greatest sports moments. Reed and the Knicks manipulated the MSG throngs during pre-game warmups as the injured star remained hidden in the locker room, appearing to a thunderous ovation only moments before the opening tipoff. With a hobbled Reed back in the lineup the Knicks owned a psychological edge: the gutsy but immobile center leaned on and shoved at Chamberlain to distract his offense and also inflamed passions of the locals with the opening bucket of the game, a long-ranger jumper from the head of the key. Reed's harrassing defense against Wilt, and his inspirational presence on the floor, were all the Knicks seemed to need. Precision shooting in the second half provided a 113–99 victory and a long-awaited NBA title for basketball's showcase city. The Los Angeles version of the Lakers had now extended their NBA Finals losing streak to seven straight; the New York Knicks, however, had now ended their own losing streak in their fourth crack at the league title.

After the 1971 post-season collapse against Baltimore by the defending champion Knicks, the team was again beaten in the NBA Finals of 1972. This time the Lakers would have their revenge against New York and would finally end their own post-season losing skein against DeBusschere, Bradley, Frazier and company. It was essentially the same New York club two seasons later; the starting line-up that won in '70 was still intact and had been strengthened by '72 with the acquisition of superb bench strength in the persons of Earl Monroe (from Baltimore, for Mike Riordan) and Jerry Lucas (from San Francisco, for Cazzie Russell). But Willis Reed went down again in mid-season with another knee injury, and Jerry Lucas had to assume the starting center role. Los Angeles had finally lost Baylor to retirement but had added Gail Goodrich (reacquired from Phoenix) and Jim McMillan (from the '70 collegiate draft). Los Angeles was seemingly a mistake-free ballclub under new coach Bill Sharman and signalled their invincibility in mid-season with a new NBA win-streak that stretched to an incredible 33 games and obliterated the Knick's 2-year-old mark (and the Milwaukee record of 20, which immediately followed) by almost doubling it.

Once the title matchup arrived, it was apparent that the aging Knicks front line could no longer handle the seemingly ageless Wilt Chamberlain, especially with Lucas subbing in the post for Reed. With Wilt concentrating on clearing the boards and defending the lane as Boston's Russell had once done, and with Goodrich and West lighting up the scoreboard, the Lakers easily won their first west coast title with a four-game sweep, soiled only by an opening night loss.

But the great Knicks ballclub of the early '70s was not quite done yet. There would be one more glorious hurrah. The Knicks were back in the NBA Finals once more in 1973 and they were loaded with new ammunition. Monroe had now moved into the starting lineup as replacement for Barnett, and Jerry Lucas had returned to a valuable bench role when Reed healed enough to again man the post. John Gianelli (6–10 rookie from College of the Pacific) and Phil Jackson (with the team since '67–'68) were also increasingly important contributors. And the result would now be the Knickerbockers' second (and so far last) NBA championship banner. The Lakers were, of course, a slight favorite in the '73 title affair, based on their domination of New York a season earlier. But the balance was not the same when New York had Reed instead of Lucas and DeBusschere battling Wilt under the boards. The pattern thus reversed itself completely: Los Angeles drew first blood, but then fell four straight—just as the Knicks had previously done. The measure of this rematch series was a pressing New York defense which held the Lakers talented shooters under the century mark in all four championship victories.

The Knicks dropped off the championship pace in the late '70s as the handful of available stars aged and no new ones took their place. Walt Frazier paced the ballclub with his sixth-straight 20-plus scoring season in '74–'75, then enjoyed two more productive seasons (19.1 and 17.5 ppg.) as the team's "senior stateman" before departing to Cleveland as compensation for the Knicks' signing of free-agent Jim Cleamons in October, 1977. After arriving in mid-season of '71–'72 from Baltimore, Earl Monroe remained a club offensive star for much of the '80s, yet even "The Pearl's" productivity slid drastically during his final campaigns of 1979 and 1980. Bradley retired after the '76–'77 season, but had played effectively for the final time in '74–'75. Bob McAdoo (acquired from Buffalo in December, 1976) was the team's high scorer for three straight years before a questionable trade sent the fluid-shooting big man on to Boston. But with McAdoo—for all his offensive production—the team never climbed out of the middle of the pack and thus never shed their image as hopeless also-rans.

Bernard King was another league scoring star in the early '80s. Three years of pacing the New York ballclub in point-making (1983–1985) were the hallmark career seasons for the former Tennessee All-American who had battled alcohol problems early in his checkered career before becoming one of the league's most potent offensive stars with New York, Washington and New Jersey. King owed perhaps the quickest shot-release of any forward of his generation, and narrowly missed the coveted 20,000-point career barrier (19,655) before several severe knee injuries forced retirement in 1993. But the year King won his single NBA scoring crown ('84–'85) was the very season the Hubie Brown-coached team bottomed out with only 24 victories. And with that low ebb came the lucrative consolation prize of a number one pick in the NCAA draft lottery. Patrick Ewing—who had taken Georgetown University to three NCAA title matches and built a personal reputation as one of the most dominant collegiate big men of all-time—was now on the way to New York and the Knicks fans again dreamed of glories lost and glories never yet achieved.

But the promise of a powerhouse Ewing-led team was painfully slow to develop. Ewing was an immediate impact scorer as well as a shot-blocking defensive presence that almost reminded older fans of the long-armed and omnipresent Bill Russell. The ballclub struggled for several seasons, nonetheless, until former Providence College mentor Rick Pitino coached a run to a divisional title in 1989. Pitino had reversed five back-sliding seasons under Hubie Brown with a 38–44 mark and a second-place Atlanta Division finish in '88; then the '89 Pitino club soared to the top of the Atlantic Division and trailed only Central Division pacesetters Detroit and Atlanta in total victories. What seemed the final gelling of a true contender quickly proved little more than another false start, however, as Pitino soon left for the college ranks (the University of Kentucky) and another brief sag inevitably followed. It was only with the arrival of successful Lakers bossman Pat Riley to start the '91–'92 season that there could be serious hopes for a championship club built around a maturing Patrick Ewing.

With Riley running the ship and teaching the same team-oriented concepts he had practiced with Magic, Kareem and James Worthy out in Los Angeles, the Knicks now faced the same challenge as all other serious contenders of the early '90s. They had to find a way to climb over, around, or under Michael Jordan and the reigning NBA champion Chicago Bulls. For several years, however, the Bulls put a quick end to New York championship dreams, and always with resounding and unambiguous finality. In the final pre-Riley season the Bulls had swept a first-round matchup in three easy games, as Jordan dominated the scoring and the tone of each contest. Riley's debut campaign brought a more respectable standoff as the rivals battled to seven full games in the Eastern Conference Semi-Finals. The rubber match was a crushing 110–81 Chicago romp, however, with Jordan (42) doubling Ewing's (22) offensive output. A rematch in '93 waited for the Eastern Finals, but this time the three-peat Bulls had even less difficulty with New York, at least after escaping a two-game hole at the series outset. Jordan exploded for 54 points in game four and Chicago roared home with four uninterrupted victory celebrations.

Once Jordan was gone, the road seemed suddenly and surprisingly clear. But like so many clearly marked thoroughfares anywhere in Gotham, somebody had forgotten about the hidden potholes. One of those potholes was the inadequate support that now surrounded the untiring Ewing. The backcourt was especially vulnerable. Three-point gunner and playmaker John Starks could light it up in spurts, but was almost always inconsistent with his shooting and play-making. A classic case of Stark's unreliability would arrive with the seventh game in the 1994 Finals against Houston: the New York guard went stone cold at the worst time imaginable, yet wouldn't give up his shooting role (firing 20 straight costly misses from long range) as the team fell into deeper and deeper trouble down the stretch. Derek Harper had also been brought in from Dallas to fill a back-court gap and the veteran Harper actually performed well above his team-mates throughout the Eastern Finals and league Finals. But Harper was aging and couldn't be counted on for the future. And the other pothole—

the biggest of all—was the upstart Indiana Pacers and the Hakeem-led Houston Rockets. Or was it merely—as New York media pundits might have one believe—that teams wearing New York Knicks colors were simply forever doomed to be unable to handle post-season NBA pressure?

Chicago sports fans have built a reputation of national proportion by learning to love not one, but two baseball losers. Of course baseball, more than any other sport, seems to romanticize and mythologize such glorious failure and such gallant losing. Basketball fans in New York have also had to learn how to love a persistent loser. For years they have remained loyal to a Knicks ballclub that is usually either a hopeless also-ran or (in the very best of years) a title-bound upset victim. In those rare seasons, like '93–'94, when all signs point to easy New York victory, these prognostications never quite materialize, and the bitter pill is just a little more difficult to swallow. In recent years, under the coaching of Pat Riley and the post-play of the nearly-great but never quite fulfilled Patrick Ewing, the Knicks have remained a most bitter pill for most of their legions of loyalists.

Suggested Readings on New York Knicks

Berger, Phil. **Miracle of 33rd Street—The New York Knickerbockers' Championship Season**. New York: Simon and Schuster, 1970.

Bradley, Bill. **Life on the Run**. New York: Times Books (Quadrangle Books), 1976.

Cole, Lewis. **Dream Team—The Candid Story of the Champion 1969–1970 Knicks**. New York: William Morrow and Company, 1981.

DeBusschere, Dave (Edited by Paul D. Zimmerman and Dick Schaap). **The Open Man: A Championship Diary**. New York: Random House, 1970.

Frazier, Walt and Joe Jares. **Clyde**. New York: Holt, Rinehart and Winston (Rutledge Books), 1970.

Frazier, Walt (with Neil Offen). **Walt Frazier—One Magic Season and a Basketball Life**. New York: Times Books, 1988.

Pepe, Phil. **The Incredible Knicks**. New York: Popular Library (Associated Features), 1970.

Salzberg, Charles. **From Set Shot to Slam Dunk—The Glory Days of Basketball in the Words of Those Who Played It**. New York: Dell Publishing (Bantam Doubleday), 1987.

New York Knicks Retired Uniform Numbers (8)

Walt Frazier (10)
Dick Barnett (12)
Earl Monroe (15)
Dick McGuire (15)
Willis Reed (19)
Dave DeBusschere (22)
Bill Bradley (24)
Red Holzman (613*, Coach) *Number of his career coaching victories

Year-by-Year New York Knicks Summary

Season	Record	Finish	Coach(es)	Scoring Leader(s)	Playoffs (W-L Record)

Key: * = Tied for Position; # = League Scoring Leader

Basketball Association of America

Season	Record	Finish	Coach(es)	Scoring Leader(s)	Playoffs (W-L Record)
1946–47	33–27	3rd	Neil Cohalan	Bud Palmer (9.5)	Lost in 2nd Round (2–3)
1947–48	26–22	2nd	Joe Lapchick	Carl Braun (14.3)	Lost in 1st Round (1–2)
1948–49	32–28	2nd	Joe Lapchick	Carl Braun (14.2)	Lost in 2nd Round (3–3)

National Basketball Association

Season	Record	Finish	Coach(es)	Scoring Leader(s)	Playoffs (W-L Record)
1949–50	40–28	2nd	Joe Lapchick	Carl Braun (15.4)	Lost in 2nd Round (3–2)
1950–51	36–30	3rd	Joe Lapchick	Vince Boryla (14.9)	Lost in NBA Finals (8–6)
1951–52	37–29	3rd	Joe Lapchick	Max Zaslofsky (14.1)	Lost in NBA Finals (8–6)
1952–53	47–23	1st	Joe Lapchick	Carl Braun (14.0)	Lost in NBA Finals (6–5)
1953–54	44–28	1st	Joe Lapchick	Carl Braun (14.8)	Lost in Round Robin (0–4)
1954–55	38–34	2nd	Joe Lapchick	Carl Braun (15.1)	Lost in 1st Round (1–2)
1955–56	35–37	4th	Joe Lapchick Vince Boryla	Carl Braun (15.4)	Lost in Tie Breaker (0–1)
1956–57	36–36	4th	Vince Boryla	Harry Gallatin (15.0)	Did Not Qualify
1957–58	35–37	4th	Vince Boryla	Kenny Sears (18.6)	Did Not Qualify
1958–59	40–32	2nd	Fuzzy Levane	Kenny Sears (21.0)	Lost in 1st Round (0–2)
1959–60	27–48	4th	Fuzzy Levane Carl Braun	Richie Guerin (21.8)	Did Not Qualify
1960–61	21–58	4th	Carl Braun	Willie Naulls (23.4)	Did Not Qualify
1961–62	29–51	4th	Eddie Donovan	Richie Guerin (29.5)	Did Not Qualify
1962–63	21–59	4th	Eddie Donovan	Richie Guerin (21.5)	Did Not Qualify
1963–64	22–58	4th	Eddie Donovan	Len Chappell (17.3)	Did Not Qualify
1964–65	31–49	4th	Eddie Donovan Harry Gallatin	Willis Reed (19.5)	Did Not Qualify
1965–66	30–50	4th	Harry Gallatin Dick McGuire	Walt Bellamy (23.2)	Did Not Qualify
1966–67	36–45	4th	Dick McGuire	Willis Reed (20.9)	Lost in 1st Round (1–3)
1967–68	43–39	3rd	Dick McGuire Red Holzman	Willis Reed (20.8)	Lost in 1st Round (2–4)
1968–69	54–28	3rd	Red Holzman	Willis Reed (21.1)	Lost in 2nd Round (6–4)
1969–70	60–22	1st	Red Holzman	Willis Reed (21.7)	**NBA Champion** (12–7)
1970–71	52–30	1st	Red Holzman	Walt Frazier (21.7)	Lost in 2nd Round (7–5)

Season	Record	Finish	Coach(es)	Scoring Leader(s)	Playoffs (W-L Record)
1971–72	48–34	2nd	Red Holzman	Walt Frazier (23.2)	Lost in NBA Finals (9–7)
1972–73	57–25	2nd	Red Holzman	Walt Frazier (21.1)	**NBA Champion** (12–5)
1973–74	49–33	2nd	Red Holzman	Walt Frazier (20.5)	Lost in 2nd Round (5–7)
1974–75	40–42	3rd	Red Holzman	Walt Frazier (21.5)	Lost in 1st Round (1–2)
1975–76	38–44	4th	Red Holzman	Earl Monroe (20.7)	Did Not Qualify
1976–77	40–42	3rd	Red Holzman	Bob McAdoo (26.7)	Did Not Qualify
1977–78	43–39	2nd	Willis Reed	Bob McAdoo (26.5)	Lost in 2nd Round (2–4)
1978–79	31–51	4th	Willis Reed / Red Holzman	Bob McAdoo (26.9)	Did Not Qualify
1979–80	39–43	4th	Red Holzman	Bill Cartwright (21.7)	Did Not Qualify
1980–81	50–32	3rd	Red Holzman	Bill Cartwright (20.1)	Lost in 1st Round (0–2)
1981–82	33–49	5th	Red Holzman	M.R. Richardson (17.9)	Did Not Qualify
1982–83	44–38	4th	Hubie Brown	Bernard King (21.9)	Lost in 2nd Round (2–4)
1983–84	47–35	3rd	Hubie Brown	Bernard King (26.3)	Lost in 2nd Round (6–6)
1984–85	24–58	5th	Hubie Brown	Bernard King (32.0)#	Did Not Qualify
1985–86	23–59	5th	Hubie Brown	Patrick Ewing (20.0)	Did Not Qualify
1986–87	24–58	4th*	Hubie Brown / Bob Hill	Patrick Ewing (21.5)	Did Not Qualify
1987–88	38–44	2nd*	Rick Pitino	Patrick Ewing (20.2)	Lost in 1st Round 1–3)
1988–89	52–30	1st	Rick Pitino	Patrick Ewing (22.7)	Lost in 2nd Round (5–4)
1989–90	45–37	3rd	Stu Jackson	Patrick Ewing (28.6)	Lost in 2nd Round (4–6)
1990–91	39–43	3rd	Stu Jackson / John MacLeod	Patrick Ewing (26.6)	Lost in 1st Round (0–3)
1991–92	51–31	1st*	Pat Riley	Patrick Ewing (24.0)	Lost in 2nd Round (6–6)
1992–93	60–22	1st	Pat Riley	Patrick Ewing (24.2)	Lost in 3rd Round (9–6)
1993–94	57–25	1st	Pat Riley	Patrick Ewing (24.5)	Lost in NBA Finals (14–11)

Individual Career Leaders and Record Holders (1946–1994)

Scoring Average	Bob McAdoo (26.7 ppg., 1976–79)
Points Scored	Patrick Ewing (16,191, 1985–1994)
Games Played	Walt Frazier (759, 1967–77)
Minutes Played	Walt Frazier (28,995, 1967–77)
Field Goal Pct.	Bill Cartwright (.552, 1979–88)
3-Pt. Field Goals	Trent Tucker (504)
Free Throws Made	Walt Frazier (3,145)
Free-Throw Pct.	Kiki Vandeweghe (.886, 1988–92)
Rebounds	Willis Reed (8,414, 1964–74)
Rebound Average	Willis Reed (12.9 rpg., 1964–74)
Personal Fouls	Willis Reed (2,411)
Assists	Walt Frazier (4,791)
Steals	Michael Ray Richardson (810, 1978–82)
Blocked Shots	Patrick Ewing (1,984)

Individual Single-Season and Game Records (1946–1994)

Scoring Average	Bernard King (32.9 ppg., 1984–85)
Points Scored (Season)	Patrick Ewing (2,347, 1989–90)
Points Scored (Game)	Bernard King (60, 12-25-84 vs. New Jersey Nets)
Minutes Played (Season)	Walt Frazier (3,455, 1970–71)
Field Goal Pct. (Season)	Bernard King (.572, 1983–84)
Free-Throw Pct. (Season)	Kiki Vandeweghe (.899, 1990–91)
3-Pt. Field Goals (Season)	Trent Tucker (118, 1988–89)
3-Pt. Field Goals (Game)	John Starks (8, 3-31-92 vs. Chicago Bulls)
Rebounds (Season)	Willis Reed (1,191, 1968–69)
Rebounds (Game)	Willis Reed (33, 2-2-71 vs. Cincinnati Royals)
	Harry Gallatin (33, 3-15-53 at Fort Wayne Pistons)
Assists (Season)	Mark Jackson (868, 1987–88)
Assists (Game)	Richie Guerin (21, 12-12-58 vs. St. Louis Hawks)
Personal Fouls (Season)	Lonnie Shelton (363, 1976–77)
Steals (Season)	Michael Ray Richardson (265, 1979–80)
Steals (Game)	Michael Ray Richardson (9, 12-23-80 at Chicago Bulls)
Blocked Shots (Season)	Patrick Ewing (327, 1989–90)
Blocked Shots (Game)	Joe Meriweather (10, 12-12-79 at Atlanta Hawks)

Best Trade in Franchise History

There have been many over the years, such as the 1960s deals that brought guard Dick Barnett from Los Angeles for Bob Boozer, and center Walt Bellamy from Baltimore for Johnny Green, Johnny Egan, and Jim Barnes. Or the 1970s deals which obtained Earl Monroe from Baltimore (for Mike Riordan and Dave Stallworth) and Jerry Lucas from San Francisco (for Cassie Russell). But each of these blockbuster deals shipped away almost as much as was received in return. The best deal of this vintage seems to be the one in which the Knicks acquired Dave DeBusschere from Detroit in exchange for Walt Bellamy and Howie Komives. DeBusschere provided the final necessary element required to make the 1970 championship team run as a fine-tuned basketball machine. And Dave DeBusschere, of course, would later ably served the franchise in other important front office capacities as well.

Worst Trade in Franchise History

Bob McAdoo was only halfway through his long career as a productive scorer when the Knicks peddled him to the Boston Celtics after three high-scoring late–'70s campaigns. The return on the February, 1979, deal was three draft choices and an unheralded role player named Tom Barker, whose two-year career total of 639 NBA points was but a couple of months' work for the talented McAdoo. It hardly seemed to be enough in exchange for such a marquee player as a recent three-time league scoring champion. And, of course, it certainly wasn't. McAdoo netted better than 5,000 additional career points in the league after he departed New York for Boston, Detroit, New Jersey, Los Angeles and Philadelphia (before retiring to brief Europe league play in 1986).

New York Knicks Historical Oddity

Here is pro basketball's grandaddy franchise, the longest surviving member of the pro basketball world as we know it today. Only the Boston Celtics have been around in the same league and in the same city for as many years. But it was the Knicks that played the very first game in the history of what was soon to become the NBA. And ironically, that first game occurred on Canadian, and not American soil. On November 1, 1946, the Toronto Huskies would play host to the New York Knickerbockers at Toronto's Maple Leaf Gardens. It was the season's lidlifter for a new venture known as the Basketball Association of America. Just over 7,000 spectators turned out to watch an exciting hard-fought contest won 68–66 by New York largely on the clutch shooting of forward Max Zaslofsky. The very first basket in the new league would be scored by New York guard Ossie Schectman only seconds after the opening tipoff. The league that would soon (three years later) be known as the NBA had been formally launched, and it was the still-existing New York Knicks ballclub that owned the first appearance, the first basket, and the first league victory as well.

Knicks All-Time Number One Draft Picks List

New York Knicks
1947 Walt Misaka (Utah)
1948 Harry Gallatin (NE Missouri State)
1949 Dick McGuire (St. John's)
1950 Irwin Dambrot (CCNY)
1951 Ed Smith (Harvard)
1952 Ralph Polson (Whitworth)
1953 Walter Dukes (Seton Hall)
1954 Jack Turner (Western Kentucky)
1955 Kenny Sears (Santa Clara)
1956 Ronnie Shavlik (North Carolina State)
1957 Brendon McCann (St. Bonaventure)
1958 Mike Farmer (USF)

1959 Johnny Green (Michigan State)
1960 Darrell Imhoff (California)
1961 Tom Stith (St. Bonaventure)
1962 Paul Hogue (Cincinnati)
1963 Art Heyman (Duke)
1964 Jim Barnes (Texas Western)
1965 Bill Bradley (Princeton)
1966 Cazzie Russell (Michigan)
1967 Walt Frazier (Southern Illinois)
1968 Bill Hosket (Ohio State)
1969 John Warren (St. John's)
1970 Mike Price (Illinois)
1971 Dean Meminger (Marquette)
1972 Tom Riker (South Carolina)
1973 Mel Davis (St. John's)
1974 None
1975 Eugene Short (Jackson State)
1976 Lonnie Shelton (Oregon State)
1977 Ray Williams (Minnesota)
1978 Michael Ray Richardson (Montana)
1979 Bill Cartwright (USF)
1980 Mike Woodson (Indiana)
1981 None
1982 Trent Tucker (Minnesota)
1983 Darrell Walker (Arkansas)
1984 None
1985 Patrick Ewing (Georgetown)
1986 Kenny Walker (Kentucky)
1987 Mark Jackson (St. John's)
1988 Rod Strickland (DePaul)
1989 None
1990 Jerrod Mustaf (Maryland)
1991 Greg Anthony (UNLV)
1992 Hubert Davis (North Carolina)
1993 None

Chapter 4

CHICAGO BULLS

Long and Painful Prelude to Air Jordan

All-Time Franchise Record: 1197–1088, .524 Pct. (1966–1994)
NBA Championships (3): 1990–91, 1991–92, 1992–93
Greatest Franchise Player: Michael Jordan (1984–1993)
All-Time Leading Scorer: Michael Jordan (21,541 Points, 1984–1993)
Most Successful Coach: Phil Jackson (295–115, .720 Pct., 1989–1994)
All-Time Franchise Team: Artis Gilmore (C), Scottie Pippen (F), Bob Love (F), Jerry
  Sloan (G), Michael Jordan (G).

The '50s opened with the reign of basketball's first great dynasty franchise in Minneapolis, and its first great superstar in bulky George Mikan; it closed with the rise of Auerbach's juggernaut Cousy-led Celtics. The sixties were colored through and through with Boston Celtic kelly green and walled from end to end with Bill Russell and Wilt Chamberlain. In the pro basketball void that was the "forgotten seventies" there was little enough to cheer about except perhaps the resurrection of the Celtics under Coach Tom Heinsohn and the coming of age of an oversized youngster named first Alcindor, and later Jabbar. Then, in the revival of the eighties, it was all Bird and Magic and the fourth consecutive decade of titanic struggles between the Lakers and the Celtics. And finally in the nineties, Air Jordan took off as the game's greatest media celebrity. With Jordan carrying the Chicago franchise on his shoulders (and on the coattails of his endorsements portfolio) a new dynasty team wore the colors of the long lackluster Chicago Bulls.

For those who have only discovered the NBA in the johnny-come-lately age of Turner Broadcasting and Magic, Larry and Michael, the Bulls may indeed seem one of pro basketball's most glorious success stories. Yet in the larger perspective of the league's near half-century history, this current three-time championship club has more often been a colorless doormat than a distinguished leader of the pack.

The Bulls franchise started on an upbeat note with a surprising playoff appearance during the club's maiden season under NBA Coach-of-the-Year, Johnny "Red" Kerr. Most of the first decade featured solid teams under diminutive and scholarly Dick Motta that four times won 50 games, and even took a division title in the club's ninth season. The Bulls' rise to the top of the Midwest Division might have been even quicker but for the presence of another expansion club a few miles to the north in Milwaukee that had the extreme good fortune to own Kareem Abdul-Jabbar (née Lew Alcindor). But then the Chicago club grew old and collapsed entirely for the second half of the '70s and post-season playoff appearances became a true rarity for the Windy City outfit. Just before the drafting of Michael Jordan, the team under coach Kevin Loughery even suffered through one of the worst seasons in franchise history, winning only 27 ballgames and escaping the NBA cellar by only a single-game margin over the lackluster Indiana Pacers.

We modern-day sports fans (and basketball fans in particular) have a remarkably inconsistent attitude toward historical interpretation of our favored national games. Basketball fans come to their sport, after all, with little or no historical perspective. This is inevitably the case because there are surprisingly few hoops fans around who have carried the game with them for decades; few basketball fanatics inherited their passion from fathers, or grandfathers, or uncles. Most fans are thirty-ish "youngsters"— or their juniors—with no access to stars of earlier generations. And to complicate matters, little has been written about the earlier generations of NBA play; and what *has* been written molders on library shelves, since hoop fans—unlike baseball fanatics—tend to have little patience with, or fondness for, the literary treatments of their game.

Yet with little reverence or seeming need for historical perspective, we are at the same time in desperate need of sanction for current events from the archives of the past. Hardly is a new champion crowned than we wish to compare present glories with those of yesteryear. Each new championship series must be "the greatest ever played" and each repeating champion must be measured as the most invincible of all-time. The '92–'93 Blue Jays versus the '50s Yankees or the '40s Cardinals; the three-peat Bulls aligned against the Cousy Celtics. And each new star player must surpass in reputation all who have gone before. Mantle and Mays must outstrip Ruth and Speaker and then give way to Barry Bonds and Ken Griffey, Jr. Larry Bird was simply the greatest ever, until Jordan was even greater. My heroes must be far superior to anyone else's. And while this predilection for such self-justification through our athlete-champions has always been part and parcel of the sporting scene, it has only intensified in an age in which athletes have become TV pitchmen for everything from beer to toothpaste to designer fashions. It is the inevitable fallout of an age of constant hype and unmatched hyperbole.

Thus the ink was hardly dry on the headlines proclaiming the Chicago Bulls' third straight NBA title when every sports columnist in the land worth his mettle took up the common theme—were not the Bulls the greatest basketball team of all-time? Clearly, to win three-straight in an era when repeating at all had been almost unheard of for two decades (no one repeated after the 1968–1969 Celtics until the 1987–1988 Lakers and 1989–1990 Pistons) should be worth more than a Celtics' string in the '60s, earned when Boston was the only decent team. This is the line that got repeated time and again without any balanced assessments of the competition actually faced year-in and year-out by Cousy and Russell and company. It seemingly wasn't enough for fans that the Bulls were an entertaining championship outfit that provided plenty of joy in the watching. Chicago fanatics and sportswriters alike somehow needed an "all-time best" lapel to feel themselves whole and justified.

The best way to assess the Bulls' place in the history book, of course, would be to open the history book itself. But cold hard fact hardly stands a chance against biased rationalizing. Yes, the Celtics won eight straight titles, we were told by today's commentators, but they played in a primitive league consisting of only eight (and later ten) teams, a seeming cakewalk by today's standards. Air Jordan is the greatest media celebrity in sports history and thus obviously the greatest player as well. If fans and media love Jordan as they have never loved anyone save Babe Ruth, then isn't Jordan exactly the same in hoopdom's world as the Babe once was on the diamond? None of the records of the past (and this is usually said or written without remembering that Wilt and Russell scooped nearly 25 rebounds nightly, that Wilt once averaged 50 ppg. for a full season, that Oscar Robertson also **averaged** a triple-double for the same full year) can possibly compare with today's achievements since the players of the '90s are far superior to earlier generations of NBA stars. Can't today's athletes leap higher, run faster and dunk more resoundingly than their predecessors? Since slam dunks make more thrilling "sight-bite" TV highlights, don't they also reflect far better basketball? And so the reasoning disturbingly goes.

What is overlooked here, unfortunately, is the true nature of the evolution of NBA play over the past four decades. Just as it is foolish to argue that baseball stars of the past must be superior to present-day stars because of the numbers they put up (viz., Ruth's 60 homers, Williams's .400 average, dead-ball epoch pitching ERAs, etc.), so is it equally foolish to assume that ancient NBA players are weaker for the same reason (greater individual achievements in the past, like Wilt's scoring averages and the Celtics uninterrupted championship string). But it is equally shortsighted to assume that the general size, speed and leaping abilities of modern hoopsters—along with changes in the game which glorify dunking and have almost totally removed "traveling" as a rules violation—indicate that today's game and its stars are far superior to the best from a generation or two back. The unalterable fact is that the number of select superstar players has likely neither increased nor decreased; nor have their overall playing abilities—as opposed to playing *styles*, which is quite another matter altogether.

Evolutionist and articulate baseball fan Stephen Jay Gould has artfully demonstrated this for the diamond sport in a series of cogent articles (e.g. "Why No One Hits .400 Anymore" in *Baseball & the Game of Ideas*, edited by Peter C. Bjarkman, 1993). Gould argues persuasively that general evolutionary principles and not the superiority or inferiority of past or present stars is what explains why there are no further .400 hitters in baseball today. The simple fact of the matter is that a very small percentage (perhaps 1% or less) of truly exceptional athletes remain about equal in talent from one generation to the next; but as any sport (or any activity, for that matter) progresses, its vast majority of other players hone their skills and close the gap between themselves and the Ruths, and Cobbs, and Williamses. In short, Wee Willie Keeler "hit 'em where they ain't" in the 19th century simply because fielders didn't yet know where to be. In baseball, the equipment has improved, as have the techniques of fielding, positioning and pitching. The gap between the "greats" and the journeymen necessarily evens out. The strong deviations from the standard bell-shaped curve of performance lessen; there are no more .400 hitters, but there are fewer .150 or .200 hitters as well. The lack of .400-hitting today is not found because Boggs is not as great as Williams; rather it comes about because Boggs is surrounded by a greater level of talent (as well as better equaipment and playing conditions) than Williams, and thus the extremes of performance have been virtually eliminated.

The same reasoning can be applied to the NBA as well. It is often jokingly observed that no one will ever score 100 again in an NBA contest like Wilt did, simply because no one will play against as many white men as Wilt did. The racist implications of such an observation are inexcusable; yet behind such a joke lies a certain logic, once stripped of interpretations based on skin color. No one will ever face as many marginal players as Wilt faced, simply because the gap between "average" and "great" in the NBA has been reduced drastically over the past two decades. Clearly overall talent in the NBA is today far greater, if one assesses abilities of the marginal players who today fill out roster spots. But there is no shread of evidence that the handful of a dozen or so superstars of the '60s (Wilt, Russell, West, Robertson, Baylor) were anything but the full equal of Jordan. Ewing, Olajuwon and David Robinson. Indeed there is evidence— in the consistency of their performance and the multiplicity of their skills— that the '60s stars may indeed have been a bit better.

This argument about talent levels—especially the assumption that the average NBA player today (say Scott Williams of the Bulls) is better than the average player of times past (say Howie Komives of the mid-'60s Knicks)—might indeed seem to suggest that Michael Jordan's achievements against modern competition are even greater than were Chamberlain's and Cousy's in some distant age. It might persuade us as well that the Bulls' dynasty should outstrip that of the Beantowners in merit. There *is* a grain of truth in such reasoning—Jordan is indeed a phenomenon in an age when great players seem rarer than they were in the '60s—but this is not admissible evidence that Jordan is necessarily any more talented than Oscar or Russell or Wilt. For one thing, it is like comparing apples and oranges. As a guard Jordan can not be reasonably compared with towering centers or even bulky power forwards—their roles, styles and purposes are far too different. And as a player whose game was built largely on flashy one-on-one showmanship—i.e. "moves"—MJ can not be compared with "The Big O" either. Robertson shunned showy displays a lá Jordan. Instead he was the "prototype all-around guard" and a conservative playmaker who avoided flashy offense in favor of an unmatched economy of productive scoring, passing and rebounding that has never been seen in another backcourt performer since.

The argument in fact works in precisely opposite ways. The very claim that the Celtics played in a league of but eight teams is tribute to the *superiority*, and not the inferiority, of their achievement. There were just as many superstars in the '60s—Wilt, Oscar, West, Baylor, Pettit, Walt Bellamy, Hal Greer and Nate Thurmond were the match of any half-dozen of today's best. And their impact on the outcome of a game was far greater, since it was the rest of the league's more average players who were clearly inferior by today's standards. And because there were the same dozen great players as in almost any epoch, but only eight teams to house them, the better teams (each with a couple of these superstars or more) were even stronger, more balanced and harder to beat. Imagine the Bulls facing a playoff final or semifinal against a team (let's say the Knicks) that featured Ewing, Barkley *and* David Robinson all in the same starting lineup. This is what the Celtics of the '60s faced, season after championship season, in taking the floor numerous times during the year against the Lakers, Royals, Hawks, Warriors and Sixers.

One must also remember that the true test of a dynasty team is its miraculous ability to consistently win in the face of insurmountable odds, strange bounces, injuries, and fluke occurrences of all kinds. To survive is the mark of greatness, and the longer a champion lasts the greater it is. Two momentary slips by the opposition in 1993 (Charles Smith's missed layups at the buzzer in the pivotal game 5 of the Eastern Finals, and poor Phoenix floor strategy in the final seconds during game 6 of the NBA Finals) allowed Chicago to survive as if by divine intervention. But would they repeat this time and again throughout yet another five playoff summers (as did Boston two decades earlier)? The answer was soon forthcoming that they of course would not. In a tension-packed game 7 of the 1994 Eastern Semifinals, the ball would bounce New York's way instead. At this point the Celtics of Auerbach stand unchallenged as durable champions for all ages. The Bulls are not yet even close.

And other measures of "greatest team ever" might also work against the Chicago Bulls as well. The 1971–'72 Lakers won only a single title, yet they strung together 33 straight regular-season victories, perhaps the most remarkable team feat in all NBA history—if not all American sports history. The Sixers of 1982–'83 marched through the entire playoff season with but a single loss, something the Bulls have fallen short of matching (their best post-season record being 15–2 in 1993). And the Lakers clubs of the early '70s (with Baylor, West, Hairston, Goodrich, Jim McMillan and Chamberlain) were personnel-wise the most talented outfit ever crammed onto the same floor, save perhaps the Celtics, who always somehow beat them out in late spring and early summer.

The facts have now clustered to mandate that the Chicago Bulls of the early 1990s were hardly a team that stood above all others in NBA annals. One of the five or six most memorable NBA championship outfits, perhaps, but hardly a true candidate for ultimate king of the mountain. Comparisons with the '60s Celtics simply don't hold up: Boston's domination was over a league packed with many more serious contenders (Pettit's Hawks, Oscar's Royals, Wilt's Warriors and Sixers, and the powerhouse Lakers of West, Baylor and again, finally, Wilt) if not more quality teams overall, and the skein also stretched four times as long as the Bulls' title string. Jordan's early retirement and the failures of the 1994 Bulls in their Eastern Conference shootout with the Knicks have put a quick end to any further talk of a Chicago dynasty. Yet this is not to say that the Bulls have not been one of the most colorful and exciting teams of the modern NBA era. It is only that their many oncourt achievements cry out for far more balanced historical assessment than has usually been given by today's over-enthusiastic and short-sighted fans and media.

Tale of Two Contrasting Decades

The Bulls of the 1990s are, all the above quibbles aside, a basketball team of considerable achievement. And that achievement is in every sense tied up with the individual performances of Michael Jordan. Jordan *was* the 1990s Chicago Bulls, just as Russell was the '60s Celtics, and Mikan was the '50s Lakers. Two decades of Bulls basketball before Michael Jordan, however, today stand in history like odd-fitting bookends. The teams taking the floor in Chicago Stadium for the first nine years of Bulls history were never exactly shoddy, although none of these teams were spectacular either. There are no embarrassing 15-win seasons to be buried here; but there are no sudden and miraculous rises to the upper regions of post-season play to be wistfully recalled and celebrated, either.

The very first Bulls team of '66–'67 did send some shock waves around the NBA, however. Never before had an expansion team played quite so well as the one wearing red and black and representing the Windy City. That is, of course, if one rules out ABA transfers Denver and San Antonio in 1977. Neither of those clubs, of course, were expansion teams in any true sense. Under coach Johnny "Red" Kerr—former iron-man center with the Syracuse Nats and Philadelphia 76ers—Chicago won an amazing 33 games. This remains to date a record for a neophyte ballclub. It was indeed a pleasing turn of events for NBA movers and shakers who were making their third attempt to establish a successful franchise in Chicago. Twice before Chicago teams had failed—first the Chicago Stags (an NBL holdover that lasted exactly one season in the newly reorganized NBA of 1949–'50) and later the Packers, who changed their name to the Zephyrs in 1962, then packed up and moved to Baltimore (as the second edition of the Baltimore Bullets) in 1963–'64. When the Bulls under Kerr enjoyed such a propitious start it looked like this time around success was assured for a team in the nation's second largest city.

Kerr, for his part, was the Coach-of-the-Year award winner. The team's winning tear assured a playoff spot in the very first season out of the gate. Yet the Chicago ballclub was not exactly a box office smash, though it did draw its share of fans. An average throng of 4,772 patrons attended games in Chicago Stadium that year. They were entertained by a strong expansion lineup of Don Kojis and Bob Boozer at the forwards, Erwin Mueller at center, and Jerry Sloan and Guy Rodgers in the guard slots. Boozer and Rodgers led the scoring parade at 18.0 ppg. Boozer then upped his average to 19.7 ppg. in the 3–0 playoff sweep which Chicago suffered at the hands of the St. Louis Hawks.

The Bulls made gradual if not spectacular improvement over the next four seasons. Kerr was around only one more winter before Dick Motta came on board to direct the holding-pattern ballclub. The Chicago team then drew its first attention as a legitimate challenger in the first season of the '70s. Motta's third edition of the Bulls posted a 51–31 mark, which was good enough for a second-place slot in the Midwest Division, 15 full games behind another fast-starting expansion team in Milwaukee—a team that featured young Lew Alcindor (Kareem Abdul-Jabbar). Motta's surprising Bulls team could boast two future NBA coaches—Jerry Sloan and Bob Weiss—at the guards, and another—Matt Guokas—on the bench. Chet Walker, Bob Love and Tom Boerwinkle provided an imposing front line. What the Bulls put out on the floor nightly was a devastatingly physical outfit, if not necessarily a smooth-running offensive unit. And though they trailed the Bucks by a mile, they nonetheless owned the third best record in the entire league, only a game behind second-ranking New York. In the playoffs, however, the Bulls lost a tough seven-game first-round series to the Los Angeles Lakers.

The next four seasons under Motta were easily the best of the pre-Jordan era. The victory totals for these years stood at 57, 51, 54, and 47 for an average of better than 52 victories a season. While the first three of these campaigns brought second-place finishes (all three times behind the powerful Milwaukee Bucks), the lowest victory total actually represented a climb to a first-ever division title in 1974–'75. The Bulls seized an opportunity to move up when Milwaukee suddenly sank from prominence: Jabbar had broken his hand in the pre-season (slamming it against a backboard in a fit of anger) and Oscar Robertson had finally retired. Chicago now had enough firepower after Bob Love returned from an early season holdout to top the second-place Kansas City-Omaha Kings by three full games. Nate Thurmond had been acquired from Golden State (in a swap of centers involving Clifford Ray) and despite the veteran all-star's surprise drop in offensive production (7.9 ppg.) the Bulls now boasted a potent starting five that also included Chet Walker, Jerry Sloan and Norm Van Lier. And for the second straight year this Bulls team reached the second post-season round, this time actually posting a winning 7–6 play-off ledger.

During the successful string of seasons under Motta a host of new talent came on board. Gar Heard was a fourth future NBA mentor who joined the roster in 1972–'73. But these upscale teams also included memorable players like Bob Love (6–8 slender quick-shooting forward), Chet "The Jet" Walker (who earlier starred with the champion '67 Philadelphia Sixers), Norm Van Lier (6–1 playmaker who was a defensive specialist and also logged over 5,000 career assists) and Jerry Sloan (6–6 guard who would, a decade later, serve as Bulls head coach). Love was the biggest drawing card and the first scoring hero for Chicago, more than a full decade before Michael Jordan would come along. The Southern University star had been a 1966 draft pick of the Cincinnati Royals, where he played two seasons before joining the Bulls. Overcoming a severe stuttering problem to succeed as a pro athlete, the courageous Love established a club mark by pacing the team in scoring seven straight seasons, a standard that Jordan would later only tie. Twice (1971 and 1972) Love was sixth in the entire league in scoring while averaging over 25 ppg.

Motta's division-winning team of '74–'75 was a high-water mark that would not be soon matched. There was an immediate dropoff the next season to 24 wins, and the bottom rung in the division standings. Chet Walker had retired and another crucial personnel loss occurred when Jerry Sloan injuried a knee after only 22 games. With Love in his last full season (but still averaging 19.1 ppg.) the aging team was now ineffectual and a losing habit was already starting to set in.

And that losing habit soon stuck to the Chicago team like glue. Like super glue! The entire second half of the decade would see increasing incompetence reign in Chicago Stadium. The club which dropped to a record-low 24 victories in 1976 would make the playoffs only twice (1977 and 1981) over the next nine years. Ed Badger was on board only two seasons as Motta's ineffectual coaching replacement, and 7-footer Artis Gilmore had come from the ABA as the club's new big gun. But if Gilmore racked up points (22.9 in '78 and 23.7 in '79) and rebounds, he garnered few victories. After Larry Costello and Scotty Robertson split coaching duties in '78–'79 former star guard Jerry Sloan took the controls in the fall of 1979. Sloan would remain only until partway through the '81–'82 campaign. And the long losing skein did not finally bottom out until an embarrassing 27–55 fifth-place year in 1983–'84 under new coach Kevin Loughery.

But then everything changed drastically on the Bulls' horizon, and the catalyst for such change was a fortuitous college draft at the conclusion of Loughery's maiden campaign. The 1984 draft lottery was the deepest in many years—raw but awesome Nigerian native Hakeem Olajuwon at Houston, injury-prone but coveted Kentucky center Sam Bowie, collegiate player-of-the-year Michael Jordan out of North Carolina, Jordan's UNC teammate Sam Perkins, and Auburn's All-American wide-body Charles Barkley. Houston's Rockets had won an earlier coin flip and owned the first pick, which they expended as expected on local favorite Olajuwon. Portland grabbed risky Bowie, the potential franchise player other teams also wanted, including Chicago. It seems that 7-footers bring out a special hunger in general managers, whether they are healthy or exceptionally talented or not. Owning the third selection, Bulls GM Jerry Krause was somewhat dismayed at losing Bowie and thus reluctantly weighed the selection of Jordan, Perkins or Barkley. The Bulls gambled on Jordan and the choice would evermore rank as one of the wisest in NBA drafting history.

Taking Off With Air Jordan

A few rare players have an immediate impact on the teams they join as raw rookies. Certainly Jabbar (then Alcindor) turned things around overnight for the expansion Milwaukee Bucks. And Wilt and Oscar both reshaped the league in a hail of scoring their first seasons in action. And no one has perhaps taken the NBA by bigger storm than Bill Russell— an eleven-time world champion in only thirteen seasons of action. But Michael Jordan took awhile to grow on Chicago and on the league. It wasn't exactly slow growth; but it wasn't overnight mania either. In fact, not only did Jordan not turn the Bulls into immediate winners and into the media darlings of the NBA they later became, but for awhile, despite his own high level of performance, MJ was actually blamed for the Bulls' continued lack of progress toward NBA elite status. He was seen (perhaps unfairly) as a ball-hog who ruined team cohesiveness, and a prima donna who undermined a winning spirit.

It was, of course, not a matter of Air Jordan himself starting slowly— not by any standard imaginable. Basketball's greatest "air show" took off down the runway during his earliest weeks in the league. It was obvious to most that the NBA's "future" after Magic and Larry Bird was already wearing uniform number "23" for the Chicago Bulls. Jordan had an abso- lutely huge rookie season. He averaged 28.2 ppg. (one of the highest figures ever for a rookie, though not in the class with Wilt or Oscar) and he also showed impressive numbers in other categories: 6.5 rebounds, 5.9

assists, 2.39 steals. He was named for the All-Star Game and would be the last rookie to boast that honor until Shaquille O'Neal came along nearly a decade latter. And he easily outdistanced number one draft pick Akeem Olajuwon for Rookie-of-the-Year honors.

Jordan's All-Star Game appearance in the Indianapolis Hoosier Dome was one of the big stories of the year, although not an entirely positive one. Veteran stars like Isiah Thomas, Larry Bird and Bernard King on the East squad were apparently mifted by the media attention lavished on the Chicago rookie, and made certain during the game that Michael had very little opportunity to actually handle the ball (Jordan attempted but nine shots and scored but seven points). But all this hype surrounding Michael Jordan did not immediately rescue and revive the Chicago Bulls as a mediocre team. The ballclub plugged along six games under .500 for the season and sold out only seven home games in dingy Chicago Stadium. All that, of course, would be changing dramatically in the very near future.

But there would be at least one faltering step back before the imminent giant leap forward. The second year for Michael Jordan and his Bulls teammates was a total disaster. Kevin Loughery had been replaced by Stan Albeck in hopes of an upgrade in team image and performance. But rarely has a new coach gotten a worse welcome-on-board present. Only a few games into the first month of his sophomore campaign Michael Jordan went down in a west coast game and had suffered a broken left foot. The star would be lost for much of the remainder of the season (he made only a few token rehabilitation appearances with restricted playing time at season's end) and it would now overnight become obvious to everyone how great MJ's impact on the Bull's lineup had actually been. The team waffled and finished 18 games under the break-even point. Stan Albeck, of course, didn't personally survive the massacre.

Jordan was back as strong as ever in '82, but Albeck wasn't—both events delighting Bulls faithful and management. The new coach was a former flashy ballhandler and playmaker with the Philadelphia 76ers, Doug Collins, who obviously knew something about stylish guard play. And Collins knew enough to give Jordan the ball and let him do his own thing ninety percent of the time. Jordan's thing, of course, was to immediately tear up the league on his way to the first of his seven straight scoring titles. MJ's average of 37.1 ppg. that season would be the highest of his career and the highest ever recorded by anyone other than Wilt Chamberlain and Elgin Baylor (whose one injury-shortened 38.3 season stretched over only 48 games). The Bulls star also recorded 236 seals and blocked more shots (125) than thirteen of the league's starting centers. While Magic Johnson was that year's NBA MVP it was clear that Jordan—a superstar at both the offensive and defensive ends of the court—was now already the league's MAP—"most amazing" player. Jordan alone was enough to pull the Bulls back to just shy of the .500 mark. He was not enough, however, to prevent a first-round sweep at the hands of Larry Bird's Celtics. The Celts simply let Jordan do his thing (which included a record

63 point game) and closed down everything else Chicago had to offer. It was another classic case of a good team triumphing handily over a good player.

With Jordan now clearly in charge of his team and of most of the league as well, and Doug Collins handling the details of the bench and keeping his superstar happy, the Bulls soon leaped to the next plateau with 50 wins and a trip to the second round of post-season playoffs. The improved record also meant new respectability in the form of a second-place (tied with Atlanta) finish in the Central Division, four games behind Detroit. Jordan had no serious challengers for scoring honors as Dominique Wilkins finished almost five points behind MJ's 35.0 ppg. average. And Michael was now both the Edge NBA MVP and the Master Lock NBA Defensive Player of the Year. No player—not even the versatile Oscar Robertson—had ever achieved such a "double" before (although, in fairness to Oscar, who was versatile on offense but concentrated less as a defender, NBA Defensive All-Star Teams were not even named until the final six seasons of his career). In the playoffs the Bulls dispensed with Cleveland (3–2) but simply couldn't cope with the depth of the Detroit Pistons team headed for a final showdown with the Lakers. Detroit simply wore down the Bulls in five games (4–1), despite the playoff-best 36.3 average of the sensational Jordan.

Chicago's overall record dropped in '88–'89 as the team sank to 47 wins and trailed Cleveland, Atlanta, and Milwaukee, as well as first-place Detroit, in the top-heavy divisional race. But Jordan's maturity and the jelling of a unit around him now became more evident when post-season again rolled around. Once more the Cavs were overcome in a tight five-game series when Jordan's own 16-footer at the buzzer shocked Cleveland in the deciding fifth game. MJ and company had gained momentum and next climbed over the New York Knicks, who had reigned in the Atlantic Division, but couldn't shut down Air Jordan. A rematch with Detroit—this time in the Conference Finals—was enough, however, to prove that Chicago still didn't have enough horses to compete at the true championship level. Scottie Pippen (14.4 ppg.) and Horace Grant (12.0 ppg.) had supplemented Jordan along the front wall with fine sophomore seasons. But the Bulls, as a legitimate contender, had not yet fully arrived. A running mate for Jordan at the guard slot remained a special problem since B. J. Armstrong's talented play was still one season away. The Chicago Bulls were indeed up and running, but they were still largely marking time and running in place.

Saga of the Three-Peat

The exciting saga of Chicago's reign as NBA world champions actually begins with the season before the Bulls made it all the way into the NBA Finals. This would be a year of major transition at Chicago Stadium. First,

Doug Collins was suddenly and surprisingly out as coach, reportedly canned because of ongoing squabbling with franchise-player Jordan. The replacement would be a most fortuitous choice, however—Collins's assistant Phil Jackson. In their first year under the former reserve NBA center—a no nonsense coach who brought out the best in team-oriented play—the Bulls kept up momentum with 55 regular-season victories. But once again when the month of May rolled around, Jordan and the Bulls couldn't manage to step over Bill Laimbeer, Isiah Thomas, and the rest of those Bad-Boy Detroit Pistons.

A second straight loss at the hands of Detroit (this time in seven games) in the conference finals proved a hard pill to swallow for the growing legions of Bulls fans. There was a growing sense of frustration, and even a gloomy feeling that perhaps it was true that Jordan, for all his spectacular play, was simply not a reliable winner when the championship chips were on the line. But the 93–74 pasting, delivered to the Bulls by Detroit in game seven of the 1990 conference finale, was to be a significant point of departure. For it would now prove to be the last post-season series the Chicago team would lose over a lengthy stretch that included the next four calendar years.

The Chicago team under Phil Jackson started slowly in '90–'91 by winning just 12 of their first 20. Not a bad start for other teams perhaps, but not what overconfident Chicago fans now expected. But things righted themselves in a hurry and the Bulls were 49–13 for the remainder of the season. Next the Central Division champions proved that they had finally arrived at the next level of excellence when they mowed down, in quick succession, the Knicks (with Patrick Ewing), the Sixers (with Charles Barkley), and Pistons (with Isiah Thomas). The 1991 post-season run toward a title had started in most impressive fashion as the Bulls posted an 11–1 record throughout the first three rounds and thus entered their first-ever NBA Finals as a somewhat surprising concensus favorite.

The matchup of the Bulls and Lakers in the 1991 NBA Finals would soon prove to be the end of one dynasty and the launching of another. Magic Johnson and his Los Angeles Lakers had long owned the 1980s. Jordan and the Bulls were about to place their own personal stamp on the 1990s. Yet when the Lakers, under new coach Mick Dunleavy, and with European import Vlade Divac rather than Jabbar stationed at center, won the series opener in the Bulls' own backyard, it looked like the Chicago Bulls' inheritance was on hold and Magic was still the post-season NBA king. The thrilling win for the Lakers and wrenching loss for Chicago had come about when Los Angeles escaped with a seeming miracle—a desperation three-pointer by veteran Sam Perkins just seconds before the final buzzer.

The Bulls soon caught fire, however. They rebounded when spurred on by a wild Chicago Stadium crowd and took game 2 in lopsided fashion (107–86) to knot the series. The NBA Finals were still being played under the old format of 2–3–2 and thus when the Bulls next travelled to the west coast they made quite sure a return trip home wouldn't be necessary. Game 3 was an overtime thriller (104–96 for Chicago), but the final two contests were all Chicago (97–82 and 108–101) as a supporting cast of Pippen, Paxson and Horace Grant stepped forward to control the action. Jordan paced all scorers with a 31.1 post-season average and easily captured playoff MVP honors. By sweeping three straight at the LA "Fabulous Forum" the Chicago Bulls had officially ended the era of Magic Johnson and formally launched the epoch of Air Jordan. Jordan was now not only the king of hoopdoom and thus the monarch of corporate merchandizing, but he was at long last also a ring-wearing champion. And for the long-suffering fans of Chicago he was now the one true savior and all-time idol of a city that had so desperately craved a big-time sports championship and had been, for so many long seasons, always disappointed in the end by the football Bears, hockey Blackhawks, baseball Cubs and White Sox, and basketball Bulls. But thanks to Michael Jordan Chicago was no longer "the second city"—not, at least, in the glamorous pro basketball world.

The Bulls had very few hurdles to master on their way to repeating their NBA title. First the confident and talented club ran off a team-record 67 regular-season wins. Included in that total were a record-tying 36–5 homecourt ledger and a franchise-record 31 road victories. Air Jordan stretched his string of scoring titles to six, one short of Wilt's quarter-century-old record, though his 30.1 ppg. average was the lowest of the entire skein. Michael was also league MVP for a second year running, plus a first-team selection on the mythical All-NBA squad and the All-Defense Team as well. It was in the post-season's second round that the New York Knicks, in their first year under Pat Riley, provided the only small hurdle for Jordan and his mates, but it was hardly an insurmountable one. Not for a team with Michael Jordan at his peak. New York did force seven games by stealing the Chicago Stadium opener (94–89) and hanging on for Madison Square Garden victories in games four (93–86) and six (100–86). But the Bulls cruised by a 110–81 count in the deciding match, then disposed of Cleveland in six.

Fans of NBA drama could not help but salivate over a championship series like the one which offered itself in 1992, between Portland with "Phi Slamma Jamma" alumni Clyde Drexler and Chicago with the incomparable Jordan. Drexler had come into the league a year before Michael, after leading the University of Houston to the NCAA Finals; Drexler had started slowly for three seasons but by his fifth NBA campaign he had hit full stride and emerged as one of the NBA's top scorers (27.0 ppg. in 1988 and 5th in the league) and certainly its top artistic dunker behind Jordan and Dominique Wilkins of Atlanta.

Drexler and the Trail Blazers had enjoyed a previous crack at the NBA Finals only two years earlier, but had fallen flat against Isiah Thomas and the Pistons. Now Drexler (fourth leading scorer in '92 and second in the MVP balloting behind Jordan) would again have the center stage to test his high-flying game directly against Jordan. Many believed that given either a more glamorous media market (say New York) to play in, or perhaps a stellar outing against Air Jordan in the championship round, now Drexler could forever shed his "Rodney Dangerfield" image. In the end, however, the touted matchup was nothing more than a glorified mismatch. Michael Jordan reached new heights that might previously have been thought impossible and was never any better than in his championship showdown with Clyde Drexler, pouring in 46 points in game five and 35 during a single opening half of game one. Drexler did acquit himself well enough, posting impressive numbers in scoring (26.8), minutes played (39.7), rebounding (7.8) and assists (5.3) throughout the Finals. But in the all-important ledger of game victories the final tally stood Jordan's Bulls four and Drexler's Blazers but two.

The road traveled by the Chicago Bulls to a third title was nowhere near as smooth as the first two title trips. In fact, at times it was downright rocky and treacherous along the booby-trapped route. The club did manage once more to capture a division pennant during regular-season play, although 57 victories trailed both New York in the East and Phoenix in the West for overall best-record honors (and the post-season homecourt positioning that went with it). But the margin was now tighter (three games ahead of Cleveland) and the win column didn't reach the lofty sixty-plus level of the two previous campaigns.

As a result the Bulls lost home court advantage for the third and fourth rounds of post-season play. Yet this was obviously a team on a mission, and one seemingly marked by the hand of destiny. Playing with obvious confidence the Bulls swept into the Finals with relative ease, home court advantage or no. Atlanta was swept aside in three games (3–0) and Cleveland in a mere four (4–0). Forced to open on the road against the Knicks and Patrick Ewing in the Conference Finals, Jordan and company fell twice against a New York pressure defense that kept the champions under 100 points in both contests. But then it was again four straight victories for Chicago, paced by Pippen with 29 in game three and of course by Jordan, who was closing out his career with one of the finest post-season runs ever. Before the championship chase was over Air Jordan would become the first player ever named NBA Finals MVP three straight times (Magic Johnson was the only other three-time winner of the honor) and also join Elgin Baylor and Rick Barry as the only players ever to score at least 30 points in each game of a championship series.

The championship shootout with the Phoenix Suns was indeed a series for all ages, one filled with colorful stories as well as exciting hardwood action. There was of course the best-selling script of the Bulls chasing down a "three-peat" string of titles behind the leadership of America's most popular all-time athlete. There was Charles Barkley, in indomitable "Round Mound of Rebound" and the sport's true anti-hero, adding color and controversy as he always managed to do. And it was a most unpredictable series, as well, one where the usual perk of homecourt advantage (owned this time by Phoenix) didn't seem to mean anything. And at the very end it was a series that also had a most surprising last-minute hero who would emerge at just the right instant to earn his own measure of lasting Bulls' "three-peat" fame.

If the Bulls would soon earn a rare spot in history as only the third three-time title defender, they would grab an even rarer distinction at the outset of the title series by taking back-to-back games on the road in Phoenix. No previous team had ever opened 2–0 on the road in an NBA Finals. Phoenix soon proved just as tough a road team, however, collecting two of three in Chicago Stadium, including a dramatic 129–121 triple-overtime victory in game three. It was the second triple-overtime game of Finals history and the Phoenix ballclub had now participated in both elongated affairs. Only a 111–105 game-four win by Chicago (the only home-court victory of the series) prevented the Bulls from needing another sweep when the series returned to Phoenix for the final showdown. Game six stretched to the wire in a tight defensive battle which left the Bulls trailing 98–96 with 4 seconds remaining on the clock. In the past it had always seemed to be Michael Jordan who had the ball, and thus the glory, when games and championships were on the line. But now Phil Jackson and his staff unveiled one of the great surprise moves of NBA Championship history, freeing veteran guard John Paxson for the final shot while all eyes and defenders remained glued upon Jordan. With 3.9 seconds remaining Paxson cut the nets with a memorable three-pointer and the Chicago Bulls' long-anticipated "three-peat" dream was finally a reality.

The Chicago Bulls three-championship run will long stand proud as a rare moment in NBA history. Only twice before had a team won three titles in a row. It had been done by Mikan and the Minneapolis Lakers when the league itself was just a fledgling affair. And of course the Celtics had run off an untouchable eight straight in the halcyon-era sixties. Thus only once had the Bulls' string been surpassed. With so much apparent balance (and some might even say overall weakening compared to the heyday '80s with the Bird Celtics, Magic Lakers and Isiah Pistons) now restored to the NBA scene it may indeed be some time before we see such a thing again.

Suggested Readings on Chicago Bulls

Aaseng, Nathan. **Sports Great Michael Jordan**. Hillside, New Jersey: Enslow Publishers, 1992.

Bjarkman, Peter C. **Sports Great Scottie Pippen**. Hillside, New Jersey: Enslow Publishers, 1996 (to appear).

Clary, Jack. **Michael Jordan**. New York and London: Smithmark (Brompton Books), 1992.

Gutman, Bill. **Michael Jordan: A Biography**. New York and London: Archway Publishers (Pocket Books), 1991.

Krugel, Mitchell. **Michael Jordan**. New York: St. Martin's Press, 1988.

Logan, Bob. **The Bulls and Chicago: a Stormy Affair**. Chicago: Follett Publishing Company, 1975.

Naughton, Jim. **Taking to the Air—The Rise of Michael Jordan**. New York: Warner Books, 1992.

Smith, Sam. **The Jordan Rules—The Inside Story of a Turbulent Season with Michael Jordan and the Chicago Bulls**. New York: Simon and Schuster, 1992.

Chicago Bulls Retired Uniform Numbers (1)

Jerry Sloan (4)

Year-by-Year Chicago Bulls Summary

Season	Record	Finish	Coach(es)	Scoring Leader(s)	Playoffs (W-L Record)
Key: * = Tie for Position; # = League Scoring Leader					
1966–67	33–48	4th	Johnny Kerr	Bob Boozer (18.0) Guy Rodgers (18.0)	Lost in 1st Round (0–3)
1967–68	29–53	4th	Johnny Kerr	Bob Boozer (21.5)	Lost in 1st Round (1–4)
1968–69	33–49	5th	Dick Motta	Bob Boozer (21.7)	Did Not Qualify
1969–70	39–43	3rd	Dick Motta	Bob Love (21.0)	Lost in 1st Round (1–4)
1970–71	51–31	2nd	Dick Motta	Bob Love (25.2)	Lost in 1st Round (3–4)
1971–72	57–25	2nd	Dick Motta	Bob Love (25.8)	Lost in 1st Round (0–4)
1972–73	51–31	2nd	Dick Motta	Bob Love (23.1)	Lost in 1st Round (3–4)
1973–74	54–28	2nd	Dick Motta	Bob Love (21.8)	Lost in 2nd Round (4–7)
1974–75	47–35	1st	Dick Motta	Bob Love (22.0)	Lost in 2nd Round (7–6)
1975–76	24–48	4th	Dick Motta	Bob Love (19.1)	Did Not Qualify
1976–77	44–38	2nd	Ed Badger	Artis Gilmore (18.6)	Lost in 1st Round (1–2)
1977–78	40–42	3rd	Ed Badger	Artis Gilmore (22.9)	Did Not Qualify
1978–79	31–51	5th	Larry Costello Scotty Robertson	Artis Gilmore (23.7)	Did Not Qualify
1979–80	30–52	3rd	Jerry Sloan	Reggie Theus (20.2)	Did Not Qualify
1980–81	45–37	2nd	Jerry Sloan	Reggie Theus (18.9)	Lost in 2nd Round (2–4)
1981–82	34–48	5th	Jerry Sloan Rod Thorn	Artis Gilmore (18.5)	Did Not Qualify
1982–83	28–54	4th	Paul Westhead	Reggie Theus (23.8)	Did Not Qualify
1983–84	27–55	5th	Kevin Loughery	Orlando Woolridge (19.3)	Did Not Qualify
1984–85	38–44	3rd	Kevin Loughery	Michael Jordan (28.2)	Lost in 1st Round (1–3)
1985–86	30–52	4th	Stan Albeck	Orlando Woolridge (20.7)	Lost in 1st Round (0–3)
1986–87	40–42	5th	Doug Collins	Michael Jordan (37.1)#	Lost in 1st Round (0–3)
1987–88	50–32	2nd*	Doug Collins	Michael Jordan (35.0)#	Lost in 2nd Round (4–6)

Season	Record	Finish	Coach(es)	Scoring Leader(s)	Playoffs (W-L Record)
1988–89	47–35	5th	Doug Collins	Michael Jordan (32.5)#	Lost in 3rd Round (9–8)
1989–90	55–27	2nd	Phil Jackson	Michael Jordan (33.6)#	Lost in 3rd Round (10–6)
1990–91	61–21	1st	Phil Jackson	Michael Jordan (31.5)#	**NBA Champion** (15–2)
1991–92	67–15	1st	Phil Jackson	Michael Jordan (30.1)#	**NBA Champion** (15–7)
1992–93	57–25	1st	Phil Jackson	Michael Jordan (32.6)#	**NBA Champion** (15–4)
1993–94	55–27	2nd	Phil Jackson	Scottie Pippen (22.0)	Lost in 2nd Round (6–4)

Individual Career Leaders and Record Holders (1966–1994)

Scoring Average	Michael Jordan (32.3 ppg., 1984–93)*
Points Scored	Michael Jordan (21,541, 1984–1993)
Games Played	Jerry Sloan (696, 1966–76)
Minutes Played	Michael Jordan (25,842)
Field Goals Made	Michael Jordan (8,079)
Field Goal Pct.	Artis Gilmore (.587, 1976–82, 1987–88)
Free Throws Made	Michael Jordan (5,096)
Free-Throw Pct.	Craig Hodges (.900, 1988–92)
Rebounds	Tom Boerwinkle (5,745, 1968–78)
Rebound Average	Tom Boerwinkle (9.1 rpg.)
Assists	Michael Jordan (3,935)
Steals	Michael Jordan (1,815)

* = NBA Record

Individual Single-Season and Game Records (1966–1994)

Scoring Average	Michael Jordan (37.1 ppg., 1986–87)
Points Scored (Season)	Michael Jordan (3,041, 1986–87)
Points Scored (Game)	Michael Jordan (69, 3–28–90 at Cleveland Cavaliers)
Field Goal Pct. (Season)	Artis Gilmore (.670, 1980–81)
Free-Throw Pct. (Season)	Ricky Sobers (.935, 1980–81)
3-Pt. Field Goals (Season)	Craig Hodges (87, 1989–90)
3-Pt. Field Goals (Game)	Michael Jordan (7, 1–18–90 vs. Golden State Warriors)
Rebounds (Season)	Tom Boerwinkle (1, 133, 1970–71)
Rebounds (Game)	Tom Boerwinkle (37, 1–8–70 vs. Phoenix Suns)
Assists (Season)	Guy Rodgers (908, 1966–67)
Assists (Game)	Guy Rodgers (24, 12–21–66 vs. New York Knicks)
Steals (Game)	Michael Jordan (10, 1–29–88 vs. New Jersey Nets)
Blocked Shots (Game)	Nate Thurmond (12, 19–18–74 vs. Atlanta Hawks)

Best Trade in Franchise History

Forward Bob Love ruled the decade of the '70s for the Chicago Bulls, leading the ballclub in scoring for seven straight seasons, a club record eventually tied but not surpassed by Michael Jordan. Love still ranks as one of the club's all-time great forwards. He was obtained, along with guard Bob Weiss, from the Milwaukee Bucks on November 7, 1968, in exchange for forward Flynn Robinson. Robinson had proved solid for Chicago in the club's second expansion season (16.0 ppg.), but he was in the end no Bob Love.

Worst Trade in Franchise History

This wasn't even a trade per se. And it certainly wasn't a front office transaction that left the franchise in shambles, or even weakened the club in any noticeable way. But sometimes you just have to wonder about the logistics of some pro ballclub transactions. Phil Hicks, for example, was a particularly mediocre 6'7" forward who appeared in 57 games for Houston, Chicago and Denver over two seasons in the late 1970s. But in early 1977 Hicks must have himself felt like a loose ball in a mid-court scramble. Consider the following chain of events. January 11th: Bulls sign Hicks as free agent; January 21st: Bulls waive Hicks, then resign him the same day. February 1st: Bulls waive Hicks again. February 3rd: Bulls resign Hicks as free agent. Later that year, on October 6th, Hicks would be waived by the club for the third and final time in less than a year. All this for a guy who poured in 132 career NBA points.

Chicago Bulls Historical Oddity

Everyone knows that Michael Jordan may well have been the single greatest player in the history of the indoor roundball sport—or, at the very least, the most "hyped" and "merchandized" athlete in basketball history. What is sometimes forgotten is that coming off his exciting collegiate career Jordan was only the third player selected in the deep 1984 college draft. Hoping to build a winner overnight, the Houston Rockets had selected the nation's most promising big man and potential "franchise player" in Akeem (later Hakeem) Olajuwon, out of the University of Houston. Jordan was not even the second choice, falling behind often-injuried yet talented Kentucky center Sam Bowie. Furthermore, the Portland team that might well have taken Jordan ahead of the Bulls could have done so with a draft pick they never even should have had in the first place. If Indiana had not traded that pick away for journeyman center Tom Owens several years earlier, the Pacers (unlike Portland) might well have grabbed Michael Jordan.

Bulls All-Time Number One Draft Picks List

Chicago Bulls
1966 Dave Schellhase (Purdue)
1967 Clem Haskins (Western Kentucky)
1968 Tom Boerwinkle (Tennessee)
1969 Larry Cannon (LaSalle)
1970 Jimmy Collins (New Mexico State)
1971 Kennedy McIntosh (Eastern Michigan)
1972 Ralph Simpson (Michigan State)
1973 Kevin Kunnert (Iowa)
1974 Maurice Lucas (Marquette)
1975 None
1976 Scott May (Indiana)
1977 Tate Armstrong (Duke)
1978 Reggie Theus (UNLV)
1979 David Greenwood (UCLA)
1980 Ronnie Lester (Iowa)
1981 Orlando Woolridge (Notre Dame)
1982 Quintin Dailey (USF)
1983 Sidney Green (UNLV)
1984 Michael Jordan (North Carolina)
1985 Keith Lee (Memphsis State)
1986 Brad Sellers (Ohio State)
1987 Olden Polynice (Virginia)
1988 Will Perdue (Vanderbilt)
1989 Stacey King (Oklahoma)
1990 Toni Kukoc (Yugoslavia)
1991 Mark Randall (Kansas)
1992 Byron Houston (Oklahoma State)
1993 Corie Blount (Cincinnati)

Chapter 5

GOLDEN STATE WARRIORS and PHILADELPHIA WARRIORS

Two Coasts, Two Identities, Two Heroes

All-Time Franchise Record: 1816–1902, .488 Pct. (1946–1994)
NBA Championships (3): 1946–47, 1955–56, 1974–75
Greatest Franchise Player: Wilt Chamberlain (1959–1965)
All-Time Leading Scorer: Wilt Chamberlain (17,783 Points, 1959–1965)
Most Successful Coach: Neil Johnston (95–59, .617 Pct., 1959–1961)
All-Time Franchise Team: Wilt Chamberlain(C), Nate Thurmond (C-F), Paul Arizin (F), Rick Barry (F-G), Guy Rodgers (G)

Through the first four decades of pro basketball history no franchise can boast a greater collection of fan-pleasing sharpshooters. Nowhere does a longer list of league scoring champions line up in the uniform of the same franchise, even if that uniform occasionally underwent a change of city affiliation on the logo. In the late 1940's it was the amazing "Jumpin' Joe Fulks who lit up the scoreboards in the old BAA as the first scoring phenomenon of the hardcourt sport. When the BAA overnight matured into the NBA, the mantle of league scoring ace was passed from Fulks to a pair of gunners also wearing the Warriors colors. Paul Arizin was a nine-time All-Star who averaged 22.8 ppg. for his career and unleashed the revolutionary jump shot as basketball's prime offensive weapon. Arizin's teammate, center Neil Johnston—who once gathered 39 rebounds in a game and another time scored a Madison Square Garden record 50—was the greatest exponent of the hook shot until the indefensible sky-hooking arch-shots of Kareem Abdul-Jabbar came along. With his sweeping lefty hooks the 6–8 Johnston (a towering center who today would stand shorter than some guards) won three scoring titles in succession in the mid-fifties.

But such early path-blazing sharpshooters were just a foreshadowing of the scoring machines the Warriors franchise would eventually unleash on the basketball scene of the '60s and '70s. First came the incredible Wilt Chamberlain, basketball's most intimidating force ever, especially on the offensive end of the game. Chamberlain would not win any team championships until he moved on in late career to the 76ers and finally the Los Angeles Lakers. But with his rookie 1959–60 season in Philly, Wilt unleashed the greatest string of individual scoring domination the sport has ever known. He averaged an unheard of 37.6 ppg. as a rookie and amassed a previously unthinkable 2,707 points. Then for six more seasons Wilt unleashed scoring totals that were truly unthinkable, before or since. Before he was done Wilt's scoring average would climb above forty and then even above fifty! His seasonal point totals would soon top the 3,000-point barrier and then scale the mountain peak of 4,000 as well.

Michael Jordan would eventually equal Wilt Chamberlain's string of seven uninterrupted scoring titles. And Jordan, not Wilt, would one day wear the badge of retiring with the highest lifetime ppg. average, due mainly to the fact that a switch in style and motivation eroded Wilt's totals during the second phase of "The Dipper's" uneven 14-year career. Jordan's career point totals don't even come close to reaching those of Chamberlain and Jabbar (or Oscar Robertson, Jerry West, Alex English, Julius Erving and a host of others for that matter). This is because Air Jordan walked away from the game at the zenith of his career and at the apex of his scoring string. Had he played on, Jordan was an even bet to surpass Wilt's seven-straight titles. But MJ's average also would likely have fell off eventually, just like Wilt's later in his career. Or had Wilt, like Jordan, simply quit at the end of his seven scoring titles, he would have recorded a career average (39.6) far superior to that owned by the Bull's star of the 1990s.

Chamberlain Versus Jordan at End of Seven-Year Scoring Strings

	Years	Games	Points	PPG	Scoring Titles
Wilt Chamberlain	1959–66	543	21,486	39.6	7
Michael Jordan	1986–93	567	18,820	33.1	7

For all his personal milestones, Chamberlain was not a happy camper with the Warriors once the club transfered its operations from Philadelphia on the east coast to San Francisco on the west coast. Wilt's scoring rampages continued largely unabated, but so did his growing discontent. Finally he would be dealt back east to the replacement Philadelphia club in mid-season of 1964–65 by a transplanted Warriors team that had overnight fallen on hard times. Yet even without Wilt, the Warriors' now well-established tradition of big-time scorers would miraculously continue unchecked. In the 1965 draft the San Francisco club used a fourth overall pick to select yet another phenomenal gunner from the University of Miami named Rick Barry. As a rookie Barry popped in an impressive 25.7 ppg. and then in his sophomore campaign he revved up his shooting a notch further and restored the Warriors' grip on the league individual scoring title.

Barry would be lost a year later to the rival American Basketball Association which claimed the Warriors' hotshot as their single early badge of legitimacy. But eventually a faltering ABA—plus a welcomed court decision ending a long legal hassle over Barry's contract—would bring the "Golden Boy" dead-eye back to the Bay area and back to the NBA. Returning after a five-year absence, the player who some still call the greatest forward ever to lace up sneakers would soon enjoy his second great "debut" run with the same Warriors he had earlier left. This time Rick Barry teamed with a talented lineup (Keith Wilkes, Clifford Ray, Butch Beard, Charlie Johnson) to lead the Warriors back to the NBA mountain top and a 1975 NBA Championship victory over the Washington Bullets.

In all, the Warriors would boast 14 individual regular-season scoring titles during the first 22 years of league play. No other team comes close, with the Lakers capturing three (all by George Mikan) and the Pistons (Yardley and Bing) and St. Louis Hawks (Bob Pettit twice) claiming two apiece.

INDIVIDUAL SCORING TITLES FOR WARRIORS PLAYERS (1946–68)

Joe Fulks	Philadelphia Warriors	1946–47	23.2 ppg.	BAA
Joe Fulks	Philadelphia Warriors	1947–48	22.1 ppg.	BAA
Paul Arizin	Philadelphia Warriors	1951–52	25.4 ppg.	NBA
Neil Johnston	Philadelphia Warriors	1952–53	22.3 ppg.	NBA
Neil Johnston	Philadelphia Warriors	1953–54	24.4 ppg.	NBA
Neil Johnston	Philadelphia Warriors	1954–55	22.7 ppg.	NBA
Paul Arizin	Philadelphia Warriors	1956–57	25.6 ppg.	NBA
Wilt Chamberlain	Philadelphia Warriors	1959–60	37.6 ppg.	NBA
Wilt Chamberlain	Philadelphia Warriors	1960–61	38.4 ppg.	NBA
Wilt Chamberlain	Philadelphia Warriors	1961–62	50.4 ppg.	NBA
Wilt Chamberlain	San Francisco Warriors	1962–63	44.8 ppg.	NBA
Wilt Chamberlain	San Francisco Warriors	1963–64	36.9 ppg.	NBA
Wilt Chamberlain	San Francisco/ Philadelphia*	1964–65	34.7 ppg.	NBA
Rick Barry	San Francisco Warriors	1966–67	35.6 ppg.	NBA

*Traded to Philadelphia 76ers at mid-season

Once Rick Barry departed for the ABA in 1967, the Warriors incredible string of scoring titles—like all good things—came abruptly to an end. No one wearing a San Francisco or Golden State Warriors uniform has taken a league point-making title in the 27 seasons that have transpired since; nor has any Warrior come tantalizingly close. Barry *did* finish distant second to Bob McAdoo of the Buffalo Braves during the Warriors championship year of 1975, and ten years later in 1986 Purvis Short of the Warriors trailed Bernard King, Larry Bird and Michael Jordan in fourth place. And since the Warriors title in 1975 there has been equally as large a drop off in championship contenders as there has been in those prodigious individual pointmakers. Never again has the ballclub made it out of the second round of the playoffs, and for one stretch of nearly a decade (1977–1987) the Warriors never even visited post-season play.

The very name "Warriors" is, of course, one that recalls a most glorious NBA tradition. And it is a tradition, after all, that boasts quite a few feathers in the franchise cap besides the run of productive big-scoring frontline stars. There are also other bold personalities who have enlivened the game in Philly and Frisco—Eddie Gottlieb, Tom Gola, Guy Rodgers, Nate Thurmond, Al Attles, George Lee, Jeff Mullins, Chris Mullin, Phil Smith. And this is a team that can also always crow about a winning feat never again to be duplicated for as long as the great game of basketball is played. It is the Celtics alone that have long reigned as basketball's most successful championship franchise; the Warriors' West Coast rivals, the Los Angeles Lakers, may also brag of 11 league titles; and even the one-time patsy Chicago Bulls can now cheer about the only three-peat outside of Celtics and Lakers history. Yet none have accomplished something that was once achieved by the ancient Warriors ballclub. For it was the Philadelphia Warriors, we should remember, who once won what is today recognized by most historians as the sport's first true NBA title.

This last point remains somewhat controversial. At the end of the very first season in which the established pro circuit began calling itself by the NBA call-letters, it was the Minneapolis Lakers and Syracuse Nationals who met in the championship round, the Lakers claiming the title. The NBA, however, was the product that year of merger between the BAA and NBL circuits. The majority of the teams entering and completing the '49–'50 campaign were those that had been playing for several years under the BAA logo. Thus careful historians of the pro version of Dr. Naismith's sport are in general accord that it was, in fact, the inaugural year of the BAA that was the true start for the NBA as we would later come to know it. What happened in 1949 was merely a name change and not a bonafide inauguration like the one when the BAA launched play three years earlier. And herein lies the claim for the Philadelphia Warriors. For it was a Philadelphia outfit coached by Eddie Gottlieb that walked off with the first championship crown in the league known as the BAA.

After the merger of pro circuits in 1949 the Warriors remained one of the strongest clubs of the first decade, alongside the Lakers and Syracuse

Nats and possibly even the Rochester Royals. The Boston Celtics, without Bill Russell, were as yet nowhere in sight. Gottlieb's team would once again play in the championship round at the end of the second BAA season. This time they would lose out in the title matchup with the original Baltimore Bullets, however. And then a prolonged slump would follow that would eventually cause Gottlieb to step aside after seven more seasons of steadily diminishing status for the Warriors. But the Warriors clubs of the mid-fifties were not yet entirely done-for. Behind the prolific scoring duo of Paul Arizin and Neil Johnston, and under the new coaching leadership of George Senesky, the Philadelphia Warriors would rebound from a brief dry spell and jump from last place in 1954 to the NBA title the very next year. With two championships in the first ten seasons of the combined BAA and NBA the Philadelphia Warriors were the only dual-championship team, besides the Lakers, during pro basketball's first decade.

The original Philadelphia Warriors ballclub of the BAA was largely the brainchild and personalized product of one of basketball's most talented early promoters, Eddie Gottlieb. Gottlieb first made his lasting mark in the sport as organizer and coach of one of the early barnstorming outfits which rivaled the pioneering "Original Celtics" out of New York City. Gottlieb's SPHAs (South Philadelphia Hebrew Association) made a distinctive mark on the "dance hall days" of the young and growing game in the '30s and early '40s. And he also assisted Abe Saperstein with the promotion and European touring of the Harlem Globetrotters, basketball's most famous barnstorming franchise. Then Gottlieb entered the BAA with his Warriors and coached the game's first explosive shooter, Joe Fulks. Today Gottlieb is remembered appropriately by having the league's "Rookie of the Year" trophy named in his honor and memory.

The first BAA edition of the Warriors hardly looked like champions during the league's first regular season. Gottlieb's club did finish ten games above .500 but was a distant second in their division to the Washington Capitols, owners of a 17-game winning streak early in the season and coached by an unheralded high school mentor named Red Auerbach—*the* Red Auerbach. Yet in the playoff title chase the Philly team rode the unparalleled scoring of Joe Fulks (22.2 ppg. in post-season) to mini-series victories over the St. Louis Bombers and New York Knicks. The high-flying Capitols in the meantime were upset by the surprising Chicago Stags. This set up a championship series between Philadelphia and Chicago which Gottlieb's team won going away (4–1) with Fulks twice topping the 30-point barrier.

The Warriors were even stronger in regular-season action the second time around the BAA circuit, and posted a division title with a 27–21 ledger, a record which left them a single game ahead of the New York Knickerbockers in the Eastern Division race. Fulks also led the club with enough scoring (22.1 ppg.) to earn himself another individual title. Again the Gottlieb-coached club worked its way to the Finals despite the somewhat bizarre playoff round robin: it was a system which matched the two division winners head-to-head in the first round, while second and third place teams of each division also squared off. Philadelphia survived the mayhem by edging the St. Louis Bombers in a seven-game set between division pacesetters. The Warriors were once again in the championship round and this time they faced a Baltimore Bullets team that was pro basketball's first somewhat embarrassing "no-name" team (their best performer was veteran player-coach Buddy Jeannette). With no star players and a rough style of play the Bullets were acknowledged as a dull team to watch and a crude throwback to rugged dance-hall and barnstorming vintage play. But their style was good enough to put away the Warriors for the league championship in a less-than-artistic six-game set. The turning point of the embarrassing finale was game two, in which Gottlieb's team led 41–20 at halftime and then fumbled away the huge lead in a sloppy 66–63 defeat.

Gottlieb's Warriors slipped to a sub-.500 team (28–32) during the final season of play under the BAA banner and remained there during the first NBA campaign (26–42) as well. Paul Arizin arrived from the campus of Villanova University for the '50–'51 season and a revamped lineup of Arizin, Fulks, Bill Closs, Andy Phillip and George Senesky brought the club a surprising 14-game improvement and an Eastern Division title. Fulks enjoyed his last top scoring season (18.7 ppg.) and Arizin (17.2 ppg.) was right on his heels. But the team was shocked in the opening round of post-season warfare when it suffered a quick two-game elimination at the hands of Dolph Schayes and the Syracuse Nats.

Paul Arizin was one of the rarest talents of early NBA days—one of the ugly-duckling gangly ballplayers of basketball's pioneer era, cut in the mold of Joe Fulks and later, George Yardley. An apparent asthmatic condition (Arizin himself claimed it was only sinus problems) kept "Pitchin' Paul" huffing and puffing as he labored up and down court and made him the only ballplayer around who made a racket while simply running in sneakers. But his uncanny sense of timing (allowing him to exploit any momentary relaxation by a defender) and quick-release-jumper allowed him to drill points in machine-gun-like fashion from all over the floor. He had led the nation in scoring (26 ppg.) as a senior at Villanova and once cranked in 85 against the Philadelphia Naval Air squad. And with Gottlieb's Warriors Arizin was soon exploiting his quick mind and even quicker jump shot to compete effectively up front with the big boys, despite his 6–4 height and his frail and even unathletic body.

Neil Johnston, the 6–8 hook-shot specialist from Ohio State, arrived in time for the following season. But despite the high-scoring front line of Johnston and Arizin (with four straight league scoring titles between them) the Warriors fell on very hard times during the final four seasons under Eddie Gottlieb's direction. Johnston and Arizin now made a personal possession out of the league scoring race. Arizin nipped Mikan for the 1952 scoring prize and then left town for two years of military duty; Johnston then took up the slack as league pacesetter for three straight winters. But the Warriors team as a whole was no longer intimidating anybody in a far more balanced league. The '52–'53 edition of the Warriors even set a league standard for futility which still stands among the all-time worst NBA team performances. Here was a club that boasted the league scoring champ (Johnston) but could somehow only win 12 games. For one thing Philly had been badly crippled by the forced loss of Arizin. The 12-win season would stand for quite a few years as an NBA record low until surpassed by another hapless team out of the same city but representing a different franchise. The '72–'73 Philadelphia 76ers would eventually bury memories of the hapless '52–'53 Warriors by winning a mere nine games exactly two decades later.

There were two new faces on the Philadelphia pro basketball scene for the 1955–56 season and together they worked some astounding minor miracles. Veteran Warriors player George Senesky had taken over as head coach from Eddie Gottlieb and he inherited a rebuilt Warriors lineup that promised a surge in the standings. Most important in the rebuilding was the arrival of local collegiate star Tom Gola from LaSalle College. The 6'6" All-American forward made a smooth transition to the guard slot in the pros and was one of the game's first big-yet-smooth backcourt performers. And an old face had also returned in the person of Paul Arizin. Arizin (24.2) and Johnston (22.1) finished two-three in the scoring race behind St. Louis ace Bob Pettit (25.7). Together the Arizin-Johnston tandem now gave the Philly club an unstoppable inside-outside scoring combo. And the rest of the supporting cast was also quite formidable. Veteran forward Joe Grabowski (13.2 ppg. and a club second-best 94 rebounds) added considerable muscle in the forecourt. Guard Jack George (13.6 ppg.) developed into a first-rate playmaker and finished second in the league in assists behind Boston's Bob Cousy.

This was perhaps the greatest club in Warriors history. And Senesky's first Philadelphia team wasted little time in proving just that. The Warriors outdistanced Boston's improving Celtics for an Eastern Division title by posting a league-best 45 wins. They next got by the tough Syracuse Nats and Dolph Schayes by taking three of five to win an Eastern Division playoff crown. In the final round of post-season play Arizin, Johnston, Gola and company had little enough difficulty with the Fort Wayne Pistons led by Larry Foust and George "The Bird" Yardley. The series ended after only five games with Fort Wayne managing only a single one-point victory in game two. Thus the Philadelphia Warriors were the second champion under the NBA's new 24-second-clock format. And they would soon prove to be the final league champions before the arrival of Bill Russell and the birth of the Boston Celtics dynasty. Whatever aging and other factors might do to slow the Warriors in years to come, it would be mainly the presence of the Boston juggernaut that would henceforth always keep the Philadelphia Warriors at bay.

It turned out that the Philadelphia Warriors had made two fortuitous decisions in the summer of 1955. The first had been to hire George Sen-

esky which resulted in an immediate championship turnaround—from Eastern Division tailender to NBA champ in a single year. The second and
less noted at the time was the use of the club's territorial draft rights to
reserve local high school phenom Wilt Chamberlain out of Philadelphia
Overbrook High. This move would never bring the club an NBA title. But
it would result in the most exciting and dominant single ballplayer in
franchise history—and perhaps even in NBA history for that matter.

Chamberlain would not become eligible to play for the Warriors for
four more seasons. (Wilt split these between a short collegiate career with
Kansas and a limited tour with the Harlem Globetrotters.) In the meantime
the club would flounder as a mediocre outfit after its championship year
and George Senesky would be replaced on the bench by first Al Cervi, and
then scoring star Neil Johnston. When Wilt did hit the league, however, he
did it in a dramatic and record-busting fashion never witnessed before
or since.

Chamberlain's presence did immediately improve the Philadelphia franchise by immense proportions; the Warriors rode Wilt's rookie season to
a 17-game jump in the win column and a leap from fourth to second
place. But his impact could not overhaul the team's Eastern Division
nemesis, the Boston Celtics. During three final seasons in Philly the club
would finish a strong second all three times, and yet never get closer than
ten games at season's end to the Cousy-led team. And two of those three
years they would make it all the way to the Eastern Division playoff finals
only to be gunned down by none other than Boston.

The final season in Philadelphia was to be one of epic proportions. And
that epic had Wilt Chamberlain written all over it. Wilt did things in
'61–'62 that will never be done again. He would send individual scoring
records soaring through the roof. And he would make it look so easy that
he was almost immediately being charged with playing at only half speed
and performing nightly with little dedication or enthusiasm. Actually it
was a season that also carried many seeds of disappointment and many
signs of distress for pro basketball as a whole. A team had been placed
in Chicago as the NBA's first-ever expansion franchise. But with one great
rookie star named Walt Bellamy and a bunch of castoffs surrounding him,
the Chicago Packers drew no support from fans in the nation's second
largest city. This was not a good sign for a league still struggling for
national attention and facing the heat of a new rival pro circuit now being
formed by Abe Saperstein and called the American Basketball League.

The new circuit in the end didn't prove much of a threat, as only a
handful of unimportant veteran players (like Dick Barnett and Kenny
Sears) abandoned ship to enter the new league. And fans paid almost no
attention at all. The NBA meantime drew a publicity bonanza from the
truly awesome scoring displays unleashed by Chamberlain, who was now
outdoing even himself. On March 2nd, Wilt poured in an unthinkable 100
points in a game with the New York Knicks played, surprisingly, in Hershey, Pennsylvania. It seems that NBA teams were still performing in odd

roadside venues from time to time to fill up the league's still meager coffers. Wilt's explosion against New York was part of a season in which "The Dipper" also crossed the 70-point barrier three additional times and the 60-point mark fifteen more times. In all, Wilt knocked down a fabulous 4,029 points for the season which meant a 50.4 ppg. scoring average. 50.4 ppg.! Chamberlain's unprecedented scoring feat in 1962 must unquestionably still rank as the most unapproachable mark in all of major sport—it could perhaps only be equated to Babe Ruth or Roger Maris hitting 100 homers in a season (since Wilt passed all previous high scoring marks before or since by almost 40%). The fans of Philadelphia (and backwater towns like Hershey) that year saw something truly unique in sports history. And it was a bittersweet sight, indeed, since Wilt and the Warriors would be on their way out of town that very summer, bound for hopefully greener pastures at a new west coast home in San Francisco.

The Warriors' abandonment of Philadelphia in 1962 was the telltale sign of a new era (already blooming fully in baseball a few years earlier) in which owners of professional sports franchises no longer saw their ballclubs as public trusts and community fixtures but as business properties to be bought and sold for a bottom line of personal profit. Philadelphia had been a pro basketball fixture since the earliest barnstorming days and, since the coming of the NBA, had also been home to such great stars as Joe Fulks, Paul Arizin, Neil Johnston and Wilt Chamberlain. But Ed Gottlieb, who had operated teams out of the city since the earliest days of his Philadelphia SPHAs, was tiring of the grind and now found an opportunity to sell a showcase ballclub featuring Chamberlain to a group of eager California investors. And thus the Warriors would follow the Lakers west in the same manner that the baseball Giants had recently followed the baseball Dodgers. There was no sentiment here, just a huge profit margin.

Fittingly for hardline traditional fans, perhaps, the first year in San Francisco for the Warriors was a complete disaster. Opposing teams had now found a way to neutralize the leading scorer with pressing defenses applied against his weakened contingent of supporting teammates. Paul Arizin had retired rather than make the west coast trek. Tom Gola had been traded early in the season to New York for Willie Naulls and Kenny Sears. Al Attles and Guy Rodgers were aging and therefore had to accept reduced playing time in the backcourt. Furthermore, rookie coach Bob Feerick had no magic formula for melding Wilt into a team concept. The result was a Warriors team that slumped to 31 victories and a fourth-place finish in its new Western Division home. Chamberlain averaged a modest 44.8 ppg to again pace the circuit. But the transplanted Warriors and their new west coast fans watched the playoffs from the sidelines that first transition year.

It was only a temporary setback in '62–'63. Or perhaps viewed somewhat differently, it was only a view of things to come that was then followed by only a temporary revival in '63–'64. At any rate, a second year on the West Coast brought a great turnaround for a Warriors club that still had plenty of horses in Chamberlain, Guy Rodgers, Tom Mesch- ery and Wayne Hightower. Wilt's average dropped another 10 points, but was still lofty enough to outdistance everyone else in the league. Wilt may no longer have been outscoring complete teams but he was still outdistanc- ing mere mortals among the opposition. Under new coach Alex Hannum the Warriors also fashioned a new approach that quickly paid big divi- dends. Wilt was convinced to concentrate more on shot-blocking defense *a la* Bill Russell; the rest of the team concentrated on a more deliberate offensive style and a tightened hard-nosed team defense. As a result the Warriors found themselves back atop the Western Division standings. They also found themselves in the championship series with Boston at season's end. Chamberlain and Russell were matched for another titanic slugfest and, as usual, Wilt won the offensive end of matters. But Russell's defense and the other dimensions of the balanced Celtics club meant a short five- game series win for the now six-peat Auerbach Celtics.

It was becoming apparent by now that the club could seemingly never win it all with Wilt as the focal point of team attack. Year three in Frisco thus brought with it a great turning point in ballclub history. By the time of the league's All-Star Game break on January 13th the defending champion Warriors had already dropped 16 of 21 games and, despite Wilt's 38.9 ppg. average, had already fallen completely out of the regular season race. What made matters worse for Alex Hannum's team was the fact that they already possessed another potentially potent center who was far more ori- ented toward a team concept, but who was playing out of position at forward simply to accommodate Wilt. Club management rightfully felt that Nate Thurmond could unquestionably carry the load in the pivot. Besides, San Francisco's fans had not warmed up to Wilt and were staying away from the Cow Palace in droves. Unloading Wilt and turning his big salary into working capital might allow the building of a truly attractive team that would click at the box office. Thus on the eve of the All-Star Game in St. Louis the biggest NBA story in years hit the front pages. The greatest scorer in basketball history had been traded and the San Francisco Warriors would now have to face the short-term bleak effects of their bold move toward the future.

The avalanche of losses for the Warriors in the first half of the '64–'65 campaign became an uncheckable landslide once Wilt was peddled away at the All-Star intermission. Thurmond paced the club the rest of the way with a 16.5 average that wasn't even close to half of Wilt's earlier totals. The miniscule victory count at season's end stood at a mere 17—bad enough for a new club futility record. But there was also a silver lining to all this losing as things turned out. Owning the fourth pick in the post- season college draft the San Francisco team selected Rick Barry, the NCAA scoring champion out of the University of Miami. And what they got was as immediate impact player who surpassed management's wildest dreams. Barry was deemed in most quarters to be too frail to succeed in the NBA trenches. But few had apparently noted Barry's quick shooting release or unfailing radar-like outside shooting touch. Nor his uncanny ability to make free-throws with an ancient underhanded shooting style that almost never missed.

Rick Barry joined the Warriors in the fall of 1965 and plunked down a rookie scoring average of 25.7 (fourth best in the league) that played a major role in doubling the team's victory total. After bagging rookie-of-the-year honors Barry kept up his scoring onslaught and the Warriors climbed all the way to a division title during Barry's sophomore trek around the league. Rick pumped in 35.6 ppg. to end the seven-year domination in league scoring by the man he had replaced with the Warriors, Wilt Chamberlain. With plenty of help from a lineup that included Thurmond (limited to 65 games by a broken hand), Paul Newman, Jeff Mullins and Fred Hetzel, along with strong bench support from Al Attles and Tom Meschery, the Bill Sharman-coached Warriors eliminated Los Angeles and St. Louis to earn a spot in the NBA Finals.

In a great piece of irony, the resurgent 1967 San Francisco Warriors team would now face in the championship round the very player who had earlier taken them to the brink and then disappointed them so very often. Wilt had sacrificed his high-scoring center-stage role back with the Philadelphia 76ers and was now the role-playing centerpiece of a 68–13 Philadelphia juggernaut that had just posted the best season's record in league history. While Wilt as a scoring machine could never win it all for the Warriors, Wilt the revamped team-player would now finally have his own championship ring at the expense of his old team, the selfsame Warriors. Philadelphia's balanced lineup—one of the greatest ever with Chet Walker, Luke Jackson, Hal Greer and Wally Jones flanking Wilt—was more than Barry's scoring and Thurmond's adroit pivot play could ever hope to offset. The Warriors thus went down to a gallant but nonetheless decisive defeat in six quick games.

The biggest blow of summer 1967 in Warriorland was not the revenge of Wilt Chamberlain and the near-miss in pursuit of an NBA championship. It was the loss of franchise-player and number-one drawing card Rick Barry. One of the sport's pioneering exemplars of a new breed of mercenary athletes who were now entering the American sporting scene, Barry took his high priced act elsewhere when he signed a huge contract to play for the across-the-bay Oakland Oaks of the new rival American Basketball Association. The deal would eventually be voided and Barry would be forced back to the NBA and the Warriors five seasons down the road. But in the interim the loss of the high-scoring forward was a near-fatal blow to the continued health of the San Francisco Warriors.

As the tumultuous sixties finally evolved into the more sedentary seventies across the face of the entire nation, an upscale lifestyle complete with escape from past nightmares and broadening prospects for a bright future also seemed to come to the northern California pro basketball franchise. The Warriors moved across the bay from San Francisco to Oakland and were rechristened as the Golden State Warriors for the 1971–72 campaign.

And a long-awaited act of the legal courts a season later also sent wayward scoring star Rick Barry back to the Warriors camp after a lengthy and painful absence. Barry had been lighting up the nets in the ABA for four seasons (one right there in Oakland and three on the east coast in Washington and New York) and he now seemed to take right up where he had left off back in the Bay area. Former Warriors mainstay Al Attles was now the head coach, and a healthy supply of veteran talent also included Nate Thurmond, Jeff Mullins, Cazzie Russell and Jim Barnett. With this contingent the Warriors reeled off three straight second place finishes in the Pacific Division.

The NBA was rapidly evolving by the mid-'70s into a circuit which emphasized total team balance and a talent for aggressive defense. Clubs built around a single star or two who were expected to carry the load with free-wheeling offense were no longer in vogue. And no franchise had taken better advantage of the new direction toward team defense than Al Attles's Warriors by the time the '74–'75 season had rolled around. The franchise had squarely faced the need for wholesale dismantling and retooling and had thus shipped veteran Nate Thurmond to Chicago in exchange for cash and a promising young aggressive pivot defender named Clifford Ray. Golden State also succeeded in signing two prized rookies. The first was Keith Wilkes out of UCLA and the second was a local collegiate star named Phil Smith from the University of San Francisco. Cazzie Russell in turn had also left the team as a free-agent and signed with Los Angeles. Barry was now the only holdover from the best Warriors team of the '60s and Rick promptly took over the scoring burden with a league second-best 30.6 ppg. average.

The fresh-look Warriors team rode a new offensive and defensive style to the top of the Pacific Division (48–34) and then also to a berth in the NBA Finals. Attles utilized a team-unit concept of constant substitution which meant constant pressing defensive pressure on opponents and thus many games won by mere attrition of the enemy forces. After bumping Seattle (4–2) and Chicago (4–3) on the road to the finals the Warriors ran roughshod over the worn-down Washington Bullets (4–0) in the title series. It was only the third-ever four-game championship sweep and Barry led the way with a 28.2 post-season average. The swarming Golden State defense held the surprised Bullets to less than 100 points in three of the four title games.

The bleak period of more than a decade which stretched from the '77–'78 season through the '87–'88 campaign was truly the darkest in all of Warriors history. The stretch which opened to Rick Barry's final season with the team included a spate of losing seasons and a more-or-less regular berth in 4th, 5th or 6th slot in the division standings. There were also precious few individual stars. Purvis Short was the only big scorer of the period (28.0 ppg. in 1985) who remained with the team for more than a year or two. The club experimented with a couple of spindly 7-foot centers, but both Joe Barry Carroll and Ralph Sampson proved large disappointments. The pivot position became a true sore point with Warriors fans after Robert Parish was traded to Boston in order to obtain the 1980 draft rights to Purdue's Joe Barry Carroll. While Carroll seemed to sleepwalk through a number of seasons (his best year was '82–'83 when he averaged 24.1) Parish was building a Hall-of-Fame career and collecting a handful of championship rings with Larry Bird and the Boston Celtics. Parish would provide part of a durable front line in Boston (Bird, Parish and McHale) that one over-zealous Boston analyst and writer (Peter May in his book **The Big Three**, 1994) has even called the best in basketball history.

The long-suffering Warriors turned a new page in their rollercoaster history with the arrival of Don Nelson as the new head coach and part club owner. Nelson came on board in the summer of 1988 and immediately set in motion to rebuild the Warriors into the kind of year-in and year-out competitive Milwaukee team he had recently directed throughout the entire previous decade. Nelson's earliest teams out in Oakland featured a trio of high scorers in Chris Mullin, Tim Hardaway and Sarunas Marciulionis. Mitch Richmond (a 22.5 scorer over five NBA seasons) was also a big gunner until he was traded to Sacramento in exchange for the largely disappointing rookie Billy Owens (15.0 ppg. in two seasons with Golden State). But these initial Nelson-coached teams started slowly (two 4th-place finishes and one 5th) until improving to 55–27 in '91–'92. By the 1992–93 season, however, a rash of injuries would strike throughout the lineup and seemingly cancel any further immediate progress. In limping through a dreadful 34–48 season this fourth edition of the Nelson-coached Warriors would lead the NBA in games missed due to injury as 14 players were sidelined for a mind-boggling total of 312 games. A projected starting lineup of Mullin, Hardaway, Marciulionis and Owens were on the court at the same time for a grand total of 2 minutes and 37 seconds during the entire season (and that rare event occurred during the second quarter of a January 12th game versus Atlanta). With all or part of his starting lineup missing most of the time, Nelson had little hope for competing successfully against such strong Pacific Division foes as Portland, Phoenix and the Seattle SuperSonics.

Desperate for a quick upturn in fortunes the Warriors took a large gamble with the collegiate draft that took place in June, 1993. Owning the third overall pick in the lottery, the Warriors selected a stellar guard out of Memphis State with "can't-miss star quality" written all over him. But the player that Don Nelson and his staff really coveted was the one taken with the overall first selection by Orlando's Magic and this was Michigan's 6–10 power forward-center, Chris Webber. The Magic had themselves enjoyed the good fortune of drawing the first overall pick two straight years and now wanted backcourt help to support giant Shaquille O'Neal, their 1992 first choice. Thus Nelson and the Warriors were able to swing the deal which peddled Hardaway and three future first-round picks to Orlando in exchange for Webber. Nelson saw Chris Webber as being the key to the Warriors' future improvement. And the Warriors' coach didn't mince words in his assessment: "Chris Webber deserved the honor of being the number-one pick in the draft. He has a lot of skills and is going to help us right away. We think he will continue to grow throughout his NBA career. With some work he's going to be an excellent offensive player on the low block as well as a dominating rebounder.''

Chris Webber did not disappoint as he scored at a 17.5 ppg. pace, blocked 164 shots (9th best in the league), and edged out Anfernee Hardaway for the league's Rookie-of-the-Year honors. Even stronger play came from surprise sophomore Latrell Sprewell as the 6–5 guard paced the club in scoring (21.0, 11th best in the league). Chris Mullin was now fading somewhat (16.8 ppg.) but did provide support in 62 games after returning from an early-season injury. But the bad luck continued in double doses as top stars Tim Hardaway and Sarunas Marciulionis sat out the entire campaign on the injured list. Nonetheless Golden State was able to rebound with Webber and Sprewell to post a surprising 50–32 mark and gain a third-place finish in the tough Pacific Division. It seems now that with a return to top form by Hardaway and Marciulionis and continued development by Sprewell and Webber the Golden State Warriors could well be among the NBA surprises of the 1994–1995 upcoming campaign.

Suggested Readings on Golden State (Philadelphia) Warriors

Barry, Rick (with Bill Libby). **Confessions of a Basketball Gypsy: The Rick Barry Story**. Englewood Cliffs, New Jersey: Prentice-Hall Publishers, 1972.

Sullivan, George. **Wilt Chamberlain**. Grosset Sports Library Series. New York: Grosset and Dunlap Publishers, 1966.

Golden State Warriors Retired Uniform Numbers (4)

Tom Meschery (14)
Al Attles (16)
Rick Barry (24)
Nate Thurmond (42)

Year-by-Year Golden State (Philadelphia) Warriors Summary

Season	Record	Finish	Coach(es)	Scoring Leader(s)	Playoffs (W-L Record)

Key: * = Tie for Position; # = League Scoring Leader
Philadelphia Warriors
Basketball Association of America

1946–47	35–25	2nd	Ed Gottlieb	Joe Fulks (23.2)#	**BAA Champion** (8–2)
1947–48	27–21	1st	Ed Gottlieb	Joe Fulks (22.1)#	Lost in BAA Finals (6–7)
1948–49	28–32	4th	Ed Gottlieb	Joe Fulks (26.0)	Lost in 1st Round (0–2)

Season	Record	Finish	Coach(es)	Scoring Leader(s)	Playoffs (W-L Record)
National Basketball Association					
1949–50	26–42	4th	Ed Gottlieb	Joe Fulks (14.2)	Lost in 1st Round (0–2)
1950–51	40–26	1st	Ed Gottlieb	Joe Fulks (18.7)	Lost in 1st Round (0–2)
1951–52	33–33	4th	Ed Gottlieb	Paul Arizin (25.4)#	Lost in 1st Round (1–2)
1952–53	12–57	5th	Ed Gottlieb	Neil Johnston (22.3)#	Did Not Qualify
1953–54	29–43	4th	Ed Gottlieb	Neil Johnston (24.4)#	Did Not Qualify
1954–55	33–39	4th	Ed Gottlieb	Neil Johnston (22.7)#	Did Not Qualify
1955–56	45–27	1st	George Senesky	Paul Arizin (24.2)	**NBA Champion** (7–3)
1956–57	37–35	3rd	George Senesky	Paul Arizin (25.6)#	Lost in 1st Round (0–2)
1957–58	37–35	3rd	George Senesky	Paul Arizin (20.7)	Lost in 2nd Round (3–5)
1958–59	32–40	4th	Al Cervi	Paul Arizin (26.4)	Did Not Qualify
1959–60	49–26	2nd	Neil Johnston	W. Chamberlain (37.6)#	Lost in 2nd Round (4–5)
1960–61	46–33	2nd	Neil Johnston	W. Chamberlain (38.4)#	Lost in 1st Round (0–3)
1961–62	49–31	2nd	Frank McGuire	W. Chamberlain (50.4)#	Lost in 2nd Round (6–6)
San Francisco Warriors					
1962–63	31–49	4th	Bob Feerick	W. Chamberlain (44.8)#	Did Not Qualify
1963–64	48–32	1st	Alex Hannum	W. Chamberlain (36.9)#	Lost in NBA Finals (5–7)
1964–65	17–63	5th	Alex Hannum	W. Chamberlain (38.9)#	Did Not Qualify
1965–66	35–45	4th	Alex Hannum	Rick Barry (25.7)	Did Not Qualify
1966–67	44–37	1st	Bill Sharman	Rick Barry (35.6)#	Lost in NBA Finals (9–6)
1967–68	43–39	3rd	Bill Sharman	Rudy LaRusso (21.8)	Lost in 2nd Round (4–6)
1968–69	41–41	3rd	George Lee	Jeff Mullins (22.8)	Lost in 1st Round (2–4)
1969–70	30–52	6th	George Lee	Jeff Mullins (22.1)	Did Not Qualify
1970–71	41–41	2nd	Al Attles	Jeff Mullins (20.8)	Lost in 1st Round (1–4)
Golden State Warriors					
1971–72	51–31	2nd	Al Attles	Jeff Mullins (21.5)	Lost in 1st Round (1–4)
1972–73	47–35	2nd	Al Attles	Rick Barry (22.3)	Lost in 2nd Round (5–6)
1973–74	44–38	2nd	Al Attles	Rick Barry (25.1)	Did Not Qualify
1974–75	48–34	1st	Al Attles	Rick Barry (30.6)	**NBA Champion** (12–5)
1975–76	59–23	1st	Al Attles	Rick Barry (21.0)	Lost in 2nd Round (7–6)
1976–77	46–36	3rd	Al Attles	Rick Barry (21.8)	Lost in 2nd Round (5–5)
1977–78	43–39	5th	Al Attles	Rick Barry (23.1)	Did Not Qualify
1978–79	38–44	6th	Al Attles	Phil Smith (19.9)	Did Not Qualify
1979–80	24–58	6th	Al Attles	Robert Parish (17.0)	Did Not Qualify
1980–81	39–43	4th	Al Attles	Lloyd Free (24.1)	Did Not Qualify
1981–82	45–37	4th	Al Attles	Bernard King (23.2)	Did Not Qualify
1982–83	30–52	5th	Al Attles	Joe Barry Carroll (24.1)	Did Not Qualify
1983–84	37–45	5th	John Bach	Purvis Short (22.8)	Did Not Qualify
1984–85	22–60	6th	John Bach	Purvis Short (28.0)	Did Not Qualify
1985–86	30–52	6th	John Bach	Purvis Short (25.5)	Did Not Qualify
1986–87	42–40	3rd	George Karl	Joe Barry Carroll (21.2)	Lost in 2nd Round (4–6)
1987–88	20–62	5th	George Karl Ed Gregory	Eric Floyd (21.2)	Did Not Qualify
1988–89	43–39	4th	Don Nelson	Chris Mullin (26.5)	Lost in 2nd Round (4–4)
1989–90	37–45	5th	Don Nelson	Chris Mullin (25.1)	Did Not Qualify
1990–91	44–38	4th	Don Nelson	Chris Mullin (25.7)	Lost in 2nd Round (4–5)
1991–92	55–27	2nd	Don Nelson	Chris Mullin (25.6)	Lost in 1st Round (1–3)
1992–93	34–48	6th	Don Nelson	Chris Mullin (25.9)	Did Not Qualify
1993–94	50–32	3rd	Don Nelson	Latreell Sprewell (21.0)	Lost in 1st Round (1–3)

Individual Career Leaders and Record Holders (1946–1994)

Scoring Average	Wilt Chamberlain (41.5 ppg., 1959–65)
Points Scored	Wilt Chamberlain (17,783, 1959–65)
Games played	Nate Thurmond (757, 1963–74)
Minutes Played	Nate Thurmond (30,729)
Field Goal Pct.	Bernard King (.577, 1980–82)
3-Pt. Field Goals Made	Tim Hardaway (349, 1989–94)
Free Throws Made	Paul Arizin (5,010, 1950–62)
Free-Throw Pct.	Rick Barry (.896, 1965–67, 1972–78)
Rebounds	Nate Thurmond (12,771)
Assists	Guy Rodgers (4,855, 1958–66)
Steals	Chris Mullin (1,101, 1985–94)
Blocked Shots	Joe Barry Carroll (837, 1980–88)
Personal Fouls	Paul Arizin (2,764)

Individual Single-Season and Game Records (1946–1994)

Scoring Average	Wilt Chamberlain (50.4, 1961–62)*
Points Scored (Season)	Wilt Chamberlain (4,029, 1961–62)*
Points Scored (Game)	Wilt Chamberlain (100, 3-2-62 vs. New York Knicks)*
Field Goal Percentage (Season)	Bernard King (.588, 1980–81)
Free-Throw Pct. (Season)	Rick Barry (.924, 1977–78)
3-Pt. Field Goals (Season)	Tim Hardaway (127, 1991–92)
Rebounds (Season)	Wilt Chamberlain (2,149, 1960–61)*
Rebound Average	Wilt Chamberlain (27.2, 1960–61)*
Rebounds (Game)	Wilt Chamberlain (55, 11–24–60 vs. Boston Celtics)*
Assists (Season)	Eric "Sleepy" Floyd (848, 1986–87)
Assists (Game)	Guy Rodgers (28, 3–14–63 vs. St. Louis Hawks)
Steals (Season)	Rick Barry (228, 1974–75)
Blocked Shots (Season)	Manute Bol (345, 1988–89)
Blocked Shots (Game)	Manue Bol (13, 2-2-90 vs. New Jersey Nets)
Personal Fouls (Season)	Rudy LaRusso (337, 1967–68)
* = NBA Record	

Best Trade in Franchise History

The deal that brought number one 1994 draft selection Chris Webber to Golden State in exchange for Anfernee Hardaway will take some time to evaluate fully, especially in light of Hardaway's exceptional rookie season in Orlando. But the deal was certainly one of the most spectacular in club history.

Only a handful of times has an NBA team selected a number one overall pick only to immediately trade him elsewhere. The Warriors are confident, however, that Webber will fill a gaping whole and turn them onto the road back to respectability. And the first season with Webber manning the post position seemed an indication that exactly this may indeed already be happening.

Worst Trade in Franchise History

No doubt about this one. The Warriors buried themselves for several seasons and brought an end to a glorious era in franchise history when they traded away Wilt Chamberlain in mid-season 1965. The deal sending Wilt back to Philadelphia came on January 15, 1965, and brought journeymen Connie Dierking, Paul Newman, and Lee Schaffer, plus cash, in return. But this shameless transaction only nudges out by a fraction the 1980 trade of center Robert Parish (and a 1980 first round choice that led directly to Kevin McHale) to Boston for the first pick in the 1980 college draft. That pick was used to acquire Joe Barry Carroll, a giant multi-season disappointment who never matched either Parish or McHale for either career longevity or career productivity.

Golden State Warriors Historical Oddity

The Warriors ballclub that began in Philadelphia and eventually settled in San Francisco and Oakland as the NBA's second west coast franchise is owner of a unique franchise trophy. It is the Celtics in Boston with 16 NBA banners who can lay claim to the most world titles. The Los Angeles Lakers out west can boast of 11 championships as well. Yet it is the Warriors franchise that in its infancy won the very first NBA championship. Or at least the inaugural championship of the league that was the recognized forerunner of the NBA, the Basketball Association of America. Although the Celtics' stranglehold on "most" will likely never be challenged, it is nonetheless theoretically possible for a more prolific champion to someday emerge. But there can always be only one *first*. And that distinction rests forever in the record books with Eddie Gottlieb's original Philadelphia Warriors.

Warriors All-Time Number One Draft Picks List

Philadelphia Warriors
1947 Francis Crossin (Pennsylvania)
1948 Phil Farbman (CCNY)
1949 Vern Gardner (Utah)
1950 Paul Arizin (Villanova)
1951 Don Sunderlage (Illinois)

1952 Bill Mlkvy (Temple)
1953 Ernie Beck (Pennsylvania)
1954 Gene Shue (Maryland)
1955 Tom Gola (La Salle)
1956 Hal Lear (Temple)
1957 Len Rosenbluth (North Carolina)
1958 Guy Rodgers (Temple)
1959 Wilt Chamberlain (Kansas)
1960 Al Bunge (Maryland)
1961 Tom Meschery (St. Mary's)
1962 Wayne Hightower (Kansas)

San Francisco Warriors

1963 Nate Thurmond (Bowling Green)
1964 Barry Kramer (NYU)
1965 Fred Hetzel (Davidson)
1966 Clyde Lee (Vanderbilt)
1967 Dave Lattin (Texas Western)
1968 Ron Williams (West Virginia)
1969 Bob Portman (Creighton)
1970 Traded (to Detroit Pistons) for Dave Gambee
1971 Darnell Hillman (San Jose State)

Golden State Warriors

1972 Traded (to Portland Trail Blazers) for Jim Barnett
1973 Kevin Joyce (South Carolina)
1974 Keith Wilkes (UCLA)
1975 Joe Bryant (LaSalle)
1976 Robert Parish (Centenary)
1977 Rickey Green (Michigan)
1978 Purvis Short (Jackson State)
1979 Traded (to Boston Celtics) for Jo Jo White
1980 Joe Barry Carroll (Purdue)
1981 Traded (to Portland Trail Blazers) for 1978 1st Round Pick
1982 Lester Conner (Oregon State)
1983 Russell Cross (Purdue)
1984 Traded (to Los Angeles Clippers) for World B. Free
1985 Chris Mullin (St. Johns)
1986 Chris Washburn (North Carolina State)
1987 Tellis Frank (Western Kentucky)
1988 Mitch Richmond (Kansas State)
1989 Tim Hardaway (Texas El Paso)
1990 Tyrone Hill (Xavier)
1991 Chris Gatling (Old Dominion)
1992 Latrell Sprewell (Alabama)
1993 Anfernee Hardaway (Memphis State) (Traded to Orlando Magic for Chris Webber)

Part II

Traditional Franchises

Chapter 6

PHILADELPHIA SIXERS (76ers) and SYRACUSE NATS

One Giant, One Magician, and One Magical Season

All-Time Franchise Record: 2078–1637, .559 Pct. (1946–1994)
NBA Record: 1993–1555, .562 Pct.; NBL Record: 85–82, .509 Pct.
NBA Championships (3): 1954–55, 1966–67, 1982–83
Greatest Franchise Player: Julius Erving (1976–1987)
All-Time Leading Scorer: Hal Greer (21,586 Points, 1958–1973)
Most Successful Coach: Alex Hannum (130–33, .798 Pct., 1966–1968)
All-Time Franchise Team: Wilt Chamberlain (C), Dolph Schayes (F), Charles Barkley (F), Hal Greer (G), Julius Erving (G)

A few teams like the Celtics, the Lakers, and perhaps the Milwaukee Bucks have set the standard for consistent excellence. A few more like the Sacramento Kings, Los Angeles Clippers or Indiana Pacers can be counted on to disappoint regularly as year-in and year-out losers. Most teams that have called the NBA home, however, float across the decades somewhere in between such extremes. An occasional glory run or back-slide is always balanced by dozen of seasons somewhere in the middle of the heap. But one NBA team has swung most wildly from one giddy or god-awful extreme to another, providing both the very best and very worst the NBA has to offer. The only thing consistent about the Philadelphia Sixers and their forerunners the Syracuse Nats is that they could usually always be found dangling out on one limb or the other, finding their home at the extremes of fortune or infamy.

The Syracuse Nats—ancient forerunners of the present-day Sixers—began their NBA sojourn near the very zenith of franchise performance. And despite all their eventual ups and downs the Nats could boast one thing in the end that no other team could ever lay claim to. This was the

137

team that walked away with a championship banner in the very first season of NBA competition played under a truly modern guise. The Syracuse Nats were thus the first true champions of pro basketball as we now know it.

The Nats' memorable title run came in a season during which the Syracuse franchise held a major role off the court as well as on—it was a role in staking out the 1954–55 campaign as the sport's most revolutionary season ever. Mere days after the close of a 1953–54 campaign which had seen the unsightly tactics of excessive fouling and strategic stalling making a true mockery of post-season play, NBA owners had decided to take some drastic action. Two radical rule adjustments were voted into effect, one limiting the time a team could possess the ball without shooting (the 24-second shot clock) and the other introducing bonus free throws after teams exceeded a limit of six fouls in any quarter. It was the first rule change, of course, that completely revolutionized the appearance of the young professional game. And it was this rule which had been the original brainchild of Syracuse Nats owner Danny Biasone.

Playing under Biasone's newly-shaped game, the Syracuse team proved the class of the souped-up league. The Eastern Division champion Nats tied the Western Division-leading Fort Wayne Pistons for the league's best record, then won an eventual title showdown with the Pistons in a tightly contested seven-game shootout. With the new fast-paced league action brought by a forced shooting tempo and less fouling game scores soared and 100-point games became common. Dolph Schayes led the Syracuse scoring parade throughout the championship series, and guard George King secured the title with a crucial free throw and steal in the final seconds of the closing came. When Syracuse bested Fort Wayne 92–91 in the final day's action, the NBA had its first champion of the modern pro basketball era.

The Nats quickly deflated from their championship run and were, for their final Syracuse years, little more than a largely mediocre team. Schayes poured in tons of points and ranked with Paul Arizin of the Philadelphia Warriors and Bob Pettit of the St. Louis Hawks as the game's three most unstoppable frontcourt scorers. There was little else in Syracuse to brighten the cause, however, and annual playoff trips always ended abruptly in the first or second round. But when they finally moved southward in search of a larger market and landed in the City of Brotherly Love, the *real* roller coaster ride arrived. This would become a franchise that could soon boast the very best NBA team—in personnel as well as in won-lost records—that has ever been pasted together. The 1966–67 Philly team that finally broke the Celtics sixties strangle-hold on the rest of the league was not only for a single season the most dominant ballclub ever seen. It was also, man-for-man, perhaps the most balanced and potent team ever put on a basketball floor—anywhere or anytime.

It is hard to recall today just how talented the Sixers outfit of 1967 truly was. Somehow the memory of that 68–13 team has been buried under an avalanche of nostalgia about the Russell-and-Cousy Celtics, which so dominated the rest of the era. But no Celtics team could match the one the Sixers fielded in 1966–67. That year's Russell-led team had itself captured 60 games—its second-best total of the decade—yet still trailed Philadelphia by eight full games in the standings. And when it came to a nightly lineup, the Celts with Russell, Havlicek, and Sam and K.C. Jones had nothing on Wilt and his supporting cast of all-star teammates. Chamberlain, for starters, was the most dominant player in the game. His first seven seasons in the league the seven-foot "Dipper" had led the circuit in scoring with totals (once in the 50s and once in the 40s) never previously dreamed of. Despite Russell's prowess on the boards, Wilt annually led the NBA in caroms as well by posting numbers that rivaled his scoring totals. In 1962 he had swept the boards at a 25.7 per game rate; the total was 24.6 in 1966. And now back in Philadelphia after a stint with the Warriors in San Francisco, and inspired by Coach Hannum to think of team sacrifice and championship pride, Wilt had modified his game to complement the team around him. Now passing to open mates Wilt saw his scoring average dip to 24.1 and for the first time failed to win an individual scoring title. Yet he still paced the circuit in shooting accuracy, led in rebounds, finished an amazing third in assists, and matched Russell in blocked shots. With Wilt dishing off and clearing out the scoring lanes, the results for league rivals were truly devastating.

But there was indeed more to the 1967 championship Sixers than merely Wilt Chamberlain. Teams with Chamberlain alone always seemed to lose at playoff time to the balanced attack of Russell and a diversified fast-breaking Boston offense. This team, however, was potent beyond belief from top to bottom and featured more than its own share of speed and diversity. Chet Walker (19.3 ppg.) and Billy Cunningham (18.5 ppg.) were two power-packed scorers anchored in the front court. Luke Jackson at 6'9" could spell either one, or fill in for Wilt at center, and also contributed mightily off the bench as a rebounder (8.9 rpg.). The corps of guards was headed up by Hal Greer (eventually a 21,000-point career scorer) who had few peers in Boston or elsewhere as a playmaker. And Hal Greer had no peers as a jump shooter either, contributing 20-plus scoring seasons the first seven years the club was in Philadelphia. Wally Jones (13.2 ppg.) filled the other guard slot adequately and then some and matched Greer's total with 303 assists. The bench, to round things out, was the strongest in the league. Rookies Matt Guokas and Bill Melchionni and experienced hand Dave Gambee had impressive years as reserves while second-year man Bob Weiss rounded out the roster with token duties. Veteran Larry Costello had returned from retirement and also played a sound fill-in role in reserve (7.8 ppg.) until felled with a knee injury at mid season.

But if the Celtics under Auerbach were outclassed by the Sixers of Alex Hannum for one year, nonetheless Boston still owned a championship characteristic that the Sixers sorely lacked. In Boston they preached consistency and parlayed that consistency into unflinching performance year after year. In Philly they always let their better clubs disintegrate all too rapidly.

And none seemingly dismantled faster than the once-in-a-lifetime 1967 championship team. Only six years later the Sixers would parade onto the floor not only the worst team of the season or the decade, but actually the worst ballclub in the long scope of league history. Everything the 1967 team of Chamberlain, Walker and Greer had, the 1973 team of Manny Leaks, Fred Carter and Freddie Boyd totally lacked—and then in spades.

Both before and after the two extreme seasons posted in 1967 and 1973, the name of the game for Philadelphia pro basketball has always been rapid-fire ups and downs. The 1955 champion Nats were replaced in Syracuse by eight seasons of hopeless losers. The two decades that have followed the dark pit of 1973 have seen the Philadelphia franchise climb all the way back up to the mountain peak, only to collapse back, and then do it all again several times over. Under Bill Cunningham who starred on the court with the 1967 team, the Sixers rebuilt into a winner in the late seventies. Twice in the early 1980s Philadelphia challenged in the NBA Finals. Then they climbed over the top with another "team for the ages" in 1983, one that featured two of the NBA's respected elder statesmen bidding for a final crack at a championship ring. The subsequent decade has seen another rapid decline and a tumble in the most recent seasons all the way back to the league's lowest rungs.

The first franchise championship team in Syracuse in 1954–55 had been built around Dolph Schayes. Through all their failed title runs in the early and late '50s the Nats had always boasted one of basketball's greatest success stories of the NBA's first decade, and perhaps of any NBA decade for that matter. Dolph Schayes clearly was one of the games' greatest early stars and he now remains one of basketball's greatest forgotten legends as well.

Schayes was also one of the most rugged and consistent players in all basketball history. He was also the sport's first great three-point man— not a long-range bomber who measured his treys in yards from the hoop but instead a powerful lane-driver who could shoot with either hand and from any angle, and took his three points in two distinct stages. Schayes was a relentless driver who drew defenses and thus fouls like honey draws flies and winners draw bandwagons. He excelled with this type of game, both before the 24-second shot-clock innovation and after. In addition to his shooting ability, the 6–8, 220-pound muscular forward was also an adept rebounder and probably the best passing big man around; there was no more versatile all-around player to be found anywhere in the early days of the NBA. And as one of the most proficient free-throw shooters of his era (he shot .904 pct. in 1957 and 1958 and trailed only dead-eye Bill Sharman in this category) Schayes compiled points at a rate that made him the first player in history to cross the career 15,000 point barrier. Most of Dolph Schayes' records have been dwarfed in the modern era (including his career-length standard of 16 seasons), but his stature as one of the early legends will always remain among fans with a sensitive eye to true landmarks of NBA history.

Twice the Schayes-led Nats challenged for the league title immediately before their breakthrough in 1954–55. The Syracuse NBA title in 1955 came on the heels of a failed trip to the finals just one year earlier. In that final pre-shot-clock campaign Cervi's Nats swept both New York (2–0) and Boston (4–0) to get at Mikan and his Lakers for the title waltz. The Lakers would make it in three-straight with a hard-earned seven-game triumph, but not before the scrappy Nats captured a must-win road game in Minneapolis on a Jim Neal bucket in the final four seconds, to force a game-seven showdown. For several seasons Syracuse had played in the shadows of Minneapolis (NBA champs in '50, '52, '53 and '54) and Rochester (winner of the '51 title). And after their single title triumph in '55 they would largely remain back in the shadows once again. Al Cervi coached the club for eight years and posted only two losing seasons (both only two games under). Cervi was then replaced by Paul Seymour, whose three full campaigns brought two more winning seasons and yet another year when the record again slipped only two games under. Seymour soon gave way to Alex Hannum who kept the team on a winning note in 1962 and 1963. But none could quite recapture the special magic of 1955.

The 1954 season, however, would be one in which near misses would finally be avoided. The victory over Fort Wayne's Pistons in the league finals was a somewhat tainted one by most accounts written at the time. But it was a cherished championship nonetheless. Syracuse and Fort Wayne had seemed to be on a collision course from the season's opening week. With George Mikan now voluntarily retired, the Minneapolis domination of the infant NBA seemed certain to end and these two smaller market teams slugged it out throughout the regular season to lead their respective divisions with identical 43–29 records. While the Pistons polished off the Lakers in four games (3–1) in the league's championship tourney, the Nats made short work of Boston and Bob Cousy by an identical 3–1 count. Yet when the two faced off with a title on the line, Fort Wayne suffered an immediate psychological blow when it was forced to move its share of home contests to a smaller arena in Indianapolis; it seems that the still-lowly NBA had to play second fiddle to a national bowling tournament earlier scheduled for the same dates in Fort Wayne's Coliseum. In retrospect it his hard to fairly pin the Pistons' loss to Syracuse in a rugged series that went the distance on any change in playing sites, however, since the four Syracuse victories all came in upstate New York, while Fort Wayne captured each of the three "home" games it played in Indianapolis. What brought Syracuse the championship in the end was a typically clutch game-six performance by Schayes—whose 28 points allowed the Nats to survive for a seventh game—and the clutch free-throw shooting of George King, which preserved the championship victory in the closing seconds of game seven.

The Nats wallowed in mediocrity after the 1954 season and saw little improvement until the move into Philadelphia at the end of the 1963 campaign. With Schayes now coaching and with a fresh name and image, the club was not able to do much more than hold its own in its first season as the 76ers, beating out the hapless Knicks by a dozen games to avoid the Eastern Division cellar. Then in the second season Wilt Chamberlain triumphantly returned to his home in Philadelphia and fortunes began to change almost overnight. Chamberlain's arrival back in Philly was indeed the biggest story of an otherwise colorless 1964–65 NBA season—perhaps even the biggest story (next to the Celtics' incredible run of championships itself) of the entire NBA decade.

Fan interest seemed to be slipping a bit in the NBA as Boston predictably rolled to title after title with all the finesse of a steamroller. Then, on the very date (January 13th) of the mid-season All-Star Game in St. Louis, came shocking developments that restored balance to the Eastern Division of the league, provided a legitimate threat to Boston's reign, and set up a welcomed renewal of one of pro basketball's biggest-ever head-to-head rivalries. The East had just nipped the West 124–123 in the All-Star classic and yet newspaper stories everywhere the very next day featured only a single basketball story regarding events surrounding All-Star play. The league's perennial scoring champion Wilt Chamberlain had been traded by the defending champion San Francisco Warriors for cash and a handful of journeymen (Paul Neumann, Connie Dierking, and Lee Shafer). With Wilt's return to Philadelphia the Russell-Chamberlain head-knocking would now be re-established on a regular basis within the same division. And the team Wilt was joining was one that had already been breathing heavily down Boston's neck and seemingly lacked only size to complement its balanced scoring, aggressive defense, stable of shooting stars, fast-breaking offense, and reputation for the tightest brand of team play.

Despite the 76ers great newfound strength with Chamberlain and other newcomers like Hal Greer (1958), Chet Walker (1962) and Luke Jackson (1964), it would be several seasons before a breakthrough against the mighty Celtics would be possible. But the Sixers were bent on proving time and again that they weren't lagging very far behind. Wilt's first half-season with the Sixers featured a post-season run which pushed Boston all the way to seven games in the Eastern Division finals, collapsing only when John Havlicek executed basketball's most famous steal of an in-bounds pass in the closing second of a one-point game. Schayes' team had the best record in the NBA in 1966 (55–25, a game better than Boston) but still couldn't crack the Celtic grip in the playoffs. After sitting out a first-round bye they appeared rusty and tentative and were again swept aside by Russell and company with far greater ease and in only five contests. Many blamed Chamberlain for simply not playing hard enough once playoff money was squarely on the line.

The breakthrough finally came with the return of Alex Hannum. Hannum had directed the ballclub in the final Syracuse seasons and then had led the San Francisco Warriors and Wilt Chamberlain to an NBA Finals showdown with Boston in 1964. Although Chamberlain's own return to Philly had allowed the Sixers to wrest first place from Auerbach's men by 1966, post-season collapses against Boston for two straight seasons had spelled the end as coach for franchise legend Dolph Schayes. Hannum returned in the fall of 1966 to Philadelphia and took up where he had left off in Frisco in converting Wilt from a one-dimensional scorer to the anchor of a title contender. Under Hannum and the converted Wilt every challenge was now swept aside, including Boston in the regular-season round robin for the second straight year. And then the post-season riddle was finally solved by Hannum as well. A huge mountain peak was scaled when Boston was mowed down in five games with Chamberlain dominating Russell and his supporting cast, leaving no doubt about the better overall team. In an anticlimactic championship round Hannum and Chamberlain faced their former San Francisco team now rejuvenated by Rick Barry and Nate Thurmond. It was little contest with Philadelphia building an unsurmountable 3–1 lead and coasting in six games. Wilt Chamberlain had finally traded in his once-endless string of scoring titles for the real prize—a coveted NBA championship ring.

The 76ers were still impressive at 62–20 the year after their championship and also remained a first-place outfit. But then Boston rebounded from a regular-season eight-game deficit, clipped the Sixers in seven, then stopped the Lakers in six to earn still another Boston Garden banner. And the following campaign was a repeat performance. Philly was nipped by Baltimore for the Eastern Division crown; the Celtics sagged to fourth place with less than 50 wins; then Boston turned on the post-season heat to crush the Sixers in the opening playoff round. A few weeks later the Boston Celtics were champs yet again, now for the tenth time in eleven tries, and once again the league looked like it had returned to business as usual. And "usual" in Philly always meant another wild pendulum swing of some sort. Unfortunately, this time the cycle was again pointing downward. Chamberlain was gone at the end of the decade, now off to Los Angeles, and Luke Jackson and Darrall Imhoff were huge busts as his replacements. Jack Ramsay maintained momentum for one first-place season (1969) but soon could work little magic with a team obviously coming apart at the seams. Three straight first-round playoff exits under Ramsay were followed by a 1972 dip to 22 games under the break-even level. Mediocrity and much worse had once again come calling.

The 1972–73 season was every bit as bad for Philly as it today looks on paper. The depths of lackluster performance by a team that gave up an average 116.2 points and was outscored nightly by better than a dozen were again recently underscored when even the horrendous Dallas Mavericks clubs of the past two seasons under Rich Adubato and Quinn Buckner could not match such a strenuous record of losing. At one point the team stood 0–15, later 4–58; finally 9–73. They would not only lose 15 to open the campaign but also drop 13 to close it. In the end they trailed the division-leading Boston Celtics by 59 full games after taking to the court only 82 times.

Few coaches in basketball history, or in all of sports history for that

Peter C. Bjarkman

matter, have been dealt a worse deck of cards at the outset than Roy Rubin, first-year coach with the '72–'73 Philadelphia NBA team. After a long and largely successful tenure at Long Island University, Rubin was enticed into taking an open coaching slot with the fast-fading 76ers team that had slipped into mediocrity under Jack Ramsay. Over the past six seasons a Philadelphia club that had been the toast of the league had fallen into the hardest of times. A series of poor deals had shipped away most of the stars of the 1967 title winner. And to make matters worse, the collegiate draft had resulted in a string of poor decisions which further minimized the vital flow of young talent onto the team. It was obviously a huge task that Rubin had been handed. But then it suddenly got much worse when the courts ruled that star Billy Cunningham was bound to a contract he had signed with the ABA and was obligated to report to that upstart league's Carolina Cougars club. The Cunningham decision was the proverbial straw breaking the camel's back and Rubin's first pro team was left with miserable talent, almost no speed or board strength, and a raft of inexperienced ballplayers prone to numerous and repeated mental errors.

Veteran Hal Greer had been the Philly mainstay along with Cunningham, but was now relegated to the bench by nagging injuries and an aging body. Rookie Fred Boyd was thus handed the playmaking chores by default and soon failed miserably at the task. Boyd did average double figures (10.5 ppg.) in scoring for the only time in his six-season career. He also chipped in a career-best 310 assists (25% less than forward Bill Cunningham's team-leading total in this department a year earlier) but committed costly turnovers on a regular basis and provided little inspirational floor leadership. Management had, of course, expected a lost season under a rookie coach and prepared for a winter devoted largely to rebuilding. But the losses soon became so embarrassingly frequent and by such embarrassingly large margins that Rubin was clearly destined not to make it through the full season. The ballclub was 4–47 by the time the coaching reins were finally handed over to reserve guard (and long-time future NBA mentor) Kevin Loughery. Loughery made his own coaching debut hardly a memorable one by coaxing only the slightest improvement out of the battle-weary and outmanned Philly squad. At season's end the club had achieved a near-impossible badge of dishonor. In a league filled with numerous other patsies (like Buffalo and Portland, with only 21 wins apiece) the Rubin-Loughery team had somehow managed to play badly enough consistently enough to win less than ten ballgames in 82 excruciating outings.

After the 1973 fiasco Gene Shue appeared on the scene as the new 76ers coach and the always-present pendulum began to swing upward once more. Five straight seasons of marked improvement followed with the team jumping to 25 victories (still 4th in a four-team Atlantic Division), then 34 (4th again), and then 46 (second-place tie). And the real sign of franchise upgrade game when Philly landed the prize catch of the now-defunct ABA and perhaps the prize catch in all of basketball. Julius Erving—the *one* showcase player that allowed the shaky ABA to claim the smallest measure of legitimacy in its head-to-head competition with the NBA—came on board in a Sixers uniform and the team that had so long banged around the basement once again had instant credibility and instant appeal everywhere around the league. Erving himself had reached loggerheads with New York Nets owner Roy Boe over a promised salary increase which the struggling former ABA outfit could now ill-afford—especially in view of the stiff entrance fee the club was now being assessed for admission into the NBA (along with Indiana, Denver and San Antonio). To the rescue (of Erving, the Nets, the Sixers, and perhaps the entire NBA) came new Philly owner Fitz Eugene Dixon. In a deal which sent shock waves through the entire sports world Dixon was reportedly parting with an unheard-of $6 million in cold cash ($3 million in compensation to Boe and another $3 million in signing bonus to Erving himself) to acquire basketball's biggest headliner. If one single deal could not assure an immediate return to glory days it could certainly put plenty of luster back on a very tarnished franchise.

The Sixers were clearly back in business in the late '70s when they were able to team Erving with George McGinnis as the league's best pair of high-scoring forwards. The resurrection of club fortunes had actually begun a season before Erving's arrival, during Gene Shue's third season at the helm, when the team climbed back over the .500 ledger for the first time in five years. McGinnis, an ABA star with the Indiana Pacers, had signed on with the NBA in Philadelphia preceding that turn-around 1975–76 season and had quickly paced the club's climb into a second-place Atlantic Division tie with Buffalo. McGinnis and Erving had actually shared ABA MVP honors only two seasons earlier in 1975, and with the two of them now in the same front-court lineup Philly suddenly boasted a front wall second to none in the league. With Doug Collins, Lloyd Free, and Henry Bibby filling out the backcourt duties the 1977 team won 50 games, outdistanced the Celtics by six games in the Atlantic Division, and advanced all the way through post-season minefields into the NBA finals.

It was indeed fitting that the Philly ball club should revive so dramatically with its new power-packed lineup and with the acquisition of McGinnis and the debut of Dr. J., all in the very season that mirrored the ballclub's patriotic nickname. It might have been another title for the 76ers beginning in the fall of 1976, but the Portland Trail Blazers and Bill Walton had also upgraded their act and were eventually to prove even more of a charmed team during that very same season. Portland had won but 49 games in regular season action (trailing the Lakers and Denver as well as Philly) and had chased the Los Angeles Lakers over in the Pacific Division. But when post-season tipped off Walton—slowed by injuries his first two seasons—finally rose to the prominence expected after his brilliant collegiate career. After toying with Chicago and Denver in earlier rounds Walton's crew blew past the Lakers and Kareem Abdul-Jabbar in four straight. This set up a championship showdown with the heavily favored

76ers which would in the end prove one of the most surprising in several seasons.

With Dr. J. having more than lived up to expectations all year long and with Erving (21.6) and McGinnis (21.4) providing double-barrelled offense, Gene Shue's team had reason for full confidence entering the final round of championship play. McGinnis had slumped badly in the early playoff rounds (he would eventually average only 14.2 ppg. through 19 post-season contests) yet Philadelphia got off on sound footing with two immediate victories on the home hardwood. Then suddenly everything seemed to change for the worse for the Atlantic Division champs. Revving up their game against an effectual Philly defense out in Portland, the Blazers knotted the series with laughably easy victories of 22 and 32 points. Back in the Spectrum the confident Blazers built another huge second-half lead and withstood a furious 76ers rally to move within a game of an unexpected NBA title.

There was still a spark of life left in Erving (who scored 40 points) and McGinnis (who finally returned to mid-season shooting form) during game six, played in Portland, but it was not nearly enough to stem the rush of Walton. Basketball's famed redhead was finally proving his meddle as the post-season MVP. Another large lead almost evaporated for Portland down the stretch when Philadelphia cut a 12 point deficit to 109–107 with 18 seconds remaining. Yet when McGinnis and Erving both missed game-tying medium range shots in the closing seconds, it was the Portland team which celebrated a league title in only its seventh NBA season. The league's 31st season had begun with a huge trade which had apparently guaranteed Philadelphia a league championship in exchange for nearly $6 million spent to acquire basketball's most celebrated player. Yet when Dr. J.'s final shot of the season rolled harmlessly off the rim as the clock ran down nine months later in Portland, it was once again demonstrated that— in basketball as in life—the best-laid plans often have a way of going suddenly awry, and sometimes in the most ironic of ways.

The Sixers were not quite ready for another total collapse on the heels of the frustrating title loss to Portland. Former backcourt hero Bill Cunningham returned to the fold when he took over the coaching reins in the early weeks of 1977–78 and steady improvement was still the order of the day from that point forward. Things didn't appear very bright at the season's outset, to be sure, and when a rude stumble out of the gate resulted in a 2–4 start, Gene Shue suddenly found himself on the sidelines. But under Cunningham the 1978 team actually improved five games (55–27) in the win column and thus trailed only the defending-champion Trail Blazers in regular-season victories.

While that 1978 Cunningham team collapsed in the Eastern Conference finals against the Cinderella Washington Bullets, the 1980 contingent raised the victory total to 59 games (second best in franchise history) and again earned a spot in the NBA championship round. This time the opposition was the Los Angeles Lakers and the star enemy player was sensational Lakers rookie Earvin "Magic" Johnson. While Erving was again spectacular in the championship round the magical LA rookie named Earvin was even moreso as the playoffs wore on, shifting to center from his normal guard spot when Kareem Abdul-Jabbar was floored by injury for a crucial game six. With Johnson inspiring the Lakers and pouring in 42 points from the unfamiliar post slot the LA club easily won the only one-sided game of the title series. And with a six-game title triumph that staked out the 1980s as the Lakers' own personal playground, the first LA title of the decade left the Sixers a bridesmaid for the second time in the past four years.

The final move over the top for Cunningham's team came with the acquisition of rugged pivotman Moses Malone. Philadelphia would make three vital trades in club history and each would miraculously result in a surge to the league's top rung. The first such deal had returned Wilt to his home city in January 1965 and thus provided the pillar around which to build the greatest single-season team ever. The second, bringing Dr. J. into the fold, launched the modern era in Sixers basketball history. And the third was indisputably a deal which inked Malone and therefore almost assured a league title to crown Julius Erving's brilliant ABA/NBA career.

Malone arrived from Houston in a September 1982 deal for cash plus lanky center Caldwell Jones. And he immediately combined with Erving and with a talented backcourt of Andrew Toney and Maurice Cheeks to power the team all the way to the top. For awhile it looked like the 1983 Sixers might even equal the records amassed by the 1967 club on which Cunningham himself had played. In the end the Sixers won 65 games (three short of '67) and Malone repeated his 1982 MVP season with the Rockets by duplicating the award for Philly. In the process, Malone would also become the last center to win the MVP trophy until Hakeem Olajuwon would finally earn the honor eleven seasons later.

The 1983 finals with the Los Angeles Lakers and Magic Johnson was one of the NBA's all-time post-season classics. The old guard and new guard faced off as Magic and Dr. J. now again battled head-to-head and spectacular move to spectacular move for a title. And in the end Erving finally had his championship laurels. But if the drama was high because of the protagonists, the action on the court itself was rather one-sided. There were no routs, and LA never lost a contest by more than ten points. But they didn't win a game against the Sixers either. With James Worthy out with a broken leg and Bob McAdoo and Norm Nixon also slowed by injury the Lakers could hardly contain the Sixers, despite veteran Kareem Abdul-Jabbar's brilliant 27 ppg. playoff average. When the four-game mini-series was over, Moses Malone had added a post-season MVP, as well, to his two trophies as regular-season most valuable player.

The Sixers were strong for several more years, but gradually injuries and retirements took their toll. Two more 50-plus-win seasons under Cunningham meant playoff appearances but no advance farther than the third round. Matt Guokas was at the helm by the middle of the decade and the victory totals slid from 54 to 45 to 36 (and an exit from playoff competition) by 1988.

Despite the presence of Charles Barkley as one of the game's true stars in the late '80s the Sixers had again descended on particularly hard times.

Barkley was not only a huge force on the playing floor for more than a decade but also one of the most outrageous and outspoken athletes in all basketball history. The portly battler challenged foes and teammates alike and usually backed up every threat and complaint with a show of relentless strength and fury on the court. "Sir Charles" cajoled his teammates periodically for lackluster play and scolded tauting fans near courtside by returning barbs and insults of his own. More than once Barkley threatened to enter the stands after personally-abusive fans and involved himself in several off-court altercations that resulted in legal charges against the star player. And Barkley also accused Philly owner Harold Katz on more than one occasion, and in public statements released to the press, of having very little interest in building another winner for Sixers faithful and for the players themselves. Regarding this last charge there seemed to be much evidence stacked up on Barkley's side of the issue.

During this period a great basketball icon disappeared from the Philadelphia sporting scene. He was a long-time living legend virtually unknown to the wider national audiences, yet one who inspired fierce love and loyalty from usually-fickle Philly sports fans everywhere. Dave Zinkoff had been a fixture for years at the public address microphone in Philadelphia's Spectrum and had entertained Sixers crowds for decades before his death. His intonation of "Errrrrr-ving" every time Dr. J. canned a bucket was as familiar a sound on the Philly sporting scene as the boos and catcalls with which the city's fans greet almost every unpopular action. Zinky was permanently remembered by the NBA club with a most fitting tribute—a unique permanent retirement of his trademark microphone.

By the early '90s the Sixers were again clearly stuck in rebuilding mode. Barkley had worn out both his best seasons and his personal welcome while hanging around the Philly clubhouse; few were thus shocked when "The Round Mound of Rebound" was traded to Western Conference tenant Phoenix in exchange for Jeff Hornacek, Andrew Lang and Tim Perry. A series of coaches came, and went as well—Matt Guokas, Jim Lyman, Doug Moe, Fred Carter. Seven-foot-six Shawn Bradley out of Brigham Young University was a high draft choice and a huge reclamation project, to boot; yet Bradley spent much of his rookie year on the injured list and offered few immediate dividends. The team itself promised little in the early '90s but sideshows like the towering Bradley and the spindly Manute Bol, the latter a Dinka tribesman who had acted as Bradley's unschooled forerunner. Winning basketball had again fled the City of Brotherly Love.

Once again there is little at present to buoy the spirits of faithful Sixers fans in Philly or elsewhere. Shawn Bradley may mend and slowly-but-surely develop into a huge roadblock around the opponents' bucket, yet Bradley will never be a second coming of Wilt Chamberlain or even of Robert Parish. Clarence Weatherspoon shows few signs of withering after two productive career-launching seasons; but Weatherspoon has yet to record a 20 ppg. season and seems more of a stop-gap performer than a superstar. A dismal 1994 record has assured a quality draft pick from one of the richest lottery talent pools in years. On the other hand, history itself holds out the strongest hope for a Sixers' future. Perhaps it will again be time for yet another rapid pendulum swing by basketball's most roller-coaster franchise.

Suggested Readings on Philadelphia Sixers and Syracuse Nats

Barkley, Charles (with Roy S. Johnson) **Outrageous! The Fine Life and Flagrant Good Times of Basketball's Irresistible Force**. New York: Simon and Schuster, 1992.

Bell, Marty. **The Legend of Dr. J**. New York: Coward, McCann & Geoghegan, 1975.

Bjarkman, Peter C. **The History of the NBA**. New York and Avenel, New Jersey: Crescent Books (Outlet Books, Random House), 1992.

Koppett, Leonard. **24 Seconds to Shoot: An Informal History of the National Basketball Association**. New York and London: Collier-Macmillan, 1968 (1970).

Salzberg, Charles. **From Set Shot to Slam Dunk—The Glory Days of Basketball in the Words of Those Who Played It**. New York: Dell Publishing (Bantam Doubleday), 1987.

Philadelphia Sixers Retired Uniform Numbers (5)

Julius Erving (6)
Wilt Chamberlain (13)
Hal Greer (15)
Bobby Jones (24)
Bill Cunningham (32)
Dave Zinkoff (Microphone, Announcer)

Year-by-Year Philadelphia Sixers (Syracuse Nats) Summary

Season	Record	Finish	Coach(es)	Scoring Leader(s)	Playoffs (W-L Record)

Key: * = Tie for Position; # = League Scoring Leader
Syracuse Nats (Nationals)
National Basketball League

Season	Record	Finish	Coach(es)	Scoring Leader(s)	Playoffs (W-L Record)
1946–47	21–23	3rd*	Benny Borgmann	Mike Novak (11.2)	Lost in 1st Round (1–3)
1947–48	24–36	4th	Benny Borgmann	Jim Homer (12.5)	Lost in 1st Round (0–3)
1948–49	40–23	2nd	Al Cervi	Dolph Schayes (12.8)	Lost in 2nd Round (3–3)

Season	Record	Finish	Coach(es)	Scoring Leader(s)	Playoffs (W-L Record)
National Basketball Association					
1949–50	51–13	1st	Al Cervi	Dolph Schayes (16.8)	Lost in NBA Finals (6–5)
1950–51	32–34	4th	Al Cervi	Dolph Schayes (17.0)	Lost in 2nd Round (4–3)
1951–52	40–26	1st	Al Cervi	Dolph Schayes (13.8)	Lost in 2nd Round (3–4)
1952–53	47–24	2nd	Al Cervi	Dolph Schayes (17.8)	Lost in 1st Round (0–2)
1953–54	42–30	2nd*	Al Cervi	Dolph Schayes (17.1)	Lost in NBA Finals (9–4)
1954–55	43–29	1st	Al Cervi	Dolph Schayes (18.5)	**NBA Champion** (7–4)
1955–56	35–37	3rd	Al Cervi	Dolph Schayes (20.4)	Lost in 2nd Round (4–4)
1956–57	38–34	2nd	Al Cervi	Dolph Schayes (22.5)	Lost in 2nd Round (2–3)
			Paul Seymour		
1957–58	41–31	2nd	Paul Seymour	Dolph Schayes (24.9)	Lost in 1st Round (1–2)
1958–59	35–37	3rd	Paul Seymour	Dolph Schayes (21.3)	Lost in 2nd Round (5–4)
1959–60	45–30	3rd	Paul Seymour	Dolph Schayes (22.5)	Lost in 1st Round (1–2)
1960–61	38–41	3rd	Alex Hannum	Dolph Schayes (23.6)	Lost in 2nd Round (4–4)
1961–62	41–39	3rd	Alex Hannum	Hal Greer (22.8)	Lost in 1st Round (2–3)
1962–63	48–32	2nd	Alex Hannum	Hal Greer (19.5)	Lost in 1st Round (2–3)
Philadelphia Sixers (76ers)					
1963–64	34–46	3rd	Dolph Schayes	Hal Greer (23.3)	Lost in 1st Round (2–3)
1964–65	40–40	3rd	Dolph Schayes	Wilt Chamberlain (30.1)#	Lost in 2nd Round (6–5)
1965–66	55–25	1st	Dolph Schayes	Wilt Chamberlain (33.5)#	Lost in 1st Round (1–4)
1966–67	68–13	1st	Alex Hannum	Wilt Chamberlain (24.1)	**NBA Champion** (11–4)
1967–68	62–20	1st	Alex Hannum	Wilt Chamberlain (24.3)	Lost in 2nd Round (7–6)
1968–69	55–27	1st	Jack Ramsay	Bill Cunningham (24.8)	Lost in 1st Round (1–4)
1969–70	42–40	4th	Jack Ramsay	Bill Cunningham (26.1)	Lost in 1st Round (1–4)
1970–71	47–35	2nd	Jack Ramsay	Bill Cunningham (23.0)	Lost in 1st Round (3–4)
1971–72	30–52	3rd	Jack Ramsay	Bill Cunningham (23.3)	Did Not Qualify
1972–73	9–73	4th	Roy Rubin	Fred Carter (20.0)	Did Not Qualify
			Kevin Loughery		
1973–74	25–57	4th	Gene Shue	Fred Carter (21.4)	Did Not Qualify
1974–75	34–48	4th	Gene Shue	Fred Carter (21.9)	Did Not Qualify
1957–76	46–36	2nd*	Gene Shue	George McGinnis (23.0)	Lost in 1st Round (1–2)
1976–77	50–32	1st	Gene Shue	Julius Erving (21.6)	Lost in NBA Finals (10–9)
1977–78	55–27	1st	Gene Shue	Julius Erving (20.6)	Lost in 3rd Round (6–4)
			Bill Cunningham		
1978–79	47–35	2nd	Bill Cunningham	Julius Erving (23.1)	Lost in 2nd Round (5–4)
1979–80	59–23	2nd	Bill Cunningham	Julius Erving (26.9)	Lost in NBA Finals (12–6)
1980–81	62–20	1st*	Bill Cunningham	Julius Erving (24.6)	Lost in 3rd Round (9–7)
1981–82	58–24	2nd	Bill Cunningham	Julius Erving (24.4)	Lost in NBA Finals (12–9)
1982–83	65–17	1st	Bill Cunningham	Moses Malone (24.5)	**NBA Champion** 12–1)
1983–84	52–30	2nd	Bill Cunningham	Moses Malone (22.7)	Lost in 1st Round (2–3)
1984–85	58–24	2nd	Bill Cunningham	Moses Malone (24.6)	Lost in 3rd Round (8–5)
1985–86	54–28	2nd	Matt Guokas	Moses Malone (23.8)	Lost in 2nd Round (6–6)
1986–87	45–37	2nd	Matt Guokas	Charles Barkley (23.0)	Lost in 1st Round (2–3)
1987–88	36–46	4th	Matt Guokas	Charles Barkley (28.3)	Did Not Qualify
			Jim Lyman		
1988–89	46–36	2nd	Jim Lyman	Charles Barkley (25.8)	Lost in 1st Round (0–3)
1989–90	53–29	1st	Jim Lyman	Charles Barkley (25.2)	Lost in 2nd Round (4–6)
1990–91	44–38	2nd	Jim Lyman	Charles Barkley (27.6)	Lost in 2nd Round (4–4)
1991–92	35–47	5th	Jim Lyman	Charles Barkley (23.1)	Did Not Qualify
1992–93	26–56	6th	Doug Moe	Hersey Hawkins (20.3)	Did Not Qualify
			Fred Carter		
1993–94	25–57	6th	Fred Carter	C. Weatherspoon (18.4)	Did Not Qualify

Individual Career Leaders and Record Holders (1946–1994)

Scoring Average	Wilt Chamberlain (27.6 ppg., 1965–68)
Points Scored	Hal Greer (21,586, 1958–1973)
Games Played	Hal Greer (1,122, 1958–73)
Minutes Played	Hal Greer (39,788)
Field Goal Pct.	Wilt Chamberlain (.583, 1965–68)
3-Pt. Field Goals Made	Hersey Hawkins (476, 1988–93)
3-Pt. Field Goal Pct.	Hersey Hawkins (.406)
Free Throws Made	Dolph Schayes (6,979)
Free-Throw Pct.	Scott Brooks (.881, 1988–90)
Rebounds	Dolph Schayes (11,256, 1948–64)
Assists	Maurice Cheeks (6,212, 1978–89)
Steals	Maurice Cheeks (1,942)
Blocked Shots	Julius Erving (1,293, 1976–87)
Personal Fouls	Hal Greer (3,855)

Individual Single-Season and Game Records (1946–1994)

Scoring Average	Wilt Chamberlain (33.5 ppg., 1965–66)
Points Scored (Season)	Wilt Chamberlain (2,649, 1965–66)
Points Scored (Game)	Wilt Chamberlain (68, 12–16–67 at Chicago Bulls)
Minutes Played (Season)	Wilt Chamberlain (3836, 1967–68)
Field Goal Pct. (Season)	Wilt Chamberlain (.683, 1966–67)
3-Pt. Field Goal Pct. (Season)	Al Wood (.448, 1985–86)
3-Pt. Field Goals (Season)	Hersey Hawkins (122, 1992–93)
Free-Throw Pct. (Season)	Mike Gminski (.938, 1987–88)
Free Throws Made (Season)	Moses Malone (737, 1984–85)
Rebounds (Season)	Wilt Chamberlain (1,957, 1966–67)
Rebounds (Game)	Wilt Chamberlain (43, 3–6–65 vs. Boston Celtics)
Assists (Season)	Maurice Cheeks (753, 1985–86)
Assists (Game)	Wilt Chamberlain (21, 2–2–68 vs. Detroit Pistons)
	Maurice Cheeks (21, 10–30–82 vs. New Jersey Nets)
Steals (Season)	Steve Mix (212, 1973–74)
Blocked Shots (Season)	Manute Bol (247, 1990–91)
Personal Fouls (Season)	George McGinnis (334, 1975–76)

Best Trade in Franchise History

Some clubs have a history of always trading badly. A few have the Midas Touch and always seem to work blockbuster deals which fall squarely in their favor. The Sixers franchise has worked deals that brought them Wilt Chamberlain in 1965, Julius Erving from the ABA in 1976, and Moses Malone in 1982. And each deal led to a championship run and a mini-dynasty of sorts. Perhaps the best of the lot was the transaction to get Erving, since he remains to this very date the franchise's and perhaps the game's most glamorous player ever. But the other two deals were vital franchise-builders as well.

Worst Trade in Franchise History

The trade of Wilt Chamberlain to the Los Angeles Lakers in 1968 was one that probably made some modicum of sense at the time. Wilt had been a league force for years and did pack in paying fans. But it was also evident that the Sixers were never going to challenge the league's top teams like the Celtics and Lakers at playoff time with a team built around Chamberlain alone. Wilt had plenty of opportunities to deliver championships in Philly and had failed on all previous occasions but one. It was therefore seemingly time for a change and that change had to be dramatic. Yet the Sixers management simply didn't get enough in return. The Chamberlain deal and those which soon followed involving stars of the 1967 world championship outfit contained the seeds, if not the full-blown shrubs, of ballclub self-destruction. The dismantling was complete after a few short seasons and the team was soon a laughingstock of the entire NBA. With Wilt, on the other hand, the Sixers would have always been at least respectable and attendance-rich. And they might have also been these things without Wilt, as well, had the seven-footer only brought them at least a fair market value when traded to LA.

Philadelphia Sixers Historical Oddity

In a rare oddity of sports history the Philadelphia Sixers can legitimately boast of owning both the best and the worst single seasons in all of NBA history. The 1966–67 team is rivaled for the title of "all-time best" only by the 1971–72 Lakers. Its starting lineup—Chet Walker, Luke Jackson, Wilt Chamberlain, Hal Greer and Wally Jones—was as solid top to bottom as any ever put out on the floor for regular league action. This unit might even have held its own with any imaginable NBA All-Star squad drawn from any era, ancient or modern. And the worst team of all-time is also, hands-down, the 1972–73 Philadelphia outfit that came along only six seasons later. Here was a team comprised of a starting five—Tom Van Arsdale, Manny Leaks, Leroy Ellis, Fred Carter and Freddie Boyd—and bench (lowlighted by Kevin Loughery, Dale Schlueter and John Block) both so bad that it is almost inconceivable that they ever played as a unit in the high-profile NBA.

Sixers All-Time Number One Draft Picks List

Philadelphia Sixers

1964 Lucious "Luke" Jackson (Pan American)
1965 Bill Cunningham (North Carolina)
1966 Matt Goukas (St. Joseph's)
1967 Craig Raymond (Brigham Young)
1968 Shaler Halimon (Utah State)
1969 Bud Ogden (Santa Clara)
1970 Al Henry (Wisconsin)
1971 Dana Lewis (Tulsa)
1972 Fred Boyd (Oregon State)
1973 Doug Collins (Illinois State)
1974 Marvin Barnes (Providence)
1975 Darryl Dawkins (Evans High School, Orlando, Florida)
1976 Terry Furlow (Michigan State)
1977 Glenn Mosley (Seton Hall)
1978 Maurice Cheeks (West Texas State)
1979 Jim Spanarkel (Duke)
1980 Andrew Toney (SW Louisiana)
1981 Franklin Edwards (Cleveland State)
1982 Mark McNamara (California)
1983 Leo Rautins (Syracuse)
1984 Charles Barkley (Auburn)
1985 Terry Catledge (South Alabama)
1986 David Wingate (Georgetown)
1987 Chris Welp (Washington)
1988 Charles Smith (Pittsburgh)
1989 Kenny Payne (Louisville)
1990 None
1991 None
1992 Clarence Weatherspoon (Southern Mississippi)
1993 Shawn Bradley (Brigham Young)

Chapter 7

DETROIT PISTONS AND FORT WAYNE PISTONS

Somehow the Wheels Always Manage to Fall Off

All-Time Franchise Record: 1754–1880, .483 Pct. (1946–1994)
NBA Championships (2): 1988–89, 1989–90
Greatest Franchise Player: Isiah Thomas (1981–1994)
All-Time Leading Scorer: Isiah Thomas (18,822 Points, 1981–1994)
Most Successful Coach: Chuck Daly (538–313, .632 Pct., 1983–1992)
All-Time Franchise Team: Bob Lanier (C), George Yardley (F), Bailey Howell (F), Dave Bing (G), Isiah Thomas (G)

"They got a big shaggy dog about to bite them in the rear end, and the name of the dog is the present."

—Isiah Thomas

Nowhere in sports can one find a better example of how quickly the worm can turn or how rapidly the mighty may fall. For a brief three-year flourish at the end of the 1980s the Detroit Pistons rode unchallenged on the top of the basketball world. The team known as basketball's "Bad Boys" was the toast of the popular NBA and perhaps the toast of the entire sporting scene. The club rode a rough style of play and a perfect blend of team personalities to two straight NBA titles, thus becoming only the second repeat-champion in more than two full decades. They had appeared in three straight NBA finals when they swept aside the Lakers in 1990 and Daly's club thus stood on the verge of the league's first three-peat since the glorious Boston Celtics dynasty of the turbulent sixties.

But then the Chicago Bulls suddenly jelled with Michael Jordan and Scottie Pippen and a new champion brushed aside the Bad Boys and overnight launched their own three-peat string of world titles. And as the

154

Chicago Bulls rose to prominence the Pistons just as quickly unravelled. A close-fought divisional finals loss to the Bulls in 1991 signalled the changing of the guard and marked a key transition in fortunes of the Detroit team. Two final seasons under Chuck Daly revealed steady if not overnight decline. A transition season under Ron Rothstein brought clear signs of growing mediocrity. Daly's departure was followed by trades of John Salley and Dennis Rodman. Bill Laimbeer and Isiah Thomas limped down the road to retirement. And then the bottom completely fell out in 1994, one of the worst seasons in Detroit Pistons history.

The 1993–94 season marked the final curtain call for a giddy era of Detroit basketball. Daly's powerhouse outfit was on its last legs with only Isiah Thomas, Bill Laimbeer and Joe Dumars remaining from the nucleus of the recent repeat championship club. But days were clearly numbered in Detroit for both Laimbeer and Thomas. First Laimbeer retired during the early weeks of the campaign, admitting that his body could no longer measure up to his rough-house style of play. But Laimbeer did not go without a final moment of controversy. A practice-session confrontation with Isiah led to a hand injury for the senior-statesman star guard.

Thomas himself was clearly nearing the end of his career. A severe injury in the closing weeks of the campaign brought an unfitting conclusion to Thomas' hall-of-fame career. The team itself was a shambles and tumbled to the worst record in thirteen years. The 60 losses and 6th place tie represented the first time that those marks of futility had been reached since the back-to-back 60-loss campaigns of 1979–80 and 1980–81. Through the club's first several decades Pistons fans were used to such losing. But on the heels of Thomas's glorious career it was now a lot tougher to take.

Isiah Thomas retired at the conclusion of the 1994 season as clearly the greatest player in franchise history. It was possible that Isiah would remain a fixture with the Pistons front office. But his replacement on the floor would be impossible. The imaginative playmaker had established a laundry list of milestones and club and league records over his thirteen seasons in the NBA. He was the all-time club leader in points, assists and steals in both regular-season and post-season play. He had climbed above 18,000 career points, and in the final month of his final season became only the third NBAer (along with Magic Johnson and Oscar Robertson) to reach above the 9,000 plateau in career assists. His honors included NBA Finals MVP (1990), twelve straight All-Star game selections, and two All-Star Game MVP awards (1984 and 1986). With assists as the true hallmark of his game, Thomas now rates as the all-time All-Star game leader in that department and also once held the league single-season assists standard (since broken by John Stockton of Utah). During the 1984–85 campaign Thomas piled up a then-record 1,123 assists for a 13.1 per game average.

The crowning jewels of Thomas's career, however, were the three seasons at the end of the 1980s when the club roared to three consecutive appearances in the league's championship finals. The club averaged 59 wins per season over that stretch. Two of the three seasons the Lakers *did* edge out the Pistons for the best regular-season record, and the two power-house clubs led by Magic and Isiah split their two head-on collisions in the championship final round. But the Lakers' stumble in the second play-off round in 1990 allowed the Pistons to sail past Portland for a repeat championship and thus match the Los Angeles repeat titles of '87 and '88. Isiah was at the peak of his game during this stretch, even though his scoring average had fallen off slightly from his back-to-back 20 ppg. seasons in 1986 and 1987. Isiah was still the club scoring leader during the two championship years and teamed with Joe Dumars to provide the league's most potent and versatile backcourt combo in more than a decade. And Thomas turned his game up a notch for the post-season, earning a playoff MVP in 1990 with his averages of 27.6 points, 7 assists and 5.2 rebounds in the final series against the Portland Trail Blazers.

The glory-run years under Chuck Daly actually began in 1987 with a swift climb up the ladder of the competitive Central Division. Daly's first Piston's club in 1983–84 had turned the city's first winning record (49–33) and playoff appearance in seasons. His 1985 and 1986 clubs had both checked in at an identical 46–36 mark and thus served notice that the Pistons were no longer divisional doormats, as they had been under Scotty Robertson, Richie Adubato and Dick Vitale.

But it was in the 1987 season that Detroit really caught fire under Daly and recorded the first franchise 50-win season since the Bob Lanier era back in the mid-seventies. Scoring-machine Adrian Dantley (acquired in the off-season from Utah for Kelly Tripucka) provided the needed offensive thrust with a 21.5 average his first season in Detroit. Dumars (11.8 ppg.), Thomas (20.6) and Laimbeer (15.4) were other starters averaging in double figures, and bench scoring support was provided by sixth-man star Vinnie Johnson (15.7). Rookies Dennis Rodman and John Salley also provided solid rebounding and defensive play off the bench, as did rugged veteran Rick Mahorn. The bruising image of the "Bad Boy" line-up was already being earned on the court with a no-holds-barred scrappy style of rough-and-tumble play. The talented young Detroit club trailed Atlanta by five full games during the regular campaign, yet steamrolled those same Hawks in five games during second-round post-season play. Daly's club served sufficient notice of a bright future by extending the Larry Bird-led Boston Celtics to the maximum seven contests of the Eastern Division finals.

Chuck Daly's fourth season at the helm, buoyed by the trade for Adrian Dantley and the drafting of Rodman and Salley, had been a huge step in the right direction for the Detroiters. The 52 victories tied a club record and a trip to the divisional finals was the first venture into the playoff third round since the club had shifted from Fort Wayne over to the Motor City.

It was the 1987–88 season, however, that trumpeted the Pistons full arrival as a legitimate potential championship force. Adrian Dantley (20.0 ppg.) continued to pace a balanced scoring attack in which all five starters, as well as Rodman and Vinnie Johnson off the bench, now averaged in double figures. A two-game improvement in the won-lost column was enough to vault the Pistons over Atlanta and into their first regular-season first-place finish since the 1956–57 finale season back in Fort Wayne. Under a full head of steam the club next charged past Washington (3–2), Chicago (4–1) and Boston (4–2), and into a final-round championship showdown with Isiah's off-court friend and on-court rival, Magic Johnson, and his Los Angeles Lakers. The Boston series for the divisional title was especially hard fought and featured two overtime contests (split between the teams) and no victory margin on either side of greater than eight points. It was the physical nature of this particular Boston series which first earned Chuck Daly's team its reputation for rugged—if not at times even unsportsmanlike—ferocious play. Detroit's "Bad Boys" contingent of Laimbeer, Rodman, Salley, and Mahorn simply wore out an aging Larry Bird, Robert Parish and Kevin McHale.

The Los Angeles Lakers club that matched up in the championship final with Detroit in spring, 1988 was the dominant franchise of the 1980s by any imaginable standard. No team since the Celtics had been able to garner back-to-back crowns, yet the Lakers had barely failed to do so after their championships in 1982 and 1985. The Lakers team of Johnson, Abdul-Jabbar and James Worthy was riding its final crest, and this was clearly perceived as their last probable shot at repeat titles. And the Lakers were perhaps carting extra baggage as a result of the promise made by coach Pat Riley on the heels of the 1987 Los Angeles championship. Looking for a psychological edge to motivate his team in 1988, Riley had guaranteed LA fans the first NBA repeat since the Auerbach Celtics.

Detroit grabbed the early lead in the series and, for a short while at least, it looked like the Lakers might not bear up well under their own self-inflicted pressure of Riley's prediction. Worse for Pat Riley's crew, however, than the specter of boasts about repeating a championship, were the physical and psychological bruises suffered in an unexpectedly difficult previous series that had stretched out to seven games against the upstart Dallas Mavericks. Detroit split the two road games in LA, then took the final two of three on the home floor to grab a 3–2 series advantage heading back to the west coast. The crucial sixth game swung to the now-desperate Lakers, who staved off elimination by the narrowest of margins, 103–102. Playing on a badly-sprained ankle, Isiah Thomas nonetheless poured home 43 in a losing effort. By game seven momentum had shifted to the defending champs who held on tenaciously for a slim 108–105 title-clinching victory. With 36 points and 16 rebounds, playoff MVP James Worthy was more than even a scrappy group of "Bad Boys" could hope to handle.

The Lakers had crested in the 1988 finals, but the Pistons were only just now peaking. That became readily apparent as another season began to unfold in the fall of the year. The Pistons again stormed through the regular season, this time with the best record in the NBA and the best in club history at 63–19. The key to success was a balanced lineup, as no

Piston cracked the 20 ppg. barrier yet four starters (Dantley, Laimbeer, Dumars and Thomas) and two reserves (Vinnie Johnson and Mark Aguirre, acquired in mid-February from Dallas for Dantley and a first-round draft selection) averaged in double figures. Post-season didn't slow the well-primed Daly machine the least bit. The Detroiters would run roughshod over the playoff opposition with a 15–2 record, which included first and second round sweeps over Boston and Milwaukee. The Chicago Bulls, with Jordan sporting a playoff-best 34.8 average, rose up momentarily in the conference finals to capture two of the first three matches before crumbling. And Magic and the Lakers were little obstacle this second time around. It was Jabbar's final season and the Lakers might thus have had a slight emotional edge. Yet, when hamstring injuries slowed Byron Scott and Magic Johnson, there was nothing left on Pat Riley's bench to match up adequately with the Detroiters' powerful backcourt. It was a four-game sweep for Daly's outfit, with Joe Dumars averaging 27 ppg. and carting off an MVP plaque as well as an NBA championship ring.

It was now the Pistons who were primed for talk of repeats, three-peats, and even dynasties—dynasties, of course, being of generally short duration in the world of the NBA. The 1989–90 season brought little if any loss of momentum for Daly's charges. A record of 59–23 was solid enough to bring with it a third straight Central Division first-place slot. Age had now relegated Mark Aguirre to a permanent sixth-man role and it was thus up to Thomas (18.4) and Dumars (17.8) to take up much of the slack left by Adrian Dantley's departure. Rick Mahorn had also been left unprotected in the spring expansion draft and thus had been plucked by Minnesota's Timberwolves. But Rodman (792 rebounds) and veteran center James Edwards (14.5 ppg.) were more than adequate replacements for Mahorn on the front line. Detroit sprinted through a 13-game win streak in mid-season and by year's end truly *did* seem on the verge of boasting a dynasty ballclub. Daly had solid performers at every position and the look of the Pistons team was still very much that of an exceedingly young squad.

With the Lakers out of the way early (a second-round loser to Portland) the path was now also suddenly wide open for the Pistons to fashion a repeat title of their own. Indiana was swept in three games and New York pushed aside in four before the Pistons and Bulls met head-to-head for the Conference title for the second year running. This time it took Isiah and company the full compliment of seven contests to dispense with Michael Jordan's crew and earn a third straight trip to the NBA finals. The rugged series featured a string of low-scoring games which left the Pistons' game average at only 96 points for the series and the Bulls' at only 93. As is often the case with such evenly matched teams, the home squad captured all seven contests. Michael Jordan was easily the big weapon for Chicago with 47 and 42 points respectively during the third and fourth games.

Western Conference champ Portland (a 4–2 victor over Phoenix) offered little true opposition to Detroit's seasoned Bad Boys once Jordan had been conquered and the championship round began. The series would stretch no longer than five games, and it went that long only after Portland eked out an overtime road win in game two. But this was to be a series of road victories, however, and Detroit answered with three consecutive back in Portland to slam an early door on the 1990 post-season chase.

Detroit had now become only the sixth team in forty years to repeat as NBA champion, joining Minneapolis in 1949–1950, the Lakers again in 1952–54 (three straight), Auerbach's Celtics in 1959–1966 (eight in a row), Boston once more in 1968–1969, and the recent Lakers (1987–1988). And the team had not only become the best in the league, and one of the best of all-time, but one of the most universally hated in NBA history to boot. Bill Laimbeer was viewed by fans everywhere as a spoiled whiner who always bent the rules himself during rugged scuffling around the hoop (shoving, leaning, uniform tugging, and continuous elbowing) and then howled at all officials' calls that went against him. Before his departure Rick Mahorn had also fashioned the reputation of a brute who would use every physical trick to gain an advantage at either end of the floor. And Dennis ("The Worm") Rodman, already one of the league's toughest if also crudest rebounders, was well on the way to building his own reputation for non-stop trash talking and taunting of the opposition forces.

But the reputation for physical play and rough-and-tumble scrappiness also accounted for a second interpretation of the most famous team nickname of the early '90s—as in Black English street talk and ghetto slang, "bad" also meant "good" or "cool" or "tough," and thus also carried positive connotation. And the "Bad Boy" image in the end seemed to be something that pulled the team together in a common cause and motivated their run at a repeat title. It was thus a strange enough image, but a most effective one indeed.

The championship drive in 1989, and again in 1990, was led by "Zeke" Thomas but made possible by a strong supporting cast. Laimbeer, for all his official baiting and opponent baiting, was a solid big man who ranked in the league's top ten with 700–plus rebounds and also shot effectively away from the basket when left unguarded. Joe Dumars knocked down better than 17 ppg. in both championship seasons and took much of the defensive pressure off Thomas. The Pistons may have lost out on the Dantley-for-Aguirre trade, and yet Mark Aguirre did contribute as a double-figure scorer who could provide solid bench relief. And while most quality teams can boast a solid sixth man, the Pistons owned the luxury of three. John Salley, Vinnie Johnson and Dennis Rodman seemed to come off the bench in waves night after night to harass and bury weary opponents in the latter stages of tight contests.

It is indeed a most fitting chapter of Detroit Pistons history, then, that even during the club's glory years of the late '80s and early '90s the franchise should foster a thoroughly blue-collar image. It was the image of a team that could effectively blend flashy star-quality play by Thomas and Dantley and Dumars with a widespread reputation for grind-it-out defense and gang rebounding cut squarely in a blue-collar mold.

This blue collar "down and-dirty" image surrounding Pistons basketball stretches back all the way, perhaps, to the ballclub's roots in midwestern industrial league play. Fred Zollner's original Pistons were a barnstorming outfit founded just before Pearl Harbor in 1941, and later this same team represented Zollner's piston-manufacturing plant in the old National Basketball League, well before that circuit became a full-fledged pro loop after World War II. And during the early NBA years, this strictly blue-collar team also headlined a strictly blue-collar player. George Yardley was probably the least glamorous and thus the most overlooked among the league's first decade of truly talented scoring stars like Paul Arizin, Joe Fulks, Neil Johnston and Bob Pettit.

Yardley was a skinny 6'5" forward out of Stanford University, built like "a human flamingo" (in one scribe's apt description) and appropriately nicknamed "The Bird" (mostly for his stork-like appearance, and not at all for any abilities to "fly" or "sky" in the fashion of modern players). Neither fans or opponents were ever very impressed with a basketball player who was almost bald, had unsightly knobby knees and spindly legs, and ran with the deceptive lopping gait of a weekend schoolyard ballplayer and not a genuine professional. Yet while Yardley was hardly a graceful athlete, he *did* have a workman-like ethic and an uncanny ability simply to put the basketball through a hoop. George Yardley played only seven NBA seasons, yet he finished with a career 19.2 average and even earned for himself a lasting place in league history. During his most spectacular season—1957–58, when he averaged 27.8 ppg. and copped a league scoring title—George Yardley became the first man in pro history to toss in a then-unheard-of total of 2,001 points in a single league season. Pro basketball's first 2,000-point man never won any accolades for polished or stylish play; nonetheless George Yardley was one of the most inventive scorers ever to lace up a pair of sneakers and take to the hardwood floor.

Beyond the scoring sideshow of George Yardley, the Pistons had little to boast of during this last decade before Bill Russell and the Celtics brought NBA-style basketball into the modern age. Larry Foust was a formidable big man who manned the post in Fort Wayne for seven seasons and always averaged near 15 points per game while muscling opponents away from the bucket. Max Zaslofsky closed out his career in Fort Wayne after proving to be one of the more productive scorers of the league's first decade. And ex-Illinois star Andy Phillip provided four productive seasons at the guard slot as well. The club was just barely good enough with such dependable veterans as Yardley, Foust and Phillip to struggle out of the first round of post-season play on three different occasions.

The best season for the Pistons in Fort Wayne would be the campaign which opened in the fall of 1954. The club would post its highest victory total to date (43) and garner the first of three-straight Western Division first-place finishes. The regular season divisional title was likely all the more savory, given the fact that it was the Mikan-less Lakers who trailed the Pistons of rookie coach Charlie Eckman by three full games. To underscore their newly-found superiority over Minneapolis, the Pistons also rolled through a three-games-to-one second-round playoff bashing of the defending champions. Then would follow a dramatic playoff series against the Syracuse Nats for ultimate NBA bragging rights.

The arrival of Fort Wayne in the league title series in 1955 was something of a shock since owner Fred Zollner had fuelled considerable controversy and criticism at the season's outset when he named ex-referee Eckman as his bench boss. For Eckman to earn the spot over more experienced pro coaches, and then to enjoy such immediate success, was a sore point with many in the league family. And such controversy swirling around the off-court affairs of the Piston's club would soon be matched and then some by the controversy that eventually raged at playoff time. For this was a series that would have a most ironic conclusion, one which robbed the Fort Wayne team of any possible homecourt advantage against Dolph Schayes and company.

Paced by a potent backcourt of Max Zaslofsky, Andy Phillip and Frankie Brian and a hefty frontcourt of George Yardley, Larry Foust, Mel Hutchins, and Bob Houbregs, Eckman's club bounced back from two opening defeats to run off an impressive string of three victories, and thus shove Dolph Schayes and the Nats to the very brink of destruction. Syracuse gamely bounced back for the series-tying victory and then the championship clincher on their home floor. Under the new 24-second shot clock the title game was finally free from endless fouling and stalling tactics down the stretch and concluded in dramatic fashion when guard George King sank a go-ahead free throw and then executed a game-saving steal.

While the Pistons won all three home contests of the championship series with Syracuse, Zollner's team nonetheless had to feel itself at an emotional disadvantage when it was forced to move its home playoff dates into a smaller gymnasium located two-hours away in Indianapolis. Since no one in Fort Wayne had expected the usually lackluster Pistons to survive the first playoff round (and since pro basketball was hardly a marquee event at the time, anyway, even in its more showcase venues like Fort Wayne), city officials had embarrassingly rented out the Fort Wayne Coliseum for a revenue-producing bowling tournament.

The two seasons which followed the disappointing loss of a championship to Syracuse would see the Pistons remain a competitive bunch under coach Eckman and behind the scoring onslaughts of Yardley. The team would drop back to the .500 mark, but would register two more first-place finishes within an admittedly weak division. Again in 1956 they would work their way to the finals of post-season play. This time around, however, they would provide little challenge to the Philadelphia Warriors featuring a front line of Neil Johnston and Paul Arizin.

Unfortunately, the Fort Wayne Pistons will perhaps always be remembered by hoops history buffs more for a single moment of basketball infamy than for that narrowly-unsuccessful title run at the end of the 1955 season. More prominent in club history than the early championship charge is a single dark night of November 22, 1950 in which the desperate Fort Wayne ballclub conspired to stage what may well have been the most embarrassing act in all of league history. The results of this better-to-be-forgotten game were hardly artistic. But as a piece of basketball strategy the game plan was akin to a stroke of pure genius. And in the annuals of pro basketball history it still stands as perhaps the most famous single game ever played. Certainly no other game ever had quite such a far-reaching effect on the makeup of any team sport.

The colossal event in question transpired on the very night when the Piston's unveiled a radical new strategy for overcoming the powerhouse Minneapolis Lakers and their monster of the middle, George Mikan. Clearly a radical strategy for contending with Mikan and his teammates was not unexpected at the time. The Lakers were coming off a 51–17 record a season earlier, which had also seen them convert 11 playoff games into nine victories and the first championship of the newly named NBA. The Lakers were already beating a path toward another Western Division league crown and before season's end would capture 29 of 31 home-floor contests. That very same season Fort Wayne, by contrast, would prove capable of only five road victories in 32 tries. Against such odds the Piston's bench decided to adopt an old if unsightly strategy. They would stand around holding the ball as long as they could in each and every possession and only shoot the nearly impossible-to-miss shot from ultra-close range.

The result was predictable if largely coma-producing. The count was 9–7 Pistons at the quarter and then 13–11 Lakers at the half. Fort Wayne edged ahead once more 17–16 at the three-quarter mark. With officials Stan Stutz and Jocko Collins calling the game tightly, the resulting free-throws proved in the end to be the determining factor since each team buried only four field goals for the entire contest (the four Minneapolis baskets were all by Mikan).

In the modern era of 24-second shot clocks and racehorse offenses, it is indeed hard to visualize the spectacle that unfolded before dazed fans on the night the Pistons attempted to put a lid on Mikan and the Lakers. To the astonishment and eventual outrage of the partisan crowd, Fort Wayne controlled the opening tip and stationed center Larry Foust at midcourt with the ball tucked under his arm. There Foust stood firm and the Piston's novel strategy was very quickly apparent to all in attendance. Occasionally there would be a surprise pass and a flurry of movement, yet Fort Wayne continued the slowdown to its own advantage. With the Lakers finally in the lead during the second half, the Minneapolis players saw little reason to press their stalling opponents and force the action. Coach Mendenhall's game plan, by contrast, was to keep the score tight even when behind. With the Lakers tallying but a single charity throw by Jim Pollard in the final quarter, and still leading 18–17 with seconds remaining, the Fort Wayne plot suddenly hatched its bizarre results. Curly Armstrong drove toward the hoop and then fed Foust for a last-second desperation heave which Mikan actually deflected—straight up into the goal! Fort Wayne was the winner—19 to 18—in the lowest scoring contest of NBA history. And it would be this game more than any other—along with the increasingly brutal hacking and shoving defenses employed throughout the league—which resulted, a couple of seasons down the road, in a shot-clock rule which has remained an NBA staple for four full decades.

Zollner's embarrassment over home court playing sites in the 1955 NBA playoffs was unfortunately not just an isolated incident. Such difficulty in acquiring an acceptable local venue would eventually force the Fort Wayne club to be moved out of its original Indiana home altogether. Of course, owner Fred Zollner was also hoping to expand his revenue through a much larger population base from which to draw his paying fans. This same enticement had also convinced Les Harrison to move his Rochester Royals to a larger urban center in Cincinnati the very same season.

There were plenty of fireworks on the basketball front in Detroit throughout the final years of the fifties, but that excitement always translated into stellar individual performers and never even the mildest case of championship fever. Yardley, Gene Shue, Dick McGuire, Walter Dukes, Bailey Howell, Terry Dischinger and Dave DeBusschere were all talented players who wore the Pistons uniform. Gene Shue was a five-time NBA All-Star guard who ranked high among the league's free-throw shooters and held his own for several seasons with the likes of Cousy, Sharman, Slater Martin and Larry Costello. Walter Dukes was one of the NBA's first seven-footers and, despite his disappointments as a scorer (10.4 for a 500 game career), remained a solid rebounder even against Russell, Bellamy and Chamberlain. Bailey Howell was a bruising physical forward under the boards who could score (17,000 career points) and rebound with the all-time greats. In multi-talented two-sport star Dave DeBusschere (who also pitched briefly in the big leagues) Detroit also had a defensive stalwart who was a six-time member of the league's all-defensive unit during his 12-year pro career. But all this talent was seemingly squandered on teams that never seemed to have the right chemistry, the crucial depth, or the defensive strength necessary to win consistently. The Detroit Pistons (formerly Fort Wayne Pistons) would thus sleepwalk through fifteen long seasons between 1956 and 1970 without tasting a single winning season.

Detroit Pistons blahs would unfortunately stretch from end-to-end of the turbulent 1960s. If life was explosive in Detroit's inner city during the decade of Kennedy's assassination and Johnson's Great Society, little of that explosiveness found its way into Cobo Arena. And while the country experienced political upheaval and social change of previously unknown proportions over the next several years, there was very little changing on the basketball scene in Detroit. Dick McGuire directed the Pistons' bench during the first three seasons of the decade and the club consistently hov-

ered at ten games under .500. Dave DeBusschere was a player-coach for
almost three seasons and produced the lowest victory total of the decade
with only 22 victories in '65–'66. Dave Bing came on the scene as 1967
NBA rookie of the year and was, for several seasons, almost the only
thing Pistons fans had to work up much of a sweat over.

With the first full season of the 1970s came a distinct upswing in
ballclub fortunes. Two of the greatest players in club history—Bing and
Bob Lanier—were now about to lead a resurgence that would last through
most of the coming decade. The '70–'71 campaign (45–37) not only saw
the first non-losing season in a decade and a half but a rise in competitiveness as well. While the ballclub still stood last in the strong Midwest
Division, they nonetheless could boast of the fifth best record among nine
Western Conference clubs. Leading the charge were fluid scorer Dave
Bing, now in his fifth straight 20-plus ppg. season with the club, and
rookie center Bob Lanier, who broke in with a 15.6 1971 scoring average
but would average 20 or more with the Pistons for the next eight seasons.
Jimmy Walker was an explosive guard who also contributed mightily on
offense by chipping in 20-plus scoring seasons in both '70 and '71.
Walker, however, would be peddled to Houston in 1972 for Stu Lantz and
thus his impact in Detroit was unfortunately short-lived.

As the two leading scorers in Pistons history before Isiah Thomas,
Lanier and Bing would both top 15,000 points in Detroit, and together
they owned the 1970s chapter in the Detroit NBA saga. The 6'3" guard
from Syracuse and 6'11" center from St. Bonaventure together brought the
club at least a new respectability, if not wholesale success, and engineered
three winning seasons during the next seven campaigns under a parade of
coaches including Butch Van Breda Kolff, Ray Scott and Herb Brown.

But progress was sporadic at best, and the Pistons would soon hit the
wall and fall into another painful lull by the end of the decade. Under the
loose reins of Dick Vitale, the Detroiters suffered through the worst dry
spell in club history in 1979 and 1980. The first campaign under Vitale
saw a 14-game dropoff from only two seasons earlier and a dip from
second in 1977 back to fourth in the conference. Vitale was dealt an
increasingly bad hand by mid-season of 1980 when Lanier was shipped
to Milwaukee for Bucks center Kent Benson. Two number-one draft picks
and guard M.L. Carr had been also handed to Boston at the season's outset
for high-scoring forward Bob McAdoo, whose only full season in Detroit
would be his last as a productive NBA point producer. This combination of
shifting personnel and Vitale's ineffectual bench leadership spelled certain
disaster. Detroit's sixteen victories that lackluster season would be the
lowest anywhere in club annals.

The 1980s were little more than a holding pattern for the ballclub that
had disintegrated under Dick Vitale and his replacements Rich Adubato
and Scotty Robertson (whose 1981 club was not much better at 21–61).
Only the arrival of Daly would save the day and launch an era of consistent
winning after 1983. While improvement would be seemingly instantaneous

under Daly, whose first team was 49–33 and a second-place finisher, the nucleus of Tripucka, Thomas, Laimbeer, Vinnie Johnson and John Long which he inherited had already been together for more than a season and had already begun to exhibit considerable firepower in '82–'83. Daly would provide the iron hand of leadership that quickly matured potential into gritty achievement.

Detroit's new firepower was especially evident in one 1983 contest which seemed to look more like an image of basketball as it may someday be played deep into the 21st century. Ten years ago, on December 13, 1983, the Pistons visited McNichols Arena in the Mile High City of Denver for a marathon affair with the host Nuggets, which would go down in history as the highest-scoring game in pro history. The contest would last 3 hours and 11 minutes and before its three overtime sessions had been completed the teams had racked up an incredible 370 points in a 186–184 Piston victory. Bushels of scoring marks fell by the wayside as six players totalled more than 25 points, topped by career highs for Denver's Kiki Vandeweghe (51) and Detroit's Isiah Thomas (47). League records were set for most points and field goals by one team and by two teams jointly, as well as for most combined assists (93 in all). It was indeed a memorable night that wore out fans and scorekeepers as well as the shot-weary players themselves.

In the end, Pistons club history is neatly compartmentalized into three distinct eras and only one of those lays claim to much in the way of bragging rights. During eleven seasons as the Fort Wayne Pistons (in the NBL, BAA, and NBA) the club, owned and operated by Fred Zollner, posted five winning records but won only four playoff series and stood 22–34 in post-season play. In the first twenty-six years of Detroit residence the club won only three more playoff series and managed a 23–45 post-season ledger. Yet during one nine-year span filling the eighties and early nineties under the tutelage of Coach Chuck Daly, the Detroit club put on an entirely new face—the face of a formidable winner. Daly's teams never won fewer than 46 games nor slipped lower than a third-place divisional birth. They won 16 playoff series and racked up a 71–42 post-season mark. And they bagged the only two world titles known to club history.

Now that Daly has departed for other greener coaching challenges, the Detroit Piston's seem to have quickly converted back to the lackluster also-rans they were for most of the three and a half decades before his arrival. One questions now has to hang heavily over the Detroit NBA franchise and cloud the horizons of every diehard Pistons booster. Was the reign of Chuck Daly a landmark shift in the fortunes of a team that so long floundered as a league doormat? Or was Daly's tenure a mere aberration dropped into a long saga of hopeless losing? Will the Pistons again rebound and soar, or did Daly take every last bit of magic with him on his way out of town?

Suggested Readings on Detroit (Ft. Wayne) Pistons

Green, Jerry. **The Detroit Pistons—Capturing a Remarkable Era**. Chicago: Bonus Books, 1991.

Thomas, Isiah (with Matt Dobek). **Bad Boys! An Inside Look at the Detroit Pistons' 1988–89 Championship Season**. Grand Rapids, Michigan: Masters Press, 1989.

Stauth, Cameron. **The Franchise—Building a Winner With the World Champion Detroit Pistons, Basketball's Bad Boys**. New York: William Morrow, 1990.

Detroit Pistons Retired Uniform Numbers (2)

Bob Lanier (16)
Dave Bing (21)

Year-by-Year Detroit (Ft. Wayne) Pistons Summary

Season	Record	Finish	Coach(es)	Scoring Leader(s)	Playoffs (W-L Record)

Key: * = Tie for Position; # = League Scoring Leader; @ = Player/Coach

Fort Wayne Zollner Pistons
National Basketball League

Season	Record	Finish	Coach(es)	Scoring Leader(s)	Playoffs (W-L Record)
1946–47	25–19	2nd	Carl Bennett Paul Armstrong @Bobby McDermott	Chuck Reiser (9.0)	Lost in 2nd Round (4–4)
1947–48	40–20	3rd	Carl Bennett	Bob Kinney (10.8)	Lost in 1st Round (1–3)

Fort Wayne Pistons
Basketball Association of America

Season	Record	Finish	Coach(es)	Scoring Leader(s)	Playoffs (W-L Record)
1948–49	22–38	5th	Carl Bennett Curly Armstrong	Bruce Hale (10.5)	Did Not Qualify

National Basketball Association

Season	Record	Finish	Coach(es)	Scoring Leader(s)	Playoffs (W-L Record)
1949–50	40–28	3rd	M. Mendenhall	Fred Schaus (18.5)	Lost in 2nd Round (3–2)
1950–51	32–36	3rd	M. Mendenhall	Fred Schaus (15.1)	Lost in 1st Round (1–2)
1951–52	29–37	4th	Paul Birch	Larry Foust (15.9) Frankie Brian (15.9)	Lost in 1st Round (0–2)
1952–53	36–33	3rd	Paul Birch	Larry Foust (14.3)	Lost in 2nd Round (4–4)
1953–54	40–32	3rd	Paul Birch	Larry Foust (15.1)	Lost in Round Robin (0–4)
1954–55	43–29	1st	Charlie Eckman	George Yardley (17.3)	Lost in NBA Finals (6–5)
1955–56	37–35	1st	Charlie Eckman	George Yardley (17.4)	Lost in NBA Finals (4–6)
1956–57	34–38	1st*	Charlie Eckman	George Yardley (21.5)	Lost in 1st Round (0–3)

Detroit Pistons

Season	Record	Finish	Coach(es)	Scoring Leader(s)	Playoffs (W-L Record)
1957–58	33–39	2nd*	Charlie Eckman Red Roche	George Yardley (27.8)#	Lost in 2nd Round (3–4)
1958–59	28–44	3rd	Red Roche	Gene Shue (17.6)	Lost in 1st Round (1–2)
1959–60	30–45	2nd	Red Roche Dick McGuire	Gene Shue (22.8)	Lost in 1st Round (1–2)

Season	Record	Finish	Coach(es)	Scoring Leader(s)	Playoffs (W-L Record)
1960–61	34–45	3rd	Dick McGuire	Bailey Howell (23.6)	Lost in 1st Round (2–3)
1961–62	37–43	3rd	Dick McGuire	Bailey Howell (19.9)	Lost in 2nd Round (5–5)
1962–63	34–46	3rd	Dick McGuire	Bailey Howell (22.7)	Lost in 1st Round (1–3)
1963–64	23–57	5th	Charles Wolf	Bailey Howell (21.6)	Did Not Qualify
1964–65	31–49	4th	Charles Wolf @Dave DeBusschere	Terry Dischinger (18.2)	Did Not Qualify
1965–66	22–58	5th	@D. DeBusschere	Eddie Miles (19.6)	Did Not Qualify
1966–67	30–51	5th	@D. DeBusschere Donnis Butcher	Dave Bing (20.0)	Did Not Qualify
1967–68	40–42	4th	Donnis Butcher	Dave Bing (27.1)#	Lost in 1st Round (2–4)
1968–69	32–50	6th	Donnis Butcher Paul Seymour	Dave Bing (23.4)	Did Not Qualify
1969–70	31–51	7th	B. Van Breda Kolff	Dave Bing (22.9)	Did Not Qualify
1970–71	45–37	4th	B. Van Breda Kolff	Dave Bing (27.0)	Did Not Qualify
1971–72	26–56	4th	B. Van Breda Kolff Terry Dischinger	Bob Lanier (25.7)	Did Not Qualify
1972–73	40–42	3rd	Earl Lloyd Ray Scott	Bob Lanier (23.8)	Did Not Qualify
1973–74	52–30	3rd	Ray Scott	Bob Lanier (22.5)	Lost in 1st Round (3–4)
1974–75	40–42	3rd	Ray Scott	Bob Lanier (24.0)	Lost in 1st Round (1–2)
1975–76	36–46	2nd	Ray Scott Herb Brown	Bob Lanier (21.3)	Lost in 2nd Round (4–5)
1976–77	44–38	2nd*	Herb Brown	Bob Lanier (25.3)	Lost in 1st Round (1–2)
1977–78	38–44	4th	Herb Brown Bob Kauffman	Bob Lanier (24.5)	Did Not Qualify
1978–79	30–52	4th*	Dick Vitale	Bob Lanier (23.6)	Did Not Qualify
1979–80	16–66	6th	Dick Vitale Richie Adubato	Bob McAdoo (21.1)	Did Not Qualify
1980–81	21–61	6th	Scotty Robertson	John Long (17.7)	Did Not Qualify
1981–82	39–43	3rd	Scotty Robertson	John Long (21.9)	Did Not Qualify
1982–83	37–45	3rd	Scotty Robertson	Kelly Tripucka (26.5)	Did Not Qualify
1983–84	49–33	2nd	Chuck Daly	Kelly Tripucka (21.3) Isiah Thomas (21.3)	Lost in 1st Round (2–3)
1984–85	46–36	2nd	Chuck Daly	Isiah Thomas (21.2)	Lost in 2nd Round (5–4)
1985–86	46–36	3rd	Chuck Daly	Isiah Thomas (20.9)	Lost in 1st Round (1–3)
1986–87	52–30	2nd	Chuck Daly	Adrian Dantley (21.5)	Lost in 3rd Round (10–5)
1987–88	54–28	1st	Chuck Daly	Adrian Dantley (20.0)	Lost in NBA Finals (14–9)
1988–89	63–19	1st	Chuck Daly	Isiah Thomas (18.2)	**NBA Champion** (15–2)
1989–90	59–23	1st	Chuck Daly	Isiah Thomas (18.4)	**NBA Champion** (15–4)
1990–91	50–32	2nd	Chuck Daly	Joe Dumars (20.4)	Lost in 3rd Round (7–8)
1991–92	48–34	3rd	Chuck Daly	Joe Dumars (19.9)	Lost in 1st Round (2–3)
1992–93	40–42	6th	Ron Rothstein	Joe Dumars (23.5)	Did Not Qualify
1993–94	20–62	6th	Don Chaney	Joe Dumars (20.4)	Did Not Qualify

Individual Career Leaders and Record Holders (1946–1994)

Scoring Average	Bob Lanier (22.7 ppg., 1970–80)
Points Scored	Isiah Thomas (18,822, 1981–94)
Games Played	Isiah Thomas (979, 1981–94)
Minutes Played	Isiah Thomas (35,516)

Field Goal Pct.   Dennis Rodman (.537, 1986–93)
Field Goals Made   Isiah Thomas (7,194)
Free Throws Made   Isiah Thomas (4,036)
Free-Throw Pct.   Joe Dumars (.848, 1985–94)
Rebounds   Bill Laimbeer (9,430, 1982–93)
Assists   Isiah Thomas (9,061, 1981–94)
Steals   Isiah Thomas (1,861)
Blocked Shots   Terry Tyler (1,070, 1978–85)

Individual Single-Season and Game Records (1946–1994)

Scoring Average   George Yardley (27.8 ppg., 1957–58)
Points Scored (Season)   Dave Bing (2,213, 1970–71)
Points Scored (Game)   Kelly Tripucka (56, 1–29–83 vs. Chicago Bulls)
Field Goal Pct. (Season)   Dennis Rodman (.595, 1988–89)
3-Pt. Field Goals (Season)   Joe Dumars (112, 1992–93)
Free-Throw Pct. (Season)   Joe Dumars (.900, 1989–90)
Rebounds (Season)   Dennis Rodman (1,530, 1991–92)
Rebounds (Game)   Dennis Rodman (34, 3–4–92 vs. Indiana Pacers)
Assists (Season)   Isiah Thomas (1,123, 1984–85)
Assists (Game)   Kevin Porter (25, 3–9–79 and 4–1–79)
                                 Isiah Thomas (25, 2–23–85 vs. Dallas Mavericks)
Steals (Season)   Isiah Thomas (204, 1983–84)
Steals (Game)   Earl Tatum (9, 11–28–78 at Los Angeles Lakers)
                                 Ron Lee (9, 3–16–80 vs. Houston Rockets)
Blocked Shots (Season)   Bob Lanier (247, 1973–74)
Blocked Shots (Game)   Edgar Jones (10, 12–17–81 vs. Indiana Pacers)
Personal Fouls (Season)   Joe Strawder (344, 1966–67)

Best Trade in Franchise History

When Bill Laimbeer was acquired from the Cleveland Cavaliers in February, 1982, few could have imaged how durable and potent basketball's leading "Bad Boy" would actually become by the end of the decade. Laimbeer was acquired along with Kenny Carr for Phil Hubbard, Paul Mokeski and a couple of high-round draft picks. Soon the ex-Notre Dame star would develop into the quintessential role player, the anchor of the Piston's versatile offense under Chuck Daly, and the blood-and-guts inside player that everyone loved to hate. "Bad Bill" also, by the time of his retirement in early 1993, had registered the second most games played (behind Zeke Thomas) in franchise history. While Laimbeer would later in the decade develop a wide reputation as a whiner and a somewhat dirty player under the boards, he was at the same time one of the most dependable clutch ballplayers to be found anywhere around the league.

Worst Trade in Franchise History

Micheal Williams might well have been the versatile point guard to inherit the Detroit backcourt leadership role from Isiah Thomas. Seemingly guard-rich with Thomas and Dumars, the Pistons, however, let Williams go to the Phoenix Suns (along with Kenny Battle) for draft rights to Anthony Cook in June, 1989. Several seasons later, Williams would emerge as a skilled point guard with the expansion Minnesota T-Wolves (after also being overlooked by the Suns, Dallas Mavericks, and finally the Indiana Pacers). Williams would set an all-time NBA consecutive free-throw record at the end of the 1993 season. Cook, it turns out, was subsequently traded away for more draft picks before even another six months had expired.

Detroit Pistons Historical Oddity

The modern-day ''Bad Boys'' Pistons of Isiah Thomas and Bill Laimbeer have long had a reputation for rough play that seems somewhat outside the true spirit of the hardwood sport—a non-contact game, in theory. But this distinction for rough and unconventional play goes back to the very roots of franchise history in Fort Wayne. For this is the team whose unconventional and almost unsportsmanlike stalling tactics once forced the invention, back in 1954, of the league's first shot clock restrictions on ball possession. The contest between the Fort Wayne Pistons and Minneapolis Lakers on November 22, 1950 was only the most extreme example of the fouling and stalling tactics that the Pistons and other league clubs had begun to adopt in an effort to neutralize the massive advantage that an unfettered Mikan had over his opponents. But the lowest scoring game in NBA history was also one of the ugliest spectacles in pro basketball annals. The Pistons had shown their penchant for rough and quasi-legal play decades before the basketball world would romanticize a group of rugged Pistons known as ''Bad Boys'' for their hatchet-style of play.

Pistons All-Time Number One Draft Picks List

Detroit Pistons
1957 Charles Tyra (Louisville)
1958 Mike Farmer (USF)
1959 Bailey Howell (Mississippi State)

1960 Jack Moreland (Louisiana Tech)
1961 Ray Scott (Portland)
1962 Dave DeBusschere (Detroit)
1963 Eddie Miles (Seattle)
1964 Joe Caldwell (Arizona State)
1965 Bill Buntin (Michigan)
1966 Dave Bing (Syracuse)
1967 Jimmy Walker (Providence)
1968 Otto Moore (Pan American)
1969 Terry Driscoll (Boston College)
1970 Bob Lanier (St. Bonaventure)
1971 Curtis Rowe (UCLA)
1972 Corky Calhoun (Pennsylvania)
1973 Dwight Jones (Houston)
1974 Al Eberhard (Missouri)
1975 Bill Robinzine (DePaul)
1976 Leon Douglas (Alabama)
1977 Ben Poquette (Central Michigan)
1978 Terry Tyler (Detroit)
1979 Greg Kelser (Michigan State)
1980 Larry Drew (Missouri)
1981 Isiah Thomas (Indiana)
1982 Cliff Levingston (Wichita State)
1983 Antoine Carr (Wichita State)
1984 Tony Campbell (Ohio State)
1985 Joe Dumars (McNeese State)
1986 John Salley (Georgia Tech)
1987 Freddie Banks (UNLV)
1988 Fennis Dembo (Wyoming)
1989 Kenny Battle (Illinois)
1990 Lance Blanks (Texas)
1991 Doug Overton (LaSalle)
1992 Don MacLean (UCLA)
1993 Lindsey Hunter (Jackson State)

Chapter 8

ATLANTA HAWKS AND ST. LOUIS (MILWAUKEE) HAWKS

Penthouse to Low Rent District—Basketball's Tale of Two Cities

---

All-time Franchise Record: 1796–1754, .506 Pct. (1949–1994)
NBA Championships (1): 1957–58
Greatest Franchise Player: Bob Pettit (1956–1969)
All-Time Leading Scorer: Dominique Wilkins (22,096 Points, 1983–1993)
Most Successful Coach: Ed Macauley (89–48, .650 Pct., 1958–1960)
All-Time Franchise Team: Bob Pettit (C), Dominique Wilkins (F), Lou Hudson (F-G), Slater Martin (G), John Drew (G)

The city of Atlanta, Georgia, has carved its permanent niche in the sporting world by stealing proud franchises at their peak of performance from other cities and then sending those same franchises straight into the dung heap. First came the saga of baseball's Milwaukee Braves, a thirteen-year unparalleled success story in the Wisconsin city during the '50s and early '60s and a ballclub which set standards for winning and for fan support that were baseball's biggest story during the diamond sport's last true Golden Age. Yet when the lure of a potential untapped television market beckoned from the deep south, Lou Perini wasted little time in selling off his team lock, stock and barrel to Atlanta interests; soon enough the fans of Milwaukee were left out in the cold with the dust bin of their memories, while at the same time Atlanta fans largely stayed home and ignored their new team for most of the next quarter century. For twenty-five seasons after their trek to the promise land of mid-Georgia the Atlanta Braves remained baseball's most colorless and consistently mediocre also-ran.

171

Basketball, too, has its parallel version of the "Atlanta Saga" and this NBA version of Atlanta ballclub pillaging is an equally disarming tale of busted franchise dreams in the hunt for quick-fix expansion riches. Next to the Boston Celtics outfit built by Auerbach and led by Cousy and Russell, the NBA of the latter '50s and early '60s could boast no prouder and more exciting team that the St. Louis Hawks of Bob Pettit, Cliff Hagan, Slater Martin and company. This was a team that seemed to have just as many free passes to the NBA Championship Finals of that era as did Auerbach and his dynasty Celtics. Indeed it was the Hawks that sat right on Auerbach's heels at the start of the Boston dynasty run; it was also the ongoing rivalry between Russell and company and Pettit and company that provided the bulk of NBA excitement between the retirement of George Mikan in 1954 and the coming of Wilt, Oscar and Jerry West at the beginning of the tumultuous sixties. They may have changed coaches more frequently in St. Louis (Holzman, Hannum, Macauley and Seymour) than they did in Boston (Auerbach), but no amount of tinkering at the top seemed to derail the St. Louis Hawks' annual playoff express.

For a string of years between 1955 and 1961, the St. Louis Hawks terrorized NBA opponents every bit as much as the Boston Celtics. But for a few breaks along the way the true dynasty team for basketball's Golden Era might well have been the one playing in Kemper Arena on the banks of the Mississippi and not the one housed in Boston Garden near the Charles. Under the guidance of coach Red Holzman and in Pettit's second season the transplanted Hawks of St. Louis (they had played in Milwaukee a season earlier) first made their presence known in the '55–'56 campaign when they pulled together a post-season run that catapulted them into the third round of playoff action. Pettit established himself as a bright offensive star that very year with his first scoring title and with league-leading numbers in field goals (made and attempted), free throws (made and attempted), rebounds and total points.

Then came five straight Western Division titles and an incredible string of post-season triumphs that resulted in four appearances in the NBA Finals over that same five seasons. Red Holzman was eventually replaced by Alex Hannum (33 games into the '56–'57 season), who in turn gave way to Ed Macauley (after ten games of '58–'59) and then Paul Seymour (at the start of '60–'61). It didn't seem to matter who was on the bench with the clipboard. As long as Pettit and Hagan were filling up the nets with two-point buckets, and Slater Martin was directing the offense, the Hawks were a persistent undeniable force.

St. Louis admittedly won only a single NBA title over that glorious five-year stretch—hardly the stuff of a dynasty. But that was as much due to Lady Luck as to the defensive genius of Bill Russell or the fast-breaking offenses devised by Auerbach and Cousy. Had Pettit's desperation tip rolled an inch or so in the other direction in 1957, or had a Boston blitz been better controlled over a short stretch in the first half of game seven in 1960, then the championship banners in St. Louis might easily have numbered three and not one.

The Hawks team that posed such a threat to the Celtics and came so close to short-circuiting Auerbach's reign didn't actually begin life in St. Louis. The team first played in the NBL as one of those small-town midwestern industrial league teams with few fans and an identity crisis hidden behind multi-city affiliation (as the Tri-Cities Blackhawks). Then came a temporary relocation to Milwaukee and only slightly greener pastures. It was during the four Milwaukee seasons that the club picked up its greatest star—Bob Pettit. The team ultimately arrived in St. Louis the very year that it began its five-season period of unparalleled greatness.

And as great as the St. Louis Hawks were for the half-dozen seasons after the NBA first introduced modern-style play with its shot-clock innovation, indeed except for the dastardly reign of Lady Luck once again, the team might have been even greater than it was. For the greatest victories of the Celtics over the Hawks came at the trading table and in smoky executive offices and not on the basketball court at all. The telling blow, of course, was the trade that Red Auerbach orchestrated to pry the draft rights to Bill Russell away from the Hawks. But Auerbach himself might have been directing fortunes in St. Louis and not in Boston at all had the cards fallen just a little differently. Auerbach had first coached the Tri-Cities Blackhawks in the year of BAA-NBL merger, before he abandoned that ship and signed on with Boston. Had Walter Brown not convinced Auerbach to come to Beantown, the history of the NBA during the '50s and '60s might have had a very different look to it indeed.

And then there was the saga of Bob Cousy. As a college All-American, Cousy was immensely popular in Boston and the press clamored for the Celtics and their new coach Red Auerbach to draft the flashy Holy Cross playmaker. But Auerbach and Boston passed, and the Tri-Cities Blackhawks ended up signing the man who would singlehandedly change the slow-paced game into a fast-breaking one. But the talent scouts working for the Hawks were as myopic of view as were those in the Celtics organization, and Tri-Cities immediately dished off Cousy to the Chicago Stags for established backcourt star Frankie Brian. Things then got worse for the Hawks and the rest of the league when Boston recovered from its mistake and, in spite of Auerbach's instincts, acquired Cousy as its playmaker. (This happened when the Chicago club folded and its players went into a lottery to be divvied up by the league's other club's; Boston had the final pick and was stuck with the unwanted Cousy.) A little better planning and foresight here and there and the Hawks would have settled into St. Louis owning Auerbach, Cousy and Bill Russell to compliment the versatile Bob Pettit. One can only fantasize about what a team that one might have been.

The Hawks opened their inaugural NBA season under the unique Tri-Cities logo (representing Moline and Rock Island, Illinois, and Davenport, Iowa) in the fall of 1949, the first year of the new sprawling NBA conglomeration which had resulted from the BAA-NBL merger. Actually, the Hawks ballclub (known as Blackhawks during Tri-Cities days) had started out in the northern port city of Buffalo (as the original Buffalo Braves), a National Basketball League franchise which transferred from upstate New York to its split Illinois-Iowa home in the early stages of the '46–'47 season. The team was respectable enough during its first NBA year, especially after Red Auerbach (fired by the Washington Caps after losing the BAA finals to Minneapolis the previous year) was hired by owner Ben Kerner to take up the coaching reins. The club had started badly with a single victory in its first seven games under Roger Potter, and Kerner didn't hesitate to go after the colorful Auerbach to right his ship. As a .500 club under coach Auerbach the rest of the way, the Tri-Cities team finished in third place and advanced to a second playoff round. Jack Nichols (13.1), Dick Eddleman (12.9) and Mike Todorovich (12.2) were the top players. But the bad news of the opening NBA campaign was that Auerbach was gone shortly after season's end, lured back to the East by Boston Celtics owner Walter Brown.

After a stumblebum second season (25–43, 5th place) the Hawks sought friendlier environs (as well as a potentially bigger gate) and settled into Milwaukee in '51–'52 as one of the league's marginal franchises of the early NBA era. The ballclub struggled on the floor under Doxie Moore and won but 17 games in 1952. Moderate improvement marked the next two seasons under coach Andrew Levane as the victory total climbed to 27 and then slid back again to 21. But the turnaround for the struggling franchise came in 1954 with two grand personnel coups. First, Red Holzman was hired to coach late in the '53–'54 campaign; and then the Hawks picked up Bob Pettit in the collegiate draft, and a bright outlook was seemingly assured.

The club remained one final season in Milwaukee, dressed up with a couple of stellar rookies who now promised a glowing future. The first of these freshman phenoms was 1954 NCAA scoring champion Frank Selvy out of Furman College, who had made headlines a year earlier with a 100–point undergraduate game. Selvy had actually been drafted by the Bullets and had started his season in Baltimore. The Baltimore Bullets franchise folded in November, however, and a special dispersal draft made Milwaukee the lucky recipient of the dead-eye forward-guard. (As it turned out, Selvy would never better his 19.0 ppg. rookie scoring standard and would be dealt to the Lakers two seasons later.) If Selvy was the more touted rookie, a slim 6'9" battler out of LSU named Bob Pettit would quickly become the more productive catch. During his rookie season the LSU All-American took the league's freshman honors and showed his great scoring talents with a 20.4 average (the lowest of his brilliant career). The new shot-clock rule was designed to the benefit of players like Pettit and Paul Arizin in Philadelphia (since it neutralized less mobile centers, cut in the George Mikan mold) and Pettit would now be an unstoppable force under the basket for a full decade to come.

When the Hawks and owner Ben Kerner set up shop in St. Louis in 1955–56, the solid lineup featured Pettit (league scoring champ at 25.7 ppg.) and Jack Coleman up front, Charlie Share at center, and Jack Stephens and Bob Harrison at the guards. During the season, an important trade brought Coleman and Jack McMahon in from the Rochester Royals and they together added considerable firepower (averaging a joint 20.1 ppg. for the season). The Hawks were a force on the floor as they tied for second in the Western Division (with Minneapolis, which won the tie-breaking game for playoff home-court advantage) and visited the playoffs for the first time since the club's maiden season. While they didn't get past the second playoff round the team, coached by Red Holzman, did climb over the Minneapolis Lakers, and then pushed Fort Wayne to the limit in a tight five-game semi-final series. And the transplanted ballclub was a smash at the box office in its new home as well.

Kerner's Hawks would again post a losing record in '56–'57, yet benefit from imbalanced divisions to finish first in the West. The St. Louis 34–38 ledger actually meant a three-way tie with Western rivals Minneapolis and Fort Wayne, and a three-way round-robin at season's end to determine post-season matchups. After defeating both rivals to earn the first-place bye, the Hawks easily swept past Minneapolis in three games to earn a spot in the championship round with Boston's upsurging Celtics. This was the year that the fateful deal had been made with Boston, the one that lost Russell in the draft but did bring in Ed Macauley and Cliff Hagan to team on the front line with Pettit. And the Hawks had added another talent as well, picking up Slater Martin at mid-season from New York to feed Pettit and Hagan from the backcourt. Even without Russell, the pieces were now seemingly in place for a great St. Louis team. A slow start, however, brought the ouster of Holzman and led to a short coaching stint by Martin before Alex Hannum took over on the bench. And Pettit pulled off a seemingly amazing feat with his second-place finish in the scoring race, which came despite a broken wrist that demanded a bulky cast on his shooting hand from February on. Despite all the upheavals of this chaotic season, the Hawks nonetheless jelled late in the year and announced their future presence by taking Boston all the way to seven games in the stirring series for the league championship.

But for another fluke of luck seemingly aimed against the Hawks in the final playoff game of 1957, perhaps St. Louis and not Boston might have celebrated a first championship during the debut year of Bill Russell and Tom Heinsohn. The Hawks indeed had a clear shot (quite literally) at winning both a deciding seventh game and a championship in what turned out to be one of the most exciting games of NBA history. This was, in fact, the single game that as much as any other established the NBA's nationwide appeal for a new audience of basketball television viewers. And it was also the game which seemed to tip the balance of favor for the next half dozen or so seasons in the direction of Russell and company, and thus away from Pettit and his equally talented teammates.

The rubber match of the 1957 title series had itself been set up by a heart-stopping contest in game six. Trailing 3–2 in the series and facing elimination, the Hawks were able to stay alive when Cousy missed a free-throw with 12 seconds remaining; Pettit missed a potential game-winning bucket, but Cliff Hagan then tapped in the errant shot to steal a 96–94 series-tying victory. But this was only a prelude to an even more stirring finale. The two heavyweights battled to the wire before Pettit's two free throws knotted the game at 103 with time expired in regulation play. Again the Hawks somehow staved off defeat as Jack Coleman's desperation shot, with nine seconds remaining, clinched a second overtime frame. The Celt-ics again stood poised for victory yet a third time with a 125–123 lead and but two seconds remaining in overtime period two. But now luck had finally turned to the kelly green Celtics. St. Louis inbounded to Pettit under the hoop, who tapped the ball against the rim with the buzzer already sounding. Time seemed to stop as the ball rolled along the rim and then dropped harmlessly out. Boston's Celtics were NBA champions for the first time and bedlam exploded throughout Boston Garden.

If the St. Louis Hawks were a step behind Boston in 1957, they were determined to remain second to no one in '57–'58 and thus battled toward a championship from the earliest games of the fall season. Boston and St. Louis seemed indeed bent on a collision course toward a rematch right from the season's opening toss, and the league's two best teams jockeyed for position throughout the long campaign and throughout the early rounds of the playoffs as well. Each club boasted a single 20–point scorer (Pettit at 26.6 and Sharman at 22.3) and a solid balanced supporting lineup as well. Boston won 49 contests and outdistanced Syracuse by 8 games in the East; St. Louis won only 41 in the West, but also outdistanced their rivals by a margin of the same eight games. When post-season festivities began it was the Celtics crushing Philadelphia in a short five-game series (4–1) while the Hawks eliminated Detroit in similar fashion.

Then in the 1958 finals it was the Hawks' turn, at long last, for some unexpected and tide-turning luck. The long-anticipated rematch with Bos-ton turned one-sided when, in game three, disaster struck suddenly and without warning for Boston. For a rare time in their dynasty years the Celtics were now kayoed by a freak injury; Russell's ankle gave way in game three and with it the Boston hopes seemingly collapsed as well. With the Hawks up three games to two, Russell made a desperate come-back attempt in game six, but the giant Boston center simply couldn't compete to normal standards on but one healthy leg. St. Louis suddenly enjoyed a huge rebounding edge and an open alley around the basket for Pettit's uncanny shooting. And Pettit also had the game of his life that day, pouring in 50 points, 19 in the fourth quarter alone. In the end it was still a squeaker, but with Pettit relentlessly filling the nets, St. Louis came out on top by a single point, 110–109. Boston thus had its eventual dynasty string interrupted after only one season. The NBA now had its fifth different champion in five years, and with only an eight-team league.

And the St. Louis Hawks owned their first and only championship in four-and-a-half decades of club history.

Pettit remained brilliant until his retirement in 1965, never slipping below 1,000 points or a 20–ppg. average. He would eventually be an eight-time league all-star selection in only 11 seasons of NBA play. Twice he would be the regular season MVP and four times an all-star game MVP as well. And Bob Pettit would also establish one of the sport's great milestones in 1964 when he became the first ever to cross the career threshold of 20,000 NBA points scored. Two times he would win a scoring championship (1956, 1959) and once a rebounding title (1956). As a rebounder he would consistently finish in the league's top three or four and actually posted much higher totals (1,540 in 1961) in seasons following the rebound title he won in his sophomore campaign; but after 1956 Bill Russell was in the league and after 1959 Wilt Chamberlain was there as well. Over the first ten seasons of his career, in fact, Pettit would never finish lower than fifth among league scorers or rebounders. Bob Pettit's domination as a scorer came to an end when Wilt arrived in 1959 and he eventually slipped behind Elgin Baylor and Oscar Robertson as well. But there were few, if any, better combination center-forwards who ever played the game, especially from the perspective of rebounding and inside scoring efficiency. And it was the playoffs and the All-Star game which seemed to be his special domains: in 88 post-season contests the Hawks star posted a 25.5 scoring average; his three outright All-Star MVP awards were supplemented by a fourth he shared with Elgin Baylor. And five years after retirement as the NBA's all-time scoring leader, Bob Pettit would be a shoo-in member of the Naismith Basketball Hall of Fame.

The Hawks did not collapse after their 1958 title, even though they would never again quite grasp the brass ring. Twice over the next three years they would be back for the Finals and thus also for a rematch with Russell and Auerbach. In 1959 Pettit and company cruised to a Western Division regular-season crown (49–23, and 16 games ahead of 2nd-place Minneapolis) behind the big forward's second scoring championship. But in the division finals of the post-season dance, St. Louis would be ambushed by Elgin Baylor and the upstart Minneapolis Lakers. While the inconsistent Lakers had been able to post no better than a 33–39 regular-season mark, they nonetheless had plenty of firepower in capturing the final three games of the six-game post-season set with the Hawks. Yet the shock was only temporary and the following season under Ed Macauley, the St. Louis club was back stronger than ever. Another regular-season crown (this time by 16 games over runner-up Detroit) was followed by a playoff run that extended all the way to the seventh game of a championship showdown with Boston. But even with Pettit and Hagan teaming up for a 50.3 joint playoff scoring average, there would be no beating the Celtics this time around. Although the teams traded victories through the first six games, the seventh and deciding match wasn't even close as Russell grabbed 35 rebounds and scored 22 points in a 122–103 Celtics cakewalk. Boston was now clearly the better team and thus earned the first repeat title since the Minneapolis Lakers and George Mikan had relinquished their championship reign earlier in the decade.

St. Louis captured its fifth straight divisional crown in 1961, this time behind new coach Paul Seymour. And in post-season play the team earned its fourth title-round matchup with Auerbach, Russell, and the rest of the dynasty-in-the-making Celtics. While the Hawks seemed to roll on without substantial change, the league around them was now beginning to take on a somewhat different look. For one thing the Lakers had relocated from Minneapolis to Los Angeles, and the league had thus ushered in the era of coast-to-coast play. And this was also the season that Oscar Robertson and Jerry West hit the circuit as rookies, pushing Bob Pettit down yet another rung among the league's showcase scorers. But at season's end, for all the topsy-turvy change, it was old rivals Boston and St. Louis once again squaring off with the league title on the line. And Boston once again dominated, taking care of a slipping Hawks team in five largely one-sided games. While Pettit (28.6) and Hagan (22.0) provided proficient post-season scoring, they were no match for a balanced Celtics attack that had all five starters (Ramsey, Heinsohn, Russell, Sharman, Cousy) averaging between 16.7 and 19.7 ppg. Red Auerbach was able to light up his victory cigar early in all but the third game of the series.

A weak performance in the 1961 NBA Finals was a clear sign that the end was beginning to close in on this particular edition of the Hawks. Pettit would be around for a few more seasons, yet the team now slid into fourth slot with an embarrassing mirror-image record in 1962 of only 29–51. For the first time since coming to St. Louis, Pettit and the Hawks were left sitting on the sidelines for the post-season playoffs. The next five seasons also saw the club hover in the middle of the pack, playing well enough each winter to make it out of the first playoff round but never well enough to advance beyond the third round. A final St. Louis spurt did occur in '67–'68 when a run-and-gun team featuring Zelmo Beaty, Lenny Wilkens, Joe Caldwell, Paul Silas, Bill Bridges and Lou Hudson emerged as a legitimate title contender. Success came that year despite the early season threats by 1967 scoring leader Lou Hudson to jump to the ABA and then the eventual loss of Hudson part way through the year to the military draft. This final great St. Louis outfit, coached by Richie Guerin, won the Western Division race for the first time since 1961 (edging the Lakers by four games) yet were quickly eliminated by San Francisco (4–2) in the opening round of post-season play.

Interest surrounding the Hawks had steadily waned in St. Louis over the second half of the '60s (an era which also saw a major revival for the city's baseball franchise during the glory seasons of Bob Gibson) and after the final hurrah of the promising '67–'68 team, the ignored franchise was altogether ready to pack its bags and head off to greener ground in Atlanta. Ben Kerner was ready for retirement and finally sold out his interests in the club he had founded back in the barnstorming National Basketball

League days (1946–47), three seasons before the BAA-NBL merger. With this fourth move of the Hawks (born in Buffalo, succored in the Tri-Cities region, reared in Milwaukee, and matured in St. Louis) would come a transition—difficult to see at the time—which would eventually take one of basketball's proudest franchises on a much more perilous journey than the one marked by mere miles between Missouri and Georgia. This would be a journey—rapid beyond expectation—straight from the attic penthouse to the dreaded basement junk pile. For once the Hawks starting receiving their mail in Atlanta franchise glory days had already come to a more-or-less permanent demise.

The Atlanta Hawks were a mediocre team throughout the entire decade of the seventies and thus a far cry from the St. Louis powerhouse clubs that once featured Pettit, Hagan, Zelmo Beaty and Slater Martin. Four seasons with ex-Knick backcourt star Richie Guerin at the helm *did* bring a pair of identical 48–34 records (the first two seasons in Atlanta) followed by a pair of 36–46 marks, all good for one first-place and three second-place divisional finishes. Four subsequent seasons under the guidance of Cotton Fitzsimmons (1973–1976) meant three more losing campaigns and three more years outside the post-season playoffs. Hubie Brown (1977–1981) then closed out the decade in the coach's seat with a trio of similarly lackluster campaigns.

One "highlight" of the 1970s, however, was the acquisition of high-scoring "Pistol Pete" Maravich, who had been the third overall selection in the 1970 draft (after Bob Lanier and Rudy Tomjanovich) and who played with Atlanta for four generally lackluster seasons. For all his record-breaking scoring feats at LSU, Pistol Pete would play second fiddle to Lou Hudson his first three NBA seasons and would not emerge as the leading Atlanta pointmaker until his fourth year in the league. Maravich would, however, be the NBA's second leading scorer (27.7) during his final year in Atlanta and would prove his further worth by also pacing the Hawks in assists that winter. But Maravich had quickly worn out his welcome as a largely one-dimensional player and would be traded off to the New Orleans Jazz (for Dean Meminger, Bob Kauffman and future draft choices) before the start of yet another campaign.

The Atlanta ballclub would be acquired by cable television mogul Ted Turner (also owner of Atlanta's baseball Braves) in 1977, and during the next decade the Georgia NBA team would become a fixture on the nation's cable airwaves. A significant upswing in club oncourt fortunes did not occur until 1983, however, when Mike Fratello began a seven-year coaching stint that would produce one divisional title and four seasons of better that 50 victories. The team's best season under Fratello would be '86–'87, when the revitalized Hawks soared to a club-record 57 victories on the way to a first-place Central Division finish. But despite Fratello's modest successes the Atlanta teams he coached somehow never made it out of the second round of post-season playoffs.

Dominique Wilkins was the true steal of the 1982 collegiate draft. Wilkins, indeed, may well have been the ultimate steal (if one discounts perhaps only the Chicago Bulls' pilfering of Scottie Pippen from Seattle on draft day five years later) of the entire decade. The all-time leading scorer at the University of Georgia, despite leaving school as a hardship case (now called "early entry") at the end of his junior season, Wilkins was the first-round pick (third overall) of the Utah Jazz. Somehow Dominique managed to slip through the fingers of a careless Jazz front office, however, being traded to the Hawks in September on the eve of fall training camp for high-scoring veteran guard John Drew, Freeman Williams, and an undisclosed amount of cash. And with this single transaction Atlanta was on its way back to respectability, if not to a string of NBA championships.

Much of the story of Atlanta Hawks basketball in the 1980s was the story of basketball's "Human Highlight Film"—Dominique Wilkins. Wilkins was the club's first truly great player since Bob Pettit, and in an era when the sport had now come of age as an entertainment spectacle, Wilkins actually reached heights of national celebrity never available to Pettit in the game's infant days. Maravich had also flashed as a brief one-dimensional star during his four Atlanta seasons at the outset of the seventies. And guard John Drew had been the scoring pacesetter throughout much of the late '70s, leading the team in point-making seven straight years (1975–1981). But in Wilkins the ballclub now owned one of the most exciting basketball showmen who ever graced the hardwood floor. Wilkins unarguably ranks behind only Michael Jordan as the most spectacular showman and most thrilling offensive player of the past decade (1984–1994). Even a career-threatening Achilles tendon rupture in mid-season, 1992, could not short-circuit Dominique from soaring above the career 20,000-point plateau. In 1986 Wilkins would be the league's last scoring champion before Air Jordan's run of seven straight titles. Three times it would be Wilkins who would finish second to Jordan in the league scoring derby. And by reaching the 20,000 point barrier in 1992, Dominique Wilkins would join basketball's first 20,000–point scorer, Bob Pettit, as the only two players in franchise history to scale one of the sport's most difficult individual landmarks.

Seven up-and-down seasons under pint-sized mentor Mike Fratello brought five playoff trips for the one-dimensional Hawks ballclub between 1984 and the end of the decade. But with little backcourt consistency to match and even enhance the forecourt power of Wilkins and seven-footer Kevin Willis, the Hawks were doomed to be easy playoff pickings year-in and year-out for their Eastern Conference rivals. Milwaukee would twice (1984, 1989) dispense with the Hawks in round one action over this stretch; and when Atlanta did advance into the second round three times, between 1986 and 1988, Boston (with Larry Bird) and Detroit (with Isiah Thomas) were waiting as most effective roadblocks.

One memorable máno-a-máno duel between Dominique Wilkins and Boston's Larry Bird provided both the crowning high point and the ultimate frustration-filled symbol of the Atlanta Hawks' disappointment-laced 1980s post-season sojourn. The setting was the final game of the 1988 Eastern Conference semi-finals, held in Boston Garden. The result was a blistering one-on-one duel between two NBA greats which author Jack Clary (**Basketball's Greatest Moments**, 1988) would later call ''basketball's ultimate shoot-out'' and which Celtics forward Kevin McHale would also describe as being ''like two gunfighters waiting to blink'' in the icy ''stare-down'' between two unflinching rivals. Bird for his part made nine of ten shots and scored 20 points (of his 34) in the last ten minutes of the breathtaking fourth quarter; Wilkins answered with 16 of his 47 over the same tension-packed period. McHale (who himself scored 33) later observed that the fourth quarter ''was like two people standing at arm's length and ceaselessly punching each other'' into submission. But in the end Bird had McHale at his side and no matter what Wilkins had to offer it would not be quite enough. Wilkins would tally his final point from the foul line with 0:01 remaining on the time clock to bring Atlanta within two at 118–116. But when Dominique purposely bounced a second free throw off the rim in a futile attempt at a rebound and game-tying desperation shot, Robert Parish slapped the ball away and Atlanta's playoff journey again ended in the second round for a third straight season.

A colorful era ended in Atlanta when franchise star Dominique Wilkins was traded in late-season 1994 to the Los Angeles Clippers for promising young forward Danny Manning. Manning did not yet possess Wilkins' firepower, but he was six years younger than Dominique and his youth and all-around game (he has been called ''a point guard in the body of a forward'') promised to solidify an already potent and largely rebuilt Hawks team. Atlanta had already taken a bold step into the future at the outset of '93–'94 with the hiring of veteran coach Lenny Wilkens, now second on the all-time NBA win list. Under the new regime of coach Wilkens, the Hawks rebounded to a somewhat surprising division and conference lead early in the '93–'94 campaign and now hoped that the newly acquired Manning would be the crucial key element necessary for finally climbing the elusive championship ladder.

But although the Hawks charged to a division-best 57–25 record under NBA Coach-of-the-Year Wilkens, chemistry was never quite right on the revamped Atlanta ballclub after Dominique's controversial departure. A unit of Manning, seven-footer Kevin Willis, third-year forward Stacey Augmon, Mookie Blaylock and veteran guard Craig Ehlo struggled with their opening-round playoff opponent, the Miami Heat, then fell quickly out of contention against the surprising Indiana Pacers in post-season round two. An upgrade in Hawks' fortunes had thus slowly begun under Lenny Wilkens; but measurable improvement was seemingly still very far from complete at the end of the largely disappointing 1993–'94 campaign.

Suggested Readings on Atlanta (St. Louis) Hawks

Bjarkman, Peter C. **Sports Great Dominique Wilkins**. Hillside, New Jersey: Enslow Publishers, 1996 (to appear).

Gutman, Bill. **Pistol Pete Maravich—The Making of a Basketball Superstar**. New York: Grosset and Dunlap Publishers, 1972.

Harris, Merv. **On the Court with the Superstars of the NBA**. New York: The Viking Press, 1973.

Pettit, Bob (with Bob Wolff). **Bob Pettit: The Drive Within Me**. New York: Prentice-Hall Publishers, 1966.

Webb, Spud (with Reid Slaughter). **Flying High**. New York: Harper and Row Publishers, 1988.

Atlanta Hawks Retired Uniform Numbers (2)

Bob Pettit (9)
Lou Hudson (23)

Year-by-Year Atlanta (St. Louis) Hawks Summary

Season	Record	Finish	Coach(es)	Scoring Leaders	Playoffs (W-L Record)
Key: # = League Scoring Leader					
Tri-Cities Blackhawks					
National Basketball League					
1946–47	19–25	5th	Nat Hickey	Don Otten (12.9)	Did Not Qualify
1947–48	30–30	2nd	Nat Hickey	Don Otten (13.7)	Lost in 2nd Round (3–3)
			Bob McDermott		
1948–49	36–28	2nd	Bob McDermott	Don Otten (14.0) #	Lost in 2nd Round (3–3)
			Roger Potter		
National Basketball Association					
1949–50	29–35	3rd	Roger Potter	Jack Nichols (19.7)	Lost in 2nd Round (1–2)
			Red Auerbach		
1950–51	25–43	5th	Dave McMillan	Frankie Brian (16.8)	Did Not Qualify
			John Logan		
			Mike Todorovich		
Milwaukee Hawks					
1951–52	17–49	5th	Doxie Moore	Don Otten (12.0)	Did Not Qualify
1952–53	27–44	5th	Andrew Levane	Jack Nichols (15.8)	Did Not Qualify
1953–54	21–51	4th	Andrew Levane	Don Sunderlage (11.2)	Did Not Qualify
			Red Holzman		
1954–55	26–46	4th	Red Holzman	Bob Pettit (20.4)	Did Not Qualify
St. Louis Hawks					
1955–56	33–39	3rd	Red Holzman	Bob Pettit (25.7)#	Lost in 3rd Round (4–4)
1956–57	34–38	1st	Red Holzman	Bob Pettit (24.7)	Lost in NBA Finals (8–4)
			Slater Martin		
			Alex Hannum		

Season	Record	Finish	Coach(es)	Scoring Leaders	Playoffs (W-L Record)
1957–58	41–31	1st	Alex Hannum	Bob Pettit (24.6)	**NBA Champion** (8–3)
1958–59	49–23	1st	Andy Phillip	Bob Pettit (29.2)#	Lost in 3rd Round (2–4)
			Ed Macauley		
1959–60	46–29	1st	Ed Macauley	Bob Pettit (26.1)	Lost in NBA Finals (7–7)
1960–61	51–28	1st	Paul Seymour	Bob Pettit (28.6)	Lost in NBA Finals (5–7)
1961–62	29–51	4th	Paul Seymour	Bob Pettit (31.1)	Did Not Qualify
			Andrew Levane		
			Bob Pettit		
1962–63	48–32	2nd	Harry Gallatin	Bob Pettit (28.4)	Lost in 3rd Round (6–5)
1963–64	46–34	2nd	Harry Gallatin	Bob Pettit (27.4)	Lost in 3rd Round (6–6)
1964–65	45–35	2nd	Harry Gallatin	Bob Pettit (22.5)	Lost in 2nd Round (1–3)
			Richie Guerin		
1965–66	36–44	3rd	Richie Guerin	Zelmo Beaty (20.7)	Lost in 3rd Round (6–4)
1966–67	39–42	2nd	Richie Guerin	Lou Hudson (18.4)	Lost in 3rd Round (5–4)
1967–68	56–26	1st	Richie Guerin	Zelmo Beaty (21.1)	Lost in 2nd Round (2–4)
Atlanta Hawks					
1968–69	48–34	2nd	Richie Guerin	Lou Hudson (21.9)	Lost in 3rd Round (5–6)
1969–70	48–34	1st	Richie Guerin	Lou Hudson (25.4)	Lost in 3rd Round (4–5)
1970–71	36–46	2nd	Richie Guerin	Lou Hudson (26.8)	Lost in 2nd Round (1–4)
1971–72	36–46	2nd	Richie Guerin	Lou Hudson (24.7)	Lost in 2nd Round (2–4)
1972–73	46–36	2nd	L. Fitzsimmons	Lou Hudson (27.1)	Lost in 2nd Round (2–4)
1973–74	35–47	2nd	L. Fitzsimmons	Pete Maravich (27.7)	Did Not Qualify
1974–75	31–51	4th	L. Fitzsimmons	John Drew (18.5)	Did Not Qualify
1975–76	29–53	5th	L. Fitzsimmons	John Drew (21.6)	Did Not Qualify
			Gene Tormohlen		
1976–77	31–51	6th	Hubie Brown	John Drew (24.2)	Did Not Qualify
1977–78	41–41	4th	Hubie Brown	John Drew (23.2)	Lost in 1st Round (0–2)
1978–79	46–36	3rd	Hubie Brown	John Drew (22.7)	Lost in 2nd Round (5–4)
1979–80	50–32	1st	Hubie Brown	John Drew (19.5)	Lost in 2nd Round (1–4)
1980–81	31–51	4th	Hubie Brown	John Drew (21.7)	Did Not Qualify
			Mike Fratello		
			Brendan Suhr		
1981–82	42–40	2nd	Kevin Loughery	Dan Roundfield (18.6)	Lost in 1st Round (0–2)
1982–83	43–39	2nd	Kevin Loughery	Dan Roundfield (19.0)	Lost in 1st Round (1–2)
1983–84	40–42	3rd	Mike Fratello	Dominique Wilkins (21.6)	Lost in 1st Round (2–3)
1984–85	34–48	5th	Mike Fratello	Dominique Wilkins (27.4)	Did Not Qualify
1985–86	50–32	2nd	Mike Fratello	Dominique Wilkins (30.3)#	Lost in 2nd Round (4–5)
1986–87	57–25	1st	Mike Fratello	Dominique Wilkins (29.0)	Lost in 2nd Round (4–5)
1987–88	50–32	3rd	Mike Fratello	Dominique Wilkins (30.7)	Lost in 2nd Round (6–6)
1988–89	52–30	3rd	Mike Fratello	Dominique Wilkins (26.2)	Lost in 1st Round (2–3)
1989–90	41–41	6th	Mike Fratello	Dominique Wilkins (26.7)	Did Not Qualify
1990–91	43–39	4th	Bob Weiss	Dominique Wilkins (25.9)	Lost in 1st Round (2–3)
1991–92	38–44	5th	Bob Weiss	Kevin Willis (18.3)	Did Not Qualify
1992–93	43–39	4th	Bob Weiss	Dominique Wilkins (29.9)	Lost in 1st Round (0–3)
1993–94	57–25	1st	Lenny Wilkens	Danny Manning (20.6)	Lost in 2nd Round (5–6)

Individual Career Leaders and Record Holders (1949–1994)

Scoring Average	Dominique Wilkins (26.5 ppg., 1982–93)#
Points Scored	Dominique Wilkins (22,096, 1982–93)#
Games Played	Dominique Wilkins (833, 1982–93)#
Minutes Played	Dominique Wilkins (30,850)#
Field Goal Pct.	Mike Glenn (.533, 1981–85)
3–Pt. Field Goals	Dominique Wilkins (439, 1982–93)#
Free Throws Made	Bob Pettit (6,182, 1954–65)
Free-Throw Pct.	Clyde Lovellette (.832, 1958–62)
Rebounds	Bob Pettit (12,851, 1954–65)
Rebound Average	Bob Pettit (16.2 rpg.)
Assists	Glenn "Doc" Rivers (3,866, 1983–91)
Steals	Dominique Wilkins (1,182, 1982–93)#
Blocked Shots	Wayne "Tree" Rollins (2,283, 1977–88)
Personal Fouls	Wayne "Tree" Rollins (2,924)

= Wilkins' partial 1993-94 season with Atlanta not included

Individual Single-Season and Game Records (1949–1994)

Scoring Average	Bob Pettit (31.1 ppg., 1961–62)
Points Scored (Season)	Bob Pettit (2,429, 1961–62)
Points Scored (Game)	Dominique Wilkins (57, 12–10–86 and 4–10–86)
	Lou Hudson, (57, 11–10–69 vs. Chicago Bulls)
	Bob Pettit (57, 2–18–61 at Detroit Pistons)
Field Goal Pct. (Season)	Mike Glenn (.588, 1984–85)
3–Pt. Field Goals (Season)	Dominique Wilkins (120, 1992–93)
Free-Throw Pct. (Season)	Tom McMillen (.891, 1978–79)
Rebounds (Season)	Bob Pettit (1,540, 1960–61)
Rebounds (Game)	Bob Pettit (35, 3–3–58 and 1–6–56)
Assists (Season)	Glenn "Doc" Rivers (823, 1986–87)
Assists (Game)	Mookie Blaylock (23, 3–6–93 vs. Utah Jazz)
Steals (Season)	Mookie Blaylock (203, 1992–93)
Blocked Shots (Season)	Wayne "Tree" Rollins (343, 1982–83)
Blocked Shots (Game)	Wayne "Tree" Rollins (12, 2–21–79 vs. Portland Trail Blazers)
Personal Fouls (Season)	Dan Roundfield (358, 1978–79)

Best Trade in Franchise History

Sometimes unpopular deals have a way of turning out to prove the best of transactions in the hindsight of history. Thus the much-celebrated trade sending franchise star Dominique Wilkins to the Los Angeles Clippers for

Danny Manning in mid-season 1994 may have been precisely one of those deals that will look more and more positive for the Hawks as the next couple of seasons slowly unfold. Wilkins need take a seat second to no one (save possibly Hall-of-Famer Bob Pettit) in five decades of Hawks history. But Wilkins's days in the NBA now seem definitely numbered and Manning, by contrast, is a rising young star who can perhaps revive team chemistry and even lead a series of championship charges over the next half decade or more. Hawks fans may grouse for awhile, but it is nothing a post-season charge won't cure.

Worst Trade in Franchise History

Bill Russell and the Boston Celtics owned the late '50s and most of the '60s and the only team that mounted much of a challenge to their reign over that stretch was the St. Louis Hawks led by Bob Pettit and Cliff Hagan. But can you imagine a front line stacked with both Pettit *and* Russell? That might well have been the case had the Hawks not sealed their own doom when they traded off draft rights for Russell to Boston in 1956 in order to obtain all-star center "Easy Ed" Macauley and rookie forward Cliff Hagan. It is true enough that St. Louis received much talent in return during this celebrated swap. But never has a team given up quite so much either, especially to their single rival for league supremacy.

Atlanta Hawks Historical Oddity

Dominique Wilkins will probably always be remembered as the answer to a popular trivia question: Who was the last player to win an NBA scoring title before Michael Jordan took over the throne for seven straight seasons? It is fitting, if sad, that "Human Highlight Film" Wilkins is so linked to "Air" Jordan. If it hadn't been for Michael, after all, Dominique might well have been himself an unforgettable scoring legend of unsurpassed magnitude. Wilkins has to know exactly how Jerry West (or Elgin Baylor and Oscar Robertson) felt in the shadow of Wilt Chamberlain. Wilkins and West will remain among the half-dozen greatest scorers in league history and yet rarely do they show up in listings of the league's yearly leaders. West, in fact, ranks fourth (27.0) on the list of highest career scoring averages, while Wilkins currently stands fifth (26.5, after the 1993 season). And each owns but a single scoring title. Baylor (3rd, 27.4) and Robertson (9th, 25.7) were, surprisingly, never league scoring champions.

Hawks All-Time Number One Draft Picks List

Atlanta Hawks
1968 Skip Harlicka (South Carolina)
1969 Butch Beard (Louisville)

1970 Pete Maravich (LSU)
1971 George Trapp (Long Beach State)
1972 None
1973 Dwight Jones (Houston)
1974 Tom Henderson (Hawaii)
1975 David Thompson (North Carolina State)
1976 Armond Hill (Princeton)
1977 Wayne "Tree" Rollins (Clemson)
1978 Butch Lee (Marquette)
1979 James Bradley (Memphis State)
1980 Don Collins (Washington State)
1981 Al Wood (North Carolina)
1982 Keith Edmonson (Purdue)
1983 Randy Wittman (Indiana)
1984 Kevin Willis (Michigan State)
1985 Jon Koncak (SMU)
1986 Billy Thompson (Louisville)
1987 Dallas Comegys (DePaul)
1988 Anthony Taylor (Oregon)
1989 Roy Marble (Iowa)
1990 Rumeal Robinson (Michigan)
1991 Stacey Augmon (UNLV)
1992 Adam Keefe (Stanford)
1993 Doug Edwards (Florida State)

Chapter 9

WASHINGTON (CAPITAL) BULLETS AND BALTIMORE BULLETS

Finally They Made the Fat Lady Sing

All-Time Franchise Record: 1274–1421, .473 Pct. (1961–1994)
NBA Championships (1): 1977–78
Greatest Franchise Player: Elvin Hayes (1972–1981)
All-Time Leading Scorer: Elvin Hayes (15,551 Points, 1972–1981)
Most Successful Coach: K.C. Jones (155–91, .630 Pct., 1973–1976)
All-Time Franchise Team: Walt Bellamy (C), Wes Unseld (C-F), Elvin Hayes (F), Jeff Malone (G), Earl Monroe (G)

Each NBA decade seems to have its dominant team or two. The 50's were equally carved up between the George Mikan Minneapolis Lakers, Bill Russell Boston Celtics and Bob Pettit-led St. Louis Hawks. The 60's were owned from end to end by the Auerbach-coached Celtics alone. The 80's were divided down the middle between the Lakers with Magic Johnson and modern-era Boston Celtics with Larry Bird. And so far the '90s have belonged almost exclusively to the Chicago Bulls. But the '70s— where there was perhaps more balance and parity than in any other NBA decade—nonetheless was largely owned by the Washington Bullets.

Over the first five years of the '70s the Bullets would amass five straight Central Division titles. These would ironically come with three different ball-club names—they were known variously as the Baltimore Bullets ('70–'71, '71–'72, '72–'73), Capital Bullets ('73–'74) and Washington Bullets ('74–'75). In the second half of the same decade the divisional titles would slide a bit as the Bullets took only one first alongside three seconds and a third. But the team would rise during this stretch to even greater post-season

187

heights, winning one NBA crown outright in 1977–78 and barely losing another in the NBA Finals a year later. Three times, in fact, would the 1970s Washington Bullets make it all the way into the NBA Finals.

The remainder of Bullets history slopes away from the mountain peak that was the 1970s like two giant slalom courses—replete with plenty of zigs and zags for excitement. It took the franchise nine long years with three different team names and two different cities before the Bullets finally became contenders under coach Gene Shue in the final two seasons of the '60s. And after the peak seasons of 1978 and 1979 the Bullets— nestled at long last into a permanent home in Washington's Capital Center (actually located in Lanham, Maryland)—have almost never been heard from again. During fifteen seasons since 1980 and under three different coaches (Shue back for a second try, Kevin Loughery, and Wes Unseld) the ballclub has finished as high as second in a divisional race only a single time. This occurred in 1987–88, the transition year when Unseld replaced Loughery in mid-stream and fashioned a 30–25 record down the stretch run. It would be Unseld's only winning ledger as a Bullets coach. For six straight years now Unseld's teams have remained on the sidelines during post-season play. Over the past decade the lackluster Washington ballclub has, in fact, been as impotent as any other NBA ballclub any- where, including any of the league's latest expansion add-ons.

Despite the narrow focus of franchise glory on a single decade, the Bullets can boast their handful of all-time greats and even a few of the sport's loftiest superstars. As a matter of fact, no other NBA franchise has ever had three past stars inducted into the Naismith Basketball Hall of Fame in the exact same year. This happened for the Bullets back in 1989 when Elvin Hayes, Earl Mon- roe, and Dave Bing shared the same induction ceremony in Springfield, Massa- chusetts. Hayes was the team's greatest offensive star and played with the Bullets throughout all but the first two seasons of their most glorious decade. Monroe joined the club in Baltimore as a sterling rookie out of Winston Salem State in the late '60s and enjoyed four great years in the Chesapeake Bay City before moving on to a second illustrious career with the New York Knicks. And while Bing earned greater fame with the Detroit Pistons as one of that franchise's greatest scorers ever, he was nonetheless a memorable star with the Bullets for a few short seasons near the twilight of his 18,000-point career.

Yet perhaps the greatest franchise star—if not, objectively speaking, the most talented all-around player in club history—was the rotund and massive enforcer who came to Baltimore as the second overall choice of the 1968 collegiate draft. Wes Unseld was a 6–7 245–pound muscleman who owned the boards and cut down opponents with vicious picks for 13 seasons, in both Baltimore and Washington. By career's end Unseld would hold a slot in the record books as basketball's eighth greatest rebounder ever (Elvin Hayes, who played three more seasons ranks fourth). During the peak Washington seasons it was Elvin Hayes who always lit up the scoreboard; but during that same great stretch it was Wed Unseld who consistently won close ballgames in the trenches, and thus won divisional and post-season championships as well.

Unseld would begin his fabulous career as only the second man in league history to simultaneously reign as rookie of the year and NBA MVP to boot. His MVP selection that year was indeed unique because it was not earned through the more glamorous route of scoring, but rather through board play and defense. Unseld's 13.8 rookie-year scoring average was the lowest ever for a league MVP and still remains so today. But in that noble first season Wes Unseld also posted two other stats of far greater impact. He hauled down 18.2 rpg. to trail only annual leader Wilt Chamberlain. And he was clearly the most significant factor in hiking up the Bullets' won-lost total by an amazing 21 games. Few rookies have ever had such clear-cut overnight impact in the league standings.

The Bullets franchise first saw the light of day far from its current home in the nation's capital or even its previous abode a few miles to the north in Baltimore. The team was instead christened as the first "expansion team" in NBA history and was brought into existence by the league's great recent successes with new stars and thus burgeoning public attention in 1958–59 (Elgin Baylor), 1959–60 (Wilt Chamberlain) and 1960–61 (Oscar Robertson and Jerry West). The league's first new club since the BAA-NBL merger would be called the Chicago Packers. In a unique instance of unguarded irony surrounding a staid pro sports franchise, the name for the first-year Chicago club originated from the site of its home court, the Chicago Amphitheater, located right next door to the aromatic Chicago Stockyards. But much of the unpleasant smell surrounding this team—wags might have contended at the time—surely emanated from the first-year club's ragged play on the floor, as the Packers limped to an extremely ugly 18–62 inaugural campaign.

There was one extremely bright success story in the single season of a team known as the Chicago Packers. Walt "Bells" Bellamy was a towering yet extremely mobile center drafted out of Indiana University, who would have perhaps been the year's unrivaled headline story had this been almost any other year. But Bells had the extreme misfortune of debuting in the very season in which Wilt Chamberlain was busy accomplishing absolutely superhuman feats like scoring 100 points in one game, averaging an unheard of 50.4 points for the entire season, and never missing a single minute of on-floor action during the course of an entire year's schedule of games. In short, Wilt in 1961–62 enjoyed the greatest individual season of all time, in any sport, and by any measure. Chicago's overshadowed rookie, Walt Bellamy, would nonetheless finish a distant yet respectable second to Wilt in the scoring race by averaging 31.6 ppg. Only Elgin Baylor a year earlier had ever posted a loftier figure and still not won an individual scoring title. Bellamy (.519) would even lead Chamberlain (.506) and all others that season in field goal percentage. He would also trail only Wilt (25.7 rpg.) and Bill Russell (23.6 rpg.) in rebounding, and then by only a respectably narrow margin. Bellamy was also, as a mere matter of course, the runaway league rookie-of-the-year selection.

In still another fine touch of careless irony the Chicago team decided a name change was in order for season number two. This time around management—presumably tongue rooted deeply in cheek—settled casually on Chicago **Zephyrs**. With yet another archly appropriate name for a team playing adjacent to the infamous stock yards, the Chicago team thus cleaned up its act a bit, as well as sanitizing its humorous name. Terry Dischinger was another fine rookie now on board, this time out of Purdue University. In a year which saw such other stellar newcomers as John Havlicek of Boston, Zelmo Beaty in St. Louis, and Dave DeBusschere of Detroit, it was Dischinger who would rule as top rookie selection. And Walt Bellamy continued his stratospheric scoring as well, although falling to fifth in the point race due to increased competition from sharpshooters like Baylor, Robertson, and Pettit, who all passed him by. Dischinger's rookie honors would thus provide a rare moment of franchise history. For this marked the first and only time that a new expansion club would own the rookie-of-the-year selection in both of its first two NBA seasons.

By the following year—1963–64—it had become clear that the Packers/ Zephyrs wished to escape the stockyard atmosphere of their current location through more than mere cosmetic name changes. Team management demanded a new playing arena and, unable to locate a satisfactory one anywhere in the Chicagoland area, decided to take the team all the way to Baltimore. Bellamy and Dischinger were not seemingly affected by this move out of a midwest venue, where they had both been college stars. Both remained among the league leaders in scoring, field goal accuracy and rebounding. And the team (now known as Bullets) inched up to 31 wins and even climbed over Detroit to escape the basement. It was the basement of the Western Division and not the Eastern Division, however, as the team's move into a different sector of the country had not caused any reshuffling of the divisional alignments. And the constantly shifting Baltimore ballclub now owned another unique and trivial distinction as well. No other NBA franchise has ever used a different team nickname and logo for each and every one of its first three league seasons.

The Bullets were now apparently done revolving club nicknames, but some other significant administrative changes were still in store. The ballclub was soon sold during its first Baltimore season to a group of neighboring Washington, D.C. investors which included successful construction contractor Abe Pollin, a farsighted entrepreneur and philanthropist who remains the current club owner three decades later. It would be Pollin who would bring the team into the modern age nine years later by moving it into the D.C. area and building the first new plush arena of the modern NBA era. Today known as the USAir Arena, the D.C. beltway Capital Center featured a number of forward-looking features when Pollin opened its doors in the fall of 1973. Among these were the first large luxury skyboxes, the first giant four-sided video screen hanging over center court, and the first fully-computerized system for event ticketing.

For five years during the mid-sixties, the Packers-turned-Bullets had shown a steady improvement in the number of games won as the totals climbed from 18 to 25 to 31 and then to 37 and 38. Then suddenly there was a major on-floor setback in 1966–67, the first season the Baltimore team had been reassigned to the NBA's Eastern Division. This Baltimore edition was largely colorless and extremely ineffectual as it posted the lowest division scoring average (115.5) and also gave up more points nightly (122.0) than any club in either circuit. Gus "Honeycomb" Johnson—a 6–6 jumping jack forward—added perhaps the only air of excitement with his career-high 20.7 ppg. average. Three seasons earlier the colorful Johnson had earned lasting notoriety as a rookie when he accounted for the NBA's first smashed backboard with a thundering dunk shot in a pre-season exhibition game against San Francisco. Bellamy had already been unwisely unloaded a season earlier to New York, and Terry Dischinger had departed the same year for Detroit. The stable was now indeed thin and a starting lineup of Jack Marin, Gus Johnson, Leroy Ellis, Kevin Loughery and Don Ohl did little to intimidate any Eastern Division foes. But in the end the dreadful season also provided a silver lining within the gathering storm clouds. For out of the league's worst record came the summer's number one draft pick and a ticket back to immediate respectability. The choice of Earl "The Pearl" Monroe from tiny unheralded Winston Salem College (where he had electrified the collegiate scene with a 41.5 ppg. average his senior season) was undoubtedly among the wisest draft choices in all of Bullets club history.

Earl Monroe would shine as NBA Rookie of the Year in 1967–68. The Pearl would not only dazzle with a breathtaking display of every offensive move in the book but would also pour in enough points to tie Chamberlain for fourth spot in the league's scoring derby. In one game Monroe bagged 56, the third highest rookie single-game total ever. And another newcomer would be coach Gene Shue, who had finished out the preceding campaign but now celebrated his first full season on the job with a noticeable Bullets revival. With Monroe shooting and Shue drawing the x's and o's the team improved a solid 16 games in the won-lost columns. But this would not be enough improvement to deprive them of still another number one pick in the 1968 collegiate draft. And with Wes Unseld from the University of Louisville as that year's first selection, the Bullets would now assure themselves of a second straight NBA rookie of the year candidate.

With Unseld's inside game joining Monroe's outside firepower in Baltimore the team jumped this next season even further up the ladder of progress. In fact the Baltimore ballclub jumped right out of the basement and into the penthouse. There was little argument that the Bullets of coach Gene Shue were the most shocking development of a 1968–69 season that also saw the Celtic's dynasty wind down with a final championship in Boston, and Wilt Chamberlain take his bridesmaid act on the road one final time to the Los Angeles Lakers.

Baltimore had already stockpiled plenty of shooters in Monroe, Kevin Loughery and Jack Marin; with Unseld's ferocious rebounding and pin-point outlet passes now joining the mix, the Bullets were instantly turned into a devastating fast-breaking unit. The victory total soared up to 57 and brought with it a division title for a team that had a year earlier been the pasty of the Boston-dominated Eastern Division. The playoffs would prove a rude shock and quick exit, however, as New York blitzed the Bullets in four straight and Boston wound its way through the mine-fields toward another championship showdown with the Lakers. But nonetheless dramatic progress was now underway and moving full steam ahead. There would indeed be a brief slump into third slot the very next season, but this was only apparently a holding-pattern year as New York (the league's new champion) and Milwaukee enjoyed brief runs at the top. Despite a second straight loss to the Knicks in round one of the playoffs, the Baltimore season was anything but disappointing in view of 50 more wins and another season of true championship contention.

Three final seasons in Baltimore—also the final three of Gene Shue's first tenure—were the beginning of the greatest period in team history. It started with a loud bang in 1970–71 as Shue's club headed up a newly-formed and obviously weak Central Division (at 42–40 the Bullets were the only team above .500) and then finally earned some post-season revenge against the New York Knicks. Just about everyone had expected at Milwaukee-New York Final that would pit veteran center Willis Reed against second-year youngster Lew Alcindor. But Unseld and Gus Johnson controlled the boards against New York in the Eastern Conference finals and New York reeled under the pressure of injuries which slowed star Willis Reed. New York built a cushion with two early victories but Baltimore won games three, four and six to force an unexpected seventh-game showdown. Then the Bullets pulled off the upset of the season with a stunning 93–91 victory in Madison Square Garden which left Knicks faithful limp when Bill Bradley missed a tying jump shot at the buzzer. The final-game upset of defending champion New York in the conference finals was one of the darkest moments in Knicks history but also the pinnacle moment of the Baltimore franchise. It almost seemed an anticlimax when Wes Unseld couldn't control Alcindor in the Finals, and Milwaukee roared to a four-game sweep over Baltimore to salt away the NBA title that should have belonged to the Knicks.

The playoffs continued to be a stumbling block under Shue, whose teams sandwiched four round-two defeats around their one trip to the league finals. But if the playoffs were seemingly an insurmountable hurdle, the brief interruptions of a relocation to the nation's capital and a coaching switch to former Celtics great K.C. Jones (both occurring in 1973) were mere minor distractions. The renamed and resettled Capital Bullets were now maturing into a veteran and talented ballclub and were to all indications on a fast train back toward the top.

The summer immediately before the final Baltimore season had brought a most crucial change in the team chemistry. Elvin Hayes was acquired from the Houston Rockets for the league's 1971–72 free throw champion, Jack Marin. With Hayes penciled into the lineup that now also boasted Mike Riordan at forward and Phil Chenier in the backcourt, it took only a handful of seasons for the ballclub to break loose. That jump over the top came in

1974–75 when the K.C. Jones-coached team recorded the league's best record (also a franchise record 60 wins) and advanced all the way to the NBA championship finals. Bullets teams seemed to have a way of throwing in the towel if and when they made it all the way to championship face-offs, however, and this time Washington—like Baltimore a handful of seasons back— was again a loser in four straight. Now it was Golden State and Rick Barry that applied the whitewashing, only the third in the 26–year history of the NBA Finals. Unfortunately for Baltimore and Washington loyalists, the Bullets themselves had twice been the victims of those blankings.

The Bullets were at least now banging lustily on the front door and only minor tinkerings seemed to stand between the current team and a collection of NBA championship rings. One final adjustment in blending the perfect chemistry of a championship team would come just a couple of seasons later under K.C. Jones's successor Dick Motta. Jones had once again failed to get his talented team out of the second round of playoffs in 1976 and thus sealed his own fate. Motta suffered the same post-season failure in 1977 when Central Division rival Houston nipped the Bullets by a single game during regular-season action and then shot down Washington once again during the Eastern Conference semis. Motta's first team ironically had posted the exact same regular-season ledger of 48 wins as the final team under K.C. Jones. But the ballclub still anchored by Hayes and Unseld was now respected everywhere as one of the best veteran units in either conference, and thus eyed warily on all fronts as a potential title contender.

Everything finally fell perfectly into place for 1978 and 1979 as the Bullets enjoyed two of the finest years of franchise history. And since Hayes had now turned 34 and Unseld 33 this final maturing probably didn't come a single moment too soon. The '77–'78 season didn't start off so spectacularly; Washington logged a regular-season won-lost mark just six-games over break-even level. Bob Dandridge and Hayes both topped 19 ppg. and Hayes and Unseld both cracked the elite top ten in rebounding. The team trailed San Antonio by a country mile, however, during regular season divisional play. But the Bullets were now a dangerous veteran team and they got hot just when it counted—at playoff time. While Seattle's SuperSonics were turning heads out west by trimming the Lakers and derailing defending titlest Portland, Hayes and company advanced past Atlanta and San Antonio. The 1978 NBA Finals thus brought an unlikely matchup of the second-place Bullets with a third-place club from the Pacific Division. It was an extremely exciting series even if the big-name division winners were nowhere in evidence. Before it was over NBA fans saw the Bullets climb out of a 3–2 deficit to capture their only NBA world title.

Wes Unseld capped his considerable career with perhaps his finest performance during the 1978 Finals. The only remaining member of the 1975 Finals runner-up, Unseld was tabbed unanimously as NBA Finals MVP yet was only one of a handful of Washington post-season heroes. Charles Johnson and Bob Dandridge each fired home 19 points as the Bullets clinched the title with a seventh-game 105–99 triumph before 39,547 hostile fans in the Seattle Kingdome. The victory had been set up in game six at the Cap Center when Motta's inspired Bullets had posted the most one-sided Finals victory in league history—117–82. "It isn't over until the Fat Lady sings," Motta had cautioned disappointed Bullets fans when the team had slipped behind earlier in the series. Now at long last the legendary fat lady was singing loud and clear everywhere in the nation's capital.

If the Bullets and SuperSonics didn't seem to belong in the NBA Finals in 1978 they both broke from the gate early in the following season to prove a point—that they *did* belong there beyond any shadow of a doubt in 1979. And by season's end the return matchup was virtually assured: Washington owned the East's best record at 54–28 while Seattle dominated the West at 52–30. Atlanta and San Antonio both extended the Bullets to seven-game series while Seattle's Sonics needed two comeback victories to wrest a seven-game Conference finals from Phoenix. This time the Sonics were able to master the aging Bullets head-to-head, however. Key reserve Mitch Kupchak was hobbled by injury and, after surviving a 99–97 opening victory, the tired and outmatched Bullets faded badly in the second half of each of the four remaining games. A short era of greatness for Washington basketball was now apparently coming to an abrupt end.

The Bullets dropped under .500 for Motta's final year and then hung around almost no time at all in the playoffs, suffering a two-game white-washing by Philadelphia in round one of post-season. Under the returning Gene Shue the Washington team next became a mediocre (sometimes worse) also-ran for the next five long seasons. Hayes returned to Houston to play out his swan-song campaigns; Jeff Ruland took up the scoring slack for two winters of an injury-shorten career; Jeff Malone launched a high-scoring sojourn that would vault him onto the all-time top ten NBA career list for free-throw-shooting accuracy.

One-time Baltimore Bullets shooting guard Kevin Loughery took over in mid-season 1986 and was gone by mid-season 1988. Nothing else much changed as the fortunes of the Bullets continued to drift aimlessly. It now seemed as though the long-deteriorating situation in Washington needed a miracle-working savior. Bullets fans and management (and probably players also) hoped against hope that this miracle-worker would be former long-time team hero and Hall-of-Famer Wes Unseld. Unseld seemed to know what it took to win; at least that had to be the judgment based on his highly successful playing days. The Bullets, after all, had never experienced a winning season before Unseld's appearance with them as a player; with this wide-body center in the lineup, however, the team recorded ten winning campaigns. But coaches don't rebound and set bone-crushing picks; with Unseld at the end of the bench the Bullets had now come full circle back to the pre-Unseld playing days.

Six years under an often-frustrated Unseld brought no miracles. It brought instead only a steep downward spiral to new embarrassing lows. For all six seasons of the Unseld experiment, the team was completely out of the picture when it came to playoff qualification. Only Jeff Malone provided some bright play and some scoring punch at the guard slot for seven seasons (1983–90) before being traded to Utah in a three-team transaction that brought disappointing Pervis Ellison to Washington. Three seasons of 25 wins or less didn't even bring any outstanding recruits from the draft lottery. Calbert Chaney (Indiana University All-American) is one of the most recent picks who flashed promise his rookie year (12.0 ppg.) but is hardly a franchise maker. And the only trades that brought much help were those which secured three-point specialist Michael Adams from Denver and shooting guard Rex Chapman from Charlotte.

As much as anything the Bullets of the late '80s and early '90s seemed to be a depository for strange basketball personalities and bizarre basketball experiences. Two of the league's largest and least-talented giants—7'6" Manute Bol ('85–'88) and 7'7" Gheorghe Muresan ('93–'94)—would perform their sideshow acts here. Moses Malone ('86–'88) would attempt to extend his career and his numerous statistical records (including his relentless march toward 30,000 career points) while actually contributing little beyond a 22.2 scoring average. Bernard King ('87–'91) would also play on well past his prime in Washington where he could contribute little beyond a growing set of numbers beside of his own name in the *Basketball Encyclopedia*. But if they weren't very good, the Bullets managed to find ways to remain at least interesting: this would be one of the clubs involved, for example, in a fiasco head-to-head pairing of the two towering imports—Bol (now with Miami) and Muresan—both posing, largely unsuccessfully, as legitimate basketball players. When Boll and Muresan faced off for eight minutes in a November matchup, in which neither scored or rebounded, the duel marked the tallest one-on-one confrontation anywhere in league annals.

At end of 1994 the Bullets were again mired deep in basketball's basement. Rex Chapman (18.2) and Don MacLean (18.2) had emerged as new talents, but were not enough to carry the team very far. The 6–10 MacLean, who had come from the LA Clippers along with William Bedford in exchange for John Williams, was the biggest surprise; the leading scorer in PAC–10 and UCLA history (2,608 points) tripled his rookie scoring average during a vastly improved sophomore campaign. Detroit and Milwaukee of the Central Division and Minnesota and Dallas of the Midwest were the only clubs that didn't top Washington's win total of 24 games. Wes Unseld had finally had enough and stepped down at season's end, leaving behind a six-year coaching legacy that averaged less than 30 wins per year. Ex-Sixers coach Jim Lyman would inherit this sagging team in 1995, but Lyman would apparently have to work near miracles to bring the Bullets back to the prominence they once knew in Unseld's own long-lost playing days.

Suggested Readings on the Washington (Baltimore) Bullets

Allen, Woody. "A Fan's Notes on Earl Monroe" in: **Take it to the Hoop: A Basketball Anthology**. Edited by Daniel Rudman. Richmond, California: North Atlantic Books, 1980, 241–247.

Bjarkman, Peter C. **The History of the NBA**. New York and Avenel, New Jersey: Crescent Books (Outlet Books, Random House), 1992.

Monteville, Leigh. **Manute—The Center of Two Worlds**. New York and London: Simon and Schuster, 1993.

Washington Bullets Retired Uniform Numbers (3)

Elvin Hayes (11)
Gus Johnson (25)
Wes Unseld (41)

Year-by-Year Washington (Baltimore) Bullets Summary

Season	Record	Finish	Coach(es)	Scoring Leader(s)	Playoffs (W-L Record)
Key: * = Tie for Position; # =League Scoring Leader					
Chicago Packers					
1961–62	18–62	5th	Jim Pollard	Walt Bellamy (31.6)	Did Not Qualify
Chicago Zephyrs					
1962–63	25–55	5th	Jack McMahon Bob "Slick" Leonard	Walt Bellamy (27.9)	Did Not Qualify
Baltimore Bullets					
1963–64	31–49	4th	Bob Leonard	Walt Bellamy (27.0)	Did Not Qualify
1964–65	37–43	3rd	Buddy Jeannette	Walt Bellamy (24.8	Lost in 3rd Round (5–5)
1965–66	38–42	3rd	Paul Seymour	Don Ohl (20.6)	Lost in 2nd Round (0–3)
1966–67	20–61	5th	Mike Farmer Buddy Jeannette Gene Shue	Gus Johnson (20.7)	Did Not Qualify
1967–68	36–46	6th	Gene Shue	Earl Monroe (24.3)	Did Not Qualify
1968–69	57–25	1st	Gene Shue	Earl Monroe (25.8)	Lost in 2nd Round (0–4)
1969–70	50–32	3rd	Gene Shue	Earl Monroe (23.4)	Lost in 2nd Round (3–4)
1970–71	42–40	1st	Gene Shue	Earl Monroe (21.4)	Lost in NBA Finals (8–10)
1971–72	38–44	1st	Gene Shue	Archie Clark (25.1)	Lost in 2nd Round (2–4)
1972–73	52–30	1st	Gene Shue	Elvin Hayes (21.2)	Lost in 2nd Round (1–4)
Capital Bullets					
1973–74	47–35	1st	K.C. Jones	Phil Chenier (21.9)	Lost in 2nd Round (3–4)
Washington Bullets					
1974–75	60–22	1st	K.C. Jones	Elvin Hayes (23.0)	Lost in NBA Finals (8–9)
1975–76	48–34	2nd	K.C. Jones	Phil Chenier (19.9)	Lost in 2nd Round (3–4)
1976–77	48-34	2nd	Dick Motta	Elvin Hayes (23.7)	Lost in 2nd Round (4–5)
1977–78	44–38	2nd	Dick Motta	Elvin Hayes (19.7)	**NBA Champion** (14–7)
1978–79	54–28	1st	Dick Motta	Elvin Hayes (21.8)	Lost in NBA Finals (9–10)
1979–80	39–43	3rd	Dick Motta	Elvin Hayes (23.0)	Lost in 1st Round (0–2)
1980–81	39–43	4th	Gene Shue	Elvin Hayes (17.8)	Did Not Qualify
1981–82	43–39	4th	Gene Shue	Greg Balland (18.8)	Lost in 2nd Round (3–4)
1982–83	42–40	5th	Gene Shue	Jeff Ruland (19.4)	Did Not Qualify
1983–84	35–47	5th	Gene Shue	Jeff Ruland (22.2)	Lost in 1st Round (1–3)
1984–85	40–42	4th	Gene Shue	Gus Williams (20.0)	Lost in 1st Round (1–3)
1985–86	39–43	3rd	Gene Shue Kevin Loughery	Jeff Malone (22.4)	Lost in 1st Round (2–3)

Season	Record	Finish	Coach(es)	Scoring Leader(s)	Playoffs (W-L Record)
1986–87	42–40	3rd	Kevin Loughery	Moses Malone (24.1)	Lost in 1st Round (0–3)
1987–88	38–44	2nd	Kevin Loughery Wes Unseld	Jeff Malone (20.5)	Lost in 1st Round (2–3)
1988–89	40–42	4th	Wes Unseld	Jeff Malone (21.7)	Did Not Qualify
1989–90	31–51	4th	Wes Unseld	Jeff Malone (24.3)	Did Not Qualify
1990–91	30–52	4th	Wes Unseld	Bernard King (28.4)	Did Not Qualify
1991–92	25–57	6th	Wes Unseld	Pervis Ellison (20.0)	Did Not Qualify
1992–93	22–60	7th	Wes Unseld	Harvey Grant (18.6)	Did Not Qualify
1993–94	24–58	7th	Wes Unseld	Don MacLean (18.2)	Did Not Qualify

Individual Career leaders and Record Holders (1961–1994)

Scoring Average	Walt Bellamy (27.6 ppg., 1961–66)
Points Scored	Elvin Hayes (15,551, 1972–81)
Games Played	Wes Unseld (984, 1968–81)
Field Goal Pct.	Jeff Ruland (.564, 1981–86)
3-Pt. Field Goals	Michael Adams (276, 1986–87, 1991–94)
Free Throws Made	Elvin Hayes (3,046)
Free-Throw Pct.	Jeff Malone (.869, 1983–90)
Rebounds	Wes Unseld (13,769, 1968–81)
Rebound Average	Walt Bellamy (16.6 rpg., 1961–66)
Assists	Wes Unseld (3,822, 1968–81)
Steals	Greg Ballard (762, 1977–85)
Blocked Shots	Elvin Hayes (1,558)
Consecutive Games Played	Jack Marin (349)

Individual Single-Season and Game Records (1961–1994)

Scoring Average	Walt Bellamy (31.6, 1961–62)
Points Scored (Season)	Walt Bellamy (2,495, 1961–62)
Points Scored (Game)	Earl Monroe (56, 2–3–68 vs. Los Angeles Lakers)
Field Goal Pct. (Season)	Jeff Ruland (.579, 1983–84)
3-Pt. Field Goals (Game)	Michael Adams (6, 12–18–91 vs. San Antonio Spurs)
Free-Throw Pct. (Season)	Jack Marin (.894, 1971–72)
Rebounds (Season)	Walt Bellamy (1,500, 1961–62)
Rebounds (Game)	Walt Bellamy (37, 12–4–64 vs. St. Louis Hawks)
Assists (Season)	Kevin Porter (734, 1980–81)
Assists (Game)	Kevin Porter (24, 3–23–80 vs. Detroit Pistons)
Steals (Season)	Gus Williams (178, 1984–85)
Steals (Game)	Gus Williams (9, 10–30–84 vs. Atlanta Hawks)
	Michael Adams (9, 11–1–91 at Indiana Pacers)
Blocked Shots (Season)	Manute Bol (397, 1985–86)
Blocked Shots (Game)	Manute Bol (15, 2–26–87 and 1–25–86)
Personal Fouls (Season)	Rick Mahorn (358, 1983–84)

Best Trade in Franchise History

Elvin Hayes was as much of a franchise player as just about any high-scoring power player ever has been or ever could be. And few such marquee players have ever been acquired in the early stages of a budding career for a lesser price. On June 23, 1972 the Baltimore Bullets plucked Hayes from the Houston Rockets for Jack Marin (just off a 22.3 ppg. scoring season) and some soon-forgotten future considerations. But the future in this case belonged to the Bullets, for whom Hayes was an immediate club scoring pacesetter in 1972–73 and in seven of the next nine seasons as well.

Worst Trade in Franchise History

Walt Bellamy was the club's first high profile star and set a team single-season scoring mark in the first year of franchise history that still stands today. After pacing the team in scoring in each of the first four franchise seasons (two in Chicago and two in Baltimore), the number-one pick of the 1961 draft was sent to the New York Knicks on the eve of the 1965 season for Johnny Egan, Jim Barnes, Johnny Green and cash. Bellamy would eventually extend his 20,000-point career another full decade after leaving the Baltimore Bullets.

Washington Bullets Historical Oddity

Induction ceremonies during the fall of 1989 at the Naismith Memorial Basketball Hall of Fame saw three of the four inductees representing a single NBA franchise—the Washington (neé Baltimore) Bullets. It was the proudest of days for Bullets fans everywhere when Elvin Hayes, Earl Monroe and Dave Bing were all sanctioned as immortals of the game with the same memorable celebration. For this was the first and only time that as many as three players from a single team have simultaneously been accepted into basketball's primary shrine at Springfield, Massachusetts.

Bullets All-Time Number One Draft Picks List

Chicago Packers
1961 Walt Bellamy (Indiana)
Chicago Zephyrs
1962 Billy McGill (Utah)
Baltimore Bullets
1963 Rod Thorn (West Virginia)
1964 Gary Bradds (Ohio State)
1965 Jerry Sloan (Evansville)

1966 Jack Marin (Duke)
1967 Earl Monroe (Winston-Salem)
1968 Wes Unseld (Louisville)
1969 Mike Davis (Virginia Union)
1970 George Johnson (Stephen Austin)
1971 Stan Love (Oregon)
1972 None

Capital Bullets
1973 Nick Weatherspoon (Illinois)

Washington Bullets
1974 Len Elmore (Maryland)
1975 Kevin Grevey (Kentucky)
1976 Mitch Kupchak (North Carolina)
1977 Greg Ballard (Oregon)
1978 Roger Phegley (Bradley)
1979 None
1980 Wes Matthews (Wisconsin)
1981 Frank Johnson (Wake Forest)
1982 None
1983 Jeff Malone (Mississippi State)
1984 Mel Turpin (Kentucky)
1985 Kenny Green (Wake Forest)
1986 John Williams (LSU)
1987 Tyrone "Muggsy" Bogues (Wake Forest)
1988 Harvey Grant (Oklahoma)
1989 Tom Hammonds (Georgia)
1990 None
1991 LaBradford Smith (Louisville)
1992 Tom Gugliotta (North Carolina State)
1993 Calbert Cheaney (Indiana)

Chapter 10

SACRAMENTO KINGS AND CINCINNATI (ROCHESTER) ROYALS

If At First You Don't Succeed, Move and Move and Move Again

All-Time Franchise Record: 1728–1989, .465 Pct. (1946–1994)
NBA Record: 1953–1960, .458 Pct.; NBL Record: 75–29, .721 Pct.
NBA Championships (1): 1950–51
Greatest Franchise Player: Oscar Robertson (1960–1970)
All-Time Leading Scorer: Oscar Robertson (22,009 Points, 1960–1970)
Most Successful Coach: Les Harrison (295–181, .620 Pct., 1948–1955)
All-Time Franchise Team: Sam Lacey (C), Jack Twyman (F), Jerry Lucas (F), Oscar
  Robertson (G), Nate Archibald (G)

"Traveling" is a distinct rules violation in the sport of basketball (though one that is at best loosely interpreted in this age of the Michael Jordan "three-steps-and-a-glide" flights toward the bucket). But no one apparently ever told that to the people who, over the years, have owned and transported around the country the professional basketball team variously known as the Rochester Royals, Cincinnati Royals, Kansas City-Omaha Kings, Kansas City Kings, and finally Sacramento Kings. Perhaps one should not be quite so confident about "finality" here, for the Honolulu Regals may be only a few more losing seasons down the road.

All this endless searching for the perfect basketball homeland has, in the end, meant but a single championship banner. It is an ultimate irony staring this franchise smack in the face, but that single title was garnered several years before the club packed up its trunks in Rochester and began its endless westward odyssey. The rest of the Royals/Kings story is a tale of almost incessant losing. Over a stretch of 48 years one of the league's remaining original eight franchises has posted 30 losing campaigns, including the last eleven in a row. They have sat on the post-season sidelines 26 times, more than any of the other five-decade NBA franchises. They have never made it back to the championship round since their 1951 title and have escaped the playoff first round a mere five times over that same lengthy span. First the Royals, and then the Kings, have given basketball losing a new definition.

Yet despite this penchant for dismal play the Royals and Kings have nonetheless had their share of proud courtside moments and their spate of boasting points as well. This club can, after all, still claim the sport's greatest all-time player (sorry Chicago Bulls fans). It also owns basketball's strangest all-time trade and its darkest individual player tragedy. And all across the sport's first legitimate pro decade, only the Minneapolis Lakers franchise with George Mikan could boast of more stars, victories, or year-in and year-out on-court success.

The Rochester Royals, it should today be remembered, were once something of a phenomenal basketball success story during the growing-pain era of pro basketball's miraculous start-up. The first four years of club history witnessed four straight first-place divisional finishes and regular-season ''best-record'' titles in three different leagues. During its first eight years, the Rochester club never failed to win less than 41 contests and thus never slipped below second place at the end of any campaign.

Two obstacles beyond their control would eventually sabotage the ongoing efforts of the Royals' to climb to the pinnacle as basketball's first true pro dynasty team. For one thing, they never could seem to survive when it came to post-season play. For another, they were doomed by the very town that so enthusiastically supported them. As the new pro circuit grew in popularity throughout the fifties, the Rochester franchise simply outgrew its small-town backwater home. Basketball would soon become a sport demanding large arenas and large crowds and national media attention to fill the coffers. Once the ballclub headed westward to Cincinnati and entered a big-time venue, however, Royals basketball never again seemed to be quite the same.

Rochester Royals—Playing in the Shadow of the Lakers

The history of the team once known as ''Royals'' certainly started out on a high enough note. The Rochester Royals were not only a treasured part of the original NBA family, but the Rochester outfit was, in early seasons, one of the league's most potent clubs as well. They stormed through three different leagues—the NBL, the BAA, and eventually, the renamed NBA—trailing in the wake of no one except their bitter rivals, the Minneapolis Lakers. And but for a few post-season bad breaks and the lack of a dominant big man to compete successfully against towering George Mikan or with Philadelphia's hook-shooting Neil Johnston, Rochester might well have been the biggest story from the first decade of NBA basketball. As it was the team led by backcourt aces Bob Davies and Bobby Wanzer was certainly one of the biggest stories.

If Mikan was pro basketball's first big-man hero, then Rochester's Bob Davies was the sport's first true backcourt hero. A decade before Cousy it was Bob Davies who was displaying dazzling backcourt artistry and entertaining small if enthusiastic pro basketball crowds with his scoring and wizard-like ballhandling. Known as "The Harrisburg Houdini," the two-time All-American from Seton Hall displayed remarkable dribbling abilities and pioneered the behind-the-back dribble and pass which Bob Cousy would popularize a few seasons later. And Davies had a talented backcourt partner to complement his often spectacular play. Bobby Wanzer filled the other guard spot for Rochester and teamed with Davies and 6'9" center Arnie ("Stilts") Risen as one of the team's three consistent double-figure scorers.

The infant Rochester Royals launched their earliest success run under the careful tutelage of Ed Malanowicz and posted a 30–13 ledger in the National Basketball League's first post-World War II season. With the addition of veteran Dolly King (a 6'4" center-forward) and rookie Arnie Johnson (6'5" forward-center) to a lineup of Bob Davies, George Glamack, Al Cervi and Red Holzman, the Royals seemed to have no peer in the league throughout much of the season. The Chicago American Gears team enjoyed a sudden revival in late season, however, when George Mikan joined the club after sitting out six weeks in a contract dispute, and player-coach Bobby McDermott joined the team as well in a trade, after wearing out his welcome with a series of locker room brawls while playing for the Fort Wayne Pistons. Mikan and McDermott gave Chicago one of the sport's first great inside-outside combinations that was enough to over-power Oshkosh and Indianapolis on the way to a post-season championship showdown with the suddenly not-so-dominant Royals. A tough Rochester defense held Mikan in check for a single game and keyed a 71–65 opening victory. Then the Chicago "monster of the middle" exploded for 27 and 23 points and Chicago was off to a three-game sweep and the league title. Rochester had tasted Mikan's dominance for the first, but certainly not the final time, and Bob Davies and company probably already sensed that the new big man would be a thorn in their sides for many seasons to come.

The NBL season which followed had to be greeted with enthusiasm by Rochester fans, since the Royals returned to the fray every bit as strong as a year earlier, while George Mikan and his Chicago Gears outfit were now taken out of the league and out of the title running. Gears' owner Maurice White was so inspired by his club's immediate NBL successes that he decided to form a 24-team circuit of his own to showcase his star Mikan and control more of the anticipated profits for himself. The over-ambitious plans collapsed almost immediately, to the surprise of few observers of the infant sport. The unanticipated result of all this over-expansion was the awarding during the season's first month of George Mikan to a first-year club known as the Minneapolis Lakers. Minneapolis already possessed former Sanford star Jim Pollard and was an immediate title threat with the addition of Mikan.

Rochester seized the opportunity presented by the dismantling of the Chicago Gears to post a league-best 44–16 record and edged out the strengthened Minneapolis team by a single game. The Royals were doomed in post-season tournament play, however, when leading scorer Arnie Risen was sidelined with a broken jaw and Bob Davies slowed by a lame ankle. Rochester could manage to capture but one game in the finals, against Minneapolis, and did little to contain their nemesis Mikan who poured in 110 points for a series average of 27.5 ppg.

Mikan again left the NBL in the fall of 1948, this time taking his act over to the rapidly growing east coast-based Basketball Association of America. This of course left the championship door wide open for clubs remaining behind in the crippled National League. But unfortunately for Rochester fans coveting a championship banner, the Royals moved right along with Mikan into the tougher, younger, yet more profitable league.

If the Royals were still intimidated by Mikan and his mates in their new home with the BAA, they hardly showed it at the outset of the new campaign. Les Harrison now had control from the bench for an entire season and guided his talented club to a league-best 45–15 record and a narrow one-game Western Division lead over the Minneapolis team. The Royals seemed on fire down the stretch when they captured 27 of the season's final 32 contests. Post-season play brought an immediate cool down, unfortunately, and Mikan's scoring and rebounding was enough to brush Rochester aside in two straight games of the Western Division finals. Stellar guard Bob Davies was the league's leader in assists during that third season of BAA play (Rochester's first in the league) while center Arnie Risen paced the circuit in field goal percentage (.423) and the ballclub in point making (16.6 ppg).

The BAA would take a giant step forward in the fall of 1949 as it changed both its name and its image and accepted several new teams into the circuit as a result of a merger with the suddenly moribund rival National League. Playing in their third different league in three seasons, the Royals under Les Harrison simply continued their pattern of winning despite the novel surroundings and stronger rivals. The key to a 51-victory season was clearly the club's outstanding homecourt play which saw the team roll off 23 consecutive home court victories for a still-standing franchise mark. League standards would also fall to this home floor streaking as the club's .971 (33–1) home winning percentage would remain the second best in NBA history behind the 1985–86 Boston Celtics (.976, 40–1). Yet, if most clubs in the league couldn't match up successfully with Harrison's Royals, one team definitely could. Finishing in a flatfooted tie with Rochester at 51–17, George Mikan's Minneapolis Lakers were awarded the division flag after a one-game, 78–76 tie-breaker in Rochester at season's end. When post-season play opened the following week Rochester fell quickly in a surprising two-game mini-series with Fort Wayne, clearing the way for Minneapolis to cop the first-ever official "NBA" crown.

The Royals had now been knocking on the door for four straight seasons; it was time to break through to victory or seriously consider some kind of drastic overhaul of team personnel. Fortunately for long-frustrated Royals boosters as well as veteran Royals players, the breakthrough would precede the overhaul in a most timely fashion. For one of the rare times in the club's first half-dozen seasons the Royals did not top all challengers for the best regular-season mark. But the team that had trailed the champion Lakers down to the regular-season wire was ready to sweep aside repeated Laker challenges throughout their Western Division title matchup. Reversing the fortunes of the past two seasons, it was Rochester which swept three straight close games after dropping the series opener.

The championship series matching two old rivals—the Royals and Knicks—was the best yet seen in the youthful NBA. The deciding seventh-game matchup is still mentioned four decades later as one of the most exciting title games of NBA history. The series looked like a runaway at the outset as the Royals routed the Knicks twice in Rochester and then took a commanding 3–0 lead on the strength of a 78–71 road victory. New York fought back to claim three straight of their own and force a deciding contest in Rochester. The nip-and-tuck rubber match was not to be decided until the final minute of play, when two free throws by Davies and a layup by Jack Coleman provided the only NBA title in Royals-Kings history. The 79–75 title victory had been a true team triumph with the "big three" of Davies, Risen and Wanzer combining for 57 points and 27 rebounds, to pace the most memorable victory in franchise annals.

Rochester basketball of this vintage had more to offer the sport than a single isolated championship run. The ballclub over the years would also be involved in some of the young league's most memorable individual contests. It was the Royals, for example, who participated in one unforgettable outing that still reigns as the roundball sport's longest game. On the evening of January 6, 1951 3,300 patrons in Rochester's Edgerton Sports Arena sat through an unparalleled marathon contest which stretched out for six overtime sessions before the hometown club eventually fell victim to the Indianapolis Olympians, 75–73. In an era before the institution of the 24-second shot clock, these two ball control teams increasingly slowed the tempo in the strategic moments of overtime play. Two of the extra sessions had no points scored at all. Red Holzman, later of New York Knicks coaching fame, played seventy-six of the game's seventy-eight minutes at guard for the losers.

The Royals were simply not destined to repeat as champions in 1952. This was still a formidable enough team to return to another resting place in first spot throughout the winter-long campaign. A regular-season record of 41–25 was nearly identical to the title-winning campaign. But again the playoffs would prove an insurmountable stumbling block. Fort Wayne was swept aside in two games with little resistance. But Mikan and the Lakers were back on championship track and not to be headed off two years in a row. Minneapolis picked up the needed road victory in game-two at Rochester and then followed up with two rugged homecourt wins to close out the overmatched Les Harrison team during the Western Division showdown. Davies, Wanzer and Risen all finished the year among the league's top ten point-makers and Wanzer reigned as the circuit's leading free throw shooter. A highlight of an only slightly disappointing season was a then league-record 124 points, scored by the Royals in a late February game against the Baltimore Bullets.

One story of true tragedy and another of lasting inspiration also highlight the final years of the Rochester Royals. And the two tales, along with their teammate protagonists, are forever linked one with the other. Maurice Stokes, a black 6'7" forward out of St. Francis College of Pennsylvania, had been an immediate sensation as NBA Rookie of the Year in 1956, then had continued his front-court power game during the club's final Rochester year and its first Cincinnati season as well. Jack Twyman was a hardworking 6'6" white University of Cincinnati star who joined the league the same year as Stokes, and teamed with the rookie sensation to provide one of the league's most potent inside combos. While a lesser star his first several seasons, Twyman would hit full stride by the end of the '50s, and eventually evolve into one of the best pure-shooting forwards from the first two decades of the NBA. Fate stepped in to join Stokes and Twyman forever, when a sudden horrible turn of events left Maurice Stokes crippled for life at the very height of his budding basketball career.

In mid-March of the first Royals season in Cincinnati, Maurice Stokes would crash to the floor during the final regular season game at Cincinnati Gardens and receive a severe blow to the head, which rendered him unconscious. Three nights later, the star forward would again collapse on a plane flight returning the team to Cincinnati immediately following an opening playoff loss to Detroit. A once-graceful athlete, Mo Stokes had been struck down and left a life-long invalid by a rare form of brain damage to his motor control centers. Teammate Jack Twyman would soon be named legal guardian of Stokes and would, for years, tirelessly organize an off-season charity game designed to raise funds for the crippled ex-star (and later for other needy former players from the game's earliest days). The tragic fate of Maurice Stokes was a truly dark moment that would soon cast a long shadow over the ballclub's next stop in Cincinnati.

Cincinnati Royals—Stage for the Game's Greatest Player

One has to search long and wide to find any pro sports franchise more thoroughly associated in fans' minds with a single player. Not only was Oscar Robertson the mainstay of the usually lackluster Cincinnati team for most of their fifteen-year history—the team's one single showcase feature—but the Big O was, in point of fact, the very reason the Royals were no longer in Rochester in the first place.

The deal that brought the Royals to Cincinnati was a deal that had Oscar Robertson's name written all over it from the outset. The Royals and Pistons both escaped small-market cities at the beginning of the 1957 season, opting for larger venues with newer arenas and potentially larger crowds. Three years earlier, the young NBA suffered from the fact that exactly half its franchises were located in metropolitan centers with populations of less than a million; after the relocation of the Pistons to Detroit and the Royals to Cincinnati, only the Syracuse Nats were now left in such a market. But the Royals had their eye on something other than the box office when they pulled up stakes and headed west. The NBA's territorial draft ruling would allow the Royals first crack at the sensational Oscar Robertson, who would complete his collegiate eligibility in the spring of 1960. Never before or since—not even in the case of the expansion Milwaukee Bucks and Lew Alcindor—has any NBA team leaped through quite so big a hoop in order to obtain the coveted rookie of their choice. The Bucks would later deal off nearly a full starting five to get Alcindor; the Royals traded away a city to assure a crack at Oscar. As it would ironically transpire two years down the road, Cincinnati finished dead last in the entire NBA in 1960 and the Royals thus were guaranteed the first draft selection—and thus Oscar—without any need to invoke territorial prerogative.

The case has often been made—and with good reason—that Oscar Robertson was the finest and most complete player in all of basketball history. The argument still seems reasonable, even in the wake of the career of media-hero Michael Jordan. Those who will not consider Oscar in Michael Jordan's league simply never saw the game's greatest ''complete player'' in action. Robertson not only had all the tools, he also had to play nightly against a bevy of superstars that were among the game's finest. Night after night he faced the likes of Russell, Chamberlain, etc. There was nothing like coasting against the Mavericks or Clippers or Pacers back in 1965.

And Oscar Robertson's statistical achievements are simply outstanding and make the achievements of almost any modern-era superstar—save only Michael Jordan—pale by comparison. While broadcasters and sportswriters today rave endlessly about players achieving a ''triple-double'' (double figures in scoring, rebounding and assists) it seems to escape notice that Oscar came dangerously close to **averaging** a triple-double for the entire first decade of his career, before slowing in the rebound department across four final seasons. And in a rookie season that may have been the finest ever, he missed the feat of a full season's triple-double by only a hairline fraction in the rebound department.

Robertson also had an amazing overnight impact on both the Cincinnati Royals and the league as a whole. His rookie campaign was the third in a string of the three greatest debut seasons in league history, all strung out back-to-back as the '50s opened up into the '60s. First Elgin Baylor, then Wilt Chamberlain, and finally Oscar—each swept into the league as though there was no such thing as a strenuous adjustment to the high-notch professional game.

Basketball's Three Greatest Rookie Seasons

Year	Player	Team	PPG	Points	Rebounds	Assists
1958–59	Elgin Baylor	Minneapolis	24.9	1742	1050	287
1959–60	Wilt Chamberlain	Philadelphia	**37.6**	**2707**	**1941**	168
1960–61	Oscar Robertson	Cincinnati	30.5	2165	716	**690**

Oscar had not only previous-year rookie sensation Wilt Chamberlain to pursue in the battle for individual scoring honors, but fellow freshman Jerry West as well. The Big O would never quite overall Chamberlain, but when it came to his former collegiate rival and Olympic teammate, West Virginia sharpshooter Jerry West, the Cincinnati backcourt ace barely managed the upper hand. West would eventually amass 25,192 career points (eighth all-time) over his 14 seasons (and would have posted a ton more had the three-point line been in effect); Oscar finished a couple of rungs up the ladder, with 26,710 total points (5th) over a career that spanned exactly the same years as West's (1960–1974). West would win a single scoring title and thus nip Oscar in this category, as well as in lifetime scoring average (27.0 to 25.7). A rookie scoring battle never materialized, however, as the Lakers' "Mr. Outside took a back seat to LA's Mr. Inside, Elgin Baylor, and averaged only 17.6 in his first NBA campaign. Robertson also trailed Baylor as well as Chamberlain in the league scoring race, but outdistanced all rookies in just about every statistical category imaginable.

The Royals did not qualify for any post-season action in Oscar's first year, but they were there like clockwork over the next half-dozen. Under second-year coach Charles Wolf, the team climbed above .500 and into second slot in the division in '61–'62. Oscar had meant an improvement of 14 victories for the Royals in his rookie campaign and another upswing of ten victories by 1962. Cincinnati did not last long against the Pistons in only its second playoff appearance in seven years. Two of the Royals' four losses were by one point, however, and the only blowout contest of the five-game matchup was the one in which Cincinnati triumphed 129–107. The 1962 season as a whole was remarkable for the fact that five individuals (Chamberlain, Bellamy, Pettit and West besides Robertson) averaged better than 30 ppg. and the entire league scored at a clip (118.9) not to be matched again until the final winter of the 1970s.

Over his ten years in the Queen City of Cincinnati, the Big O averaged only an eyelash below 30 ppg. across nearly 800 contests. He was an All-Star fixture for the duration and also the league's unanimous MVP selection in 1963–64. It was that 1964 season that was, by all measures, Oscar's finest and the one in which the Cincinnati Royals briefly peaked. The club's 55 wins were the most in franchise history (a record that still stands) and thus topped any of the best Rochester years. Everyone around the NBA circuit— including the players in the Royals locker room, knew that Oscar was surrounded by the most talented and balanced NBA team. But championships are always won on hardwood and not on paper, and just as Wilt was always there to bar Oscar from individual scoring titles, so too were the Celtics a championship roadblock that was, in the end, always insurmountable.

It was the clearcut Boston dominance over the Royals and everyone else in the league that would once again turn Oscar Robertson's "Golden Year" into yet another campaign destined to end in failure and frustration. The Royals had been primed for a title as the '63–'64 season unfolded and to a man felt that this was the season that, at long last, should belong to them alone. Jerry Lucas was in his rookie season and now gave Oscar a big man to work with, and thus created for Cincinnati a "Mr. Inside-Mr. Outside" pair of their own. Lucas would average above 17 points and 17 rebounds per contest and trail only Chamberlain and Russell in the league's rebounding derby.

The Royals would stay on Boston's heels all season long, finishing a mere four paces back at the end of regular season play. Then while the Celtics, for the first time without Bob Cousy, waited through the bye round, the Royals and Oscar swapped games across a five-game set with the newly transplanted Syracuse Nats, now known as the Philadelphia 76ers. When the Boston-Cincinnati showdown materialized in round two, the now more potent Royals—with a frontcourt of Lucas, Jack Twyman, Wayne Embry and Tom Hawkins—were able to give the Celts a true run for their money. All but the lid lifter were close games turning on clutch fourth-quarter nail-biting action. But the Celtics were simply too deep and cruised to a five-game domination during the Eastern Conference finals. Boston would move on to a sixth straight world championship under Auerbach, while the Cincinnati Royals licked the wounds of a championship dream quickly derailed.

Cincinnati would never again come so close to an NBA title during the Robertson era, or during any of the eight years remaining in a short-lived franchise history. Three more first-round playoff losses would soon follow for the team now coached by veteran mentor Jim McMahon. Philadelphia would do the honors of eliminating Oscar and his mates in only four games on two of these occasions; a hard-fought loss to the Celtics in a series-stretching full five contests was sandwiched in between. When McMahon moved on to a combined coaching-GM slot with the expansion San Diego Rockets, Oscar's former college coach Ed Jucker took the helm and presided over a couple of break-even seasons, which featured near-misses in post-season play and a noticeable slide in Robertson's scoring totals from the stratospheric to the mere mortal (24.7 in '68–'69). Guard-forward Tom Van Arsdale, acquired in a late-season 1968 exchange with the Detroit Pistons, did pick up some of the scoring slack from the Big O in his first two full campaigns, averaging 19.4 and then 22.8 ppg. and providing rebounding help for veteran Jerry Lucas as well.

By the time Hall-of-Fame Boston Celtics star Bob Cousy took the coaching reigns in Cincy in May, 1969, the talent around Oscar Robertson and Jerry Lucas had thinned and the two franchise stars of the sixties had themselves began to lose a bit of their luster, if not their overall effectiveness. Ironically,

Cousy had been elected that same season for induction into the club Hall of Fame as the all-time favorite opponent, but his achievements as coach on the home team side would be hardly as lustrous. Oscar chaffed from the beginning under Cousy's handling and an era came crashing to an end when the all-time franchise player was traded off to Milwaukee in late-season, 1970, for guard Flynn Robinson and forward Charlie Paulk. Robertson's trade was actually the second blockbuster of the campaign, as Jerry Lucas had also been dealt to San Francisco only ten days into the season.

Cousy's first Royals edition, stripped first of Lucas and then of Oscar, wallowed in fifth place with an embarrassing 36–46 won-loss tally. And that was actually the best of the final three campaigns in Cincinnati Gardens. With its two showcase players now gone, local interest in the ballclub seemed to plummet almost as fast as the victory totals. Perhaps a single bright spot of the Cousy curtain-call years was the 1970 collegiate draft, which brought two players who rank inclusion on any all-time franchise all-star club. New Mexico State center Sam Lacey was grabbed with the fifth overall pick while Texas El Paso guard Nate "Tiny" Archibald was plucked from the second round. Few ballclubs have ever enriched themselves quite so quickly in a single afternoon of drafting, as these two rookies would combine the next season to average jointly 29.5 ppg., 14.2 rpg., and 6.9 assists-per-game.

On the 26th of March, the Cincinnati club would play its final contest under the label of its original namesake—the Royals. It would be a 135–122 season-ending victory at Cleveland. And it was a final hurrah for the time-honored franchise which would, next season, begin a journey westward on the nation's map, as well as a two-decade journey southward to the bottom of the NBA standings.

Kansas City Kings—Lost Years in America's Heartland

Thirteen seasons of the renamed "Kings" in Kansas City brought very little to cheer about for lower midwest fans who had once enjoyed the glory years of the St. Louis Hawks and Bob Pettit. These were certainly not the Hawks of the Pettit-era; and unfortunately they were no longer even the Royals of the Robertson-era. The Royals had been tantalizing near-misses in Rochester; in Cincinnati they were a high-profile disappointment featuring the league's best player and its largest penchant for underachievement. But once the club crossed the Mississippi there were no more near-misses and no more superstars. In retrospect, the late-season failures and underachievement had to look good in contrast to what followed.

If there was one truly ironic twist to the first season spent by the ex-Royals in Kansas City, it had to be the performance of guard Nate "Tiny" Archibald. Enjoying a career year, Archibald became the first franchise player to earn first-team all-NBA honors since Oscar had turned the trick in each of his first nine seasons in the league and in Cincinnati. Archibald also won a league scoring title, something that Oscar for all his weighty point totals had never done. In fact Tiny Archibald's one-year explosion in '72–'73 was nothing short of a season for all ages. Running the court like an unstoppable dervish, Tiny became the first player in history to pace the NBA (or NBL, BAA or ABA for that matter) in both scoring and assists at one and the same time. Thus in their first season in a new city the club again briefly owned the league's showcase player. But it would not last long, as Archibald quickly proved to be no second coming of the incomparable Big O.

The first several seasons for the former Cincinnati Royals in their new home west of the Mississippi was definitely a case of split franchise personality. First off the team would split their home playing dates between the Municipal Auditorium in downtown Kansas City and Omaha Civic Auditorium located 190 miles away in Nebraska. And the Kings turned out to be something of a Jekyll-and-Hyde outfit on their two home floors, posting a break-even 14–12 mark in K.C. but playing more like league leaders at 10–5 (.666 pct.) over in Omaha. The club hovered near playoff contention under Cousy, until the final 18 games of the season. They then went only 3 and 13 down the stretch run to finish ten games under .500 and dead last in the Midwest Division. More on the strength of bringing basketball to a new league venue in the Missouri valley than on any solid franchise building, General Manager Joe Axelson received a nod from *The Sporting News* as NBA Executive of the Year.

And if the club was now divided between Missouri and Nebraska, it also stood with one foot planted deeply in a proud past and another anchored tentatively within a mediocre present. There was the burden of the regal-sounding club name and lofty achievements in Rochester as well as the crowning jewel of Oscar Robertson's undying legend in Cincinnati. And there was now a new image and name as "Kings" transported to unfamiliar surroundings and hung with new colors, logo and traditions. Unfortunately the image proved anything but regal as the ballclub quickly dressed itself in the cloak of losers.

The Kings did finally settle on a permanent home in Kansas City in 1975. Omaha was dropped from the club name, although a few games were still played at the team's second residence up in Nebraska. There they would remain for exactly a decade of more or less uninspired play. Phil Johnson (155–196, 4 seasons plus) and Cotton Fitzsimmons (248–244, 6 seasons) would handle the bulk of he coaching duties across this stretch. And Ron Boone (former ABA standout with the Utah Stars) along with Otis Birdsong (with 20 ppg. plus in three of his four seasons) would follow Tiny Archibald as showcase backcourt players. Sam Lacey would play the bulk of his games in the pivot during this era and compile numbers that would leave him the all-time franchise leader in games played, rebounds, steals and blocked shots, as well as in personal fouls. But seven of ten seasons would be losers between the mid-seventies and mid-eighties. And four playoffs appearances would do little to wash out the losers image with only one trip past the first round of action.

The Kings did enjoy one brief run at prosperity at the very end of he '70s and the outset of the 1980s. Back in 1975 Phil Johnson had engineered the club's first trip to post-season play in eight seasons and had captured NBA Coach of the Year honors for his surprising success with the also-ran franchise. But Johnson could produce only one winning campaign in four years at the helm and it would be left to Cotton Fitzsimmons to light a fire under the Kings in 1979 (48–34, first place) and again in 1980 (47–35, second place). If Fitzsimmons had any measurable advantage over his immediate predecessors on the Kings' bench it had to be the arrival of flashy backcourt performer Phil Ford. Ford stormed into the league from the campus of the University of North Carolina and earned rookie-of-the-year honors on the strength of balanced scoring and skillful floor generalship. One highlight of Phil Ford's stellar rookie campaign was a record-breaking performance against the Milwaukee Bucks on February 21, 1979, an outing which saw the Kings' newest floor leader tie Oscar Robertson's franchise single-game standard of 22 assists.

In 1980–81, the third campaign under Fitzsimmons, the team dropped back to more familiar sub-.500 surroundings yet somehow managed to limp home once again as a divisional runner-up. An upset first-found playoff triumph over Portland in three hard-fought games seemed somehow to coalesce a starting lineup of Scott Wedman, Reggie King, Sam Lacey, Ernie Grunfeld and Phil Ford into one of the true surprises of one of the league's most topsy-turvy post-season round-robins in years. Wedman and King both averaged above 20 ppg. for the tournament duration and the upstart Kings lasted all the way to the Western Conference finals before elimination by Houston put an end to the Cinderella spree.

Four final seasons in Kansas City would bring another particularly arid stretch of play and only one additional winning compaign. The 1983 club managed to keep its head barely above water, but despite a Midwest Division runner-up spot and a ledger eight games above .500 KC still didn't manage to make it into the post-season round robin. Ironically enough, the following year's edition would slip below a break-even record and fall two notches to fourth place and yet become a post-season invitee under the NBA's imbalanced playoff format. Cotton Fitzsimmons was gone at the conclusion of 1984 after six seasons at the helm. While Fitzsimmons' tenure had been the lengthiest since Les Harrison in the early fifties, his successor, Jack McKinney, would fail to make it ten games into the new campaign. McKinney saw the handwriting on the wall with the inept '84–'85 Kings and relinquished the reins back to former Kings mentor Phil Johnson before the final Kansas City season was even off the ground.

Sacramento Kings—A Continuous Legacy of Losing

Some things never seem to improve noticeably, no matter how much tinkering is invested in them. The story of professional basketball in the city of Sacramento, for example, so far remains one of the losingest sagas in all of American sport. This is a franchise that has not enjoyed a single winning season nor won a single post-season game since way back in 1983, two seasons before the club's move over to the west coast. Nor have there been any mega-stars wearing the powder blue colors of the doormat Sacramento Kings. One has to search quite long and hard to find anything colorful about this team that has finished fifth, sixth or seventh in every divisional race they have ever entered.

If little upbeat can be said about the Sacramento Kings franchise, it is nonetheless true that the city's support for this team is a surprising gage to the overall health of the modern-era NBA. As long as the Michael Jordans or Patrick Ewings or David Robinsons are wearing uniforms for the visitors, local fans will pour through the gates to see the celebrity stars of the league perform. It seems to make little difference whether the home team wins very often or ever itself puts quality stars on the floor. After all, even benchwarmers are celebrity stars in today's high profile NBA; and there simply aren't any NBA clubs who suffer much at the turnstiles.

Sacramento is a special NBA success story, however. Fans in the California capital city have witnessed in person just one playoff game through the span of nine full years. They have missed out on post-season play entirely for the past eight. Yet entering the '93–'94 campaign, those same long-suffering fans had packed Arco Arena (capacity 17,014) for 329 consecutive sellouts, beginning with the arena inaugural on November 8, 1988. Only the Portland Trail Blazers and Boston Celtics can currently boast longer home sellout strings.

While Kings fans have not had many victories to cheer over the last decade, they have nonetheless been treated to homecourt displays of athleticism by a number of talented young performers. Scoring guard Mitch Richmond has been the franchise jewel of recent years since being acquired from Golden State in early 1992. The Kings sent their number one draft pick (third overall) Billy Owens to the Warriors for the 1989 NBA Rookie of the Year. Since coming to Sacramento Richmond has paced the club in scoring three straight seasons and reached a high of 23.4 ppg. in 1994. Mitch Richmond is also the first leading NBA rookie since the Kings own Phil Ford in 1979 to actually improve his personal scoring totals during his second and third seasons in the league. Besides Richmond, Lionel Simmons and Walt Williams have also flashed moments over the past three seasons. Simmons is a 6'7" forward and first round draft pick (1990) who has scored 30 or more points fifteen times; Williams posted the fourth highest first year scoring totals (17.0, behind Oscar Robertson, Lionel Simmons and Jerry Lucas) in franchise history during his 1993 debut year.

The remainder of the Kings' roster over the past decade has reflected the club's seemingly inherent mediocre status. Wayman Tisdale reigned as the club scoring leader for several seasons before Mitch Richmond but has never quite lived up to his early promise with the Indiana Pacers. Spud Webb remains a novelty who earns admiration for remaining in the league at his diminutive 5'7" stature, yet rarely challenges point guards from the better clubs around the league. Indeed the important point guard slot has remained largely a wasteland for the Kings until the 1994 Draft brought hope with Duke All-American Bob Hurley (seventh player picked), owner of two collegiate national championships and a much-needed winning attitude.

If Hurley offered a glimmer of hope to end the long Sacramento doldrums, it was a brief hope indeed. For the 1993–94 season was yet another gloomy winter for the hapless Kings in their never-ending west coast journey through one catastrophe after another. This time the tragedy was truly one befitting the often over-used term. Hurley was barely out of the starting gate for his heralded debut season when a November automobile accident less than a mile from Arco Arena nearly ended the player's life. Bob Hurley was thrown from his truck and lay in a hospital bed in guarded condition for weeks after the crash. With Hurley out of the lineup and his basketball career now in serious jeopardy, the Kings could boast nothing but the solo scoring of yeoman guard Mitch Richmond (23.4 ppg.). The team thus limped to another 28–54 marker, escaping the cellar by a single game in the standings. While prospects did seem improved by the end of the long campaign that Hurley might someday return to basketball, there was little optimism surrounding such speedy recovery for the franchise itself. There was, after all, sufficiently little reason to believe that the Kings could rebound quite as quickly to anything that remotely resembled solid basketball health.

Suggested Readings on Cincinnati Royals (Sacramento Kings)

Berkow, Ira. **Oscar Robertson—the Gold Year, 1964**. New York: McFadden-Bartell Books, 1972.

Bjarkman, Peter C. **The History of the NBA**. New York and Avenel, New Jersey: Crescent Books (Outlet Books, Random House), 1992.

Koppett, Leonard. **24 Seconds to Shoot: An Informal History of the National Basketball Association**. New York and London: Collier-Macmillan, 1968 (1970).

Sacramento Kings Retired Uniform Numbers (5)

Bob Davies (11)
Maurice Stokes (12)
Oscar Robertson (14)
Jack Twyman (27)
Sam Lacey (44)

Year-by-Year Sacramento Kings (Cincinnati Royals) Summary

Season	Record	Finish	Coach(es)	Scoring Leader(s)	Playoffs (W-L Record)

Key: * = Tie for Position; # = League Scoring Leader

Rochester Royals
National Basketball League

Season	Record	Finish	Coach(es)	Scoring Leader(s)	Playoffs (W-L Record)
1946–47	31–13	1st	Ed Malanowicz	Al Cervi (14.4)	Lost in NBL Finals (6–5)
1947–48	44–16	1st	Ed Malanowicz Les Harrison	Arnie Risen (14.5)	Lost in NBL Finals (6–5)

Basketball Association of American

| 1948–49 | 45–15 | 1st | Les Harrison | Arnie Risen (16.6) | Lost in 2nd Round (2–2) |

National Basketball Association

1949–50	51–17	1st*	Les Harrison	Bob Davies (14.0)	Lost in 1st Round (0–2)
1950–51	41–27	2nd	Les Harrison	Arnie Risen (16.3)	**NBA Champion (9–5)**
1951–52	41–25	1st	Les Harrison	Bob Davies (16.2)	Lost in 2nd Round (3–3)
1952–53	44–26	2nd	Les Harrison	Bob Davies (15.6)	Lost in 1st Round (1–2)
1953–54	44–28	2nd	Les Harrison	Bobby Wanzer (13.3)	Lost in 2nd Round (3–3)
1954–55	29–43	3rd	Les Harrison	Bobby Wanzer (13.1)	Lost in 1st Round (1–2)
1955–56	31–41	4th	Bobby Wanzer	Maurice Stokes (16.8)	Did Not Qualify
1956–57	31–41	4th	Bobby Wanzer	Jack Twyman (16.3)	Did Not Qualify

Cincinnati Royals

1957–58	33–39	3rd	Bobby Wanzer	Clyde Lovellette (23.4)	Lost in 1st Round (0–2)
1958–59	19–53	4th	Bobby Wanzer Tom Marshall	Jack Twyman (25.8)	Did Not Qualify
1959–60	19–56	4th	Tom Marshall	Jack Twyman (31.2)	Did Not Qualify
1960–61	33–46	4th	Charles Wolf	Oscar Robertson (30.5)	Did Not Qualify
1961–62	43–37	2nd	Charles Wolf	Oscar Robertson (30.8)	Lost in 1st Round (1–3)
1962–63	42–38	3rd	Charles Wolf	Oscar Robertson (28.3)	Lost in 2nd Round (6–6)
1963–64	55–25	2nd	Jack McMahon	Oscar Robertson (31.4)	Lost in 2nd Round (4–6)
1964–65	48–32	2nd	Jack McMahon	Oscar Robertson (30.4)	Lost in 1st Round (1–3)
1965–66	45–35	3rd	Jack McMahon	Oscar Robertson (31.3)	Lost in 1st Round (2–3)
1966–67	39–42	3rd	Jack McMahon	Oscar Robertson (30.5)	Lost in 1st Round (1–3)
1967–68	39–43	5th	Ed Jucker	Oscar Robertson (29.2)	Did Not Qualify
1968–69	41–41	5th	Ed Jucker	Oscar Robertson (24.7)	Did Not Qualify
1969–70	36–46	5th	Bob Cousy	Oscar Robertson (25.3)	Did Not Qualify
1970–71	33–49	3rd	Bob Cousy	Tom Van Arsdale (22.9)	Did Not Qualify
1971–72	30–52	3rd	Bob Cousy	Nate Archibald (28.2)	Did Not Qualify

Kansas City-Omaha Kings

1972–73	36–46	4th	Bob Cousy	Nate Archibald (34.0)#	Did Not Qualify
1973–74	33–49	4th	Bob Cousy Draff Young Phil Johnson	Jimmy Walker (19.8)	Did Not Qualify
1974–75	44–38	2nd	Phil Johnson	Nate Archibald (26.5)	Lost in 1st Round (2–4)

Kansas City Kings

1975–76	31–51	3rd	Phil Johnson	Nate Archibald (24.8)	Did Not Qualify
1976–77	40–42	4th	Phil Johnson	Ron Boone (22.2)	Did Not Qualify
1977–78	31–51	5th*	Phil Johnson Larry Staverman	Ron Boone (17.7)	Did Not Qualify
1978–79	48–34	1st	L. Fitzsimmons	Otis Birdsong (21.7)	Lost in 1st Round (1–4)
1979–80	47–35	2nd	L. Fitzsimmons	Otis Birdsong (22.7)	Lost in 1st Round (1–2)
1980–81	40–42	2nd*	L. Fitzsimmons	Otis Birdsong (24.6)	Lost in 3rd Round (7–8)

Season	Record	Finish	Coach(es)	Scoring Leader(s)	Playoffs (W-L Record)
1981–82	30–52	4th	L. Fitzsimmons	Cliff Robinson (20.2)	Did Not Qualify
1982–83	45–37	2nd*	L. Fitzsimmons	Larry Drew (20.1)	Did Not Qualify
1983–84	38–44	4th	L. Fitzsimmons	Eddie Johnson (21.9)	Lost in 1st Round (0–3)
1984–85	31–51	6th	Jack McKinney Phil Johnson	Eddie Johnson (22.9)	Did Not Qualify
Sacramento Kings					
1985–86	37–45	5th	Phil Johnson	Eddie Johnson (18.7)	Lost in 1st Round (0–3)
1986–87	29–53	5th	Phil Johnson Jerry Reynolds	Reggie Theus (20.3)	Did Not Qualify
1987–88	24–58	6th	Bill Russell Jerry Reynolds	Reggie Theus (21.6)	Did Not Qualify
1988–89	27–55	6th	Jerry Reynolds	Wayman Tisdale (17.5)	Did Not Qualify
1989–90	23–59	7th	Jerry Reynolds	Wayman Tisdale (22.3)	Did Not Qualify
1990–91	25–57	7th	Dick Motta	Antoine Carr (20.1)	Did Not Qualify
1991–92	29–53	7th	Dick Motta Rex Hughes	Mitch Richmond (22.5)	Did Not Qualify
1992–93	25–57	7th	Garry St. Jean	Mitch Richmond (21.9)	Did Not Qualify
1993–94	28–54	6th	Garry St. Jean	Mitch Richmond (23.4)	Did Not Qualify

Individual Career Leaders and Record Holders (1946–1994)

Scoring Average	Oscar Robertson (29.3 ppg., 1960–70)
Points Scored	Oscar Robertson (22,009, 1960–70)
Games Played	Sam Lacey (888, 1970–82)
Minutes Played	Oscar Robertson (33,068)
Field Goal Pct.	Johnny Green (.575, 1969–73)
3-Pt. Field Goals Made	Harold Pressley (208)
Free Throws Made	Oscar Robertson (6,583)
Free-Throw Pct.	Ron Boone (.848, 1976–78)
	Anthony "Spud" Webb (.843, 1991–94)
Rebounds	Sam Lacey (9,353, 1970–82)
Assists	Oscar Robertson (7,731)
Steals	Sam Lacey (950)
Blocked Shots	Sam Lacey (1,098)
Personal Fouls	Sam Lacey (3,127)

Individual Single-Season and Game Records (1946–1994)

Scoring Average	Nate Archibald (34.0 ppg., 1972–73)
Points Scored (Season)	Nate Archibald (2,719, 1972–73)
Points Scored (Game)	Jack Twyman (59, 1-15–60 vs. Minneapolis Lakers)
Field Goal Pct. (Season)	Steve Johnson (.624, 1982–83)
Free-Throw Pct. (Season)	Bobby Wanzer (.904, 1951–52)
3-Pt. Field Goals Made (Game)	Ricky Berry (7, 2-9–89 vs. Golden State Warriors)
Rebounds (Season)	Jerry Lucas (1,668, 1965–66)
Rebounds (Game)	Jerry Lucas (40, 2–29–64 at Philadelphia Sixers)

Assists (Season)	Nate Archibald (910, 1972–73)
Assists (Game)	Oscar Robertson (22, 10–29–61 and 3–5–66)
	Phil Ford (22, 2–21–79 vs. Milwaukee Bucks)
Steals (Season)	Brian Taylor (199, 1976–77)
Steals (Game)	Sam Lacey (8, 2–5–75 vs. Portland Trail Blazers)
	Danny Ainge (8, 4–22–89 vs. Los Angeles Clippers)
Blocked Shots (Season)	Duane Causwell (215, 1991–92)
Blocked Shots (Game)	Duane Causwell (9, 4–18–91 vs. Denver Nuggets)

Best Trade in Franchise History

This club hasn't made very many good deals, especially since they left the Queen City of Cincinnati. They did seem to come out on the top end, however, in a February 1989 transaction which brought high-scoring forward Wayman Tisdale from the Indian Pacers in exchange for LaSalle Thompson and Randy Wittman. Wittman was already at the end of the road, and LaSalle Thompson would prove to be even more unproductive and unmotivated in Indiana than he had been in Sacramento.

Worst Trade in Franchise History

Otis Thorpe is one of the most underrated frontcourt players in the NBA. The leaper can rebound with anyone and has been one of the yearly league leaders in field goal percentage throughout much of the past decade. Thorpe was certainly underrated by the Kings, who peddled him in October, 1988, to Houston for washed-up guard Rodney McCray and unproductive forward Jim Peterson. Thorpe had just been signed by Sacramento to a long-term free agent deal before he was sent to his new home in Houston.

Sacramento Kings Historical Oddity

Only once in sports history has a franchise actually relocated from one city to another for the sole purpose of acquiring a future star player. Other teams have traded away coaches for players, dealt whole rosters for a single player, or offered the equivalent of Fort Knox in gold to purchase a franchise-anchoring star. But it was the Kings (nee Royals) alone who traded a home city itself to get the single "franchise player" they once desired. The acquisition of Oscar Robertson through the territorial draft clause of the NBA constitution was the real reason why the successful Rochester Royals took their act on the road to the midwestern city of Cincinnati, Ohio. The club was sadly fated never again to be as successful with "The Big O" as they had always been with a roster of mere no-names in upstate New York. Nonetheless, it was the "Big O" who not only changed a ballclub's physical map site, but in the end also put the Royal's franchise squarely on the basketball map in the imagination of '60s NBA fans from coast to coast.

Kings (Royals) All-Time Number One Draft Picks List

Cincinnati Royals
1963 Tom Thacker (Cincinnati)
1964 George Wilson (Cincinnati)
1965 Nate Bowman (Wichita State)
1966 Walt Wesley (Kansas)
1967 Mel Daniels (New Mexico)
1968 Don Smith (Abdul Aziz) (Iowa State)
1969 Herm Gilliam (Purdue)
1970 Sam Lacey (New Mexico State)
1971 Ken Durrett (LaSalle)
1972 Nate Williams (Utah State)
Kansas City-Omaha Kings
1973 Ron Behagen (Minnesota)
1974 Scot Wedman (Colorado)
1975 Bill Robinzine (DePaul)
Kansas City Kings
1976 Richard Washington (UCLA)
1977 Otis Birdsong (Houston)
1978 Phil Ford (North Carolina)
1979 Reggie King (Alabama)
1980 Charles "Hawkeye" Whitney (North Carolina State)
1981 Steve Johnson (Oregon State)
1982 LaSalle Thompson (Texas)
1983 Ennis Whatley (Alabama) (Acquired in trade from Chicago Bulls)
1984 Otis Thorpe (Providence)
1985 Joe Kleine (Arkansas)
Sacramento Kings
1986 Harold Pressley (Villanova)
1987 Kenny Smith (North Carolina)
1988 Ricky Berry (San Jose State)
1989 Pervis Ellison (Louisville)
1990 Lionel Simmons (LaSalle)
1991 Billy Owens (Syracuse)
1992 Walt Williams (Maryland)
1993 Bobby Hurley (Duke)

Chapter 11

HOUSTON ROCKETS and SAN DIEGO ROCKETS

Manchild, The Twin Towers, and Mr. T

All-Time Franchise Record: 1073–1141, .485 Pct. (1967–1994)
NBA Championships (1): 1993–94
Greatest Franchise Player: Hakeem Olajuwon (1984–1994)
All-Time Leading Scorer: Calvin Murphy (17,949 Points, 1970–1983) and Hakeem Olajuwon (17,899 Points, 1984–1994)
Most Successful Coach: Rudy Tomjanovich (129–65, .665 Pct., 1992–1994)
All-Time Franchise Team: Hakeem Olajuwon (C), Moses Malone (C–F), Rudy Tomjanovich (F), Elvin Hayes (F), Calvin Murphy (G)

A handful on NBA teams are so completely wedded to the personality or career achievement—or perhaps both—of a single outstanding individual that one can not possibly think of the ballclub without thinking simultaneously of that ballplayer or club executive as well. Red Auerbach and the Boston Celtics are almost entirely synonymous terms. Chicago Bulls discussions will likely henceforth always conjure up Michael Jordan, no matter what else transpires with the history of the NBA ballclub in the Windy City. Nor will one ever again think of the Lakers without seeing images in the mind's eye of Magic Johnson or Kareem Abdul-Jabbar. And when the Houston Rockets are the topic of conversation it is impossible not to start, end, and fill up the space in between, with Rudy Tomjanovich.

Rudy "T" has been there for just about every moment of franchise history—he has seen both good and bad and played just about all the imaginable roles in team annals. Tomjanovich played for the club in a starring capacity for a dozen seasons (1970–81); he has also been a scout (1981–83) and he has subsequently coached as both an assistant (1983–92) and as the head man (1992–present). The five-time all-star, whose number

218

45 is one of two retired by the Rockets (along with Calvin Murphy's "23"), has thus been connected in one capacity or another with the ball-club in 24 of 27 seasons. He remains the third leading scorer in team history (his 13,383 points trail only Hakeem Olajuwon and Calvin Murphy who now stand in a virtual deadlock at the top of the list). Only Murphy and Olajuwon surpass him in career minutes logged in Houston, and Murphy alone played more games with the Rockets. And he is also the patient coach who has most recently led the 1993–94 edition of the Houston Rockets into the NBA finals in pursuit of their first-ever NBA championship crown.

The Houston Rockets were the surprise team of the early part of the season in '93–'94. With Hakeem establishing his reputation as a prime-time defensive enforcer and a veteran backcourt tandem of Vernon Maxwell and Kenny Smith directing a ball-control offensive, the Rockets left the Midwest Division in shock as they raced to 18 straight season-opening victories. An aggressive Houston defense keyed the victory skein with a new NBA record for consecutive games holding opponents to under 100 points. In a year which saw defense return to the NBA with a vengeance (ten clubs held opponents' scoring averages below 100 over the course of the season) Houston ultimately finished only fifth overall in point-average allowed, yet rode their early streak to a divisional title and second-best overall NBA record (58–24, which trailed only Pacific Division leader Seattle at 63–19). The club's second divisional title in a row was clinched in large part by Hakeem's first-ever league MVP season (27.3 ppg., 955 rebounds, 297 blocks). But Otis Thorpe (14.0 ppg.) Mario Elie (9.3 ppg.) and Robert Horry (9.9 ppg.) provided plenty of front-court strength and rookie guard Sam Cassell (192 assists) joined Maxwell and Smith to anchor one of the strongest backcourts in the league.

In post-season play, the Rockets again found themselves not receiving much respect from opponents or national media, especially after blowing a 20–point lead on their home floor at the Summit during the fourth quarter of conference semi-final Game Two with Phoenix. Down 0–2 after only two games with the defending conference champion Suns, the Rockets did show plenty of character, however, as they roared back with two hard-fought road victories and an eventual 4–2 series triumph. Over the long post-season haul this edition of Rudy T's Houston Rockets would finally prove their tenaciousness and their talent by sweeping past Karl Malone and the Utah Jazz in five games to claim a third franchise trip into the final round of NBA championship play.

A seven-game championship series with the Pat Riley-coached New York Knicks would prove a distinct disappointment for a new generation of NBA fans weaned in recent seasons on the spectacular post-season showmanship of Michael Jordan, Magic Johnson, Larry Bird and Isiah Thomas. The sequence of low scoring and sloppily played games featured tenacious defense that was effective, if not at all glamorous, as well as inconsistent shooting and erratic playmaking which convinced many observers that the league's two best teams could not actually be the ones still on the floor at season's end. A seventh game in Houston found the Rockets finally on top by a 90–83 mark in a game that was perhaps most memorable for the ineffectual second half shooting of the Knicks backcourt, especially point-guard John Starks, who suffered through a nightmarish 3-for-20 shooting performance. Even league MVP Hakeem Olajuwon seemed to disappear from view for long stretches of the "ugly" Finals series, which saw the lowest television ratings for NBA championship play in over a decade. But Olajuwon in the end was just effective enough to earn post-season MVP honors to go with his regular-season plaudits. And when the unartistic series finally wound down, it left fans wildly celebrating a first-ever NBA title in Houston, even if the majority of the nation's remaining hoop faithful seemed to share no other emotion than a sense of relief that one of the NBA's dullest championship rounds ever was at last mercifully over.

It was fitting that perhaps the best Houston team ever assembled had been directed and molded by Rudy Tomjanovich. Rudy T had been the pillar of many Houston clubs in the past as a high-scoring forward on every Rockets team that took the floor during the seventies and first two years of the eighties. He had been the Rockets' scoring leader four or five seasons in the mid-seventies with a career best 25.4 in 1974. And he had played nearly 800 games in a Houston uniform. But Rudy T was not around when the club started up in 1967–68, and when it launched its first opening-night lineup it was in San Diego, California, not in Houston, Texas. Robert Breitbard had acquired the expansion rights for the team that began operations as the San Diego Rockets and Breitbard had hired NBA veteran Jack McMahon to coach an expansion roster that included castoffs and journeymen like Don Kojis, Dave Gambee, Jon McGlocklin, John Barnhill and Toby Kimball. The team not only finished at the bottom of the Western Division with a league-high 67 losses but also managed to trail its fellow expansion entry, the Seattle SuperSonics, by eight full games in the last-place derby.

The Rockets made a huge jump for their second season, however. And that jump was the result largely of one superb draft selection out of the University of Houston named Elvin Hayes. Hayes took the league by storm with a 28.4 league-leading scoring average and 2327 points; the latter number would stand as a franchise record until cracked by Moses Malone in the early 1980s. Two future NBA coaches of note also played prominent roles on that early San Diego roster. Rick Adelman and Pat Riley both provided quality play off the bench, although the latter was limited to 56 games by injury. With increased firepower the Rockets leapfrogged by not only Seattle, but Phoenix and Chicago as well. The final ledger was 37–45 and a fourth-place finish. Even a first-round playoff loss to the newly relocated Atlanta Hawks could hardly dim what had been a most surprising upbeat season.

The presence of Hayes gave the team considerable respect, but it didn't translate into very much winning after the sudden step up in 1969. The third edition of the Clippers won but 27 games and took up a more accustomed address back in the Western Division basement. Elvin Hayes was still ripping up the nets (27.5 ppg.) as the league's third most productive scorer behind Jerry West and a rookie Lew Alcindor. And the Rockets' agile 6–9 center also paced the league in rebound average (16.9) and total boards (1386) and field goal attempts (2020) as well as minutes played (3665). But number-two scorer Don Kojis (15.3) broke an ankle, bench strength was nonexistent with Adelman and Riley also sidelined, and coach McMahon was replaced by Alex Hannum only 27 games into the campaign.

The final year in San Diego brought several bright spots even if Southern California fans would not be able to savour them for very much longer. The first piece of bright news came in the form of the best record (40–42) in four years of San Diego residence. Another plus was a couple of roster additions which finally brought some reinforcements to the aid of beleaguered Elvin Hayes. Rudy Tomjanovich made his debut appearance as the second overall pick (after Bob Lanier in Detroit) of the 1970 college draft. Admittedly Rudy didn't score much as a bench player his rookie season (5.3 ppg.) but was an important piece of the long-range puzzle soon to be patched together out in Houston. A smaller but hardly less significant addition came when pint-sized Calvin Murphy was plucked out of the second round of the same draft after other teams looked more at the 5'9" guard's physical stature than his incredible 48.9 ppg. Wilt-Chamberlain-like 1967 scoring average at Niagara University. Calvin Murphy would of course one day become one of the most popular players in club history, a Hall-of-Famer, and also one of the very best shooters (especially at the free-throw line) in all of hoops history.

Just when it appeared that rookies like Murphy and Rudy T, and a scoring machine like Hayes, would be enough to begin "taking over" most Western Division rivals, the San Diego ballclub fell surprise victims to a "corporate takeover" of a more ominous sort. On June 23, 1971, owner Breitbard announced the shocking news—his team was being sold to a group headed by real estate developer Wayne Diddleston, attorney Billy Goldberg, and sportswriter Mickey Herskowitz, all based in Houston. The whole deal took less than three weeks to transact and carried a now-modest price tag of $5.6 million. One benefactor thrilled by the imminent move, of course, was Rockets star Elvin Hayes, who would now return to the city where he built his fabled collegiate career. But for the rest of the team, a first season in a new home meant largely being without a permanent home at all. The move had been transacted with such haste that the new Houston club was left with the west coast schedule designed for San Diego (meaning sometimes playing in San Francisco or LA one night and then back in Houston the next) and no permanent home arena had been arranged. The resettled Rockets thus played on three "home floors" in Houston (Hofheinz Pavilion, the Astrodome, Astrohall) and three more around the rest of the state (Waco, El Paso, San Antonio) on the way to a 34–48 fourth-place finish.

No one was more overjoyed by the Rockets resettlement in Houston than franchise centerpiece Elvin Hayes. "It's a dream come true," remarked the stunned Hayes at the time. "It's a thrill right up there with the victory over UCLA and Lew Alcindor in the Astrodome." But Hayes would have little time to celebrate this homecoming to the scene of collegiate triumphs. He would, in fact, play just one season with the Rockets (to whom he would also return briefly late in his career) and then be dealt to the Baltimore Bullets in a surprise move during June, 1972. The return prize was not earthshaking at the time and proves less so in retrospect since the Rockets received only Jack Marin, a 6'6" forward-guard who had just enjoyed his only 20 ppg. scoring average of an eventual eleven-year career. The trade of Elvin Hayes at the outset of the club's Houston sojourn may indeed have been one of the biggest mistakes of Rockets' history. The Rockets, after all, would acquire a young and bulky Moses Malone just three seasons down the road. Hindsight now assures us that with both Hayes and Malone, the Rockets would already have enjoyed a potent Twin Towers lineup a full decade before Olajuwon and Sampson were on the scene.

Over the first five years in Houston, the Rockets only twice came close to a winning season, and those challenges at respect both came in the final two years under coach and ex-player Johnny Egan. The '74–'75 campaign, Egan's second in Houston, brought a .500 record (41–41) which meant second place in the Central Division but nonetheless a 19-game deficit to the runaway Washington Bullets. It was this Houston team which made a first post-season appearance since leaving San Diego, and pulled off a game playoff run which saw a mini-series victory over the New York Knicks followed by a five-game whipping at the hands of the Atlantic Division champion Boston Celtics. A season later Egan's club would fall to third and miss the playoffs again, yet they would dip only a single game in the won-lost columns.

The first truly significant upturn in club history came with the 1976–77 season which also happened to be the initial year under Tom Nissalke. This was, first of all, the year two significant players were added—John Lucas and Moses Malone. Lucas, a flashy guard who dribbled and shot from the left side, had been plucked off the campus of the University of Maryland in the first round of the collegiate draft. Malone, unique because he had never played college basketball, came shortly thereafter, during the season's first week, via a trade made with the Buffalo Braves and involving two future first round draft picks. As a result of such roster padding this also turned into a year when the club won its first divisional title ever. It came by a narrow margin of a single game over Washington, yet was all the sweeter for its tense race to the wire. Tomjanovich was the scoring leader (21.6) of this much-improved unit and was ably assisted by Moses Malone who paced the entire circuit in offensive rebounds. Tomjanovich had started out modestly enough in San Diego six years earlier but had now paced the ballclub in scoring during four of the past five seasons.

The first division-winning season also brought the first serious run in post-season by a Houston ballclub. The young Rockets first beat up on a veteran Washington team which was still led by ex-Rocket Elvin Hayes. The six-game set saw only one contest (the opener won by Washington) with a ten-point spread and found Houston roaring toward the finish with three straight closeout victories. In the Eastern Conference finals the tables were turned completely, however, when a Philadelphia Sixers contingent featuring Julius Erving and George McGinnis prevailed in six. Philadelphia actually had the series wrapped up by game five, only to blow a huge lead and let the reeling Rockets off the hook for one more game.

Rudy T was hurt the next year and missed much of the season after a regrettable altercation on December 9th in the Los Angeles Forum. As a result, the club slumped horribly (28–54) and tumbled directly from first place into last place. Tomjanovich's injury not only ruined the Rockets' season but nearly ended Rudy T's career, and it might well have proven far worse than it did, had not a bit of luck intervened in the midst of potential tragedy. The ugly events were triggered when a fight broke out under the basket between Kermit Washington of the Lakers and Houston center Kevin Kunnert. When Tomjanovich raced to the action to act as peacemaker, an enraged Washington wheeled unexpectedly and delivered a terrifying blow to the face of the onrushing enemy player. The frightening result was a badly smashed face for the Houston star, who nearly became pro basketball's first oncourt fatality. Rudy T's recovery would be painful and slow but his career would thankfully resume right where it left off the following season. Kermit Washington, for his part, was fined $10,000 and suspended for 60 days of game action. The Lakers player was also traded away to Boston, yet his regrettable actions had left a permanent cloud which would always hang darkly over the remainder of his career.

Despite a welcomed rebound the next year—when the Houston club stayed healthy and edged twelve games above .500—coach Tom Nissalke was nevertheless replaced by Del Harris in time for the 1979–80 campaign. Harris's first two clubs were solid but didn't impress overly much until a late-season hot-streak in '80–'81 carried over into the 1981 post-season derby. The champion Lakers had slipped behind Phoenix in the Western Division race during the 1981 late-season going, yet still figured to be a major contender during the playoff title chase. That was until Magic Johnson and his teammates ran into a buzz saw called the Houston Rockets. Houston had peaked at exactly the right time in late 1981 and shocked the basketball world by eliminating LA 2–1 during the opening-round mini-series. To prove it was no fluke the Rockets also cut down San Antonio in a seven-game series and then blew right past Kansas City in the Western Conference finals. Suddenly the upstart Rockets were sitting in the championship series across the ring from Larry Bird and the Boston Celtics.

The biggest factor in Houston's surprise post-season run was obviously Moses Malone, who had finished the year as the league's second best scorer (27.8) and had more importantly won his second straight rebounding title. By the end of the playoffs Malone was deservedly being touted as the NBA's best all-around center. And an additional force for the Rockets was tiny Calvin Murphy who was now a 33 year-old, 11-season veteran, but was still shooting free throws with the deadliest eye in league history. It was in this campaign that Murphy niched his eternal fame with two remarkable records at the charity stripe. Early in the year the future Hall-of-Famer sank a record (since broken) 78 straight free throws which surpassed Rick Barry's mark of 60 set in 1976. By season's end, Murphy had also surpassed Barry's record standard for free throw accuracy by netting charity tosses at a .957 rate. Barry had ironically set the old mark (.947) in 1979 when he was still Murphy's teammate with these same Houston Rockets.

The 1981 NBA finals saw Houston throw a mild scare into the Celtics. Boston prevailed without too much difficulty by winning four of six including the final two. Houston, however, was now showing signs of respectability and the Rockets put up a gallant fight, holding Boston under 100 points in each of four tight games and earning a 2–2 split before wilting under the scoring onslaught of series MVP Cedric Maxwell in game five.

After one more decent season (46–36) the bottom somehow seemed to fall out completely for Del Harris's previously stable program in Houston. A season below 20 wins was easily enough to sabotage coach Harris, who had chafed under a team that could boast no 15 ppg. scorer and found Calvin Murphy and Elvin Hayes closing out their Hall-of-Fame careers in embarrassing fashion. Bill Fitch couldn't do much better a year later as the Rockets climbed to 29 victories yet remained anchored to a basement slot. But the two bleak seasons had a huge payoff for the Houston fans and management in the long run. First the club won a crucial coin flip with Indiana to earn rights to Ralph Sampson, who was bringing his famed act from the University of Virginia to the NBA via the 1983 draft. The following year another fortuitous flip (with Portland) left Houston picking first once again and now selecting local University of Houston star Akeem (later Hakeem) Olajuwon. Two lucky coin flips and 121 losses in but two seasons had been enough to turn a significant page in NBA basketball history—Houston's famed "Twin Towers" were now set firmly in place.

Few could have predicted during Hakeem's rookie season that Olajuwon and not Sampson would one day become perhaps basketball's most versatile pivot man ever. Sampson, after all, had once earned raves with several All-American seasons in the prestigious Atlantic Coast Conference. Despite leading Houston's Cougars to three straight NCAA Final Four appearances, Olajuwon was a mere basketball novice during his own All-American collegiate years. The former Nigerian soccer goalie had taken up the sport only three years before enrolling at Houston. He was still in the process of learning basketball fundamentals at the same time he was earning his first NBA paychecks. But Olajuwon seems to learn faster than almost anyone who has ever dribbled a ball.

With the Twin Towers boosting offense and defense, the Houston club was again on the upbeat during the next couple of years. The experiment of playing two seven-footers on the same front wall gave all the initial signs of a stroke of pure coaching genius on the part of Bill Fitch and his staff. In their first year together Sampson (22.1 ppg., 10.4 rpg., 2.1 blocks) and Olajuwon (20.6 ppg., 11.9 rpg., 2.7 blocks) became the first pair since Wilt Chamberlain and Elgin Baylor of the 1970 Lakers to average better than 20 points and 10 rebounds in the same lineup. Over their first two seasons the Towers would author a 99–65 record, surpassed only by a handful of two-year teams in recent decades. A 48-win campaign meant only a short playoff visit in 1985 with a five-game first-round loss to Utah, despite 22.1 playoff scoring averages from both Towers. Then came another post-season trip a year later, and this one carried all the way to the NBA Finals. Again Houston's championship opponent would be Boston and again the result would be largely the same as in 1981. But things would now be a little more fun at the zenith of the short-lived Twin Tower era.

The 1986 NBA Finals were one of the Rockets' greatest hours. It was a six-game series that saw six players average in double figures for Houston (Olajuwon 23.5, Sampson 18.9, Lewis Lloyd 16.9, John Lucas 15.5, Robert Reid 12.0, Rodney McCray 10.0). A fifth-game bench-clearing brawl involving Sampson and Boston's Danny Ainge spiced the festivities. But Boston, in the end, was just too strong and deep and boasted its own "towers" of strength in Larry Bird (25.9) and Kevin McHale (24.9). And the Celtics 82 combined regular season and post-season victories would establish a new all-time NBA mark for single-season winning. For Houston's part, perhaps the most thrilling post-season moment didn't come in the Finals at all, but instead in the finals seconds of Western Conference action. Ralph Sampson took an inbounds pass from Rodney McCray and corkscrewed home a 10-foot jumper to seal a victory at the buzzer and eliminate the heavily favored Los Angeles Lakers. The play soon become known to every Houston fan as "The Shot" and to date remains the single most memorable moment of ballclub history.

The Twin Towers already seemed to be paying big dividends, but their two-pronged attack was not meant to last very long. After only three more-than-adequate seasons with an overall 20.6 scoring average, disaster struck for 7'4" tower Ralph Sampson. The slimmer half of the Twin Towers combo was rendered ineffective by two ankle sprains and an injury to his left knee which followed in quick succession during 1986–87 and kept the 1985 All-Star Game MVP out of 39 games that season. The team wouldn't be the same after Sampson proved injury prone and almost immediately the Rockets began another downward slide. Sampson himself would be traded 19 games into the 1987–88 campaign (along with Steve Harris) to the Golden State Warriors for replacement center Joe Barry Carroll (number one overall selection in the 1980 draft) and guard Eric "Sleepy" Floyd. The Sampson-Carroll trade made NBA history as the first swap ever of two players who had both been number one picks in the NBA draft. But it was a trade that did precious little to enhance the immediate fortunes of either ballclub involved.

It took a slow rebuilding process once the team had to be restructured around only one remaining and isolated tower—Olajuwon. Sampson's final partial season in Houston would also prove to be the curtain call for coach Bill Fitch as well. In three subsequent years under Fitch's replacement, Don Chaney, there would be nothing resembling an all-out collapse, yet little measurable forward progress either. Four straight playoff visits (counting the last under Bill Fitch) lead to four quick first-round exits for the holding-pattern team from Houston. About the only event in this stretch to inspire real excitement from the heart of Texas was the league's 1989 All-Star Game, played before a record throng of 44,735 in the Houston Astrodome.

There were some record-setting performances during Chaney's third season—the team actually set or tied 63 individual franchise marks that year in compiling the best-yet regular season of the city's NBA history. And all this came despite a 25-game absence of Olajuwon, who was felled with a severe eye injury. Don Chaney not only captured NBA Digital Coach of the Year plaudits, but also became the first in league history to win consecutive Coach-of-the-Month honors when he turned the trick in February and March. One of the more noteworthy rewritten records was Vernon Maxwell's new standard for 3-point goals in a season (172). Two vital trades had seemingly kick-started the rebuilding Rockets and they were the deals that had provided the most potent starting backcourt combo since Calvin Murphy and Mike Newlin a decade earlier. Maxwell had been obtained from San Antonio for cash in February 1990. And in a deal with even greater impact, Kenny Smith was acquired in September from Atlanta in exchange for Tim McCormick and John Lucas. Smith was soon providing excellent generalship from the point guard slot and also won a handful of games himself with clutch last-second baskets. But for all the records and improvements the Rockets in Chaney's best year were still no more than a third-place finisher in the loaded Midwest Division and an easy three-game victim of the Los Angeles Lakers in playoff round one.

The spurt under Don Chaney in '90–'91 had sent expectations, if not Rocket fortunes, soaring, and the predictable result was the firing of the even-tempered Chaney once the '91–'92 ballclub faltered in early going. Rudy Tomjanovich took over in time for a hopeless 1992 stretch run, yet was able to salvage the final 30 games of a campaign which found the ballclub dipping to a 42–40 record, yet steadfastly maintaining its slot behind San Antonio and Utah in basketball's most competitive division. But the rebuilt foundation had now largely been laid with Smith and

Maxwell in the backcourt, Otis Thorpe and Olajuwon still in place along the front wall, and within a year Tomjanovich was leading the club back to a divisional title.

This set the stage for the memorable 1994 season—one which basketball historians will probably always refer to as "the year after Air Jordan" and which they will underscore as marking a needed return to competitive balance in the NBA. It was also a season that would feature a multi-faceted Rockets team still built around Olajuwon yet now displaying a maturity always lacking in earlier contenders out of Houston. Otis Thorpe played a major role with the third highest field goal percentage (.561) in the league and a quiet leadership in the clubhouse. But the backbone of the team was the guards—Vernon Maxwell (the club's third leading scorer), Kenny Smith (in the league's top ten in 3–point accuracy and free throw percentage), and rookie and 1993 first-round pick Sam Cassell. Robert Horry was also a huge factor, especially in post-season contests where he exploded for 22 points during the 94–83 victory over Utah, which clinched a berth in the NBA Finals.

And it was the 1994 NBA Finals themselves that proved two things above all others about the directions the NBA might now take in the post-Michael Jordan era. First off, there would apparently now be room for surprise teams like the Indiana Pacers, featuring little in the way of name-recognition superstars, but stocked with plenty in the way of defensive tenaciousness and team chemistry. And secondly, Hakeem Olajuwon had wasted little time in rising to the head of the class among a new crop of centers who were threatening to turn the sport back over to long-ignored big men who banged heads in traffic and applied a power game rather than a finesse game. It was true that Olajuwon had advanced farther in post-season than David Robinson or Patrick Ewing or Shaquille O'Neal, in large part because his team featured guards capable of taking pressure off the pivot man, and also capable of delivering the ball to their aircraft carrier inside. But Hakeem also demonstrated that as a defensive force (and defense, remember, is the staple of post-season play) he was a clear cut above Ewing, Robinson or the "Shaq Attaq" in Orlando.

Olajuwon has evolved into one of the finest players in NBA history. He nailed that evaluation even more firmly in place, of course, with his spectacular MVP season of '93–'94 and with a preceding campaign, which left him touted as the NBA Defensive Player of the Year. Many an NBA rim has been rattled by a jarring Olajuwon dunk, sending defenders back on their heels and inspiring pure crown frenzy. Hakeem has the advantage against almost any of his oversized rivals—David Robinson, Shaq O'Neal, Patrick Ewing—as none can match his quickness or raw leaping ability. Few have ever played with Olajuwon's night-in and night-out intensity at both ends of the floor. And no center since Wilt Chamberlain has owned the same soft touch on jump shots taken a dozen or more feet from the basket.

Suggested Readings on Houston Rockets

Bjarkman, Peter C. **Slam Dunk Superstars**. New York and Avenel, New Jersey: Crescent Books (Outlet Books, Random House), 1994.

Bjarkman, Peter C. **The History of the NBA**. New York and Avenel, New Jersey: Crescent Books (Outlet Books, Random House), 1992.

Houston Rockets Retired Uniform Numbers (2)

Calvin Murphy (23)
Rudy Tomjanovich (45)

Year-by-Year Houston Rockets Summary

Season	Record	Finish	Coach(es)	Scoring Leader(s)	Playoffs (W-L Record)

Key:* # = League Scoring Leader

San Diego Rockets

Season	Record	Finish	Coach(es)	Scoring Leader(s)	Playoffs (W-L Record)
1967–68	15–67	6th	Jack McMahon	Don Kojis (19.7)	Did Not Qualify
1968–69	37–45	4th	Jack McMahon	Elvin Hayes (28.4)#	Lost in 1st Round (2–4)
1969–70	27–55	7th	Jack McMahon Alex Hannum	Elvin Hayes (27.5)	Did Not Qualify
1970–71	40–42	3rd	Alex Hannum	Elvin Hayes (28.7)	Did Not Qualify

HOUSTON ROCKETS

Season	Record	Finish	Coach(es)	Scoring Leader(s)	Playoffs (W-L Record)
1971–72	34–48	4th	Tex Winter	Elvin Hayes (25.2)	Did Not Qualify
1972–73	33–49	3rd	Tex Winter John Egan	Rudy Tomjanovich (19.3)	Did Not Qualify
1973–74	32–50	3rd	John Egan	Rudy Tomjanovich (24.5)	Did Not Qualify
1974–75	41–41	2nd	John Egan	Rudy Tomjanovich (20.7)	Lost in 2nd Round (3–5)
1975–76	40–42	3rd	John Egan	Calvin Murphy (21.0)	Did Not Qualify
1976–77	49–33	1st	Tom Nissalke	Rudy Tomjanovich (21.6)	Lost in 3rd Round (6–6)
1977–78	28–54	6th	Tom Nissalke	Calvin Murphy (25.6)	Did Not Qualify
1978–79	47–35	2nd	Tom Nissalke	Moses Malone (24.8)	Lost in 1st Round (0–2)
1979–80	41–41	2nd	Del Harris	Moses Malone (25.8)	Lost in 2nd Round (2–5)
1980–81	40–42	2nd	Del Harris	Moses Malone (27.8)	Lost in NBA Finals (12–9)
1981–82	46–36	2nd	Del Harris	Moses Malone (31.1)	Lost in 1st Round (1–2)
1982–83	14–68	6th	Del Harris	Allen Leavell (14.8)	Did Not Qualify
1983–84	29–53	6th	Bill Fitch	Ralph Sampson (21.0)	Did Not Qualify
1984–85	48–34	2nd	Bill Fitch	Ralph Sampson (22.1)	Lost in 1st Round (2–3)
1985–86	51–31	1st	Bill Fitch	Hakeem Olajuwon (23.5)	Lost in NBA Finals (13–7)
1986–87	42–40	3rd	Bill Fitch	Hakeem Olajuwon (23.4)	Lost in 2nd Round (5–5)
1987–88	46–36	4th	Bill Fitch	Hakeem Olajuwon (22.8)	Lost in 1st Round (1–3)
1988–89	45–37	2nd	Don Chaney	Hakeem Olajuwon (24.8)	Lost in 1st Round (1–3)
1989–90	41–41	5th	Don Chaney	Hakeem Olajuwon (24.3)	Lost in 1st Round (0–3)
1990–91	52–30	3rd	Don Chaney	Hakeem Olajuwon (21.2)	Lost in 1st Round (1–3)
1991–92	42–40	3rd	Don Chaney R. Tomjanovich	Hakeem Olajuwon (21.6)	Did Not Qualify
1992–93	55–27	1st	R. Tomjanovich	Hakeem Olajuwon (26.1)	Lost in 2nd Round (6–6)
1993–94	58–24	1st	R. Tomjanovich	Hakeem Olajuwon (27.3)	**NBA Champion** (15–9)

Individual Career Leaders and Record Holders (1967–1994)

Scoring Average	Moses Malone (24.0 ppg., 1976–82)
	Hakeem Olajuwon (23.6 ppg., 1984–94)
Points Scored	Calvin Murphy (17,949, 1970–83)
	Hakeem Olajuwon (17,899, 1984–94)
Games Played	Calvin Murphy (1,002)
Minutes Played	Calvin Murphy (30,607)
Field Goal Pct.	Otis Thorpe (.559, 1988–94)
3-Pt. Field Goal Pct.	Scott Brooks (.414, 1992–93)
Free Throws Made	Calvin Murphy (3,445)
Free-Throw Pct.	Rick Barry (.941, 1978–80)
Rebounds	Hakeem Olajuwon (9,464)
Rebound Average	Moses Malone (15.0 rpg.)
Assists	Calvin Murphy (4,402)
Steals	Hakeem Olajuwon (1,448)
Blocked Shots	Hakeem Olajuwon (2,741)

INDIVIDUAL SINGLE-SEASON AND GAME RECORDS (1967–1994)

Scoring Average	Moses Malone (31.1 ppg., 1981–82)
Points Scored (Season)	Moses Malone (2,520, 1981–82)
Points Scored (Game)	Calvin Murphy (57, 3–18–78 vs. New Jersey Nets)
Field Goal Pct. (Season)	Otis Thorpe (.592, 1991–92)
Free-Throw Pct. (Season)	Calvin Murphy (958, 1980–81)
Free Throws Made (Season)	Moses Malone (630, 1981–82)
Free Throws Made (Game)	Eric "Sleepy" Floyd (22, 2–3–91 vs. Golden State Warriors)
3-Pt. Field Goals (Season)	Vernon Maxwell (172, 1990–91)
3-Pt. Field Goals (Game)	Vernon Maxwell (8, 4–5–91 at Denver Nuggets)
	Rick Barry (8, 2–9–80 vs. Utah Jazz)
Rebounds (Season)	Moses Malone (1,444, 1978–79)
Rebound Average (Season)	Moses Malone (17.6 rpg., 1978–79)
Rebounds (Game)	Moses Malone (37, 2–9–79 at New Orleans Jazz)
Assists (Season)	John Lucas (768, 1977–78)
Assists (Game)	Art Williams (22, 12–28–68 and 2–14–70)
	Allen Leavell (22, 1–25–83 vs. New Jersey Nets)
Steals (Season)	Hakeem Olajuwon (213, 1988–89)
Blocked Shots (Season)	Hakeem Olajuwon (376, 1989–90)

Best Trade in Franchise History

With Elvin Hayes removed from the Houston scene by a questionable 1972 trade with Washington, the door was left open for Moses Malone to become the first true NBA franchise player down in Texas. Malone—the first of the handful of NBA'ers to come straight to the league without benefit of college playing time—was acquired from the Buffalo Braves in a blockbuster deal executed in October, 1977. Shipped to the Braves were two first-round draft picks (resulting in Wesley Cox and Michael Ray Richardson) and a truckload of cash. It was obviously a small price to pay for basketball's most dominant rebounder since the days of Russell and Chamberlain.

Worst Trade in Franchise History

Elvin Hayes must rate a position on any all-time Houston Rockets team. This would mean, of course, that any "Dream Team" for the frontcourt-rich Rockets must contain Olajuwon, Malone, Tomjanovich and Hayes, making room for only one backcourt player. It also means that Elvin Hayes earns a spot even though his most glorious Hall-of-Fame years were played elsewhere. For on June 23, 1972, Hayes was somehow traded away to the Washington Bullets for journeyman forward Jack Marin. Marin was a respectable player who survived for eleven season in the NBA; but he also scored 14,772 fewer points than Hayes. The result of the Hayes deal in the end was several runs to the NBA finals for Washington and a string of lackluster seasons for Rockets faithful. One can only dream about what the Houston team might have accomplished throughout the remainder of the '70s with Rudy T, Moses Malone and Elvin Hayes all terrorizing enemy teams across the front line.

Houston Rockets Historical Oddity

Only one general manager has ever led two different NBA franchises to the league Finals and that GM is a man whose name and career are now almost as synonymous with the Houston Rockets as the more publicized figure of Rudy Tomjanovich. Ray Patterson first led Milwaukee's Bucks to the top of the NBA heap when he won a famous coin flip that landed Lew Alcindor as a franchise-building prize for the Wisconsin expansion club. Later, this same Ray Patterson would join the Houston Rockets organization in 1972 and become the front office leader who constructed powerhouse Houston Rocket outfits of the early and mid eighties. Patterson—who earned NBA Executive-of-the-Year plaudits in 1977—remained the GM in Houston until his son Steve succeeded him upon retirement in 1989.

ROCKETS ALL-TIME NUMBER ONE DRAFT PICKS LIST

San Diego Rockets
1967 Pat Riley (Kentucky)
1968 Elvin Hayes (Houston)
1969 Bobby Smith (Tulsa)
1970 Rudy Tomjanovich (Michigan)
Houston Rockets
1971 Cliff Meely (Colorado)
1972 John Gianelli (Pacific)
1973 Ed Ratleff (Long Beach State)
1974 Bobby Jones (North Carolina)
1975 Joe Meriweather (Southern Illinois)
1976 John Lucas (Maryland)
1977 Larry Moffett (UNLV)
1978 Buster Matheny (Utah)
1979 Lee Johnson (East Texas State)
1980 John Stroud (Mississippi)
1981 Ed Turner (Texas A & M)
1982 Terry Teagle (Baylor)
1983 Ralph Sampson (Virginia)
1984 Akeem (Hakeem) Olajuwon (Houston)
1985 Steve Harris (Tulsa)
1986 Buck Johnson (Alabama)
1987 Doug Lee (Purdue)
1988 Derrick Chievous (Missouri)
1989 None
1990 Alec Kessler (Georgia)
1991 John Turner (Phillips)
1992 Robert Horry (Alabama)
1993 Sam Cassell (Florida State)

Chapter 12

SEATTLE SUPERSONICS

Slow Train For the Jet Age

All-Time Franchise Record: 1132–1082, .511 Pct. (1967–1994)
NBA Championships (1): 1978–79
Greatest Franchise Player: "Downtown" Fred Brown (1971–1984)
All-Time Leading Scorer: Fred Brown (14,018 Points, 1971–1984)
Most Successful Coach: George Karl (145–61, .704 Pct., 1992–1994)
All-Time Franchise Team: Jack Sikma (C), Spencer Haywood (F), Dale Ellis (F), Fred
 Brown (G), Gus Williams (G)

Some teams seem to have unalterably perfect names. "Sixers" in Philadelphia—to cite one example—captures the patriotic spirit for which the
city of the Liberty Bell and Independence Hall is perhaps most famous.
What is better associated with the car-making capital of Detroit and also
better reflects the plodding workmanlike nature of most yearly renditions
of the Detroit NBA team than the name "Pistons." And who could argue
the appropriateness of Nuggets in Denver, Celtics in Boston, Suns in Phoenix, or Heat in Miami.

Other team nicknames seem to remain a complete mystery, however—
like Cleveland Cavaliers, Milwaukee Bucks or Sacramento Kings. And
then there are those ballclubs that are simply grossly misnamed. "Jazz"
may have played well in New Orleans but hardly seems to fit the temper
and mind-set of a predominantly Mormon state in Utah. And most egre-
gious of all seems to be the moniker adopted for the Seattle NBA team.
It is true enough that the Washington city is the home of the Boeing
Aircraft Corporation and thus the producer of the nation's huge aluminum
and steel jet-propelled birds. But otherwise there has been absolutely nothing "SuperSonic" about the professional basketball team that has now
played in Seattle for a little over a full quarter century.

The Seattle team hovered in the middle of the pack for all of the first

232

ten years of franchise history. It was never a dreadful team, not even as a lackluster first-year expansion outfit capable of winning but 23 games. But it was never a good one either, especially not in its maiden season— 35 games off the division-winning pace, a record better than only the expansion bedfellow San Diego Rockets, a no-name roster featuring one 20 ppg. scorer. And for nine seasons that followed the Sonics mustered but two playoff appearances (1975, 1976), garnered only three winning seasons (1972, 1975, 1976), and enjoyed only one short-lived franchise superstar in the person of high-scoring forward Spencer Haywood.

Then in one shocking season of 1977–'78 the Seattle SuperSonics would emerge unannounced and unanticipated into the NBA Finals. This happened, of course, in a year when the team placed only third in the regular season (47–35), split the season between two coaches (Bob Hopkins and Lenny Wilkens), and then went on a post-season hot streak that caught opponents and fans by total surprise. Los Angeles, Portland (the defending champion now weakened by the injury loss of Bill Walton) and Denver all fell to Wilkens's hot-shooting team in several series that were all one-sided. Never has there been a better example of the pitfall and beauty of the NBA post-season system—one team (or perhaps two, as was actually the case in 1978) getting hot at just the right time and completely overreaching itself. In the end luck ran out against an even hotter and more underrated Washington Bullets team, which walked off with the league title. But the Sonics had nonetheless sprung seemingly from nowhere to prominence at the very end of an otherwise mediocre first decade of franchise history.

Seattle did then hold on for one more season under Lenny Wilkens and ultimately won the championship it was now finally supposed to win. For the '78–'79 season, at least, the Seattle club was almost "super" if not quite "sonic" with its controlled playing style. Both Washington and Seattle were now pre-season picks on the basis of their late-season runs of a year earlier, and both justified the oddsmakers with the league's top regular season records, and with a dual return trip to the championship round. Seattle dominated the Bullets this time around in a five-game set which showcased a cohesive Sonics seven-man unit consisting of John Johnson, Lonnie Shelton, Jack Sikma, Dennis Johnson, Gus Williams, Paul Silas and Freddie Brown. But the label of "SuperSonics," as well as the label of champions, didn't seem to fit too comfortably out in the far northwest. Thus the Seattle ballclub would immediately drop far back into the pack after their single title celebration and manage to stay buried there ever since.

Ever since, that is, until the '93–'94 season under third-year coach George Karl. The Seattle club had shown signs of dramatic improvement under Karl the previous season with a surge in the victory column from 47 to 55 wins. Yet they hardly seemed ready to challenged powerful Western Conference clubs like San Antonio with David Robinson, Houston with Hakeem Olajuwon, or Utah with Karl Malone. Then a crucial trade was made with the Indiana Pacers on the eve of a new season to fit in the last important missing piece of the puzzle. Detlef Schrempf had compiled a host of NBA Sixth Man awards in Indiana and seemed the perfect complement to Kemp, Perkins, Payton and Pierce. He was brought to Seattle at a stiff price (defensive ace Derrick McKey) but seemed to be worth any such gamble at the trading block. High-scoring guard Kendall Gill (20.5 ppg. in 1992) was also acquired from Charlotte for Dana Barrios, Eddie Johnson and some future draft considerations. House cleaning had occurred and a jigsaw puzzle of promise had been hastily pasted together. Now Karl had a team seemingly ready to blast off for some serious space-aged flying.

Seattle roared from the gate in '93–'94 and was never headed in the six-month Pacific Division race. Defending conference champion Phoenix would finish a distant seven games behind. Although jockeying with the equally fast-starting Houston Rockets in the early going for the NBA's overall best record, there was little contest in the latter portions of the year as Houston faded and Seattle (63–19) remained several lengths ahead of both Eastern Conference division leaders (New York and Atlanta) as well. With a balanced attack led by the ferocious play of Shawn Kemp (10.8 rpg., .538 field goal percentage, 18.1 ppg.) the Sonics were easily the cream of the NBA during the first "parity year" after Jordan's retirement had broken up the three-time champion Chicago Bulls. It was clearly a matter of team balance and cohesiveness in Seattle, as superstars and league leaders were nowhere to be found on George Karl's talented roster; Kemp's fifth-ranking field goal percentage was the only Sonics performance to rank among the top dozen in any of the league's important individual statistical categories. The question everywhere around the NBA at season's end was whether or not the Sonics—despite their 37–4 home record—were truly for real?

Post-season brought a quick and disturbing answer. Against a game but lowly Denver Nuggets team, which held the eighth seed in the west, the Sonics coasted to two homecourt victories. Then midnight struck, the carriage turned into a hollow pumpkin, and the Cinderella Sonics lost more than just a glass slipper. The Nuggets roared back for three straight wins, two in Denver, including an overtime thriller. The clincher was an emotional second-straight overtime defeat of the Sonics, this time on their home floor where they had lost only four times all year. It was Denver's unheralded Brian Williams and not Seattle's Shawn Kemp who seemed to rule the boards; and Denver's heretofore disappointing center Dikembe Mutombo came of age during the shocking upset series with an new NBA post-season record for blocked shots. This "SuperSonic" outfit thus proved to be no more glamorous than any past editions. Here, apparently, was yet another broken down DC-3 and not at all a modern airbus or unstoppable space missile. The Sonics had once again proven pretenders rather than contenders for an NBA championship crown.

It was probably only fitting that a Seattle front office memo had already announced—shortly before this playoff debacle of '94—that during the coming 1994–1995 season the ballclub would be officially shortening its name to "Sonics" and finally dropping the superfluous "super" appendage. Of course, management could hardly have been intending an early signal to its players, who nonetheless quickly also dropped "super" from their own level of performance, before post-season had even hardly gotten out of the box. It looks now like yet another major rebuilding job is due to begin in Seattle during still another long off-season of reflection and retooling. By draft day, 1994 Seattle was already discussing a potential trade with Chicago involving Shawn Kemp and the Bulls' Scottie Pippen. Will Kemp, and Gary Payton, and Schrempf, and still others now be thrown on the trading block in a massive purge? Or will the shocking loss of 1994 simply be taken as a minor setback for a team that is legitimately already on its way to the top for 1995? If past history is any guide on this matter, the fans of Seattle can't be too optimistic at present.

The pattern of repeated disappointment that has defined Seattle basketball was first launched with the announcement of an NBA expansion ballclub for the Pacific Northwest on December 20, 1966. The league was now expanding to an even dozen teams and thus also adding a franchise in San Diego. The latter novice ballclub would be rather short-lived, and would soon depart for Texas to become the Houston Rockets. But Seattle's franchise was destined to be at least more stable in its original home, if not any more successful in building an early winner and crowd-pleaser.

The first Seattle ownership group was headed up by Sam Schulman, and Schulman and his partners in turn selected Al Bianchi as their debut head coach. The first player to see his name on the new Seattle roster was San Francisco Warriors veteran forward and free spirit, Tom Meschery. Other experienced players acquired in the first expansion draft for the Sonics included Rod Thorn (St. Louis Hawks), Bob Weiss (Philadelphia Sixers) and Walt Hazzard (a three-year Lakers reserve who would soon change his name to Mahdi Abdul-Rahmad). And the first collegian drafted was a 6'8" forward named Al Tucker, while the second was 6'9" Colorado State center Bob Rule. The sharpshooting Tucker came out of tiny and unheralded Oklahoma Baptist, yet he bore a large enough reputation as a collegiate star; Rule would prove the biggest catch, however, and would twice lead the club in scoring during early expansion seasons.

The first Seattle NBA season was largely the standard fare as far as inaugural seasons go. It included the obligatory opening night pounding, a 144–116 drubbing in San Francisco. Also included was a second defeat— in the home opener with expansion rival San Diego (121–114)—before the first club victory could be earned eight nights later. That also came against fellow also-ran San Diego, this time on the road and in a 117–110 overtime thriller. The inaugural Seattle team did lose eight straight in early going and later dropped twelve of thirteen during a February-March dry spell. But Bianchi was able to string together a respectable first two years that witnessed first 23 victories in season number one (eight more than

San Diego) and then 30 more wins in year two. It was hardly fever-pitch improvement, but hardly a complete disaster either.

The first major player transaction came less than a week before the opening of a second franchise season. Leading scorer Walt Hazzard was peddled to Atlanta's Hawks in a one-for-one swap that radically altered the direction of the young Seattle ballclub. Coming over in exchange for Hazzard was an all-star guard named Lenny Wilkens, who would soon become one of the central figures of club history. Wilkens debuted in Seattle with a club-best 674 assists (8.2 apg., second in the entire league) and a club-runner-up 22.4 scoring mark (ninth in the league). Bob Rule would surprise as well that second season with a league fourth-best 24.0 ppg. scoring performance of his own. But it was the newly acquired Wilkens who would now be the club mainstay. Before the beginning of a third season Wilkens would also be installed in the post of player-coach, one of the last players of the modern era to hold such a responsibility. The team improved steadily under Wilkens for three seasons and cracked the .500 barrier for the first time in '71–'72—the fifth season of Seattle franchise history.

The big jump in 1972 (47–35, third in the Pacific Division) could be partially attributed to Wilkens who averaged 18.0 ppg. while directing the bench strategy and also trailing only the Lakers' Jerry West in total assists. But another newcomer played perhaps an even larger role. Controversial but multi-talented Spencer Haywood had been grabbed from the ABA Denver Nuggets in time for the '70–'71 campaign. The free-agent signing of Haywood turned out not only as a milestone in Seattle's club fortunes but also soon stood as one of the most important transactions in NBA history—at least from a legal and policy-forming standpoint. Haywood had earlier starred on the 1968 Olympic team, and then had decided to leave college as a sophomore and try his hand at the challenge (and the paychecks) of pro basketball. The NBA's rules preventing a player from signing before his collegiate class had graduated shut off Haywood's NBA options and left him no option but to ink a contract for a year with the ABA Nuggets. But the unstoppable 6'8" pivotman who ate up the ABA for one season in Denver soon longed for an NBA opportunity, and could hardly refuse the huge deal Schulman and Seattle were willing to dangle in front of him.

Other clubs naturally objected loudly to Spencer Haywood entering the NBA without passing through the normal draft process. The draft would give them all (or at least those at the bottom of the standings and thus top of the draft heap) a proper crack at the former University of Detroit star. The legal battle which ensued kept Haywood on the sidelines for half a season in '70–'71 but was soon settled in Seattle's favor. This off-court victory was probably the landmark moment of ballclub history. The ruling of a federal judge that the NBA restriction against undergraduates was improper, simply because it prevented certain players from determining if and when they wished to become professionals, sent immediate shock waves throughout the league.

The overnight result was institution of a new league "hardship" drafting policy for undergraduates. The ruling had an impact in basketball parallel to that of the Curt Flood case, which legally brought free agency to baseball. The game would never again look quite the same. Nor would the earning potential of most, if not all, of its players.

Haywood joined the Sonics in the league's 25th anniversary year—a year that saw perhaps the best crop of NBA rookies ever. They included Pete Maravich (Atlanta), Dave Cowens (Boston), Bob Lanier (Detroit), Calvin Murphy (San Diego), and Geoff Petrie (Portland). While Haywood's first season in Seattle started too late (he reported to the ballclub on New Year's Day) for his debut to have much impact on the league standings that rookie season, the next few years proved his full worth and sent the stock of under-graduate "hardship" players soaring for decades to come. Haywood would leap into fourth slot in league scoring in 1972, as the Sonics coached by Wilkens would leap into the middle of the pack in the Pacific Division. The following season he would post a team-record 51 points in a January game against Kansas City. Wilkens himself would be traded over to Cleveland in the summer of 1972—this time again as a player, along with Barry Clemens, for Butch Beard—and fortunes would dip predictably the following season. But by '74–'75, under new coach Bill Russell, the Sonics were able to ride Haywood's scoring to a first-ever playoff appearance.

In a bold move in October, 1975, general manager and coach Bill Russell would trade Spencer Haywood to the New York Knicks for a first round draft selection (which later turned out to be Vinnie Johnson) and considerable cash. While mildly shocking at the time, the deal was probably a good move in the long run as Haywood never again achieved the high scoring totals posted for several seasons in Seattle. Only once in his final seven seasons, in fact, would Spencer Haywood be able to crack the 20 ppg. plateau while playing with New York, New Orleans, Los Angeles and finally Washington. And there was a new gunner now on board for Seattle in "Downtown" Freddie Brown. Brown (23.1 ppg.) would pace the club that year to an identical record (43–39), another second-place Pacific Division finish, and a second-straight playoff visit.

Russell lasted just four seasons before wearing out his welcome in Seattle with a caustic front-office and coaching style (Seattle players found him both distant and overbearing) and a failure to move his teams beyond the second round of post-season play. Lenny Wilkens would eventually be rehired as coach (no longer a playing-coach, however) 22 games into the slow-starting '77–'78 season. And with the return of Wilkens would come the launching of the two-year stretch that represents the only true franchise highpoint of a quarter-century NBA sojourn.

Wilkens's "inherited" 1978 Seattle team would turn very few heads as a third-place finisher during regular-season play. But then the lineup of John Johnson, Jack Sikma, Marvin Webster, Dennis Johnson and Gus Williams would catch fire and shock first Los Angeles, and later defending champion Portland in the opening rounds of post-season festivities. Finding themselves a surprise entrant in the NBA Finals, and lining up against another over-achieving team from Washington, the Sonics battled gamely against the Bullets and seemed to have an unexpected championship now firmly within their grasp. Wilkens's Sonics were not yet "Super" enough, however, and back-to-back road and home losses eventually handed the title over to Elvin Hayes, Wes Unseld, and the equally unheralded Washington Bullets.

When the '78–'79 campaign opened, both Seattle and Washington were clearly bent on immediately correcting any lingering image that they were both undeserving flukes as post-season combatants a season earlier. The two clubs ran and hid from their divisional opponents as they charged forward on a championship collision course throughout the '78–'79 campaign. And when they again inevitably met in the NBA Finals, it was a generally-held opinion that this time around the two best NBA teams were indeed still there, shooting and rebounding, when it came time to sort out a deserving league champion.

Coach Lenny Wilkens had an especially cohesive seven-man unit at his disposal as Seattle approached the NBA final round in 1979. John Johnson (11.0 ppg. and 358 assists) and Lonnie Shelton (13.5 ppg.) now anchored the forward slots. Jack Sikma (15.6 ppg. and 12.4 rpg.) was a pillar of strength plugging the center. Guard play was handled superbly by Dennis "DJ" Johnson (280 assists) and Gus Williams (307 assists). And veterans Paul Silas (575 rebounds) and Freddie Brown (14.0 ppg.) provided one of the most experienced bench tandems the NBA Finals had ever known. After losing the opening game (99–97) the Sonics got straight down to business and swept to their only franchise championship by beating Washington in four straight games. Only game four—a two-point overtime thriller—was all that close at the final buzzer. The guard tandem of DJ and Gus Williams both averaged above 20 for the post-season and Dennis Johnson was a runaway choice as the finals MVP.

The defending champion Sonics did seem to have at least one good year left in them as they charged to a 56–26 record in 1979–'80. It was, in fact, the best overall record in club history. But it was also only good enough for a second-place Pacific Division finish behind the revived Los Angeles Lakers ballclub which now had a rookie named Earvin "Magic" Johnson on its side. The Johnson-led LA Lakers team soon demonstrated that their season-long dominance (4–2 in head-to-head matchups) over Seattle's defending champions was hardly an aberration. Exhausted by a tough see-saw seven-game series with Milwaukee, the Sonics were simply no match for the re-charged Lakers. Seattle did muster enough to cop an opening game in the LA Forum by a single point (108–107) in the Western Conference Finals; but the Lakers then answered with a convincing five-game elimination of Seattle on their way to a first title of the Magic Johnson era.

Seattle and Washington were both slightly above-average teams that were able to pluck a couple of championships during the late-'70s in a league devoid of any truly dominant teams. Once Magic Johnson arrived in Los Angeles and Larry Bird took flight in Boston the same season, however, the NBA took on an entirely new complexion. LA would now own the west for the full decade ahead, and Boston would rule unchallenged in the east. An immediate result was that Washington's Bullets and Seattle's SuperSonics both fell like lead weights back into mediocrity.

The next ten years for the Sonics would be split equally between two coaches—Lenny Wilkens and Bernie Bickerstaff. Only once in the long stretch would the Seattle club make it out of the second round of the playoffs. In 1987 a sub-.500 Bickerstaff balllclub ruined the post-season for two Texas teams with a sudden playoff spurt of their own, reminiscent of the one back in 1978. First the revved up Sonics disposed of the Midwest Division champion Dallas Mavericks by taking the final three of four without breaking much of a sweat. Then they shot down an equally over-achieving Houston Rockets team (42–40 in regular season play) that was attempting to make their own surprising post-season run. But in the third round Seattle luck ran completely dry, and the Sonics would tumble in four straight to the eventual champions, Magic Johnson's Los Angeles Lakers.

Former Boston Celtics backcourt great K. C. Jones would put in two seasons on the Seattle bench in the early 1990s but the presence of Jones would do little to greatly revive team fortunes. Muscular leaper Shawn Kemp did join the team during this stretch and would carve a great success story as one of a small handful of players ever to by-pass college competition on a fast track straight into the NBA. A 6'10" dunker and ferocious rebounder who possessed perhaps the finest power forward's body in the entire league, Shawn Kemp seemed loaded with almost limitless potential as a future league superstar. Kemp would also bring attention to himself and the team with two proud performances (runner-up in 1991 and 1994) in the league's new showcase Gatorade Slamdunk competition, held annually on All-Star Weekend. But it was only when veteran coach George Karl arrived near the end of the 1992 season that Seattle fortunes again began to take a noticeable upward swing.

Over the years the Seattle SuperSonics have boasted 30 players in the showcase NBA All-Star Game. And they have owned two All-Star Game MVPs as well. Lenny Wilkens earned that distinction at San Diego in 1971 (21 points and a stellar all-around performance) and Tom Chambers on the Seattle home floor in 1987 (34 points, 4 in the deciding overtime period). The team has also featured three first-team all-pros in Haywood in 1972 and 1973 and Gus Williams in 1983. But all the big honors seem to have eluded the club, which has remained, despite its upbeat name, a rather earthbound and even colorless outfit. There has been no scoring champion, or league MVP, or NBA Coach of the Year ever coming out of Seattle. The team has never garnered a league Rookie of the Year, despite coming close with Spencer Haywood (whose 20.6 ppg. scoring might have garnered the honor had not the ABA renegade joined the league, after a court-battle, with the '70–'71 season already half gone). But the most painful gap in the trophy case is the one where they put the NBA championship trophies. Only one lonely momento adorns that particular sparsely decorated shelf.

Suggested Readings on Seattle SuperSonics

Bjarkman, Peter C. **Slam Dunk Superstars.** New York: Smithmark (W.H. Smith Publishers), 1994.

Johnson, Blaine. **What's Happenin'? A Revealing Journey Through the World of Professional Basketball.** Englewood Cliffs, New Jersey. Prentice-Hall, 1978.

Seattle SuperSonics Retired Uniform Numbers (2)

Lenny Wilkens (19)
Fred Brown (32)

Year-by-Year Seattle SuperSonics Summary

Season	Record	Finish	Coaches	Scoring Leader(s)	Playoffs (W–L Record)
Key: * = Tie for Position; $ = Player Coach					
1967–68	23–59	5th	Al Bianchi	Walt Hazzard (24.0)	Did Not Qualify
1968–69	30–52	6th	Al Bianchi	Bob Rule (24.0)	Did Not Qualify
1969–70	36–46	5th	Lenny Wilkens$	Bob Rule (24.6)	Did Not Qualify
1970–71	38–44	4th	Lenny Wilkens$	Spencer Haywood (20.6)	Did Not Qualify
1971–72	47–35	3rd	Lenny Wilkens$	Spencer Haywood (26.2)	Did Not Qualify
1972–73	26–56	4th	Tom Nissalke Buck Buckwalter	Spencer Haywood (29.2)	Did Not Qualify
1973–74	36–36	3rd	Bill Russell	Spencer Haywood (23.5)	Did Not Qualify
1974–75	43–39	2nd	Bill Russell	Spencer Haywood (22.4)	Lost in 2nd Round (4–5)
1975–76	43–39	2nd	Bill Russell	Fred Brown (23.1)	Lost in 1st Round (2–4)
1976–77	40–42	4th	Bill Russell	Fred Brown (17.2)	Did Not Qualify
1977–78	47–35	3rd	Bob Hopkins Lenny Wilkens	Gus Williams (18.1)	Lost in NBA Finals (13–9)
1978–79	52–30	1st	Lenny Wilkens	Gus Williams (19.2)	**NBA Champion** (12–5)
1979–80	56–26	2nd	Lenny Wilkens	Gus Williams (22.1)	Lost in 3rd Round (7–8)
1980–81	34–48	6th	Lenny Wilkens	Jack Sikma (18.7)	Did Not Qualify
1981–82	52–30	2nd	Lenny Wilkens	Gus Williams (23.4)	Lost in 1st Round (7–8)
1982–83	48–34	3rd	Lenny Wilkens	Gus Williams (20.0)	Lost in 1st Round (0–2)
1983–84	42–40	3rd	Lenny Wilkens	Jack Sikma (19.1)	Lost in 1st Round (2–3)
1984–85	31–51	4th*	Lenny Wilkens	Tom Chambers (21.5)	Did Not Qualify
1985–86	31–51	5th	B. Bickerstaff	Tom Chambers (18.5)	Did Not Qualify
1986–87	39–43	4th	B. Bickerstaff	Dale Ellis (24.9)	Lost in 3rd Round (7–7)
1987–88	44–38	3rd	B. Bickerstaff	Dale Ellis (25.8)	Lost in 1st Round (2–3)
1988–89	47–35	3rd	B. Bickerstaff	Dale Ellis (27.5)	Lost in 2nd Round (3–5)
1989–90	41–41	4th	B. Bickerstaff	Xavier McDaniel (21.3)	Did Not Qualify
1990–91	41–41	5th	K.C. Jones	Eddie Johnson (17.4)	Lost in 1st Round (2–3)
1991–92	47–35	4th	K.C. Jones Bob Kloppenburg George Karl	Ricky Pierce (21.7)	Lost in 2nd Round (4–5)

Season	Record	Finish	Coaches	Scoring Leader(s)	Playoffs (W–L Record)
1992–93	55–27	2nd	George Karl	Ricky Pierce (18.2)	Lost in 3rd Round (10–9)
1993–94	63–19	1st	George Karl	Shawn Kemp (18.1)	Lost in 1st Round (2–3)

Individual Career Leaders and Record Holders (1967–1994)

Scoring Average	Spencer Haywood (24.9 ppg., 1970–75)
Points Scored	Fred Brown (14,018, 1971–84)
Games Played	Fred Brown (963)
Minutes Played	Fred Brown (24,442)
Field Goal Pct.	James Donaldson (.584, 1980–83)
3-Pt. Field Goals	Dale Ellis (476, 1986–91)
Free Throws Made	Jack Sikma (3,044, 1977–86)
Free-Throw Pct.	Ricky Pierce (.908, 1991–94)
Rebounds	Jack Sikma (7,729)
Rebound Average	Jack Sikma (10.8 rpg., 1977–86)
Assists	Nate McMillan (4,080, 1986–94)
Steals	Fred Brown (1,149)
Blocked Shots	Jack Sikma (705)
Personal Fouls	Jack Sikma (2,473)

Individual Single-Season and Game Records (1967–1994)

Scoring Average	Spencer Haywood (29.2 ppg., 1972–73)
Points Scored (Season	Dale Ellis (2,253, 1988–89)
Points Scored (Game)	Fred Brown (58, 3–23–74 at Golden State Warriors)
Field Goal Pct. (Season)	James Donaldson (.609, 1981–82)
3-Pt. Field Goals (Season)	Dale Ellis (162, 1988–89)
3-Pt. Field Goals (Game)	Dale Ellis (9, 4–20–90 vs. Los Angeles Clippers)
Free-Throw Pct. (Season)	Ricky Pierce (.925, 1990–91)
Rebounds (Season)	Jack Sikma (1,038, 1981–82)
Rebounds (Game)	Jim Fox (30, 12–26–73 vs. Los Angeles Lakers)
Assists (Season)	Lenny Wilkens (766, 1971–72)
Assists (Game)	Nate McMillan (25, 2–23–87 vs. Los Angeles Clippers)
Steals (Season)	Slick Watts (261, 1975–76)
Steals (Game)	Gus Williams (10, 2–22–78 vs. New Jersey Nets)
	Fred Brown (10, 12-3-76 at Philadelphia Sixers)
Blocked Shots (Season)	Alton Lister (180, 1986–87)
Blocked Shots (Game)	Shawn Kemp (10, 1–18–91 at Los Angeles Lakers)

Best Trade in Franchise History

Not much attention was paid at first to the deal in July, 1986, that brought three-point bomber Dale Ellis from Dallas to Seattle in exchange for dependable guard Al Wood. Over the next several seasons, however, Ellis would quietly prove himself one of the greatest offensive threats in club history and one of the finest three-point-range shooters in NBA annals. But perhaps the best trade ever for the Sonics in the end will prove to be the one they didn't make. This was the reported blockbuster deal that would have sent Shawn Kemp and Ricky Pierce to Chicago for Scottie Pippen on the eve of draft day, 1994. Thus the Sonics narrowly avoided the mistake once made by baseball's Cleveland club, which first blundered in a huge way by trading away popular slugger Rocky Colavito smack in his prime, and then committed an even bigger gaffe in trading to get him back at a time when Colavito was clearly far over the hill. Scottie Pippen (fifth overall pick in a draft which also earned Seattle Derrick McKey) was a player the Sonics brass never should have let slip through their fingers on draft day of 1987; but Pippen (saddled with a reputation for clubhouse moodiness) was hardly a prize worthy of Kemp by draft day, 1994.

Worst Trade in Franchise History

Scottie Pippen was just the player the Chicago Bulls needed to supplement Jordan at the end of the '80s and to shape a good Chicago team into a very great one. Thus only three years after the Portland Trail Blazers had passed on an opportunity to draft Michael Jordan in 1984, it was now the Seattle SuperSonics' turn to hand Chicago a franchise player they never should have had. Pippen was drafted by the Seattle club as a 1987 first round pick (5th overall, behind David Robinson, Armon Gilliam, Dennis Hopson, and Reggie Williams), then shipped to Chicago for mediocre center Olden Polynice. This single move would eventually launch a three-peat reign at the top for Chicago and again postpone Seattle championship hopes for at least several seasons down the line.

Seattle SuperSonics Historical Oddity

The Sonics make NBA history in December, 1970, when they openly defied the league's ban on signing collegiate underclassmen whose original classes had not yet graduated. The Seattle signing of Spencer Haywood brought instant respectability to a heretofore lackluster Sonics ballclub; and it also undercut the single recruiting advantage the upstart ABA might have had over the more established NBA. Furthermore, the controversial move launched a new type of bidding war soon to be known rather euphemistically as the NBA's "hardship clause" for undergraduates interested in entering the lucrative pro ranks after only a year or two of collegiate seasoning. It might also be mentioned here that it was the self-same Haywood whose career in Seattle was almost tragically and prematurely ended in another odd moment of franchise history. A leaky Seattle Center Coliseum roof in 1972 was responsible for an avoidable accident which saw Haywood slip on the dampened court and severely damage a knee ligament. The sieve-like Coliseum continued to provide problems in Seattle for years to come, despite $2 million in building repairs. In 1986, the same building was site for the NBA's first-ever "postponed due to rain" game, when additional rain-induced roof repairs caused suspension of game action which then had to be concluded the following night.

Sonics All-Time Number One Draft Picks List

Seattle SuperSonics
1967 Al Tucker (Oklahoma Baptist)
1968 Bob Kauffman (Guilford)
1969 Lucious Allen (UCLA)
1970 Jim Ard (Cincinnati)
1971 Fred Brown (Iowa)
1972 Bud Stallworth (Kansas)
1973 Mike Green (Louisiana Tech)
1974 Tom Burleson (North Carolina State)
1975 Frank Oleynick (Seattle)
1976 Bob Wilkerson (Indiana)
1977 Jack Sikma (Illinois Wesleyan)
1978 None
1979 James Bailey (Rutgers)
1980 Bill Hanzlik (Notre Dame)
1981 Danny Vranes (Utah)
1982 None
1983 John Sundvold (Missouri)
1984 None
1985 Xavier McDaniel (Wichita State)
1986 Nate McMillan (North Carolina State)
1987 Scottie Pippen (Central Arkansas)
1988 Gary Grant (Michigan)
1989 Dana Barros (Boston College)
1990 Gary Payton (Oregon State)
1991 Rich King (Nebraska)
1992 Doug Christie (Pepperdine)
1993 Ervin Johnson (New Orleans)

Chapter 13

MILWAUKEE BUCKS

Quite Fast at the Gate, Even Faster in the Homestretch

All-Time Franchise Record: 1212–920, .568 Pct. (1968–1994)
NBA Championships (1): 1970–71
Greatest Franchise Player: Kareem Abdul-Jabbar (Lew Alcindor) (1969–1975)
All-Time Leading Scorer: Kareem Abdul-Jabbar (14,211 Points, 1969–1975)
Most Successful Coach: Larry Costello (540–344, .611 Pct., 1976–1987)
All-Time Franchise Team: Kareem Abdul-Jabbar (C), Bob Lanier (C-F), Terry Cummings (F), Oscar Robertson (G), Sidney Moncrief (G)

On May 22, 1994, the Milwaukee Bucks basketball club and their fans celebrated a moment of rare good fortune. Under the NBA's new complex lottery system, the Bucks heard their name called out for the top choice in the 1994 college player draft. And thus, waiting for them a month down the road on the night of the formal draft party in Indianapolis was Glenn "Big Dog" Robinson, one of the most touted undergraduate prospects to come along in many a year. Robinson had played at Purdue University in the Big Ten, and had just finished his junior season with a nation-best 30.3 scoring average. There wasn't a scout anywhere on the NBA circuit who wasn't calling him the next Elgin Baylor or perhaps the second coming of Bob McAdoo. The "Big Dog" appeared to be a franchise player, one built along the lines of Jordan a decade earlier, or Magic or Bird before that. The Bucks now seemed ready to turn several years of misery into a sharp swing up the league ladder of prosperity.

Yet, surprising as it may now seem to often short-sighted modern NBA fans, this was not at all the biggest draft day news in the history of the Milwaukee NBA franchise. This is a franchise, after all, that had once received the biggest draft day bonus of all time. In fact, as many a scribe has put it in the past, the whole history of this NBA expansion club seems to rest on a single fateful flip of the coin way back in March, 1969. It was that flip that brought Lew Alcindor to Milwaukee and thus turned an expansion deadbeat into an NBA champion in only the third season of ballclub history. It was the biggest and most surprising success story that pro basketball has ever known.

Milwaukee was back in the NBA in the fall of 1968 after a thirteen-year absence (the Hawks had relocated to St. Louis in 1955) and the year of their debut was a transition year for the league as a whole. Phoenix would join Milwaukee that season as an expansion franchise and the old Milwaukee tenant, the Hawks, would move once again, this time from St. Louis to Atlanta. And more importantly, the great dynasty of the Auerbach-Russell Celtics would finally play itself out with a final Boston championship of the '60s and the retirement of center Bill Russell.

The Bucks themselves would experience a perfectly typical expansion first-year season. Milwaukee's last-place entrant in the Eastern Division was largely dreadful and completed the year with 55 defeats and a 30-game deficit between themselves and the division-leading Baltimore Bullets. Flynn Robinson, picked up from Chicago for Bob Love and Bob Weiss in the early weeks of the season, provided much of the offense (20.3 ppg.) and veteran Wayne Embry, playing his final season, anchored the center slot. A single high spot was an NBA attendance record (6,246 per game in Milwaukee Arena) for a first-year expansion club. Of course the Bucks were not quite as dreadful as their expansion rivals in Phoenix, who posted a 16–66 record despite the high-scoring presence of former LA Lakers star guard Gail Goodrich (23.8 ppg.) And if the fledgling Milwaukee ballclub was actually a good deal better than the one in Phoenix, it would soon prove to be a good deal luckier at the craps table as well.

The fateful day of franchise history was thus set up by the events of an altogether undistinguished maiden campaign. The NBA draft is the mechanism that maintains balance in the league by rewarding also-rans with a chance at over-the-summer immediate improvement. But only on the rarest of occasion does the type of acknowledged franchise player come along who can truly reverse the fortunes of a ballclub almost by himself—as great as they were, neither Chamberlain nor Oscar Robertson (nor even Michael Jordan) made immediate winners out of their new pro clubs. Bird and Magic would both do it a decade later, in the same season, but almost no one else has.

This was one of those occasions, however, and by the logic of the draft principle the lowly Phoenix Suns (16–66, with eleven less wins than the Bucks) should have now owned that magical player. Still another wrinkle had been written into the draft procedure, however. To prevent teams from simply losing games to garner a top pick, the league had decided on a coin flip between the two conference tailenders. And thus the Bucks would luck out over the doubly downtrodden Phoenix team on March 19, 1969;

Phoenix called for heads and when tails came up Milwaukee suddenly had the rights to 7-foot wonder Lew Alcindor. Once the Bucks management had won the toss they must have instantly realized they had guaranteed respectability staring them squarely in the face. All that remained was to outbid the rival ABA (it took a five-year $1.2 million contract offer) for the greatest rookie to come along in two decades of pro basketball history.

Never before in NBA history—save possibly with Russell's arrival in Boston in 1957—had a single player made such an instantaneous difference. But Boston was not a hopeless expansion team like Milwaukee; Russell joined a Celtics ballclub that could already boast Cousy and was bringing Heinsohn on board that same season. And never before, or since, in NBA annals would an expansion team turn things around quite so quickly. The Orlando Magic, for example, would jump 20 games in the won-lost columns during their own first season with touted recent rookie Shaquille O'Neal. But Orlando did not win an NBA title in Shaq's first or second year and did not even become a playoff qualifier in the Shaq's rookie campaign. In year two the Bucks, however, reversed their record completely (a 29-game improvement in victories) and made it all the way to the second round of the playoffs. For the first time ever a total doormat had become a league power in but one calendar revolution. There was no long-term building plan for this emerging powerhouse. It simply happened—literally overnight.

But the Bucks were still perhaps one player away. And just as quickly as they had gone out and gotten the franchise player they had needed, Milwaukee management would also take immediate steps to fill this one last gap as well. Simultaneous with season's end, the Bucks turned to the trade route and picked up the perfect player to complement Jabbar. In a major transaction Flynn Robinson—the club's first-year scoring leader who also averaged 21.8 ppg. in year two—was packaged with reserve forward Charlie Paulk and sent to Cincinnati for the incomparable, but now aging Oscar Robertson. And there was not just one trade to cement this promising team, but actually two. Five months later, on the eve of the new season, substitute forward Don Smith was next sent packing to Seattle for veteran starter Bob Boozer and promising rookie forward Lucius Allen. All the pieces were seemingly now in place for a true powerhouse team.

The team that had been put together almost overnight now quickly proved, in its first season featuring Alcindor alongside Robertson, to be one of the greatest outfits that pro basketball has ever witnessed. With their balanced attack Milwaukee roared through the regular season in first place in the Midwest Division under the new four-division alignment. A starting five of Lew Alcindor, Jon McGlocklin, Bob Dandridge, Oscar Robertson and Greg Smith compiled the league's best record (66–16); bench strength from Bob Boozer, Lucius Allen and Dick Cunningham provided firepower that contributed to six new league records—home wins (34), road wins (28), field goal percentage (.509), field goals made (3,972),

George Mikan, Minneapolis Lakers, the original "Mr. Basketball." (NAISMITH BASKETBALL HALL OF FAME)

Bob Cousy, basketball's greatest ballhandler. (NAISMITH BASKETBALL HALL OF FAME)

"The Big O" was by any reasonable measure the greatest basketball player of all time. (NAISMITH BASKETBALL HALL OF FAME)

Red Holzman, who coached the "Miracle on 33rd Street" in 1970. (NEW YORK
KNICKS)

Bill Russell, Boston Celtics. (NAISMITH BASKETBALL HALL OF FAME)

Basketball's greatest scorer, Wilt Chamberlain of the Los Angeles Lakers. (NAI-SMITH BASKETBALL HALL OF FAME)

Jerry West, Los Angeles Lakers. (NAISMITH BASKETBALL HALL OF FAME)

(facing pg.) Jumpshot pioneer, "Pitchin' Paul" Arizin, Philadelphia Warriors. (NAISMITH BASKETBALL HALL OF FAME)

The NBA's first 20,000-point man, Bob Pettit of the St. Louis Hawks. (NAISMITH BASKETBALL HALL OF FAME)

Willis Reed, hero of the 1970 "Miracle on 33rd Street." (NAISMITH BASKETBALL HALL OF FAME)

"The Redhead" Dave Cowens finished his career in Milwaukee. (LARRY S PHENSON)

John Havlicek, the best in a long line o Boston "sixth man" heroes. (BOSTON CELTICS)

Dr. J (Julius Erving) is the inventor of "hangtime" and basketball's greatest all-time showman. (FRANK P. MCGRATH, JR.)

David Thompson broke in with Denver of the ABA as one of the game's greatest high-flyers. (LARRY STEPHENSON)

Rick Barry, basketball's original superstar "gypsy" of both ABA and NBA fame. (HOUSTON ROCKETS)

Bob McAdoo, New York Knicks. (NEW YORK KNICKS)

Moses Malone has quietly built up rebounding and scoring stats that rank him among the all-time greats. (LARRY STEPHENSON)

Larry Bird of the Boston Celtics, perhaps the game's greatest forward. (LARRY STEPHENSON)

Darryl Dawkins, straight from high-
school to the NBA. (LARRY STE-
PHENSON)

Magic Johnson saved the pro game at the outset of the '80s. (LARRY STE-
PHENSON)

Air Jordan flies high at the 1985 NBA Slam Dunk Contest in Indianapolis.
(FRANK P. MCGRATH, JR.)

Bill Walton led a "miracle season" drive for Portland in the late '70s. (PORTLAND TRAIL BLAZERS)

Dominique Wilkins, Atlanta Hawks, basketball's "Human Highlight Film." (LARRY STEPHENSON)

Kareem Abdul-Jabbar, basketball's all-time "Iron Man." (LARRY STEPHENSON)

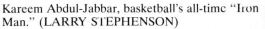

Shaquille O'Neal, the latest NBA phenomenon and possible heir to Chamberlain and Russell. (FRANK P. MCGRATH, JR.)

Micheal Williams of the Timberwolves now owns the NBA consecutive free throws record. (FRANK P. MCGRATH, JR.)

and assists (2,249, with Oscar himself accounting for a team record 668 of the total).

Next Costello's juggernaut roared through the playoffs just as easily. They mowed down first San Francisco, and then Los Angeles, by identical 4–1 margins. And then they manhandled Baltimore's Bullets (upset winners over New York in the Eastern Finals) in four straight with only one game providing a victory margin of less than ten points. Milwaukee was thus only the second club ever to sweep an NBA championship series. Only the Russell-Cousy Boston Celtics of 1958–59 had accomplished this feat by shutting down the Minneapolis Lakers and Elgin Baylor in the same one-sided fashion Alcindor and company had now become—in only the third season of franchise history—a team destined to be remembered for all the ages.

It didn't look like things would slow down the least bit for Milwaukee in season number four. Abdul-Jabbar (for he had now officially changed his name from Alcindor) continued his domination with a career-high ppg. average (34.8) and was once more scoring champion and league MVP. The season's won-loss record (63–19) was only a hair short of the previous year's championship team. But this time luck ran out when the Bucks faced the now much-improved Los Angeles Lakers in the conference finals. The renewal of the Jabbar-Chamberlain face-off found Kareem with another big offensive edge; but Oscar Robertson was slowed by muscle spasms and the Lakers pulled away after the clubs had spilt the first four contests. Earlier in the season it had been Milwaukee which put an end to the record Los Angeles 33-game winning streak, the longest in U.S. professional sports history. But in the post-season wars, the Bucks were unable to prevent the best-ever Los Angeles club from making it all the way into the league's final round.

The playoff collapse of 1972 was seemingly only a temporary setback. The '72–'73 campaign brought another year of 60 victories, another runway division title (nine full games ahead of Chicago's Bulls), and another season of Abdul-Jabbar's total domination (second in league scoring, third in field goal percentage, fourth in rebounds). Unfortunately this fourth year of Costello's juggernaut would also bring another unexpected playoff collapse as well. The Warriors this time around stunned the Bucks in round one by wrapping up Milwaukee (despite 20 ppg. post-season averages by both Jabbar and Robertson) in six games.

But the derailing again seemed to be largely temporary and more an aberration than an omen. When play opened again in the fall of 1973 the Milwaukee club showed that it had really lost nothing of its potency. Jabbar was still at the very height of his game and another division-title year brought Kareem his third MVP in five seasons. And it also brought another crack at a second NBA championship ring. This time there would be no early post-season collapse as the Bucks breezed by Los Angeles (4–1) in the opening round. Then they swept past Chicago (4–0) in the Conference Finals. But the title matchup with the tough Boston Celtics would prove another huge stumbling block. Oscar was well past his prime and incapable of carrying the entire backcourt load when Lucius Allen was felled by a knee injury. In the end, Boston won-out in a hotly contested series that went the full distance after Milwaukee's gritty double-overtime triumph in game six. Game seven found Boston's Dave Cowens outscoring Jabbar by two points (28 to 26) in an even matchup of superstars. But the Celtics won handily (102–87) to return to the championship circle after an absence of five long years.

The dream finally began to unravel in 1974–75, however. For starters, Oscar Robertson had retired at the conclusion of the previous campaign, closing the door on what may have been the most brilliant overall career of all-time. Oscar had averaged 30 ppg. six times and led the league in assists six times as well; he just missed *averaging* a triple-double (double figures in scoring, rebounds and assists) over his first *five full NBA seasons*; he never won a scoring title and yet when he retired, Oscar was the highest scoring guard of NBA history. And now he was finally gone. And if that weren't enough, Jabbar also missed the first 16 games with a broken wrist, while a knee injury also kept all-star guard Jim Price sidelined the entire second half of the season as well. The club started out 3–13 and never fully recovered on the way to a 38–44 mark, while nonetheless remaining in the playoff hunt until the final week of the season. For the first time since the franchise rookie season, however, the Milwaukee ballclub was now left on the sidelines when the post-season playoffs finally rolled around.

This first season on the downslide in Milwaukee was not to be just a year of normal transaction, but rather one of almost complete transformation. For a ballclub that had, from the first, done things in a big hurry, an era had already come to an end just seven winters into franchise history. For Jabbar was suddenly to follow Oscar out of Milwaukee as well. Kareem had for some time wanted a return to his collegiate home in Southern California, and the Bucks graciously accommodated their superstar by pulling off one of the largest transactions in NBA history. Kareem was shipped off to Los Angeles (along with center Walt Wesley) on June 16, 1975, for what amounted to a full starting team—center Elmore Smith, forward Dave Meyers, guards Brian Winters and Junior Bridgeman, and some future considerations as well. The trade was a blockbuster for its impact around the league; and it was also a curtain closer in the nation's beer capital.

Without Jabbar and the Big O, Milwaukee was just not the same team by any stretch. But the club did rebound in what would be Larry Costello's last full season. Costello's outfit duplicated its 38 victories of the previous year and again returned to the first round of the playoffs. The first real collapse would come in the following season, however, when the now punchless Bucks dropped a dozen games under .500 and fell straight into the Midwest Division basement. Three left-over ABA ballclubs had been merged into the NBA for this particular season and three (Denver, San

Antonio, and the Indiana Pacers) outstretched the Bucks in victories. Not surprisingly, Costello didn't complete the season and was replaced by ex-Celtics star Don Nelson a mere 18 games into the fall campaign.

At the conclusion of the dreadful 1977 season the Milwaukee Bucks would now, for the second time, hold the first overall selection of the collegiate draft. This time the choice was another center, 6'11" Kent Benson from the Bobby Knight-coached Indiana University Hoosiers. Benson would never develop into a first-rate NBA player, however, and would average double figures in scoring only three times over an 11-year pro career. The Bucks now stood one-and-one on their two "franchise player" picks—with one more still awaiting them some years down the road.

If the first chapter of Milwaukee Bucks basketball had been the glorious era of Kareem Abdul-Jabbar, the second epoch was the nearly as spectacular sojourn of coach Don Nelson. It took Nelson a couple of seasons to light a fire under the rebuilding Milwaukee ballclub. But slowly the pieces were put in place, one crucial player at a time. Bob Lanier was an important acquisition at the 1980 All-Star break to plug the post position inadequately manned by the disappointing Kent Benson for two break-even seasons. The trade of Benson and the top draft selection of 1980 for the long-time All-Star from Detroit, not only strengthened the ballclub immediately but also served to recoup the team's losses in the original drafting of Benson with the top overall choice in 1977. The Bucks rebounded in the victory column after the vital Lanier trade, to roar down the stretch with a 20–6 mark and capture the first of seven straight Midwest Division (later Central Division) titles.

Nelson's teams were among the best in the Eastern Conference throughout most of the 1980s. Paced by a strong nucleus of Sydney Moncrief, Terry Cummings and Paul Pressey the Bucks averaged 55 wins a year during Nelson's seven-year period of mastery. But Milwaukee's role as an Eastern Conference force always seemed to shut down by the time the month of May had rolled around. Despite an almost monotonous string of divisional titles the Bucks could never seem to get very far in post-season play. The first three years of the string they were eliminated in the opening round. During the final four seasons they dropped out in the second round twice and the third round twice. The Celtics and Larry Bird seemed to be the largest roadblock for potential Milwaukee playoff dreams. In 1984 Bird and company eliminated the Bucks in five games. And in 1986 it was an easy four-game sweep for the eventual NBA champions.

Don Nelson's tenure ended with the injury-plagued season of 1986–87. Nelson's final edition again won 50 games despite limited playing time for veterans like Paul Pressey, Sidney Moncrief and Jerry Reynolds. Moncrief did stay healthy long enough to cross the career 10,000 point plateau. Another milestone was reached when popular Junior Bridgeman rejoined the team in January from the LA Clippers and extended his franchise record for games played. But the Bucks had slipped to third in the division and were again eliminated in the second playoff round. The string of seven straight division titles (second only to a run of nine by the dynasty Bill Russell-led Celtics) was at long last over. And so was the tenure of the most successful coach in Bucks history as Don Nelson stepped down shortly after season's-end to pursue other basketball opportunities.

The post-Nelson era in Milwaukee has been witness to the club's first long period of steady decline. Teams coached by Del Harris remained over .500 for four more seasons but now never seriously challenged in either the divisional race or in the post-season tournament chase. A spanking new Bradley Center replaced Milwaukee Arena as the team's home in '88–'89 and now offered Bucks' fans one of the plushiest venues anywhere on the NBA circuit. But an upgrade in lodging spurred no similar increase in team prowess. First Detroit, and then Chicago, would instead emerge as the new Central Division powerhouse clubs. When Harris's fifth team fell twenty games below the break-even point it was a time for only the third coaching change of franchise history. Mike Dunleavy—ex-Bucks player, short-term assistant under Del Harris, and recent head coach of the LA Lakers for two seasons—signed an eight-year contract in May, 1992, that was hopefully the first step in resurrecting a once-proud Milwaukee franchise.

The first two years under Dunleavy (who also serves as general manager) have instead been the bleakest period in franchise history. For the first time since their inaugural year, the Bucks tumbled into last place during the '92–'93, 25th anniversary campaign. Seven new roster faces (Alaa Abdelnaby, Anthony Avent, Blue Edwards, Todd Day, Lee Mayberry, Eric Murdock, and Anthony Pullard) provided little stability on a 28–54 ballclub, and also represented the largest turnover in personnel from one season to the next in club history. The only consolation prize this time around would be promising 6'11" center Vin Baker (8th overall draft selection) from an unheralded basketball program at the University of Hartford.

And if the lidlifter under Dunleavy wasn't bad enough, the Bucks repeated their last-place finish in '93–'94, this time tying for the basement slot with another fallen giant, the "over-the-hill-gang" Detroit Pistons. Perhaps this time the consolation prize would be much greater. The Bucks did win the lottery pick, after all, and luck seemed to be back squarely on their side. Glenn Robinson was now waiting on the sideline and the NBA's first $100-million player was sure to draw considerable media focus for the team, as well as an upsurge in season ticket sales and hopefully also higher numbers in the win column. But even the most zealous fans of Robinson's high-powered collegiate game were not now claiming that Purdue's "Big Dog" would ever be a second coming of Kareem Abdul-Jabbar. And even Jabbar in his prime (without an Oscar Robertson to share the load) could never hope to carry on his broad shoulders the weak supporting cast that was penciled into the lineup around rookie Glenn Robinson.

Suggested Readings on Milwaukee Bucks

Cohen, Joel. **The Big A: The Story of Lew Alcindor.** New York: Scholastic Book Services, 1971.

Moncrief, Sidney (with Myra McLarey). **Moncrief—My Journey to the NBA.** Little Rock, Arkansas: August House Publishers, 1990.

Pepe, Phil. **Stand Tall: The Lew Alcindor Story.** New York: Grosset and Dunlap Publishers, 1970.

Milwaukee Bucks Retired Uniform Numbers (7)

Oscar Robertson (1)
Junior Bridgeman (2)
Sidney Moncrief (4)
Jon McGlocklin (14)
Bob Lanier (16)
Brian Winters (32)
Kareem Abdul-Jabbar (33)

Year-by-Year Milwaukee Bucks Summary

Season	Record	Finish	Coach(es)	Scoring Leader(s)	Playoffs (W-L Record)
Key: * = Tied for Position; # = League Scoring Leader					
1968–69	27–55	7th	Larry Costello	Flynn Robinson (20.3)	Did Not Qualify
1969–70	56–26	2nd	Larry Costello	Lew Alcindor (28.8)	Lost in 2nd Round (5–5)
1970–71	66–16	1st	Larry Costello	Lew Alcindor (31.7)#	**NBA Champion** (12–2)
1971–72	63–19	1st	Larry Costello	K. Abdul-Jabbar (34.8)#	Lost in 2nd Round (6–5)
1972–73	60–22	1st	Larry Costello	K. Abdul-Jabbar (30.2)	Lost in 1st Round (2–4)
1973–74	59–23	1st	Larry Costello	K. Abdul-Jabbar (27.0)	Lost in NBA Finals (11–5)
1974–75	38–44	4th	Larry Costello	K. Abdul-Jabbar (30.0)	Did Not Qualify
1975–76	38–44	1st	Larry Costello	Bob Dandridge (21.5)	Lost in 1st Round (1–2)
1976–77	30–52	6th	Larry Costello Don Nelson	Bob Dandridge (20.8)	Did Not Qualify
1977–78	44–38	2nd	Don Nelson	Brian Winters (19.9)	Lost in 2nd Round (5–4)
1978–79	38–44	4th	Don Nelson	Marques Johnson (25.6)	Did Not Qualify
1979–80	49–33	1st	Don Nelson	Marques Johnson (21.7)	Lost in 1st Round (3–4)
1980–81	60–22	1st	Don Nelson	Marques Johnson (20.3)	Lost in 1st Round (3–4)
1981–82	55–27	1st	Don Nelson	Sidney Moncrief (19.8)	Lost in 1st Round (2–4)
1982–83	51–31	1st	Don Nelson	Sidney Moncrief (22.5)	Lost in 2nd Round (5–4)
1983–84	50–32	1st	Don Nelson	Sidney Moncrief (20.9)	Lost in 3rd Round (8–8)
1984–85	59–23	1st	Don Nelson	Terry Cummings (23.6)	Lost in 2nd Round (3–5)
1985–86	57–25	1st	Don Nelson	Sidney Moncrief (20.2)	Lost in 3rd Round (7–7)
1986–87	50–32	3rd	Don Nelson	Terry Cummings (20.8)	Lost in 2nd Round (6–6)
1987–88	42–40	4th	Del Harris	Terry Cummings (21.3)	Lost in 1st Round (2–3)
1988–89	49–33	4th	Del Harris	Terry Cummings (22.9)	Lost in 2nd Round (3–6)

Season	Record	Finish	Coach(es)	Scoring Leader(s)	Playoffs (W-L Record)
1989–90	44–38	3rd	Del Harris	Ricky Pierce (23.0)	Lost in 1st Round (0–3)
1990–91	48–34	3rd	Del Harris	Dale Ellis (19.3)	Lost in 1st Round (1–3)
1991–92	31–51	6th	Del Harris Frank Hamblen	Dale Ellis (15.7)	Did Not Qualify
1992–93	28–54	6th	Mike Dunleavy	Blue Edwards (16.9)	Did Not Qualify
1993–94	20–62	6th*	Mike Dunleavy	Eric Murdock (15.3)	Did Not Qualify

Individual Career Leaders and Record Holders (1968–1994)

Scoring Average	Kareem Abdul-Jabbar (30.4 ppg., 1969–75)
Points Scored	Kareem Abdul-Jabbar (14,211, 1969–75)
Games Played	Junior Bridgeman (711, 1975–87)
Minutes Played	Bob Dandridge (22,094, 1969–77 and 1981–82)
Field Goals Made	Kareem Abdul-Jabbar (5,902)
Field Goal Pct.	Kareem Abdul-Jabbar (.547)
3-Pt. Field Goals	Brad Lohaus (267, 1990–94)
3-Pt. Field Goal Pct.	Dale Ellis (.423, 1990–92)
Free Throws Made	Sidney Moncrief (3,505, 1979–89)
Free-Throw Pct.	Jack Sikma (.884, 1986–91)
Rebounds	Kareem Abdul-Jabbar (7,161)
Assists	Paul Pressey (3,272, 1982–90)
Steals	Quinn Buckner (1,042, 1976–82)
Blocked Shots	Alton Lister (744, 1981–86)

Individual Single-Season and Game Records (1968–1994)

Scoring Average	Kareem Abdul-Jabbar (34.8 ppg., 1971–72)
Points Scored (Season)	Kareem Abdul-Jabbar (2,822, 1971–72)
Points Scored (Game)	Kareem Abdul-Jabbar (55, 12–10–71 vs. Boston Celtics)
Field Goal Pct. (Season)	Kareem Abdul-Jabbar (.577, 1970–71)
Free-Throw Pct. (Season)	Jack Sikma (.922, 1987–88)
3–Pt. Field Goals (Season)	Dale Ellis (138, 1991–92)
Rebounds (Season)	Kareem Abdul-Jabbar (1,346, 1971–72)
Rebounds (Game)	Swen Nater (33, 12–19–76 vs. Atlanta Hawks)
Assists (Season)	Oscar Robertson (668, 1970–71)
Assists (Game)	Guy Rodgers (22, 11–31–68 vs. Detroit Pistons)
Steals (Season)	Alvin Robertson (246, 1990–91)
Steals (Game)	Alvin Robertson (10, 11–19–90 vs. Utah Jazz)
Blocked Shots (Season)	Kareem Abdul-Jabbar (283, 1973–74)
Blocked Shots (Game)	Kareem Abdul-Jabbar (10, 11–3–73 vs. Detroit Pistons)

Best Trade in Franchise History

Lew Alcindor came into the NBA as the most touted rookie ever, and the soon-to-be renamed ''Kareem Abdul-Jabbar'' was almost enough of a dominating talent to single-handedly make a championship team overnight—just as Bill Russell had for the Celtics a decade and a half earlier. But it was not going to be quite that simple in reality. There was yet another needed piece for the puzzle, and that piece, it turned out, was veteran backcourt star Oscar Robertson. The Big O was pryed all too easily from Cincinnati on April 21, 1970, for forward Flynn Robinson (the club's debut-season high scorer) and bulky center Charlie Paulk. With Oscar and Kareem, the Bucks were an undeniable force before they had passed their third birthday in the league.

Worst Trade in Franchise History

The Boston Red Sox trading Babe Ruth to the Yankees. The ABA New York Nets dealing Julius Erving to Philadelphia. Anybody parting with Wilt Chamberlain or Oscar Robertson for any price. These are the most laughable transactions in the history of American sport. And the third of this tripartite collection of all-time silliest superstar giveaways is the Milwaukee Bucks shipping Kareem Abdul-Jabbar to the Los Angeles Lakers in June of 1975. It is certainly true enough that the Bucks received practically a whole starting five in return—Elmore Smith, Brian Winters, David Meyers and Junior Bridgeman, plus some cash. But Jabbar would go on to score more NBA points *after* he left Milwaukee (24,176) than all but a half-dozen players have in their entire offense-oriented careers. Whatever the Bucks might have received in return for Jabbar, it could not possibly have been anywhere near enough.

Milwaukee Bucks Historical Oddity

If the Milwaukee Bucks have not necessarily been one of pro basketball's more glamorous or high-profile franchises, they certainly have been one of the steadiest when it comes to year-in and year-out quality performance. When the Bucks tumbled to a last-place division finish in 1992–93, it represented only the second time they had ended in the basement since the team's first season, a quarter-century earlier. Furthermore, this Milwaukee franchise has averaged 48 wins per season across the entire first quarter-century of ballclub existence. It boasts a winning percentage of nearly .570, surpassed over the years only by Boston (.633) and the LA Lakers (.606). Thus only the league's two proudest franchises—the Celtics and

Lakers—can boast better all-time winning ledgers than the one owned by the Milwaukee Bucks.

Bucks All-Time Number One Draft Picks List

Milwaukee Bucks

1968 Charlie Paulk (Northeastern)
1969 Lew Alcindor (UCLA)
1970 Gary Freeman (Oregon State)
1971 Collis Jones (Notre Dame)
1972 Russell Lee (Marshall)
1973 Swen Nater (UCLA)
1974 Gary Brokaw (Notre Dame)
1975 None
1976 Quinn Buckner (Indiana)
1977 Kent Benson (Indiana)
1978 None
1979 Sidney Moncrief (Arkansas)
1980 None
1981 Alton Lister (Arizona State)
1982 Paul Pressey (Tulsa)
1983 Randy Breuer (Minnesota)
1984 Kenny Fields (UCLA)
1985 Jerry Reynolds (LSU)
1986 Scott Skiles (Michigan State)
1987 None
1988 Jeff Grayer (Iowa State)
1989 None
1990 Terry Mills (Michigan)
1991 Kevin Brooks (SW Louisiana)
1992 Todd Day (Arkansas)
1993 Vin Baker (Hartford)
1994 Glenn Robinson (Purdue)

Chapter 14

PHOENIX SUNS

One Phoenix That Couldn't Rise from the Ashes

All-Time Franchise Record: 1146–986, .538 Pct. (1968–1994)
NBA Championships: None
Greatest Franchise Player: Walter Davis (1977–1988)
All-Time Leading Scorer: Walter Davis (15,666 Points, 1977–1988)
Most Successful Coach: Paul Westphal (118–56, .720 Pct., 1992–1994)
All-Time Franchise Team: Alvan Adams (C-F), Connie Hawkins (F), Charles Barkley
   (F), Walter Davis (G), Paul Westphal (G)

Located in the heart of the old Wild West badlands, it is altogether fitting that the Phoenix NBA franchise should provide the setting, at two ends of franchise history, for the pro game's two most notorious "bad guy" superstars.

In the early '70s there was Connie Hawkins—banned from the NBA and shunned by the NCAA as well for alleged association with game-fixing gamblers. Basketball's original Prince of Darkness remained—even when his pro career was belatedly restored—a mysterious legend from the dark netherworld of New York City playground basketball, a stone-faced and side-burned high-flying dunker who first performed his magic in those back alleys of professional sport known as the American Basketball League and the American Basketball Association. And by the early '90s there was "Sir Charles" Barkley, an outrageous motormouth who hoodwinked the press to attack teammates, club owners, fans and anything else that suited his fancy. But this latest outrageous knight of the hardwood always backed up his loudest boasts with a "complete package" game that constantly kept him entrenched among the top league scorers, rebounders, and "thrill-a-minute" pure excitement generators.

Connie Hawkins might well have stood among the great legends of NBA history, an immediate successor in the mid-sixties to the crown

255

worn by Chamberlain, Russell, Baylor, Robertson and West. Instead fate legislated one of the most tragic stories associated Dr. Naismith's American sport. A phenomenal high-leaping star from Boys High School in Brooklyn, Hawkins was an unparalleled playground legend ready to burst on the NCAA and NBA scene after his final 1960 high school season. But a Brooklyn high school "education" had sadly failed to provide the tall, skinny and naturally shy youngster with proper life skills to prepare him for the dark webb that would soon entangle his life. When a second college betting and point-shaving scandal broke in New York City in the early '60s Hawkins was implicated for having accepted personal loans from accused game-fixer Jack Molinas. (There was no evidence that Hawkins—who had not yet played a moment of college basketball—ever contemplated any wrongdoing or even understood the consequences of his actions.) Once Hawkins was formally questioned by authorities at the 1961 trial of Molinas, his soaring basketball reputation and confused answers were enough to brand him as "guilty by association" in the eyes of a sanctimonious basketball world. While 250 colleges had recently clamored to offer scholarships to this Brooklyn "Wonder Boy" with almost no reading or writing skills, none now wanted anything to do with him. The University of Iowa withdrew the scholarship Hawkins had already accepted and expelled him from campus. One of the most promising careers in basketball history was seemingly over before it had ever even started.

A stunned and confused Connie Hawkins expended what might have been the glory years of his basketball youth trying to find a way back into the glamorous spotlight of the game at which he so excelled. Banned by the NBA as well as the NCAA, "The Hawk" toured briefly with the Harlem Globetrotters, who themselves had now tumbled far from the limelight they had once enjoyed. When a short-lived venture known as the American Basketball League was initiated by Globetrotters founder Abe Saperstein in the early '60s, Hawkins seemed to have found a much-needed stage for his talents as the league's MVP in his one season with the Pittsburgh Rens. Then the league suddenly collapsed, and "The Hawk" was again left without a space in which to soar. Next came the ABA, where Hawkins again played with the Pittsburgh franchise and was again a league MVP in the new circuit's inaugural season. A second ABA season saw Hawkins soar even higher, with a 30.3 ppg. average and all-league status despite a debilitating bout with the flu and an assortment of injuries that kept him sidelined for a large part of the campaign.

After years of being buffeted around by the cruel winds of fate, Connie Hawkins finally found his rich pot at the end of the rainbow once the decade of the '60s mercifully drew to a close. Early in the 1968–'69 season, a lawyer named David Litman had filed a six-million dollar suit on Hawkins' behalf against the NBA. The suit would charge that there was absolutely no basis for excluding the star player since he was never convicted of wrongdoing; it furthermore sought compensation for the career years already lost by Hawkins. The league was now quick to settle, offering immediate reinstatement of Hawkins if the suit were dropped. Primary winner would of course be the NBA—itself in need of showcase players by 1969. Russell was retiring, Baylor was gone, and Oscar, Wilt and Jerry West were all fading from prominence. And another victor would be the expansion Phoenix Suns, who had just lost out on obtaining rookie sensation Lew Alcindor, but who, in Hawkins, were given a star performer capable of winning fans as well as games. Yet Hawkins himself would enjoy only a Pyrrhic victory at best. Already 28, slowed by knee injuries, and robbed of years of top-flight competition and of much of his confidence, Connie Hawkins was no longer the totally dominating player he had once been. Of course he was good enough to leave a memorable mark on NBA history, even if that mark would only be a dim shadow of what it might have been.

In Connie Hawkins the Suns had inherited one of the sport's most unfortunate victims; with Barkley they would possess basketball's most incorrigible instigator. If Hawkins was largely a victim of media distortions which long unfairly branded him an unsavory rebel, Charles Barkley, two decades later, would become perhaps the greatest single manipulator of the sporting press that basketball has ever known. Barkley, from his earliest NBA days in Philadelphia, has drawn constant attention to himself with his colorful and sometimes shocking public statements. "Sir Charles" was at his best with the media during the spotlight of championship play in the spring of 1993. "There will never be another player like me again," Barkley warned the press. "I'm the ninth wonder of the world." And these outrageous Barkleyisms do not stop with such self-promotional boasts. Sir Charles has always been controversial both off and on the court. In Philadelphia, while playing for the Sixers, he often publicly criticized his owner and his teammates in the press for not wanting to win badly enough. Charles has always put winning and hustling at the very top of his personal goals. But the outspoken athlete has also had more important and serious messages for his legions of fans. Most recently he has made a television commercial in which he tells young fans that he should not be a hero or an idol just because he can dribble and shoot and rebound a basketball. Youngsters should idolize their own parents and teachers, Barkley warns, and not glamorous professional ballplayers like himself.

On the court, however, Barkley has always had a personal style which has made him a widely recognized star. He is one of basketball's most ferocious rebounders and has averaged more than 800 caroms for each of his nine seasons. The most memorable aspect of Barkley's play is his fierceness under the basket and around the rim. The typical Barkley maneuver is to grab a defensive rebound, lumber the full length of the court like a runaway freight train, then slam home a huge dunk that intimates his foes as well as electrifying the home crowd. Indeed, the most terrifying sight in basketball—perhaps in all of sports—has to be the image of this huge and agile 250-pound athlete roaring down the floor toward the enemy basket, determined to fly through, if not over, any defender daring to block his path. With his large but finely-tuned body, Barkley has been the most physical basketball player of the past decade. But his personal style has also made him one of the game's greatest and most glamorous modern-day stars.

If two franchise stars seemed to draw their colorful "badlands" image (one unjustly inherited and the other painstakingly created) from the Phoenix team's physical surroundings, it also seems that the larger trends of Suns history have done much the same. For this ballclub has climbed its few momentary peaks of glory like almost all other NBA franchises. But in between these short-lived "glory runs" there have been very few deep valleys indeed. From the broader perspective of a quarter-century of Phoenix Suns history, this team's fortunes seem to appear as one flat and almost endless desert. There are precious few rises above the landscape: two rare division titles a dozen seasons apart, in 1981 and 1993, two unsuccessful trips into the NBA Finals which brought much excitement, but no cherished cigar. But there are no deep gullies either. Only twice since the inaugural season have the Phoenix Suns dipped as low as fifth place; since 1975 no playoff drought has lasted more than three seasons; only once (1988) since the inaugural expansion season has the ballclub ever won fewer than 30 ballgames.

The Phoenix Suns started their remarkably even-keel history saddled with an especially bad break. In what at first appeared to be the standard fare of pro sports expansion seasons, the Suns initial ballclub crashed and burned in the final seven games of an already lackluster inaugural campaign. The result was a 16–66 ledger that left the Johnny Kerr-coached team with the worst record in the NBA—14 games worse than the closest Western Conference rival (Seattle) and 11 lengths behind fellow expansion competitor Milwaukee over in the east. At first glance, it appeared that the late-season collapse in Phoenix was actually a golden key to success, since this was one expansion franchise that had enjoyed its season of rough knocks in the very year that the league's booby prize happened to be the most touted incoming rookie in league history. Lew Alcindor of UCLA awaited in the wings and no league observer failed to predict that this was an instant "franchise" player if ever there was one.

But the NBA in 1969 was a league with an image problem, and only three seasons earlier league officials had exercised "credibility control" by ordering that cellar finishers in each conference should henceforth flip for the league's first draft pick. It would not do at all for the impression to exist that tailender teams might simply be losing games on purpose in order to guarantee a top draft selection.

Given their first-season results, the Phoenix Suns unarguably had the best claim on Alcindor. They were indeed the league's weakest team and the one most obviously in need of a huge and instantaneous talent influx. But league policy now dictated a coin flip with Milwaukee; and when the Suns called heads they had suddenly been dealt a decidedly cruel blow which sent Alcindor packing for Milwaukee and the charmed Bucks headed straight for the league's upper echelons. Phoenix, for its part, was left with the consolation prize, University of Florida center Neal Walk.

The 6'10" Walk was far from a complete bust: despite a slow rookie season (as backup to Jim Fox) he would eventually mature into a solid league performer and log five adequate campaigns for Phoenix (eventually cracking the 20 ppg. barrier in 1973). But Neal Walk was not by any stretch a Lew Alcindor; and a solid draft choice was not the same thing as a hoped-for "franchise" ballplayer.

But all the luck wasn't quite so bad in Phoenix in the summer of 1969. There was another important coin flip now scheduled for that summer as well, and this one turned more in the Suns' favor. Since the league's board of governors had decided to rectify their long-time mistreatment of Connie Hawkins (actually they were simply trying to avoid a costly lawsuit most likely destined to be settled to their own disfavor) it was now also necessary to award the banished ABA star to some lucky league ballclub. Since Milwaukee had already plucked Alcindor, it was determined that the two worst Western ballclubs (Phoenix and Seattle) should draw lots for rights to Hawkins. This time Fate smiled in a southerly direction and in acquiring the option to sign Hawkins, the Phoenix ballclub now owned the most unusual NBA rookie ever. They also had a first true franchise star thrown into the bargain. Despite his advanced age for a debut player, Connie Hawkins would log four 20 ppg. seasons with the Suns and also earn four All-Star Game berths and one valued selection for first-team all-league honors.

Hawkins wasn't the only pickup that first summer of free-wheeling drafting and trading. Gary Gregor (the initial player taken by the Suns in their first collegiate draft a year earlier) was dealt to the Atlanta Hawks for five-year veteran Paul Silas, a talented rebounder and bruising forward who would later in the decade anchor three championship teams in Boston. And with Hawkins and Silas up front, the Phoenix team already had enough horses—even without Alcindor—to pull off one of the biggest single-season turnarounds ever by an early expansion entry. First-season mentor Johnny "Red" Kerr stepped aside 38 games into the season and with GM Jerry Colangelo substituting in the coach's slot, the surprising Suns roared down the stretch for a 39–43 ledger. It was a 23-game improvement that had rarely been seen from a second-year ballclub. Strongly detracting from any premature optimism and over-enthusiastic title dreaming in Phoenix, however, was the undeniable fact that Milwaukee, with Lew Alcindor, had made an even bigger turnaround. The Bucks for their part registered a 29-game upsurge and solid second place finish in the Eastern Conference race.

The second season rebound was good enough, however, to put the Suns into post-season play alongside fellow newcomer Milwaukee, two of the earliest post-season appearances ever by NBA "new kids on the block." Again Milwaukee would have slightly the better of it behind the pacesetting 35.2 ppg. post-season average of Alcindor; the Bucks were able to sweep aside Philadelphia with Billy Cunningham and Hal Greer before being crushed in five games by the eventual champions, the New York Knicks. While Phoenix never got out of the first round, on the other hand, the Suns acquitted themselves well by giving the powerful Los Angeles

Lakers quite a run for their money. Los Angeles featured Chamberlain, Baylor (now in his final season), and Jerry West, and would soon hang on for a seven-game championship series with the talented Knicks. But not before they were also extended to the full limit of seven games in the opening round by a Phoenix team that showed plenty of grit under interim coach Colangelo, and revealed plenty of firepower in the scoring of Hawkins (25.4 ppg.) and rebounding of a front line consisting of Hawkins (13.9 rpg.), Silas (15.9 rpg.) and center Jim Fox (10.7 rpg.)

By the third and fourth seasons the team featured a totally new roster from the one it had started out with. Dick Van Arsdale was now the single original Sun from only two seasons earlier; Haskins, Walk, Silas and Hawkins now replaced names like Gary Gregor, Jim Fox, Dick Snyder and Gail Goodrich. There was also a new head coach as Cotton Fitzsimmons took the reins in the fall of 1970. The immediate result was two years of solid records as the first team under Fitzsimmons finished 14 games above .500 (48–34) and the second climbed to exactly the same level (49–33). High scoring guard Charlie Scott jumped ship with the ABA Virginia Squires (where he led the rival league in scoring) and signed on in Phoenix late in 1971–'72. But there would be no playoff appearances during this stretch to demonstrate that the Phoenix team had truly turned the corner and headed up the hill toward title contention.

Change remained the byword of early seasons in Phoenix and that change was as regular on the coach's end of the bench as it was in the nightly starting lineup. General manager Jerry Colangelo replaced Cotton Fitzsimmons before the outset of the '72–'73 seasons with Butch van Breda Kolff, then decided he had made a mistake and installed himself in the position only eight games into the campaign. But this early coach-shuffling was not to last much longer as Colangelo finally settled on John MacLeod prior to the '73–'74 campaign. Thus began the longest and most successful coaching tenure in ballclub history. MacLeod would remain at the helm for more than a dozen years and would launch in the first half of that tenure a slow but steady climb toward the elusive 50-victory plateau. Before his NBA days were over MacLeod would also climb into seventh slot among the all-time winningest coaches in league history.

The peak of the MacLeod era came early on with the 1975–'76 season, the third for the popular ex-college coach (University of Oklahoma) from the basketball-crazy state of Indiana. This was indeed the most exciting year in team history and most of that excitement was packed into the spring's "second season" of playoff mania. Only the 1993 run at the NBA Finals could rival 1976 for pure excitement and near-miss achievement. Yet this first Phoenix challenge at a league title was perhaps all the more sweet for its largely unexpected nature.

With newcomer Paul Westphal (20.5) providing the backcourt scoring punch and veterans Curtis Perry and Garfield Heard (also acquired at midseason from Buffalo for John Shumate) teaming with Rookie-of-the-Year Alvan Adams along the front line, the Suns were rugged enough to climb into third slot in the Pacific Division, a single game behind runnerup Seattle, but still 17 full games behind powerful Golden State. The team had started fast (14–9), slumped at mid-season (winning only four of their next 22), then caught fire down the home stretch to storm into the playoffs as a force to be reckoned with. Just how much of a force became quickly apparent when the upstart Suns first cruised by Seattle (4–2) and then rudely upset the World Champion Golden State Warriors in seven games to gain the NBA Finals.

If the Phoenix Suns have from the start seemed doomed to remain that one NBA franchise whose name is most synonymous with "near miss," then it is certainly the post-season climax of 1976—as much as the fateful coin flip sending Alcindor to Milwaukee—that has cemented this reputation in the public consciousness. For post-season 1976 would provide one of the greatest NBA championship matchups ever. And it would also provide the greatest single game of NBA tournament history—perhaps the greatest game of all NBA history. The combatants were the underdog West Conference winners out of Phoenix, and the tradition-bound Boston Celtics now coached by Tom Heinsohn and led into battle by John Havlicek, Dave Cowens and Jo Jo White. The setting was a crucial game five, which came on the heals of a four-game split, with each team winning twice in its home arena. The locale was fittingly the NBA's most storied playing surface—the parquet floor of ancient Boston Garden. And the undeserving last-minute loser would of course again be the ne'er-do-well Suns.

What transpired in playoff game five has been described by more than one commentator as a tension-coated marathon of endurance and pure luck. The Celtics seemed to have the game in hand down the stretch and led by five with 55 ticks of the clock remaining. Then Westphal worked playoff magic with a bucket, a steal, another bucket and a game-tying foul shot. A first nail-biting overtime would fail to resolve the issue, and a second extra session suddenly found Phoenix taking command (110–109) on a long jumper by Curtis Perry with only five seconds remaining. It was then time for Boston heroics as "Mr. Clutch" John Havlicek returned the Boston advantage on a bucket which ripped the nets with just two second showing on the time clock.

But the drama was only now heating up in perhaps the wildest championship finish ever known on a basketball court at any level of play. Phoenix called an illegal time-out to stop the clock after Havlicek's thrilling basket and a subsequent penalty shot had increased the Boston lead to 112–110. Phoenix inbounded a desperation pass to Gar Heard, who threw up a blind shot which somehow swished through the nets to clinch yet a third overtime period. As the two drained teams now struggled through the final extra session it was an unlikely hero who emerged from the Boston bench. Reserve Glenn McDonald would score six points in the final session to seal an exhausting 128–126 Boston victory. And if there was ever an anti-climax in NBA post-season annals it came next, when Boston coasted to a predictable 87–80 title-clinching victory three days later back in Phoenix.

A mere year later the team from Phoenix fell on unexpected hard times. The tumble was largely a result of that old injury bugaboo as mishaps eventually eliminated the entire starting front line for MacLeod's hard-luck team. With Curtis Perry (back, 44 games), Gar Heard (leg, 46 games) and Alvan Adams (ankle, 72 games) all restricted in playing time, the Suns collapsed all the way to the division basement, dropping 17 of their final 22 contests in the process. This team did become the answer to an obscure trivia question, however, with the first twin brothers (Dick and Tom Van Arsdale) ever to play on the same NBA roster. But injuries do heal and rosters are shuffled and soon there was another run of three straight 50-plus winning seasons for MacLeod. The biggest personnel change of this era came with the 1977 first-round draft selection of North Carolina All-American Walter Davis (5th overall selection), and one highlight of the late '70s was Davis's stellar Rookie-of-the-Year season (24.2 ppg., 1959 points, 6.0 rpg., 273 assists). With Davis and Westphal combining for nearly 50 points per contest (49.4 in 1978 and 47.6 in 1979) Phoenix could suddenly boast the best single guard-forward combo in the entire league.

Another highlight of this three-year run at respectability was an '80–'81 campaign which witnessed the club's first division title since 1976. Key to this title year was the trade of five-time club scoring leader Paul Westphal to Seattle for equally potent guard Dennis Johnson, a leader of Seattle's title team of the late '70s and post-season MVP in 1979. While "DJ" had lost popularity with coach Lenny Wilkens in Seattle, he seemed to blend perfectly with a lineup of Truck Robinson, Alvan Adams, and hot-shooting Walter Davis. But the Suns were unable to make it back to the NBA finals for all their strength during regular season competition, despite a 57–win season which topped all clubs in the Western Conference. Once the playoffs rolled around, it was Houston who ruled the West. For their own part the Suns never got past their semifinal series with surprising Kansas City, rallying from a 3–1 deficit to force a seventh game, but then losing the crucial rubber match 95–88 on their own home floor.

The only thing approaching a lengthy drought came to Phoenix in the early and mid '80s. And the slump came straight on the heels of those three uplifting 50-win seasons that had promised such a rosy immediate future. The victory totals now slid consistently from 53 (1983) to 41, to 36, to 32, and then from 37 again in 1987 all the way down to 28 in 1988. There were numerous key personnel changes as well: Truck Robinson was traded to New York for Maurice Lucas on the eve of the '82–'83 campaign; emerging star Larry Nance was plucked in the 1981 draft and became the biggest "small forward" around (at 6'10"); Jay Humphries (13th overall pick out of Colorado) was a promising rookie backcourt performer in '84–'85; and veteran center Alvan Adams retired in April, 1988. The tailspin eventually meant three straight seasons at the end of the decade without a playoff appearance and also spelled an end to the 14-year tenure of John MacLeod, who departed before the 1987 season had run its full course. The Phoenix ballclub was also rocked by a well-publicized drug scandal (five players were implicated in the press, but none drew league sanction) which sealed the need to clean house and crank up a full-scale rebuilding program for the 1990s.

The Suns eventually climbed out of the hole and were rebuilding as the decade drew to a close. Draft selections and trades brought a stock of quality players like Tom Chambers (signed as an unrestricted free agent in summer, 1988), Mark West (from Cleveland in 1988), Kevin Johnson (also from Cleveland), and Dan Majerle (14th overall 1st round pick in 1988). Cotton Fitzsimmons returned as the head coach and enjoyed considerable immediate success in the form of another four-year string of 50-win seasons. Cotton's first season at the helm was itself almost miraculous in nature, representing the third best one-season turnaround in NBA history. The biggest fortune-builder for the Suns, however, was the blockbuster trade with Cleveland, orchestrated by Fitzsimmons (as Player Personnel Director, only months before he rejoined the active coaching ranks) and designed to completely reshape the Phoenix roster. Forwards Larry Nance and Mike Sanders headed east in exchange for young guard Kevin ("KJ") Johnson, lanky center Mark West, and role player Tyrone Corbin. There had never been a bigger trade in club history (this one also involved the complicated reshuffling of at least four future draft picks); there had also never been one so clearly one-sided in favor of the near-miss Suns.

The Phoenix Suns now seemed to be only a major deal or two away from reaching the summit, perhaps even alighting upon the championship throne. And those deals were soon consummated as well, the front-office team of Jerry Colangelo and Cotton Fitzsimmons now demonstrating to fans and rivals alike that they would pull no stops whatsoever in seeking a proven winner for the franchise which had been a bridesmaid so many times in the past. The corner was seemingly turned when three Phoenix starters—Jeff Hornacek, Andrew Lang and Tim Perry—were swapped with Philadelphia on June 17, 1992, for disgruntled superstar Charles Barkley. If there was now a single true franchise player anywhere in the league beyond Michael Jordan, it had to be Barkley; "Sir Charles" had lacked nothing in his eight-year all-star career but the chance to perform for a potential winner. And to solidify the elements surrounding Barkley, onetime Suns ace floor general Paul Westphal was also brought home to Phoenix as the new head coach. Now the Suns were seemingly primed and ready for another strong run at the very top.

The season of '92–'93 was the second best of club history by any standard of measure. With Barkley in tow and solid offense production from Dan Majerle (16.9), Kevin Johnson (16.1), and surprise rookie forward Richard Dumas (drafted originally back in 1991), Phoenix was seemingly the class of the entire league, posting a franchise-record 62 victories, coasting to a seven-game margin over Pacific Division runner-up Seattle, and even outpacing the World Champion Chicago Bulls (57–25) over the course of regular-season play. Expectations were exceedingly high in Phoenix after four straight 50-win seasons and two trips to the conference finals over the past four campaigns, and such lofty hopes were hardly disappointed. Barkley's MVP season (ending Jordan's two-year reign) and Cedric Ceballos's league-best figure for field goal percentage were individual highlights of a spectacular end-to-end year. And the 62–20 Phoenix ledger also had made Paul Westphal the winningest rookie coach in the near half-century of NBA history.

Things seemed to come together in post-season as well for the Barkley-led and rejuvenated Phoenix Suns. Surprising back-to-back opening round losses to the Lakers seemed only an aberration when Phoenix swept Los Angeles aside in the next three straight contests; neither San Antonio (six games) nor Seattle (seven games) went quietly in the conference semi-finals and finals, yet neither provided a major stumbling block either, as Barkley, Johnson, Ceballos and Majerle all took turns as the club's leading scorers during these two pressure-packed series. In the end it would be only one dominant opposition player that blocked a championship for this Phoenix franchise that had already known so many near misses over the years. Two decades earlier it had been John Havlicek and the Celtics that proved invincible. This time it was Michael Jordan and the defending champion Bulls. Across a six-game championship series the inspired Jordan would rack up point totals of 31, 42, 44, 55, 41 and 33. While the Suns did battle valiantly to salvage games three and five in Chicago, the Bulls were in control from start to finish and earned Jordan a repeat championship by sweeping all three games on the Suns' own home floor.

The Suns were now confident under Westphal that they would be back to challenge again for the title. Especially after Jordan's unexpected retirement on the eve of the '93–'94 season, their prospects looked excellent, and an NBA championship for Phoenix in the minds of at least some pundits was even a foregone conclusion. But it never quite happened the way most of the pre-season gurus had envisioned it for the hardluck Suns. The team was already aging as Ainge (13), Barkley (10), Frank Johnson (10), and Mark West (11) were playing in their tenth season or better; and A. C. Green and Joe Kleine were now nine-year veterans as well. Barkley was slowed throughout the year by nagging back problems and logged only 65 games; injuries also struck other key performers as point guard Kevin Johnson played in but 67 contests and small forward Cedric Ceballos was limited to 53 largely ineffective outings. The Suns did maintain enough momentum and occasionally flashed enough talent to chase the Seattle SuperSonics (63–19) down to the wire for a second-place Pacific Division finish (at 56–26). But an aging and worn-down lineup fell short in the end against eventual league-champion Houston, and Hakeem Olajuwon during the Western Conference semi-finals.

One man has stood on center stage for the Phoenix Suns throughout a full quarter-century of franchise history. Like Auerbach in Boston, Jerry Colangelo in Phoenix has been there from the beginning and thus seen every triumph and failure of club annals from a first-hand perspective. Jerry Colangelo was named general manager of the expansion Suns on March 1, 1968, which made him at the time the youngest leading executive to be found anywhere in professional sports. Since then he has been, at one time or another, an owner, president, chief financial officer and even twice an interim coach. He has signed the paychecks, filled out the lineups, hired and fired ballplayers and coaches, directed the construction of the ballclub's gorgeous new America West Arena, basked in media praise and squirmed under journalistic criticism, and probably packed and unpacked the ball bags and swept the arena floors on more than a single occasion. But Colangelo has yet to enjoy the grandest prize of his profession—a coveted NBA title. And with Charles Barkley contemplating retirement before the opening of the '94–'95 campaign, and with the Western Conference now stacked full of quality young teams and franchise stars in Denver (Dikembe Mutombo), San Antonio (David Robinson), Houston (Hakeem Olajuwon), Golden State (Chris Webber) and Seattle (Shawn Kemp), the wait may yet continue on for quite some while.

Suggested Readings on Phoenix Suns

Barkley, Charles (with Roy S. Johnson). **Outrageous! The Fine Life and Flagrant Good Times of Basketball's Irresistible Force.** New York: Simon and Schuster, 1992.

Van Arsdale, Tom and Dick (with Joel H. Cohen). **Our Basketball Lives.** New York: G.P. Putnam's Sons, 1973.

Wolf, David. **Foul! Connie Hawkins—Schoolyard Star, Exile, NBA Superstar.** New York: Holt, Rinehart and Winston, 1972.

Phoenix Suns Retired Uniform Numbers (4)

Dick Van Arsdale (5)
Alvan Adams (33)
Connie Hawkins (42)
Paul Westphal (44)

Year-by-Year Phoenix Suns Summary

Season	Record	Finish	Coach(es)	Scoring Leader(s)	Playoffs (W-L Record)
Key: * = Tied for Position; # = League Scoring leader					
1968–69	16–66	7th	Johnny Kerr	Gail Goodrich (23.8)	Did Not Qualify
1969–70	39–43	3rd*	Johnny Kerr	Connie Hawkins (24.6)	Lost in 1st Round (3–4)
			Jerry Colangelo		
1970–71	48–34	3rd	L. Fitzsimmons	Dick Van Arsdale (21.9)	Did Not Qualify
1971–72	49–33	3rd	L. Fitzsimmons	Connie Hawkins (21.0)	Did Not Qualify
1972–73	38–44	3rd	Jerry Colangelo	Charlie Scott (25.3)	Did Not Qualify
			Bill van Breda Kolff		
1973–74	30–52	4th	John MacLeod	Dick Van Arsdale (17.8)	Did Not Qualify
1974–75	32–50	4th	John MacLeod	Charlie Scott (24.3)	Did Not Qualify
1975–76	42–40	3rd	John MacLeod	Paul Westphal (20.5)	Lost in NBA Finals (10–9)

Season	Record	Finish	Coach(es)	Scoring Leader(s)	Playoffs (W-L Record)
1976–77	34–48	5th	John MacLeod	Paul Westphal (21.3)	Did Not Qualify
1977–78	49–33	2nd	John MacLeod	Paul Westphal (25.2)	Lost in 1st Round (0–2)
1978–79	50–32	2nd	John MacLeod	Paul Westphal (24.0)	Lost in 3rd Round (9–6)
1979–80	55–27	3rd	John MacLeod	Paul Westphal (21.9)	Lost in 2nd Round (3–5)
1980–81	57–25	1st	John MacLeod	Truck Robinson (18.8)	Lost in 2nd Round (3–4)
1981–82	46–36	3rd	John MacLeod	Dennis Johnson (19.5)	Lost in 2nd Round (2–5)
1982–83	53–29	2nd	John MacLeod	Walter Davis (19.0)	Lost in 1st Round (1–2)
1983–84	41–41	4th	John MacLeod	Walter Davis (20.0)	Lost in 3rd Round (9–8)
1984–85	36–46	3rd	John MacLeod	Larry Nance (19.9)	Lost in 1st Round (0–3)
1985–86	32–50	3rd*	John MacLeod	Walter Davis (21.8)	Did Not Qualify
1986–87	36–46	5th	John MacLeod	Walter Davis (23.6)	Did Not Qualify
			Dick Van Arsdale		
1987–88	28–54	4th	John Wetzel	Larry Nance (21.1)	Did Not Qualify
1988–89	55–27	2nd	L. Fitzsimmons	Tom Chambers (25.7)	Lost in 3rd Round (7–5)
1989–90	54–28	3rd	L. Fitzsimmons	Tom Chambers (27.2)	Lost in 3rd Round (9–7)
1990–91	55–27	3rd	L. Fitzsimmons	Kevin Johnson (22.2)	Lost in 1st Round (1–3)
1991–92	53–29	3rd	L. Fitzsimmons	Jeff Hornacek (20.1)	Lost in 2nd Round (4–4)
1992–93	62–20	1st	Paul Westphal	Charles Barkley (25.6)	Lost in NBA Finals (13–11)
1993–94	56–26	2nd	Paul Westphal	Charles Barkley (21.6)	Lost in 2nd Round (6–5)

Individual Career Leaders and Record Holders (1968–1994)

Scoring Average	Charlie Scott (24.8 ppg., 1971–75)
Points Scored	Walter Davis (15,566, 1977–88)
Games Played	Alvan Adams (988, 1975–88)
Minutes Played	Alvan Adams (27,203)
Field Goals Made	Walter Davis (6,497)
Field Goal Pct.	Mark West (.621, 1988–93)
Free Throws Made	Dick Van Arsdale (3,404, 1968–77)
Free-Throw Pct.	Kyle Macy (.884, 1980–85)
Rebounds	Alvan Adams (6,937)
Rebound Average	Paul Silas (12.1 rpg., 1969–72)
Assists	Kevin Johnson (4,719, 1988–94)
Steals	Alvan Adams (1,289)
Blocked Shots	Larry Nance (940, 1981–88)

Individual Single-Season and Game Records (1968–1994)

Scoring Average	Tom Chambers (27.2 ppg., 1989–90)
Points Scored (Season)	Tom Chambers (2,201, 1989–90)
Minutes Played (Season)	Dick Van Arsdale (3,388, 1968–69)
Points Scored (Game)	Tom Chambers (60, 3–24–90 vs. Seattle Supersonics)
Field Goals Made (Season)	Tom Chambers (810, 1989–90)
Field Goal Pct. (Season)	Mark West (.653, 1988–89)
3-Pt. Field Goals (Season)	Dan Majerle (167, 1992–93)
3-Pt. Field Goals (Game)	Dan Majerle (8, 1–30–93 vs. Dallas Mavericks)

Free Throws Made (Season)	Connie Hawkins (577, 1969–70)
Free-Throw Pct. (Season)	Eddie Johnson (.917, 1989–90)
Rebounds (Season)	Paul Silas (1,015, 1970–71)
Round Average (Season)	Paul Silas (12.5 rpg., 1970–71)
Rebounds (Game)	Paul Silas (27, 1–18–71 vs. Cincinnati Royals)
Assists (Season)	Kevin Johnson (991, 1988–89)
Assists (game)	Kevin Johnson (21, 2–26–89 at Los Angeles Lakers)
Steals (Season)	Ron Lee (225, 1977–78)
Blocked Shots (Season)	Larry Nance (217, 1982–83)

Best Trade in Franchise History

It was one of the biggest blockbuster deals of the decade, and it brought the Phoenix Suns back to full respectability in the late '80s and early '90s. The Suns obtained guard Kevin Johnson, center-forward Mark West, and small forward Tyrone Corbin, plus three high draft picks from Cleveland in exchange for Larry Nance, Mike Sanders, and a Detroit Pistons first round draft selection to boot. Nance was the marquee player of the February, 1988 deal, but the inconsistent rebounding and dunking star would soon be spending most of the rest of his career moving on and off the disabled list, felled by an assortment of nagging injuries. Johnson and West, on the other hand, formed the backcourt-frontcourt nucleus which had already propelled Phoenix to the top of the west by early 1992.

Worst Trade in Franchise History

Gail Goodrich started his career unspectacularly with the Los Angeles Lakers in the mid-sixties, before being plucked by Phoenix in the 1968 expansion draft. After two 20-point-plus seasons with the Suns, the high-scoring guard was unwisely returned to Los Angeles in what proved to be a one-sided exchange if there ever was one. Goodrich quickly became a Lakers standout, burning the nets for almost 20,000 points in a career that stretched all the way to the end of the '70s. The return for Goodrich in that ill-fated May, 1970 mis-deal was hulking 7-foot center Mel Counts. Counts would more than disappoint with two altogether mediocre seasons in Phoenix, averaging only 5.2 ppg. for the 1971–'72 campaign.

Phoenix Suns Historical Oddity

When the term "near-miss" was added to the sports lexicon someone must have had the NBA's Phoenix Suns in mind. Many (perhaps most) sports franchises can point to that one player or deal that got away and forever turned franchise history hopelessly in the wrong direction. But none can do it with more justification, perhaps, than basketball's Suns. Reverse a single coin flip back in March, 1969, and the Phoenix franchise would have owned rookie sensation Lew Alcindor, fresh from the campus of UCLA and from one of the greatest collegiate careers in NCAA basketball history. With Lew Alcindor, not Neal Walk, at the center post, surrounded by a lineup of Connie Hawkins and Paul Silas in the frontcourt and Dick Van Arsdale and Clem Haskins in the backcourt, the Suns and not the Milwaukee Bucks would likely have pulled off the fastest conversion from expansion chump to league champ in basketball history. And oh how very different it all might have been from that point on down Arizona way.

Suns All-Time Number One Draft Picks List

Phoenix Suns
1968 Gary Gregor (South Carolina)
1969 Neal Walk (Florida)
1970 Greg Howard (New Mexico)
1971 John Roche (South Carolina)
1972 Corky Calhoun (Pennsylvania)
1973 Mike Banton (St. Joseph's)
1974 John Shumate (Notre Dame)
1975 Alvan Adams (Oklahoma)
1976 Ron Lee (Oregon)
1977 Walter Davis (North Carolina)
1978 Marty Byrnes (Syracuse)
1979 Kyle Macy (Kentucky)
1980 None
1981 Larry Nance (Clemson)
1982 David Thirdkill (Bradley)
1983 Rod Foster (UCLA)
1984 Jay Humphries (Colorado)
1985 Ed Pinckney (Villanova)
1986 William Bedford (Memphis State)
1987 Armond Gilliam (UNLV)
1988 Tim Perry (Temple)
1989 Anthony Cook (Arizona)
1990 Jayson Williams (St. John's)
1991 None
1992 Oliver Miller (Arkansas)
1993 Malcom Mackey (Georgia Tech)

Chapter 15

LOS ANGELES (SAN DIEGO) CLIPPERS and BUFFALO BRAVES

Staying Afloat in a Rudderless Ship

All-Time Franchise Record: 732–1236, .372 Pct. (1970–1994)
NBA Championships: None
Greatest Franchise Player: Bob McAdoo (1972–1977)
All-Time Leading Scorer: Randy Smith (12,753 Points, 1971–1983)
Most Successful Coach: Larry Brown (64–53, .547 Pct., 1991–1993)
All-Time Franchise Team: Swen Nater (C), Bob McAdoo (F), Danny Manning (F),
  Norm Nixon (G), Randy Smith (G)

This franchise has boasted but one headline solo act—a high scoring gunner on almost every yearly edition of the ballclub. This is a player who will likely fill up the nets with a ton of points, night after night, while a second rate team around him limps along to a truckload of losses and a spot deep in the standings. First there was three-time scoring champ Bob McAdoo, with a 30-plus scoring average in Buffalo. When the scene shifted to San Diego, it was World B. Free and then Terry Cummings and Freeman Williams who came onto the scene to burn the nets but usually get burned on defense themselves to an equal or higher count. In Los Angeles the revamped version of the prime-time Clippers has boasted free wheeling offensive machines like Marques Johnson, Danny Manning, and most recently Dominique Wilkins. But there has been very little else positive in the offering—17 different coaches, but only five winning records and four playoff appearances in 24 long years.

Beyond a few bulky scorers, there is not much to take pride in with this club that has now known two different west coast homes and one shaky berth in the upper northeast over its near quarter-century history. Of all NBA teams whose birthright stretches back before the 1980s, it is the Clippers franchise that sports the worst won-lost record by far (an average of but 30 wins per season over the entire span). This is a club that missed out on the playoffs for fifteen straight seasons between its earliest years in Buffalo and its most recent campaigns out in Los Angeles. There have been only five winning seasons in club history and only two of these (1979 with Gene Shue and 1992 under Larry Brown) have come since the team left Buffalo.

And there are other measures of ineptitude as well. The 1986–87 season for the Los Angeles Clippers was one of the worst overall team performances in NBA history. The 12 wins (.146 winning percentage) for Don Chaney's hapless club that year has been surpassed for ineptitude only in Philadelphia in 1973, and Dallas in 1993. Perhaps only the 9–73 Philadelphia Sixers and the most recent two editions of the Dallas Mavericks put worst excuses for an NBA club onto the floor. The Los Angeles entrant in the "worst team ever" derby would capture but four road games, and only two after the second week of the season. Mike Woodson would be the offensive star with a mediocre 17.1 scoring average. While Magic and the Lakers were winning another NBA championship across town, the lowly Clippers were finishing 24 full games behind the fifth place team (Phoenix) in the same Pacific Division.

One of the few badges this club can wear—at least in terms of individual performances—is the iron man streak amassed by team career scoring leader Randy Smith. Smith today reigns as the NBA's original "iron man" with the longest consecutive games streak in league history. Smith's career began with the second season of the expansion Buffalo Braves and eventually included 976 total contests spread across a dozen seasons, with subsequent stops in San Diego (when the Braves transfered there in 1978), Cleveland, and New York, before a return to San Diego at career's end. The 976 games were not exceptional in themselves, as a hefty number of NBA players (30 to be exact) have topped the lofty 1,000-game mark over their careers. What was remarkable was that from the tail end of his rookie season until the end of the '82–'83 campaign 12 years later, the speedy 6' 3" guard ran off a record string of 906 straight appearance, eventually overhauling the league's previous iron-man mark of 844 games set between 1954 and 1965 by Philadelphia 76ers (Syracuse Nats) center Johnny "Red" Kerr.

NBA Iron Man Consecutive-Game Streaks

Player (Years of Streak)	Total Games	Primary Team
1. Randy Smith, 1972–83	**906 Games**	Buffalo Braves
2. Johnny "Red" Kerr, 1954–65	844 Games	Philadelphia 76ers
3. Dolph Schayes, 1952–61	706 Games	Syracuse Nats

4. Bill Laimbeer, 1981–89	685 Games	Detroit Pistons
5. Harry Gallatin, 1948–58	682 Games	New York Knicks
6. A.C. Green, 1986–1994*	**649 Games**	Los Angeles Lakers
7. Jack Twyman, 1955–63	609 Games	Cincinnati Royals
8. James Donaldson, 1981–88	586 Games	Seattle SuperSonics
9. Terry Tyler, 1978–85	574 Games	Detroit Pistons
10. Otis Thorpe, 1986–92	542 Games	Sacramento Kings
11. Bob Weiss, 1968–74	538 Games	Chicago Bulls
12. Jo Jo White, 1972–78	488 Games	Boston Celtics
13. Don Nelson, 1967–72	465 Games	Boston Celtics
14. Artis Gilmore, 1971–79	420 Games**	Chicago Bulls
15. Ron Boone, 1976–81	379 Games #	Kansas City Kings

#Ron Boone actually played in 1,041 consecutive games if his record 662 ABA streak is added to his NBA totals

**Artis Gilmore total 670 consecutive games in all, 420 in ABA action and then 250 NBA games

* A.C. Green's streak is still active at the end of 1993–94 season

---

Randy Smith had actually been brought back to San Diego in the twilight of an exceptional career by a Clippers ballclub that had unloaded him four seasons earlier, but now hoped to benefit by the small fervor over Smith's record-approaching streak. Yet little hoopla in the end surrounded Smith when he overtook the mark early in the '82–'83 campaign in Philadelphia (exactly where Kerr had set it 19 seasons earlier). But although the Clippers didn't make much of the feat at the time, it was nonetheless fitting that Randy Smith should cross his milestone in a Clippers uniform. He had logged enough games with the Braves and then the Clippers to become the club's all-time point-producer. And he was noted in his earlier Buffalo days for far more than mere iron man play. His surprising career total of 16,262 points would eventually top more publicized shooters such as Pete Maravich and Walt Frazier; he would be a 1987 NBA All-Star Game MVP with 27 points; and he would develop into arguably the fastest and quickest backcourt player of all time.

In addition to Randy Smith's rare record, the Braves and Clippers franchise has also been distinguished by several front office transactions that rate among the strangest in all of NBA history. For one thing, this franchise can boast of being the only one in professional sports history (at least in the history of major US team sports) to be sold before it ever played its first game. Original ownership transfered control of the ballclub to Freezer Queen entrepreneur Paul Snyder on October 13, 1970, one day before the team's first-ever game (a 107–92 home victory over the expansion rival Cleveland Cavaliers). And then, at the end of the same decade, the Buffalo club would also be the centerpiece of perhaps the most bizarre professional sports trades ever witnessed. In mid-summer, 1978, the Buffalo and Boston clubs actually traded owners. John Y. Brown, who by then controlled the Braves, saw an opportunity for bigger and betters things when he was able to hand over his ballclub in an even swap with Irv Levin for the Boston Celtics. As an absentee owner of the once-proud Celts, Levin was involved deeply in the west coast motion picture industry and had for some time hoped to combine his twin interests closer to home. Knowing full well that the NBA governors would likely never approve an uprooting of the Boston club, Levin did the next best thing by acquiring the Braves with the sole motive of trucking them cross-country to his California back-yard in San Diego.

The team now known as Clippers were launched at the outset of a wave of NBA expansion in the early '70s, and were first known as the Buffalo Braves. Buffalo actually joined the league at the same time as Cleveland and Portland, to launch a new four-division format of regular-season play. Portland would capture the most first-season games of the three (29) and Cleveland the fewest (15) with Buffalo tallying a 22–60 record that meant last place in the new Atlantic Division. Dolph Schayes, one-time iron-man star of the Syracuse Nats, just up the road from Buffalo, was the club's first coach, and center Bob Kauffman (20.4) and forward Don May (20.2) launched the Buffalo (and later San Diego) tradition of high-scoring free shooters on usually under-staffed tailender ballclubs.

But the spate of truly phenomenal scoring binges came along only when Bob McAdoo finally joined the team as a number two overall pick in the 1972 collegiate draft out of North Carolina. A skinny 6'10" stilt-like speci-men when he joined the club, McAdoo would soon prove to be the best pure-shooting center ever to play the game, preferring to pop long-range jumpers rather than muscle with other post-men under the boards. And Mac was part of a general upgrade which sent team prospects skyrocketing over the next couple of seasons. Jack Ramsay was brought over from the Philadelphia 76ers as head coach for the start of season number three; Randy Smith surprised as an unheralded seventh round selection in the 1971 draft out of Buffalo State College; guard Ernie DiGregorio upgraded the playmaking when he was plucked with the third overall 1973 pick; forwards Jim McMillan (Los Angeles Lakers) and Gar Heard (Chicago Bulls) came via the trade route to shore up the front wall around the All-Star Bob McAdoo.

McAdoo would win three straight league scoring titles beginning with his sophomore season (with averages of 30.6, 34.5, and 31.1 ppg.) and actually proved enough of a force to put his expansion team squarely on the basketball map. Three 40-win seasons followed behind the tutelage of Ramsay and the net-ripping of McAdoo, and Buffalo fans pinched them-selves and cheered to three straight playoff appearances. This flurry of post-season activity brought one first-round loss to Boston (4–2, 1974) and two second-round trimmings by Washington (4–3, 1975) and Boston again (4–2, 1976). While the 1975 ballclub had earned an opening-round playoff bye with its second-place Atlantic Division regular-season finish (49–33, behind Boston), the 1976 team earned the first franchise victory in a playoff series when McAdoo and company ousted Philadelphia in a three-game set.

But sadly enough for sparse Buffalo Braves fans, neither McAdoo nor Jack Ramsay would be around in upstate New York for very much longer. Ramsay pulled up stakes first, at the end of the '75–'76 season, to seek greener pastures with a rival expansion team, the Portland Trail Blazers. It would of course be a bonanza move for Ramsay, who would benefit from Bill Walton's presence in the Northwest and utilize his newly-devised control offense to capture an NBA title his first season on the job with the Blazers. Tates Locke spelled Ramsay in Buffalo and had much less luck, lasting only 46 games through his first season. And if one change at the top wasn't enough in Buffalo, Snyder also sold 50% interest in the ballclub to John Y. Brown, current owner of the Kentucky Fried Chicken empire and former owner of the ABA Kentucky Colonels. And the biggest shake-up of all as far as fans were concerned came when star McAdoo was peddled away after 20 games of this topsy-turvy '76–'77 campaign to the down-state New York Knickerbockers (along with Tom McMillen for John Gianelli, and cash).

With both a drastic new look and an entirely new regime, the Buffalo Braves ballclub nonetheless fell upon increasingly hard times during the final two seasons in Buffalo. Of course no one knew precisely that these would be the last two seasons at the time. After the 30–52 season that started under Tates Locke and finished with Joe Mullaney controlling the bench, came the 27–55 season under one-year boss Cotton Fitzsimmons. Marvin Barnes and Swen Nater had now arrived from Detroit (for center John Shumate) and Randy Smith was left as the team's scoring leader. The winds of change were also increasingly in the air as John Y. Brown assumed sole ownership of the ballclub just before the close of the 1976–77 season.

It was little more than a year after seizing complete control that Brown stunned the pro basketball world by engineering the biggest change of all in the fortunes of his Buffalo Braves. First a highly successful coach with a talent for producing playoff-worthy teams had been stolen away by one of the competing neophyte clubs. Next a superstar named McAdoo had been lost to an in-state rival, with no readily apparent improvement of the team as a consequence. Now with John Y. Brown's high-stakes dealings to obtain a more glitzy Boston team for himself, the entire city would be sold down the drain and Buffalo and up-state New York would say fare-well to pro basketball for the final time (or at least until the coming of the nearby expansion Toronto Raptors more than a decade and a half later).

Once ensconced in the sunny climes of southern California, the San Diego Clippers would prove from the very beginning one of the NBA's saddest stories and most unredeeming franchises. There was, of course, the usual optimism surrounding a new ballclub married to a new venue; there was a new coach in former NBA player Gene Shue; and there had

also been a massive trade with Boston that accompanied the unique swap-
ping of franchise owners. Boston had culled Nate Archibald, Billy Knight
and Marvin Barnes from the Buffalo roster; the renamed Clippers in return
received Kermit Washington, Kevin Kunnert, and rookie scoring sensation
Freeman Williams. This atmosphere of optimism was rewarded at the
outset, at least, with a winning first winter in San Diego. Another newcomer in the backcourt, Lloyd (World B.) Free (acquired from the Philadelphia Sixers) provided the most offensive punch since McAdoo, with a
28.8 ppg. average. And yet the team was no better than a distant 5th-place
finisher in a loaded Pacific Division, and the substantial crowds of 9,000-
plus in San Diego Coliseum had little to cheer nightly beyond the joys of
a first-hand look at NBA basketball.

And the San Diego Clippers never got any closer to modest success
than this first break-even season. It would be all down hill, in fact, from
this point on. Down hill, and eventually right out the door! Portents of
the future would even attach themselves to a bold move made in May,
1979, when the transplanted franchise gambled heavily with the signing
of injured free-agent star Bill Walton. Walton had led Portland to a world
title only two seasons back, then missed a full season when a broken foot
received late in 1978 action refused to heal properly. Walton was soon
quarrelling with Trail Blazers' management over handling of the injury,
claiming the team had pressured him to return to action far too early and
that he thus had no intention of again playing for Portland when his
contract expired. San Diego gambled that Walton would recover, but had
to pay a heavy price by shipping Kevin Kunnert, Kermit Washington and
a first-round draft selection to Portland as compensation. But the recovery
never came and Walton contributed precious little by playing in only 169
total games for the Clippers over the next six full seasons.

A second fifth-place finish in '79–'80 quickly ended Gene Shue's brief
tenure as the team dropped back below .500 and fell eight games off the
previous year's surprising pace. Under replacement Paul Silas, another
former NBA playing star of a decade earlier, club fortunes dipped still
further over three succeeding campaigns. A collapse to only 17 victories
during the second year under Silas established a franchise low that had
not been previously approached, even in the first several expansion years
back in Buffalo. World B. Free also took his rim-rattling act on the road
after two seasons when traded to Golden State in an August, 1980, deal
for guard Phil Smith. But Freeman Williams (19.3 ppg. in 1981), Tom
Chambers (17.2 in 1982) and Terry Cummings (23.7 in 1983) continued
to lead a free-shooting attack. Cummings, a second overall 1982 first-
round pick from DePaul, was the most promising, and garnered outstanding
rookie honors for the '82–'83 NBA season.

Paul Silas was also done in San Diego after the 1982–83 slipshod season
which logged 25 victories and a second sixth-place standing and boasted
nothing beyond Terry Cummings' stellar debut. And the Clippers themselves were just about done by now as well. Jim Lyman took the reins

and did no better during the final San Diego season. The club jumped five digits in the win column, yet remained anchored to their basement address in the Pacific Division. The only-modest help for forward Terry Cummings (22.9 ppg.) came from veteran guard Norm Nixon (17.0 ppg. with a league-best and club-record 914 assists) who had played in the Los Angeles Lakers backcourt alongside Magic Johnson during the previous half-dozen seasons.

Another ownership transfer had already taken place with Don Sterling purchasing the franchise during the summer of 1981. After three years of steady backsliding, Sterling now longed for a drastic image upgrade and revamped environment that no coaching replacements or roster fine-tuning could apparently accomplish. Doing what most owners of sinking-ship franchises seem to do in such situations, Sterling next petitioned the league for approval of another franchise shift, this time northward into Los Angeles Sports Arena, smack in the very backyard of the highly successful Lakers. The fourth owner of the Clippers ballclub now had his environment change, but outside of new red, white, and blue playing uniforms, one could detect little that would separate the image of the Los Angeles Clippers from that of the San Diego Clippers. Two water-treading seasons, each 20 games under .500, only proved that a cabbage is still a cabbage no matter the type of cellophane wrapping. The only effort to change the contents of this slow-rotting package was a major trade, which sent current team star Terry Cummings (along with guards Craig Hodges and Ricky Pierce) to the Milwaukee Bucks for guards Marques Johnson and Junior Bridgeman, center Harvey Catchings, and a banana-boat load of cash.

As bad as the Buffalo Braves had been in the earliest expansion season, and as hopeless as the San Diego Clippers were a decade later in '81–'82, LA's version of the Clippers would now plunge to new and even darker depths than anything that had come before. At least the 1971 and 1982 teams had owned excuses for overall incompetence: the first-year expansion club had a no-name roster befitting such first-year lame ducks, and the 1982 outfit had sacrificed a bundle of role players to get Walton, who then sat out the full campaign. The 1987 and 1988 teams were simply horrendous, however, without much excuse. Benoit Benjamin was a seven-foot center who rarely imitated an animate object, Mike Woodson was an acknowledged bench player cast in the role of a scoring leader; Marques Johnson often scored like his forerunner Terry Cummings, but never matched Cummings as a rebounder or defender.

As the downtrodden ''other team'' from Los Angeles finally entered the 1990s, there would thankfully be a few glimmering sparks of life that began to show themselves cautiously. Ron Harper was acquired from Cleveland and brought much-needed 20 ppg. firepower as well as a star-quality the club now desperately lacked. Danny Manning was the first player taken in the 1988 draft (thus the only compensation for the awful 1988 showing) and had superstar quality written all over him. While an early season knee injury would wipe out much of his rookie campaign,

Manning was fully recovered and playing like an All-Star a few seasons down the road. Miracle-worker but transient coach Larry Brown was hired midway through the '91–'92 season, and triggered a 23–12 stretch run that landed the Clippers in their first playoff action since Year Six back in Buffalo.

For the first time in years it was looking as though the Los Angeles Clippers now sported a hopeful future, if not exactly a bright one. Across town the Lakers were entering a tailspin of their own that had already taken some of the luster off of one of basketball's brightest clubs of the 1980s and levelled the playing field in the competition for paying customers. With young stars like Danny Manning, Ron Harper and Mark Jackson (a former NBA Rookie of the Year with the Knicks) this team could now generate interest at the box office from league fans and respect on the hardwood from league opponents. And the roster had been fleshed out with other promising young players like Loy Vaught and Gary Grant from Michigan, and Kenny Norman out of the University of Illinois. And in Larry Brown's first full season at the helm there would be another .500 season and even a second straight trip to the playoffs.

Yet it was all seemingly a delusion that soon crashed and burned. Coach Brown—who never seemed to stay in any one spot long enough to wear out his welcome—was having communications problems with the front office and departed to seek other coaching employment. Manning also started to make noises about wanting to move to greener pastures. By the latter part of the last-place '93–'94 campaign (27–55 record) Danny Manning got his wish in the form of an even swap with the Atlanta Hawks for fading superstar Dominique Wilkins. Wilkins would provide some luster at the end of 1994 when he unleashed his still potent "Human Highlight Film" act in the L.A. Sports Arena. But 'Nique also left little doubt that he would turn his back on the Clippers and seek to renew his free-agent contract elsewhere for the coming campaign.

With Wilkins now packing his bags for a final career stop (reportedly with the Celtics) and with coach Bob Weiss dismissed after only a single last-place season, the Los Angeles Clippers were once more at sea without a captain, ship's rudder, or even a decent sailing breeze. The NBA's least-successful long-term franchise was still searching for an identity, for a divisional title, for a trip beyond the second round of the playoffs, and for a big star or headline coach. Without any of these vital ingredients, the number-two LA NBA franchise would certainly always seem little more than second rate in Los Angeles, and third rate just about everywhere else they play or discuss the nation's new favorite sport.

Suggested Readings on Los Angeles (San Diego) Clippers

Bjarkman, Peter C. **The History of the NBA**. New York: Crescent Books), 1992.

Strasen, Marty (et. al.) **Basketball Almanac, 1993–94**. New York: Publications International (Signet Sports Library), 1994.

Year-by-Year Los Angeles (San Diego) Clippers Summary

Season	Record	Finish	Coach(es)	Scoring Leader(s)	Playoffs (W-L Record)
Key: *=Tied for Position; #=League Scoring Leader					
Buffalo Braves					
1970–71	22–60	4th	Dolph Schayes	Bob Kauffman (20.4)	Did Not Qualify
1971–72	22–60	4th	Dolph Schayes	Bob Kauffman (18.9)	Did Not Qualify
			Johnny McCarthy		
1972–73	21–61	3rd	Jack Ramsay	Elmore Smith (18.3)	Did Not Qualify
1973–74	42–40	3rd	Jack Ramsay	Bob McAdoo (30.6)#	Lost in 1st Round (2–4)
1974–75	49–33	2nd	Jack Ramsay	Bob McAdoo (34.5)#	Lost in 2nd Round (3–4)
1975–76	46–36	2nd*	Jack Ramsay	Bob McAdoo (31.1)#	Lost in 2nd Round (4–5)
1976–77	30–52	4th	Tates Locke	Bob McAdoo (23.7)	Did Not Qualify
			Bob MacKinnon		
			Joe Mullaney		
1977–78	27–55	4th	L.Fitzsimmons	Randy Smith (24.6)	Did Not Qualify
San Diego Clippers					
1978–79	43–39	5th	Gene Shue	World B. Free (28.8)	Did Not Qualify
1979–80	35–47	5th	Gene Shue	World B. Free (30.2)	Did Not Qualify
1980–81	36–46	5th	Paul Silas	Freeman Williams (19.3)	Did Not Qualify
1981–82	17–65	6th	Paul Silas	Tom Chambers (17.2)	Did Not Qualify
1982–83	25–57	6th	Paul Silas	Terry Cummings (23.7)	Did Not Qualify
1983–84	30–52	6th	Jim Lyman	Terry Cummings (22.9)	Did Not Qualify
Los Angeles Clippers					
1984–85	31–51	4th*	Jim Lyman	Derek Smith (22.1)	Did Not Qualify
			Don Chaney		
1985–86	32–50	3rd*	Don Chaney	Derek Smith (23.5)	Did Not Qualify
1986–87	12–70	6th	Don Chaney	Mike Woodson (17.1)	Did Not Qualify
1987–88	17–65	6th	Gene Shue	Mike Woodson (18.0)	Did Not Qualify
1988–89	21–61	7th	Gene Shue	Ken Norman (18.1)	Did Not Qualify
			Don Casey		
1989–90	32–50	6th	Don Casey	Ron Harper (22.8)	Did Not Qualify
1990–91	31–51	6th	Mike Schuler	Charles Smith (20.0)	Did Not Qualify
1991–92	45–37	5th	Mike Schuler	Danny Manning (19.3)	Lost in 1st Round (2–3)
			Mack Clavin		
			Larry Brown		
1992–93	41–41	4th	Larry Brown	Danny Manning (22.8)	Lost in 1st Round (2–3)
1993–94	27–55	7th	Bob Weiss	Dominique Wilkins (26.0)	Did Not Qualify

Individual Career Leaders and Record Holders (1970–1994)

Scoring Average	World B. Free (29.4 ppg., 1978–80)
Points Scored	Randy Smith (12,735, 1971–83)
Games Played	Randy Smith (715, 1971–83)
Minutes Played	Randy Smith (24,393)
Field Goal Pct.	Swen Nater (.542, 1977–83)
3-Pt. Field Goals	Ron Harper (248, 1989–94)
3-Pt. Field Goal Pct.	Brian Taylor (.376, 1978–82)
Free Throws Made	Randy Smith (2,986)
Free-Throw Pct.	Ernie DiGregorio (.906, 1973–77)
Rebounds	Bob McAdoo (4,229, 1972–77)
Assists	Randy Smith (3,498, 1971–83)
Steals	Randy Smith (1,072)
Blocked Shots	Benoit Benjamin (1,117, 1985–91)
Personal Fouls	Randy Smith (2,018)

Individual Single-Season and Game Records (1970–1994)

Scoring Average	Bob McAdoo (34.5 ppg., 1974–75)
Points Scored (Season)	Bob McAdoo (2,831, 1974–75)
Points Scored (Game)	Charles Smith (52, 12-1-90 at Denver Nuggets)
	Bob McAdoo (52, 3-17-76 and 2-22-75)
Field Goal Pct. (Season)	James Donaldson (.637, 19874–85)
Free-Throw Pct. (Season)	Ernie DiGregorio (.945, 1976–77)
Rebounds (Season)	Swen Nater (1,216, 1979–80)
Rebounds (Game)	Swen Nater (32, 12-14-79 vs. Denver Nuggets)
Assists (Season)	Norm Nixon (914, 1983–84)
Assists (Game)	Ernie DiGregorio (25, 11-1-74 at Portland Trail Blazers)
Steals (Season)	Randy Smith (203, 1973–74)
Steals (Game)	Doc Rivers (9, 11-6-91 vs. Phoenix Suns)
Blocked Shots (Season)	Bob McAdoo (246, 1973–74)
Blocked Shots (Game)	Benoit Benjamin (10, 3-31-89 and 1-29-88)
Personal Fouls (Season)	Tom Chambers (341, 1982–83)

Best Trade in Franchise History

Although there were a few more odds and ends thrown into the November, 1989, deal, the Clippers acquired flashy scoring guard Ron Harper from the Cleveland Cavaliers for Reggie Williams and the draft rights to Duke All-American Danny Ferry. Ferry had been a highly touted collegian (1989 collegiate player of the year) who had opted to play first in Italy for a large-dollar contract rather than spend his rookie season with the lowly Clippers. The Clippers subsequently gambled that Ferry was over-rated as an NBA prospect, and they clearly won that huge gamble. The 6'10" Ferry has been largely a bust with the Cavs, and while Harper has not been a superstar in Los Angeles, he has nonetheless put in several solid offensive years for the Clippers (never dipping below 18.0 ppg. during four seasons in LA and twice exceeding 20 ppg.)

Worst Trade in Franchise History

For nearly twenty-five seasons the Braves and Clippers escaped the fate of trading away a franchise player, largely because this doormat franchise never possessed such a player to squander. Once one came along, it was only a matter of time until he was peddled in some get-rich-quick scheme that would backfire. Danny Manning was indeed the closest thing to a franchise-type player ever to come the Clippers way. Frustrated with seasons of little progress (and also seemingly in a rare position to grab fickle fans from a struggling LA Lakers franchise across town) the Clippers peddled Manning in mid-season, 1994, for a marquee player of the past decade—Dominique Wilkins. While the deal may have secured the future for the rebuilding Hawks, the Clippers had to come out the losers. Wilkins was clearly near the end of his career. Furthermore, as a free agent at the end of the 1994 season, he early declared he would have absolutely no interest in re-signing with the Clippers organization after only a half season in Los Angeles.

Los Angeles Clippers Historical Oddity

The Buffalo Braves, forerunners of the current Los Angeles Clippers, were prime participants in one of the zaniest trades in all of sports history. In the summer of 1978, the Buffalo club got together with the Boston Celtics and actually traded, not players or managers or coaches, or even radio announcers, but franchise owners. John Y. Brown exchanged his ownership rights to the Buffalo Braves with Irv Levin, for ownership rights to Levin's Boston Celtics. Levin seemed to be getting the far shorter end of the stick here, but did have an ulterior motive. The west-coast-based film producer had his eye on a ballclub which he could move into California without objection from other owners or from the NBA commissioner and governors. The strange result, when the dust cleared, was the birth of the west coast San Diego (and later Los Angeles) Clippers.

Clippers (Braves) All-Time Number One Draft Picks List

Buffalo Braves
1970 John Hummer (Princeton)
1971 Elmore Smith (Kentucky State)
1972 Bob McAdoo (North Carolina)
1973 Ernie DiGregorio (Providence)
1974 Tom McMillen (Maryland)
1975 None
1976 Adrian Dantley (Notre Dame)
1977 None
1978 None

San Diego Clippers
1979 None
1980 Michael Brooks (LaSalle)
1981 Tom Chambers (Utah)
1982 Terry Cummings (DePaul)
1983 Byron Scott (Arizona State)
1984 Lancaster Gordon (Louisville)

Los Angeles Clippers
1985 Benoit Benjamin (Creighton)
1986 None
1987 Reggie Williams (Georgetown)
1988 Danny Manning (Kansas)
1989 Danny Ferry (Duke)
1990 Bo Kimble (Loyola Marymount)
1991 LeRon Ellis (Syracuse)
1992 Randy Woods (LaSalle)
1993 Terry Dehere (Seton Hall)

Chapter 16

CLEVELAND CAVALIERS

Hardwood Follies in the Topsy-Turvy Land of the Cavaliers

All-Time Franchise Record: 863–1105, .439 Pct. (1970–1994)
NBA Championships: None
Greatest Franchise Player: Brad Daugherty (1986–1994)
All-Time Leading Scorer: Brad Daugherty (10,389 Points, 1986–94) and Austin Carr (10,265 Points, 1971–1980)
Most Successful Coach: Lenny Wilkens (316–258, .551 Pct., 1986–1993)
All-Time Franchise Team: Brad Daugherty (C), Mike Mitchell (F), Jim Chones (F), Austin Carr (G), Mark Price (G)

Every city and even every sports franchise is entitled to a bad century now and then. And for the past nine decades the often-maligned city of Cleveland, Ohio—with its handful of professional sports franchises—has been stuck right smack in the middle of one of the worst centuries imaginable. The city's foremost pride—baseball's Indians—have disappointed and discouraged fans for almost as long as any living soul can remember. The cloud may finally be lifting for Cleveland's devotees of the national pastime, however, after a full half-century of second-rate second-division play. There is now a spanking new stadium to boost local civic pride, and the young Cleveland Indians team, boasting slugging stars like Carlos Baerga and Joey Belle, has shown encouraging signs of crawling at long last out from under "the curse of Rocky Colavito" that has hung over northern Ohio like industrial pollution since the mid-fifties.

When it comes to basketball, on the other hand, the Cleveland entry in the professional ranks has hardly been around long enough to move generations of rooters to near distraction. But this has not excused those owners, coaches, and players associated with the NBA Cleveland Cavaliers from working overtime to make up for lost opportunities in the disappointment department. Here, after all, is an expansion franchise from the early '70s which has won only slightly more than 40% of its games over almost a quarter century; which has qualified for post-season competition in but 10 of 24 seasons, with a half dozen of those coming in the seven most recent campaigns; which has never made it into the NBA finals and which has enjoyed exactly one divisional title (and that came two full decades ago); and which has fielded perhaps fewer glamorous headline players than any NBA franchise of the modern era. It hasn't been any more fun being a Cavs fan than it has been rooting for the lackluster baseball Indians.

Much of the history of professional basketball in Cleveland boils down to painful sagas of two separate Herculean efforts, both aimed at pulling a disabled and distraught franchise up by the boot straps and digging a floundering ballclub out of a huge and seemingly bottomless pit. The first of these inescapable pits was one that team management had altogether little to do with creating. It was merely the unfortunate inheritance of a lowly expansion team given all-too-few tools with which to compete against more established NBA clubs. The second hopeless hole, however, was one the ne'er-do-well club had recklessly dug for itself and one which could be expected to generate altogether little sympathy from fans—either those in Cleveland or elsewhere around the league. This was the near-fatal situation created in the early '80s by meddling franchise owner Ted Stepien. For Stepien was that breed of sports entrepreneur who took special delight in exercising his personal incompetence through running the club's hands-on daily basketball operations. Outdoing even egotistical owners like baseball moguls George Steinbrenner and Marge Schott, Stepien hired inappropriate coaches and unleashed a series of improvident trades which nearly wiped out the ballclub's future and bankrupted its present oncourt operations as well.

If things have thus looked bleak for the Cleveland Cavaliers throughout most of franchise history, they certainly started out on the worst possible foot. The 1970 expansion roster that joined the NBA alongside two other newcomers in Buffalo and Portland was about as thin on talent as any first-year lineup since the very earliest days in league history. On being tabbed by owner Nick Mileti as the expansion club's first coach, former University of Minnesota mentor Bill Fitch would wisecrack that the press should always try and remember that his name was "Fitch, not Houdini!" Fitch's quip was great for a press conference laugh but also provided an ominous prediction of just where things would stand before this first-year expansion nightmare was over.

The most notable players culled by Cleveland from the NBA dispersal draft of 1970 comprised a group of NBA journeymen with truly limited pedigrees. Walt Wesley was a 6'11" center with shamefully little mobility, who had never even averaged double figures in scoring during his previous four NBA seasons in Cincinnati and Chicago. Forward Bobby "Bingo" Smith was coming off a mediocre rookie season in San Diego, and guard

John Warren was another 1970 rookie who had averaged just 2.5 ppg. in 44 games as a New York Knicks reserve. Other veterans selected included guards Butch Beard, Don Ohl and Johnny Egan and forward McCoy McLemore. But Beard would have to spend the year completing military service, Ohl would announce his retirement rather than join the lowly Cavaliers, and Egan and McLemore would be dealt away in minor trades before the first season was complete. John Johnson of Iowa and Dave Sorenson of Ohio State—both forwards—would be the first two prospects selected from a collegiate draft which also provided precious little true talent.

A question on the lips of NBA fans around the country during the opening month of the 1970–71 expansion season soon became whether or not these Cleveland Cavaliers would ever win a game. The patchwork roster handed to Coach Fitch managed to lose fifteen straight before tasting victory. Included was a dreadful 141–87 pasting in Philadelphia during game eleven, which still stands as a ballclub record for humiliation. Finally able to eke out a first victory on the road over fellow expansion stumble-bum Portland, the Cavs then raced to a dozen more defeats before finally capturing an inaugural home victory—predictably against the other expansion rival from Buffalo. At one point, the Cleveland team had slid to 2 and 34 and only once (in December versus Cincinnati, Buffalo and Philadelphia) did they manage to string together three victories in a row. Mere incompetence eventually gave way to true slapstick as guard John Warren on one occasion scored two points for the opponents (Portland) by making a layup at the wrong end of the floor. The final count for the nightmarish season was a 15–67 record that assured a basement slot in the Central Division. John Johnson did register a fine rookie season with a 16.6 scoring average and represented Cleveland in the annual NBA All-Star Game. The biggest miracle, however, was that coach Bill Fitch somehow managed to hold onto his job throughout not only this disastrous initial season but for eight more to follow.

Fitch's eight-year tenure would be marked largely by slow but steady improvement as Cleveland painfully inched its way out of a subterranean home inherited with the hand dealt to an expansion franchise. The victory total climbed first to 23 games in season two and 32 in '72–'73; after a holding-pattern season (29–53) in year four the team finally climbed out of the basement with 40-plus wins four seasons in a row. Much of the improvement was due to the continuing development of John Johnson, one solid trade which shipped Butch Beard to Seattle in exchange for sharpshooting forward Barry Clemens and stellar playmaking guard Lenny Wilkens, and the drafting, in season two, of phenomenal Notre Dame scorer Austin Carr. With their increased firepower the '72–'73e Cavs finished only a single game behind the Houston Rockets in their quest to escape the Central Division's bottom rung.

Austin Carr provided the Cleveland ballclub with its closest thing to a legitimate superstar during two opening decades of franchise history. Arriving in time for the club's second season, the hard-driving Carr would have an immediate impact. An unstoppable scoring machine during three NCAA seasons with the University of Notre Dame, Carr had averaged 34.5 as a collegian, one of the loftiest career pointmaking marks ever recorded. Although he would be limited to just 43 games as a rookie by a broken foot bone, nonetheless the stellar freshman would pace the club with a 21.2 average. Carr's 20-point scoring would continue for only three total seasons with the Cavs, as his NCAA promise never seemed to fully materialize under the weight of several nagging NBA injuries. Yet the sharpshooting guard would remain a contributing team member for nine seasons and function admirably as a role player when new talent eventually pushed him out of the starting lineup.

The first "glory season" for the Cavaliers was now just around the corner and would arrive with the 1975–76 campaign. It would indeed be a memorable year, and one that would result in the only divisional title ever garnered by this usually lackluster ballclub. Off-season activity a year earlier, on the eve of the '74–'75 campaign, had been spectacular as the Cavs solved their desperate pivot problem with the acquisition of Jim Chones, who had been playing in the ABA, but whose NBA rights were owned by the Los Angeles Lakers. Another trade, with Seattle, brought over veteran guard Dick Snyder and a first-round draft pick used to select "Campy" Russell out of Michigan. And just after the '75–'76 season opened, a final piece of the puzzle was fortuitously inserted when Fitch acquired veteran center Nate Thurmond from the Chicago Bulls as a needed backup for Chones.

A bolstered lineup paid big dividends as Fitch guided his upgraded 1976 team to 49 victories and a one-game Central Division margin over Washington. Then against those same Washington Bullets Dick Snyder sank a five-foot running bank shot in the closing seconds of game seven to send the dizzy Cavs into the post-season third round. The Cinderella Cleveland club now faced stiff odds indeed in a conference finals shootout with Boston. A Tom Heinsohn-coached Celtics juggernaut was on its way to its second title in three seasons and boasted a lineup (John Havlicek, Charlie Scott, Paul Silas, Dave Cowens, and Jo Jo White) that was as good as any during the Cousy-Russell era. And when Jim Chones broke his ankle in a practice session prior to the Boston series, an easy Celtics victory (in six games) was virtually assured.

Bill Fitch claimed NBA Coach-of-the-Year honors for his bang-up season of 1976. But Fitch's successes in '75–'76 were unfortunately never to be repeated—not while he remained in Cleveland at any rate. The team leveled off with identical 43–39 records over the next two seasons. Youngster Campy Russell and aging Austin Carr shared the scoring burden and veteran New York Knicks backcourt star Walt Frazier came aboard to finish out his career as a part-time player in Cleveland. But after two holding-pattern seasons Bill Fitch's ninth and final year would bring a near-total collapse. The 1979 club slumped into a fourth-place tie in the

Central Division and missed the playoffs for the first time in four years. After coaching Cleveland through its first 756 regular-season and playoff games, Bill Fitch finally announced his resignation on May 21, 1979. Two days later Fitch was tabbed to head up the more prosperous Boston Celtics, where he would soon enough inherit Larry Bird and thus his only NBA championship ring. Stan Albeck, in turn, earned the unenviable task of becoming only the second head coach of the less-promising Cleveland Cavaliers.

Several discouraging seasons at the end of the '70s were only a small harbinger of how bad things would soon become. The fate of the sinking ballclub was soon sealed when original owner Nick Mileti sold his remaining interests in the struggling franchise to Joe Zingale, who in turn peddled his majority stock to Ted Stepien just prior to the 1980–81 season. Before Cavs fans had a chance to catch their collective breath the unpopular Stepien had begun dismantling their ballclub wholesale.

Stepien began his disfiguration of the Cleveland NBA franchise by hiring coach Bill Musselman, and then sending three coveted number-one draft picks to the up-and-coming expansion Dallas Mavericks for the undistinguished trio of guard Mike Bratz, and forwards Richard Washington and Jerome Whitehead. Another number-one pick soon went to the overjoyed Dallas Mavericks for journeyman guard Geoff Huston. The result at the end of a single season was a 28–54 record (worst since the club's second year) and a ledger now missing four first-round draft selections. But even before all the damage reports were in, Stepien continued his whirlwind dealing and tinkering throughout '81–'82: first Don Delaney took over as head coach, and soon Chuck Daly had that title as Delaney's mid-season replacement; leading scorer Mike Mitchell and flashy guard Roger Phegley were next traded to San Antonio for Reggie Johnson and Ron Brewer; Johnson was then immediately off to Kansas City for Cliff Robinson, while promising center Bill Laimbeer and Kenny Carr were peddled to Detroit for lumbering ineffectual center Paul Mokeski. In all, 23 players wore the Cleveland uniform in 1982 and their combined efforts resulted in but 15 victories.

The 1982–83 season was one that saw the mammoth fire sale continue to unfold and the club's performance continue to unravel at a record rate. Tom Nissalke was the new head coach, and veteran center Sam Lacey was signed as a free agent. Another leading scorer was then dispensed with as Ron Brewer was offered to the Golden State Warriors for free-shooting free spirit Lloyd (World B.) Free. About the only fun in Cleveland for most of the 23–57 season was that garnered from watching World B. Free unleash his non-stop array of long-range shots from all over the court. Cavs fans could finally take some solace, however, when owner Stepien eventually tired of his own meddling and unloaded his entire ballclub to local ownership, headed by George and Gordon Gund.

It took a long time for the Cavaliers franchise to recover from the extensive damage that Stepien's two years of dealing and wheeling had ultimately done. The league even helped out some by awarding the Cavaliers four bonus first-round draft selections over the next four years. But nonetheless the progress was slow as two of the next three seasons under Nissalke and George Karl brought victory totals under 30 games. But slowly the record crept up and up, reaching first the 40 plateau and then the 50 plateau, before the decade was out. The truest sign of a reversal of fortunes came when ex-NBA great Wayne Embry took control of the club as general manager for the 1986–87 season. Embry brought Lenny Wilkens back as head coach and then engineered several draft choices and trades that solidified a team that would soon contend for years to come.

The team built at the draft table by Wayne Embry became a serious divisional challenger in the early seasons of the 1990s. A single draft on June 19, 1986, reaped a harvest like few ever known in franchise, or even league history. This was indeed the most pivotal single moment of franchise history for the long-suffering Cavaliers. On the very eve of the crucial draft, the Cavs had received exciting news that 1985 first-round selection John Williams had been found innocent of game-fixing charges at Tulane University and was finally cleared by the league to play. Then on draft day itself a major trade was announced, one that had shipped Roy Hinson to Philadelphia in exchange for the number-one selection later that morning. With this pick, Cleveland selected North Carolina seven-footer Brad Daugherty, a certain franchise player. Promising Miami University scoring guard Ron Harper would also be taken, with a first-round number eight selection. And the day's activities would be concluded in most fitting fashion when a second trade was announced which would bring in stellar Georgia Tech playmaker Mark Price, that day's 25th overall draft selection, from the Dallas Mavericks. The only two things that now seemed to stand in the way of the Cavs were the Chicago Bulls and a series of devastating injuries which would eventually wipe out Daugherty for much of the 1990 and 1994 seasons and then fell Mark Price as well for almost the entire 1991 campaign.

But the Bulls, and the nagging injuries, were in the end enough to keep the ballclub from ever quite climbing over the hump and capturing that long-elusive divisional title. A second-ever trip to the conference finals in March, 1992, ended in a six-game loss to the defending NBA champion Bulls, despite a surprising game two 107–81 romp for the Cavs in Chicago Stadium. A year later Wilkens and company would meet the Bulls in the playoffs for the fourth time in six years, this time in the conference semifinals. Jordan's jumper at the buzzer would steal game four in the Richmond Coliseum and seal a four-game sweep of the outmanned Cavs. Finally, even Lenny Wilkens would be a victim of these continuing frustrations and would step down in May as an admission of his failure to achieve the team's post-season goals. Wilkens would soon be off to direct the Atlantic Division's Atlanta Hawks in his continuing quest to dethrone the three-peat champion Chicago Bulls. And in a strange version of coaching musical chairs, former Atlanta coach Mike Fratello would now come over to Cleveland toting the very same mission that Wilkens had been desperately pursuing throughout the first third of the 1990s.

The season which marked Fratello's debut in Cleveland was another injury-plagued session (47–35, tied for third in the Central Division) showing only moderate successes and finally ending in familiar post-season failures. Brad Daugherty logged but 50 regular season games and sat on the side-lines while the Jordan-less Bulls once more scuttled the Cavs playoff hopes in three straight. And things were somehow all the more somber this time around. With the team rapidly aging (Daugherty would be 28 and Price 30 for the coming season) and with a desperate need for fresh blood, it seemed as though this edition of the Cavs might be enjoying a last hurrah as a team of great promise that never quite made it all the way to the top. Unfortunately it now also looked as though another long rebuilding process would soon be in the offering.

Suggested Readings on Cleveland Cavaliers

Ryan, Bob and Terry Pluto. **Forty-Eight Minutes: A Night in the Life of the NBA**. New York: Macmillan, 1987.

Strasen, Marty (et. al.). **Basketball Almanac, 1993–94**. New York: Publications International (Signet Sports Library), 1994.

Cleveland Cavaliers Retired Uniform Numbers (3)

Bingo Smith (7)
Austin Carr (34)
Nate Thurmond (42)

Year-By-Year Cleveland Cavaliers Summary

Season	Record	Finish	Coach(es)	Scoring Leader(s)	Playoffs (W-L Record)
Key: *=Tied for Position					
1970–71	15–67	4th	Bill Fitch	Walt Wesley (17.7)	Did Not Qualify
1971–72	23–59	4th	Bill Fitch	Austin Carr (21.2)	Did Not Qualify
1972–73	32–50	4th	Bill Fitch	Lenny Wilkens (20.5)	Did Not Qualify
				Austin Carr (20.5)	
1973–74	29–53	4th	Bill Fitch	Austin Carr (21.9)	Did Not Qualify
1974–75	40–42	3rd	Bill Fitch	Bingo Smith (15.9)	Did Not Qualify
1975–76	49–33	1st	Bill Fitch	Jim Chones (15.8)	Lost in 3rd Round (6–7)
1976–77	43–39	4th	Bill Fitch	Campy Russell (16.5)	Lost in 1st Round (1–2)
1977–78	43–39	3rd	Bill Fitch	Campy Russell (19.4)	Lost in 1st Round (0–2)
1978–79	30–52	4th*	Bill Fitch	Campy Russell (21.9)	Did Not Qualify
1979–80	37–45	5th	Stan Albeck	Mike Mitchell (22.2)	Did Not Qualify

Season	Record	Finish	Coach(es)	Scoring Leader(s)	Playoffs (W-L Record)
1980–81	28–54	5th	Bill Musselman Don Delaney	Mike Mitchell (24.5)	Did Not Qualify
1981–82	15–67	6th	Don Delaney Bob Kloppenburg Chuck Daly Bill Musselman	Ron Brewer (19.4)	Did Not Qualify
1982–83	23–59	5th	Tom Nissalke	World B. Free (24.2)	Did Not Qualify
1983–84	28–54	4th	Tom Nissalke	World B. Free (22.3)	Did Not Qualify
1984–85	36–46	4th	George Karl	World B. Free (22.5)	Lost in 1st Round (1–3)
1985–86	29–53	5th	George Karl Gene Littles	World B. Free (22.9)	Did Not Qualify
1986–87	31–51	6th	Lenny Wilkens	Ron Harper (22.9)	Did Not Qualify
1987–88	42–40	4th	Lenny Wilkens	Brad Daugherty (18.9)	Lost in 1st Round (2–3)
1988–89	57–25	2nd	Lenny Wilkens	Brad Daugherty (18.9) Mark Price (18.9)	Lost in 1st Round (2–3)
1989–90	42–40	4th	Lenny Wilkens	Mark Price (19.6)	Lost in 1st Round (2–3)
1990–91	33–49	6th	Lenny Wilkens	Brad Daugherty (21.6)	Did Not Qualify
1991–92	57–25	2nd	Lenny Wilkens	Brad Daugherty (21.5)	Lost in 3rd Round (9–8)
1992–93	54–28	2nd	Lenny Wilkens	Brad Daugherty (20.2)	Lost in 2nd Round (3–6)
1993–94	47–35	3rd*	Mike Fratello	Mark Price (17.3)	Lost in 1st Round (0–o3)

Individual Career Leaders and Record Holders (1970–1994)

Scoring Average	World B. Free (23.0 ppg., 1982–86)
Points Scored	Brad Daugherty (10,389, 1986–94)
	Austin Carr (10,265, 1971–80)
Games Played	Bingo Smith (720, 1970–80)
Minutes Played	Bingo Smith (19,221)
Field Goals Made	Austin Carr (4,272)
Field Goal Pct.	Mark West (.553, 1984–88)
3-Pt. Field Goals	Mark Price (699)
Free Throws Made	Brad Daugherty (2,741)
Free-Throw Pct.	Mark Price (.906, 1986–94)
Rebounds	Brad Daugherty (5,227)
Assists	Mark Price (3,871)
Steals	Clarence "Foots" Walker (722, 1974–80)
Blocked Shots	Larry Nance (1,087)
Personal Fouls	Bingo Smith (1,752)

Individual Single-Season and Game Records (1970–1994)

Scoring Average	Mike Mitchell (24.5 ppg., 1980–81)
Points Scored (Season)	Mike Mitchell (2,012, 1980–81)
Points Scored (Game)	Walt Wesley (50, 2-19-71 vs. Cincinnati Royals)
Minutes Played (Season)	Mike Mitchell (3,194, 1980–81)
Field Goal Pct. (Season)	Brad Daugherty (.571, 1992–93)

Free-Throw Pct. (Season)	Mark Price (.948, 1992–93)
3-Pt. Field Goals (Season)	Mark Price (152, 1989–90)
Rebounds (Season)	Jim Brewer (891, 1975–76)
Rebounds (Game)	Rick Roberson (25, 3–4–72 at Houston Rockets)
Assists (Season)	John Bagley (735, 1985–86)
Assists (Game)	Geoff Huston (27, 1–27–82 vs. Golden State Warriors)
Steals (Season)	Ron Harper (209, 1986–87)
Blocked Shots (Season)	Larry Nance (243, 1991–92)
Personal Fouls (Season)	James Edwards (347, 1981–82)

Best Trade in Franchise History

If Mark Price isn't Cleveland's all-time franchise player (he probably loses out by only a nod to center Brad Daugherty) he is certainly the second best ever to wear a Cavs' uniform. Price was stolen from the Dallas Mavericks on June 17, 1986, in perhaps the best single draft day pilfering ever engineered. In exchange for basketball's current leading point guard the Mavericks received only a second round draft selection for 1989 (used to acquire no-name guard Jeff Hodge).

Worst Trade in Franchise History

This has to be the deal that shipped Kevin Johnson and Mark West to Phoenix in February, 1988, in exchange for Larry Nance and Mike Sanders. Although Sanders later provided some yeoman sixth-man duty over several seasons, Nance was a disappointment in Cleveland from the very first, despite his double-figure scoring and shot blocking abilities (he holds all Cleveland franchise records in this latter category). Nance has never returned to the scoring levels he displayed briefly in Phoenix and injuries have slowed him considerably in the two most recent seasons. Nance played only 33 games in 1993–94 and also missed the entire playoff round this past season.

Cleveland Cavaliers Historical Oddity

It seems hard to believe in today's cut-throat and competitive market, but the NBA once felt so sorry for the Cleveland franchise and the damage it had been dealt by a previous owner, that the league's governors actually awarded the Cleveland team a supply of extra draft selections. It was Ted Stepien who had squandered a decade worth of first-round draft choices (most of them directed toward the Dallas Mavericks) in misguided deals throughout the early 1980s. George and Gordon Gund, co-owners of the

Ritchfield Coliseum, had agreed to purchase the ballclub from Stepien in April, 1983, once it was announced that Cleveland would get four "bonus" first round selections spread over a four-year period between 1983 and 1986. Two of these bonus selections would eventually themselves be traded away and the other two used to pluck Stewart Granger (1983) and Ron Harper (1986) from the collegiate ranks.

Cavaliers All-time Number One Draft Picks List

Cleveland Cavaliers
1970 John Johnson (Iowa)
1971 Austin Carr (Notre Dame)
1972 Dwight Davis (Houston)
1973 Jim Brewer (Minnesota)
1974 Campy Russell (Michigan)
1975 John Lambert (USC)
1976 Chuckie Williams (Kansas State)
1977 Ed Jordan (Rutgers)
1978 Mike Mitchell (Auburn)
1979 Bruce Flowers (Notre Dame)
1980 Chad Kinch (UNCC)
1981 Mickey Dillard (Florida State)
1982 John Bagley (Boston College)
1983 Roy Hinson (Rutgers)
1984 Tim McCormick (Michigan)
1985 Charles Oakley (Virginia Union)
1986 Brad Daugherty (North Carolina)
1987 Kevin Johnson (California)
1988 Randolph Keyes (Southern Mississippi)
1989 John Morton (Seton Hall).
1990 Sefano Rusconi (Ranger Varese)
1991 Terrell Brandon (Oregon)
1992 None
1993 Chris Mills (Arizona)

Chapter 17

PORTLAND TRAIL BLAZERS

At Least They Always Fill the Arena

All-Time Franchise Record: 1041–927, .529 Pct. (1970–1994)
NBA Championships (1): 1976–77
Greatest Franchise Player: Clyde Drexler (1983–1994)
All-Time Leading Scorer: Clyde Drexler (17,136 Points, 1983–1994)
Most Successful Coach: Rick Adelman (291–154, .654 Pct., 1989–1994)
All-Time Franchise Team: Bill Walton (C), Maurice Lucas (F), Clyde Drexler (F),
   Geoff Petrie (G), Dave Twardzik (G)

For Portland Trail Blazers fanatics it will always be 1977. At least in that perfect frozen world of nostalgic memory, where past glories are endlessly relived and present shortcomings melt before the rich triumphs of those halcyon days. This one single season in Portland, after all, looms as one of the greatest Cinderella tales of all basketball history. It was a year when a hopeless underdog, led by a single charismatic giant of a hero, emerged from a half dozen seasons of mediocrity to unaccountably find itself alone atop the basketball universe as unexpected NBA world champion. And fans in Portland have never stopped rubbing their eyes since.

For their six initial franchise seasons, the Portland Trail Blazers had suffered the indignities of predictable and all-too-familiar expansion-era blues. Only once had the second NBA entry from the Pacific Northwest been anything but a fifth-place finisher. The team had already known turmoil and transition in the form of three regular coaches (along with one interim bench boss), two moderate stars beloved on the home floor (Geoff Petrie and Sidney Wicks) but hardly household names around the rest of the league, and no playoff appearances or winning records. Then a veteran college coach (200 wins and a 76% winning ledger) who had also logged eight NBA seasons (four with the Philadelphia Sixers and four more in Buffalo) came on the scene and reversed ballclub fortunes in the span of but a single season. Overnight the Blazers soared to a winning record (49–33) and a solid second place Pacific Division finish. Even before local fans could absorb such unaccustomed success the Blazers, by early summer, were unaccountably the reigning NBA champions. Before he was done with his profession, Jack Ramsay would amass 864 coaching wins, second in the NBA only to Boston's Red Auerbach. But nothing in his legendary career outstripped the one-season miracle Ramsay had once pulled off for the fans of Portland.

When Jack Ramsay signed on in Portland on June 1, 1976, he seemed to own just the type of winning attitude desperately needed by a franchise entering a seventh season with no climb higher than six games below the .500 benchmark of respectability. Here, after all, was an experienced and innovative mentor who had recently directed Buffalo's Braves into the playoffs for three straight seasons with little more than machine-gun scorer Bob McAdoo to work with. In Portland, by contrast, Ramsay was inheriting plenty to build on. For starters, he had Bill Walton. Walton had been an unparalleled collegiate legend at UCLA, where he had inherited the mantle from Lew Alcindor and led John Wooden's Bruins in the final two years (1972 and 1973) of an incredible seven-year championship run; he was a three-time collegiate All-American, a three-time college player of the year, twice NCAA tournament MVP, and the first overall selection of the 1974 collegiate player draft. But injuries had already clouded Walton's first two NBA seasons (he had played but 35 games during his rookie season and averaged 12.8 ppg.) and left Portland faithful wondering if they had been gypped in a draft lottery that had also offered Marvin Barnes, John Shumate, Tom Burleson, Bobby Jones, Maurice Lucas and Campy Russell. But by 1976 Walton seemed finally healthy; furthermore, he would fit perfectly into Ramsay's solid team-oriented approach that was much like the one Wooden had taught during Walton's collegiate heyday. Bill Walton was a great physical talent on a basketball floor, but he was also one of the most intelligent big men ever to play the game, and precisely the kind of heady ballplayer that Ramsay could most fully exploit.

And there was a strong supporting cast in Portland in 1976 as well. Maurice Lucas was the enforcer up front who had just signed on from the now defunct ABA, where he had trailed only Artis Gilmore in the junior league's individual rebounding race. Lionel Hollins and Dave Twardzik were pencilled in to handle the guard play at the opening of the '76 campaign, the former coming off a solid Portland rookie season (10.8 ppg., 306 assists) and the latter also an ABA veteran of four seasons with the Virginia Squires. And there were other key players as well in Herm Gilliam (seven-year veteran guard just acquired from Seattle), Bobby Gross (a second-year forward with potential as a streak scorer), and Larry Steele (a five-year veteran who doubled at guard and forward off the bench).

Paced by the huge redhead in the center slot, the revamped Blazers opened their first campaign under Jack Ramsay by finally living up to their colorful team moniker. The Portland club blazed from the starting gate in November, and had already posted a sterling 23–12 mark by New Year's Day. There were indeed some rough spots scattered throughout the second half of the season, as Ramsay's team eventually settled back to earth. One of the roughest would be a five-game losing skid in mid-February. But with Walton averaging a career second-best 18.6 ppg. and Lucas pacing the club offensively with 20.2 ppg., Ramsay's charges finished strong in the stretch run. A 49 victory total left them in runner-up slot a mere four games behind the powerful Los Angeles Lakers. And besides the Lakers, Portland would trail only Atlantic Division leader Philadelphia and Midwest Division pacesetter Denver in the race for best overall season's record.

But it was post-season tournament play (called simply "the playoffs" in the NBA) that provided the true joyride for the suddenly upsurging Portland team and their fans. The Blazers first demonstrated they were for real—even when the chips were down in post-season's fight for survival—by beating both Chicago and Denver. A close three-point defeat at Chicago was sandwiched between two convincing wins on the home floor against a Bulls team that received surprising scoring strength (27.3 ppg. over three contests) from unheralded 6–10 forward Mickey Johnson. The Denver series again found the Walton-led Blazers dominant on their home court, combining a 3–0 mark in Portland with a single road victory to end the Western Conference semifinals in six games. This set up the conference title match with Los Angeles, the league's strongest team and one featuring Kareem Abdul-Jabbar (the league's third leading scorer) at the post, proficient scorer Cazzie Russell in the power forward's slot, and Don Chaney and Lucius Allen as a talented backcourt combination.

But for all the power in the lineup of the Jerry West-coached Lakers, Portland was seemingly a young team of destiny and certainly not a team to be easily denied. And before it was over, the 1977 Western Conference Finals would provide one of the major shocks of NBA post-season history. The upstart Blazers not only climbed quickly over the hurdle of the Los Angeles Lakers; they altogether embarrassed one of basketball's proudest franchises with a four-game sweep which, while not entirely one-sided (three of four games were decided by five points or less), was nonetheless altogether decisive in its outcome. Walton and Jabber both performed superbly in the post positions and before the matchup of UCLA successors was concluded the press was drooling about a future decade of Walton-Jabbar confrontations that might resurrect the titanic struggles of Chamberlain-Russell. Just as Wilt always seemed to dominate Russell, yet come out on the losing end, so too Jabbar had held the statistical edge over his younger rival (121–77 in scoring, and an advantage in rebounding and blocked shots as well). But like Russell, Walton was simply surrounded by the better teammates as Gross and Lucas handled Cazzie Russell, and the guard trio of Hollins, Twardzik and Johnny Davis controlled the backcourt action. For the first time in the modern era of the NBA a team would now be heading into the championship finals in their very first trip into post-season play.

The dramatic NBA Finals that matched surprise Portland and a Philadelphia team now featuring ABA transfers Julius Erving and George McGinnis was hardly an anti-climax to what had already preceded. Philly had also been a surprise throughout most of the season, riding the double-barreled offense of the newcomer Erving (21.6) and front-court partner McGinnis (21.4) to an easy Atlantic Division title (six games over Boston) and hard-fought playoff victories over the still-potent Celtics with Jo Jo White and Dave Cowens (4–3), and Central Division leader Houston (4–1) with Moses Malone and Calvin Murphy. Now an elite team of individual superstars, the Sixers showcased not only the best two holdovers from the ABA (Erving and McGinnis had shared ABA MVP honors in 1975) but other weapons as well. Supporting the best forward tandem in years was also a solid backcourt combo of reliable Doug Collins and free-spirited streak-shooter Lloyd Free. Caldwell Jones was the defense-oriented center, and bench strength came in the form of power-dunker Darryl Dawkins, rugged forward Steve Mix and classy guard Henry Bibby.

Philadelphia's proven stable of luminous individual stars would now confront Portland's still largely untested, and thus suspect team-oriented style of play. And for the first few days it looked as if star play would outreach team play. Portland's "dream season" indeed seemed to be coming apart at the seams quickly when Philly took the first two games on their home floor in the Spectrum. In game one Dr. J rattled the nets for 33 while Collins rifled in 30; the key was Bibby's pressure defense which intimidated Hollins and forced a disastrous 34 Portland turnovers. Things didn't get any better for Ramsay's charges in a fight-marred and generally ugly game two. Caldwell Jones and Darryl Dawkins threw a blanked over a frustrated Walton, whose shooting was stone cold. But the lasting memory of one of the NBA's most embarrassing post-season tussles was one of bench-clearing brawls, player ejections (Maurice Lucas and Darryl Dawkins) and general mayhem hardly befitting championship play.

The Blazers quickly bounced back with two much-needed victories before a frenzied home crowd in Portland's Memorial Coliseum. A 27–point performance by Lucas and a hot-shooting 42–point Portland third quarter sparked the 129–107 game-three rout. Lucas continued to pace the offense in a second straight blowout (130–98) while Walton unleashed a shot-blocking flurry which kept the cold-shooting George McGinnis largely in check. Then came the pivotal game five back in Philadelphia. The Sixers had lost only nine times in the home arena all season, and momentum might well have been expected to once again reverse. But Jack Ramsay's team-oriented offense had now regained control and the Portland starters had regained lost inspiration. Bobby Gross now stepped forward and led the way with 25 points, while Walton continued to supplement the scoring of his teammates with 24 rebounds. Portland would return home with a

110–104 upset victory, a 3–2 series lead, and a squad now oozing with plenty of confidence.

The ultimate moment of Portland NBA history came next in game six of the 1977 Finals. This single June 5th game would also mark the crowning achievement of Bill Walton's Hall-of-Fame career. The emotional Walton would now ride Blazermania to an exceptional and dominating performance which saw him post 20 points, 23 rebounds, 8 block shots and 7 assists. It was barely enough, however, as the unstoppable Erving scored 40 for the visitors, McGinnis finally clicked on offense as well, and a 12 point Trail Blazer lead with five minutes remaining shrunk to a final margin of 109–107. When Erving, Free and McGinnis all drew iron with crucial shots in the final tense seconds of play, the Portland-mania finally broke into uncontrolled euphoria. The seven-year old franchise suddenly owned its one and only basketball world championship.

If the Portland "dream" had simply refused to die throughout the charmed '76–'77 season, it would soon enough suffer a shocking cardiac arrest before the end of the next full season. The Blazers and Ramsay certainly seemed well on their way to defending their surprise title as they improved nine games in the won-lost columns, surged to the top of the Pacific Division, and enjoyed a career high 18.9 scoring average from star center and 1977 post-season MVP Bill Walton. With little more than a month of play remaining, Portland had stood at 50–10 and was seemingly staking their claim on another title season. But then the injury-prone Walton went down with what was first diagnosed as a stress fracture of the foot, and with Walton's fall so too collapsed any glimmer of dynasty hopes in the city of Portland.

Bill Walton's injury was clearly as much an evil omen as it was a true lineup wrecker. His replacement, veteran Lloyd Neal, would disastrously suffer a career-ending knee injury of his own only three games later. And it was all the crippled Portland outfit could now do to hold on to the division lead with a dismal 8–14 stretch-run finish. And with Walton hobbling through only 49 minutes of two playoff games, the Blazers fell quickly enough to Seattle (4–2) in their opening round of post-season title defense.

By all practical measure, Bill Walton's ill-fated career was now largely over, at least in Portland. And so were any further dreams of future serious title contention in the expansion city of Portland. The franchise center would sit out the entire 1978–79 season when the earlier-diagnosed stress fracture proved to be a more serious bone break which responded to neither therapy nor extended rest. For his own part, Walton now complained loudly about the team's handling of his injury and especially about being forced into an early return to action for the 1978 playoffs. Such was Walton's displeasure with management that he eventually announced he would not return to the court in Portland when his contract expired at season's end, soon making good on his threats by signing on as a free agent with the San Diego Clippers. Stripped of both Walton and Lloyd

Neal (who had set a single-season club rebounding record in 1973 which still stands twenty years later) Portland quickly slipped into the middle of the pack and seemed to take up residence there for the long haul. Only twice in the next dozen years, in fact, would the Blazers advance out of the first round of post-season play.

After Walton's departure, the Portland franchise was seemingly right back where it had started. It was once again time to rebuild for the unknown future. Of course the Blazers had not actually slid all the way back to those early expansion years in the wake of Walton's injuries; a team with players like Bobby Gross, Maurice Lucas, Lionel Hollins and Mychal Thompson was not at all the same thing as an expansion roster filled with hopefuls like Stan McKenzie, Ed Manning, Rick Adelman and Dale Schlueter.

The first several expansion seasons had indeed been far bleaker than any moderate tumble at the end of the 1970s. The Portland ballclub originally had been welcomed into the circuit in fall, 1970, alongside the Cleveland Cavaliers and Buffalo Braves, and had managed to outstrip the rival newcomers if no one else during that first season. Rolland Todd had been hired off the campus of western collegiate powerhouse UNLV as the team's first head coach, and guard Geoff Petrie out of Princeton was the first collegiate draft choice. Leroy Ellis, a 6–10 center, had also been lifted from the roster of the Baltimore Bullets as the first prize of the league expansion draft. Petrie would quickly emerge as the singular team star, becoming only the second rookie guard in league history (Oscar Robertson was of course the first) to register above 2,000 points. And Petrie would tie Boston's Dave Cowens for league Rookie-of-the-Year honors. Beyond Geoff Petrie, however, there was precious little to cheer about in Portland that first long season of uninterrupted losing.

And things would get a good bit worse before they got very much better. The second Portland season was easily the bedrock of franchise history. Head coach Rolland Todd (12–44, .214 Pct.), for one, didn't survive very long at the helm once season number two was underway; Stu Inman (6–20, .234 Pct.) would fill in as interim coach after 56 games, yet bring little change in direction for the season's final third. Only 18 victories in Portland were few enough to drop the new ballclub below both their expansion rivals in Cleveland and Buffalo, and to leave them 16 full games in arrears of the next closest team within the Pacific Division. This was indeed a year of numerous changes in the NBA, as the San Diego Rockets ballclub relocated to Houston, the San Francisco Warriors sought a new identity as the rechristened Golden State Warriors, and the league's top individual star—Milwaukee's Kareem Abdul-Jabbar (earlier Lew Alcindor)—underwent a surprising name change. But the only thing suggesting motion out in Portland seemed to be a further slide into the depths of the league basement.

There was room for a little optimism, however, especially regarding the stockpile of young playing talent. Sidney Wicks was the number two overall selection from the collegiate player draft (sandwiched between Cleveland's selection of Austin Carr and Buffalo's choice of Elmore Smith) and the UCLA All-American quickly teamed with last year's choice, Geoff Petrie, for a high-scoring frontcourt-backcourt combination. Wicks would score often enough (24.5 ppg.) to earn Portland a second straight Rookie-of-the-Year selection and duplicate Petrie's rare first-year feat of 2,000 points; Petrie himself (18.9) was slowed by injury and limited to but 60 games. But the combination of Wicks and Petrie would indeed remain most of the show in Portland over the next four seasons; each paced the Portland club in scoring three times during the first six years of franchise history. Ironically, both would be peddled on the very eve of the club's most successful season, Petrie heading to Atlanta and Wicks to Boston. Petrie would bring the largest dividend (and even contribute indirectly to the club's championship surge) when he was traded along with forward Steve Hawes for rights to Maurice Lucas in the 1976 ABA dispersal draft.

On the coaching front there were several unsuccessful experiments as well, before Ramsay arrived to cement the team's hold on progress. Jack McCloskey suffered through almost identical 20–odd-win seasons and failed to budge the club out of its basement home. Player-coach Lenny Wilkens inherited both the ballclub and the league's top draft choice when he came on board in 1974, but only partially fulfilled soaring expectations surrounding the acquisition of Bill Walton. Walton, signed to a $2.5 million contract, seemed the franchise player capable of making the expansion club an immediate title contender. Yet the more-than-promising prospect suffered immediate injury problems (bone spurs in his foot) and played in but 35 rookie games. While Wilkens did get enough mileage out of Walton, and out of an improved lineup featuring Wicks and Petrie alongside John Johnson and Larry Steele, to engineer a climb to 38 victories in 1975 and 37 in 1976, it was not quite enough to satisfy club ownership and local faithful. Wilkens was therefore already packing his bags by the time Walton's sore feet had largely recovered on the eve of the 1976–'77 campaign.

Jack Ramsay provided more than just a single high point of ballclub history when he took over, just in time for the championship run of 1977. Ramsay would also provide the longest-running act ever to hit town. Ramsay's tenure in Portland eventually stretched a full ten years before it was over in 1986, and thus doubled the stay of the next most stable coach in club history, Rick Adelman. What is perhaps now easily forgotten about Ramsay's sojourn in Portland is the input that the wily 19–year veteran coach actually had in crafting the '76–'77 breakthrough ballclub. It remains a popular misconception that Coach Ramsay was merely the fortunate recipient of a team already built by Wilkens and player personnel director Stu Inman. Yet it was Ramsay himself who directed a major face-lift for the Blazers upon his arrival by first trading away leading scorers Wicks and Petrie, acquiring Maurice Lucas to supplement Walton, and then in-

stalling the running offense and swarming team defense that were keys to
a dramatic shift in oncourt fortunes.

After the two great Walton years, Ramsay's teams always remained
respectable and competitive if never again quite so unbeatable. Over the
next eight campaigns there would be only two losing seasons in Portland
(1980 and 1986) and only one dismal drop into fifth place (1982). But
stability is not often a true measure of success in the goal-oriented NBA
and it was Ramsay's misfortune that there were also only two visits to
the second round of the playoffs during this comfortable stretch of above-
.500 play. After his second losing campaign in '85–'86 Coach Ramsay
had simply had enough and announced his retirement from the game (a
retirement that would be broken only a few weeks later when the second
winningest coach in NBA history signed on as head mentor of the Indiana Pacers).

A model of management consistency, the Portland Trail Blazers would
know only two head coaches in the eight seasons that followed Jack Ramsay's departure. Mike Schuler replaced Ramsay in 1986 and earned immediate Coach-of-the-Year plaudits as the Blazers improved to 49 wins and
a second-place divisional finish behind the inspired play of center-forward
Kiki Vandeweghe (the league's fifth-leading scorer at 26.9) and fourth-year
guard Clyde "The Glide" Drexler (21.7). In Schuler's two full seasons at
the helm, the Trail Blazers shot back directly into the Western Conference
title hunt; one second-place campaign was quickly followed by another as
the team victory total shot to 53 (at the time second best in club history),
and the gap behind Pacific Division leader Los Angeles was narrowed
slightly from 16 games to nine. But for all the rapid regular-season improvement, Schuler's teams would suffer the same curse that had plagued
Ramsay's editions; the Blazers simply couldn't find a way to climb out
of the first round of post-season play. In 1987 it was the Houston Rockets
who closed the door on the Blazers in a short four-game series; and in
1988 it was the Utah Jazz who administered the knockout punch in a
parallel four-game set.

The brightest spot in the Mike Schuler reign in Portland was, clearly,
the development of Clyde Drexler as the largest star in franchise history.
Drexler had been the club's top pick (14th overall) in the 1983 draft and
had finally emerged into a showcase player by the 1988 and 1989 seasons.
But there was obviously a key ingredient still missing from the Portland
lineup. The Blazers, after all, should have had Michael Jordan, but instead
had gambled on fragile Sam Bowie; and the fateful choice had been a
disaster from both perspectives—that of Jordan's incredible brilliance and
that of Bowie's unanticipated failures. Vandeweghe (acquired from Denver
in 1985 for Lafayette Lever, Calvin Natt, Wayne Cooper and a first round
selection that turned out to be Blair Rasmussen) had emerged as a proficient scorer but didn't complement Drexler in a balanced offense, and was
eventually shipped to New York for a 1989 first round pick (Byron Irvin).

Then, on the eve of the 1989 draft, the Blazers management at least partially recouped their losses with Sam Bowie.

A huge and haunting mistake of the past was indeed at least partially rectified when the disappointing pivot man from Kentucky was finally traded away to the New Jersey Nets for established power forward and ace rebounder Buck Williams. Williams, despite his eight years of heavy-duty service and potentially aging legs, was precisely the missing piece of the puzzle. Drexler would now be turned loose to do most of the scoring; Terry Porter had emerged as a skilled point guard capable of doing the playmaking and the dishing off of basket-producing passes; and Buck Williams now provided one of the best rebounding and shot-blocking forces in the league. Williams had corralled over 1,000 caroms in five of his first eight seasons, would soon become only the 20th man in league history to claim both 10,000 boards and 10,000 points, and now stands third all-time in NBA offensive retrievals. And to supplement Drexler, Porter and Williams, the Blazers also had forward Jerome Kersey and 7–foot center Kevin Duckworth to round out one of the strongest lineups in the league.

Another important change had also occurred in Portland late in the '88–'89 campaign, and it came in the form of an altogether uncharacteristic mid-stream coaching change. A mysterious slide (despite the same starting lineup of Kersey, Vandeweghe, Duckworth, Porter and Drexler) had left the Blazers unaccountably floundering slightly beyond the midway point of the season and Schuler was quickly replaced by assistant Rick Adelman in a desperate attempt to at least stop the bleeding. There was little in the way of a quick-fix, however, as victories were even scarcer under Adelman (14–21) than they had been under Schuler (25–22) and the ballclub limped home a most surprising 5th-place also-ran. Yet the slump was nothing that the replacement of the offense-minded Vandeweghe with the defense-minded Buck Williams wouldn't seemingly cure, and by late '90 the team, now coached by Adelman, was again entrenched in the familiar surroundings of a second-place Pacific Division finish. Drexler and company not only rebounded, but actually soared in Rick Adelman's first full campaign, and a strong stretch drive resulted in a smart 59–23 ledger—the best Portland season to date.

Pundits had the 1990 NBA playoffs all figured out long before the opening post-season tip, and a Los Angeles Lakers and Detroit Pistons final-round match seemed about as certain as another Michael Jordan scoring title. The Lakers spoiled the scenario early on, however, stumbling against the Phoenix Suns, a team that had beaten them but once over the course of the entire regular season. The other strong Pacific Division entry from Portland faired a bit better than the Lakers, escaping a second-round tussle with San Antonio. But it took the Blazers a tough seven games (including two overtime victories) to move into the conference finals for the first time in thirteen long years. Against Phoenix in the conference championship round, Adelman's team had an easier time of it, winning three times at home and closing out the six-game series with a 112–109 nail-biter back in Phoenix.

For the second time in club annals, the Portland Trail Blazers had now rewarded the league's most fanatic followers with a trip into the NBA Finals. The party would be quickly ruined this time around by a one-sided five-game stumble against the powerful Detroit Pistons, a team headed for only the second title repeat of the past two decades. The starting teams in Detroit and Portland seemed even enough, but Portland simply couldn't match the bench strength of a Pistons lineup supplemented by John Salley, Vinnie Johnson and veteran Mark Aguirre. The Blazers lost three straight at home to seal their own fate, and Detroit's Isiah Thomas emerged as post-season MVP with point totals of 33, 23, 21, 32, and 29 against the outmanned Trail Blazers.

Despite being humbled by Isiah Thomas's Pistons, Adelman's mature team was now seemingly back on top to stay for awhile. In '90–'91, the Blazers would even post their best-ever regular season mark with a league-leading 63–19 ledger, two games better than Michael Jordan's eventual champion Chicago Bulls. But the Blazers were once again seemingly snakebit when it came to getting through the tough test of post-season play. First a mediocre Seattle team (41–41) extended the Pacific Division champs to a tougher-than-necessary five-game set, with Portland taking all three matches (including the rubber game) on their home floor, yet failing to win at all on the road. A much easier series followed with Utah (4–1), but by the conference finals the Portland season had clearly already run its course. A six-game series loss to the final Magic Johnson-led edition of the Los Angeles Lakers meant that Portland would once again fail to make the NBA Finals; and they would again fail in the very year during which they seemed, for eight long months, to have been the league's undisputed premier team. A 1977 NBA title had been followed with a best-ever Portland club unable to defend their championship laurels. It now seemed like instant replay when the second-ever Portland entry in the NBA Finals returned a mere season later to improve in every imaginable category, yet collapse once the post-season title chase heated up in June.

Portland bounced back quickly enough to register yet a third super season under the guidance of Rick Adelman. With Clyde Drexler providing a Western Conference version of Chicago's Michael Jordan, the '91–'92 Portland edition would once again repeat as the "best in the West" and ride a 57–25 record to a second straight Pacific Division first-place finish. Drexler was the NBA's fourth-best scorer with his 25.0 average, while veteran Buck Williams paced the entire league in field goal percentage with his .604 shooting efficiency. And this time there would be no stumbling blocks along the way to the Finals as the Lakers (3–1), Suns (4–1) and Jazz (4–2) offered only a series of minor hurdles en route to a championship showdown with Jordan's Bulls.

Pro basketball fans everywhere were truly excited about the 1992 NBA

Finals match-up between the Chicago Bulls and Portland Trail Blazers. Not only would the league's two most potent teams lock horns in the best-of-seven series to crown a new champion, but for the first time in several seasons—since Larry Bird had battled Magic Johnson in '84, '85 and '87—the game's two most spectacular individual players would square off head-to-head as well. Michael "Air" Jordan would carry the banner for the Bulls in their attempt to repeat as NBA world champions. And although the Portland ballclub was returning to only its third final round ever, this time they were equipped with an almost equally spectacular athlete to lead a true championship charge. Clyde Drexler would finally have the chance to show that he was every bit the center stage act that Air Jordan had long been. Drexler, after all, had waited a long time for this chance to showcase his talents before the widest possible basketball audience. For years he had been a headline player in one of the league's smallest media markets. Many nights he had been truly spectacular and almost no one beyond those in that particular arena had paid any notice. But a stellar performance against Jordan would be the final stamp of approval on Drexler's spectacular game. A team championship would even further enhance his reputation as one of basketball's brightest stars.

Drexler would not win his championship against the powerful Chicago Bulls. Yet he would have several chances to test his talent on Jordan's own stage. And in the end Drexler was indeed gracious in his defeat by the incomparable Air Jordan: "I don't compete against Michael and I don't play for recognition. What I can do for Portland is all that matters." In the 1992 NBA Finals, however, Drexler had done all three, despite his modest denials to the contrary. He had competed head-to-head with Michael and held his own, averaging 25 points per contest for the series and exploding for 32 points in game three. He had shown the entire NBA world what fans in Portland already knew, that here was one of the league's most skilled and glamorous players. And he had indeed carried his Portland Trail Blazers all the way to the doorstep of an NBA world championship.

The Rick Adelman-coached Blazers had gotten all the way back to the brink in 1992, and yet they would never get over the top. Drexler would suffer leg damage in the early fall of 1992 and would therefore be limited to 49 games for the defending Western Conference champs in '92–'93 action. Jerome Kersey (65 games, tendonitis and pleurisy) and Kevin Duckworth (74 games, traded to the Washington Bullets at season's end) were also slowed considerably by nagging illness and injury. Portland was doomed to discover in a hurry the extreme challenge of defending a title, even a division title or a conference title. The team still managed to capture 51 games, good enough for a third-place division finish. Yet this time there would be no getting past San Antonio and David Robinson in the opening playoff round. A slip to 47 victories, fourth place, and another quick opening-round playoff exit in 1994 would soon be enough to seal the fate of a five-year coaching skein for popular Rick Adelman. A victim of unfulfilled expectations, Adelman stepped down in June, 1994, to be replaced by veteran college coach P. J. Carlesimo from the campus of Seton Hall. And once again the task of rebuilding was the order of the day for the Portland NBA franchise.

Portland's Trail Blazers have remained, from the mid-seventies, a competitive franchise year-in and year-out and have made it all the way to the NBA Finals on three separate occasions, and twice in the last five-year stretch. And this success has come despite a series of noteworthy draft day blunders which have no parallel in the saga of any other NBA ballclub. At the dawn of franchise history, back in 1972, Portland owned the first overall player selection and stood poised to benefit by huge measure from a draft lottery which included the likes of Bob McAdoo (2nd pick, Buffalo), Corky Calhoun (4th pick, Phoenix), Freddie Boyd (5th pick, Philadelphia) and Paul Westphal (10th pick, Boston). The Blazers gambled on 6–11 center LaRue Martin out of Loyola-Chicago, who proved a major bust, logging four NBA seasons and posting a anemic 5.3 ppg. career scoring mark. And then a decade later there was the embarrassing choice of Sam Bowie over Michael Jordan, Charles Barkley, or even Sam Perkins.

1977 has always remained the single magical year for Portland Trail Blazer basketball fans and the single cornerstone season for Portland franchise history. And the number 12,666 (the seating capacity of always sold-out Portland Memorial Coliseum, until recent campaigns when the number was elevated to 12,888) has long remained the most automatic number found anywhere in the NBA. By the end of the '93–'94 season, the remarkable string of homecourt sellouts had stretched all the way to 769, with no reason to believe that anything less than a full house could be expected in Portland for years to come. The remarkable Portland run of full-house games is in fact the longest such string to be found anywhere in professional sports. Ironically enough, the last non-sellout came back on April 5th, 1977, in the closing weeks of the team's great championship season itself. And all those faithful patrons in Portland have indeed been waiting for something like 1977 to return ever since.

Suggested Readings on Portland Trail Blazers

Halberstam, David. **The Breaks of the Game**. New York: Ballantine Books, 1981.

Scott, Jack. **Bill Walton—On the Road with the Portland Trail Blazers**. New York: Thomas Y. Crowell Publishers, 1978.

Portland Trail Blazers Retired Uniform Numbers (6)

Dave Twardzik (13)
Larry Steele (15)
Maurice Lucas (20)
Bill Walton (32)
Lloyd Neal (36)
Geoff Petrie (45)

Year-by-Year Portland Trail Blazers Summary

Season	Record	Finish	Coach(es)	Scoring Leader(s)	Playoffs (W-L Record)
1970–71	29–53	5th	Rolland Todd	Geoff Price (24.8)	Did Not Qualify
1971–72	18–64	5th	Rolland Todd	Sidney Wicks (24.5)	Did Not Qualify
			Stu Inman		
1972–73	21–61	5th	Jack McCloskey	Geoff Petrie (24.9)	Did Not Qualify
1973–74	27–55	5th	Jack McCloskey	Geoff Petrie (24.3)	Did Not Qualify
1974–75	38–44	3rd	Lenny Wilkens	Sidney Wicks (21.7)	Did Not Qualify
1975–76	37–45	5th	Lenny Wilkens	Sidney Wicks (19.1)	Did Not Qualify
1976–77	49–33	2nd	Jack Ramsay	Maurice Lucas (20.2)	**NBA Champion** (14–5)
1977–78	58–24	1st	Jack Ramsay	Bill Walton (18.9)	Lost in 2nd Round (2–4)
1978–79	45–37	4th	Jack Ramsay	Maurice Lucas (20.4)	Lost in 1st Round (1–2)
1979–80	38–44	4th	Jack Ramsay	Calvin Natt (20.4)	Lost in 1st Round (1–2)
1980–81	45–37	3rd	Jack Ramsay	Jim Paxson (17.1)	Lost in 1st Round (1–2)
1981–82	42–40	5th	Jack Ramsay	Mychal Thompson (20.8)	Did Not Qualify
1982–83	46–36	4th	Jack Ramsay	Jim Paxson (21.7)	Lost in 2nd Round (3–4)
1983–84	48–34	2nd	Jack Ramsay	Jim Paxson (21.3)	Lost in 1st Round (2–3)
1984–85	42–40	2nd	Jack Ramsay	Kiki Vandeweghe (22.4)	Lost in 2nd Round (4–5)
1985–86	40–42	2nd	Jack Ramsay	Kiki Vandeweghe (24.8)	Lost in 1st Round (1–3)
1986–87	49–33	2nd	Mike Schuler	Kiki Vandeweghe (26.9)	Lost in 1st Round (1–3)
1987–88	53–29	2nd	Mike Schuler	Clyde Drexler (27.0)	Lost in 1st Round (1–3)
1988–89	39–43	5th	Mike Schuler	Clyde Drexler (27.2)	Lost in 1st Round (0–3)
			Rick Adelman		
1989–90	59–23	2nd	Rick Adelman	Clyde Drexler (23.3)	Lost in NBA Finals (12–9)
1990–91	63–19	1st	Rick Adelman	Clyde Drexler (21.5)	Lost in 3rd Round (9–7)
1991–92	57–24	1st	Rick Adelman	Clyde Drexler (25.0)	Lost in NBA Finals (13–8)
1992–93	51–31	3rd	Rick Adelman	Clyde Drexler (19.9)	Lost in 1st Round (1–3)
1993–94	47–35	4th	Rick Adelman	Cliff Robinson (20.1)	Lost in 1st Round (1–3)

Individual Career Leaders and Record Holders (1970–1994)

Scoring Average	Kiki Vandeweghe (23.5 ppg., 1984–89)
Points Scored	Clyde Drexler (17,136, 1983–94)
Games Played	Clyde Drexler (826, 1983–94)
Minutes Played	Clyde Drexler (28,068)

Field Goal Pct.	Buck Williams (.564, 1989–94)
3-Pt. Field Goals	Terry Porter (729, 1985–94)
Free Throws Made	Clyde Drexler (3,591)
Free-Throw Pct.	Kiki Vandeweghe (.881, 1984–89)
Rebounds	Clyde Drexler (5,105)
Assists	Terry Porter (5,186)
Steals	Clyde Drexler (1,721)
Blocked Shots	Mychal Thompson (768, 1978–86)
Personal Fouls	Clyde Drexler (2,582)
Consecutive Games Played	Cliff Robinson (410, 1989–94)#

= Streak in progress at end of 1993–94 season

Individual Single-Season and Game Records (1970–1994)

Scoring Average	Clyde Drexler (27.2 ppg., 1988–89)
Points Scored (Season)	Clyde Drexler (2,185, 1987–88)
Points Scored (Game)	Geoff Petrie (51, 1–20–73 and 3–16–73 vs. Houston Rockets)
Field Goal Pct. (Season)	Dave Twardzik (.612, 1976–77)
Free-Throw Pct. (Season)	Kiki Vandeweghe (.896, 1984–85)
3-Pt. Field Goals (Season)	Terry Porter (143, 1992–93)
Rebounds (Season)	Lloyd Neal (967, 1972–73)
Rebounds (Game)	Sidney Wicks (27, 2–26–75 at Los Angeles Lakers)
Assists (Season)	Terry Porter (831, 1975–76)
Assists (Game)	Terry Porter (19, 4–14–88 at Utah Jazz)
Steals (Season)	Larry Steele (217, 1973–74)
Steals (Game)	Larry Steele (10, 11–16–84 vs. Los Angeles Lakers)
	Clyde Drexler (10, 1–10–86 at Milwaukee Bucks)
Blocked Shots (Season)	Bill Walton (211, 1976–77)
Personal Fouls (Season)	Steve Johnson (340, 1986–87)

Best Trade in Franchise History

If the Blazers had made the worst player move in their history when they drafted Sam Bowie ahead of Michael Jordan, they may have actually recovered a little of the damage from that disastrous decision a few seasons later when they were able finally to deal Bowie (along with draft choice Mookie Blaylock) to the New Jersey Nets in exchange for remarkable rebounding forward Buck Williams (on June 24, 1989). While the loss of Jordan had probably cost Portland a handful of trips to the NBA Finals, Williams at least was enough compensation to help propel the Blazers into two NBA title matchups during his first three seasons on the west coast.

Worst Trade in Franchise History

It was not a trade at all, but rather a draft pick which remains the lasting albatross of the Portland pro basketball franchise. Yet it has to be marked down in the always-clear hindsight of history as perhaps the poorest player transaction to be found anywhere in basketball annals. Losing a coin flip for the 1984 draft day first pick to the Houston Rockets (the Blazers called tails and the coin came up heads), the Blazers had to sit by patiently while the Rockets selected Hakeem Olajuwon. Then, with the plum second pick, the Blazers went for potential franchise center Sam Bowie, the oft-injured giant from the University of Kentucky. Bowie had already been frequently sidelined by leg problems during his collegiate career (he missed most of two seasons) and represented a huge gamble at best. As it turned out, he would be injury-riddled at the pro level as well, and provided little payoff for Portland in the long run. In five seasons on the Portland roster, Sam Bowie would miss one entire year ('87–'88) with a broken foot, log but 38, 5 and 20 games respectively in three other campaigns, and average exactly 10 ppg. during his one complete year of service. But this is not the real story, for sitting available in that 1984 draft was also a player which Chicago grabbed with the number three selection—basketball's greatest performer of the modern era, Michael Jordan. And the rest, as they say, is merely history!

Portland Trail Blazers Historical Oddity

There is one glorious NBA record at least that is not owned by either the Boston Celtics or the Los Angeles Lakers, and that record belongs to the basketball-crazy city of Portland, Oregon. And it is a record, ironically, set not on the court of play but rather in the grandstands of the home arena—it is the fans and not the team that owns this particular piece of the NBA record book. Every home game of the Portland Trail Blazers in the city's Memorial Coliseum—all regular season and playoff contests included—has been a sellout since the late part of the 1977 season—a remarkable string of 769 straight contests heading into the 1994–1995 season. On November 27, 1990, the 10 millionth Blazer fan passed through the home portals to watch Portland play the Phoenix Suns. The string of full-house crowds in Portland now stretches for 17 complete seasons, and first included a nightly attendance of 12,666, which jumped to 12,854 with a small addition of courtside seats in 1988, and then to 12,884 in 1989 and 12,888 in 1992. The scheduled opening of a plush new arena for the 1995 campaign (with an increased seating capacity of 20,340) seems no threat at all to the ongoing string which now seems certain to continue on and on in basketball's most successful ''small town'' market ever.

Blazers All-Time Number One Draft Picks List

Portland Trail Blazers
1970 Geoff Petrie (Princeton)
1971 Sidney Wicks (UCLA)
1972 LaRue Martin (Loyola-Chicago)
1973 Barry Parkhill (Virginia)
1974 Bill Walton (UCLA)
1975 Lionel Hollins (Arizona State)
1976 Wally Walker (Virginia)
1977 Rich Laurel (Hofstra)
1978 Mychal Thompson (Minnesota)
1979 Jim Paxson (Dayton)
1980 Ron Lester (Iowa)
1981 Jeff Lamp (Virginia)
1982 Lafayette Lever (Arizona State)
1983 Clyde Drexler (Houston)
1984 Sam Bowie (Kentucky)
1985 Terry Porter (Wisconsin-Stevens Point)
1986 Walter Berry (St. John's)
1987 Ronnie Murphy (Jacksonville)
1988 Mark Bryant (Seton Hall)
1989 Byron Irvin (Missouri)
1990 Alaa Abdelnaby (Duke)
1991 None
1992 Dave Johnson (Syracuse)
1993 James Robinson (Alabama)

Chapter 18

UTAH JAZZ and NEW ORLEANS JAZZ

Out of Tune in Salt Lake City

All-Time Franchise Record: 855–843, .504 Pct. (1974–1993)
NBA Championships: None
Greatest Franchise Player: Karl Malone (1985–1994)
All-Time Leading Scorer: Karl Malone (19,050 Points, 1985–1994)
Most Successful Coach: Jerry Sloan (304–171, .640 Pct., 1988–1994)
All-Time Franchise Team: Mark Eaton (C), Karl Malone (F), Adrian Dantley (F), John Stockton (G), Pete Maravich (G)

From the outset, the history of the Utah (née New Orleans) Jazz has been a seemingly relentless saga of misguided trades and squandered draft picks. First came the celebrated deal which brought local hero Pete Maravich to New Orleans from Atlanta before the ball club even had a nickname or a head coach. Maravich gave the expansion franchise instant credibility in Louisiana and everywhere around the NBA but provided little else beyond a marquee name plate. Next came an ill-starred deal with the Los Angeles Lakers that brought in guard Gail Goodrich and left the Lakers holding a 1979 first-round draft choice that would one day materialize into Earvin "Magic" Johnson. Then there was the fortuitous selection of prolific scorer Dominique Wilkins in the 1982 collegiate draft and the immediate squandering of Wilkins in a brainless trade with Atlanta which rates among the league's all-time worst. (Using career points scored, as only a single measure, Utah came out about 21,000 points short on the Wilkins deal alone.) After unloading Wilkins the Jazz (by now in Utah) scored big in three subsequent years of drafting, acquiring Thurl Bailey and Bob Hansen in 1983, John Stockton in 1984, and (biggest of all) Karl Malone in 1985. Fortunately the Jazz had learned something from past mistakes and kept both Stockton and Malone long enough for them both to develop into first-rate all-stars. But having traded away Wilkins now left the Salt Lake City club with only part of what might have been the most dominant team of the mid-'80s and late-'80s. The end result of all these deals was to put the Utah Jazz always on the outside looking in when it came to the final rounds of post-season play over the past two decades.

Jazz history, both literally and figuratively, begins with the flamboyant ballhandler and magical shooter named Pete Maravich. New Orleans had been granted an expansion franchise in March 1974 and the nine-man original ownership which paid $6.15 million for the team was determined to get off to a successful start—at least at the ticket gate if not in the league standings. The formula seemed simple enough—a tried and true principle of the pro hoop sport—a single "name player" to provide excitement and plenty of charisma. And no name was bigger in New Orleans and the state of Louisiana than that of Atlanta Hawks star Pistol Pete Maravich. From the outset the deal to bring Maravich back to New Orleans in time for NBA opening night seemed a natural by any measure.

Pete Maravich had been a legendary figure at Louisiana State University. In the late '60s Maravich dismantled just about all existing career, season and game scoring records lodged in the NCAA record book while playing for his father, Press Maravich at the Baton Rouge, Louisiana campus. And he was a colorful and flashy ballplayer as well, specializing in no-look and behind-the-back "blind" passes that took up where Bob Cousy had left off. But it was as a prodigious scorer—the most prodigious in history—that Pistol Pete left his lasting collegiate mark. He ripped the nets for better than 50 points 28 times, scored 66 once and 69 in yet another outing, once drilled 30 field goals in a single game, and averaged 44.2 for his entire fairy-tale career.

Maravich had actually started slower than expected in the NBA after being the third overall selection of the 1970 draft (Bob Lanier and Rudy Tomjanovich went ahead of him). But he was now a big scorer in the NBA as well, just like he had been in college, and Jazz management simply had to have him as a hometown drawing card. Atlanta was seemingly more than willing to accommodate, since Maravich had proven a rather one-dimensional player during four seasons with the Hawks. A May, 1974, deal seemed to satisfy both ballclubs. Atlanta got Dean Meminger, Bob Kauffman and future draft selections. The Jazz, for their part, now had Maravich to sell tickets. It was only then that the expansion club turned to the business of naming a coach, selecting a nickname (a more natural or obvious choice could not possibly have been made), and filling out a roster for a season only several months away.

The first New Orleans roster was filled out with 15 players added in the expansion dispersal draft. The group of veteran players included Jim Barnett, Walt Bellamy (who appeared in just one Jazz game before retiring), John Block, Lamar Green, Tony Kimball, Stu Lantz and Bud Stallworth. Also brought on board was Aaron James of Grambling, plucked in the college draft held only weeks later. Scotty Robertson was soon added as the inaugural coach. Robertson's first task was not at all an easy one: to paste together a respectable or nearly respectable lineup built around Maravich. For much of the first season that lineup consisted of James and Coleman at the forwards, Otto Moore at center (acquired mid-season as a free agent from Detroit), and Maravich and Louie Nelson at the guards. Only Nelson and James managed to join Maravich as double-figure scorers.

If Maravich had started slowly with the Hawks in Atlanta over his first several NBA seasons, so too did the Jazz start slowly with Maravich over the first several months of their own debut season. The new club lost by a wide margin on opening night of the '74–'75 season (89–74 to the New York Knicks) and continued to lose over the next ten outings. Finally the first franchise victory came in the twelfth game of the season. That win was against the Portland Trail Blazers by a single point (102–101) at home, with Maravich scoring 30. But the team continued to bungle over the course of its first full month and the season (and franchise history as well) was only fifteen games old when the Jazz were already making a coaching change. No other expansion club of the modern era would ever turn over its bench leadership any earlier than the New Orleans Jazz were doing when they canned Scotty Robertson after a 1–14 season's start.

Long-time NBA star and Jazz assistant coach Elgin Baylor filled-in for Robertson on a most temporary basis (one game) and then college coaching veteran Bill (Butch) van Breda Kolff (Princeton) took more permanent control. Halfway through an inaugural season the newly-minted Jazz franchise had already experienced three different head coaches. And the results showed, as the team skidded to a 24–59 opening season record.

The Jazz surprised everyone and perhaps even themselves when they improved by leaps and bounds during their second NBA season. Maravich provided heavy scoring (25.9) despite a shoulder separation that knocked him out for 20 games. Starting forward Ron Behagen was also an injury victim with a broken cheekbone and 16 games missed. Yet the club won an amazing 38 games for all their woes and escaped the cellar by outdistancing Maravich's old team, the Atlanta Hawks, by nine full games. The New Orleans victory total also matched that of Midwest Division leader Milwaukee (thus besting Detroit, Kansas City and Chicago in the win column) and equalled the output of the New York Knicks and Portland Trail Blazers as well.

If things seemed to be on the definite upbeat when the Jazz launched season number three it certainly didn't stay that way for very long. With the team getting off to a respectable start, though one that didn't meet heightened expectations, another coaching change was made 26 games into the season. Bill van Breda Kolff was out and Elgin Baylor was back in. Under Baylor the team came close enough to equaling the previous season's record (winning 35). But fans were certainly entertained as Maravich (31.1 ppg.) finally unleashed his game and won his only league scoring title. In one outing (February 25 against the Knicks) Pistol Pete chalked up an eye-opening 68 points. And he was not just a ball-hogging shooter, but also led the club in both assists and steals that year as well.

Maravich was rapidly proving a box office attraction, if not exactly the kind of franchise player that would provide a one-man championship team. The original trade several seasons earlier already seemed to be paying sufficient dividends. Now in 1976 the Jazz front office swung another major deal which this time was aimed at an immediate upsurge in the victory column. They traded with the Los Angeles Lakers for guard Gail Goodrich, an 11-year veteran who had been averaging 20 ppg. or better for the previous half-dozen campaigns. And the deal seemed to bomb for New Orleans on almost all counts. Goodrich would remain in a Jazz uniform for three seasons and average only 14.8 ppg., far less than management had hoped for. And his presence hardly meant oncourt improvement either, as the team continued to wallow in either 5th or 6th place during his temporary visit. Yet the biggest sting from the Goodrich deal would come four seasons later, when the Lakers front office parlayed the draft pick they had received from New Orleans into the selection of Earvin "Magic" Johnson. Johnson would, of course, put on a Lakers uniform to become the most outstanding all-around player (and proven winner) of the entire '80s decade.

While the Jazz struggled for two more seasons in New Orleans, the record continued to sag and attendance continued to ebb. The team did win 39 games in '77–'78 but was still not a playoff qualifier. Maravich was now tired of all the losing and was making noises about wanting a trade to a contender. Baylor's second full-time season at the helm saw the record plummet to 26–56, the worst ledger in the entire league. It was also a year of instability in the clubhouse. Spencer Haywood came over from the Knicks, but couldn't pick up the slack created by Maravich's continued injury woes. Pistol Pete suffered from chronic knee problems and played only 49 games in another shortened season. And Goodrich was now only a bench player averaging a disappointing 12.7 ppg. And the team's other quality player (Truck Robinson with a club-best 24.2 average) was shipped off to Phoenix for guard Ron Lee. The team was so desperate for media coverage and fan notice by this time that management even resorted to the ploy of selecting a woman (Lucy Harris from nearby Delta State) in the end-of-the-year collegiate draft.

The franchise had run its course in New Orleans and fresh ownership alongside a fresh venue now seemed necessary to save it. Both materialized when the majority interest in the club was sold to restauranteur Sam Battisone and computer magnate Larry Hatfield. The new ownership acted quickly to pump life into the dying ballclub, and started by transferring the entire operation into Salt Lake City during the summer of 1979. One immediate result was a team that now seemed to sport the most anachronistic nickname in NBA annals. It was hard to figure out just what a sports team named "Jazz" was doing representing the politically, religiously and socially-conservative Mormon state of Utah.

The new Jazz ownership made more moves than the one that affected franchise name and mailing address. They began to overhaul the club roster in dramatic fashion as well. In another deal with Los Angeles—this one a little more stacked in their own favor, as things would turn out—Spencer Haywood was exchanged for Adrian Dantley in a swap of high-scoring forwards. Tom Nissalke was also brought in as the new head coach. And management also granted the unhappy Maravich his wish by allowing him to buy out his contract and take his now fading act over to the Boston Celtics.

The first three years in Salt Lake City would provide little enough immediate relief from regular losing. The victory totals stood at 24, then 28, then 25. The club remained at or near the bottom of the division (5th twice and 6th once) and stretched the string of years without a playoff appearance to eight. Twenty games into the 1981–82 season, Nissalke was gone and replaced by General Manager Frank Layden.

There were two upbeat stories surrounding the Jazz during these early seasons of the '80s and earliest campaigns in Utah. Adrian Dantley emerged as a super scorer and launched a string of four straight seasons when his average remained slightly above 30 ppg. Two of these years saw Dantley as the league's scoring champion. And the lowly last-place finish of '79–'80 resulted in a coin flip between Utah and Golden State (tied for the worst West Conference record) for the number-one selection of the 1980 college draft. Golden State celebrated victory in the important coin toss, but Utah ironically seemed to be the true winner of the draft lottery in the long run. Golden Sate expended its selection on Purdue's seven-foot center Joe Barry Carroll. Carroll would never live up to expectations with the Warriors, however, or in any of his other stops around the league in subsequent seasons. Left holding the number-two pick, the Jazz then opted for "Dr. Dunkenstein"—Darrell Griffith, the talented jumper and shooter from the University of Louisville. And it was Griffith, not Carroll, who would burst on the NBA scene with an outstanding Rookie-of-the-Year season in 1981.

With Darrell Griffith demonstrating electrifying rookie play and Adrian Dantley (30.7 ppg.) pacing the league in scoring, the 1980–'81 Jazz team would appear to have been well stocked with talent. But a supporting cast was lacking entirely and the club won only 28 games in Tom Nissalke's final season in the coach's seat. And Frank Layden's arrival the next season didn't seem at first to signal any prospects for immediate positive change. A jovial heavyweight with a love of media attention, Layden was popular with fans and players alike, and had served as general manager since the team's founding. Layden particularly loved to join the Jazz broadcast team for halftime game analysis and was a first-rate ambassador for the game. His fun-loving approach to the sport did raise some serious questions, however, about his eventual overall effectiveness as a bench coach in the highly competitive and stress-filled league.

The draft selection of Louisville's Darrell Griffith in June, 1981, was

the first volley in what soon turned into a rather amazing run of draft day
good fortune for the Utah franchise. This run would extend throughout
the early and mid 1980s and provide several of the most outstanding new
players to enter the pro circuit during this recent era. If the Jazz didn't
get the player they had wanted in 1981 (they undoubtedly would have
selected Joe Barry Carroll had they won the fateful coin toss that had
fallen to the Golden State Warriors), they instead got the player they most
desperately needed. Darrell Griffith was an outstanding 6'4" leaper destined
for Rookie-of-the-Year status, 12,000-plus career points, and four 20-plus
ppg. seasons during his decade with Utah. Dr. Dunkenstein had been best
known for his "hangtime" displays while leading Louisville to the 1980
NCAA championship, but he proved a three-point shooter deluxe as well,
once his game diversified in the pro ranks. He didn't handle the ball
particularly well for a guard and thus was a scorer, period, but Griffith
provided enough Midwest Conference fireworks to make Jazz fans and
management quickly abandon any regretful thoughts about Joe Barry
Carroll.

And the following June brought still more of the same kind of draft
day bungling into and out of unwanted selections. This time the Jazz
again grabbed off precisely the player they unquestionably needed—but
apparently also thought they didn't want. Dominique Wilkins was a third
overall pick and it seemed almost a no-brainer assessment that Wilkins—
with his wide array of unparalleled free-lance moves and uncanny shooting
and jumping abilities—was a guaranteed NBA superstar in the making.
But the Jazz and Layden soon fell for a deal with Atlanta, a team also on
the rise and one which obviously coveted the player who was not only
the closest thing to Dr. J in years, but also had starred at the nearby
University of Georgia in Athens. The Hawks would part with guards John
Drew and Freeman Williams—essentially "damaged" merchandise, as it
soon turned out. Both Drew and Williams already suffered from age as
well as personal adjustment problems and both were out of the league in
almost no time flat. Drew did average better than the benchmark standard
of 20 ppg. for one Jazz season, but eventually lost a career-long battle
with substance abuse. Williams had once shown promise as a brilliant
scorer and had even racked up one 51-point game several seasons earlier
with the Clippers; but Williams had already been reduced to ineffectiveness
by injury and saw action in only 27 more games (18 with Utah) after the
fateful trade. Wilkins, by startling contrast, was soon lighting up the entire
league as the sensational "Human Highlight Film" one-man act, which
was still playing very strong more than a full decade later.

The 1983 draft would also add Thurl Bailey and Bob Hansen to the
bulging Utah roster. Bailey was a 6'11" forward who had starred with the
1983 North Carolina State national championship team and who would
twice finish second in balloting for the NBA "Sixth Man" award during
an eight-year sojourn in Salt Lake City. Hansen, an-All-Big-Ten" selection
out of Iowa, would never be an All-Star and would never average double-

figures as a Utah guard; during his seven seasons with the Jazz, however, he was a key contributor defensively and did develop eventually into a quality starting backcourt performer. And then in 1984 would come John Stockton with the 16th overall pick in the collegiate draft. Stockton had played out of the limelight at small-school Gonzaga University, and thus attracted little notice early on. But after cracking the starting lineup in 1986, Stockton quickly became one of the greatest assists-men in basketball history. The "Dream Team" point guard is now simply the best playmaker of the current era (perhaps of all-time); he is quick and adroit with the ball and has an unmatched ability to take the ball toward the hole and then create easy shot openings for his trailing teammates. Not even Magic Johnson did it any better than John Stockton, night in and night out. And Stockton's NBA resume now reads like a Hall-of-Fame induction plaque: he is the first player in history to record five straight seasons of 1,000 or more assists; he holds the single-season record (1,164 in '90–'91) and has now led the league seven straight times.

The string of magical draft selections then ran one more year as 1985 found the Jazz acquiring an underrated Karl Malone out of Louisiana Tech with the 13th pick of the first round. Malone would do nothing more than hover near the 30 ppg. mark over the past seven seasons and is now probably the most unstoppable player five feet from the bucket in the entire league (rookie sensation Shaquille O'Neal and NBA scoring champ David Robinson included). Had the Jazz only kept Wilkins they might now have featured a lineup clearly better than anything to be found anywhere else around the league. That lineup would have offered the scoring power of Wilkins, Dantley and Malone up front, complemented by the game's greatest assists artist of the next decade, John Stockton, operating out of the backcourt. The victory potential of such a lineup would have seemed almost limitless to even the casual NBA observer.

Without Wilkins, however, the Jazz—for all their over-talented ballplayers—were now always at least one quality player away from rising straight to the top. Frank Layden coached for seven full seasons and his teams were always respectable, but never exactly awe-inspiring. No Frank Layden team won more than 47 games, for example, and none rose more than eight games above the .500 level. But five years in a row his ballclubs were nevertheless playoff participants. Before Layden took the helm Jazz teams had gone the first nine seasons of franchise history without a single playoff visit. Beginning with Layden's second full season, Utah would now launch a post-season string that has stretched through the past eleven seasons, right up to the present. And with several years hopefully left in the legs of Stockton and Malone, there should be no obvious reason to expect anything approaching a severe fall-off in the near future.

Layden's best club was his '83–'84 outfit which clinched a first Midwest Division title flag for Utah and also made the maiden franchise playoff appearance. Adrian Dantley won a second scoring title this season as he soared above the 30 ppg. mark for the fourth straight year (and the last as well). Towering center Mark Eaton at 7'4" and 280 pounds emerged as the league's most effective shot blocker (351) and defensive weapon. Eaton virtually clogged the middle and thus rejected all enemy penetration near the basket. Griffith and Rickey Green brought scoring and speed to the backcourt as both averaged double-figures in scoring, and together they accounted for 1,000 assists. And Thurl Bailey was a talented rebounder and defender from the forward slot. The club squeaked out a division win over Dallas by a mere two games. Then in the playoffs they defeated Denver (3–2) but lost out in a hard fought series against the talented Phoenix Suns which stretched to six games.

More a public relations star than an x's and o's wizard, Frank Layden finally returned to the front office during the '88–'89 season and appointed Jerry Sloan to succeed him on the bench. And it proved one of the best selections that Layden ever made. That season of transition—with Sloan taking over only 17 games into the campaign—resulted in the loftiest club record to date, with 51 victories and a second-ever divisional title. Thurl Bailey (19.5 ppg.) supported Karl Malone's (29.1 ppg.) scoring onslaughts, and Stockton was the league leader for the first time in both assists and steals. The year ended on a sour note, however, with a quick first-round exit from the playoffs as the result of three one-sided losses to Golden State.

With the inside-outside duo of Karl Malone and John Stockton now clicking with machine-like efficiency, Sloan's Utah teams would emerge as a Western Conference powerhouse over the next five seasons. In four of those five years, Utah would top the 50-victory mark; twice they would capture 55 games (1990 and 1992); never would they slip below third slot in the divisional standings. In 1991–'92, the Jazz would claim a third Midwest Division title with a comfortable 8-game margin over runner-up San Antonio. In 1992 and again in 1994, they would advance to the conference finals before bowing out of post-season play. Jeff Malone would be acquired from Washington in 1990 and prove a high-scoring guard for several seasons, drilling 20.2 ppg. in '91–'92. And Karl Malone would consistently average close to 30 ppg. yearly, yet somehow never win a scoring title due to the presence of first Michael Jordan and later (upon Jordan's retirement in 1993) David Robinson in San Antonio and Shaquille O'Neal in Orlando. Finally, John Stockton would remain the finest point guard in the league—at least after Magic Johnson's 1991 retirement—and would launch an all-out assault on Johnson's numerous NBA assist records.

The duo of Malone and Stockton—both almost certain Hall-of-Famers— has provided the Utah Jazz over the past half dozen or more seasons with one of the finest teammate-duos in all of NBA history. Few tandems have ever been so good for so long without winning an NBA title, or at least advancing to the championship round. Yet Malone and Stockton hardly stand alone as the only such miraculous pair devoid of a supporting cast to be found down through league history. There was, of course, the trio of Chamberlain, West and Baylor in Los Angeles in the late '60s and early '70s. This combo indeed formed one of the greatest teams in league history in 1972, yet inexplicably they didn't leap the hurdle of the Boston Celtics and win a league title until the year of Baylor's retirement. There was also Bob Lanier and Dave Bing with the Detroit Pistons in the first half of the seventies. Lanier might well have been the finest big man never to win an NBA championship ring. There also was Oscar Robertson and Jerry Lucas with the Cincinnati Royals, neither of whom won titles until Lucas moved on to the Knicks alongside Willis Reed and Oscar went to the Milwaukee Bucks where he teamed with Abdul-Jabbar. And there were other such combos as well—Nate Thurmond and Rick Barry with the San Francisco Warriors, Ed Macauley and Bob Cousy with the early pre-Russell Celtics, Artis Gilmore and George Gervin with the ABA-refugee San Antonio Spurs, and the Twin-Towers pair of Olajuwon and Sampson with the Houston Rockets during a more recent decade.

The 1994 loss to Houston in the Western Division Finals may indeed have been a last hurrah for Malone (now 30) and Stockton (now approaching 33). Both men are still seemingly operating near full strength, but the years are now piling up against them to be sure. And the talent around these two great stars seems to be thinning and not at all improving. Mark Eaton is now gone from the scene and his shot blocking defense is sorely missed in the lanes. Guard Jeff Hornacek (recently acquired from Philadelphia) and forward-center Tom Chambers were the only other double-figure scorers on the 1994 team and both are themselves now aging veterans. The Utah Jazz may well threaten to win 50 games again in 1995 and even in 1996. But unless more talent is found to shore up an aging team with two aging superstars, whatever muscle the Jazz offers probably won't be quite enough to provide championship rings for Stockton and Malone, and cheers for the patient Utah fans.

Suggested Readings on Utah (New Orleans) Jazz

Bjarkman, Peter C. **Slam Dunk Superstars**. New York and Avenel, New Jersey: Crescent Books (Outlet Books, Random House), 1994.
Gutman, Bill. **Pistol Pete Maravich—The Making of a Basketball Superstar**. New York: Grosset and Dunlap Publishers, 1972.

Utah Jazz Retired Uniform Numbers (2)

Frank Layden (1, Coach)
Pete Maravich (7)

Year-by-Year Utah (New Orleans) Jazz Summary

Season	Record	Finish	Coach(es)	Scoring Leader(s)	Playoffs (W-L Record)
Key: *=Tied for Position; #=League Scoring Leader					
New Orleans Jazz					
1974–75	23–59	5th	Scotty Robertson	Pete Maravich (21.5)	Did Not Qualify
			Elgin Baylor		
			Butch Van Breda Kolff		
1975–76	38–44	4th	Van Breda Kolff	Pete Maravich (25.9)	Did Not Qualify
1976–77	35–47	5th	Van Breda Kolff	Pete Maravich (31.1)#	Did Not Qualify
			Elgin Baylor		
1977–78	39–43	5th	Elgin Baylor	Pete Maravich (27.0)	Did Not Qualify
1978–79	26–56	6th	Elgin Baylor	Truck Robinson (24.2)	Did Not Qualify
Utah Jazz					
1979–80	24–58	5th	Tom Nissalke	Adrian Dantley (28.0)	Did Not Qualify
1980–81	28–54	5th	Tom Nissalke	Adrian Dantley (30.7)#	Did Not Qualify
1981–82	25–57	6th	Tom Nissalke	Adrian Dantley (30.3)	Did Not Qualify
			Frank Layden		
1982–83	30–57	5th	Frank Layden	Adrian Dantley (30.7)	Did Not Qualify
1983–84	45–37	1st	Frank Layden	Adrian Dantley (30.6)#	Lost in 2nd Round (5–6)
1984–85	41–41	4th*	Frank Layden	Adrian Dantley (26.6)	Lost in 2nd Round (4–6)
1985–86	42–40	4th	Frank Layden	Adrian Dantley (29.8)	Lost in 1st Round (1–3)
1986–87	44–38	2nd	Frank Layden	Karl Malone (21.7)	Lost in 1st Round (2–3)
1987–88	47–35	3rd	Frank Layden	Karl Malone (27.7)	Lost in 2nd Round (6–5)
1988–89	51–31	1st	Frank Layden	Karl Malone (29.1)	Lost in 1st Round (0–3)
			Jerry Sloan		
1989–90	55–27	2nd	Jerry Sloan	Karl Malone (31.0)	Lost in 1st Round (2–3)
1990–91	54–28	2nd	Jerry Sloan	Karl Malone (29.0)	Lost in 2nd Round (4–5)
1991–92	55–27	1st	Jerry Sloan	Karl Malone (28.0)	Lost in 3rd Round (9–7)
1992–93	47–35	3rd	Jerry Sloan	Karl Malone (27.0)	Lost in 1st Round (2–3)
1993–94	53–29	3rd	Jerry Sloan	Karl Malone (25.2)	Lost in 3rd Round (7–4)

Individual Career Leaders and Record Holders (1974–1994)

Scoring Average	Karl Malone (26.0 ppg., 1985–94)
Points Scored	Karl Malone (19,050, 1985–94)
Games Played	Mark Eaton (875, 1982–93)
Minutes Played	Karl Malone (27,562, 1985–94)
Field Goal Pct.	Adrian Dantley (.562, 1979–86)
3-Pt. Field Goals	Darrell Griffith (530, 1980–91)
Free Throws Made	Karl Malone (4,956)
Free-Throw Pct.	Jeff Malone (.888, 1990–93)
Rebounds	Karl Malone (8,058, 1985–94)
Assists	John Stockton (9,383, 1984–94)
Steals	John Stockton (2,031)
Blocked Shots	Mark Eaton (3,064)

Individual Single-Season and Game Records (1974–1994)

Scoring Average	Pete Maravich (31.1 ppg., 1976–77)
	Karl Malone (31.0 ppg., 1989–90)
Points Scored (Season)	Karl Malone (2,540, 1989–90)
Points Scored (Game)	Pete Maravich (68, 2-25-77 vs. New York Knicks)
Field Goal Pct. (Season)	Adrian Dantley (.576, 1979–80)
Free-Throw Pct. (Season)	Jeff Malone (.917, 1990–91)
3-Pt. Field Goals (Season)	Darrell Griffith (92, 1984–85)
Rebounds (Season)	Len "Truck" Robinson (1,288, 1977–78)
Rebounds (Game)	Truck Robinson (27, 11-11-77 at Los Angeles and 12-7-77 at Indiana)
Assists (Season)	John Stockton (1,164, 1990–91)*
Assists Average (Season)	John Stockton (14.5 apg., 1990–91)*
Assists (Game)	John Stockton (28, 1-15-91 vs. San Antonio Spurs)
Steals (Season)	John Stockton (263, 1988–89)
Steals (Game)	Ricky Green (9, 11-10-82 and 11-27-82 at Philadelphia)
	John Stockton (9, 2-12-91 vs. Houston Rockets)
Blocked Shots (Season)	Mark Eaton (456, 1984–85)*
Blocked Shots (Game)	Mark Eaton (14, 1-18-85 vs. Portland and 2-18-89 vs. San Antonio)
Personal Fouls (Season)	Ben Poquette (342, 1980–81)

*=NBA Record

Best Trade in Franchise History

The Jazz made their first trade stand up as their very best, and it occurred at the dawn of ballclub history. On May 7, 1974, the newly admitted NBA expansion team (the 18th franchise in NBA history), traded first-round draft picks for 1974 and 1975 and second-round picks for 1975 and 1976 to the Atlanta Hawks to acquire one of basketball's greatest offensive showmen ever—Pistol Pete Maravich. Pete Maravich had a special appeal in the state of Louisiana, of course, having four years earlier concluded a brilliant career at LSU marked by just about every NCAA scoring record conceivable. This trade would therefore give the fledgling club a marquee name player, and thus instant credibility at home as well as around the rest of the league.

Worst Trade in Franchise History

In September, 1980, the Jazz unloaded a troubled Bernard King to the Golden State Warriors for center Wayne Cooper and a second-round draft choice. Plagued by personal problems (including an ongoing battle with alcohol) King had appeared in only 19 games the previous season and averaged less than double figures for the only time in his productive career. Bernard King was soon to turn his troubled career around 180 degrees, of course, becoming one of the league's greatest offensive threats throughout the decade of the '80s and even pacing the NBA in scoring in 1984–'85 for the New York Knicks. But as foolhardy as the Bernard King trade may have been, it still rates close competition from another deal gone sour. For the Jazz also traded away their draft rights to Dominique Wilkins in September of 1982. One can only now dream idly—as a Jazz diehard— of watching night-in and night-out a frontline composed of Karl "Mail-man" Malone and Dominique "Human Highlight Film" Wilkins.

Utah Jazz Historical Oddity

This was the first ballclub in pro basketball history to own its greatest franchise player (or at least one of its very greatest franchise players) even before a team nickname had been selected or announced and before a coach had been hired or a logo unveiled. The New Orleans franchise was formally welcomed by the league on March 7, 1974, and within two months the new ownership group (without a general manager yet on board to handle the transaction for them) was shipping four draft choices to the Atlanta Hawks for local college legend "Pistol Pete" Maravich. And even more strangely, this is a ballclub marked by a rare kind of ongoing roster consistency. Over two decades of team history, only four men have ever paced the Jazz ballclub in scoring. Leonard "Truck" Robinson snuck in only once in 1979 to capture this honor with the 43 games he played for the Jazz that year, before being dealt in mid-season to Phoenix (Robinson's season-long average was actually 21.1 ppg.) All other team scoring titles belong to Maravich (4), Adrian Dantley (7), and Karl Malone (8). If nothing else the Jazz have always held onto their big guns. If you don't count the year they let Dominique Wilkins slip away, that is.

Jazz All-Time Number One Draft Picks List

New Orleans Jazz
1974 Aaron James (Grambling)
1975 Rich Kelley (Stanford)
1976 Jack Dorsey (Georgia)
1977 Essie Hollis (St. Bonaventure)
1978 James Hardy (USF)
1979 Larry Knight (Loyola-Chicago)
Utah Jazz

1980 Darrell Griffith (Louisville)
1981 Danny Schayes (Syracuse)
1982 Dominique Wilkins (Georgia)
1983 Thurl Bailey (North Carolina State)
1984 John Stockton (Gonzaga)
1985 Karl Malone (Louisiana Tech)
1986 Dell Curry (Virginia Tech)
1987 José Ortiz (Oregon State)
1988 Eric Leckner (Wyoming)
1989 Theodore Edwards (East Carolina)
1990 None
1991 Eric Murdock (Providence)
1992 None
1993 Luther Wright (Seton Hall)

Part III

Expansion-Era Franchises

Chapter 19

INDIANA PACERS

Middle-of-the-Road Franchise in America's Heartland

All-Time Franchise Record: 1060–1160, .477 Pct. (1967–1994)
NBA Record: 592–802, .425 Pct.; ABA Record: 427–317, .574 Pct.
NBA Championships: None; ABA Championships (3): 1969–70, 1971–72, 1972–73
Greatest Franchise Player: Mel Daniels (1968–1974)
All-Time Leading Scorer: Reggie Miller (10,879 Points, 1987–1994)
Most Successful Coach: Bob "Slick" Leonard (529–456, .537 Pct., 1968–1980)
All-Time Franchise Team: Mel Daniels (C), Roger Brown (F), Billy Knight (F), Reggie Miller (G), Billy Keller (G)

Antonio Davis, Haywoode Workman, Dale Davis, Reggie Miller, Derrick McKey, Rik Smits. They were hardly household names in the NBA world. And except for Miller, none even approached star status. But for long-starved Indiana Pacers fans, they had to seem like a lineup of Havlicek, Russell, K.C. Jones and Sam Jones. Or for fans whose memories didn't stretch that far back, then at least a lineup of Bird, McHale, Parish and Dennis Johnson.

For this Pacers team shocked the NBA (and the network television gurus as well) as they roared through the Jordan-less playoffs of 1994. They took a usually lackluster franchise all the way to the brink of an unlikely appearance in the NBA Finals. In the end, however, they could not quite exterminate Patrick Ewing, Pat Riley, and the erratic New York Knicks. And more importantly—while they indeed provided a welcomed brief joy-ride—neither could they quite exterminate a quarter-century of woeful team history that had gone before them.

Pacers fans could hardly contain themselves as the 1994 NBA playoffs progressed through early rounds, and then later rounds. Larry Brown seemed to have worked miracles in his first rollercoaster season in Indianapolis. A long moribund Indiana NBA team now actually breathed life and was still around and kicking in the post-season chase long after such playoff veterans as Portland, Chicago, Utah, Atlanta and San Antonio had been sent limping to the sidelines. The Pacers had charged down the home stretch of the regular season, posting the best record in their NBA team history and winning their final eight straight games. They had roared into the playoffs and crushed expansion upstart Orlando with its superstar center Shaquille O'Neal. Then they survived Atlanta's Hawks and had thus proven that their playoff run was no mere inexplicable fluke. Post-season had finally lasted longer in Indianapolis than the accustomed token series which always seemed only to fuel the playoff drive of some other wealthier rival like Boston, or Chicago, or New York.

In the end it wasn't anything all that extraordinary. Other perpetual NBA losers had risen up for a year and lasted deep into the playoffs before, always finally slumping back again in subsequent seasons. Denver had done it much earlier in their franchise history than the Pacers—in only their second winter in the league, in fact. The Phoenix Suns had once made such a run, as had the Portland Trail Blazers and the Milwaukee Bucks (who, with Lew Alcindor, were NBA World Champs by season number three). Dallas (1988, in their eighth season) had also known such an uplifting campaign. And Kansas City had also once played this role in 1981, nine years after relocating from Cincinnati. Indeed, much time would now be needed to assess whether or not this Indiana franchise was actually for real, or only another pretender in the deceitful guise of a legitimate contender.

At the end of a full quarter-century of franchise history, this is one big league ballclub with surprisingly little to brag about. The fandom of any hometown club is prone to such flights of loyalty, however, that even baseball's ne'er-do-well St. Louis Browns, football's doormat New England Patriots, or basketball's Indiana Pacers, find their share of immoveable diehards.

The stark truth is that the Indiana Pacers were once a fleeting powerhouse only within an unstable and imbalanced glorified minor league circuit—the American Basketball Association—which featured more franchise surnames and "gone-out-of-business" postings than legitimate roundball stars. And this Indiana ballclub has rarely ever been colorful, unless that color was largely black and blue from the bruises inflicted by two-plus decades of NBA warfare. Indeed, the Pacers have almost never been promising either, unless promise is measured merely by the expectations of a split-even season and a brief visit to the league's first round of meaningless playoff contests.

One anonymous member of the Indiana sporting press—tongue firmly in cheek—has best characterized this drifting NBA franchise. This wag was not far off the point in suggesting that, within a state and city known most widely for its springtime automobile race, the new Indiana pro basketball franchise might more appropriately have been referred to from the start not as "Pacers" (an oblique acknowledgement of the famed 500-mile auto test) but rather as the "Indianapolis 500's". That seems, after all, to be the high-water mark that Pacer management has unimaginatively grasped as a measure of ballclub success. And not to disappoint, the under-achieving NBA ball club played at a perfect .500 clip (164–164) over the first four campaigns (1990–1993) of the current decade.

Too often rooting for the Pacers has been quite similar to rooting for Bill Veeck's lackluster baseball Brownies of a half-century ago. Love those hometown boys, but be well prepared for endless bouts of disappointment and uninspired play. No other NBA ballclub in a half-century of league history has so consistently lacked a true franchise superstar to inspire the locals (save recent arrivals Minnesota and Miami, who have hardly had the chance). Even an infant Orlando Magic franchise already boasts a Shaquille O'Neal, and the young Charlotte team also has a franchise player-in-the-making in powerful Alonzo Mourning.

No NBA club owns a more dismal long-term post-season record (never advancing outside the playoff first round in nearly two decades before the just-concluded 1994 campaign). And no other club is embarrassed by a more dismal record at the trading block either. In fact it is hard to think of a pro team in any sport which has so consistently been sabotaged season after disappointing season by such an endless chain of disastrous front-office deals. For starters there was the swap of promising super-scorer Alex English, pawned off on Denver for washed up ex-Pacer George McGinnis. Earlier there was an equally unwise loss of future offensive machines Dan Roundfield and Adrian Dantley, again for little or no return. Roundfield was allowed to escape (to Atlanta) as a free agent and Dantley went (to Los Angeles with Dave Robisch) in exchange for James Edwards and Earl Tatum. Then came the dismissal of the precious lottery draft choice which would eventually bring Michael Jordan to Chicago, merely to obtain journeyman center Tom Owens in 1981 from the Portland Trail Blazers. Productive if uncooperative talents like Herb Williams, Wayman Tisdale, Chuck Person and Micheal Williams were, by contrast, held for several seasons past their optimum market value, then dumped for marginal talent under the guise of improving team chemistry. But the watchword of chemistry—in Indiana at least—never translated very readily into the yardstick of measurable improvement, either in the league standings or at the all-important turnstiles.

What has consistently deflated the Pacers over the seasons, then, has been a string of weak-willed ownerships and vacillating club executives who have shouted many a slogan about commitment to long-term franchise improvement, yet had little talent or motivation for actually executing the difficult task. Sam Nassi (1979–1983) saved the ballclub from near extinction at one juncture and then quickly lost interest in the rising sea of red ink. Later the Simon brothers, Mel and Herb, would carry out similar salvage operations with much more glitter and gold, yet enjoy very little return on their investments. George Irvine, a dedicated basketball veteran, would struggle with limited resources in the front office and on the coach's bench during the disastrous seasons of the early '70s. Veteran NBA mentors Jack McKinney (1980–1984) and Jack Ramsay (1986–1988) never had the tools to work their magic in Indianapolis either. Donnie Walsh (1986 to present, as first general manager and then president) has now directed the team for a decade with the watchword of patience. But the history of the Walsh tenure would eventually convince the faithful that patience does little to rescue a sinking ship.

Also hurting the Pacers has been a lack of much true fan support from the city of Indianapolis, or the supposedly basketball-crazy farm-belt region of the American heartland. Consistently, the Pacers are among the poorest home draws in the league, not averaging 10,000 on a regular basis until 1985, and never posting more than 9 sellouts in a single season since ABA days at the Indiana Fairgrounds Coliseum. And in this case the slim fan presence across the past decade and more is not something that is purely a product of high-priced NBA tickets and losing NBA seasons. While hoops fans in Indianapolis today wax nostalgic about the early glory days of an ABA franchise, in reality the team wasn't even a very big story in town at the very hour of its earliest and greatest successes. Eleven sellouts (25% of the season's games) was the best ever for an ABA ballclub in Indianapolis, and this occurred only during the fourth and fifth seasons; not a single ABA game sold out in '73–'74 or '74–'75, and only one during the league's farewell campaign. It took a while, indeed, for even the ABA to fire the local imagination.

Even the original birth of the city's pro basketball franchise back in January 1967, was anything but front-page news. When stories began to leak into the local press that a new pro basketball circuit called the American Basketball Association was in the works and Indianapolis might be in line for a franchise, these seemingly unimportant news items were buried in a lower corner of the local sports page. And when the original investors group attended the first organizational meeting of the new loop and plunked down cash for an entry fee, the Indianapolis *Star* fittingly gave the story secondary billing to the local small college basketball results of the previous evening. Two nights later, a banner headline did pronounce considerably more interest—"Indianapolis Back in Big League Basketball: New Pro Loop Formed"—as it was formally announced that the Indiana capital city would be rejoining the pro ranks for the first time since 1953, the year the scandal-ridden Indianapolis Olympians (stripped of accused point-shavers Alex Groza and Ralph Beard) had closed up shop in the fledgling NBA.

Early ABA years in Indianapolis were filled with their share of colorful events, proud victories, and a strange twist or two. This was especially true of an opening campaign which witnessed a 38–40 record, third-place finish in the league's Eastern Division, and a quick, three-game playoff drubbing at the hands of the eventual champion Pittsburgh Pipers, led by league star Connie Hawkins. The opening game of franchise history was a home victory over the Kentucky Colonels (117–95); but surprisingly no record today exists concerning who scored the first franchise points, although the local press did record that guard Jimmy Rayl pumped in the points which put the home team over the century mark.

But the truly indelible memories of a first franchise season involve one spectacular shot, one showcase game, and one of the most colorful characters ever to don an Indiana Pacers uniform. The shot was one sunk in early November, when reserve guard Jerry Harkness canned the longest field goal in the history of pro basketball play. Harkness's left-handed desperation buzzer-beating hook (a game-winner against the Chapparrals in Dallas) had been uncorked from just inside the opposite endline, and was quickly measured at an incredible 88–feet. The memorable contest, in turn, was the first ABA All-Star Game, staged in the Butler University Field House in January and featuring an MVP performance by later Pacers coach Larry Brown (then with the New Orleans Buccaneers) and also a sterling outing by future Pacers all-around star Mel Daniels (then a rookie center with the Minnesota Muskies). The colorful player, finally, was a troubled seven-foot center named Reggie Harding. Harding (who would later be shot to death on an Indianapolis street corner in 1972) appeared in only 25 late-season games with Indiana, but left behind a legacy of lasting legends all built upon the most bizarre off-court behavior (including once incident when he pulled a handgun on teammate Rayl in a New Orleans hotel room).

It didn't take long for a first blockbuster event in Pacers franchise history and it was an event that would shape ballclub destiny for several seasons to come. The monumental failures of Harding late in the first season had left the club searching for a legitimate pro center. Bob Netolicky (a six-foot-nine second-round 1967 draft pick out of Drake) had played the post for much of the inaugural season, and was successful enough to earn all-rookie-team honors, but Netolicky was a more natural forward. Opportunity quickly came knocking, however, in the form of the shaky Minnesota franchise which was already in the process of relocating to Miami (Florida) for year number two and thus was in desperate need of a large cash transfusion. A modest payment of $125,000 and two castoff players who would never suit up for Miami was enough to pry loose rugged 6'9" powerhouse post-man Mel Daniels, the league's leading rebounder and the outstanding rookie of the first ABA campaign. No other trade in the entire history of the ABA would prove quite so one-sided as this one which provided the cornerstone for future Pacers title-winning teams. Daniels would soon prove a two-time league MVP, as well as a three-time all-league first-team choice. And a quarter-century later he remains the Pacers all-time franchise rebounds leader and arguably the best player in all of franchise history. In one outstanding March, 1969, game, Daniels would score 56 points and grab 31 rebounds in a single night's work against the New York Nets.

With Daniels inserted in the lineup alongside offense-minded Roger

Brown, the Pacers team racked up an Eastern Division title in each of the next two years. Brown had been an outstanding schoolboy star in New York City and played briefly with the University of Dayton before fallout from the 1961 collegiate basketball betting scandals cost him a shot at the NBA. Brown had actually been working in a Dayton factory when signed on by the new league's Indiana ballclub. He had come to the attention of the Pacers when the founders of the new team had tried to lure Indiana native Oscar Robertson away from his contract with the NBA Cincinnati Royals; Oscar was not at all interested in joining the suspicious new league, but did urge the Pacers to locate and sign Roger Brown. Another important change also came in the second season with a coaching switch that brought in former Indiana University star and ex-NBA guard Bob "Slick" Leonard (who had already piloted the NBA Baltimore Bullets) as permanent replacement for Larry Staverman. It was a lackluster 2–7 season's start that cost Staverman his job and thus launched the career of Leonard, eventually the most successful coach in ABA league history.

By the end of their second season the Pacers, under the intense Slick Leonard, were already an emerging league powerhouse. They recovered promptly from the disastrous first weeks under Staverman, eventually responded to Leonard's frantic coaching style, and roared down the stretch with a solid 42–27 record after the new coach's arrival. This momentum carried straight into post-season combat, as well, as the Indiana club first bounced back from a 3–1 deficit to eliminate Kentucky's Colonels in round one, then stormed by the improved Miami Floridians (the former Minnesota Muskies) 4–1 during the Eastern Conference Finals.

But championship dreams were still a year away for the league's most improved outfit. Indiana finally dropped a five-game set in the ABA title matchup against an Oakland Oaks team led by a backcourt duo of future NBA coaches Larry Brown and Doug Moe. Oakland (60–18) had been the league's showcase team from the outset of year two, with Rick Barry pacing the Oaks during the regular season as the circuit's top scorer, averaging 34.0 ppg. for the half-season he played. But Barry had suffered a season-ending knee injury after only 35 games, and had thus left a large void in an offense also featuring Warren Armstrong (21.5 ppg.) and ex-Ohio State star Garry Bradds (18.7 ppg). Bradds at forward, and Armstrong at guard, more than filled the scoring void in post-season for Oakland, however, as the Oaks prevailed in a wild-scoring series featuring two overtime tussles. It was also a series providing no game in which the winner scored less than 123 points or the loser less than 114.

The building momentum that carried Leonard's team through the 1969 post-season was equally evident the following campaign as well. With rookie Billy Keller (Purdue University) now joining veterans Tom Thacker, John Barnhill and Freddie Lewis in the backcourt, the strong Pacers outfit compiled what later proved the best record in ballclub history (either ABA or NBA), finishing 59–25 as a runaway Eastern Conference titlest. The victory margin was 14 games over the runnerup Kentucky Colonels and the Pacers also stood 8 games better than the leading Western Division team, Denver. This high scoring Indiana contingent also posted team and league records with a 177–135 romp over Pittsburgh in April, a game in which Indiana registered an incredible 51 points in the fourth quarter alone. A first championship now seemingly loomed on the horizon as playoffs again opened at the close of the 1969–'70 season. The Pacers swept through Carolina (4–0) and Kentucky (4–1) and then battled the Los Angeles Stars (coached by ex-Celtics great Bill Sharman) for a league title. And the championship series was one-sided from the beginning, with Indiana jumping to leads of 2–0 and 3–1 before ending the title chase after six games. Roger Brown pumped home 53 points (along with grabbing 13 rebounds) in game four at Los Angeles, then poured in another 45 in the deciding match out in the City of Angels as well.

At the time, the Indiana Pacers 1969–'70 club—capable of such firepower behind Daniels, Brown and backcourt rookie star Billy Keller—seemed something of a "dynasty team" in the making. But in a league marked by its constantly shifting franchises and constantly shifting fortunes, the Pacers were somehow unable to defend their title a mere year later. ABA "Year Four" ironically represented the first time that the league's defending champ would actually return to play in the same city (since, before Indiana, both Pittsburgh and Oakland had relocated before championship celebrations had barely wound down). The Pacers themselves seemed little changed at first, again ruling a regular season which saw them shift over to the Western Division but remain a division winner nonetheless. This time the competition—mainly the Utah Stars, the transplanted team they had beaten a year earlier in Los Angeles—was stiffer, and the divisional margin was only a scant two games. The Pacers lineup had seemingly been strengthened by the drafting of a second straight local Purdue University standout, Rick Mount. But post-season play brought a surprise stumbling block, as the transplanted Stars waylaid the Pacers this time around in seven games during the Western Division Finals. NBA transfer Zelmo Beaty now supplied needed strength in the middle for Utah and the eventual champs (Utah beat Kentucky in the Finals) also had added considerable guard strength by trading for Glen Combs and Ron Boone. It was just enough for Utah to prevail in an exciting rubber game (108–101) played in the Pacers' own backyard at the Fairground Coliseum.

The glorious back-to-back championship seasons of 1972 and 1973 which would next unfold today remain the unrivalled highlight of Indiana Pacers history. Under Slick Leonard the Pacers still owned the most potent lineup in the circuit, despite the post-season loss to Utah that had ended a first attempt at a title defense. The lineup was now even further strengthened with the surprise signing of college sophomore George McGinnis off the campus of Indiana University. This was an era and a league, after all, which knew no tight restrictions on the drafting of available college talent. Desperate for drawing cards, the ABA simply sanctioned a Pacers' raid on the collegiate ranks that was guaranteed to bring another showcase player into league arenas. And if the Pacers now seemed to have the best team on paper (Daniels, Brown and McGinnis up front and Mount, Keller and Lewis at the guards) they would soon prove they were the unrivalled best on playing courts as well. And they would prove it not merely once, but twice.

If the Pacers were the strongest ABA team in both 1972 and 1973, they showed this strength in post-season combat, however, and not during regular season's play. Twice they trailed the Utah Stars from November through April, finishing 13 games off the pace during a tumult-filled '71–'72 season, and then four games behind the following year as well. The '71–'72 season, in particular, was one of much consternation in Indianapolis. Rick Mount had been disappointing as a rookie (6.6 ppg. in a reserve roll after three seasons as a phenomenal college shooter) and now battled for playing time with former Purdue mate Billy Keller. Both Mount and Keller complained bitterly to the press about reduced playing time, while an exasperated Leonard attempted to shuffle his lineup to find just the right backcourt combination. The team seemed knocked off course by such dissention and hobbled to a 47–37 record, which was viewed as nothing but schockingly disappointing by hometown fans.

Yet in the 1972 playoffs the Pacers were in complete command from the very start. The three superb frontcourt stars rose to the occasion as Brown, McGinnis and Daniels combined for better than 50 points per game in back-to-back seven-game series against Denver and Utah. The Pacers seemed at a slight disadvantage, since they were forced by booking conflicts to lose home court advantage and play all home contests on the nearby campus of Indiana University in Bloomington. But the distraction was minor at best, and in a drama-filled finals shootout with the Rick Barry-led New York Nets, the Pacers soon reclaimed both their season and their ABA title. The crucial match was a game-five encounter in which Indiana battled back from several large deficits to squeak out victory on clutch last-minute shots by Keller (a three-pointer) and Freddie Lewis (two foul shots with time already expired). Roger Brown took command of the final contest with a 32 point effort in a title clinching 108–105 win. And Freddie Lewis rode a 19 ppg. playoff average to a post-season MVP trophy. With their hard-fought triumph over New York the Pacers had now become the first two-time champion in the short span of ABA history.

Post-season play of 1973 offered a similar scenario. Bob Netolicky and Rick Mount had been sold before the season began to Dallas and Kentucky respectively, and a revamped Pacers lineup now featured Donnie Freeman (acquired from Dallas) sharing the backcourt chores with Freddie Lewis and rookie Don Buse (Evansville). Brown, Daniels, and McGinnis (runner-up in the regular-season scoring race to Julius Erving) again led the way during the spring championship charge. And again there was a classic Division Finals shootout with arch-rival Utah which stretched for six exciting games. And in the ABA Finals the victim this time around was the Kentucky Colonels with all-around league star Dan Issel. It was a colorful series which even featured a first-game protest by Kentucky resulting from a time-clock dispute, and a game-four bench-clearing brawl initiated by Donnie Freeman and ex-Pacer Rick Mount. The heated series stretched the distance with Indiana finally taking an 88–81 title clincher on the road in Louisville. Now the league's first two-time champ had become its first back-to-back champ as well.

Almost before the magic had fully sunk in for local patrons, the glory days were now over in Indiana. The last few seasons of the ABA saw both the ballclub and the league slump badly and slump repeatedly. While the Pacers were eventually rebuilding, in 1974 and 1975, the league itself was already dying, as fan interest shriveled without a television contract and weaker clubs began to fall rapidly by the wayside. A second-round playoff loss in 1974 to San Antonio brought a formal end to the championship era in Indiana. Star players were now quickly unloaded as the team began to retool for a doubtful future. Daniels, Brown and Lewis were all shipped to Memphis, and Donnie Freeman was peddled to San Antonio. Only McGinnis remained in Leonard's camp, and the bruising forward continued to excel with a 1975 co-MVP season, sharing the coveted award with New York's Julius Erving. Rookie Len Elmore and Billy Knight were now brought in to fill the growing void. But the rest of the league obviously wasn't retooling along with the Pacers. By the end of the 1976 season the dying circuit was down to but seven remaining teams—Denver, New York, San Antonio, Kentucky, Indiana, St. Louis and Virginia. When the dust cleared that summer the league was finally gone and in its wreckage stood but four orphaned franchises—the Indiana Pacers, New York Nets, San Antonio Spurs and Denver Nuggets—now ready for resurrection as NBA expansion bumpkins.

It would eventually be a negotiated settlement between the two leagues which saved the Pacers for the first time—but unfortunately, not for the last time. The Indiana Pacers—like the Nets, Spurs and Nuggets who made the trip with them—arrived in the NBA as complete and desperate paupers. The cost of admission had been exceedingly high in both entry fees and imposed sanctions. And nothing was done to provide these new teams with star players—or even with a competitive roster. Indeed, the Nets were forced to sell their only star, Julius Erving, to the Philadelphia Sixers in order to absorb the cash cost of their NBA admission. The Nuggets retained David Thompson and the Spurs kept George Gervin. But the new clubs on the block were even stripped of a crucial college draft choice the first time around. It was therefore surprising that the Nuggets and Spurs faired as well as they did in their first NBA outings; and it was not surprising that the Nets and the Pacers seemed to take forever to get off the ground.

The entry of the four ABA teams into the NBA also meant considerable shuffling of NBA operating structure. With the number of teams now up to 22, divisions had to be realigned. The schedule also had to be reshuffled—each team would now play each other team four times (twice home and twice away), but each club would face two opponents only three times in order to keep the league schedule at 82 games. And the playoff system would also be reshuffled—four division leaders would now get a first-round bye; four remaining qualifiers in each conference would be ranked by record, regardless of division, and face off in a best-of-three format to provide four added survivors; three remaining rounds of playoffs would then be best-of-seven series. There was also the matter of a dispersal draft to redistribute players from defunct ABA teams not now entering the league. Moses Malone thus ended up in Houston, Maurice Lucas went to Portland, Sidney Wicks found a home in Boston, Artis Gilmore went to Chicago and Brian Taylor to Kansas City. And of course Erving was sold to Philadelphia in a separate deal. Only Denver (with Paul Silas) and New Jersey (with Nate Archibald) among the four new ABA clubs reaped any benefit from this dispersal.

The Pacers seemingly suffered the most from the pauper status imposed by established NBA teams upon their four new ABA arrivals. Indiana was forced to pay the same $3.2 million entry fee imposed on the other three clubs, and was also required to forfeit television revenues for four seasons and to sit out the college draft of 1976. With little operating cash and less on-court talent, the club was immediately forced into mortgaging its future for the sake of short-term survival. The Pacers now had to trade future draft choices for desperately needed players (Melvin Bennent, John Williamson, John Neumann, Johnny Davis) and to swap some current players (Adrian Dantley, Dave Robisch, Earl Tatum) for even more desperately needed cash. And to make matters worse in Indiana, two ABA holdovers were lost on the eve of an opening NBA season; Billy Keller was forced into retirement by a pre-season injury and Len Elmore was sidelined as well, by a severely damaged knee.

The first four Pacers seasons as an NBA entrant were all played out under long-time ABA mentor Bob "Slick" Leonard. The first two were almost carbon copies, laced with identical futility. The Pacers ballclub that entered the NBA in 1976 owned the weakest roster in franchise history. The opening game in Market Square Arena was itself memorable, however, as the debuting Pacers extended the proud Boston Celtics and John Havlicek into overtime before losing 129–122. Veteran Boston star Havlicek would hit eight consecutive jumpers down the closing stretch of the most memorable game of early franchise history. The team led by Billy Knight's scoring (26.6 ppg.) and Don Buse's generalship (Buse actually led the entire league in assists with an 8.5 per game average) did fair well enough to finish only ten games under .500. But for the first time the Pacers were not in post-season playoff action, and this itself was a hard pill for local fans to swallow. Accustomed to winners, the fans didn't warm to an NBA loser the way they had to an ABA pacesetter; an average of 10,500 showed up at Market Square Arena, which represented a 3,000-fan increase over recent ABA draws at the smaller Fairgrounds Coliseum, but nonetheless placed the club only 13th in the league attendance derby.

That summer the front office was forced to resort to a city-wide telethon to raise necessary operating funds, boost ticket sales, and keep the now-struggling franchise afloat.

The next two campaigns did bring a climb from the basement, but no major advancement toward respectability in the stronger established league. While fellow ABA clubs from San Antonio and Denver demonstrated immediately that they had real NBA stuff, the teams in New Jersey and Indianapolis (ironically those that were once the true ABA powerhouses) continued to spawn questions about their major-league worthiness. In fact, the Pacers were a stark contrast to the Nuggets when it came to comparing NBA debuts. The Indiana team's 38–44 mark in 1979 was sufficient for a third-place Midwest Division finish. But it was not good enough to buy a ticket to the playoffs. After the 1980 season, veteran Slick Leonard was fired, ending the dozen-year reign for a coach who had already won 526 games and would always remain synonymous with the Pacers' ABA glory years.

The close of the '70s and dawn of the '80s brought a flurry of activity surrounding the Indiana NBA franchise. In the end, however, it was all so much sound and fury and signalled very little of true substance. In the summer of 1979 (the summer that brought Bird and Magic into the league and thus launched a new era of NBA growth) Californian Sam Nassi bought the Indiana ballclub and thus brought new hope for financial stability if not necessarily for on-court prosperity. The Pacers also grabbed a few off-season headlines when a woman, Ann Meyers of UCLA, was brought in for a tryout during summer rookie camp. Meyers was not the first female ever drafted by an NBA club (Denise Long in 1969 and Lusia Harris in 1977 also shared that distinction), but she was the first actually to sign a genuine professional contract and to attend an NBA rookie tryout camp. Owner Sam Nassi inked Meyers to a guaranteed $50,000 deal under which she was to collect her money as a broadcaster if cut from the team roster—which she quickly was. Meyers's broadcasting career with the Pacers was almost as short-lived as her playing career, however, as the talented female player left after only a few early season NBA games, to play for the New Jersey Gems of the newly formed Women's Professional Basketball League. In several player-personnel events that had far greater impact for most Pacers' fans, a soon-to-prove-infamous deal which sent talented prospect Alex English to Denver for the now-veteran George McGinnis followed fast on the heals of the earlier losses of promising offensive stars Dan Roundfield (departed as a free agent to Atlanta) and Adrian Dantley (traded to the Los Angeles Lakers).

A turn in the right direction came in 1980–'81 with the arrival of Jack McKinney. McKinney had suffered an unfortunate accident and an unfortunate fate with the Los Angeles Lakers on the eve of his arrival in Indianapolis. As a rookie Lakers coach, McKinney had suffered a near-fatal bicycle accident during the first month of the '79–'80 season; when his temporary replacement Paul Westhead won an NBA title with newcomer Magic Johnson, McKinney was simply not rehired. Now he had a second chance, and wasted little time in taking full advantage. Under its new mentor, the ballclub turned in a first-ever NBA winning season (44–38) and Jack McKinney got the bulk of the credit. Billy Knight (17.5 ppg.) was also a leader on the floor and balanced team play came from several other quarters also—especially from forward Mike Bantom, guard Johnny Davis, and reserve Louis Orr.

At season's end Jack McKinney was tabbed the only NBA coach-of-the-year in franchise history. Luck seemed to be suddenly shifting for both the Pacers and for McKinney himself. And for the briefest of moments hope flared up in Indianapolis. The team had improved enough to enjoy their first taste of NBA post-season. They didn't hang around long, of course, as they dropped two quick games against Philadelphia to exit from the opening playoff round. But a major step forward had indeed been taken, and it looked like the Pacers were finally about to make the kind of noise in the NBA they had once made a decade earlier, during the ABA wars.

A single year of unexpected prosperity under Jack McKinney unfortunately proved to be largely an aberration. The team fell back to 35 victories in 1982, then 20 in 1983, and settled deep in the middle of the Central Division pack. It hadn't taken long for the McKinney Pacers to self-destruct, aided by bad luck (injuries to promising forward Clark Kellogg), front-office ineptitude (trades for McGinnis and Tom Owens), and rampant fan apathy. Then the bottom fell out altogether during the '82–'83 winter, when McKinney's team crashed and burned hopelessly with a 20–victory season that represented one of the worst end-to-end performances found anywhere in NBA history. It was during this period as well that the ballclub was again on shaky financial footing and seemed to be headed out of Indiana for some more lucrative venue. Rumors had the Pacers relocating, under the ownership of Sam Nassi, to Sacramento or elsewhere on the west coast. The situation was salvaged only when brothers Melvin and Herb Simon—Indianapolis shopping mall developers—purchased the ballclub in May, 1983, from absentee owner Nassi. The Pacers now at least seemed to have a long-term local ownership commitment that would keep them in the state of Indiana. They seemed to have precious little else going for them.

Matters were also not at all helped on the court by a couple of ill-conceived trades that rank near the top of a whole long history of Pacer deals turned sour. Right before the 1981 season the Pacers had unloaded a future first-round pick to Portland for aging center Tom Owens. It all seemed harmless enough at the time, and generated little more than a collective yawn from fans and press. Owens provided little help during his single season with the Pacers, however. And then the disastrous final season under McKinney in '84 meant a further complication; the squandered draft selection was suddenly found to be near the top of the heap at the very time of an exceedingly deep draft which featured Akeem

Olajuwon, Michael Jordan, Sam Bowie, Charles Barkley, Sam Perkins, Melvin Turpin, and Alvin Robertson. Translation: In effect, the Pacers had swapped a year of Tom Owens for either Jordan, Barkley or Olajuwon— the game's superstars for the remainder of the decade.

Portland expended their second overall pick in 1984 (the one acquired for Owens) on Bowie instead of on Jordan, and thus probably saved the Indiana Pacers (when they engineered the original Owens deal) from making the same embarrassing mistake themselves. Equally unsettling, however, was the mid-season, 1980, trade which had shipped Alex English off to Denver in an effort to re-obtain one-time ABA Pacers star George McGinnis. McGinnis was now clearly finished as a star player (and as a gate attraction) and was a mere shadow of himself as he played out his final two seasons in Indiana. English, by contrast, quickly became one of the NBA's all-time great scorers. One can only speculate on what Jack McKinney's teams of the early 1980s might have looked like with Alex English and either Jordan or Barkley in the lineup alongside Clark Kellogg and Herb Williams.

There was one additional bright spot of the McKinney years, and this was the arrival via the draft route of two talented frontcourt players from Ohio State University. Clark Kellogg enjoyed a superb rookie season despite knee problems that were already casting a shadow over his potential future worth. Kellogg scored profusely (20.1 ppg.) was adept at other phases of the game (860 rebounds), and provided needed on-floor leadership. At season's end he lost Rookie-of-the-year honors by only an eyelash to Terry Cummings of San Diego. The stellar rookie was simply too fragile to last, however. Kellogg had been potentially the best player in franchise history at the time he was drafted and certainly was among the most popular (he would remain with the club as a popular broadcaster when his playing days prematurely ended). And during his rookie season he received a boost from second-year center Herb Williams, and veteran Billy Knight as well. Herb Williams, for his part, was a workmanklike and mobile post player who was unfortunately expected by fans to be far more than he was, on a team without other legitimate stars. Williams (still around as a reserve with the New York Knicks a decade later) and Kellogg simply couldn't carry the team load alone, but they did provide some short-lived excitement during their brief three-year (1983–1985) span together in Indianapolis.

McKinney lasted one more year after the dismal 1983 campaign. His 1984 team would improve only slightly in the win column (26–56). But there was no movement out of the basement for the overmatched Pacers. Clark Kellogg did enjoy the second of three solid seasons before career-killing injury struck in the form of tired knees. But there were almost no reinforcements for Kellogg and the somewhat erratic Herb Williams. With little support from his anemic lineup, Coach McKinney's hands were tied. The veteran coach had no choice but to step aside at season's end.

The crash landing of McKinney, Kellogg, and finally the Nassi ownership, ushered in a epoch of malaise which would eventually extend well beyond the ten-year mark. While the Spurs, Nets and Nuggets would continually grow in fan following and league stature, the Pacers would largely languish in the backyard of a state devoted to the college version (Indiana University, Purdue University, Notre Dame) of the hoop sport. Fan support continued to wither, even under the new Simons ownership and Indianapolis (although the nation's tenth largest city) continued to provide one of the league's worst fan markets. Rock bottom came in the '82–'83 campaign, when the Pacers' home attendance slid to a 4,814 per-game average (21st in the league) and the club completed a second straight season without a single capacity house. The Pacers, in fact, remained one of the few NBA teams that rarely played to a home sellout: attendance hovered at around the 11,000 mark throughout the second half of the '80s (Market Square Arena boasts a seating capacity of 16,500 for basketball) and 29 home capacity crowds were announced for the entire decade. Rumors of team relocation were never very long out of the press as the early '80s stretched into the late '80s and then into the '90s.

With his own two years at the helm George Irvine succeeded only in duplicating McKinney's final two disastrous seasons. The '84–'85 campaign, for example, brought only 22 victories (tying Golden State for the league's worst record). And 1986 was hardly any improvement as the Pacer victory total climbed to 26, three better than the Atlantic Division New York Knicks, but still three worse than Cleveland, the closest Central Division rival. Attendance stabilized (ranking 13th in the league for '84–'85–'86) but didn't improve greatly, and serious questions were now being raised about the viability of a lackluster NBA franchise located in the heart of the midwest's acknowledged collegiate and scholastic basketball capital. And if lengthy seasons of losing before sparse crowds weren't bad enough, the Indiana franchise soon proved to be an ill-starred loser on other important fronts as well. Post-season lottery selections earned with several seasons of dismal won-lost totals proved to be something of a hollow victory, for starters, and not at all the source of instant rebuilding that management and fans had hoped for. First the Pacers lost out via an ill-fated coin-flip for Ralph Sampson (in the 1983 draft lottery) and had to settle for Missouri's Steve Stipanovich. Stipanovich, ironically, almost turned out a better NBA player than Sampson, although few would have guessed so at the time. But while lack of desire seemingly took care of short-circuiting the lackadaisical Sampson's career, injuries would quickly kill the future of 7–foot center Stipanovich (5 seasons, 13.2 ppg.).

If the coin-flip loss of Ralph Sampson would quickly be mollified by Sampson's failures as part of the Twin Towers in Houston, a missed shot at Patrick Ewing two years later wasn't so easily forgotten. Here the league mogals breathed a sigh of relief when the touted giant from Georgetown ended up in the NBA media capital of New York, and not in the hinterlands of Indiana. The Pacers had to settle for 6–8 Oklahoma forward Wayman Tisdale, whom they selected with the overall second pick, after losing the 1985 coin flip for rights to Ewing. And Tisdale was an even larger disappointment than first-round picks Williams, Kellogg, and Stipanovich had been. Tisdale had no injury excuse, but his scoring average never soared above 16.1 ('87–'88) in three and a half seasons before he was dealt to Sacramento for LaSalle Thompson and Randy Wittman. There had been great hopes for Tisdale, the team's best natural talent since Daniels, Brown and McGinnis of ABA days, and supposedly a flashy scorer with big-time offensive moves. But the three-time All-American simply never matured into the primetime player Pacers fans had so long coveted.

Things did take a small upturn for the Pacers in '86–'87. It all started when veteran coach Jack Ramsay tired of his long and now stale tenure in Portland and agreed to take up residence with Indiana. The team returned to the .500 level under Ramsay, an event which, in Pacer Country, almost seemed like an injection of championship mania. Chuck Person (4th overall 1986 pick out of Auburn) surprised many around the league— as well as the home fans in Indiana—with a solid Rookie-of-the-Year performance (18.8 ppg. 8.3 rpg.). It was a year that the showboating and trash-talking Person would never again duplicate in his career, however. Chuck Person was thus repeating a pattern already seen with Kellogg, Williams, Stipanovich and even Tisdale—all showed much promise but all burned out quickly under the burden of starring for a division tailender. But with Person's first-year hot streak, the Pacers were suddenly good enough in a balanced league to make their first playoff appearance in a half-dozen years.

Jack Ramsay—for all his credentials, experience, and past successes (785 NBA coaching wins before coming to Indiana)—soon suffered the same fate as McKinney and Irvine before him. The Indiana Pacers indeed seemed to be building an unparalleled reputation as a sure-fire coaching graveyard. Without any renewed supply of talent, the initial upswing in record under Ramsay simply couldn't be sustained for long. Oncourt production first fell way off in '87–'88 with a slide to 38 victories, a tumble to 6th place in the division, and a drop back out of the post-season playoff picture. And then during the 1988–'89 season (28–54, last in the Central Division, 7th worst record overall) the bottom fell out altogether and the wheels seemed to come flying off once again. It was all enough for the veteran Ramsay (now the second all-time winningest NBA coach) who packed his bags permanently seven games into the disastrous campaign. Interim mentors Mel Daniels (0–2) and George Irvine (6–14) and permanent replacement Dick Versace (23–31) did little to reverse the trend the rest of the way.

While the Pacers didn't improve much under the colorful Versace, at least the massacre of 1989 had ended once the former Detroit Pistons' assistant was in full command. Much of the bleeding had stopped by the following campaign (Versace's first full season) as the Pacers spurted back to the winning side of the ledger (42–40) and even climbed back into the post-season circus. It was a short post-season visit, with three straight first-round pastings at the hands of repeat-champion Detroit. Yet for Pacers fans there was again room for at least some guarded optimism. Three-point bomber Reggie Miller (24.6 ppg.) and 7–footer Rick Smits (15.5 ppg.) had meant, if nothing else, that there was some exciting new fire-power now on board.

Dick Versace was out of the coaching picture early in the 1990–'91 season as the coaches' revolving door continued to whirl endlessly in Indianapolis. Replacement Bob (''Bo'') Hill (a Versace assistant) led the still underachieving Indiana Pacers squad he had inherited after 25 games to a second straight playoff first-round visit. And for the first time in NBA post-season competition the Pacers actually put up a fight, extending the Boston Celtics a full five games before dropping a 124–121 rubber-match decision in Boston Garden. Guard Reggie Miller—hot-shooting and hot trash-talking former first-round selection from UCLA—continued to pursue the club's all-time scoring leadership and to provide the team with its first league All-Star in years. Miller would appear in the All-Star contest in Miami in 1990 (scoring 4 points in 14 minutes). More importantly, Reggie Miller would eventually overhaul a large collection of individual team scoring records: most points in a game (57, November, 1992, in Charlotte), single-season free-throw percentage (.918 in '90–'91), single-season 3-point field goals (167 in '92–'93), career 3-point fields (840), and career points scored (10,879). It was late in the 1993 season that Miller finally surpassed Billy Knight (10,780), Roger Brown (10,058), and George McGinnis (9,554) for the all-time (ABA-NBA) club scoring record.

New coach Bo Hill would lead a return to repectability over the next two years. During these two break-even seasons Detlef Schrempf (acquired from Dallas for Herb Williams in 1989 and winner of the NBA Sixth-Man-of-the-Year award in 1991 and 1992) was the club's true backbone, despite Miller's continued record scoring onslaughts. Unpopular forward Chuck Person and underrated point guard Micheal Williams had been cleaned out of the clubhouse in a break-even trade with Minnesota that brought in guard Pooh Richardson and journeyman forward Sam Mitchell. This was a trade that also brought largely mixed reviews from frustrated Pacers fans. Most thought that it was wise indeed to deal Person, and yet opinion was also strong that the often-trade-foolish Pacers should have received far more in exchange for their controversial former Rookie-of-the-Year. At the very least, however, the team now featuring Pooh Richard-son at the point guard slot and Sam Mitchell assisting off the bench was a good deal better defensively than any recent Pacers editions.

The final corner in a long episodic struggle to build a contender finally came with the replacement of Bo Hill by much-travelled Larry Brown in time for the '93–'94 season. Brown brought a new enthusiasm and spirit to the long-languishing club, as well as a new taste for team play and tight defense. Brown's first year was also helped ironically by a controver-sial trade which sent popular sixth man Detlef Schrempf packing to Seattle and brought in Derrick McKey to even further tighten the defense. McKey blended with Dale Davis and super-sub Antonio Davis to provide a potent set of slashing and rebounding forwards. Smits picked up his level of offensive production with a career-best 15.7 ppg. average. Castoff guard Haywoode Workman provided a pleasant backcourt surprise and handled the playmaking. With Miller also now contributing more to team play under Coach Brown's system and Vern Fleming (all-time franchise leader in games played) still giving quality time off the bench, the Pacers even surprised themselves and their long-suffering fans by the end of the 1994 season. As the playoffs kicked into high gear, the Pacers were suddenly one of the most promising young teams in the league, owners of a club NBA-high 47 victories and 31–12 record over the season's final three pressure-packed months. For the first time during their NBA saga the Pacers were now finally a truly hot item in the city of Indianapolis and everywhere else around the league as well.

Post-season play in 1994 provided a highlight matched only by the three championships racked up two decades earlier, at the height of the team's best ABA years. Early round eliminations of Orlando (3–0) and then Atlanta (4–2) had thrust the Pacers into the Eastern Division championship round for the first time in club history. The opponents were the rugged New York Knicks of Pat Riley who had clawed their way through a tough seven-game series with defending champion Chicago, a still-potent team with Scottie Pippen and Horace Grant, despite the loss of Michael Jordan. Having escaped the Bulls, New Yorkers (and NBA fans everywhere else) expected an easy ticket into the NBA Finals for the defense-oriented Knicks. And two opening wins in New York (100–89 and 89–78) seemed to set the stage for a one-sided series. But the Pacers bounced back with two low-scoring victories (88–68 and 83–77) of their own in Market Square Arena. Game three had actually seen the befuddled Knicks post an unenviable NBA record for lowest post-season single-game output. And then a crucial game-five upset victory for Indiana at Madison Square Garden almost turned the entire series in the direction of the Cinderella Pacers. With a stunning 25–point fourth quarter shooting performance by Reggie Miller (who scored 39 for the game), the Pacers put away the shocked Knicks for the first time in three years at MSG. Stunned Knicks observers quickly compared the unexpected 93–86 defeat to one against Baltimore's Bullets, which had killed New York title hopes way back in 1971.

The Pacers next returned home to Market Square Arena for their first June home game in franchise history, as the entire NBA and the league's network sponsors held their collective breath. The Pacers were now standing on the verge of entering the NBA Finals for a no-name title matchup with Western Division champion Houston. But, like all true Cinderella substitutes, the Pacers would never quite escape the stroke of midnight. New York roared back behind Ewing and Starks for a convincing Market Square Arena 98–91 win which once more reversed the tables and sent momentum back in New York's direction. And then Riley's charges held on down the stretch for a heart-stopping final-second 94–90 victory in

MSG, which ended the Pacers fantasy run. The Pacers had actually held a 90–89 lead with but 25 ticks remaining, but poise left the upstarts in the closing moments as Miller missed a potential game-winning jumper and Ewing put back a missed John Starks layup which sealed victory for the New Yorkers.

The Indiana Pacers have now waffled through a quarter-century of team history, swinging like a pendulum from mountaintop to deepest valley, from brief glimpses of professional success to surprising depths of absurdity. The franchise has been, at one period of time a show piece of financial stability and has, at still another time, had to resort to community telethons to prolong its very existence. Indiana's entry in the ABA and NBA has dressed 176 players in two and a half decades—some as memorable as Mel Daniels, Alex English and Adrian Dantley, others as forgettable as Everette Stephens, Brooke Steppe and Dyron Nix—and including the only woman ever to try out officially for an NBA roster. The ballclub has boasted eight radio and television announcers (none memorable) while also featuring eight head coaches (few memorable), six general managers (few successful), five sets of owners (few farsighted), three retired jerseys (all from ABA days) and two permanent playing arenas. They have won 1,060 games while dropping 1,160 and drew their 10 millionth fan during the just concluded 1993–1994 season. They were arguably the best team in the ABA over their decade in that ill-fated circuit and just as arguably among the worst teams in the NBA during the 17 campaigns they have endured in the more stable league.

And unfortunately, throughout their NBA seasons at least, it has all been on the whole pretty dull business for Indiana Pacers fans. But nothing, of course, that wouldn't have been fixed with a Red Auerbach instead of a Donnie Walsh at the front office desk, or a Pat Riley instead of Bo Hill directing plays from the bench, or a Johnny Most instead of Mark Boyle calling radio play-by-play action—or especially a Larry Bird instead of Reggie Miller pumping up three-pointers with a ballgame on the line.

Suggested Readings on Indiana Pacers

Montieth, Mark. "Pacers History" in: **Indiana Pacers 1992–1993 Official Yearbook**. New York: Sports Media, Inc., 1993, pp. 41–51.

O'Brien, Jim. **American Basketball Association All-Stars**. New York: Lancer Books, 1972.

Pluto, Terry. **Loose Balls—The Short, Wild Life of the American Basketball Association as Told by the Players, Coaches, and Movers and Shakers Who Made It Happen**. New York and London: Simon and Schuster, 1990.

Ratterman, Dale. **Basketball Crosswords**. Indianapolis: Masters Press (Howard W. Sams), 1993.

Indiana Pacers Retired Uniform Numbers (3)

George McGinnis (30)
Mel Daniels (34)
Roger Brown (35)

Year-by-Year Indiana Pacers Summary

Season	Record	Finish	Coach(es)	Scoring Leader(s)	Playoffs (W-L Record)
Key: * = Tied for Position; # = League Scoring Leader					
American Basketball Association					
1967–68	38–40	3rd	Larry Staverman	Freddie Lewis (20.6)	Lost in 1st Round (0–3)
1968–69	44–34	1st	Larry Staverman	Mel Daniels (24.0)	Lost in ABA Finals (9–8)
			Bob Leonard		
1969–70	59–25	1st	Bob Leonard	Roger Brown (23.0)	**ABA Champion** (12–3)
1970–71	58–26	1st	Bob Leonard	Mel Daniels (21.0)	Lost in 2nd Round (7–4)
1971–72	47–37	2nd	Bob Leonard	Mel Daniels (19.1)	**ABA Champion** (12–8)
1972–73	51–33	2nd	Bob Leonard	George McGinnis (27.6)	**ABA Champion** (12–6)
1973–74	46–38	2nd	Bob Leonard	George McGinnis (25.9)	Lost in 2nd Round (7–7)
1974–75	45–39	3rd	Bob Leonard	George McGinnis (29.8)#	Lost in 3rd Round (9–9)
1975–76	39–45	5th	Bob leonard	Billy Knight (28.1)	Lost in 1st Round (1–2)
National Basketball Association					
1976–77	36–46	5th	Bob Leonard	Billy Knight (26.6)	Did Not Qualify
1977–78	31–51	5th	Bob Leonard	Ricky Sobers (18.2)	Did Not Qualify
1978–79	38–44	3rd	Bob Leonard	Johnny Davis (18.3)	Did Not Qualify
1979–80	37–45	4th	Bob Leonard	Mick Johnson (19.1)	Did Not Qualify
1980–81	44–38	3rd	Jack McKinney	Billy Knight (17.5)	Lost in 1st Round (0–2)
1981–82	35–47	4th	Jack McKinney	Johnny Davis (17.0)	Did Not Qualify
1982–83	20–62	6th	Jack McKinney	Clark Kellogg (20.1)	Did Not Qualify
1983–84	26–56	6th	Jack McKinney	Clark Kellogg (19.1)	Did Not Qualify
1984–85	22–60	6th	George Irvine	Clark Kellogg (18.6)	Did Not Qualify
1985–86	26–56	6th	George Irvine	Herb Williams (19.9)	Did Not Qualify
1986–87	41–41	4th	Jack Ramsay	Chuck Person (18.8)	Lost in 1st Round (1–3)
1987–88	38–44	6th	Jack Ramsay	Chuck Person (17.0)	Did Not Qualify
1988–89	28–54	6th	Jack Ramsay	Chuck Person (21.6)	Did Not Qualify
			Mel Daniels		
			George Irvine		
			Dick Versace		
1989–90	42–40	4th	Dick Versace	Reggie Miller (24.6)	Lost in 1st Round (0–3)
1990–91	41–41	5th	Dick Versace	Reggie Miller (22.6)	Lost in 1st Round (2–3)
			Bob Hill		
1991–92	40–42	4th	Bob Hill	Reggie Miller (20.7)	Lost in 1st Round (0–3)
1992–93	41–41	5th	Bob Hill	Reggie Miller (21.2)	Lost in 1st Round (1–3)
1993–94	47–35	3rd*	Larry Brown	Reggie Miller (19.9)	Lost in 3rd Round (9–6)

Individual Career Leaders and Record Holders (1967–1994)

Scoring Average (ABA-NBA)	Mel Daniels (19.5 ppg., 1968–74)
Scoring Average (NBA)	Reggie Miller (19.3 ppg., 1987–94)
Points Scored (NBA)	Reggie Miller (10,879, 1987–94)
Points Scored (ABA-NBA)	Billy Knight (10,780, 1974–83)
Games Played	Vern Fleming (761)
Minutes Played	Vern Fleming (22,288)
Field Goal Pct.	Billy Knight (.513)
3-Pt. Field Goals	Reggie Miller (840)
Free Throws Made	Freddie Lewis (2,511)
Free-Throw Pct.	John Long (.902)
Rebounds (ABA)	Mel Daniels (7,622)
Rebounds (NBA)	Herb Williams (4,494)
Rebound Average	Mel Daniels (15.9 rpg.)
Assists	Vern Fleming (3,929)
Steals (NBA/ABA)	Don Buse (1,284)
Steals (NBA)	Vern Fleming (858)
Blocked Shots	Herb Williams (1,094)

Individual Single-Season and Game Records (1967–1994)

Scoring Average (ABA)	George McGinnis (29.8 ppg., 1974–75)
Scoring Average (NBA)	Billy Knight (26.6 ppg., 1976–77)
Points Scored (ABA Season)	George McGinnis (2,353, 1974–75)
Points Scored (NBA Season)	Billy Knight (2,075, 1976–77)
Points Scored (Game)	Billy Knight (57, 11–28–92 at Charlotte Hornets)
Field Goal Pct. (Season)	Dale Davis (.568, 1992–93)
Free-Throw Pct. (Season)	Reggie Miller (.918, 1990–91)
3-Pt. Field Goals (Season)	Reggie Miller (167, 1992–93)
Rebounds (ABA Season)	Mel Daniels (1,475, 1970–71)
Rebounds (NBA Season)	Clark Kellogg (860, 1982–83)
Rebound Average	Clark Kellogg (10.6 rpg., 1982–83)
Rebounds (Game)	Herb Williams (29, 1–23–89 vs. Denver Nuggets)
Personal Fouls (Season)	Don Buse (685, 1976–77)
Assists (Game)	Vern Fleming (18, 11–23–90 vs. Houston Rockets)
	Micheal Williams (18, 11–13–91 vs. New York Knicks)
Steals (Season)	Don Buse (281, 1976–77)
Steals (Game)	Dudley Bradley (9, 11–10–80, 11–29–80)
Blocked Shots (Season)	Herb Williams (184, 1985–86)

Best Trade in Franchise History

Considering only the ABA portion of Pacers history, there isn't even any contest. The 1968 swap of $125,000 and two players who would never see another minute of league action (Jimmy Dawson and Ron Kozlicki) to the financially strapped Minnesota Muskies for future two-time MVP Mel Daniels was the greatest case of highway robbery in the entire annals of the wild and woolly ABA.

On the NBA side of the ledger, obtaining stellar sixth-man performer Detlef Schrempf from Dallas in exchange for Herb Williams was perhaps the one bright move in a long history of Pacers' inept dealing. Schrempf quickly developed into the best sixth man in the league during the early 1990s, and several times won the league's award as the top reserve player. And the West German native was also a 1993 All-Star selection for Indiana before himself being traded away at the outset of the '93–'94 season. The eventual trade of Schrempf to Seattle for Derrick McKey was at first widely condemned, since Detlef had turned into one of the most popular players of franchise history. But with the playoff run of late 1994 and McKey's obviously crucial role in bringing the Pacers team together, the criticisms quickly stopped. Schrempf, for his part, became a role player in Seattle who seemed to have left his best years behind in Indiana. Thus it seems that Indiana gained a huge margin of advantage, first with Schrempf's coming, and then later with his going as well. Detlef Schrempf was indeed involved in perhaps the two best franchise trades ever, and they ironically marked the bookends of his own career with the Pacers.

Worst Trade in Franchise History

Shipping Alex English to Denver for George McGinnis still has to rank as one of the most one-sided NBA swaps of all-time. Of course infamous transactions that earlier lost both Dan Roundfield and Adrian Dantley in their prime rate right up there as well. As does the embarrassing deal which sent a first round pick to Portland for journeyman center and one-year Pacer ('81–'82, 10.5 ppg.) Tom Owens. That very draft pick later rested firmly in the hands of the Trail Blazers (who wasted it on Sam Bowie) at the precise time when Michael Jordan was available for the picking.

Indiana Pacers Historical Oddity

As one of four ABA teams taken into the NBA in the summer of 1976, the Indiana Pacers quickly traded in the proud crown of an annual winner for the tattered rags of a hopeless loser. The club's inaugural NBA campaign was also the first season in the team's nine-year history in which the Pacers did not qualify for post-season playoff competition. And the ballclub, as a result, had trouble filling its new home in Market Square Arena, drawing only two sellout crowds during the entire span of its first three NBA seasons. Ironically, however, the lowest average attendance for the NBA franchise over that three-year span (8,955 in season number three) was still higher than for any single season during the ballclub's ABA glory years. Such was the difference between the "minor-league" ABA and the major-league status of the established NBA.

Pacers All-Time Number One Draft Picks List

Indiana Pacers
American Basketball Association
1967 Jimmy Walker (Providence)
1968 Don May (Dayton)
1969 None
1970 Rick Mount (Purdue)
1971 Darnell Hillman (San Jose State)
1972 George McGinnis (Indiana)
1973 Steve Downing (Indiana)
1974 Billy Knight (Pittsburgh)
1975 Dan Roundfield (Central Michigan)
National Basketball Association
1976 No Draft Selections
1977 None
1978 Rick Robey (Kentucky)
1979 Dudley Bradley (North Carolina)
1980 None
1981 Herb Williams (Ohio State)
1982 Clark Kellogg (Ohio State)
1983 Steve Stipanovich (Missouri)
1984 Vern Fleming (Georgia)
1985 Wayman Tisdale (Oklahoma)
1986 Chuck Person (Auburn)
1987 Reggie Miller (UCLA)
1988 Rik Smits (Marist)
1989 George McCloud (Florida State)
1990 None
1991 Dale Davis (Clemson)
1992 Malik Sealy (St. John's)
1993 Scott Haskin (Oregon State)

Chapter 20

NEW JERSEY NETS and NEW YORK NETS

Stepchild in Hoopdom's Biggest Market

All-Time Franchise Record: 973–1247, .438 Pct. (1967–1994)
NBA Record: 599–877, .406 Pct.; ABA Record: 374–370, .503 Pct.
NBA Championships: None; ABA Championships (2): 1973–74, 1975–76
Greatest Franchise Player: Julius Erving (1973–1976)
All-Time Leading Scorer: Buck Williams (10,440 Points, 1981–1989)
Most Successful Coach: Larry Brown (91–67, .576 Pct., 1981–1983)
All-Time Franchise Team: Derrick Coleman (C), Rick Barry (F), Buck Williams (F),
    Julius Erving (F-G), Drazen Petrovic (G)

When it comes to carting a basketball franchise around from address to address in a dusty collection of old steamer trunks, no one has a leg up on the ballclub known variously through the years as the New Jersey Americans, the New York Nets, and presently the New Jersey Nets. Granted that the Royals, who started out in Rochester, then settled in Cincinnati, and later have operated out of Omaha, Kansas City and Sacramento under the alias of ''Kings'' have logged more miles. And like the Royals-Kings, the Lakers and Warriors have also trekked from the country's eastern regions all the way out to the Pacific gold coast. The Lakers, Royals, Pistons and Syracuse Nats in earlier days can also boast of carting their act around from one league to another—NBL, BAA, NBA. But although the Nets have remained more or less anchored to the long shadows of New York City, nonetheless this refugee ABA team has had just about as many mailing addresses as any other ballclub—far more than most— and for a time in the 1970s, the team seemed bent on changing its name and its playing venue with the arrival of just about every new hoops season.

The lengthy sojourn of one of basketball's most well-travelled clubs began in Teaneck, New Jersey, in the summer of 1967, at the outset of that ambitious experiment known as the American Basketball Association. The ABA itself was hardly a prime-time act in its maiden season as ballclubs in Pittsburgh, Minnesota, Indiana, Kentucky, New Orleans, Houston, Dallas, Denver, Anaheim, Oakland and Teaneck stocked their rosters mainly with NBA rejects, a few still-kicking pro veterans (including the NBA's leading scorer, Rick Barry), a smattering of AAU industrial league players, and a handful of talented rookies like Mel Daniels, Bob Netolicky, Louie Dampier, Jimmy Jones, and Randy Mahaffey. The new circuit also brought under contract a few recognized talents (Connie Hawkins, Doug Moe, Roger Brown and Tony Jackson) who had earlier been shunned by NBA clubs due to rumored involvement with the minor 1961 college hoops betting scandals. Three features of the new circuit, however, did promise a new look, if not a bit more excitement, as the ball sped up and down the hardwood floor. Field goals from more than 25 feet out would now count for 3 points; a 30-second shot clock would allow six extra seconds for playmaking; and the ball itself would flash patriotic with its bright red, white and blue colors.

Capitalizing on this flare for the patriotic and the promotional, the ABA outfit located in the league's largest metropolitan center (New York-New Jersey) would call itself the Americans and sport red, white, and blue colors of its own. One-time pro star Max Zaslofsky from the NBA's earliest days held the coaching reigns for a team that sported a lineup of Tony Jackson (19.4 ppg. as leading scorer), Hank Whitney and Dan Anderson in the forecourt and Walt Simon and Levern Tart (acquired mid-season from the Oakland Oaks) at the guard slots. Despite a lack of name players, the first New Jersey edition posted a credible 36–42 mark which only assured a last-place tie in the stronger Eastern Division, but also tied Kentucky for the league's final playoff birth. And it was precisely that playoff tie that resulted shortly thereafter in the first bizarre happenstance in the history of this soon-to-be fortune-plagued NY-NJ vagabond ballclub.

The regular-season deadlock with the Kentucky Colonels had necessitated a one-game tiebreaker, with New Jersey holding the homecourt advance. Such a homecourt selection turned out to be more curse than blessing, however, since a circus had already been booked into the armory in Teaneck for the selected playoff date and the host club was sent scrambling for a last minute substitute arena. The best that could be arranged, with little or no notice by a league totally lacking in clout or prestige, was the Commack Arena on Long Island. Disaster struck the New Jersey franchise in a double dosage, however, when the two ABA ballclubs and a smattering of fans arrived only to find the alternate court full of missing bolts, slats and planks and thus unusable for even a rugged game of streetball. The embarrassed "home" club was left on the sidelines as the league commissioner—George Mikan of Minneapolis Lakers' fame—ruled the game a forfeit in Kentucky's favor. In their very first season out of the gate the New Jersey Americans had unwittingly become the answer to one of basketball's classic trivia questions—the only modern pro team to qualify for post-season play and then be eliminated from playoff contention without ever bouncing a single ball or taking a single shot at the hoop.

The New Jersey Americans lasted no longer than that one ill-starred season filled with its dose of expansion blues, and perhaps the most bizarre exit ever from post-season play. In year two the team was off and running—not up the ladder toward ABA prominence, but rather on a seemingly endless search over the next few seasons for a permanent home and lasting ball club identity. Even a team name that lasted for more than a season or two seemed an ungraspable goal. Over the next quarter century the team would call six different arenas their "permanent" home, sport the names of two cities or states, and trade in the title of Americans for that of Nets. This latter exchange came immediately in season number two.

Settled into the very arena that had ruined them at playoff time, the relocated Americans officially became the New York Nets for the 1968–'69 second season of ABA play. Operating out of a moderately spruced-up Commack Arena, the team discovered on opening night that the "Curse of Commack" would probably be with them for some time to come. Hockey ice, over which the basketball playing floor had been laid, began to melt during warm-up drills and the sparse crowd of 1,848 looked on in amazement as players from both teams slipped and slid on the slick and damp floor. The melting of ice was halted only by turning off the building's heat, and after an hour's delay the freezing throng and players shivered through a 99–92 Kentucky Colonels victory. And things didn't heat up much for the Nets, either, as the season progressed; the New Jersey club registered the league's worst record (17–61) in either division, trailed the Minnesota team a slot above them in the division by 19 full games, compiled only a dozen home victories, and featured only one 1,000-point scorer in guard Walt Simon (21.1 ppg.). With play like this it seemed more like a continent than a mere borough that separated Commack Arena and the ABA Nets from Madison Square Garden and the NBA New York Knicks. As yet there was no serious notion of a second legitimate pro team in the New York City metropolitan area.

In only its third season on the hardwood floor the vagabond Nets team would take on their third new location, and their third distinctively new look as well. Before the 1969–'70 campaign was ready for its first tip-off, Roy Boe purchased the team and moved it once more, this time into Island Garden in Hempstead, Long Island. It should be pointed out, of course, that such frequent movement around the map was not restricted to the New York and New Jersey ABA ballclub alone. For the second straight year the league's defending champion—previously the Pittsburgh Pipers (to Minnesota) and now the Oakland Oaks (to Washington, D.C.)—also pulled up roots and shuffled off to an entirely new city.

There was also a new coach in New York, York Larese, and a new star player, guard Bill Melchionni, who had been lured from the NBA Philadelphia 76ers. Melchionni's presence in the backcourt along with Lavern Tart (24.2 ppg.) was enough to account for a surge in the won-lost column to 39–45 and a jump in the divisional standings to fourth among six clubs. And in post-season play, the Nets once again were paired up with their nemesis the Kentucky Colonels, and this time actually even got onto the floor for seven full games of playoff action. The two clubs alternated victories across the first six games, opening with a New York 122–118 overtime victory and culminating with a series-tying 116–113 Kentucky win. The long-range shooting of Kentucky's Louie Dampier proved too much in the rubber match, however, and New York's first post-season visit ended with first-round elimination.

Season number four also saw the wheels keep up their rapid spinning (sometime backspinning) and predictably also witnessed another sharp change in ballclub appearance. This time around, however, the movement involved the comings and goings of key personnel and not the shifting of playing floors. For the first time the Nets would take the floor in the same home arena for two years running. But York Larese was out as bench boss after a single season and popular local college coach Lou Carnesecca of St. John's University-fame was in. The truest sign of a dawning respectability came, however, on September 2, 1970, when the New York Nets shipped a draft choice and cash to the Virginia Squires for high-scoring forward Rick Barry. Barry, who carries the votes of many as one of the game's greatest forwards ever, had broken Wilt Chamberlain's seven-year stranglehold as scoring champion in only his second NBA season. Skipping to the ABA in 1968, Barry had averaged 34.0 ppg. before being felled by a knee injury at mid-season. A year later, with his ABA club relocated to the nation's capital, Rick Barry was again limited to a partial season by his injured knee, yet again averaged close to 30 in the scoring column. The sharp-shooting forward would still be in recovery and thus restricted to 59 games during his first season in New York; nonetheless he would pace the team with a lofty 29.4 ppg. average. For the first time, the New York Nets could now seriously compete with the Knicks for fan interest by boasting a marquee player of unquestionably legitimate all-star status.

Stability was certainly not to be the by-word on Long Island for long. Midway through the 1971–'72 season the team, now owned by Roy Boe, relocated yet one more time, though this time to far less surprise since such shuffling was by now becoming the hallmark of both the Nets ballclub and the shaky ABA as a whole. The new venue would be the Nassau Veterans Memorial Coliseum down the road in Uniondale, Long Island. Finally getting into a full slate of contests, Rick Barry was a one-man scoring rampage as he averaged 31.5 and chased Virginia's Charlie Scott (34.6) to the wire in the individual scoring derby. While the team climbed above .500 for the first time (at 44–40) and inched into third slot in the league's Eastern Division, nevertheless they trailed a 68–16 Kentucky Colonels outfit by a country mile and then some. Post-season match-ups would tell a different tale, however, as the divisional runnerup Virginia

Squires were left gasping when scoring star Charlie Scott jumped the team for the NBA before the full season was even out (in late March), while the regular-season pacesetters in Kentucky were blitzed twice on their home court by New York as post-season play kicked off. The inspired Nets earned shocking decisions over both the Colonels (4–2) and Squires (4–3) to grab a first-ever trip into the ABA title match-up.

The final championship round of the American Basketball Association post-season in 1972 would match up some of the young rebel league's biggest stars and biggest gate attractions. The presence of a New York area team and a scorer like Barry (30.8 ppg. for the playoffs) also provided the ABA for the first time with some much-needed media attention in the nation's leading metropolitan center and elsewhere around the country as well. Roger Brown, George McGinnis, Mel Daniels, Freddie Lewis And Billy Keller rounded out the starting five for the powerhouse Indiana Pacers. Barry, backed by guard John Roche, would score at a 23.6 post-season rate. The Pacers were simply too much for the over-achieving Nets in the six-game series and with Indiana's final-round victory the ABA, for the first time, boasted a repeat champion.

The steadily improving Nets would soon suffer the first of two catastrophic personnel-related setbacks, and it came suddenly on the heels of their great 1971–'72 playoff season. Rick Barry, who had now carried the club for two seasons, was without warning ordered by the courts to return to the NBA and to the Golden State Warriors, where he had apparently signed a valid contract for future play at a time, three seasons earlier, when he had been miffed by the shift of his Oakland ABA ballclub back east to Washington, D.C. Barry again balked at a reassignment and would have preferred staying in New York. But legal authorities gave him no such choice in the matter. With Barry back in the NBA the Nets' attendance sagged, as did that of the entire ABA, and the team's fortunes sagged in the win-loss column as well. There was a drop of 14 games in the standings in what would prove to be coach Lou Carnesecca's final year on the job. George Carter offered the only heavy scoring at 19.0 while Bill Melchionni's ankle injury only further dampened a backsliding season.

But this setback, as severe as it was, was in fact only a temporary jolt. One superstar was suddenly gone but another even bigger replacement just as suddenly landed in his place. Not only the Nets but the whole league seemingly benefitted by untold measure when the foremost crowd-pleaser of the pro game transferred his dazzling act from the backwaters of Virginia (where he had, the previous season, paced the league with a 31.9 scoring average for the Squires) to the media capital of New York. Julius Erving (Dr. J.) had been demanding a contract in Virginia that was beyond that struggling club's means. A solution was found when Erving was swapped to New York on August 1st (along with Willie Sojourner) for George Carter, a pile of cash, and the ABA rights to forward and recent draft pick Kermit Washington.

With Julius Erving again pacing the ABA scoring parade in 1974 (27.4

ppg.) and with Kevin Loughery now entrenched as head coach, the Nets would next storm directly to a first league title. A 55–29 record would be the ABA's best regular-season mark in either division and Loughery's Nets would breeze through a 12–2 post-season with 4–1 victories over Virginia and Utah, plus a four-game sweep of Kentucky sandwiched in between. In the title round against the Utah Stars, the Nets were never headed after Dr. J's 47 points spurred a 89–85 opener. A title-clinching 111–100 victory before 15,934 in the Nassau Coliseum set off a wave of pure excitement surrounding the New York Nets that now almost rivalled New Yorkers' passion for the NBA champion Knicks a year earlier.

The Nets were sufficiently strong once again in the subsequent year with a 58–26 mark that co-led the Eastern Division and trailed only Denver's 65–19 as the best overall record. But this was to be a year full of surprises—and not pleasant ones. Perhaps the biggest surprise was the fact that the league was still in business at all, since rumors of its immediate collapse had run rampant all summer long. The key to survival had been a reorganization of league leadership (Ted Munchak, who had owned the Carolina franchise, was the new commissioner), new ownership for several clubs, and the relocation of the failed Carolina Cougars into the midwest as the Spirits of St. Louis. The St. Louis team would own one of the circuit's few good rookies, Marvin Barnes out of Providence College, and would provide the final surprise of the season when they knocked off the talented Nets and Julius Erving in playoff round one. New York had beaten St. Louis in eleven straight outings during regular season competition, yet found themselves overwhelmed by the rookie-laden St. Louis front court of Barnes, Maurice Lucas and Gus Gerard during four consecutive playoff loses.

By the winter of 1975–'76 the American Basketball Association was clearly on its last legs financially. But the Nets were now stronger than ever, whatever the condition of the league's troubling finances. The Nets and Denver Nuggets had actually applied formally for admission to the healthier NBA in September and were clearly now playing out their last tour through the ABA, whether the league survived the winter or not. And while clubs like Indiana (having lost McGinnis to an NBA contract in Philadelphia) and Kentucky (forced to ease its gate losses by selling Dan Issel to the Baltimore Claws) weakened around them—and others like the San Diego Sails and Utah Stars folded outright—the Nets rode Erving's scoring (best in the league at 29.3 ppg.) to 55 wins and the second-best (behind Denver) regular season mark in a circuit now reduced to seven teams.

If the ABA was playing out its last hurrah in the final rounds of post-season in May, 1976, one could hardly tell it by the size of some of the crowds that gathered to watch the championship war between the moribund league's best teams and their superstars—Erving with New York and David Thompson with Denver's Nuggets. A record ABA throng of 19,034 packed Denver's McNichols Arena to watch Dr. J. can 45, along with a game-winner at the buzzer as the Nets opened on top 120–118. Another record crowd (19,107) for game two thrilled to a home-team 127–121 series-evener, despite another 48 points from the incredible Dr. J. Erving soon put his lasting stamp on the series with eight straight points in the final ninety seconds to clinch game three at Nassau Coliseum. David Thompson finally grabbed his share of the headlines in game six with 42 points of his own, but the Nets dominated the fourth quarter despite Thompson, and clung to a 112–106 margin that assured them a second and final ABA championship celebration.

With the death knell of the ABA the following autumn, the Nets would suffer a second severe (even crippling) personnel loss. And this one would be far bigger, especially given the dramatic overall improvement in the most recent editions of the ballclub. With Julius Erving, the Nets had emerged during the final ABA seasons as the league's biggest drawing card as well as one of its more dominant teams. Stripped of basketball's greatest showman and all-around performer, Loughery's team was nothing more than another also-ran ballclub. Thus the handwriting was clearly on wall when it became increasingly clear that Dr. J.'s days with his home-town club were rapidly expiring. Erving had been demanding a salary increase, which owner Roy Boe had first promised, and then withdrew in the face of financial burdens connected with NBA-ABA merger. Julius made it clear he would not play for Boe under these conditions and the troubled club owner was left with no option but to cut his loses by accepting a handsome $3 million sale price (exactly what his club was being assessed for NBA membership) for the disgruntled star. Philadelphia owner Fitz Eugene Dixon made the transaction all the more mid-boggling at the time by also dishing out a second $3 million paycheck to Dr. J. as a promised signing bonus.

During their long first NBA season the soon-to-be-renamed New York Nets provided opponents with a nightly opportunity to face and destroy one of the worst teams the pro version of the sport had ever seen. As winners of the final ABA title hunt the New York Nets had actually entered the NBA wars with high hopes of being more competitive in the bigger league's Atlantic Division. In the final months before NBA play opened for 1976, New York had greatly improved its backcourt by shipping several players (Brian Taylor, Jim Eakins, and first-round draft choices that would eventually result in Otis Birdsong and Phil Ford) plus cash to the Kansas City Kings for talented offensive guard Nate "Tiny" Archibald. Archibald had been the league's leading point maker three seasons earlier, and promised to add firepower to Dr. J.'s existing arsenal.

But the ballclub was also reeling under a heavy financial burden of NBA admission; the four surviving clubs had first paid $3 million apiece in entry fees and next had to pool another $3 million between them as compensation to Kentucky Colonels owner John Y. Brown, who had been left on the sidelines by the merger. The Nets were even further strapped by an additional $4 million payment demanded by the Knicks in exchange for sharing of the New York territory. When Erving thus held out in pre-season camp and forced sale of his contract to Philadelphia the ballclub's financial plight was somewhat eased, despite the knockout blow suffered to its on-the-court performance. And when Archibald suffered a broken foot in January the Nets maiden NBA season turned into a complete fiasco. Denver (50 wins), San Antonio (44 victories), and Indiana (36 wins) all seemed to take NBA transition in stride, while the New York Nets won an embarrassingly low 22 ballgames, and trailed the division-leading Sixers with Erving by 28 full games.

It was now time for yet another move. For one thing, there hadn't been one in five full seasons. For another, the new upscale address in the NBA required a far better playing venue than the one the Nets had been occupying of late. The new home would be in the Rutgers Athletic Center on the campus of Rutgers University, located in Piscataway, New Jersey. Here the club would remain for four campaigns before relocating one final time into the plush new Brendon Byrne Arena at East Rutherford. The upshot of these final two address changes was that the New York Nets were now once again rechristened as the New Jersey Nets. One upbeat element of the 1977–'78 NBA season in New Jersey beyond the upscale playing quarters and window-dressing name change was the spectacular season enjoyed by Bernard King. The local Brooklyn high school product and once-troubled University of Tennessee star posted a scoring average of 24.2 (ninth in the league) and a rebound average of 9.5 for a team that finished 24–58 for the worst record in the entire league.

Not surprisingly, the wheels of change were once more spinning at an unstoppable rate. This time, however, it would be team ownership, and not an arena or a ballclub moniker, that would be traded in. A partnership group headed by Joseph Taub and Alan Cohen bought out Roy Boe's interest in the team, and under new management the club improved thirteen games in the win column, overtook both the Knicks and Celtics while finishing third in the Atlantic Division, and sprinted to its first NBA playoff appearance. Kevin Loughery was now in his 6th New Jersey season and enjoyed his best success since ABA days. King (21.6) and 6'2" guard John Williamson (22.2) split the scoring leadership, but got little offensive help after Eric Money (along with Al Skinner) was traded to Philadelphia in February for center Harvey Catchings and guard Ralph Simpson. King and Williamson also both poured in better than fifty points during the quick two-game playoff series with Philadelphia, but it was hardly enough to head off ex-Nets star Julius Erving, or slow down the Sixers easy sweep of Loughery's Nets.

The new-image Nets soon faced a most familiar pattern. Over the course of the next two seasons the team struggled severely once more. Seasons of 34 victories and then 24 victories meant a fall out of playoff contention one more time and Loughery was gone 34 games into the '80–'81 season. Next to inherit coaching duties was Larry Brown, who already sported a growing reputation for breathing life into down and out basketball clubs at both the college and professional levels. And Brown was provided with some immediate support systems in the form of high-scoring free agent guard Ray Williams (coaxed from the rival Knicks) and two productive rookies in Albert King (Bernard King's younger brother) and Buck Williams. Brown's first New Jersey team quickly surged above the .500 mark and enjoyed a brief first-round playoff visit. His second was roaring down the stretch to another five-game regular-season improvement and another playoff date when the ambitious mentor shocked Nets management and the NBA as a whole by stepping down from his responsibilities six games from the end of the season. Brown announced he was leaving to accept a post at the University of Kansas. And with him seemed to go any hopes for a long-term recovery of roller-coaster club fortunes.

The New Jersey Nets were truly a lackluster team throughout almost all of the 1980s. Ballclub scoring leaders like Otis Birdsong, Orlando Woolridge, Michael Ray Richardson, Mike Gminski and Roy Hinson were hardly household names, and also far from the catalyst ballplayers needed to spark a consistent and winning team. Rookie-of-the-Year (1982) Buck Williams, out of Maryland, proved to be the only substantial ballplayer in New Jersey for much of the '80s and certainly the only one coveted widely around the rest of the league. Williams carved out a reputation as one of the NBA's fiercest rebounders by picking up over a thousand caroms in five of his first six pro seasons.

Yet despite Buck Williams' yeoman job of board clearing and defending the lanes around the basket, the team record slipped with regularity over the next seven years and under five coaches who followed Larry Brown: the victory totals sagged from 49 to 45, 42, 39, 24, and 19 before perking up to 26 in 1989 and dipping again to a club-worst (with the 1969 expansion club) 17 by 1990. The one brief season of upswing came under coach Willis Reed, yet didn't put the Nets anywhere in striking distance of a post-season slot.

New Jersey had begun yet another rebuilding process at the outset of the '90s, this time under Coach Bill Fitch. Fitch was a veteran mentor who had been successful in both Houston and Boston and had even won an NBA title with the Celtics in Bird's sophomore campaign. Two key acquisitions were number-one draft pick (1990) Derrick Coleman out of Syracuse and Croatian ace Drazen Petrovic. Coleman had enjoyed a stellar collegiate tenure at Syracuse and earned special distinction as the first college player ever to record 2,000 points, 1,500 rebounds and 300 blocks in an NCAA career. And Coleman did not disappoint as he stormed to 1991 Rookie-of-the-Year honors and averaged 19.7 ppg. over his first three NBA winters. For years recognized as one of Europe's top guards, the 6'5" fancy-shooting but slow-footed Petrovic had adjusted slowly to NBA playing-style in his first season-and-a-half with Portland (needing to depend on teammates to set him up for open shots), then blossomed under New Jersey's more freewheeling offense. With Coleman and Petrovic providing plenty of scoring punch, the Nets were back in the playoffs, losing three of four games in the opening round to the Cleveland Cavaliers.

A second phase of slow and arduous rebuilding came with the hiring of 1992 Olympic "Dream Team" coach Chuck Daly to take over the ballclub reigns. Yet Daly has been nowhere near as charmed—or as blessed with top-to-bottom playing talent—in New Jersey as in Detroit. With Petrovic averaging 20-plus ppg. in '92 and '93, the Daly ballclubs grabbed three straight Atlantic Division third-place finishes and repeated both years the '92 playoff first-round visit (and elimination) achieved under Bill Fitch. The team would suffer a devastating blow, however, when Drazen Petrovic was tragically killed in an automobile crash in Germany during the 1993 summer months.

Prospects do not now look exceptionally bright for the New Jersey Nets as the mid-1990s rapidly approach. Derrick Coleman improved steadily, but has been surrounded with little in the way of a supporting cast. A 3–1 post-season pasting by Patrick Ewing and New York indicated that the Jersey team is still not yet ready to lock horns with the league's big boys and that Coleman is still soft against a dominating big man like Ewing. With Chuck Daly's announced resignation on the heels of the first-round playoff loss to the cross-river New York Knicks, another ill-fated phase of ballclub rebuilding seems already to have stalled and collapsed. The Nets now stand alone among the four NBA expansion clubs recruited from the ABA in 1976 as a team never having made it all the way into the post-season conference championship round. And the chances of that changing any time in the near future (under new coach Butch Beard) still seem to be very dim at best, and perhaps almost nil. Nonetheless the diehards among Nets fans still long for yet another franchise move—this time hopefully up into the NBA championship finals.

Suggested Readings on New Jersey (New York) Nets

Bell, Marty. **The Legend of Dr. J.** New York: Coward, McCann & Geoghegan, 1975.

Pluto, Terry. **Loose Balls—The Short, Wild Life of the American Basketball Association as Told by the Players, Coaches, and Movers and Shakers Who Made It Happen**. New York and London: Simon and Schuster, 1990.

New Jersey Nets Retired Uniform Numbers (4)

Wendell Ladner (4)
John Williamson (23)
Bill Melchionni (25)
Julius Erving (32)

Year-by-Year New Jersey (New York) Nets Summary

Season	Record	Finish	Coach(es)	Scoring Leader(s)	Playoffs (W-L Record)

Key: * = Tied for Position; # = League Scoring Leader

American Basketball Association

New Jersey Americans

1967–68	36–42	4th*	Max Zaslofsky	Tony Jackson (19.4)	Did Not Qualify

New York Nets

1968–69	17–61	5th	Max Zaslofsky	Walt Simon (21.1)	Did Not Qualify
1969–70	39–45	4th	York Larese	Levern Tart (24.1)	Lost in 1st Round (3–4)
1970–71	40–44	3rd	Lou Carnesecca	Rick Barry (29.4)	Lost in 1st Round (2–4)
1971–72	44–40	3rd	Lou Carnesecca	Rick Barry (31.5)	Lost in ABA Finals (10–9)
1972–73	30–54	4th	Lou Carnesecca	George Carver (19.0)	Lost in 1st Round (1–4)
1973–74	55–29	1st	Kevin Loughery	Julius Erving (27.4)#	**ABA Champion** (12–2)
1974–75	58–26	1st*	Kevin Loughery	Julius Erving (27.9)	Lost in 1st Round (1–4)
1975–76	55–29	2nd	Kevin Loughery	Julius Erving (29.3)#	**ABA Champion** (8–5)

National Basketball Association

1976–77	22–60	5th	Kevin Loughery	Robert Hawkins (19.3)	Did Not Qualify

New Jersey Nets

1977–78	24–58	5th	Kevin Loughery	Bernard King (24.2)	Did Not Qualify
1978–79	37–45	3rd	Kevin Loughery	John Williamson (22.2)	Lost in 1st Round (0–2)
1979–80	34–48	5th	Kevin Loughery	Mike Newlin (20.9)	Did Not Qualify
1980–81	24–58	5th	Kevin Loughery / Bob MacKinnon	Mike Newlin (21.4)	Did Not Qualify
1981–82	44–38	3rd	Larry Brown	Ray Williams (20.4)	Lost in 1st Round (0–2)
1982–83	49–33	3rd	Larry Brown / Bill Blair	Buck Williams (17.0)	Lost in 1st Round (0–2)
1983–84	45–37	4th	Stan Albeck	Otis Birdsong (19.8)	Lost in 2nd Round (5–6)
1984–85	42–40	3rd	Stan Albeck	M.R. Richardson (20.1)	Lost in 1st Round (0–3)
1985–86	39–43	3rd*	Dave Wohl	Mike Gminski (16.5)	Lost in 1st Round (0–3)
1986–87	24–58	4th*	Dave Wohl	Orlando Woolridge (20.7)	Did Not Qualify
1987–88	19–63	5th	Dave Wohl / Bob MacKinnon / Willis Reed	Buck Williams (18.3)	Did Not Qualify
1988–89	26–56	5th	Willis Reed	Roy Hinson (16.0)	Did Not Qualify
1989–90	17–65	6th	Bill Fitch	Dennis Hopson (15.8)	Did Not Qualify
1990–91	26–56	5th	Bill Fitch	Reggie Theus (18.6)	Did Not Qualify
1991–92	39–43	3rd	Bill Fitch	Drazen Petrovic (20.6)	Lost in 1st Round (1–3)
1992–93	43–39	3rd	Chuck Daly	Drazen Petrovic (22.3)	Lost in 1st Round (2–3)
1993–94	45–37	3rd	Chuck Daly	Derrick Coleman (20.2)	Lost in 1st Round (1–3)

Individual Career Leaders and Record Holders (1967–1994)

Scoring Average	Rick Barry (30.6 ppg., 1970–72)
Points Scored	Buck Williams (10,440, 1981–89)
Games Played	Buck Williams (635)
Minutes Played	Buck Williams (23,100)
Field Goals Made	Buck Williams (3,981)
Field Goal Pct.	Darryl Dawkins (.601, 1982–87)

3-Pt. Field Goals	Chris Morris (262, 1988–94)
Free Throws Made	Buck Williams (2,476)
Free-Throw Pct.	Mike Newlin (.886 , 1979–81)
Rebounds	Buck Williams (7,576, 1981–89)
Assists	Darwin Cook (1,870, 1980–86)
Steals	Darwin Cook (875)
Blocked Shots	George Johnson (863, 1977–80 and 1984–85)

Individual Single-Season and Game Records (1967–1994)

Scoring Average	Rick Barry (31.5 ppg., 1971–72)
Points Scored (ABA Season)	Rick Barry (2,518, 1971–72)
Points Scored (NBA Season)	Bernard King (1,909, 1977–78)
Points Scored (Game)	Mike Newlin (52, 12–16–79 vs. Boston Celtics, OT)
	Ray Williams (52, 4–17–82 at Detroit Pistons)
Field Goal Pct. (Season)	Darryl Dawkins (.644, 1985–86)
Free-Throw Pct. (Season)	Mike Gminski (.893, 1985–86)
Rebounds (Season)	Buck Williams (1,027, 1982–83)
Rebounds (Game)	Buck Williams (27, 2-1-87 at Golden State Warriors, 4OTs)
Assists (Season)	Kevin Porter (801, 1977–78)
Assists (Game)	Kevin Porter (29, 2–24–78 vs. Houston Rockets)
Steals (Season)	Michael Ray Richardson (243, 1984–85)
Steals (Game)	Eddie Jordan (10, 3–23–79 at Philadelphia Sixers)
Blocked Shots (Season)	George Johnson (274, 1977–78)
Blocked Shots (Game)	Darryl Dawkins (13, 11–5–83 vs Philadelphia Sixers)
Personal Fouls (Season)	Darryl Dawkins (386, 1983–84)

Best Trade in Franchise History

Rick Barry gets votes in some circles as the best forward in basketball history—the best pure shooting forward at any rate. During a two-year stay with the New York Nets as part of his whirlwind sojourn through several ABA franchises, Barry burned up the nets (fittingly!) at better than a 30 ppg. average. Rick Barry came to the Nets on September 2, 1970, from the Virginia Squires in one of the better most-for-least deals in basketball history. The price for Barry was merely a draft choice and several truck loads of expendable cash. A close second, of course, was the trade nearly three years later which replaced Barry by throwing more cash and journeymen players at these same Virginia Squires for another all-time great forward—Julius Erving.

Worst Trade in Franchise History

Can you imagine the Bulls trading Michael Jordan? Or what it was like when the Boston Red Sox traded away Babe Ruth? Basketball's version of the Babe Ruth deal actually transpired in 1976 when the financially-strapped New Jersey Nets owner paved the way for his club's entry into the NBA by peddling one of basketball's three greatest players ever—Julius Erving—to the established Philadelphia 76ers. And it would be a trade from which the New Jersey franchise would never quite recover to this very date. Of course there was little the Nets could do to avoid the sale of Erving, a transaction which the superstar's contract demands and the weight of NBA admissions fees had forced upon them. Only weeks before unloading Erving, however, the club had also shipped two players (Brian Taylor and Jim Eakins) and two future draft choices (used for later stars Otis Birdsong and Phil Ford) to the Kansas City Kings in exchange for 1973 NBA scoring champ Nate Archibald. Archibald would break his foot in mid-season and thus appear in only 34 games during his one unproductive season with the Nets. Indeed the bicentennial summer was not a very good one for New York's latest entry into the NBA basket-ball wars.

New Jersey Nets Historical Oddity

It remains one of those great barroom trivia questions: What pro basketball team qualified for the post-season playoffs and then was eliminated from those playoffs without ever taking to the court for a single game? Answer: the New Jersey Americans (ABA forerunner of the New Jersey Nets) and it happened to them in their very first season of existence. Of course it took the kind of bizarre circumstances peculiar only to a barnstorming circuit to bring it all about. First the team had to qualify for post-season competition in the very first ABA season by earning a tie for the final playoff slot. Then the scheduled tie-breaker contest with the Kentucky Colonels had to be dislodged from the Teaneak Armory in New Jersey by a previously booked traveling circus. If this wasn't already embarrassing enough for a basketball team laying claim to professional status, next the alternate arena in Commack (Long Island) was discovered, on game night, to be totally unplayable due to rattling floor boards and some missing nuts and bolts. The American Basketball Association began its first post-season round of 1968 with a legacy that was already seemingly destined to rival that of the old fly-by-night circuits of the immediate post-war era two decades earlier.

Nets All-Time Number One Draft Picks List

New Jersey Nets
1977 Bernard King (Tennessee)
1978 Winford Boynes (USF)
1979 Calvin Natt (Northeast Louisiana)
1980 Mike O'Koren (North Carolina)
1981 Buck Williams (Maryland)
1982 Eric "Sleepy" Floyd (Georgetown)
1983 None
1984 Jeff Turner (Vanderbilt)
1985 None
1986 Dwayne "Pearl" Washington (Syracuse)
1987 Dennis Hopson (Ohio State)
1988 Chris Morris (Auburn)
1989 Mookie Blaylock (Oklahoma)
1990 Derrick Coleman (Syracuse)
1991 Kenny Anderson (Georgia Tech)
1992 None
1993 Rex Walters (Kansas)

Chapter 21

SAN ANTONIO SPURS

The Case of the Landlocked Admiral

All-Time Franchise Record: 1171–1049, .527 Pct. (1967–1994)
NBA Record: 793–683, .537 Pct.; ABA Record: 378–366, .508 Pct.
NBA Championships: None; ABA Championships: None
Greatest Franchise Player: David Robinson (1989–1994)
All-Time Leading Scorer: George Gervin (23,620 Points, 1976–1985)
Most Successful Coach: Stan Albeck (153–93, .622 Pct., 1980–1983)
All-Time Franchise Team: David Robinson (C), George Gervin (F), Larry Kenon (F),
Johnny Moore (G), James Silas (G)

Of four American Basketball Association franchises welcomed into the NBA as outcast "poor relations" back in 1976, three suffered an immediate and lasting fate. These heavily handicapped clubs—the Indiana Pacers, Denver Nuggets and New Jersey Nets—were all left badly crippled by both the thin playing talent they inherited and the enormous financial burdens they were forced to accept as part of their admission ticket to the new league. Thus for years these three second-level teams have been largely full-fledged busts in the NBA. They had now joined the prestigious club, but they had been left standing out in the back yard and begging for their meager suppers.

Denver's Nuggets did start off in the more prestigious league with a burst of glory that earned the franchise almost immediate respectability. But the party in the NBA did not last very long for the overextended Nuggets. The Indiana franchise suffered a reverse fate. For newly two decades the Pacers remained mediocre or worse and never left the first round of the NBA playoffs. Then finally, at the more recent end of club history, the Pacers earned some overdue respect with a marvelous post-season run which took them within seconds of becoming the first ABA club to earn a spot in the NBA Finals. The New Jersey Nets, on the other hand, have merited almost no respect at all in their usually embarrassing NBA career. And none of the three has ever recaptured the glories of earlier ABA days, where Indiana won two titles, New Jersey (as the New York Nets) captured one, and the Nuggets at least advanced one time into the title round of year-end playoffs.

For the San Antonio club now known as the Spurs, however, the trek through both ABA and NBA days has revealed a far different and much more upbeat story. In the ABA the Spurs had bounced around the league like a loose rebound and found temporary homes all across the state of Texas. The franchise eventually did settle down in San Antonio and, once there, became an immediate hit with San Antonio fans hungry for any type of professional sports. But even in the final ABA years—buoyed by the coming of super scorer George Gervin—the Spurs were never more than an unglamorous also-ran ballclub.

But a move to the senior circuit brought another life altogether. The NBA, from the first, seemed to be just the proper cup of tea for the team from San Antonio and its machine-gun shooting star George Gervin. From the first season and throughout much of their history the Spurs proved to be far better in the NBA than they were in the ABA. No nostalgia for the old rival league of the 1960s and early '70s was ever expressed in this particular Texas town.

It was the Spurs and Gervin, in point of fact, that eased widespread fears about ABA impotency during the first year of the merger. It was widely held back in the autumn of 1976 that ABA teams and players would be a full disaster if not an embarrassment in the much tougher NBA. The Spurs went 44–38 in their first NBA campaign, however, and along with the equally strong Denver club (50–32) seemed to attest straight off to a pretty high level of play in the now moribund ABA. And after this smart start out of the gate, the San Antonio team soon answered any lingering questions about a first-year fluke. Once they got their feet wet the Spurs would win a division title in five of their first seven years in the league.

And if the San Antonio team performance didn't speak volumes in defense of the ABA, then the spindly 6'8" George Gervin himself personally silenced most nay-sayers. Gervin took up right where he left off in the ABA, scoring almost at will, night in and night out, against all manner of defenses. The former two-year Eastern Michigan University standout would lead the NBA in scoring four of his first six years in the older league. And in the end, of course, this refugee from the Detroit ghetto would become the second highest scoring guard in all of NBA history. Incredibly, Gervin's array of finger-rolls and high-arching bombs in both NBA and ABA seasons would leave him only 115 points short of basketball's all-time most prolific backcourt scorer, Oscar Robertson.

Today the Spurs remain the only ABA club to boast an overall winning record for combined ABA-NBA franchise histories. They are also the only team of the four to have posted a better overall NBA mark than their

ABA ledger. They were the first among ABA refugees to advance all the way to a Division Finals matchup and also remain the only one to do this on three different occasions (the Nuggets and Pacers have each made it once and the Nets never have succeeded in post-season to this date). Grant them a dry spell in the middle-aged years of their NBA sojourn, when the Spurs seemed glued to fifth and sixth place. But that aside, the San Antonio Spurs have done more damage in the NBA than all three other ex-ABA clubs combined. And just try stacking up an all-time Spurs team composed of David Robinson, Gervin, Larry Kenon, Johnny Moore and James Silas—with Artis Gilmore as a reserve—against the very best that any of the other three clubs might offer.

Rambling Around Old Texas Town

The American Basketball Association club that would eventually become the Spurs began life a considerable distance from San Antonio and a considerable distance from proven ABA respectability as well. The initial club logo—consisting of a cartoon Roadrunner bird dribbling a basketball across the map face of Texas toward a spot marked as Dallas—was one of the most ironically symbolic ever designed by a pro sports franchise. Operating as the Dallas Chaparrals, the initial team did post a winning record that first season, finishing in second spot in the Western Division at 46–32 and winning a round of playoff games before succumbing in the Divisional Finals. Cliff Hagan—Bob Pettit's old running mate with the St. Louis Hawks and one of the men Boston had originally traded for Bill Russell—was the veteran coach; but talent was thin enough for the 36-year-old forward to hold down a starring role as player as well and to finish up as the ballclub's third leading scorer at 18.2 ppg. With largely a no-name team (Cincy Powell, John and Charlie Beasley, Bob Verga, and Maurice McHartley) the Dallas outfit got by Houston in the playoffs 3–0 and were eventually ousted in the Western Division title matchup by a New Orleans Buccaneers club that starred Doug Moe, Jimmy Jones and Larry Brown. But unfortunately it would be largely downhill from there.

Dallas dropped to the middle of the pack the second year out of the starting blocks. In post-season activity the Chaps were unfortunate seventh-game losers in a close opening round division semifinal to the same New Orleans team that had slammed the door on their season a year earlier. Again this was largely a no-name team with no Dallas player to be found anywhere among the league's individual statistical leaders. Forwards Cincy Powell and John Beasley posted almost identical 19 ppg. scoring averages and future ABA-NBA ironman Ron Boone debuted with a 18.9 scoring mark. The 6'2" Idaho State alum also launched a consecutive game streak that would eventually stretch into the longest ever, at 1,042 games.

A pattern seemed to be emerging as Dallas hovered in the middle of

the pack for a third straight season. Despite a second-place official finish
(45–39) they were tightly crammed together in a dead-heat with four teams
in the Western Division that trailed after Denver. And there would be
largely a repeat performance the next two seasons as well, first under the
name Texas Chaparrals, and then as the redubbed Dallas Chaparrals. The
name changes now indicated some heavy trucking to different home courts,
spread out around the central part of the state. During the 1971 campaign
the Chaps played home matches in both Lubbock and Fort Worth as well
as in nearby Dallas.

A faltering season (28–56) in '72–'73 under veteran ABA mentor Babe
McCarthy (formerly of the New Orleans Bucs and Memphis Pros and the
league's first 200-game winner) meant a drop out of the playoffs for the
first time in club annals. It also meant a sale of the ballclub to a conglomerate of San Antonio businessmen and a relocation of the team to a final
resting place in the Alamo City. And the first year with the new affiliation
and new nickname was also, most importantly, the first season featuring
the incomparable George Gervin.

The first move of a new Spurs ownership headed by Angelo Drossos
and his associates was to bring back coach Tom Nissalke, who had been
fired two seasons earlier. A second was to part with a substantial bankroll
in order to purchase Gervin's contract from the Virginia Squires in late
January, 1974. It was the second move, of course, that paid the larger
dividends. Gervin immediately took up the scoring reins in San Antonio.
He was also immediately dubbed the "Ice Man" for his stoic look and
"ice-water-in-the-veins" shooting performances in the toughest of pressure
situations. Gervin was, in fact, almost unguardable anywhere within shooting range of the enemy basket. With Ice Man on their side, the new club
posted three successful winning records across the final three ABA seasons. And Gervin's free-wheeling style excited and entertained San Antonio fans to such an extent that a lasting love affair was quickly born
between the Texas coastal city and its professional basketball franchise.
But even with Gervin, the club never won a division flag and never got
out of the first round of the playoffs. And George Gervin never seriously
approached an individual scoring title during those final ABA winters
either. The closest he came was fourth (behind Erving of New York,
McGinnis of Indiana, and Issel of Kentucky) during the 1973–'74 season.

The Iceman Cometh

The real arrival of George Gervin in the pro ranks—the season when
he first gained wide visibility and had real impact—was the year that
merger thrust the Spurs from the disintegrating "minor league" ABA into
the stable "major league" NBA. The ABA had been only a warmup for
George Gervin. And NBA season number one was largely still part of that
warmup, as the slender Spurs guard barely cracked the top ten in league

scoring. But in season two George Gervin came of age as a big-time pro point maker.

George Gervin seemed to come out of nowhere for NBA fans in '77–'78. He popped up in the middle of a dramatic down-to-the-wire race for a scoring title that had, in recent years, featured only names like Maravich, McAdoo, Abdul-Jabbar and Rick Barry. He also pulled his Spurs directly to the top of a Central Division which had belonged to Houston, Washington and Cleveland of late. There were some other major contributors, like James Silas who already had been complimenting Gervin with some heavy scoring of his own several seasons back. But Silas was hurt for much of this particular season and the void was adequately filled with 6'9" Larry Kenon, who also gave the Spurs one of the best one-two scoring punches in the circuit. Gervin carried the bulk of the offensive load for coach Doug Moe's club himself, however. And he engaged down the stretch in one of the most exciting individual scoring races ever. Gervin and Denver's David Thompson, another ABA renegade, stood in a virtual tie on the season's final day. Thompson went out that very afternoon and apparently locked up the crown with 73 points against overmatched Detroit. It was the most ever scored by anyone other than Wilt Chamberlain. But Gervin had the last shot later that evening and he pumped home 63 himself against New Orleans. It was exactly two points more than the Ice Man needed and Gervin won the scoring title by the slimmest of possible margins. He won it, in fact—after nearly 900 baskets during the season— by but a single bucket.

Gervin's scoring title was the first of three straight and of four in five years. The tireless shooter also lead the Spurs that season to the first of back-to-back division titles. In the second season of this two-year run Gervin and his Spurs would finally hit full stride in the midst of post-season play and advance all the way to the divisional title matchup. It would be a seven-game shootout with Washington's Bullets, and one that would find San Antonio suddenly sitting on the verge of the NBA Finals by holding a commanding 3–1 lead entering game five. But the Spurs could not hang on and next dropped three straight extremely-close games (107–103, 108–100, 107–105) to the defending NBA champs. But despite their mini-collapse at the season's most decisive moment, the Spurs had become the first ABA expansion club to reach the divisional title round. And they had done it in only their third year of residence in basketball's senior circuit.

Gervin and the Spurs would have two more serious cracks over the next several seasons at getting into the NBA Finals. There would be a brief derailing in 1980 as the club fell to .500 and languished in second place. Doug Moe would be an immediate casualty of the reversal in fortunes. And ironically that same season would see Ice Man Gervin wrap up his third consecutive scoring title and post a career high 33.1 ppg. scoring mark. But with the arrival of Stan Albeck as Moe's less fiery replacement, things were seemingly back on the fast track and also back in high gear for a still potent club that then raced to three straight first-place finishes.

Finding themselves back in the divisional finals yet again in 1982, the Spurs were rudely blitzed in four straight by a Los Angeles Lakers team led by Magic Johnson—itself on a direct path toward another league championship. San Antonio had earned the match with Los Angeles by trashing Denver 4–1 in one of the highest-scoring playoff series in league annals. San Antonio's 152–133 victory on the opening night of that series still stands today as the highest scoring match of NBA post-season history. But LA proved a more difficult hurdle and the sound whipping by Magic, Kareem and company included no game closer than five points and none that was ever really up for grabs. The drubbing also came despite a barrage of 30-point games by George Gervin who bagged 39 and 38 in the two final homecourt losses. The following season, however, would bring a far better showing against the defending champion LA Lakers. While the final tally once more showed a Laker 4–2 triumph, the margin in deciding game six was but a single point. Had the Spurs only held on in that one, they might indeed have had a legitimate shot at the finals during a pivotal seventh game. As it was the team showed plenty of character by registering two convincing road wins in the hostile LA Forum. Albeck's Spurs had also enjoyed remarkable overall success in 1983 by posting the best record yet (53–29) since the transfer from the red, white, and blue days of the American Basketball Association.

The Iceman Goeth

The summer of 1983 would mark the end of an era for the San Antonio Spurs and also close the door on their seven-year successful run in the NBA. It would all begin when Stan Albeck became embroiled in a contract dispute with management that summer and left to coach the New Jersey Nets. More importantly, Ice Man Gervin was seemingly stepping over the summit and starting down the back slope of his brilliant ABA/NBA career. Gervin would put in two more seasons before being unceremoniously traded away to the Chicago Bulls. But he had by now already led the club in scoring for the final time. That role would be taken over for the next several seasons by forward Mike Mitchell, who had been acquired in a 1982 deal (for Ron Brewer and Reggie Johnson) with the Cleveland Cavaliers. Gervin was now quickly becoming a role player and the Spurs just as quickly were transforming from brash contenders into meek also-rans.

Thus the '83–'84 season would launch a slide covering six seasons which would almost exactly match in overall length both the team's first seven years as a NBA contender, and a later period of powerhouse status which would soon arrive with the acquisition of David Robinson. This losing interlude would result in one 4th-place finish, three fifths, and a pair of sixths. The only truly bright spot would be the offensive and defensive play of Alvin Robertson. Robertson was a club-leading scorer (1987, 1988) at the guard slot who was also several-time NBA Defensive Player of the Year.

This embarrassing skid in the mid-portion of Spurs NBA history would reach its eventual low point with the 21–61 record posted in 1988–'89 under Larry Brown. The well-travelled Brown had joined the club after a most recent stopover of five years at the University of Kansas, a tenure which had included a rare NCAA championship. Previously Brown had coached the ABA Carolina Cougars and Denver Rockets, the NBA Nuggets and Nets, and UCLA. But Brown's return to the NBA in 1988 was to prove a rude shock indeed. The sometimes miracle-working coach wasn't given much to work with; the Spurs featured a starting lineup of Greg Anderson, Willie Anderson, Frank Brickowski, Vernon Maxwell, and Alvin Robertson. For the first time in club history the team was without a legitimate star of any ilk. And the won-lost record was better than only that year's two brand new expansion ballclubs in Charlotte (winners of twenty games) and Miami (winners of 15).

But help was already on the way and thus club management and fans could grin and bare the poor showing with the confidence of much better days lurking around the corner. Two years earlier the Spurs had won a lottery drawing that had given them the first overall pick in the 1987 collegiate draft. With that choice they had grabbed a seven-foot superstar from the U.S. Naval Academy who had just paced the US Pan American Games squad and who owned ''phenom'' credentials as well. David Robinson had been the first player in NCAA history to score 2,500 points and garner 1,300 rebounds, while also shooting better than 60% from the field. Robinson thus had ''franchise player'' credentials written all over him. But he also faced two years of required naval duty before he could join any NBA team. The Admiral—it seemed to everyone in San Antonio at the time—would of course immediately prove in 1989 that he had been well worth the long wait.

Adrift Under the Landlocked Admiral

The Spurs team that David Robinson would join in the fall of 1989 was one that had undergone a complete makeover between seasons. Robinson would be far from the only new face to join the second edition of the Larry Brown-coached Spurs. Terry Cummings had been acquired from Milwaukee for Alvin Robertson and Greg Anderson in order to staff the forecourt; Maurice Cheeks and David Wingate arrived from Philadelphia to partially man the guard slots. Veteran free agent center Caldwell Jones had also been signed up as extra insurance and as a practice player to test Robinson. And that summer's draft had yielded another plum in athletic forward Sean Elliott, out of the University of Arizona.

The new-look team quickly put on a new game face the way none in

NBA history had ever done before them. Everyone expected the Spurs to be improved with the rusty, but nonetheless dominating, Robinson and with the talented but inexperienced rookie Sean Elliott. But no one expected them to be quite as good as they actually proved to be. The club sprinted to a 19–7 mark by New Year's, a 32–14 ledger at the All-Star break, and a 56–26 division leading final record. The 35-game turnaround in won-lost record proved to be the greatest in NBA history. The Admiral and his fleet had definitely arrived.

But despite a nearly identical record the following year, it soon became increasingly clear that the Spurs with Robinson were a good team, but not yet one ready to challenge for a post-season title. For two straight seasons with Robinson, Larry Brown's teams disappointed during the playoff season and were ousted in the very first round of competition. During the Admiral's third campaign Brown was dismissed and replaced with long-time club executive Bob Bass, but again the season ended with a collapse in post-season's round one. Jerry Tarkanian next came from the college ranks to the Spurs bench to start the '92–'93 campaign; Tark was fresh from a long and bitter squabble with NCAA and UNLV administrators and was seeking fresh stimulation in the play-for-pay league. But the outspoken UNLV coach was unprepared for the player-oriented NBA and never lasted through the first month of the season. Tark's replacement would be former Spurs guard John Lucas, who was handed the clipboard after only 20 games. Lucas was popular with his players and effected a turnaround (40–22 under Lucas) which salvaged much of the 1993 season. Yet once again the Spurs disappointed in falling by the wayside during the second round of the playoffs.

Despite post-season failures, David Robinson has emerged in the past several seasons as perhaps the premier big man in a league filled with such new pivot talent as Shaquille O'Neal, Hakeem Olajuwon, Patrick Ewing, and Alonzo Mourning. If David Robinson ranks a few notches behind Hakeem Olajuwon and Patrick Ewing as the strongest contemporary center, it is only because of a subtle difference in playing styles. Olajuwon and Ewing are traditional post-men who employ bulk and brawn to intimidate and totally control the zone that extends five to ten feet from the basket. Robinson is a more mobile big man, one who will entice his counterpart into a no-man's land near the top of the paint, and then bury him with a series of deadly jumpers, hooks, and fadeaways. It is a technique that was good enough to allow The Admiral to emerge as the first NBA scoring leader at the dawn of the post-Jordan NBA era.

Robinson had seemingly seen his opening to burst on the scene as a true league superstar with the retirement of Michael Jordan in fall 1993. Media, advertisers, and the league as a whole had pushed Orlando rookie Shaq O'Neal as Jordan's heir-apparent to the title of NBA showcase player. But Robinson overtook Shaq on several fronts when he stormed down the latter portions of the season to cop the league's scoring championship from O'Neal himself. It took a Herculean effort on Robinson's part in the end, though. The Admiral scored a club-record 71 points in the season's final game, to narrowly edge Shaq in the tight point race. It was clearly a finish reminiscent of the one between Gervin and David Thompson a decade and a half earlier. It also left David Robinson as the first center to win a scoring title since Kareem Abdul-Jabbar had done so more than twenty seasons in the past.

The Spurs had added another weapon to their arsenal for the '93–'94 campaign in the now increasingly desperate effort to reach again the upper rounds of post-season play. Sean Elliott had been dealt to Detroit in a major deal for Dennis Rodman on the eve of the season; the game plan was to obtain the NBA's premier rebounder and thus get the ball even more frequently into the hands of an offense-minded David Robinson. The deal was a huge gamble: Elliott was an outstanding defender whose offensive arsenal was also seemingly unlimited. Dennis Rodman, by contrast, brought along a reputation for colorful and intense play and often bizarre behavior as well, both on and off the court. He had been nicknamed "The Worm" by Detroit fans, strutted and taunted in front of opposition players, and had even bleached his hair an array of blond and orange colors like a circus clown. Rodman easily captured another rebound title (17.3 rpg.) and assisted a high-powered offense of Robinson, three-point shot specialist Dale Ellis, Terry Cummings and Lloyd Daniels. And the team had a spanking new venue to boast of, as well, having moved into the plush new Alamodome with its standard-fare luxury boxes and 21,372 seating capacity that could be expanded to 35,000 for overflow crowds. But despite all these perks, and despite their solid second-place finish and 55 victories in a loaded Western Conference, the Spurs would again prove one of the biggest disappointment of post-season play. The Utah Jazz, with Karl Malone outplaying Robinson, would quickly eliminate a San Antonio club which could top the 100-point mark only one time during a four-game series.

The eighteen seasons that have marked the history of the San Antonio Spurs in the NBA began on a mountain top, eventually slipped into a deep, dark valley, and have finally scaled partway back up the steep sides of the rugged peak. But the early and late phases of team history have been sufficient to leave the Spurs unchallenged as still the very best among ABA refugee teams attempting to play competitively in the NBA.

Suggested Readings on San Antonio Spurs

O'Brien, Jim. **American Basketball Association All-Stars.** New York: Lancer Books, 1972.

Pluto, Terry. **Loose Balls—The Short, Wild Life of the American Basketball Association as Told by the Players, Coaches, and Movers and Shakers Who Made It Happen.** New York and London: Simon and Schuster, 1990

San Antonio Spurs Retired Uniform Numbers (2)

James Silas (13)
George Gervin (44)

Year-by-Year San Antonio Spurs Summary

Season	Record	Finish	Coach(es)	Scoring Leader(s)	Playoffs (W-L Record)
Key: * = Tied for Position; # = League Scoring Leader; ** = Playing Coach					
American Basketball Association					
Dallas Chaparrals					
1967–68	46–32	2nd	Cliff Hagan**	John Beasley (19.7)	Lost in 2nd round (4–4)
1968–69	41–37	4th	Cliff Hagan**	Cincy Powell (19.4)	Lost in 1st Round (3–4)
1969–70	45–39	2nd	Cliff Hagan** Max Williams	Glen Combs (22.2)	Lost in 1st Round (2–4)
Texas Chaparrals					
1970–71	30–54	4th*	Max Williams Bill Blakely	Donnie Freeman (23.6)	Lost in 1st Round (0–4)
Dallas Chaparrals					
1971–72	42–42	3rd	Tom Nissalke	Donnie Freeman (24.1)	Lost in 1st Round (0–4)
1972–73	28–56	5th	Babe McCarthy Dave Brown	Rich Jones (22.3)	Did not Qualify
San Antonio Spurs					
1973–74	45–39	3rd	Tom Nissalke	George Gervin (19.4)	Lost in 1st Round (3–4)
1974–75	51–33	2nd	Tom Nissalke Bob Bass	George Gervin (23.4)	Lost in 1st Round (2–4)
1975–76	50–34	3rd	Bob Bass	James Silas (23.8)	Lost in 1st Round (3–4)
National Basketball Association					
1976–77	44–38	3rd	Doug Moe	George Gervin (23.1)	Lost in 1st Round (0–2)
1977–78	52–30	1st	Doug Moe	George Gervin (27.2)#	Lost in 1st Round (2–4)
1978–79	48–34	1st	Doug Moe	George Gervin (29.6)#	Lost in 3rd Round (7–7)
1979–80	41–41	2nd*	Doug Moe Bob Bass	George Gervin (33.1)#	Lost in 1st Round (1–2)
1980–82	52–30	1st	Stan Albeck	George Gervin (27.1)	Lost in 1st Round (3–4)
1981–82	48–34	1st	Stan Albeck	George Gervin (32.3)#	Lost in 3rd Round (4–5)
1982–83	53–29	1st	Stan Albeck	George Gervin (26.2)	Lost in 3rd Round (6–5)
1983–84	37–45	5th	Morris McHone Bob Bass	George Gervin (25.9)	Did Not Qualify
1984–85	41–41	4th	C. Fitzsimmons	Mike Mitchell (22.2)	Lost in 1st Round (2–3)
1985–86	35–47	6th	C. Fitzsimmons	Mike Mitchell (23.4)	Lost in 1st Round (0–3)
1986–87	28–54	6th	Bob Weiss	Alvin Robertson (17.7)	Did Not Qualify
1987–88	31–51	5th	Bob Weiss	Alvin Robertson (19.6)	Lost in 1st Round (0–3)
1988–89	21–61	5th	Larry Brown	Willie Anderson (18.6)	Did Not Qualify
1989–90	56–26	1st	Larry Brown	David Robinson (24.3)	Lost in 2nd Round (6–4)
1990–91	55–27	1st	Larry Brown	David Robinson (25.6)	Lost in 1st Round (1–3)
1991–92	47–35	2nd	Larry Brown Bob Bass	David Robinson (23.2)	Lost in 1st Round (0–3)
1992–93	49–33	2nd	J. Tarkanian John Lucas	David Robinson (23.4)	Lost in 2nd Round (5–5)
1993–94	55–27	2nd	John Lucas	David Robinson (29.8)#	Lost in 1st Round(1–3)

Individual Career Leaders and Record Holders (1967–1994)

Scoring Average	George Gervin (26.3 ppg., 1973–85)
Points Scored (NBA/ABA)	George Gervin (23,602, 1973–85)
Points Scored (NBA)	George Gervin (19,383, 1976–85)
Games Played	George Gervin (899)
Field Goal Pct.	Artis Gilmore (.620)
3-Pt. Field Goals (ABA)	Glen Combs (260)
3-Pt. Field Goals (NBA)	Dale Ellis (250)
3-Pt. Field Goal Pct.	Dale Ellis (.397)
Free Throws Made	George Gervin (5,096)
Free-Throw Pct.	Johnny Dawkins (.861)
Rebounds	George Gervin (4,841)
Personal Fouls	George Gervin (2,797)
Assists	Johnny Moore (3,865)
Steals	George Gervin (1,159)
Blocked Shots	David Robinson (1,473)

Individual Single-Season and Game Records (1967–1994)

Scoring Average	George Gervin (33.1 ppg., 1979–80)
Points Scored (Season)	George Gervin (2,585, 1983–84)
Points Scored (Game)	David Robinson (71, 4-24-94 at Los Angeles Clippers)
Field Goal Pct. (Season)	Steve Johnson (.632, 1985–86)
Free-Throw Pct. (Season)	Johnny Dawkins (.896, 1987–88)
3-Pt. Field Goal Pct. (Season)	Reggie Williams (.538, 1990–91)
Personal Fouls (ABA Season)	John Smith (328, 1968–69)
Personal Fouls (NBA Season)	Mark Olberding (307, 1980–81)
Rebounds (Season)	Dennis Rodman (1,367, 1993–94)
Rebound Average (Season)	Dennis Rodman (17.3, 1993–94)
Rebounds (Game)	Dennis Rodman (32, 1-22-94 vs. Dallas Mavericks)
Assists (Season)	Johnny Moore (816, 1984–85)
Assists (Game)	John Lucas (24, 4-15-84 vs. Denver Nuggets)
Steals (Season)	Alvin Robertson (301, 1985–86)

Best Trade in Franchise History

It happened early in franchise history—on January 30, 1974—way back in the midst of long-forgotten red, white, and blue ABA days. After a month of haggling and in-fighting, Angelo Drossos and his partners inked the largest deal in club history when they purchased the contract of George Gervin from the ABA-rival Virginia Squires. Before he was done, George Gervin would own just about every club record (he still possesses many of them) and would be the uncontested "all-time franchise player"—that is until David Robinson came along.

Worst Trade in Franchise History

The Spurs haven't made many deals that were pure bummers, yet the one in which they unloaded Vernon Maxwell (February, 21, 1990) to the Houston Rockets for a token cash payment comes very close. It is true that Maxwell was a problem child in San Antonio, just as he would prove to be in Houston. But this flashy trash-talking guard seemed to be enough by himself to vault the Houston Rockets over the Spurs in the 1994 regular-season standings. And if Maxwell needed to go, at least his market value might have brought another recognizable star (or at least a proven starter) in exchange for a ballhandler and three-point bomber who could star in any backcourt in the league.

San Antonio Spurs Historical Oddity

Never—at least not in pro basketball of the modern era—has a team relocated its franchise four different times and yet remained within the same state throughout all this ceaseless shifting. The early ABA days saw the club start as the Dallas Chaparrals, become the multi-housed Texas Chaparrals, return to Dallas, and then migrate to San Antonio and take on the identity of the present-day Spurs. This may indeed have once been a ballclub with a noticeable identity crisis, but it was also one that, for all is wanderlust, never strayed very far away from home.

Spurs All-Time Number One Draft Picks List

American Basketball Association
Dallas Chaparrals
1967 Matthew Aitch (Michigan State)
1968 Shaler Halimon (Utah State)
1969 Willie Brown (Middle Tennessee State)
Texas Chaparrals
1970 Nate "Tiny" Archibald (Texas El-Paso)
Dallas Chaparrals
1971 Roger Brown (Kansas)
1972 LaRue Martin (Loyola-Chicago)
San Antonio Spurs
1973 Dwight Jones (Houston)
1974 None

1975 Mark Olberding (Minnesota)
1976 Louis Dampier (Kentucky)
National Basketball Association
1977 None
1978 Frankie Sanders (Southern)
1979 Wiley Peck (Mississippi State)
1980 Reggie Johnson (Tennessee)
1981 None
1982 None
1983 John Paxson (Notre Dame)
1984 Alvin Robertson (Arkansas)
1985 Alfredrick Hughes (Loyola-Chicago)
1986 Johnny Dawkins (Duke)
1987 David Robinson (Navy)
1988 Willie Anderson (Georgia)
1989 Sean Elliott (Arizona)
1990 Dwayne Schintzius (Florida)
1991 None
1992 Tracy Murray (UCLA)
1993 None

Chapter 22

DENVER NUGGETS

Mile High and Almost Always Earthbound

All-Time Franchise Record: 1153–1067, .519 Pct. (1967–1994)
NBA Record: 740–736, .501 Pct.; ABA Record: 413–331, .556 Pct.
NBA Championships: None; ABA Champions: None
Greatest Franchise Player: Alex English (1979–1990)
All-Time Leading Scorer: Alex English (21,645 Points, 1979–1990)
Most Successful Coach: Doug Moe (432–357, .548 Pct., 1981–1990)
All-Time Franchise Team: Dan Issel (C), David Thompson (F), Alex English (F),
Lafayete Lever (G), Michael Adams (G)

For the briefest of moments at the outset of the 1994 NBA post-season festival, the Denver Nuggets finally captured the attention and respect of the entire basketball world. The team with no recognizable superstars and the NBA's youngest roster—a dozen players who barely averaged 25 years of age—had somehow pulled off one of the most dramatic upsets in a full half-century of NBA playoffs. For the first time in ten years under the new post-season format, a number-eight seed had defeated a number-one seed. A team that had limped through the campaign at .500 had embarrassed the team with the league's best record and had thus established genuine parity as the new NBA watch-word. The Denver Nuggets' no-name overachievers were, for a moment at least, basketball's biggest front-page story.

The Denver victory over the Seattle SuperSonics in the opening round of the 1994 playoffs was packed with almost as much drama and flair as it was stuffed full of surprise. The supercharged Sonics, with enforcer Shawn Kemp anchoring the front line, had posted the NBA's best record at 63–19 and had lost only four contests on their home floor all season long. And Seattle would quickly establish its role as heavy favorite with back-to-back homecourt wins (106–82 and 97–87) over the seemingly outmanned Denver club. Then the Nuggets breathed new life on their home floor in McNichols Arena, while Seattle slumped with overconfidence. The Nuggets next orchestrated a sweep of their own, keyed by a 110–93 pasting of the Pacific Division champs in game three. And to prove that these two Denver upsets were no mere flukes, the Nuggets also took care of business one final time in Seattle Coliseum, shocking the reeling Sonics 98–94 in a dramatic overtime match. In perhaps the largest win of franchise history the Issel-coached Nuggets were inspired by an offensive onslaught from journeyman guard Robert Pack, tenacious rebounding by Brian Williams, and enforcer play from improving 7–2 center Dikembe Mutombo. Mutombo proved the ultimate hero with an NBA playoff record 31 blocked shots for the five-game set.

While the Nuggets were bound to lose their Cinderella slipper and eventually fade in a seven game series against the Utah Jazz during playoff round two, the moment in Seattle was nonetheless a highwater mark of ballclub history. The Denver Nuggets remain a basketball franchise that has inexplicably always lived deep within the shadows during its 27–year NBA and ABA lifespan. Some of the obscurity under which this franchise has labored may well be deserved. The team has managed, after all, to play very close to an even .500 ledger across 18 NBA campaigns. There have been no championships to celebrate, despite some reasonably good NBA outings (1977, 1978, 1985, 1988) and a couple of spectacular ABA campaigns. Only twice have the NBA Nuggets made it as far as the conference Finals, though they were actually the first of the four clubs entering from the ABA to do so.

But there is also a rather large element of surprise to this star-crossed team's seemingly endless obscurity. The Denver franchise was, after all, a true pillar of the American Basketball Association: known as the Rockets for seven seasons, the ABA Denver club posted four winning campaigns and, more importantly, remained financially stable in a league otherwise plagued by financial failures. During two final ABA seasons—now known as the Nuggets, and under the wing of precocious young coach Larry Brown—the ballclub posted stellar won-lost marks and drew record crowds of over 19,000 to McNichols Arena to witness the dying league's last-ever championship series. And during their final ABA season, Larry Brown's team also could boast one of the circuit's biggest gate attractions in the exciting North Carolina skywalker, David Thompson.

And the Denver ballclub has also had its finger directly on the pulse of cash-paying fans, for it is Denver, more that any other franchise, that has year-in and year-out, always featured a most colorful high-powered offensive style of play. The standard line on Denver teams was always the same: ''Boy, can these guys run and shoot! But won't they ever play any defense?'' And to add to such offensive excitement, three of the game's greatest high-scoring stars have at one time or another played here—Spencer Haywood, for one brief record-breaking season in '69–'70; the aforementioned Thompson, who once poured in 73 in a single NBA game;

and Alex English, seventh all-time scorer in NBA history who bagged all but a mere handful of his 25,000 career points as a Denver Nugget. The Nuggets can also boast two of the cage sport's more colorful coaches over the years in Doug Moe (nine seasons) and his successor Paul Westhead, who together directed free-roaming offenses for more than a dozen successive seasons. Yet without much television exposure in the late rounds of post-season play, the Denver Nuggets have predictably remained a back-page story down through the years.

Even when the Nuggets made their one great run at the top of the standings in late ABA days, events seemed to conspire to keep them out of the headlines. Twice the team coached by Larry Brown stumbled in the late stages of post-season play, just when they seemed on the very verge of emerging as the cream of the league with the red, white, and blue ball. The Nuggets outdistanced everyone in sight with 65 victories in '74–'75, only to fall victim to a rejuvenated Indiana Pacers squad in the second round of the playoffs. A year later they again soared past the 60–victory mark and stood atop a weakened league now reduced to a single division, with but seven remaining teams. But the post-season derby once more brought disappointment as the second-place New York Nets with Julius Erving outlasted David Thompson and company in the six-game championship shootout. The ABA itself was now flat on its back and confined to its deathbed by this time. Thus when the Nuggets were at their very best under Larry Brown, the sad fact was that almost no one was bothering to watch anymore.

The Nuggets began their quarter-century history sporting a different league and a different nickname from the ones currently familiar to the '80s and '90s pro basketball follower. The Denver Rockets were one of the original eleven franchises of the bold, if under-capitalized experiment once known as the American Basketball Association. Colorado trucking industry executive J. W. "Bill" Ringsby had put the franchise together and was the original ballclub owner (along with his two sons) from its inaugural season in 1967–'68 through its fifth ABA campaign in 1972. The first transfer of ballclub ownership came in December, 1972, when Ringsby sold out to a pair of San Diego business partners, Frank M. Goldberg and A. G. "Bud" Fischer. And it was during these earliest seasons that the team played under the high-flying jet-age logo of "Rockets" rather than the later, more familiar, Nuggets label. With head coach Bill Bass drawing the x's and o's the Denver team got out of the gate well by posting two winning seasons (45–33 and 44–34) and logging two middle-of-the-pack third-place Western Division finishes. Much of the team's early success was due to the firepower of high-scoring forward-guard Larry Jones, who posted fifth and first place finishes of his own in the league's first couple of individual scoring derbies.

A first truly memorable year in Denver's ABA sojourn came in a third season of play and began with the landmark signing of Olympic hero Spencer Haywood of the University of Detroit. As much a relentless rebounder as he was an undefensible scorer, the 6'9" Haywood had grabbed national attention with a remarkable 1968 Olympic performance which came flush on the heels of a 32.1 ppg. freshman team scoring average at Detroit. After only a single sophomore collegiate varsity season (in which he earned All-American honors) Haywood had now decided to blaze new trails as the first athlete to leave school early and opt for a contract with the player-hungry ABA. While the lawyers and courts settled the issue of his eligibility to play in the more prestigious NBA—the established league maintained a policy forbidding its teams from signing undergraduates— the 20-year-old Haywood, for his own part, posted one of the greatest single seasons by any player in the history of professional play.

Quite simply put, Haywood proved his immediate worth by taking both Denver and the ABA by firestorm. He averaged a lofty 30 points and 16 rebounds throughout his first season and was totally unchallenged as the new circuit's showcase rookie talent of 1970. Thus the court on which Spencer Haywood would leave his most immediate mark was the one on which the leather balls were being bounced and the professional stars were showcasing their exciting action. In a rookie season without parallel Spencer Haywood was simultaneously the league MVP, scoring champ, rebounding leader, All-Star Game MVP, and also Rookie-of-the-Year for good measure.

With Haywood running the floor, the Rockets were suddenly supercharged, picked up a full head of steam, and shot off the launching pad in season number three. The launch was actually somewhat rough at first, as the team made a difficult adjustment to its new highscoring superstar and also to a rookie coach named John McLendon. After a stumbling 9–19 start McLendon was canned and replaced by former referee Joe Belmont, who seemed to work immediate magic with a new lineup of Haywood and Julie Hammond in the frontcourt, Byron Beck at center, and Larry Jones (the shooting guard) and Lonnie Wright (the playmaker) handling backcourt duties. Belmont reversed club fortunes almost overnight as the Rockets rebounded to a 17–2 spurt under their new mentor. By season's end, Denver owned its first Western Division title with a comfortable six-game cushion over runnerup Dallas. Post-season brought a first-ever trip into the second round of playoff action, reason for optimism despite a disappointing five-game losing series against the Los Angeles Stars. And the Rockets boasted not only the league's scoring leader in phenomenal rookie Spencer Haywood but the number five leading pointmaker as well in Larry Jones (24.9 ppg.).

A collective moan could be heard throughout the entire new league— most loudly in the Mile High City, of course—when Spencer Haywood opted for the NBA before the next full season had ended. Haywood would actually sit out the first half of the new campaign with a broken finger, and then demand a renegotiated (and far more lucrative) contract from the Rockets before finally signing on with the Seattle SuperSonics with slightly more than a month of 1971 play remaining. An NBA ban on undergraduates still technically stood, but not for long, once Haywood and Sonics management filed a lawsuit against the league which quickly prompted a shift in policy and an institution of special "hardship exceptions" for those qualified (to be translated as "talented enough") underclassmen ballplayers.

Haywood's loss to the Rockets and the ABA was staggering, yet not fatal. A second "hardship case" over in the ABA (where such semantic distinctions were already in full effect) had now joined the Rockets from the college ranks, to partially soften the blow of Haywood's sudden defection. Ralph Simpson, a 6'5" guard-forward with high-scoring potential, had left Michigan State to ink a contract with Denver; but Simpson broke in slowly in the fast-paced pro ranks and remained only a reserve (averaging 14.2 ppg.) during his rookie year. Other significant roster moves had brought the off-season trade of sharpshooting backcourt ace Larry Jones to the Miami ballclub (for Don Sidle) and a subsequent late-season swap of versatile frontcourt man Sidle (along with guard Wayne Chapman) to the Indiana Pacers for forward Art Becker and guard John Barnhill. Larry Cannon (26.6 ppg.) now picked up the scoring burden in the absence of Haywood and Jones, but the numerous player shifts were seemingly injurious to continued ballclub health. With their big gun now gone (Haywood) and the supporting cast (Jones and Sidle) depleted, the Rockets unraveled. Joe Belmont was replaced by Stan Albeck during the first month but this did nothing to stem a rapid downward slide. In one season, then, Denver's ballclub had managed to reverse their record by 20 full games in a negative direction.

The first of numerous top-level management changes soon to unfold in Denver occurred smack on the heals of the disappointing 1971 season. Successful NBA head coach Alex Hannum (most recently with the expansion San Diego Rockets) was hastily recruited to replace the short-lived Stan Albeck on the bench. Hannum would actually wear three simultaneous hats—those of coach, general manager and ballclub president—which perhaps left him few worries about pleasing his superiors as coach, but left precious little time to plan game strategy and coordinate scouting and player personnel activities at one and the same time.

The experiment seemed sound enough in the early going, however, as Hannum slowly but surely refueled the ABA Rockets' depleted offensive engines, and thus revved up the pace of their run-and-shoot game. In Hannum's second season, for example, the team had already climbed back over .500 at 47–37 and edged into third place in the Western Division. Warren Jabali (picked up in a dispersal draft from the defunct Miami franchise) provided important backcourt leadership which in turn sprung open the considerable scoring talents of Ralph Simpson (26.4 ppg. in 1973). But injuries to three starters (Marv Roberts, Warren Jabali and Byron Beck) perhaps cost the Rockets a legitimate shot at the league title during post-season play. The crippled Denver team was quickly eliminated in five games by the eventual champion Indiana Pacers.

Although Spencer Haywood was now gone from the scene, the Rockets still could boast a substantial offensive star in Ralph Simpson. The free-shooting Simpson soon warmed to an ABA run-and-gun style of forward-oriented fast-breaking play. He would thus lead the Denver ballclub in scoring all three seasons under Coach Hannum and even stood fourth in the individual league scoring race in '71–'72. Others also contributed, as center Dave Robisch soon cracked the ABA's top ten in field goal percentage; Julius Keye proved one of the circuit's proficient rebounders (10.7 rpg. in 1973); and Warren Jabali narrowly trailed San Diego's Chuckie Williams as the ABA's top assists producer during his first season with the team. New club ownership also contributed to a widespread feeling that the Denver Rockets were now again on the verge of returning to the lofty hopes that had once accompanied their third league season.

Yet Hannum's own third season in command only brought with it another painful reversal of fortune, both at the gate and in the league standings. When the team slipped back under .500, tumbled ten games off the previous year's pace (37–47), and thus toppled into fourth place in the division and fell out of the playoff hunt as well, further dramatic changes seemed in order. New ownership made them swiftly and decisively. Hannum gracefully stepped aside and was replaced by 37–year-old Carl Scherer as the new combined president and general manager in charge of all basketball operations. And former all-star guard Larry Brown, who had now launched a most successful coaching career as mentor of the Carolina Cougars (104–64 in his first two seasons on the bench), was also brought on board, hopefully to reverse ballclub fortunes. A new 18,500–seat plush facility was also under construction, adjacent to football's Mile High Stadium, and had already been announced to open for the '75–'76 season as McNichols Arena. And to indicate still further that the Denver team was now completely primed to follow new directions, a change of club name and corresponding team logo was also unveiled. The Denver Rockets would henceforth be prospecting for their championship ''gold'' as the rechristened Denver Nuggets.

Never before or since have such apparent cosmetic changes bought such a dramatic and immediate reversal of ballclub fortunes, or a more measurable set of substantial results. Under the bench strategy of 34–year-old Larry Brown, Denver shot to a sterling 65–19 mark—a record not matched to this day by any other Nuggets team—and to a second franchise division title as well. The Indiana Pacers would abruptly end this first Larry Brown run at an ABA championship for Denver in a thrilling Western Division championship battle. In the final ABA contest, played in Denver Auditorium, the Pacers surprised their hosts and posted a shocking seventh-game West Conference title victory right on the Nuggets' own home floor. Indiana's league co-MVP George McGinnis was just too much for Larry Brown's Denver squad as he poured in 40 points and pulled down 23 rebounds in a convincing 104–96 Pacers victory.

But things had only seemed to be starting up for Larry Brown in Denver and Mile High basketball fans were understandably estatic about their "New Nuggets" and Coach Brown, despite ominous signs that the league as a whole was now rapidly coming apart at the seams. Dave DeBusschere, a star on the 1970 and 1973 Knicks NBA championship teams, had been installed as the new ABA Commissioner in a desperate move to upgrade the struggling circuit's image. Yet just about all the remaining news surrounding the wavering league was now consistently bad. Except perhaps in Denver, where the Nuggets had succeeded in signing the first pick (David Thompson of North Carolina State) and third pick (Marvin Webster of Morgan State) among players tabbed in the recent NBA draft. With their spanking new showcase home in McNichols Arena, and with the acrobatic Thompson and shot-blocking Webster installed in the lineup, the Nuggets promised to be the only first class act the failing ABA now had left. And Larry Brown's outfit didn't disappoint as they raced to another 60–win season while outdistancing Julius Erving and the New York Nets by five full games.

Denver's only appearance in a championship final would thus ironically come in what proved to be the swansong year of the fatally stricken American Basketball Association. If crowds had shrunk to smatterings of the curious in other spots around the league, this certainly wasn't true in Denver, where an all-time league record 19,034 patrons crammed into spacious McNichols for the opening contest of the ABA's final championship series. Julius Erving stole the show that night with 45 points and a buzzer-beating game-winning hoop to pace New York to a thrilling 120–118 lidlifting victory; but a second record crowd of better than 19,107 went home happier only three nights later, as the Nuggets evened the score 127–121, despite another 48 points from the incredible Dr. J. This was to be Julius Erving's crowning ABA series. The Nets would eventually reign in six games, however, despite an answering 42 points from David Thompson during the final contest of ABA history.

The dramatic rebound of the once endangered and impotent Denver franchise under the oncourt leadership of Larry Brown, and front office leadership of a new ownership team (Bud Fischer and Frank Goldberg) was not a crowd pleaser in Denver alone. It had also been sufficient to turn heads in Chicago and New York, and thus to secure an expansion spot in the prestigious NBA at the time of inevitable ABA collapse and demise. And if the Nuggets had left the crumbling ABA as one of the ill-fated circuit's strongest performers—a young ballclub boasting a talented lineup of several potential superstars in David Thompson, Dan Issel, and Ralph Simpson—they next entered the established NBA without ever missing a step or a heartbeat. While the three other ABA interlopers (San Antonio, Indiana, and the New York Nets) struggled with their new surroundings, Brown's Nuggets ate up the NBA Midwest Division in their very first year out of the starting gate. Denver rode the high scoring of Thompson (25.9 ppg.) and Issel (22.3 ppg.) to 50 wins and a comfortable first-place finish. No other first-year NBA entrant of the modern era has, in fact, ever fared quite so well in its maiden year.

The lineup which the Denver Nuggets carried into their first-ever NBA playoff series in April, 1977, against Portland was a mix of ABA holdovers and NBA newcomers. David Thompson, Dan Issel and forward Bobby Jones had been starters in the ABA Finals a year earlier. Ralph Simpson was now gone, shipped to Detroit in a three-cornered deal which had landed forward Paul Silas from the Boston Celtics. And Ted McClain had joined the squad from the New York Nets as the second starting guard. While the Trail Blazers were able to eliminate the Nuggets (4–2) from that first taste of post-season action, Brown's club returned hungrier than ever the following season, to earn still another Midwest Division title and another crack at playoff magic. And the second time around, the Nuggets were able to hang on until the Western Conference Finals before being jettisoned by the Seattle SuperSonics in another hard-fought six-game shootout.

Dr. J may well have been the brightest star plucked from the carcass of the ABA by NBA opportunists, but David Thompson rated right up there as well, perhaps as the undisputed number two. And at moments you could hardly tell the two "hangtime" heroes apart. If Dr. J was basketball's original inventor of "hangtime" and perhaps the game's most creative high-flying dunker, then David Thompson was one of the most acrobatic scoring machines ever seen on a hardwood floor. The 1975 college "player of the year" and 1974 NCAA tournament MVP, Thompson during the late '70s was a crowd-pleasing one-man magic act who singlehandedly filled up seats and posted arena sellouts at the same rate as his contemporary Erving, or his successors Larry Bird and Michael Jordan. He also left a legacy of legendary performances that almost read like fiction. One was his manó-a-manó battle with Dr. J in McNichols Arena during the first and last ABA slam dunk contest, an event which later spawned the NBA version of an annual slamfest. And another was his explosion for 73 points (at Detroit on April 8, 1978) that remains the third highest mark (behind Chamberlain's 100 and 78) in NBA history. That single game scoring outburst was also part of the closest and most dramatic individual scoring race in NBA history as George Gervin drilled 63 himself later that same night to edge Thompson by mere percentage points for the title.

But for all his scoring pyrotechnics, David Thompson would, in the end, sadly be best remembered for his abuses of fame and his lingering personal failures. Denver's budding superstar might well have ranked right alongside Oscar Robertson, Jordan, Erving and perhaps Elgin Baylor as the greatest of all-time; instead his career and also his personal life flamed out early due to losing battles with substance abuse. Thompson's epic career was already slipping away only five years into his NBA sojourn. Slowed by injuries in '79–'80 (when he missed 43 games) and then by mounting off-court problems in 1981 and 1982, Thompson was eventually cut loose by the Nuggets at the end of the '81–'82 campaign. Two subsequent seasons in the togs of the Seattle Sonics also failed to revive David Thompson's now permanently stalled basketball career.

The true tragedy for Denver fans and league fans alike was that David Thompson's brilliant career (and his personal reputation as American sports hero to boot) were to burn out far too soon. And with the flaming crash of this high-flying superhero who had once owned the league's most impressive vertical leap (44") and greatest gift for showmanship, the entire Nuggets ballclub itself suddenly crashed and burned as well. A poor start in the fall of 1978—at the beginning of Thompson's final problem-free season—brought Larry Brown's resignation 53 games into the campaign. At the time the club was standing 28–25 and still flirting with a playoff spot. Replacement Donnie Walsh fired the reeling team to a 19–10 finish and a near first-place Midwest Division showing. Yet momentum was not sustained under Walsh, as Denver next dropped a short three-game first-round playoff series to an equally mediocre Los Angeles Lakers squad, which had little to boast itself beyond the skyhooks of Kareem Abdul-Jabbar.

Donnie Walsh, Brown's immediate replacement, proved little more than an undistinguished bridge separating two great franchise players and the ballclub's two best-ever coaches as well. Doug Moe would take over midway through the '80–'81 season after a four-year stint at the helm of the San Antonio Spurs. Moe had been an All-American guard at North Carolina and broke into the ABA with a flair as the second-leading scorer (behind Connie Hawkins) during the rebel league's very first season. His pro playing career had lasted only five season due to injuries, a tenure span he would triple as a professional coach. And it didn't hurt that Moe's arrival would coincide almost exactly with that of sweet-shooting forward Alex English who was stolen from the Indiana Pacers in a one-sided trade in February, 1980, for washed-up former ABA stalwart George McGinnis.

Moe and English would provide almost all the chapters and episodes in Denver basketball history throughout the entire span of the 1980s. For the next nine years the colorful and temperamental former ABA guard molded the ballclub in his own image. His 500-plus victories would eventually leave Doug Moe standing twelfth all-time among NBA coaches in games won. It was a fiery, and usually quite funny personality that was the lasting legacy of Coach Doug Moe, however. His colorful language (four-letter words where a post-game trademark), free-lancing style and informal approach to just about everything on and off the court were reflected throughout in high-scoring offensive-oriented teams which rarely ran set plays, rarely played defense with much dedication, and rarely failed to entertain with their end-to-end race-horse game. Moe didn't bring any championships to the Mile High City, but he *did* bring the most exciting and entertaining teams imaginable.

Over the next decade, Moe and his ballclub would average close to 45 victories a year. Denver would win a total of 432 regular-season contests during this span and claim first or second slot in the divisional standings four different times. The first-place finishes would come initially in 1985, when the club captured 52 contests, outdistanced second-place Houston by four games, then lost to the Lakers in a five-game Western Conference Finals matchup; and then again in 1988, when the victory total reached 54 (the best in the club's NBA history), the spread in the Midwest Division was a single game over Dallas, and the playoffs ended with a six-game loss to the Mavericks in the Western semifinal round. In short, despite several strong runs at the top and an overall record of excellence, Moe's teams could never find their way into (or even close to) the NBA Finals. Only in 1985, in fact, did a Moe-coached ballclub ever stick around long enough to reach a third-round shootout.

Moe's race-horse offensive style was ideally suited to the playing mode of lithe and cat-like small forward Alex English. Taking full advance of an offensive plan which got him the ball on the run and cleared out lanes to the basket, Alex English would hover above the 25 ppg. level for eight straight seasons and reign as NBA individual scoring champ in 1982–'83. He would eventually scale the 25,000 career point plateau (21,645 with Denver) and retire in 1990, as the seventh ranking scorer in NBA history (trailing only Jabbar, Chamberlain, Moses Malone, Elvin Hayes, Oscar Roberson and John Havlicek). The eight-time league All-Star was a virtual scoring machine who, like similar point-happy small forwards Adrian Dantley and Bernard King, was blessed with a lightening-like release and an unfailing nose for the basket.

With Moe's departure came a change in team leadership that hardly reflected any serious shift in ballplaying philosophy. If Coach Moe downplayed serious attention to tenacious defense, replacement Paul Westhead chucked the notion of aggressive defensive team pressure directly out the lockerroom window altogether. The former Lakers mentor arrived from his stint at Loyola Marymount College with a wide-open run-and-gun frenetic style of play that revved up scoring on both ends of the court. In the first few games of the season, Denver's new sieve-like defense gave up the incredible point totals of 173, 162 and 161 while attempting to outrun and outshoot its gleeful opponents. The result during Westheads' first season at the helm was a predictable 6–28 start and a final 20–62 ledger that ranks as the worst in franchise history. The 1990–'91 Denver club would demonstrate that scoring was indeed less than half the game as it led the circuit in points (119.9 ppg.) and yet was still outscored by its opponents by an average of more than ten points per contest.

If the Nuggets had seemingly hit rock bottom with Paul Westhead's zany and undisciplined offensive schemes, the blow—like other setbacks of the past—was not entirely fatal. Sure signs of revival, and even recovery in the club's constantly shifting fortunes could be discerned almost before ink was dry on the contract of a replacement coach. ABA Nuggets hero Dan Issel was the man of the hour, lured from his appointed post in the Kentucky state cabinet to take over the reins of the sagging NBA ballclub.

Denver benefitted not only from Issel's return put also from the on-court impact of two of the brightest prospects ever to come to the Mile High city from the collegiate basketball draft. Chris Jackson was selected as the third overall pick of the 1990 lottery and soon enjoyed a breakthrough season when he poured in over 1500 points during his third NBA session. Jackson had set three NCAA freshman records during his abbreviated LSU career, including most points (965) and highest scoring average (30.2 ppg.). And with a legal name change to Mahmoud Abdul-Rauf, the sharpshooting guard had perfected his act by the beginning of his fourth NBA campaign. Perhaps an even bigger prize, however, came in the hulking if unpolished form of Georgetown University seven-footer Dikembe Mutombo from Zaire. By only his third season Mutombo was the reigning shot blocking king of the circuit, and the second most accurate field goal shooter (behind Shaquille O'Neal) as well.

Abdul-Rauf and Mutombo now provided the Denver Nuggets with not only the strangest pair of names in all basketball, but with an unbeatable Mr. Outside and Mr. Inside combo as well. And Coach Issel's mature patience with his exceptionally young squad was already paying huge dividends by the opening round of the 1994 playoff marathon. With this combination of Issel, Abdul-Rauf and Mutombo—alongside talented contributors like Robert Pack, LaPhonso Ellis (number five overall pick in the 1992 draft), Marcus Liberty, and guard Bryant Stith—fortunes were again on the upswing in pro basketball's most neglected feature city. And Mile High fans again had reason for optimism that the up-and-down Nuggets were at long last prepared to strike gold.

Suggested Readings on Denver Nuggets

O'Brien, Jim. **American Basketball Association All-Stars**. New York: Lancer Books, 1972.

Pluto, Terry. **Loose Balls—The Short, Wild Life of the American Basketball Association as Told by the Players, Coaches, and Movers and Shakers Who Made It Happen**. New York and London: Simon and Schuster, 1990.

Denver Nuggets Retired Uniform Numbers (3)

David Thompson (33)
Byron Beck (40)
Dan Issel (44)

Year-by-Year Denver Nuggets Summary

Season	Record	Finish	Coach(es)	Scoring Leader(s)	Playoffs (W-L Record)

Key: * = Tied for Position; # = League Scoring Leader; ** = Formerly Chris Jackson
American Basketball Association

Denver Rockets

Season	Record	Finish	Coach(es)	Scoring Leader(s)	Playoffs (W-L Record)
1967–68	45–33	3rd	Bob Bass	Larry Jones (22.9)	Lost in 1st Round (2–3)
1968–69	44–34	3rd	Bob Bass	Larry Jones (28.4)#	Lost in 1st Round (3–4)
1969–70	51–33	1st	John McClendon Joe Belmont	Spencer Haywood (30.0)#	Lost in 2nd Round (5–7)
1970–71	30–54	4th*	Joe Belmont Stan Albeck	Larry Cannon (26.6)	Did Not Qualify
1971–72	34–50	4th	Alex Hannum	Ralph Simpson (27.4)	Lost in 1st Round (3–4)
1972–73	47–37	3rd	Alex Hannum	Ralph Simpson (23.3)	Lost in 1st Round (1–4)
1973–74	37–47	4th	Alex Hannum	Ralph Simpson (18.7)	Did Not Qualify

Denver Nuggets

Season	Record	Finish	Coach(es)	Scoring Leader(s)	Playoffs (W-L Record)
1974–75	65–19	1st	Larry Brown	Ralph Simpson (20.6)	Lost in 2nd Round (7–6)
1975–76	60–24	1st	Larry Brown	David Thompson (26.0)	Lost in ABA Finals (6–7)

National Basketball Association

Season	Record	Finish	Coach(es)	Scoring Leader(s)	Playoffs (W-L Record)
1976–77	50–32	1st	Larry Brown	David Thompson (25.9)	Lost in 1st Round (2–4)
1977–78	48–34	1st	Larry Brown	David Thompson (27.2)	Lost in 3rd Round (6–7)
1978–79	47–35	2nd	Larry Brown Donnie Walsh	David Thompson (24.0)	Lost in 1st Round (1–2)
1979–80	30–52	3rd	Donnie Walsh	Dan Issel (23.8)	Did Not Qualify
1980–81	37–45	4th	Donnie Walsh Doug Moe	David Thompson (25.5)	Did Not Qualify
1981–82	46–36	2nd	Doug Moe	Alex English (25.4)	Lost in 1st Round (1–2)
1982–83	45–37	2nd	Doug Moe	Alex English (28.4)#	Lost in 2nd Round (3–5)
1983–84	38–44	3rd	Doug Moe	Kiki Vandeweghe (29.4)	Lost in 1st Round (2–3)
1984–85	52–30	1st	Doug Moe	Alex English (27.9)	Lost in 3rd Round (8–7)
1985–86	47–35	2nd	Doug Moe	Alex English (29.6)	Lost in 2nd Round (5–5)
1986–87	37–45	4th	Doug Moe	Alex English (28.6)	Lost in 1st Round (0–3)
1987–88	54–28	1st	Doug Moe	Alex English (25.0)	Lost in 2nd Round (5–6)
1988–89	44–38	3rd	Doug Moe	Alex English (26.5)	Lost in 1st Round (0–3)
1989–90	43–39	4th	Doug Moe	Lafayette Lever (18.3)	Lost in 1st Round (0–3)
1990–91	20–62	7th	Paul Westhead	Michael Adams (26.5)	Did Not Qualify
1991–92	24–58	4th	Paul Westhead	Reggie Williams (18.2)	Did Not Qualify
1992–93	36–46	4th	Dan Issel	M. Abdul-Rauf (19.2)**	Did Not Qualify
1993–94	42–40	4th	Dan Issel	M. Abdul-Rauf (18.0)**	Lost in 2nd Round (6–6)

Individual Career Leaders and Record Holders (1967–1994)

Scoring Average	Alex English (25.9 ppg., 1979–90)
Points Scored	Alex English (21,645, 1979–90)
Games Played	Alex English (837)
Minutes Played	Alex English (29,893)
Field Goals Made	Alex English (8,953)
Field Goal Pct.	Kiki Vandeweghe (.541, 1980–84)
3-Pt. Field Goals	Michael Adams (630)

Free Throws Made	Dan Issel (4,214)
Free-Throw Pct.	Mahmoud Abdul-Rauf* (.921, 1990–94) (*formerly Chris Jackson)
Rebounds	Dan Issel (6,630)
Personal Fouls	Dan Issel (2,304)
Assists	Alex English (3,679)
Steals	Lafayette Lever (1,167)
Blocked Shots	Wayne Cooper (830)

Individual Single-Season and Game Records (1967–1994)

Scoring Average	Alex English (29.8 ppg., 1985–86)
Scoring Average (ABA)	Spencer Haywood (30.0, 1969–70)
Points Scored (Season)	Alex English (2,414, 1985–86)
Points Scored (Game)	David Thompson (73, 4-9-78 at Detroit Pistons)
Free-Throw Pct.	Mahmoud Abdul-Rauf (.956, 1993–94)
Rebounds (Season)	Dikembe Mutombo (1,070, 1992–93)
Rebound Average (Season)	Dikembe Mutombo (13.0 rpg., 1992–93)
Rebounds (Game)	Jerome Lane (25, 4–21–91 at Houston Rockets)
Personal Fouls (Season)	Dan Schayes (323, 1987–88)
Assists (Season)	Michael Adams (693, 1990–91)
Assists (Game)	Lafayette Lever (23, 4–21–89 at Golden State Warriors)
Steals (Season)	Lafayette Lever (223, 1987–88)
Steals (Game)	Lafayette Lever (10, 3-9-85 vs. Indiana Pacers)
Blocked Shots (Season)	Dikembe Mutombo (287, 1992–93)
Blocked Shots (Game)	Dikembe Mutombo (12, 4-18-93 vs. Los Angeles Clippers)

Best Trade in Franchise History

In the entire annals of the NBA perhaps no team has ever gotten so hefty a prize in exchange for the peddling away of a piece of damaged and unwanted merchandise. On February 1, 1980, promising third-year forward Alex English was acquired from the Indiana Pacers in exchange for NBA veteran and former Indiana University and ABA-Pacers legend George McGinnis. English would rapidly develop into a franchise-type player with Denver and prove to be one of the game's great offensive machines (25,613 career points) over the next full decade. McGinnis on the other hand was now only a shadow of his former self and contributed almost nothing after his return to the Hoosier State.

Worst Trade in Franchise History

Unlike most other NBA clubs, the Denver Nuggets have been largely able to avoid making that long-term or short-term franchise-derailing deal in which one or more established veterans are peddled in a gamble on some unproven youngster. Two deals in 1976–'77, however, did involve the firesale of a ton of proven offensive players for very little in return. In October, 1976, the newly admitted Denver NBA club worked a three-way swap with Boston and Detroit which sent proven ABA veteran Ralph Simpson on the Pistons, and in return brought Paul Silas from the Celtics to Denver. Silas, who still had miles left in him, was later that season packaged with center Marvin Webster and with another ABA legend, Willie Wise, and dealt to Seattle in exchange for seven-footer Tom Burleson and guard Bobby Wilkerson. It was largely smoke with little fire, yet Seattle did seem to reap the greater long-range benefits of this convoluted dealing.

Denver Nuggets Historical Oddity

For a brief spell in the mid and late '80s, the Nuggets franchise became widely known as the "Enver Nuggets"—since they featured absolutely no "D" for defense. Things started out this way with Coach Doug Moe, who emphasized a race-horse free-lance offense that put plenty of points on the board at both ends of the court (since Moe and his players had little taste for what happened on the defensive end of the floor). But it reached new heights of absurdity when Paul Westhead arrived on the scene and brought with him the frenzied fast-breaking game he had first developed at Loyola Marymount College. Under Westhead's approach to pushing the ball up the floor and unloading shots at a breathtaking pace, even by NBA standards, the Nuggets once actually gave up better than 160 points three times in short succession, and all within the first week of the season. It was a record for defensive breakdown that no NBA team is likely ever to approach again.

Nuggets All-Time Number One Draft Picks List

American Basketball Association
Denver Rockets
1967 Walt Frazier (Southern Illinois)
1968 Tom Boerwinkle (Tennessee)
1969 Bob Presley (California)
1970 Spencer Haywood (Detroit)
1971 Ralph Simpson (Michigan State)

1972 Bud Stallworth (Kansas)
1973 Ed Ratleff (Long Beach State)
Denver Nuggets
1974 James "Fly" Williams (Austin Peay)
1975 Marvin Webster (Morgan State)
National Basketball Association
1976 No Draft Selections
1977 Tom LaGarde (North Carolina)
1978 Rod Griffin (Wake Forest)
1979 None
1980 James Ray (Jacksonville)
1981 None
1982 Rob Williams (Houston)
1983 Howard Carter (LSU)
1984 None
1985 Blair Rasmussen (Oregon)
1986 Maurice Martin (St. Joseph's)
1987 None
1988 Jerome Lane (Pittsburgh)
1989 Todd Lichti (Stanford)
1990 Chris Jackson* (LSU) *Mahmoud Abdul-Rauf
1991 Dikembe Mutombo (Georgetown)
1992 LaPhonso Ellis (Notre Dame)
1993 Rodney Rogers (Wake Forest)

Chapter 23

DALLAS MAVERICKS

Some Teams Can't Even Lose Successfully

All-time Franchise Record: 479–669, .417 Pct. (1980–1994)
NBA Championships: None
Greatest Franchise Player: Rolando Blackman (1981–1992)
All-Time Leading Scorer: Rolando Blackman (16,643 Points, 1981–1992)
Most Successful Coach: John MacLeod (96–79, .549 Pct., 1987–1990)
All-Time Franchise Team: James Donaldson (C), Mark Aguirre (F), Roy Tarpley (F),
   Rolando Blackman (G), Derek Harper (G)

For almost two decades the 1973 Philadelphia 76ers stood unrivaled as basketball's worst team ever. That Philly team was so bad that it unwittingly earned a special stature to be recalled and discussed wherever basketball nostalgia buffs gather and relive the sport's past peaks and valleys. Sports fans love unshakable winners and sure-bet champions. But they have a special and enduring soft spot in their hearts for the most laughable among losers as well. And in the hardwood sport of basketball there has never been a loser as lovable as the 76ers outfit under freshman coach Roy Rubin, a team that won but nine of 82 games and usually looked bad even when it won. Philly's unthinkable 9–73 mark was never seriously challenged, even by such inept bunglers as the 1983 Pacers (20–62), or 1980 Detroit Pistons (16–66), or expansion 1981 Dallas Mavericks (16–67). Their cherished place in the dung heap of history was seemingly secure. Then along came the 1993 Dallas Mavericks under coach Rich Adubato. Here for the first time in nearly two decades was a team genuinely equipped to pilfer the stigma belonging to the worst team of all-time.

The lineup trucked out nightly by Adubato's Dallas team didn't—at first glance, at least—appear quite as inappropriate for successful big-time professional play as the one that had once worn Philly colors. Roy Rubin had, after all, been dealt a truly loaded deck in Philadelphia in 1972. Star

387

forward Billy Cunningham had been awarded by the courts to an ABA franchise in Carolina. Freddie Boyd was pressed into premature service at point guard and performed with ineptitude. A starting lineup of Tom Van Arsdale, Leroy Ellis, Manny Leaks, Fred Carter and Boyd was a full lineup of journeymen and has-beens.

Dallas seemed to have a much better stable of horses in fall, 1992. Derek Harper was still a quality point guard even with nine seasons already used up. Jim Jackson had been plucked from Ohio State with the fourth overall draft pick and seemed bound for immediate stardom (some were even comparing him to a rookie Jordan). Terry Davis (a 6'10" forward-center with a 10.2 ppg. average and nearly 700 rebounds a year earlier) and Sean Rooks (a 6'10" center who had just been taken in the 1992 second round out of Arizona) were multi-talented and bound to improve. Of course there was the down side of Rich Adubato, who had managed already to coach several of the worst teams in NBA history. But any team with Jim Jackson in the lineup on a daily basis seemed assured of at least 15–20 wins on the strength of the rookie's game-breaking talents alone.

Indeed, with Jim Jackson in the lineup for a full season, the Dallas record might have been quite a bit better. But things got off to an immediately bad start in and around Dallas Reunion Arena when Jackson and his agent selected to remain on the sidelines rather than accept the contract Dallas had offered. As negotiations proceeded on and off with Jackson for much of the season, the seemingly demoralized team took to the road without their prize rookie; and the path they followed was from the start one of record-pace losing.

The talent-thin Mavs would win but one of their first sixteen contests and two in their first 32. At New Years they stood 2–22; by the All-Star break the record was 4–45. A record pace was in the making and alumni of the 1973 76ers had to be looking over their shoulders as the final stretch of the season opened up. By that time Rich Adubato was no longer around for the blood-letting. Gar Heard, a star forward with several NBA clubs in the '70s and Adubato's assistant, took over as interim bench boss in the 30th game with the team standing 2–27 at the time. Although Heard's winning percentage would soar to .170 (9–44) by season's end, the new coach would start as slowly as the old by going 2–30 over his first two months on the job. Between a February 5th home victory over Indiana (the season's fourth), and back-to-back victories on March 17th and 19th (the first pair of the year) Heard's Mavericks dropped a club-record 19 straight games.

But the hapless 1993 Mavericks team under Adubato and Heard simply couldn't grab a moment in history any easier than they could grab the smallest handful of respectability. As opponents began coasting once play-off spots were secured the Mavs went on something like a tear by posting a season-closing 7–14 mark from March 17th until the season's merciful end. It was still a horse race with the ghost of the '73 Sixers, however. With only five games remaining the Mavs eked out a 99–86 yawner with

Denver that assured no worse than a tie for the record. Then they limped away from immortality with back-to-back home wins over Minnesota and Houston to close out the nightmare season.

Derek Harper stood out as the leading scorer at 18.2 ppg. by season's end. And Harper was also about the only legitimate starter the Mavs could boast before Jackson's late-season arrival from self-imposed exile. But his contributions only earned him eventual liberation in the form of a trade to the New York Knicks early in the following season. Terry Davis chipped in a club-best 9.2 rebounding average after recovering from a pre-season automobile accident which had shattered his left (shooting) elbow. Sean Rooks contributed a respectable 13.5 rookie scoring average. Jackson, on the other hand, flashed much of his anticipated brilliance once he signed a six-year contract on March 3rd and joined the club that same night. His final scoring average would stand at 16.3, but suffered from limited playing time as he worked himself into shape during much of March. By late season Jackson was on fire, averaging 28.0 in the season's final three games (two wins) and becoming one of only three 1993 rookies (alongside Shaq O'Neal, with 13, and Alonzo Mourning) to post seven straight 20-plus scoring games.

But despite the bright performances of Harper, Davis, Rooks and especially Jackson, most of the numbers in Dallas were embarrassingly bad. The club lost 58 of their games by better than ten points and the average margin of defeat was 15.2 points. They were predictably last in the league in shooting percentage (.435) as well as in opponent's shooting percentage allowed (.501). The team also established a club record for the third straight season for player games lost to illness or injury (246). But there were a few reasons for optimism as well. The dismal record had earned a lottery pick that was soon expended profitably on Kentucky junior first-team All-American Jamal Mashburn. At 6'8" and sporting two 20 ppg. seasons with the powerful Wildcats, Mashburn offered the same kind of promise as Jackson a year earlier. Davis and Rooks could be expected to improve and Murray State forward Popeye Jones was a draft-day acquisition through Houston, who was expected to contribute immediately. Quinn Buckner had been announced as coach for the new season on the same March date as Jackson's signing. Everything considered, the Mavs seemingly could go nowhere but up. Way, way up.

Yet progress wasn't quite as easy on the hardwood floor as it was on the coach's drawing board. It was almost as though returning members of the ballclub had suddenly realized that, for all their losing, they had reversed the trend just enough at season's end to miss out on a potential cherished spot in history and wanted yet another square shot at infamy. A more realistic assessment, of course, would have been to acknowledge that Buckner was simply not cut in the mold required for coaching in today's player-oriented NBA. Schooled by his old college mentor Bob Knight at Indiana (and supposedly receiving consul from the arch taskmaster and disciplinarian at points in the season), Buckner determined from the outset to be a tough taskmaster with the young Mavs team. The plan failed utterly and open mutiny hovered close to the surface as several players (especially Mashburn) publicly voiced displeasure with the coach and his tactics. One thing was certain—morale was low and losing continued under the new regime as a daily stable. The '93–'94 team for all the world looked to be worse than its near record-setting predecessor.

For all their improved talent—Jackson was now in shape and around for a full season, and Mashburn was better than anything on the front line a year earlier—the '93–'94 Mavericks equalled the inept start of the 1992–'93 team. The only two wins of the first several months came on the road and both were in Minnesota against an equally inept T-Wolves team. The Mavs again plodded into the second half of the season on a pace to overtake Philly's all-time mark for losses. In the end Buckner survived the full season (he was fired two weeks after the final regular-season game), a distinction which only brought him a record number of defeats for any freshman NBA coach. And the team won just enough in the final month to once again avoid completing the season somewhere below the ten-victory mark. Jackson and Mashburn split scoring honors at 19.2 ppg. Together they amassed 40 percent of the team's scoring total. But in a season when overall scoring was down and seven clubs failed to average 100 ppg., Dallas again limped home at the bottom of the heap with a 95.1 average. The Mavs were again the worst shooting team (.432) in the league and were beaten by better than 10 points (38 times) more than anyone else in the league save Washington (who lost 39 lopsided contests).

The Dallas Mavericks were of course not always such bumbling losers. In fact, the opposite was once the case. It has been little more than a decade, in fact, since the Dallas team stood proud as the league's model expansion franchise. Here was a place where ownership had seemingly avoided desperate quick fixes and remained focused on future excellence, assured by wise drafting, a patient ten-year plan, and confidence in a veteran coach. Throughout, the early years of normally rough sledding for any expansion franchise confidence was high, controversy low, and progress steady as a timepiece. The Dallas Mavericks somehow seemed to do everything right under owner Donald Carter, general manager Norm Sonju, and head coach Dick Motta.

The story of the Mavericks in Dallas in fact begins and ends with the astute leadership and management styles of Carter and Sonju. Norm Sonju had been in on expansion plans for Dallas from the earliest planning stages, first meeting with Dallas mayor Robert Folsum in 1978 to discuss the possible transfer of the Buffalo Braves franchise to Texas. As President and General Manager in Buffalo, Sonju moved with that club to San Diego in the summer of 1978, but continued to explore expansion possibilities for Dallas. By February, 1979, Carter had hired Sonju away from the San Diego Clippers and the two led a final push with league officials which assured a coveted Dallas franchise by April of 1980. The final deal between the league and Dallas interests underwent several modifications by NBA officials, all to the disadvantage of the infant Dallas ballclub. The team would pick 11th and not first in its first-ever collegiate draft. NBA clubs would protect eight rostered players for the dispersal draft, not seven as originally agreed. And financial details of the team's admittance were also significantly altered. Nonetheless optimism was indeed high in the Dallas and Fort Worth area when a May 1, 1980, news conference was held to announce the new team name, colors and logo.

That optimism soared further when Motta was named coach and the first roster of players was hastily assembled. Dick Motta's assistant would be former NBA player Bob Weiss. UCLA standout Kiki Vandeweghe was the first collegian selected with the 11th first-round pick the team had been granted. When Vandeweghe held out in a contract dispute, he was wisely traded to Denver in December for first-round selections in 1981 and 1985. The dispersal draft brought veterans Jim Spanarkel (Philadelphia), Tom LaGarde (Seattle), Austin Carr (Cleveland), Geoff Huston (New York), Abdul Jeelani (Portland), and Marty Byrnes (Los Angeles). While an adequate base of veterans would be sufficient to get through a respectable season or two, General Manager Sonju decided at the outset to build through the draft and avoid high-priced free-agent signees.

The Mavs won only 15 games in their first season out of the starting blocks but then quickly embarked on a path of steady and even miraculous improvement. From the second season on, Sonju's drafting policy began paying some of the highest dividends ever collected by an NBA franchise. The list of first-round and second-round choices from 1981 through 1986 was almost phenomenal—Mark Aguirre (1981), Rolando Blackman (1981), Jay Vincent (1981), Dale Ellis (1983), Ron Harper (1983), Sam Perkins (1984), Detlef Schrempf (1985), Roy Tarpley (1986), and Mark Price (1986, traded to Cleveland). All became solid NBA performers overnight, and a handful would soon be true superstars.

Motta's carefully laid building plans reached full flower during his lucky seventh season on the job. The Mavs won 55 games and stood atop the Midwest Division, a full eleven games ahead of Utah's Jazz. Motta's charges never lost more than two in a row during the regular season, but then dropped three straight in post-season after setting 11 records in a lopsided 151–129 game-one win over Seattle. It was indeed a year of milestones: two Mavs (Aguirre and Blackman) played in the same All-Star Game for the first time ever; for the fifth straight year Dallas led the NBA in fewest turnovers (14.7); a club-best home record (35–6) was established, as well as a club-best road ledger (20–21). James Donaldson was not only the best rebounding center in the Western Conference, but shattered the club record (with 11.9) in that department. Mark Aguirre was also club scoring leader (25.7) for the fifth straight year. If there was a down side to all this success, it was that veteran mentor Dick Motta—who had registered his 800th NBA career victory on March 28th—stepped down from his post shortly after the season ended.

The first year under new head coach John MacLeod was anything but a step backward. MacLeod took up where Motta had left off seemingly without missing a single beat. He became only the eighth coach in NBA annals to inherit a 50-win team and then post 50-plus wins himself. Of course such continued success is not so surprising in a league where players alone take you wherever it is that you travel in the standings while coaches are largely baby sitters and public relations men. Aguirre again paced the scorers (25.1) while Tarpley was cited for the league's best sixth man honor. MacLeod also reached a milestone of his own as the league's eighth coach ever to reach the 600-victory plateau. Overall the team didn't quite match the 1987 contingent in wins (with 53) or in the standings (slipped to second), but they nonetheless ousted Houston and Denver in the first two rounds of the playoffs by winning four road games in the process.

The true peak of franchise fortunes now lay right around the corner in the final round of post-season play during May, 1988. A surprise Western Conference championship matchup featured the world-title-bound Los Angeles Lakers with Magic and Kareem and the once-lowly expansion Mavericks with Aguirre, Perkins, Blackman and Harper. Losing two games immediately in Los Angeles, the Cinderella Mavs appeared ready for extinction. Yet Dallas roared back with consecutive wins of its own in Reunion Arena before eventually forcing a deciding seventh game at the LA Forum. MacLeod's team gamely stayed close until late in the third quarter when Laker experience took over and Magic and company pulled away down the stretch. The final tally was 117–102. While Mark Aguirre again paced the Mavs post-season offense, James Donaldson also got into the act with a .744 field goal percentage (32-of-43) in the conference finals— the best ever for an NBA seven-game post-season series.

If it was not easy at first to outline the precise reasons for a sudden collapse in Dallas, it was certainly easy enough to pinpoint a moment in franchise history when a reversal of fortunes was already at hand. The season, which began in November, 1988, was one of major transitions and disturbing reversals in fortune. The team took a step backward for the first time in club history, dropping 15 games in the win column and registering a losing record. For the first time in a half-dozen years there would be no playoff appearance to extend the season. And within the span of a single bloody week in February the previously patient GM Norm Sonju unleashed the two most shocking trades in franchise annals. First, Mark Aguirre was off to Detroit for high-scoring counterpart Adrian Dantley. Then Detlef Schrempf (yet to come into his own as a stellar impact bench player) was shipped to Indiana with a second-round draft choice for talented but underachieving center Herb Williams.

The sudden fall from respectability which began in 1989 was mostly a matter of such poor trades, coupled with some lousy draft choices, and also a measure of unavoidable bad luck thrown in as well. Thus it was an old story as far as professional sports franchises go. Another way to put it is that there was nothing so very mysterious in the long run about why the Mavs fortunes unravelled quite so quickly.

The biggest sin in the Dallas front office was as clear, after all, as the "L's" now piling up in the Dallas loss column. Mavs bosses somehow lost sight of the proven formula that had earlier taken them so far, so fast. Of the twelve rostered players who nearly toppled the champion Lakers in 1988, ten had been homegrown Dallas draft picks. Suddenly ownership set off on a course of trading future selections for the kind of quick fix that might thrust the Mavs over the top.

The Mavs after 1988 faced the talent well of the annual collegiate draft year-in and year-out with a decidedly empty hand. The 1988 first-round pick had been peddled to Miami's Heat in the expansion draft to protect roster players Bill Wennington, Uwe Blab and Steve Alford. The 1989 pick—eighth overall—was squandered on touted 6'8" forward Randy White from Louisiana Tech, who has remained with the club and never averaged double figures over five seasons. The 1990 draft selections (two first rounders) had again been dished off (along with Bill Wennington), this time to Sacramento for tarnished veteran Rodney McCray. And while little was coming in the way of reinforcement from the draft, quality talent in the club's possession was also being given away in a series of seeming fire sales. All-time scoring leader (at the time) Mark Aguirre went to Detroit for Adrian Dantley in what seemed a fair swap when it was executed. Detlef Schrempf and a second-round pick ended up in Indiana straight-up for veteran center Herb Williams. Two additional first round picks were mailed to Denver for aging point guard Lafayette "Fats" Lever. Every last deal in the end was a bust. Dantley, McCray, Williams and Lever had all lost their legs and contributed preciously little. Schrempf by contrast developed into a sixth-man star overnight with the Indiana Pacers.

Two more blows would finally scuttle the already sinking ship once and for all. Roy Tarpley, one of the best forwards in the game, was a true force on the court who might well have been one of the best rebounders ever had his game evolved. The Michigan two-time All-American flashed repeated brillance in his first couple seasons and was winner of the league's 1988 Sixth-Man Award. Yet Tarpley's seemingly boundless career self-destructed quickly after his second season, due exclusively to repeated drug and alcohol problems which kept the 6'11" forward on the sidelines most of 1989 and 1990 and all but five games in 1991. As a third-time offender of the league's drug policies, Tarpley was dismissed by the NBA on October 16, 1991, under terms of the Anti-Drug Agreement between the NBA and the league's Players' Association. The loss of Tarpley was severe by any measure, but even moreso given the earlier departure of another tower of strength off the once-talented Dallas front line. On August 6, 1990, 6'9" forward Sam Perkins was signed as an unrestricted free agent by the Los Angeles Lakers and left the Dallas camp for good. Perkins still remains the Mavs fifth all-time career scorer and second all-time career rebounder.

A sweeping overview of Dallas Mavericks franchise history in the end reveals a rise and fall that approximates a perfectly sloped pyramid. The first seven years—all under Motta—reveal a steady climb from the expected depths of a normal expansion team to the league's upper echelons. Those first seven seasons provided nothing but steady upward progress on all fronts, and that progress was almost perfectly measured by a steady elevation in the divisional standings and the win column—6th (15 wins), 5th (28 wins), 4th (38 wins), 2nd (43 wins), 3rd (44 wins), 3rd (44 wins), and 1st (55 wins). A hard-earned division title fittingly marked the exact half-way point to the club's 14-season saga. Then came the steady slippage back down the ladder, one rung at a time in an almost perfect mirror image of the previous seven seasons—2nd (53 wins), 4th (38 wins), 3rd (47 wins), 6th (28 wins), 5th (22 wins), 6th (11 wins), and 6th (13 wins). For a lucky seven seasons the ballclub was universally cited and praised around the league as basketball's model franchise. Then for seven snake-bitten seasons the Dallas Mavericks became a textbook case of self-destruction. A pillar of consistency had overnight turned into a league laughingstock.

With the continued improvement of Jim Jackson and the expected progress of Jamal Mashburn, the future of the Dallas Mavericks seems scheduled for a definite upswing. Jackson enjoyed a solid if not spectacular first full season in the pro ranks. Despite the lack of surrounding support the flashy guard jacked up his rookie scoring average from 16.3 to 19.2 ppg. Mashburn tied Jackson for club scoring honors from the forward slot, but surprised somewhat with soft rebounding (353) and shot blocking numbers (14). Mashburn was definitely a quality rookie despite his public disaffection with coach Buckner and the fact that he played in the long shadow of more touted rookies in other cities like Orlando's Penny Hardaway and Golden State's Chris Webber. Perhaps the brightest prospect of all, however, was that another miserable finish had assured another lottery pick (second overall) in one of the deepest collegiate drafts in many a year.

With the firing of coach Quinn Buckner at season's end there seemed to be another hopeful sign on the Mavericks' horizon as well. Determined to return to the path that had taken them so far in early franchise seasons, the Mavericks ownership reached back into the past to hire original coach Dick Motta, now 62 years of age and on the sidelines for the past several NBA seasons. Despite Motta's age and his recent hiatus from the NBA wars, Dallas ownership apparently felt that Motta was just the man to handle today's rich and self-centered young athletes. The hope in the Dallas camp was that under Motta the team would somehow reproduce the long and steady climb to the top that had distinguished his earlier tenure at the helm. It wouldn't be easy. But then things could hardly get much worse for basketball's greatest self-destruction act.

Suggested Readings on Dallas Mavericks

Bjarkman, Peter C. **The History of the NBA**. New York: Crescent Books (Random House, Outlet Books), 1992. (Chapter 7)

Strasen, Marty (et. al.). **Basketball Almanac, 1993–94**. New York: Publications International (Signet Sports Library), 1994.

Dallas Mavericks Retired Uniform Numbers

None (expansion franchise)

Year-by-Year Dallas Mavericks Summary

Season	Record	Finish	Coach(es)	Scoring Leader(s)	Playoffs (W–L Record)
1980–81	15–67	6th	Dick Motta	Geoff Huston (16.1)	Did Not qualify
1981–82	28–54	5th	Dick Motta	Jay Vincent (21.4)	Did Not Qualify
1982–83	38–44	4th	Dick Motta	Mark Aguirre (24.4)	Did Not Qualify
1983–84	43–39	2nd	Dick Motta	Mark Aguirre (29.5)	Lost in 2nd Round (4–6)
1984–85	44–38	3rd	Dick Motta	Mark Aguirre (25.7)	Lost in 1st Round (1–3)
1985–86	44–38	3rd	Dick Motta	Mark Aguirre (22.6)	Lost in 2nd Round (5–5)
1986–87	55–27	1st	Dick Motta	Mark Aguirre (25.7)	Lost in 1st Round (1–3)
1987–88	53–29	2nd	John MacLeod	Mark Aguirre (25.1)	Lost in 3rd Round (10–7)
1988–89	38–44	4th	John MacLeod	Adrian Dantley (20.3)	Did Not Qualify
1989–90	47–35	3rd	John MacLeod Richie Adubato	Rolando Blackman (19.4)	Lost in 1st Round (0–3)
1990–91	28–54	6th	Richie Adubato	Roy Tarpley (20.4)	Did Not Qualify
1991–92	22–60	5th	Richie Adubato	Rolando Blackman (20.7)	Did Not Qualify
1992–93	11–71	6th	Richie Adubato Garfield Heard	Derek Harper (18.2)	Did Not Qualify
1993–94	13–69	6th	Quinn Buckner	Jim Jackson (19.2)	Did Not Qualify

Individual Career Leaders and Record Holders (1981–1994)

Scoring Average	Mark Aguirre (24.6, 1981–89)
Points Scored	Rolando Blackman (16,643, 1981–92)
Minutes Played	Rolando Blackman (29,684, 1981–1992)
Field Goals Made	Rolando Blackman (6,487)
Field Goal Pct.	James Donaldson (.551, 1985–92)
3-Pt. Field Goals	Derek Harper (608, 1983–93)
Free Throws Made	Rolando Blackman (3,501, 1981–92)
Free-Throw Pct.	Jim Spanarkel (.857, 1980–84)
Rebounds	James Donaldson (4,589, 1985–92)
Personal Fouls	Brad Davis (2,040, 1980–92)
Assists	Derek Harper (4,692, 1983–93)
Steals	Derek Harper (1,414, 1983–93)

Blocked Shots   James Donaldson (615, 1985–92)

Individual Single-Season and Game Records (1981–1994)

Scoring Average	Mark Aguirre (29.5 ppg., 1983–84)
Points Scored (Season)	Mark Aguirre (2,330, 1983–84)
Points Scored (Game)	Mark Aguirre (49, 1–28–85 vs. Philadelphia Sixers)
Rebounds (Season)	James Donaldson (973, 1986–87)
Rebounds (Game)	James Donaldson (27, 12–29–89 vs. Portland in 3 OTs)
	Roy Tarpley (25, 4–1–90 vs. Milwaukee Bucks)
Assists (Season)	Derek Harper (634, 1987–88)
Assists (Game)	Derek Harper (18, 12–29–88 vs. Boston Celtics)
Blocked Shots (Season)	Kurt Nimphius (144, 1983–84)
Steals (Season)	Derek Harper (172, 1988–89)
Steals (Game)	Derek Harper (8, 11–9–85 vs. Houston Rockets)
	Jim Spanarkel (8, 3–10–81 vs. Phoenix Suns)

Best Trade in Franchise History

While James Donaldson is hardly a franchise center in the mold of Abdul-Jabbar or Bill Russell, or even Moses Malone, he is certainly the best at that position in the Mavs' short decade and a half history. And the price for obtaining Donaldson was cheap indeed. The transaction came on November 25, 1985, and it was one sending beanpole center Kurt Nimphius to the Los Angeles Clippers for Donaldson. Over the next several seasons Donaldson became the franchise career leader in several big-man categories, including career, season and single game rebounds and career blocked shots.

Worst Trade in Franchise History

On June 17, 1987, the Mavs unloaded a second round draft choice to the Cleveland Cavaliers for a 1989 second-round pick. That choice was named Mark Price, now considered by many as the premier point guard in the entire league. The compensation for Price then itself underwent a long and convoluted history. The 1989 second-round pick was later expended on Pat Durham, who remained unsigned until peddled to Milwaukee for another second-round pick in 1993. The 1993 pick was Michigan seven-footer Eric Riley, who was immediately moved to Houston for Popeye Jones. But what might Mark Price have done in the Mavs backcourt in the six years that intervened between Pat Durham and Popeye Jones?

Dallas Mavericks Historical Oddity

The Mavs did avoid becoming the worst-ever single-season team, a bullet they dodged not only once in 1993 but again in 1994. They also avoided being the first NBA club ever to suffer two consecutive 70-loss seasons. But one distinction for ineptitude was claimed during the blood letting and massacres that constituted the past two seasons in Dallas. Quinn Buckner now owns the distinction of the worst won-loss record ever for a full-season rookie NBA coach.

Mavericks All-Time Number One Draft Picks List

Dallas Mavericks
1980 Kiki Vandeweghe (UCLA)
1981 Mark Aguirre (DePaul)
1982 Bill Garnett (Wyoming)
1983 Dale Ellis (Tennessee)
1984 Sam Perkins (North Carolina)
1985 Detlef Schrempf (Washington)
1986 Roy Tarpley (Michigan)
1987 Jim Farmer (Alabama)
1988 None
1989 Randy White (Louisiana Tech)
1990 None
1991 Doug Smith (Missouri)
1992 Jim Jackson (Ohio State)
1993 Jamal Mashburn (Kentucky)

Chapter 24

CHARLOTTE HORNETS

Expansion Blues Turn Teal Green

All-Time Franchise Record: 201–311, .393 Pct. (1988–1994)

NBA Championships: None

First Draft Picks: Dell Curry (1988 Expansion Draft); Rex Chapman (1988 College Draft)

Greatest Franchise Player: Larry Johnson (1991–1994)

All-Time Leading Scorer: Dell Curry (6,214 Points, 1988–1994)

Most Successful Coach: Allan Bristow (116–130, .472 Pct., 1991–1994)

All-Time Franchise Team: Alonzo Mourning (C), Larry Johnson (F), Kelly Tripucka (F), Dell Curry (G), Tyrone Bogues (G)

From the very beginning NBA basketball and the city of Charlotte, North Carolina, seemed a perfect marriage fashioned in heaven. There have been few better success stories to be found anywhere in big-time sports. It was seemingly natural that pro basketball would someday finally invade the territory that had so long been a hot-bed of enthusism for the collegiate game. And once the NBA did arrive on Tobacco Road, the two most exacting measures of bottom-line success were quickly registered. Fan support was phenomenal as the Hornets overnight became one of the hottest ticket items anywhere in sportsdom. And in a few short seasons this expansion also-ran would feature both glamorous big-name stars and dramatic post-season successes as well.

There were, nonetheless, plenty of skeptics when Charlotte was first mentioned as a potential NBA expansion entry. For one thing the city seemed to lie well off the beaten path for prime-time sports. Charlotte, after all, did not own any other major league clubs—in football, baseball, hockey, or even pro indoor soccer. It had, granted, been home to a long-successful Class AA minor league baseball franchise and a World Football League club, but those back-page items hardly counted as big-time by any

398

stretch. And furthermore, early efforts to pull together an expansion NBA club seemed to get off to something of an ominously slow start.

For one thing, there was controversy and foot-dragging surrounding the first badge of any pro sports franchise—a marketable club nickname. In November, 1986, a local committee behind the drive to land an NBA franchise had already sanctioned one moniker—"Spirit"—by a rather wide margin in local fan polling. But after approval by the NBA expansion committee had resulted in a formal invitation to join the league, new club owner George Shinn and a vast majority of local citizenry seemed to lean towards a name which somehow held more historical significance for the Charlotte community as a whole. Shinn thus drummed up further excitement for the new club by organizing a community-wide "Name-the-Team" contest which brought 8,000 entries and gave the nod to "Hornets" in a landslide second ballot. "Hornets" was a more logical choice, and one with deep-seated regional roots. Local lore, it seems, connects the name with a derogatory comment about Charlotte reportedly uttered by British Revolutionary War General Charles Cornwallis. ("There's a rebel behind every bush," Cornwallis wrote in a message during the British invasion of the Carolinas in 1779, "It's a veritable nest of hornets down here.") And both the local minor league baseball affiliate and World Football League outfit had also borne the identical moniker.

When business soon turned from club naming to basketball planning, the novice team management also seemed to get off the ground rather slowly. The expansion dispersal draft and following NBA collegiate draft produced nothing much beyond journeymen and "no names" like Clinton Wheeler, Sedric Toney and Bernard Thompson. The collegiate talent grab did reel-in Kentucky's talented backcourt underclassman Rex Chapman. But the 6'4" Chapman (17.6 ppg. in two seasons at Kentucky) was hardly the kind of head-turning court sensation who could be considered a guaranteed "franchise" player. As the first-year roster was assembled piece by piece and countdown began in earnest for opening night, it was something of a mystery, indeed, just how the team led by coach Dick Harter was going to be at all competitive in the upcoming nightly NBA wars.

Once the larger pieces (like Chapman and NBA veterans Dell Curry, Tyrone Bogues and Kelly Tripucka) were slapped in place, however, the ball began to roll, no matter how slowly the team appeared to come out of the gate. And Charlotte management seemed to have in hand a high-powered game plan geared as much for instant success as for long-range building of an eventual NBA winner. In the first-year expansion draft the team opted wisely for selecting dependable veterans over young stars-in-the-making. The effort would clearly be to try to win (at least some) immediately, and thus to sign as many seasoned ballplayers as possible. Around Rex Chapman were put in place such unspectacular but court-tested veterans as Kelly Tripucka (obtained in a draft day deal with Utah), Kurt Rambis (free-agent signee), Earl Cureton (free agent signee) and Robert Reid (acquired from Houston). And the club's first pick in the expansion draft, Dell Curry, would still be with the club six full seasons later. Curry logged enough minutes by 1993 to become the club's all-time leading scorer at the end of the first half-dozen seasons.

Charlotte Hornets Original Draft Selections

Expansion Draft

Round	Pick	Player	Franchise (Position)	Played for Hornets
1	2	Dell Curry	Cleveland Cavaliers (Guard)	1988–94 (6 seasons)
2	4	Dave Hoppen	Golden State Warriors (Center)	1988–91 (3 seasons)
3	6	Tyrone Bogues	Washington Bullets (Guard)	1988–94 (6 seasons)
4	8	Mike Brown*	Chicago Bulls (Forward)	Did Not Play
5	10	Rickey Green	Utah Jazz (Guard)	1988–89 (1 season)
6	12	Michael Holton	Portland Trail Blazers (Guard)	1988–90 (2 seasons)
7	14	Michael Brooks	Denver Nuggets (Forward)	Did Not Play
8	16	Bernard Thompson#	Phoenix Suns (Forward)	Did Not Play
9	18	Ralph Lewis	Detroit Pistons (Guard)	1988–990 (2 seasons)
10	20	Clinton Wheeler	Indiana Pacers (Guard)	Did Not Play
11	22	Sedric Toney	New York Knicks (Guard)	Did Not Play

* Traded immediately to Utah Jazz for Kelly Tripucka
\# Traded July 18th to Houston Rockets for Robert Reid

Collegiate Draft

Round	Pick	Player	College (Position)	Played for Hornets
1	8	Rex Chapman	Kentucky (Guard)	1988–92 (4 seasons)
2	34	Tom Tolbert	Arizona (Forward)	1988–89 (1 season)
3	58	Jeff Moore	Auburn (Guard)	Did Not Play

The Charlotte formula brought rather a mixed success early on in the first season of league play. The Hornets struggled to a 20–62 expansion-year mark which earned the expected last-place berth in basketball's weakest division, the Atlantic. The opening game of that first campaign was held before a sell-out Coliseum throng on November 4, 1988. The opponents were the Cleveland Cavaliers and the game featured all the normal hoopla, excitements, and landmark moments of any such once-in-a-lifetime franchise opener. The first shot would be taken by veteran back court player Rickey Green. Workhorse forward Kelly Tripucka would then score the first-ever Charlotte points a few moments later. But the festivities largely ended shortly after the opening tipoff, as the Cavaliers drubbed the new club by an unfriendly 133–93 margin.

The remainder of the opening season brought little to match the gala opening night for thrills and hurrahs. The first victory came at the expense of the Los Angeles Clippers (117–105), on the home floor and in game three. The first road win was chalked up in San Antonio on November 19th by a narrow 107–105 margin. Two separate nine-game losing streaks marked the months of March and April, however, as the ego-bruised ball-club limped across the finish line with its final 20–62 ledger. This placed Charlotte dead last in the six-team Atlantic Division and was good enough to outpace only a lackluster group of expansion rivals, the Miami Heat of the Midwest Division. Tripucka paced the squad with a 21.6 ppg. average, followed by a rookie Chapman at 16.9 and Robert Reid at 14.7. Midget 5'3" point guard Tyrone ''Muggsy'' Bogues directed what little Charlotte offense there was with a club-best 620 assists.

A second season largely repeated the pattern of the first, though a new promising youngster had been added to the lineup via the collegiate draft, to supplement the limited firepower of Rex Chapman and the veterans Tripucka and Robert Reid. University of North Carolina standout J.R. Reid had been the fifth overall 1989 first round selection; but Reid quickly proved as much a disappointment as anything. The 6'9" forward-center seemed lethargic at times and contributed only a 11.1 scoring average, which translated into precious little additional offense along the front line. The result of a second trip through the NBA was therefore an actual dip in record—to 19 and 63—and yet another basement finish. All that seem-ingly had changed was the venue, since the league had now rotated the Hornets into the Midwest Division for Year Two, while two additional expansion clubs began the season in Orlando and Minneapolis. If Charlotte fans were to find a boasting point during the second franchise season, it could only be that their club was able to garner a handful more victories than sister expansion outfits in Miami, Orlando and Minnesota.

The first clear signs that the Hornets might indeed be headed in the right direction came with back-to-back spectacular draft hauls in 1991 and 1992. With the top pick of 1991, the club tabbed powerful front court star Larry Johnson, a certain marquee player who had recently garnered both the Wooden and Naismith awards as collegiate player of the year, while leading the UNLV Rebels of Coach Jerry Tarkanian to consecutive NCAA Final Four appearances. Then, a year later, the number-two pick brought to Charlotte further basket-fronting firepower with prize center Alonzo Mourning. Mourning had followed seven-footer Dikembe Mutombo out of Georgetown University and had gained early notoriety as a high schooler invited to the 1988 Olympic basketball trials. On the impetus of a sensa-tional senior season, Mourning had also become the first hoopster ever to be named big East Conference Player of the Year, Defensive Player of the Year, and Big East Tournament MVP in the very same season. He also became only the second player at Georgetown (after Patrick Ewing) to register 2,000 points and 1,000 rebounds for his illustrious collegiate career.

Larry Johnson owned all the tools of a franchise player when he entered the league in the fall of 1991. And Johnson did indeed enjoy a solid rookie-of-the-year season during his first NBA tour of duty. The 6'7" rock-solid small forward averaged 19.2 in scoring to pace all rookies, and also ranked second in the league in rebounding among freshman players. And Johnson's stellar rookie outing was only a prelude to a sensational sophomore campaign which saw him take over the club lead in scoring (22.1 ppg.) while earning second-team all-league honors. Most impressive of all, Larry Johnson had also joined Michael Jordan, Shaquille O'Neal and David Robinson as the only four first or second-year players during the past ten seasons to be named starters in the league mid-season All-Star classic.

Mourning came into the NBA with somewhat less fanfare than Larry Johnson simply because he had to share his debut season with Orlando's touted wunderkind Shaquille O'Neal. The media-hype surrounding the Shaq seemed unfortunately to bury Zo's equally solid and almost as spectacular rookie campaign. In any other winter Alonzo Mourning would have been the debut sensation of a new NBA year. He had scored at a 21.0 clip and ranked fourteenth in the entire league in rebounding as well as scoring. And Mourning soon showed that he was entirely for real with a second solid performance during his sophomore pro season. Slowed by injuries and limited to 60 games in 1993–94, nonetheless Zo Mourning paced the Hornets in scoring (21.5) and stood fourth in the league in the increasingly headlined defensive category of blocked shots.

A third building block for the Charlotte franchise was the arrival of Allan Bristow at the coaching helm in time for the club's fourth tour around the league. Dick Harter had lasted only a single season at the reins before being given walking papers by a front office hungry for quick improvement. Gene Littles engineered some slow upgrading in seasons two and three, yet met a similar fate. But in only his second season at the helm, Bristow—a ten-year NBA player and seven-year coaching assistant in Denver—would have the Charlotte team playing at over a break-even clip and actually contending for a playoff position.

In their fifth year in the league—Coach Allan Bristow's second at the helm—the Charlotte Hornets turned things around in the most dramatic of fashions. The team's 13-game improvement over their 31–51 ledger of 1992 tied Houston (and trailed only Orlando) for the second-best franchise overhaul in the league. With a 22–19 road mark, the young Hornets were also one of only eight league clubs that could boast more victories than defeats registered on the enemy hardwood.

The final month of the '92–'93 season was, by a stroke of good fortune, the most successful in ballclub history. Several milestones were reached in rapid succession as the season wound down toward its annual playoff frenzy. The club's 9–3 record was a new standard for victories during any single month. The Hornets also tied their own longest success string of the year by winning the final five contests of the campaign. The most memorable night, however, would be that of April 23rd at the Charlotte Coliseum, a night when the team posted a thrilling 104–103 victory over

Michael Jordan and the eventual three-peat champion Chicago Bulls. When Dell Curry stole an inbounds pass to preserve victory in the final seconds of this memorable game the upstart Hornets had prematurely achieved their first playoff trip of franchise history.

Charlotte's Cinderella Hornets were primed and prepared for their first great franchise moment during the opening playoff round against the tradition-laden Boston Celtics. Two thrilling one-point victories highlighted one of the most action-packed playoff mini-series of recent NBA seasons. The second game in legendary Boston Garden—an exciting two-overtime tussle which the Hornets captured 99–98—was the true turning point of the dramatic mini-series. This Boston team of Parish, Reggie Lewis (whose career would tragically end when he collapsed with heart problems during this series), Kevin Gamble and Xavier McDaniel was hardly the early-eighties Celtics of Bird, McHale and Dennis Johnson. But it was a formidable veteran NBA club just the same. Close-out 99–89 and 104–103 Hornet victories on home hardwood soon sent fans into a near frenzy. Alonzo Mourning applied the finishing touches with a game-clinching last-second jumper in game four and an expansion club had done what many veteran teams take many years to do. They had passed through the first playoff round as a post-season survivor.

The Charlotte Hornets had emerged as the ultimate surprise of the 1993 season, as they now entered the Eastern Conference semi-finals against the heavily favored New York Knicks and all-star center Patrick Ewing. No expansion franchise had enjoyed such post-season success in many a season. Charlotte in the end would not provide much of an obstacle for the powerful Knicks, however. New York would continue its season-long fourth-quarter domination of Charlotte and sweep the conference semi-final series in a mere five games.

If the 1993 post-season had been a three-week emotional high guaranteed to fuel rampant enthusiasm, then the developments of pre-season 1993–'94 could only further fan the fires of boundless hope. September, 1993, saw the front office pull off a doubleheader deal that was the biggest in the history of the young ballclub. The end result of the complex player shuffling was that malcontent free-agent guard Kendall Gill was now gone from the Charlotte locker room. In his place was a proven backcourt scorer who seemed to provide a key missing ingredient. Hersey Hawkins would presumably take care of weak perimeter point production with the career 19.1 ppg. scoring average he was bringing over from Philadelphia. But while the swap was simple enough on the surface, the details of the transaction were a bit more convoluted. Kendall Gill went to Seattle in the first half of the exchange with Dana Barros, Eddie Johnson and a first round draft selection coming to Charlotte. Barros and Sidney Green were then packaged with the rights to 1993 draftee Greg Graham and sent off to Philadelphia in the swap for Hersey Hawkins.

The Hornets thus entered the fall 1993 campaign with the highest expectations. But any further progress was stalled quickly by further injury problems for Alonzo Mourning and Larry Johnson. Mourning would be forced to sit out 22 contests and Johnson would lose over thirty. And although Hersey Hawkins was a welcomed addition, the ex-Sixer averaged 14.4 (well off his 20.3 in Philadelphia the previous season) and never did quite provide the backcourt fireworks management had hoped for. Mourning came roaring back in late season with a second straight solid year (21.5 ppg., 610 rebounds, a league 4th-best 188 blocked shots). The final weeks of the season would even feature a tense playoff battle with expansion rival Miami for the final Eastern Conference final post-season spot. But Charlotte fell one game short in the end and concluded the downturn year at exactly the break-even point.

In the end the club's sixth season brought distinct disappointment despite the year-end escape from total collapse. The Charlotte team remained in the playoff hunt right down to the end, and perhaps could have expected no better fate, given the injuries which slowed both Larry Johnson and Alonzo Mourning. But sitting on the sidelines once again during post-season was a bitter pill to swallow for Charlotte fans and management after the heavy playoff climb and high expectations only a single spring earlier. The first casualty of this plague of unfulfilled expectation might well be head coach Allan Bristow. Pressured by late-season second guessing from fans and media, Bristow was rumored to be near stepping down from his post immediately after the regular season's close. If Charlotte's third-year coach does indeed survive the off-season, it seems likely his fate will then rest in the hope of a fast start for the Hornets once the NBA wars have resumed for 1994–'95.

Despite the disappointments of 1994, however, the future seems bright for the Charlotte Hornets. The club is one of the most lucrative in the league with its guaranteed packed houses night after night. Alonzo Mourning shows promise of soon entering the arena with David Robinson and Shaquille O'Neal as part of the game's triumvirate of glamorous new rim-rattling big men. There is a solid cast of supporting performers in Larry Johnson, Hersey Hawkins, and veterans like Gattison, Curry, Johnson and Bogues. Perhaps the most glaring need is a backcourt overhaul to provide balance with the sterling young front line. But any team featuring Alonzo Mourning and Larry Johnson is bound to provide plenty of excitement around the league and back home on Tobacco Road over the next couple of NBA seasons.

Suggested Readings on Charlotte Hornets

Drape, Joe. **In the Hornet's Nest—Charlotte and its First Year in the NBA.** New York: St. Martin's Press, 1989.

Strasen, Marty (et. al.). **Basketball Almanac, 1993–94.** New York: Publications International (Signet Sports Library), 1994.

Charlotte Hornets Retired Uniform Numbers

None (expansion franchise)

Year-by-Year Charlotte Hornets Summary

Season	Record	Finish	Coach(es)	Scoring Leader(s)	Playoffs (W–L Record)
Key: * = Tied for Position					
1988–89	20–62	6th	Dick Harter	Kelly Tripucka (22.6)	Did Not Qualify
1989–90	19–63	7th	Gene Littles	Armon Gilliam (18.8)	Did Not Qualify
1990–91	26–56	7th	Gene Littles	Johnny Newman (16.9)	Did Not Qualify
1991–92	31–51	6th*	Allan Bristow	Kendall Gill (20.5)	Did Not Qualify
1992–93	44–38	5th	Allan Bristow	Larry Johnson (22.1)	Lost in 2nd Round (4–5)
1993–94	41–41	5th	Allan Bristow	Alonzo Mourning (21.5)	Did Not Qualify

Individual Career Leaders and Record Holders (1988–1994)

Scoring Average	Alonzo Mourning (21.2 ppg., 1992–94)
Points Scored	Dell Curry (6,214, 1988–94)
Games Played	Tyrone Bogues (481, 1988–94)
Minutes Played	Tyrone Bogues (15,166)
Field Goal Pct.	Kenny Gattison (.531, 1989–94)
3-Pt. Field Goals	Dell Curry (424)
Free Throws Made	Kelly Tripucka (902, 1988–91)
Free-Throw Pct.	Kelly Tripucka (.879)
Rebounds	Larry Johnson (2,211, 1991–94)
Rebound Average	Larry Johnson (10.3 rpg.)
Personal Fouls	Kenny Gattison (1,100)
Assists	Tyrone Bogues (4,390)
Steals	Tyrone Bogues (878)
Blocked Shots	Alonzo Mourning (459)

Individual Single-Season and Game Records (1988–1994)

Scoring Average	Kelly Tripucka (22.6 ppg., 1988–89)
	Larry Johnson (22.1 ppg., 1992–93)
Points Scored (Season)	Larry Johnson (1,810, 1992–93)
Points Scored (Game)	Johnny Newman (41, 1–25–92 vs. Indiana Pacers)
3-Pt. Field Goals (Season)	Dell Curry (152, 1993–94)
3-Pt. Field Goal Pct. (Season)	Dell Curry (.404, 1991–92)
Field Goal Pct. (Season)	Dave Hoppen (.564, 1988–89)
Free-Throw Pct. (Season)	Kelly Tripucka (.910, 1990–91)
Rebounds (Season)	Larry Johnson (899, 19991–92)
Rebounds (Game)	Larry Johnson (23, 3–10–92 vs. Minnesota T-Wolves)
Assists (Season)	Tyrone Bogues (867, 1989–90)
Assists (Game)	Tyrone Bogues (19, 4–23–89 at Boston Celtics)

Best Trade in Franchise History

Although it may be far too early to tell if the two-part deal in September, 1993, which brought high scoring guard Hersey Hawkins to Charlotte was actually the club's best transaction to date, it certain was without a doubt the biggest and most convoluted. The first phase of the two-part shuffling of players saw productive but malcontented guard Kendall Gill peddled to Seattle for Guard Dana Barros, forward Eddie Johnson and a first-round draft selection. Two days later (September 3, 1993) the Hornets shipped a huge package to Philadelphia for the coveted Hawkins. That package included Barrows, forward Sidney Green, the just-acquired first-round selection from Seattle, and the rights to recent first-round pick Greg Graham. Hawkins didn't exactly disappoint during his first year in Charlotte, providing added backcourt punch with a 14.4 scoring average.

Worst Trade in Franchise History

Guard Rex Chapman was just coming into his own after four seasons in Charlotte, which saw him average 16.7 over 220 games. Chapman had been the Hornets' first round (eighth overall) pick in the 1988 draft and had from the first been considered a future franchise cornerstone. But in February, 1992, the club was seduced by the notion of quick fixes and thus peddled Chapman off to the Washington Bullets for promising problem child Tom Hammonds. Hammonds proved a complete bust, however, playing but 19 games (2.3 ppg.) in Charlotte before being waived less than a year later. To make matters worse, Chapman's career continued its steady forward progress once the ex-Kentucky star pulled on the red, white, and blue uniform of the Washington Bullets. Despite injuries which limited him to 60 games, for example, Chapman was Washington's leading point-maker (18.2) for the just-concluded 1994 campaign.

Charlotte Hornets Historical Oddity

There has been no greater calendar coincidence in American sports history than the one that saw the National Basketball Association announce—on April Fool's Day of 1987—its awarding of a new expansion franchise to the collegiate hoop hotbed of Charlotte, North Carolina. NBA basketball in the hinterlands of North Carolina simply had to be a joke. Few took Charlotte businessman George Shinn at all seriously when he first announced his intentions back in 1985 to win an NBA slot for his hometown community. "The only franchise George Shinn and Charlotte will land is the one with the golden arches" was the comment of at least one sports columnist from an established NBA market, and his sarcastic reaction was fairly typical of attitudes around the nation. But it was hardly a joke a few years later when the NBA's newest franchise was still piling up record attendance and also putting a highly competitive team on the court after only three winters of play. Charlotte soon enough would prove its big-time professional sports worthiness. The expansion Hornets would lead the league in home attendance in four of their first five seasons and register 194 consecutive sellouts within 24,000-seat Charlotte Coliseum by the time the 1993–94 campaign arrived. This April Fool's joke was one that left businessman Shinn and his supports laughing all the way to the bank.

Hornets All-Time Number One Draft Picks List

Charlotte Hornets
1988 Rex Chapman (Kentucky)
1989 J. R. Reid (North Carolina)
1990 Kendall Gill (Illinois)
1991 Larry Johnson (UNLV)
1992 Alonzo Mourning (Georgetown)
1993 Greg Graham (Indiana) (Traded to Philadelphia Sixers for Hersey Hawkins)

Chapter 25

MIAMI HEAT

Turning Up the Heat on Basketball's Gold Coast

All-Time Franchise Record: 173–319, .352 Pct. (1988–1994)
NBA Championships: None
First Draft Picks: Arvid Kramer (1988 Expansion Draft); Rony Seikaly (1988 College Draft)
Greatest Franchise Player: Glen Rice (1989–1994)
All-Time Leading Scorer: Glen Rice (7,417 Points, 1989–1994)
Most Successful Coach: Kevin Loughery (116–130, .472 Pct., 1991–1994)
All-Time Franchise Team: Rony Seikaly (C), Glen Rice (F), Grant Long (F), Kevin Edwards (G), Sherman Douglas (G)

The Miami Heat have demonstrated a considerable flair for the off-beat and the slightly bizarre over their short five-year history. First there is the team's strange name, the first in league history not to bare the standard final "s" of the plural. A year later they would be followed by their cross-state rivals, the Orlando Magic, but the Miami club alone launched the forward-looking trend. Of course the name seems somewhat more fitting for a soccer or hockey club. But from the first the Miami ownership was determined not to do things in anything like the usual way.

This flair for the unusual was quickly demonstrated as well by Miami's seemingly unaccountable choice in the 1988 expansion draft. When Arvid Kramer was first announced as the Heat selection at the top of the dispersal draft, even the most knowledgeable among NBA fanatics must have done an extended double take. A total unknown, Kramer had already failed with the league, never making it out of an original tryout camp with the Mavericks eight seasons earlier. This was indeed a complex affair that had to be sorted out for fans and media alike. The true story was that Dallas had left unprotected a worthless washed-up player to whom they still owned rights; and all this was done in conjunction with the expansion Heat, who had secretly agreed to select Kramer and thus leave untouched several players which Dallas wanted to retain, yet could ill-afford to protect (Bill Wennington, Uwe Blab and Steve Alford). For their cooperation, the Heat would receive a Dallas-owned first-round pick in the upcoming collegiate lottery, a pick that would be spent to acquire DePaul guard Kevin Edwards. With the rest of their selections, however, the new Heat ownership suggested a clear-reasoned plan to build slowly and with an unwavering eye to the future. It was seemingly a wise way to go, yet one that would cause some rough bumps during early seasons.

Miami Heat Original Draft Selections

Expansion Draft

Round	Pick	Player	Franchise (Position)	Played for Heat
1	1	Arvid Kramer	Dallas Mavericks (Forward)	Did Not Play
2	3	Billy Thompson	Los Angeles Lakers (Forward)	1988–91 (3 seasons)
3	5	Fred Roberts	Boston Celtics (Forward)	Did Not Play
4	7	Scott Hastings	Atlanta Hawks (Center)	1989–90 (1 season)
5	9	Jon Sundvold	San Antonio Spurs (Guard)	1988–92 (4 seasons)
6	11	Kevin Williams	Seattle SuperSonics (Guard)	Did Not Play
7	13	Hansi Gnad	Philadelphia Sixers (Center)	Did Not Play
8	15	Darnell Valentine	Los Angeles Clippers (Guard)	Did Not Play
9	17	Dwayne Washington	New Jersey Nets (Guard)	1988–89 (1 season)
10	19	Andre Turner	Houston Rockets (Guard)	Did Not Play
11	21	Conner Henry	Sacramento Kings (Forward)	Did Not Play
12	23	John Stroeder	Milwaukee Bucks (Center)	Did Not Play

Collegiate Draft

Round	Pick	Player	College (Position)	Played for Heat
1	9	Rony Seikaly	Syracuse University (Center)	1988–94 (6 seasons)
1	20	Kevin Edwards	DePaul University (Guard)	1988–93 (5 seasons)
2	33	Grant Long	Eastern Michigan (Forward)	1988–94 (6 seasons)
2	35	Sylvester Gray	Memphis State (Forward)	1988–89 (1 season)
2	40	Orlando Graham	Auburn-Montgomery (Guard)	Did Not Play
3	59	Nate Johnson	Tampa University (Forward)	Did Not Play

The original building plan of the Miami Heat was a proud reflection of the solid ownership team that had successfully brought professional basketball to Miami in the late 1980s. That team started with long-time NBA executives and close personal friends Billy Cunningham and Lewis Schaffel. Cunningham had himself enjoyed a brilliant pro career as both player and coach, starring with the Philadelphia Sixers team that had registered the best NBA record ever in 1967, and later coaching the NBA Champion Sixers of 1983. Schaffel was a long-time behind-the-scenes NBA man with plenty of sterling credentials of his own when it came to front office management. Schaffel had built those credentials largely as chief operating officer with the New Jersey Nets and general manager with the New Orleans Jazz, but he had actually begun his league sojourn in the early '70s as one of the first among successful NBA player agents (launching his career with but a single client—Nate "Tiny" Archibald).

Cunningham and Schaffel first pieced together a potent ownership team which was drawn from local business giants and included theatrical producer Zev Buffman, cruise lines owner Ted Arison, and popular music entertainer Julio Iglesias. Cunningham and Buffman announced their plans to seek a franchise with a May, 1986, press conference and formally applied for admission to the league a month later. The ownership team next oversaw building of a new Miami Arena with groundbreaking taking place before the end of the same summer. The coveted franchise charter was obtained from the league (which also simultaneously announced expansion clubs for Charlotte, Minneapolis and Orlando) on April 22, 1987. The Miami and Charlotte teams would first begin play during the 1988–'89 season with Orlando and Minnesota coming on board a season later. Ron Rothstein, Detroit Pistons assistant coach under the reign of Chuck Daly, was selected as the expansion club's first head coach. Rothstein's selection was not announced by General Manager Stu Inman, however, until the month following the club's participation in both the collegiate and NBA dispersal drafts.

By staffing an expansion roster primarily through the collegiate draft, the Miami Heat knew they would be in for a rough and ego-deflating inaugural NBA season. But no one knew in advance just how rough it would actually be. The Heat lost their opening game 111–91 to the lackluster Los Angeles Clippers. In the opening lineup that first night were Rory Sparrow (a free agent signed only a week before the season), Kevin Edwards, Rony Seikaly, Pat Cummings (another free agent and battle-weary NBA journeyman) and Billy Thompson. But the opening game was only a small glimpse of far worse things to come. The Heat would proceed to lose 17 games before they would finally taste victory, the worst beginning in NBA history. The dismal streak was only ended when the Heat finally got a second crack at the Clippers and were able to return the earlier favor with an unartistic 89–88 squeaker played out in Los Angeles.

The first NBA season was indeed a long one in Miami. Besides the opening record losing streak, the Heat also went on other losing binges of ten, seven (twice), six, five and four (twice) games. The longest win-skein of the year was a brief three-game spree which came with a late-March homestand against the New York Knicks, San Antonio Spurs and New Jersey Nets. The season's final tally was a lowly 15–67, five games worse than the league's other maiden ballclub in Charlotte. Individual bright spots, however, were Edwards and Seikaly, along with four others (Long, Thompson, Sunvold, Sparrow) who all averaged in double figures.

An important product of the Heat's long first season was a top slot in the 1989 collegiate draft, a draft which saw the club pick the two most noteworthy players of the team's first five seasons. One charmed pick would bring on board the young club's best player in the immediate years to come. The other, not so charmed, would result in what is so far the biggest franchise disappointment. Glen Rice, obtained with the fourth overall pick, would soon prove to be a dependable scorer and an offensive force a full grade above first-year stars Seikaly and Long. Rice would emerge over the next four years as the team's most productive and consistent offensive weapon. Another 1989 pick (28th overall) seemed to turn quickly to disaster, however. Sherman Douglas was selected out of Syracuse in the second round and brought high hopes as the point guard of the future. While he *did* lead the club in scoring during his second season, Douglas never lived up to expectations—either those in Miami or everywhere else around the league. The Heat did not give up quickly on Sherman Douglas, however, and even matched a lucrative offer sheet extended to the restricted free agent in December, 1991, by the Los Angeles Lakers. In January of 1992, Douglas would finally be traded to Boston for Brian Shaw, an exchange of two once-promising guards who had finally worn out their welcomes with their original ballclubs.

Slow but steady improvement came in the club's second and third seasons, the final two under coach Ron Rothstein. Most of the firepower was provided by top scorer Rice, ace rebounder Seikaly, and ironman Grant Long. Appearing in less than 80 games only twice over his six-year tenure, by 1994 Long had played the most games (470) and logged the most minutes (14,797) in club history. Moved out of the Midwest Division and into the Atlantic Division after their first painful season, the Heat improved three games in the win column and climbed a single position in the standings during year two. In season number three they were once again basement-bound in their division, yet they had nonetheless improved another six games in the standings and vaulted the 20-victory plateau for the first time.

Season four brought three major changes on the Miami Heat basketball scene. The first was a new coach, as well-travelled Kevin Loughery was tabbed in June, 1991, to succeed Ron Rothstein. Under the veteran Loughery (who can now count 33 seasons as an NBA player and coach) the improving club jumped all the way to a respectable 38 victories, a leap of another fourteen games over the previous campaign. The second-change—another personnel addition—shared responsibility with Loughery for the team's sudden improvement. He was talented 6'8" guard Steve Smith, a fluid scoring machine out of Michigan State and the prize of the 1991 collegiate draft (the fifth pick overall), at least as far as Miami was concerned. Smith would be an immediate impact player, appearing in 61 games, pacing all first-year NBA players in assists average (4.6 apg.) and scoring 12.0 ppg., also fourth best on the Miami team. The biggest change, however, was the season-end appearance of the fledgling Heat in the unfamiliar territory of the NBA playoffs. Miami was quickly eliminated by

Michael Jordan and the powerhouse champion Chicago Bulls. But it now seemed that in only four seasons the Miami club had already turned the corner, well ahead of any of its three expansion rivals.

While Miami's visit to the playoffs in April, 1992, was indeed a short party, it was a festive occasion nonetheless for a young expansion outfit with but four campaigns under its inexperienced belt. It was boasting point enough that Miami was making the first trip to post-season competition of any of the new expansion ballclubs. Leave aside the fact that the Heat had only backed into post-season competition when the Atlanta Hawks lost a season's finale to Cleveland (thus leaving Atlanta and Miami in a flat tie and allowing the Heat to qualify by virtue of the second tie-breaker—a superior season-long conference record). And leave aside the fact that the post-season opposition would be Jordan and the Bulls, a modern dynasty team on its way to a repeat NBA title. Chicago indeed cruised 113–94 in the Chicago Stadium opener, blew the Heat off the floor by a 120–90 count in game two, then coasted through a 119–114 series wrap-up at the Miami Arena. But Miami looked poised in the final game of the set with all five starters (led by Rice with 25) cracking double figures. This was no match for the incomparable Jordan, however, who poured in 56 points in game three alone.

But basketball is a game of ebb and flow and the promising 1992–'93 season quickly turned from bright hope into unmitigated disaster. The key ingredient in the slide was that old basketball bugaboo of unwanted injuries. On November 6, 1992, the Heat had put a talented lineup on the floor of the Orlando Arena to face the Orlando Magic on the very night the home club would be unveiling its new rookie sensation, Shaquille O'Neal. The skilled Miami first five consisted of Brian Shaw, Glen Rice, Willie Burton (1990's top draft pick), John Salley (obtained in a trade with Detroit), and Rony Seikaly. But that opening night would be the final time this unit would play together during the entire subsequent season. Steve Smith (not even in the opening night lineup) missed half a season after undergoing training camp knee surgery. Salley missed the final third of the campaign with a stress fracture which sat him down for 27 of the final 30 contests. Burton also missed the entire second half with a severe wrist injury. Rice and Shaw were also plagued by nagging minor aches and pains, although Rice did play nightly and was the only team member to appear in all 82 games. In a league known for chronic complaining about injury, the Miami Heat were simply never able to stop the bleeding in 1992–'93. The club finished only two-games worse in the win column than a season earlier, and slid only a single notch in the division standings (still bettering Philadelphia, Washington and Milwaukee among Eastern Conference foes). But there would be no return to the playoffs this time around, and the slow franchise-building era, replete with troublesome set-backs, was still clearly far from over.

The 1993–'94 season, Miami's sixth, finally brought the hallmark of initial success for any pro sports franchise—a first climb above the break-even .500 ledger in the win-loss column. It was a season that also saw a continuation of the awful as well as the merely offbeat. At season's outset, for example, the club signed bean-pole sideshow free-agent Manute Bol, a one-dimensional player who can block shots with considerable success, yet do little else in today's physical NBA-style game. It was not clear what plans the Heat actually had for the 7'6" Dinka tribesman, however, as Coach Loughery showed little interest in playing the veteran Bol, who sat out 21 straight games during one mid-season stretch. Bol was able to establish one historical footnote in his brief Miami tenure, however, which came when he logged a six-minute stretch in mid-November versus Washington's 7'7" Gheorghe Muresan, a Rumanian import who lacks Bol's reflexes yet possesses far more bulk, muscle, and pure shooting ability. In this tallest matchup in NBA history the two behemoths lulled the audience with a completely ineffectual standoff as neither player recorded a single point, rebound or blocked shot while on the floor against each other.

The 1994 Heat fortunately could also offer fans more than such mere promotional stunts, however, and by season's end Loughery's club had posted a 42–40 ledger and also won its first post-season game ever, an opening 93–88 upset of the division-champion Hawks in Atlanta's Omni Arena. Behind the offensive displays of Rice and Seikaly, Miami would continue to play the heavily-favored Hawks close throughout the five-game, first-round, post-season series before finally succumbing 102–91 in a hotly contested rubber-match contest.

The Miami Heat are still an expansion club with a seemingly bright future. The 1993–'94 starting lineup featuring Seikaly, Long, Rice, Smith, and Shaw, is potentially one of the most promising in the league. Last year's rookie Harold Miner is an improving bench player with flair and has gained a measure of national visibility by virtue of winning a 1993 All-Star Weekend Slam Dunk championship. Loughery has enjoyed some of his greatest success in Miami after years as a middle-of-the-pack NBA coach. The Heat seem to be only a player or two away from being a legitimate yearly playoff competitor. Yet the past two seasons have also seen Miami treading water while two expansion rivals—Orlando and Charlotte—have landed big-name collegiate stars and now seem headed even more quickly to the top. Miami's Heat no longer can boast of heading the expansion derby. Yet this is a team that is still roaring down the backstretch and trailing only by a narrow length.

Suggested Readings on Miami Heat

Bjarkman, Peter C. **The History of the NBA**. New York: Crescent Books (Random House, Outlet Books), 1992. (Chapter 7)

Strasen, Marty (et. al.). **Basketball Almanac, 1993–94**. New York: Publications International (Signet Sports Library), 1994.

Miami Heat Retired Uniform Numbers

None (expansion franchise)

Year-by-Year Miami Heat Summary

Season	Record	Finish	Coach(es)	Scoring Leader(s)	Playoffs (W–L Record)
1988–89	15–67	6th	Ron Rothstein	Kevin Edwards (13.8)	Did Not Qualify
1989–90	18–64	5th	Ron Rothstein	Rony Seikaly (16.6)	Did Not Qualify
1990–91	24–58	6th	Ron Rothstein	Sherman Douglas (18.5)	Did Not Qualify
1991–92	38–44	4th	Kevin Loughery	Glen Rice (22.3)	Lost in 1st Round (0–3)
1992–93	36–46	5th	Kevin Loughery	Glen Rice (19.0)	Did Not Qualify
1993–94	42–40	4th	Kevin Loughery	Glen Rice (21.1)	Lost in 1st Round (2–3)

Individual Career Leaders and Record Holders (1988–1994)

Scoring Average	Glen Rice (18.7 ppg., 1989–94)
Points Scored	Glen Rice (7,417, 1989–94)
Games Played	Grant Long (470, 1990–94)
Minutes Played	Grant Long (14,797, 1988–94)
Field Goal Pct.	Sherman Douglas (.500, 1989–92)
3-Pt. Field Goals	Glen Rice (523)
Free Throws Made	Rony Seikaly (1,766)
Free-Throw Pct.	Glen Rice (.829)
Rebounds	Rony Seikaly (4,544)
Personal Fouls	Grant Long (1,688)
Assists	Sherman Douglas (1,262)
Steals	Grant Long (664)
Blocked Shots	Rony Seikaly (610)

Individual Single-Season and Game Records (1988–1994)

Scoring Average	Glen Rice (22.3 ppg., 1991–92)
Points Scored (Season)	Glen Rice (1,765, 1991–92)
Points Scored (Game)	Glen Rice (46, 4-11-92 vs. Orlando Magic)
Minutes Played (Season)	Glen Rice (3,082, 1992–93)
Field Goal Pct.	Matt Geiger (.574, 1993–94)
Free-Throw Pct.	Glen Rice (.880, 1993–94)
3-Pt. Field Goals (Season)	Glen Rice (155, 1991–92)
Rebounds (Season)	Rony Seikaly (934, 1991–92)
Rebounds (Game)	Rony Seikaly (34, 3-3-93 vs. Washington Bullets)
Assists (Season)	Sherman Douglas (624, 1990–91)
Assists (Game)	Sherman Douglas (17, 2-26-90 at Atlanta Hawks)

Best Trade in Franchise History

The young Miami franchise took a huge gamble when it parted with a 1993 first-round pick and the draft rights to talented Isiah Morris. Both were shipped to Detroit for veteran 6–11 forward-center John Salley, who had recently been a prime-time bench player on the Pistons' championship clubs of 1989 and 1990. Salley was a still-youthful and productive veteran and he soon proved to be a versatile frontcourt performer as well as an occasional post-position fill-in for the often injured Ron Seikaly. Salley has never been spectacular in Miami, but it is doubtful that the Heat would have been a playoff entrant in their fourth season without him.

Worst Trade in Franchise History

Sherman Douglas was always something of a disappointment in Miami. But the disappointment only grew bigger once this problem-child guard was peddled to Boston (January 10, 1992) in exchange for Brian Shaw. Shaw produced even less in the Miami backcourt than Douglas had, while Douglas, for his part, became a solid performer once he pulled on the Celtics Kelly Green uniform.

Miami Heat Historical Oddity

The Miami Heat qualify for the distinction of having made perhaps the strangest and most complicated "expansion draft" player pick of any team in American professional sports history. The unexpected draft selection of Arvid Kramer from the eligible-player list of the Dallas Mavericks turned more than a few heads and sent more than a few sports reporters shuffling for much-needed information at the time it was announced in June, 1988. Who, after all, was Arvid Kramer? It turns out that the Mavs themselves had once taken Kramer in their own expansion lottery eight full seasons earlier. Kramer had once played eight games for the Denver Nuggets but was now still property of the Dallas franchise, although he had never appeared in a single contest for either the Mavs or for any other NBA team since leaving Denver. As it would turn out Kramer would never suit up for the Miami Heat either. The true story behind the selection was that the Miami Heat had worked a deal in advance with Dallas that had allowed the Mavs to keep other unprotected but coveted players Bill Wennington, Uwe Blab and Steve Alford. In exchange for taking Kramer (who they certainly had no intention of using or even inviting to training camp) the Miami club also received from Dallas that club's first round selection in the upcoming college draft (which turned out to be guard Kevin Edwards from DePaul University).

Heat All-Time Number One Draft Picks List

Miami Heat

1988 Rony Seikaly (Syracuse)
1989 Glen Rice (Michigan)
1990 Willie Burton (Minnesota)
1991 Steve Smith (Michigan State)
1992 Harold Miner (USC)
1993 None

Chapter 26

MINNESOTA TIMBERWOLVES

A Very Ugly Baby Indeed!

All-Time Franchise Record: 105–305, .256 Pct. (1989–1994)
NBA Championships: None
First Draft Picks: Rick Mahorn (1989 Expansion Draft); Pooh Richardson (1989 College Draft)
Greatest Franchise Player: Christian Laettner (1992–1994)
All-Time Leading Scorer: Tony Campbell (4,888 Points, 1989–1992)
Most Successful Coach: Bill Musselman (51–113, .311 Pct., 1989–1991)
All-Time Franchise Team: Christian Laettner (C–F), Chuck Person (F), Tony Campbell (F), Micheal Williams (G), Doug West (G)

Some professional basketball teams—like various people, institutions or even entire nations—simply can not stand very much prosperity. Give them the slightest sign that things might be moving along the right track and they'll be certain to take immediate action to derail them. Drop an opportunity in their laps, and they'll be guaranteed either to squander it or simply not recognize it for what it is.

No pro franchise in recent memory has provided a better example of this maxim than basketball's Minnesota Timberwolves, the NBA's newest and seemingly most utterly directionless franchise. After only two years in the league, the T-Wolves gave every sign that they would leave their expansion rivals—along with a number of floundering veteran clubs as well—eating their dust at the starting gate. About twelve months later the Minnesota team and its front office poohbahs had almost entirely self-destructed—both on the court and in their relationships with the tried-and-true fans of Minnesota as well. Through their first two seasons the Wolves racked up more wins than any of the four most recent expansion teams. But over the past three seasons this same ballclub has managed to win the fewest.

417

Expansion Team Won-Loss Records (1988–1994)

Season	Minnesota	Orlando	Charlotte	Miami
1988–89	—	—	**20–62**	15–67
1989–90	**22–60**	18–64	19–63	18–64
1990–91	29–53	**31–51**	26–56	24–58
1991–92	15–67	21–61	31–51	**38–44 (0–3)**
1992–93	19–63	41–41	**44–38 (4–5)**	36–46
1993–94	20–62	**50–32 (0–3)**	41–41	42–40 (2–3)
Totals	105–305	161–249 (0–3)	**181–311 (4–5)**	173–319 (2–6)

Key: Playoff records in parentheses; Best records in boldface

Few teams, in fact, have ever debuted in the NBA with more promise for immediate success. The T-Wolves struggled in their opening campaign, of course, as absolutely everyone expected that they would. They limped to a 22–60 record in the relatively weak Midwest Division and finished 6th, 19 wins behind their closest rival, fourth-place Houston. Yet they did not rest all the way at the bottom of their divisional heap, for all their first-year ineptitude. That dubious honor belonged to a second-year expansion club—the Charlotte Hornets (19–63). And in addition to the consolation of nipping an expansion rival by three full games in the divisional standings, Minnesota's first season also saw them post a better mark than expansion teams Miami (18–64) and Orlando (also 18–64), as well as one veteran club—the New Jersey Nets (17–65). And they finished only a game worse than the Sacramento Kings to boot.

The first season of Minnesota T-Wolves basketball also showed bright signs of promise in areas other than the all-important win column. Forward Tony Campbell quickly emerged from several previous journeyman seasons in Detroit and Los Angeles to prove himself a legitimate NBA scoring star (23.2 ppg. to rank among the top fifteen in the league). Pooh Richardson not only delivered the ball to Campbell and others with regularity (554 assists) and ran the offense efficiently, but the top draft choice also proved to be an all-around adroit playmaker and an effective scoring threat himself (11.4 ppg.). Under the defense-oriented strategies of veteran coach Bill Musselman, the fledgling T-Wolves quickly became—to the surprise of almost everyone in the league, including perhaps themselves—one of the best clubs in the entire circuit at maintaining offensive tempo while also stopping opponents from effective retaliatory scoring.

Minnesota's debut squad had been patched together via dispersal and collegiate drafts and through a spattering of trades and free-agent signings. The plan implemented by coach Musselman and his front office advisers seemed to be one oriented toward immediate impact, as well as painful long-range franchise building. Little came out of the expansion draft itself, which provided a corps of veterans, yet few who would actually suit up for season number one (just Corbin, Johnson, Lohaus, and Roth) and fewer still who would be around very long (Corbin lasted three seasons and the others but one). The collegiate draft route appeared a good deal more lucrative with UCLA guard Pooh Richardson taken with the tenth overall pick, and guard Mark West from Villanova acquired as a hidden gem in round two. Five seasons later, West would still be on board as the franchise career leader in games and minutes played, as well as the team pacesetter in field goal efficiency.

Timberwolves Expansion Draft Selections (June 15, 1989)

Rick Mahorn (Detroit Pistons), 6'10" Forward (Never played with T-Wolves)
Tyrone Corbin (Phoenix Suns), 6'6" Forward (1989–92, 3 seasons)
Steve Johnson (Portland Trailblazers), 6'10" Center (1989–90, 1 season)
Brad Lohaus (Sacramento Kings), 7'0" Forward (1989–90, 1 season)
David Rivers (Los Angeles Lakers), 6'0" Guard (Never played with T-Wolves)
Mark Davis, (Milwaukee Bucks), 6'5" Guard (Never played with T-Wolves)
Scott Roth (San Antonio Spurs), 6'8" Forward-Center (1989–90, 1 season)
Shelton Jones (Philadelphia Sixers), 6'9" Forward (Never played with T-Wolves)
Eric White (Los Angeles Clippers), 6'8" Forward (Never played with T-Wolves)
Maurice Martin (Denver Nuggets), 6'6" Guard (Never played with T-Wolves)
Gunther Behnke (Cleveland Cavaliers), 7'4" Center (Never played with T-Wolves)

The T-Wolves did lose their opening franchise game at Seattle by a count of 106–94. Expansion-draft first selection Rick Mahorn, a reputed ''Bad Boy'' plucked from the champion Detroit Pistons, had refused his assignment to an expansion roster and had eventually been traded—quite reluctantly—to Philadelphia's Sixers for three future draft selections. The opening day starting lineup for coach Musselman thus consisted of Sam Mitchell and Tod Murphy at the forwards, Brad Lohaus at center, and Tony Campbell and Sidney Lowe at Guards. Sam Mitchell scored the new club's first-ever basket in Seattle. And the new team's first-ever franchise win came three games later, in Philadelphia, by a 125–118 count in overtime.

Although they didn't win with any regularity, the expansion first-year T-Wolves were immediately greeted with open arms by a midwestern metropolis which had long-coveted a return to the glories of big-time pro basketball. This is the city, after all, that had once hosted the first great NBA dynasty team, the Minneapolis Lakers with towering George Mikan, sharpshooting Jim Pollard, and scoring wizard Elgin Baylor. And although there were no Mikans or Elgin Baylors now performing for the home club, it didn't seem to matter to the city swept up by the exciting return of

NBA-style action. No first-year team was ever such a marketing success, not even the previous year's Charlotte Hornets greeted by the fanatical throngs of North Carolina basketball junkies. Minnesota fans proved even more enthusiastic, stuffing the huge Hubert H. Humphrey Metrodome night after night to the tune of more than 26,000 patrons a game. The third largest crowd in NBA history (49,551) packed the Metrodome on April 17, 1990, for Wolves Fan Appreciation night. By season's end the first-year Wolves owned a season's record attendance of well over a million, with the 1,072,572 patrons (26,160 per game) topping by 6,067 the previous single season record owned by the 1987–'88 Detroit Pistons.

It seemed at the start of things that the ownership which had brought the expansion Timberwolves to Minnesota had indeed struck pure gold. The effort to land a team had begun way back in 1984 when Minnesota Governor Rudy Perpich had established a 30-member task force headed by ex-Minneapolis Lakers great George Mikan. A formal proposal to the league came two years later from an ownership group headed by business partners Harvey Ratner and Marv Wolfenson, along with attorney and spokesman, Bob Stein. Plans for a new downtown arena were also hastily approved in February, 1987, by the Minneapolis City Council. Two weeks later the league announced its intentions to place an expansion club in Minneapolis in time for the opening of the 1989–'90 NBA season. Everything seemed in line for a triumph return of professional basketball to these Twin Cities nestled peacefully among a thousand lakes.

Much of the success of the first two seasons can be attributed to the offensive play of Tony Campbell and to the bench strategies of coach Bill Musselman. Campbell filled up the bucket with better than 20 points per game for each of his first two Minnesota seasons. While his average dipped during a third winter, he was once again the club's scoring leader. Only guard Doug West, with a surprise 19.3 average compiled in season number four, has come close to matching Campbell's two 20-point campaigns.

With the team settling into a brand new venue in the huge new Target Center in downtown Minneapolis, and with such a respectable first-year performance to build upon, everything pointed to continued successes and unstoppable progress during a second 1990–'91 campaign. And for the most part unchecked progress continued to be the first order of business. The Wolves moved up seven games in the win column and also climbed another slot in the divisional standings. Campbell was providing dependable offense, Coach Musselman's defense was clicking, and so were the all-important turnstiles. Then almost overnight all the wheels seemed to come flying off this most promising organization.

The problem suddenly seemed to be a front office that couldn't leave well enough alone and almost overnight sunk their own ship with a flurry of poorly motivated personal shifts and lackluster selections at the drafting table. First came the firing of coach Musselman immediately after the end of the second season. Musselman had proven unpopular with his players, due largely to his demanding defensive alignments and restrictive offensive style of play. Winning apparently did not seem to be a high enough priority for many of the players on the young team, and personal playing time held a much higher value for some than any less glorious measures of team progress.

Musselman was replaced by recently fired Boston Celtics mentor Jimmy Rodgers. And if Rodgers introduced a more free-wheeling offense to his players' delight, he did nothing at all to keep the club going in the right direction. Thus the third T-Wolves campaign quickly brought a tumble all the way back below the opening performance two seasons earlier. The Wolves finished 1991–'92 with the worst record (15–67) in the entire league—one of the worst in NBA annals. And they leapfrogged back behind their three expansion rivals in the process. Part of the problem was the outright failure of two huge centers the club had invested heavily in during the 1990 and 1991 college drafts. University of Louisville seven-footer Felton Spencer, a 1990 pick, spent his sophomore season on and off the injured list and contributed very little. Luc Longley, the 1991 selection out of the University of New Mexico and a native of Australia, remained a bitter holdout for the entire first month of the season. And it was all downhill from there.

An unsuccessful 1992 campaign brought in its wake a series of additional sweeping changes and each seemed only to worsen the T-Wolves plight. Tony Campbell now longed to exchange the basement play of an expansion club for the bright lights surrounding some established winner, and Campbell soon got his wish in the form of a one-way ticket to the New York Knicks for the 1992–'93 campaign. The change benefitted neither party very much, however. The Wolves, for their part, found it impossible to replace Campbell's scoring punch with a series of small forwards who followed him into town. Campbell in turn soon found himself a little-used role player languishing away on the bench in New York.

Reinforcements were indeed brought in through the drafting and trade routes, but the choices themselves were not the wisest when viewed in retrospect. First the Wolves expended their top 1992 pick (third overall) on "Dream Team" Olympian Christian Laettner of Duke. Laettner—an exceptionally quick 6'11" forward—is a most talented athlete by any standard, but his outsized ego soon proved larger than his huge salary, and Laettner was anything but a team player or a popular clubhouse fixture during his rookie season. A major deal with the Indiana Pacers at the outset of the 1992 campaign also shipped off star guard Pooh Richardson and rebounding leader Sam Mitchell. Obtained in return were flashy backcourt ace Micheal Williams and moody scorer Chuck Person, the latter a Pacers "problem child" since his Rookie-of-the-Year 1987 campaign. Williams enjoyed an effective first season in Minnesota, proving one of the league's best free-throw shooters. At the close of the season Williams recorded an all-time NBA mark for consecutive charity tosses. Person, on the other hand, continued to score about the same number of points that he nightly relinquished on defense. With Person and Laettner in the same lineup, there hardly seemed to be enough shooting opportunities to go around.

Jimmy Rodgers quickly demonstrated that his first season's inability to mold the strange hodge-podge of personnel he found in Minnesota into a winner was no one-season aberration. With the club well down the road to a second straight disastrous and backsliding campaign, Rodgers himself was fired in mid-session and replaced by inexperienced assistant Sidney Lowe. Lowe, a six-year NBA backcourt veteran and former North Carolina State star, had been in the starting lineup at point guard when the very first T-Wolves team had taken the floor four seasons earlier.

Perhaps the only true highlight during a fifth NBA season in Minnesota—the first full season under Sydney Lowe—was the NBA All-Star Weekend which came calling at mid-season on the expansion city of Minneapolis. A special hometown interest also grew up around rookie Isaiah Rider, who would carry the Timberwolves' colors in the prestigious All-Star Saturday Slam Dunk competition. The 6'5" guard-forward from UNLV indeed gave the hometown faithful something to cheer long and loud about when he parlayed a series of spinning slams into a surprise Gatorade Slam Dunk title. By outpointing Seattle's Shawn Kemp in the final round, Rider became the second straight rookie and third in four years to capture the league's coveted slam dunk trophy.

Yet Isaiah Rider and his teammates provided little else to rouse cheers from the nearly 25,000 nightly patrons who jammed into the plush Target center Arena to witness the T-Wolves' continued marathon of losing. Even the league's worst club, the Dallas Mavericks, embarrassed the Wolves twice in early season play up in Minneapolis. On a near-record losing pace of their own, the Dallas club earned only two victories over their first thirty games, and both of those came in the Target Center against their apparent cousins, the equally hapless Wolves. Rider did follow up his slam dunk success with a 16.6 ppg. average that fell a hair short of Christian Laettner (16.8) for the club leadership. Doug West logged enough games and minutes to become the all-time club leader in those often unrecognized departments; and second-year forward Marlon Maxey registered a new single-season club standard (.553) for field goal shooting efficiency.

Nonetheless, a gloomy cloud hung continually over the downtrodden franchise as rumors constantly circulated throughout the season's final weeks about the ballclub's reportedly inevitable shift of venue into either New Orleans, or possibly Memphis, Tennessee. Despite one of the league's largest nightly gate draws, club owners Marv Wolfenson and Harvey Ratner repeatedly claimed that an imbalanced lease arrangement on the Target Center was causing them to lose money at nearly intolerable levels. Only a last-minute act of the NBA Expansion Committee several weeks after the season's end (blocking a proposed sale of the team to a New Orleans outfit bent on moving the T-Wolves into the Bayou State) was able to assure at least one more season of NBA basketball for the tradition-rich city of Minneapolis.

With Lowe now established precariously as the head man in the wake of the club's fifth campaign, and with a lineup of free-shooting and free-talking individualists like Chuck Person (released at the end of the 1994 season), Christian Laettner and Micheal Williams, the T-Wolves show few signs—if any at all—of getting back any time soon upon the highroad they once seemed to be traveling during their first two winters in the league. With Charlotte, Orlando, and Miami all moving rapidly toward the league's upper echelons, Minnesota fans are still reeling under one of the earliest and fastest self-destruction acts in pro basketball history.

Suggested Readings on Minnesota Timberwolves

Bjarkman, Peter C. **The History of the NBA**. New York: Crescent Books (Random house, Outlet books), 1992. (Chapter 7)

Strasen, Marty (et. al.). **Basketball Almanac, 1993–94**. New York: Publications International (Signet Sports Library), 1994.

Minnesota Timberwolves Retired Uniform Numbers

None (expansion franchise)

Year-by-Year Minnesota Timberwolves Summary

Season	Record	Finish	Coach(es)	Scoring Leader(s)	Playoffs (W–L Record)
1989–90	22–60	6th	Bill Musselman	Tony Campbell (23.2)	Did Not Qualify
1990–91	29–53	5th	Bill Musselman	Tony Campbell (21.8)	Did Not Qualify
1991–92	15–67	6th	Jimmy Rodgers	Tony Campbell (16.8)	Did Not Qualify
1992–93	19–63	5th	Jimmy Rodgers / Sidney Lowe	Doug West (19.3)	Did Not Qualify
1993–94	20–62	5th	Sidney Lowe	Christian Laettner (16.8)	Did Not Qualify

Individual Career Leaders and Record Holders (1989–1994)

Scoring Average	Tony Campbell (20.4 ppg., 1989–92)
Points Scored	Tony Campbell (4,888, 1989–92)
Games Played	Doug West (359)
Minutes Played	Doug West (9,028, 1989–94)
Field Goals Made	Tony Campbell (1,902)
Field Goal Pct.	Doug West (.502)
3-Pt Field Goals	Chuck Person (218)

Free Throws Made	Tony Campbell (1,046)
Free-Throw Pct.	Micheal Williams (.875)
Rebounds	Sam Mitchell (1,455)
Personal Fouls	Doug West (930)
Assists	Pooh Richardson (1,973)
Steals	Pooh Richardson (383)
Blocked Shots	Felton Spencer (266)

Individual Single-Season and Game Records (1989–1994)

Scoring Average	Tony Campbell (23.2 ppg., 1989–90)
Points Scored (Season)	Tony Campbell (1,903, 1989–90)
Points Scored (Game)	Tony Campbell (44, 2-2-90 vs. Boston Celtics)
Field Goal Pct. (Season)	Marlon Maxey (.533, 1993–94)
Free-Throw Pct. (Season)	Micheal Williams (.907, 1992–93)
Rebounds (Season)	Christian Laettner (708, 1992–93)
Rebounds (Game)	Tod Murphy (20, 1-2-90 vs. Los Angeles Clippers)
Assists (Season)	Pooh Richardson (734, 1990–91)
Assists (Game)	Sidney Lowe (17, 3-20-90 at Golden State Warriors)
	Pooh Richardson (17, 3-3-92 at Washington Bullets)
Blocked Shots (Season)	Felton Spencer (121, 1990–91)
Blocked Shots (Game)	Randy Breuer (9, 4-13-90 vs. Orlando Magic)
Steals (Season)	Tyrone Corbin (175, 1989–990)
Steals (Game)	Tyrone Corbin (8, 3-30-90 at Dallas Mavericks)

Best Trade in Franchise History

Desperate for on-court glamor and some scoring punch, the Wolves traded star guard Pooh Richardson and starting forward Sam Mitchell to the Indiana Pacers on September 8, 1992, in exchange for guard Micheal Williams and high scoring forward Chuck Person. Despite his reputation for selfish play and poor defensive skills, Person battled injuries through the '92–'93 season to provide up-front strength with rookie Christian Laettner. Williams was the key to the deal, however, more than replacing Pooh Richardson as a point guard and ending the season with 84 consecutive free throws, breaking an all-time league mark held by Calvin Murphy.

Worst Trade in Franchise History

Disgruntled star forward Tony Campbell was peddled away on September 14, 1992, to the New York Knicks for future considerations. The leading scorer in franchise history was tired of playing with an expansion loser and had seemingly been made expendable by the drafting of Laettner and acquisition of Chuck Person. Campbell ended up riding the bench in New York, however, and neither Laettner (18.2) nor Person (16.8) could immediately match his 20-plus per game scoring average.

Minnesota Timberwolves Historical Oddity

The expansion Minnesota NBA franchise of 1989 had perhaps the largest and most successful community-participation contest ever held to select a professional ballclub nickname. More than 6,000 received entries put forth 1,284 different possible names, with "Timberwolves" and "Polars" far outdistancing the pack. A runoff was held between the two finalists and the "T-Wolves" moniker won out by a clear-cut 2–1 landslide margin.

Timberwolves All-Time Number One Draft Picks List

Minnesota Timberwolves
1989 Jerome "Pooh" Richardson (UCLA)
1990 Felton Spencer (Louisville)
1991 Luc Longley (New Mexico)
1992 Christian Laettner (Duke)
1993 Isaiah Rider (UNLV)

Chapter 27

ORLANDO MAGIC

Mixing Hype With Hustle in the Magic Kingdom

All-Time Franchise Record: 161–249, .393 Pct. (1989–1994)
NBA Championships: None
First Draft Picks: Sidney Green (1989 Expansion Draft); Nick Anderson (1989 College Draft)
Greatest Franchise Player: Shaquille O'Neal (1992–1994)
All-Time Leading Scorer: Nick Anderson (5,968 Points, 1989–1994)
Most Successful Coach: Brian Hill (50–32, .610 Pct., 1993–1994)
All-Time Franchise Team: Shaquille O'Neal (C–F), Dennis Scott (F), Nick Anderson (F), Scott Skiles (G), Anfernee "Penny" Hardaway (G)

In a recent sugar-coated spin-off biography of the type generated by the careers of most pop-culture heroes, author Bill Gutman waxes on for pages about how Shaquille O'Neal has overnight become the heir-apparent to a basketball celebrity throne long held by the triumvirate of Bird, Magic, and Michael "Air" Jordan. Gutman describes Shaq's omnipresent image in television commercials and his numerous celebrity appearances to perform rap music on network television shows. He informs us that recent surveys of school-aged youngsters have confirmed that Shaq is indeed a unanimous choice as today's most popular sports personality.

What Gutman does not tell his readers, of course, is that the celebrity status of Shaquille O'Neal so far has altogether little to do with the demonstrated oncourt ballplaying abilities of the NBA's latest superstar wonder. Shaq's larger-than-life image has more to do, seemingly, with the video onslaught of a multi-million dollar advertising campaign launched by the makers of Reebok athletic shoes and Pepsi-Cola soft drinks. It is the skillful handling by the O'Neal management team and NBA public relations gurus and not the skillful handling of a basketball by the Shaq himself which has built this latest NBA phenomenon, brick by brick.

Here, then, is the league's first true "manufactured" instant superstar, created to fill a perceived public relations gap in the wake of a disappearing act by the league's most recent marketing pawns. Bird surrendered all too soon to an aching body; Magic left under the cloud of the AIDS virus; Jordan chose to turn his back on further NBA stardom and pursue his own private dream in the world of minor league baseball. Jordan's unexpected retirement only seemed to underscore the immediate need for a new polished "superstar" to keep the league front-and-center in the public eye and on the public video screen.

The problem, of course, was that NBA marketing strategies of the past decade had made such a single mega-star attraction seemingly necessary to continued league health. This is probably a flaw in the image-making of a league which has far more to sell than "celebrity" players alone. And in the case of O'Neal, the whole business seems especially ludicrous. For few who gobble up Shaq memorabilia, tout his overblown praises, and select him as the league's top performer have in fact ever seen him play five minutes of live or televised basketball. Rarely did the Orlando Magic appear on national television screens during O'Neal's first regular NBA season. Ticket prices of $30 and up for NBA games assure that precious few fifth and sixth graders have ever watched O'Neal strut his stuff live in the arena. And when playoff time for the 1993 season rolled around, with its prime-time television exposure, O'Neal and the Magic had already packed up their gear and headed home for the season.

This is not to suggest that Shaquille O'Neal was not a forceful NBA rookie with plenty of potential talent oozing from his oversized seven-foot frame. He did post excellent first-year numbers for a rookie. Across his freshman campaign O'Neal led his Orlando team in just about every offensive category and a few on the defensive side as well: scoring (23.4 ppg.), rebounding (13.9 rpg.), field goal percentage (.562), and blocked shots (286). Shaq became the first NBA rookie ever to be named league player of the week in his very first week on the job. And he was the year's only NBA performer to rank in the top ten in four different categories—2nd in rebounding, 2nd in blocks, 4th in field goal percentage and 8th in scoring. He did provide some exciting moments on the court, as well, busting one backboard in New Jersey's Meadowlands Arena and still another in the Phoenix America West Arena. And he was tabbed the league's top rookie over Alonzo Mourning of Charlotte in landslide balloting. And at the start of his sophomore campaign O'Neal seemingly had replaced the retired Jordan as the league's top scorer and for much of his second season seemed positioned to become the first center to pace the NBA in scoring since Jabbar twenty years earlier.

By season's end Shaq would be edged out in the scoring race by yet another center, David Robinson of San Antonio; nonetheless Shaq had raised his scoring average to a most impressive 29.3 ppg. and silenced many of his freshman-year critics. But for all his achievements in the heat of NBA action, it still seemed that Shaq's stardom and celebrity always preceded his performances; it never seemed, more appropriately, to follow on their heels.

When biographer Gutman boasts that Shaq's "incredible" rookie season miraculously brought the Orlando Magic to a near-miss at playoff qualifications he shows a glaring ignorance of past league history. What Shaq's rookie performance did for the Magic was only to lead them to the 23rd best record in a 27-team league. Hardly an earthshaking impact in the light of even recent NBA history. Shaq's rival David Robinson, for one, launched the San Antonio Spurs on a record 35-game improvement just three seasons back. Author Gutman (and many fans along with him) fails to remember that only a decade earlier Bird and Magic both turned their teams from tailenders into true playoff contenders (champions in Magic's case) in a single season—and quite single-handedly. And several decades ago two forgotten big men—Chamberlain and Jabbar (then Alcindor)— both brought their teams to the very top of the league in a single campaign. And then there is the story of what Bill Russell did in his rookie season and thereafter for Red Auerbach's Boston Celtics. Shaquille O'Neal simply did not measure up to such earlier immediate-impact players.

The Orlando Magic, of course, are indeed fortunate to own O'Neal, as well as the horde of other young players they have stockpiled in the past two seasons and around whom they hope to construct a luminous future. The Magic have indeed enjoyed some pure "magic" when it comes to the past several lottery draft picks. First came the selection of O'Neal in the summer of 1992. Then in 1993 there was another top pick, expended on Chris Webber who was immediately traded to Golden State for Anfernee Hardaway and another secured future top selection.

From the start the new Orlando franchise has attempted to tie itself to the notion of such magic, as well as to the type of commercial promotion that has surrounded their franchise star, Shaquille O'Neal. The club has not surprisingly exploited its proximity to the Walt Disney complex from the outset. The franchise application presented to commissioner David Stern in July, 1986, was accompanied by a pair of Mickey Mouse ears. Then there is the team name and its unavoidable association with the playground world of central Florida. And also there was the design of the team's uniforms—a futuristic streamlined look featuring a star-burst itself suggestive of moviedom and pure cinematic magic.

And there was also the business of selecting the team's first roster of players. This came through the league's 1989 summer expansion draft between the Magic and the Minnesota Timberwolves. Orlando opted for a number of proven journeyman veterans like Sidney Green, Reggie Theus, and Terry Catledge, and it would be those veterans who could earn the team a small measure of first and second-year respectability until the true franchise future (O'Neal) arrived just in time for season number four.

Magic Expansion Draft Selections (June 15, 1989)

Sidney Green (New York Knicks), 6'9" Forward (1989–90, 1 season with Magic)
Reggie Theus (Atlanta Hawks, 6'7" Guard (1989–90, 1 season)
Terry Catledge (Washington Bullets), 6'8" Forward (1989–93, 4 seasons)
Sam Vincent (Chicago Bulls), 6'2" Guard (1989–92, 3 seasons)
Otis Smith (Golden State Warriors), 6'5" Guard-Forward (1989–92, 3 seasons)
Scott Skiles (Indiana Pacers), 6'1" Guard (1989–94, 5 seasons)
Jerry Reynolds (Seattle SuperSonics), 6'8" Guard-Forward (1989–92, 3 seasons)
Mark Acres (Boston Celtics), 6'11" Forward-Center (1989–92, 3 seasons)
Morton Wiley (Dallas Mavericks), 6'4" Guard (1989–92, 3 seasons)
Jim Farmer (Utah Jazz), 6'4" Guard (Never played with Magic)
Keith Lee (New Jersey Nets), 6'10" Forward/Center (Never played with Magic)
Frank Johnson (Houston Rockets), 6'3" Guard (Never played with Magic)

There has also been a good bit of "magical" luck which has unaccountably attached itself to this newest NBA franchise. When the Orlando Magic hosted the 1992 NBA All-Star contest, for example, it just happened to be the game which was to serve as the scene for Magic Johnson's much publicized final official league appearance. And one "Magic" combined with another to provide fans with a rare fantasy gala weekend of hoops and nostalgia. The 1992 All-Star Game itself was the most publicized and dramatic in league history. And all thanks to Magic Johnson and his memorable final performance in an NBA uniform.

It was perhaps the most shocking news the sporting world had received in decades when Earvin "Magic" Johnson unexpectedly announced his retirement from the game during the first week of the 1991–'92 season. Johnson had tested positive for the HIV virus and doctors had advised against the further physical stress of pro basketball competition. If Magic Johnson had disappeared from center court action by the time the league's 43rd season unfolded, his name and image nonetheless continued to dominate the NBA scene just as it had for the entire past decade. Speculation continued as to whether Magic would assume his elected spot on the summer 1992 Olympic "Dream Team" and whether he would play in the mid-season All-Star Game Classic. The latter question was quickly enough answered, and with much accompanying drama and hoopla.

The popular Los Angeles Lakers star indeed did suit up for the league's 42nd annual All-Star event—played in the expansion city of Orlando—an event for which Johnson had been the top vote-getter despite his official "retired" status. With his usual flair for the dramatic, the incomparable Johnson even topped the flood of pre-game hype by staging a remarkable MVP performance (25 points, 29 minutes played, 5 rebounds, and 9 assists) as his inspired West squad romped to a 153–113 victory. For perhaps the first time in its four-decade history—under the intense national spot-light of Magic's fabulous swan-song—the league's mid-season All-Star shootout had proven to be a true high-point moment of another action-packed NBA campaign.

Such highs have not always accompanied the on-court history of the Orlando franchise, however. In fact, the four-year team history has been a true roller coaster ride of highs and lows, rapid ascents and breakneck dips. The opening campaign brought the predictably dreadful expansion season that all might have expected. Orlando dropped its first-ever fran-chise game by a 111–106 count to the New Jersey Nets, but then re-bounded to defeat New York and Cleveland in consecutive matches. The new club surprised even diehard locals with a .500 ledger over their first 14 games. The first year was noted far more for style than substance, however. There were the flashy uniforms and also a parquet homecourt floor that imitated its counterpart in Boston Garden. But the expansion team under ex-Sixers coach Matt Guokas was hardly a passable imitation of either the old or new Boston Celtics. Reggie Theus, Sam Vincent, Otis Smith, and Scott Skiles blended with rookie Nick Anderson to form a starting lineup that was sometimes exciting, but rarely very productive by any measure.

The club improved dramatically in the win column during a second campaign. The most pleasant surprise was the solid veteran play of former journeyman Scott Skiles in the backcourt. After four mediocre seasons as an NBA bench-rider, Skiles blossomed as the league's "Comeback Player of the Year" and suddenly became the offensive force he had once been in college at Michigan State. Not only did Skiles throw in points at a career-best 17.2 clip, but he dished out assists at a record rate as well. On December 30th, in Denver, Scott Skiles accounted for an all-time NBA mark with 30 assists in a single game. Dennis Scott was the team's top rookie and pumped in better than 15 points per game. The Orlando club seemed to gel after the All-Star break and the team finished with an impressive .500 over-all mark in the season's second half and a 24–17 home record down the stretch.

But injuries quickly ruined the 1991–1992 year and ended any specula-tion that the Magic would earn overnight respectability. Just as quickly as he had arrived in the spring of 1991, Scott Skiles had fizzled in the late part of the 1992 campaign, despite continuing to pace the club in assists, free throws and minutes played. Dennis Scott was out with injury almost the entire 1991–1992 season. Without much other talent the Magic were hardly magical and finished the campaign with the worst record (21–61) in the entire Eastern Conference.

It was a different story one season later, however. Stocked with their lottery pick center, Shaquille O'Neal, and his hefty scoring average, the surprising Magic actually tied the Indiana Pacers (at 41–41 records) for an eighth and final conference playoff slot. But the technicalities of the league's tie-breaking system would then intervene to postpone a first playoff visit for at least one more season. The Pacers and Magic had split their four regular-season games (first tie-breaker) and shared an equal 27–29 mark in conference play (second tie-breaker). A third tie-breaking provision (one that considers comparative records within the division for teams which share a division) simply didn't apply to the Atlantic Division Magic and Central Division Pacers. A fourth potential standard of winning percentage against playoff opponents within the conference also left both teams in a flat-footed dead heat. Thus it was the fifth and final tie-breaking measure—point differential in head-to-head meetings—that left the Pacers (who outpointed the Magic by five) in the post-season derby, and Orlando on the sidelines.

The club's fourth season had indeed been boosted lustily by the presence of Shaq, even if the touted rookie with a mile of advanced press clippings did not prove an instant franchise savior. There were others who also pitched in around O'Neal to account for the near-playoff season in year four. Versatile Nick Anderson proved to be a solid scorer from both the shooting guard and forward positions with his second straight 19.9 ppg. average. Dennis Scott (15.9 ppg.) also doubled in both front and back court roles and added to the offensive arsenal as well. And Scott Skiles continued to run the offense efficiently from the point guard slot, performing beyond almost everyone's largest expectations. In his fourth campaign with the Magic, Skiles proved his continued worth by chipping in 40 double-digit-assists games and with a new club single-season assists mark (735).

If Shaq was "the future" in 1993 he was already "the present" a year later in 1994. The league's hottest mega-star had overnight begun the expected transition into one of its hottest on-court properties as well. Making quick work of his many nay-sayers and critics, the Shaq paced the NBA in scoring for much of the season and threatened to become the first post man since Jabbar two decades earlier to capture a league scoring title. In the end, it was another big man who would swipe scoring honors from Shaq's grasp. San Antonio's David Robinson charged down the stretch and even over-achieved with a 72-point game on the season's final afternoon to edge out O'Neal 29.8 to 29.3. The final scoring battle recalled another just like it a decade and a half earlier when George Gervin, with 63 markers on the final day, edged David Thompson, who had himself posed 71 earlier that same afternoon. O'Neal did not succumb to Robinson in the frantic scoring race, however, before he had posted a club-record 53 points of his own in Minnesota just two weeks before the end of the campaign.

And Shaq had even more reinforcements this time around. New coach Brian Hill seemed to bring a new spirit and team chemistry to the ballclub. And the acquisition of point guard Anfernee "Penny" Hardaway from Golden State on draft day had provided the backcourt help needed to balance the front-court power of O'Neal and high-scoring Nick Anderson. The draft day trade of number one pick Chris Webber had been vilified by some Orlando patrons who had hoped to see a muscular forecourt of O'Neal, Anderson and Webber. But Orlando was counting instead on Hardaway to plug the biggest gap in the team's imbalanced offense (point guard, given the advanced age of Skiles) and Penny Hardaway did not disappoint. While Webber earned Rookie-of-the-Year honors in Oakland, Hardaway also flashed brilliance with a creative floor game, a club runner-up 16.0 scoring average, and better than 500 assists. Propelled by such a backcourt boost, the Magic shot from a break-even record in 1993 to a second-place divisional finish, and even leaped over the once-distant 50-victory plateau. There would be no doubts about a first-ever playoff appearance this time around.

The seeming magic that somehow touched the like-named Orlando franchise for two straight lottery grab bags seemed to run a bit short once it came to the maiden post-season appearance of April, 1994. It was indeed ill-fortune at its worst that the Orlando playoff opponent would be the hottest late-season team in the entire NBA. Owners of a nine-game win streak at season's end, the Indiana Pacers rolled by Orlando in three straight round-one games, although two opening contests in Orlando were not completely settled until the final seconds of play. Game two, for instance, went to Indiana on a buzzer-beating three-point goal by ex-Laker Byron Scott.

One painful negative in an otherwise heady season would therefore have to be the closing note involving a stalled Shaq and an embarrassing three-game blank against the red-hot Pacers at playoff time. But everyone around the NBA knew that Shaq and Hardaway would be back again in the fall, undoubtedly better than ever and ready to take the next giant step along the championship road on which they were already seemingly embarked.

The future does indeed seem more bright than gloomy for the Orlando NBA club. After four seasons under Matt Guokas a coaching change has been made that brings novice Brian Hill and plenty of enthusiasm to the bench. Skiles will remain an adequate point guard until another draft brings in reinforcements. Anderson and Scott are on the upside of their still-promising careers. And Anfernee Hardaway may well team with O'Neal to provide one of the best young "inside and outside" combinations anywhere in the league. O'Neal is hardly a Chamberlain or a Russell, or even a Nate Thurmond, despite the tons of endless hype. But in an age of renewed league balance and with the departure of Jordan, he may well be enough to make the Orlando team a middle-of-the-pack playoff regular for years to come.

Suggested Readings on Orlando Magic

Bjarkman, Peter C. **Shaq: The Making of a Legend**. New York: Smithmark (W. H. Smith Publishers), 1994.

Castello, Bob and Matt Marsom. **Meet Shaquille O'Neal: An Unauthorized Biography**. Lincolnwood, Illinois: Publications Unlimited
International, 1993.

Gutman, Bill. **Shaquille O'Neal: A Biography**. New York and London:
Archway Paperbacks (Pocket Books), 1993.

Hunter, Bruce. **Shaq Impaq—The Unauthorized and Untold Story
Behind the NBA's Newest Superstar**. Chicago: Bonus Books, 1993.

O'Neal, Shaquille (with Jack McCallum). **Shaq Attaq!** New York:
Hyperion Books, 1993.

Orlando Magic Retired Uniform Numbers

None (expansion franchise)

Year-by-Year Orlando Magic Summary

Season	Record	Finish	Coach(es)	Scoring Leader(s)	Playoffs (W–L Record)
1989–90	18–64	7th	Matt Guokas	Terry Catledge (19.4)	Did Not Qualify
1990–91	31–51	4th	Matt Guokas	Scott Skiles (17.2)	Did Not Qualify
1991–92	21–61	7th	Matt Guokas	Nick Anderson (19.9)	Did Not Qualify
1992–93	41–41	4th	Matt Goukas	Shaquille O'Neal (23.4)	Did Not Qualify
1993–94	50–32	2nd	Brian Hill	Shaquille O'Neal (29.3)	Lost in 1st Round (0–3)

Individual Career Leaders and Record Holders (1989–1994)

Scoring Average	Shaquille O'Neal (26.4 ppg., 1992–94)
Points Scored	Nick Anderson (5,968 Points, 1989–94)
Games Played	Scott Skiles (384, 1989–94)
Minutes Played	Scott Skiles (11,940, 1989–94)
3-Pt. Field Goals	Scott Skiles (384)
Free Throws Made	Scott Skiles (1,176)
Free-Throw Pct.	Scott Skiles (.892)
Rebounds	Shaquille O'Neal (2,194)
Personal Fouls	Jeff Turner (1,055)
Assists	Scott Skiles (2,776)
Steals	Nick Anderson (502)
Blocked Shots	Shaquille O'Neal (517)

Individual Single-Season and Game Records (1989–1994)

Scoring Average	Shaquille O'Neal (29.3 ppg. 1993–94)
Points Scored (Season)	Shaquille O'Neal (2,377, 1993–94)
Points Scored (Game)	Shaquille O'Neal (53, 4–20–94 at Minnesota T-Wolves)

3-Pt. Field Goals (Season)	Dennis Scott (125, 1990–91)
3-Pt. Field Goals (Game)	Dennis Scott (9, 4–13–93 vs. Milwaukee Bucks)
Rebounds (Season)	Shaquille O'Neal (1,122, 1992–93)
Rebounds (Game)	Shaquille O'Neal (25, 4–20–93 vs. Washington Bullets)
Assists (Season)	Scott Skiles (735, 1992–93)
Assists (Game)	Scott Skiles (30*, 12–30–90 vs. Denver Nuggets)
Blocked Shots (Season)	Shaquille O'Neal (286, 1992–93)
Blocked Shots (Game)	Shaquille O'Neal (9, 2–14–93 vs. New York Knicks)
Personal Fouls (Season)	Shaquille O'Neal (381, 1992–93)

* = NBA Record

Best Trade in Franchise History

It is perhaps a bit early to judge the results, but the deal which the Magic pulled off during the 1993 draft day festivities will certainly long be remembered as one of the biggest blockbusters ever to surround an NBA lottery draft. Faced with the rare blessing of a second straight number one overall pick, the expansion club selected Michigan University's Chris Webber, then promptly dealt Webber to Golden State for desired rookie guard Anfernee Hardaway (the number three overall selection). Hardaway seemingly gave the Magic the last missing component—that much-needed point guard to team with veteran Scott Skiles and deliver the ball to franchise post-player Shaquille O'Neal. Yet throughout the early 1993–'94 season the trade remained difficult to assess as both Webber and Hardaway were plagued by injuries early in their respective rookie seasons. Both also finished strong with Webber edging Hardaway for league rookie honors. So far, however, Orlando has no reason to regret a trade that has made the Magic one of basketball's best bets for future dynasty status.

Worst Trade in Franchise History

Early in December of 1992, the Magic sought to shore-up weak guard play by waiving Chris Corchiani and then dealing a 1993 second-round draft selection to Cleveland for veteran three-point specialist Steve Kerr. Kerr contributed little in 47 games (59 assists and a 2.6 scoring average) and was no longer even with the club at the outset of the 1993–'94 campaign.

Orlando Magic Historical Oddity

Perhaps no team anywhere in sports owns a nickname that more perfectly (and without any irony) reflects the history of that particular franchise. It was something magical, indeed, that allowed the Orlando team to earn two lottery "number one" picks in the collegiate draft and thus build themselves into a powerhouse earlier in their history than any other modern-era NBA club. Owning the second worst record in the league, the Orlando club received ten of a possible 66 ping-pong balls tossed into the hopper for the 1992 post-season lottery draft. That was not exactly high odds, but it was good enough for the Magic's name to pop up with the first selection and the rights to draft the NBA's biggest prize in years—franchise player Shaquille O'Neal. A year later, the Magic with Shaq now in town had barely missed a playoff slot by the mere margin of a tie-breaker with Indiana's Pacers. This was another lucky break for the club in the long run, however, as the Magic were once again squarely in the lottery running. This time the chances were far reduced as the team holding the last lottery slot owned only one ball and a 65–1 shot at the first pick. Magically, however, the Orlando ball again came out on top, and along with it the right to draft hefty forward Chris Webber of Michigan. When the Magic subsequently traded their rights to Webber for coveted point guard Penny Hardaway, the ballclub had parlayed their good fortune into a spot as the NBA team of the future. And all this on the strength of a back-to-back set of number one lottery picks.

Magic All-Time Number One Draft Picks List

Orlando Magic
1989 Nick Anderson (Illinois)
1990 Dennis Scott (Georgia Tech)
1991 Brian Williams (Arizona)
1992 Shaquille O'Neal (LSU)
1993 Chris Webber (Michigan) (Traded to Golden State Warriors for Anfernee Hardaway)

Part IV

Other Leagues and
Forgotten
Cities

Chapter 28

AMERICAN BASKETBALL ASSOCIATION (1967-1976)

Only the Ball Was Red, White and Blue

It was a colorful experiment that never really got off the ground. For nine turbulent seasons the American Basketball Association suffered through a constantly shifting lineup of teams, cities and unrecognized stars that reminded one of the pro game's unsettled barnstorming era several decades earlier. It struggled to earn credibility in the press and struggled to gain loyal fans at the ticket windows. Against the NBA it was probably doomed to failure in the long run. But despite its shortcomings, sometimes "minor league" atmosphere, and eventual collapse, the ABA nonetheless left us a colorful legacy of basketball lore and basketball legends.

But the ABA also left hoopdom with far more than a few tinkerings and a few stars. The league and its innovations had a huge impact on the evolution of pro basketball that can only be appreciated in hindsight. Foremost, the rebel league seemed to salvage the pro game itself—especially in the wake of the ABA's own ashes. For several ABA innovations would be the very features that professional basketball now seemingly desperately needed for long-term survival. Out of its many gimmicks some—like the red, white, and blue ball—would be quickly laid to rest. But a few other unique features of the league were so successful that the NBA had no choice but to adopt them post-haste.

The most obvious legacy of the ABA was the introduction of the three-point field goal. The concept was not entirely new—it had been used back in 1961–'62 by the short-lived American Basketball League—but it now gave the new circuit a distinctly different look from the traditional NBA. And in addition to each shot from more than 25 feet now counting as three points, the new circuit also extended the shot-clock time of possession from 24 to 30 seconds, and thus gave offenses a few extra precious seconds to work the ball on the perimeter and set up the new popular

439

long-range bombs. It was these two changes that added a new dimension to offensive play and brought new excitement to a league which needed every ploy it could muster to compensate for the clear lack of competitive talent and a dearth of big-name stars. And it was an innovation that perhaps can be compared to the designated hitter which so revolutionized baseball only a few summers later. The "bomb" or "Home Run" shot (as it would soon be known) was now, and forevermore, a recognized part of basketball's growing spectator appeal.

Two other obvious features of the impact of the ABA on the more established NBA were the four franchises and several dozen marquee players contributed by the new upstart league to its more stable and success rival. The incomparable Dr. J—Julius Erving—launched his "hangtime" career here; Rick Barry, Charlie Scott, Artis Gilmore, Connie Hawkins, Dan Issel, George McGinnis were among the other giants of the '70s who either kicked off their careers in the ABA or earned their lofty reputations there. And four NBA teams with rabid built-in ABA fan support and a handful of stars of their own (like George Gervin with San Antonio and David Thompson with Denver) were also born out of the league that bounced a gaudy tri-colored basketball, changed the game's scoring rules (with the three-point goal), and pioneered the action-packed slamdunkfest.

But ABA basketball would also leave another legacy in its wake, one that is less frequently commented on today but in fact was the "real legacy" left by the rebel league to roundball posterity. For the ABA was dominated in its latter years by a handful of small, high-scoring forwards named Julius Erving, Connie Hawkins, Joe Caldwell and Charlie Scott, who together introduced to the basketball world the glamor of the highflying, thundering, crowd-pleasing dunk shot. In the NBA, the disciplined, team-oriented passing and fastbreaking game pioneered by Red Auerbach still predominated. But in the loose-knit ABA, the freewheeling and individualistic playground style of inner-city schoolyard ball seemed to take over with the arrival of Erving and a handful of other freewheeling skywalkers. The history of the post-modern pro game actually begins, then, with the history of the dunk, just as the "modern" version of Naismith's game was earlier launched in the fifties when the running one-handed jump shot replaced the stationary two-handed set shot as the sport's primary offensive strategy. And the history of the dunk itself truly begins with the history of the ABA—or at least with the history of the ABA Julius Erving help put on the map after a spectacular 1971 rookie season.

The ABA knew it had a good thing going with the innovative slam shot and its "cool" playground ambiance, and made a conscious effort to exploit this emerging individualistic style of scoring in the league's final years. The formal slam dunk contest—a much later showcase event of NBA All-Star Weekends—would, in fact, debut with the ABA during the final league season of 1976. And it would be Julius Erving—not at all surprisingly—who would be crowned as basketball's first official slam dunking champion.

The staging of the one and only ABA Slam Dunk Contest meant that the league would go out with a truly memorable bang. Five of the league's highest leapers gathered in Denver's McNichols Arena (also the site later that season for the league's final post-season showdown between Erving and David Thompson) to compete for $1,200 in prize money and bragging rights as the ABA's crown prince of dunking style. The judges would include an elderly female season ticket holder and a local concert promoter, and the rules dictated five dunks for each contestant. Two of these would be mandatory and three free-lance; the final mandatory dunk would have to start in the lane at least ten feet from the basket, but no dribbling would be required; the contestants would be judged on "artistic ability, imagination and body flow, as well as facial response." David Thompson, the sensational Nuggets rookie from North Carolina State, would wow the hometown partisans with an electrifying double-pump two-hand reverse jam that brought down the house. But the unflappable Dr. J would eventually carry the day, and basketball's first slam dunking crown as well, with a soaring slam launched from beyond the free-throw line and punctuated with the ball held by one hand high above his head before its shattering release.

ABA 1976 Slam Dunk Contest Lineup

Julius Erving, (6'7" Forward) New York Nets (Champion)
David Thompson, (6'4" Forward-Guard) Denver Nuggets (Runner-Up)
George Gervin, (6'7" Guard) San Antonio Spurs
Larry Kenon, (6'9" Forward) San Antonio Spurs
Artis Gilmore, (7'2" Center) Kentucky Colonels

The debut season of the new league was far removed from the glamorous dunking game that Dr. J and his imitators would bring into the circuit a half-dozen seasons later. The ABA startup, in fact, was anything but auspicious. There was a big-name commissioner—Mr. Basketball, George Mikan, the game's first great star—who was seemingly installed more to lend prestige to the effort than for any potential promotional and administrative skills. But there were few if any players with what could be considered household names. A handful of worn NBA veterans (Cliff Hagan, Joe Caldwell, Art Heyman) and marginal journeymen (Wayne Hightower, Ben Warley, Gary Bradds) filled out rosters alongside ex-college stars who had failed to land jobs on NBA rosters. The closest thing to a star was Connie Hawkins, shunned by the NBA because of reputed involvement in a 1961 college betting scandal, yet still considered the greatest New York City playground talent ever. And the outlawed player was enough all by himself (he paced the league in scoring with a 26.8 average) against the other talent-thin clubs, to lead the Pittsburgh Pipers to the first-ever ABA title.

Weak attendance didn't scuttle the ABA during and immediately after its first season of play. But small gate appeal did send an uncomfortable number of clubs scrambling for new and more lucrative home ports. The Anaheim Amigos were reconstituted a few miles to the north as the Los Angeles Stars; the Minnesota Muskies were moved into Miami as the Floridians; and even the first-year champion Pittsburgh Pipers relocated to Minneapolis to replace the Muskies. This migration of franchises couldn't fail to be reminiscent, for those watching closely, of the earliest shaky NBA seasons almost two decades earlier.

All the shifting led to little increased interest at the gate for a second league season. But a new recruit did join Connie Hawkins to give the struggling league a little more credibility, if precious little new fandom. NBA scoring champ Rick Barry had, a full year earlier, decided to bring his net-rippling act from the San Francisco Warriors across the bay to the ABA Oakland Oaks, a team coached by his former University of Miami coach and current father-in-law Bruce Hale. When the Warriors took legal action to block such a move, the courts had ordered Barry to sit out the final season of his San Francisco contract before reporting to the Oaks. Barry had thus spent his season doing promotional work and broadcasting for his new ABA employer. Now he was back for the 1968–'69 campaign and averaged 34 a game despite knee problems which limited him to but 35 games. Barry had to miss the entire post-season, but Oakland nonetheless boasted enough talent to surge to both regular season and playoff titles in campaign number two. Despite a lineup void of the dangerous Barry, Oakland cruised past the Indiana Pacers four-games-to-one in the title round as rookie Warren Armstrong averaged 28.8 in playoff action and Doug Moe and Gary Bradds also chipped in heavy point production.

But if Barry had brought some glamor to the league in year two, he had hardly brought much stability. Franchises continued their musical chairs in season three. Again, the defending champion abandoned its home base as the Oakland Oaks pulled up roots and moved eastward as the Washington Capitols. Also the Pipers returned to their original nest in Pittsburgh and Houston's Mavericks headed in an easterly direction to become the revamped Carolina Cougars ballclub. And another upheaval came with the ouster of Commissioner George Mikan by the club owners who now wanted much more aggressive raiding of NBA talent by the league office. While all this was transpiring, a new on-court power emerged in the guise of the Indiana Pacers ballclub. Led by Roger Brown and Bob Netolicky, both 20-point scorers, the Indianapolis team won a league-high 59 games and toyed with Los Angeles in the six-game ABA Finals. The Pacers thus became the third straight franchise to sweep both regular season and post-season titles.

And another trend continued as well—the emergence of a new high-scoring individual star to boast the ABA ratings for the third season running. This time it was Spencer Haywood, a spectacular athlete who had left college (University of Detroit) early to sign up with the Denver Rockets under the junior league's "hardship" plan. This was a clever ploy of signing undergraduate stars under the guise of assisting needy athletes; the real motive, of course, was to grab off some of the top stars before they were eligible for NBA contracts upon graduation. Haywood cruised to a league scoring title in Denver as the league's only 30 ppg. producer. But Spencer Haywood would not be around long to fill seats in empty ABA arenas. He would soon take his high-priced act into the courts and then into the more rewarding and high-profile NBA which instituted its own "hardship" clause the next season and snatched away Haywood for its own.

Rick Barry was back in the courts again as well (the ones filled with judges and not with jump shots) as he balked at accompanying his Oakland Oaks team eastward to Washington and elected to return to the NBA Warriors he had abandoned two seasons earlier. But this time ABA owner Earl Foreman sought redress and obtained a court order requiring Barry to fulfill his contract with the Washington Caps. Although still hobbled by tender knees, Barry showed little inclination to sulk over the matter as he kept pumping in points for his relocated ABA club at a 27.7 average (second to Haywood, if Barry had played enough games to qualify for the scoring race). In seven playoff games Barry also burned the nets at a 40.1 clip.

The fourth ABA season might well have been a turning point and a true watershed campaign. The Indiana Pacers, featuring rebounding king Mel Daniels and supreme power forward Roger Brown, became the circuit's top drawing card and continued their front-running act for much of the year, before stumbling in the Western Division Finals. Utah's Stars (the relocated Los Angeles Stars) emerged as another powerhouse team when post-season play again rolled around. With Kentucky and Utah upsetting divisional winners Virginia and Indiana in the conference finals, an exciting title round was set up between a pair of colorful underdogs. Utah, behind Willie Wise and Zelmo Beaty, finally prevailed in the slugfest over the Kentucky Colonels team which featured Dan Issel and Louis Dampier. And it was also significant for league health that the New York franchise for the very first time began to show some signs of actual life. Part of that life came from Rick Barry, who now took his mercenary Gypsy act over to New York. Barry was again restricted to less than 60 games by nagging injury yet maintained his scoring average (29.4) among the loftiest in the league.

But most importantly, for the first time the league had signed up a crop of first rate rookies. Dan Issel (University of Kentucky, Kentucky Colonels), Charlie Scott (North Carolina, Virginia Squires), Rick Mount (Purdue University, Indiana Pacers), Mike Maloy (Davidson College, Virginia Squires), Jim Ard (University of Cincinnati, New York Nets) and Ralph Simpson (Michigan State, Denver Rockets) were all high-profile collegians who opted to play with the newer league. A better crop of young players, however, could only partially hide the continued instability of the league. For the first time the past year's champions—the Indiana Pacers—stayed put and didn't move to a new city. Plenty of other shifting continued, however. The Washington Capitols took up residence in Norfolk as the Virginia Squires, the Los Angeles Stars were now based in Utah, and the New Orleans Buccaneers resurfaced at the Memphis Pros. The ABA was rapidly becoming a league where a scorecard was needed as much to tell vagabound teams as to identify the no-name players.

A fifth season of red, white, and blue basketball finally brought a campaign which opened with the same lineup of teams that closed the previous season. The Texas Chaparrals did undergo their third name change in as many seasons, as they were once again christened the Dallas Chaparrals; the New York Nets also enjoyed some minor tinkering as they shifted home base into the new Nassau Coliseum on Long Island; and the Memphis Pros became the property of colorful baseball owner Charles O. Finley. Another new regular season champion also emerged in the guise of last-year's post-season runner-up, the Kentucky Colonels. Kentucky's 68–13 record would in fact hold up as the best single-season mark in the nine-season history of the league.

The Indiana Pacers also remained a powerhouse and a league showcase of stability in '71–'72, as they fought their way back to a second appearance in the league finals. With their relatively easy six-game dismantling of the surprising New York Nets in the championship finals, the Pacers also became the first two-time title winner of the ABA. And this time around an even more glamorous rookie crop entered the league. Artis Gilmore (Jacksonville University, Kentucky Colonels) and Jim McDaniels (Western Kentucky University, Carolina Cougars) headlined among college seniors entering the circuit. But they were overshadowed by three spectacular underclassman who signed up for ABA play as pre-graduation hardship cases. George McGinnis (Indiana University, Indiana Pacers), Julius Erving (University of Massachusetts, Virginia Squires) and Johnny Neumann (Mississippi University, Memphis Pros) were the biggest things yet to hit the struggling new circuit, and their presence did as much as the improved play of the New York Nets in the Big Apple to garner some much needed press coverage.

Having spent his three collegiate seasons in the obscurity of the Yankee Conference, Julius Erving was an unknown quantity when he was rejected by the New York Nets, before being inked by the Squires. Erving's quiet signing with the Virginia ABA team suddenly gave the Squires the most awesome duo of hot-shooting youngsters ever to suit up in the same uniforms—in any league and at any time. Julius Erving and Charlie Scott were as good a double-barreled offense, in fact, as any coach, fan or analyst could ever fantasize about seeing on the same lineup card. Their one season together they averaged a joint 61.9 ppg. and made the Squires' offense—as one clever scribe phrased it—''as unstoppable as an impending flood seeping through a leaky dike.'' And a few seasons later George

Gervin would be putting on a Squires uniform as well. But it all went for naught, and did so in typical outrageous ABA fashion. For the Squires ownership was so intent on staying above water financially that they quickly peddled all three superstars away—even before their full market potential was ever reached or even nearly approximated.

Season number six saw the still struggling ABA circuit suffer a major blow when New York Nets star and league showcase Rick Barry was ordered by the courts to report back to the NBA Golden State Warriors. The decision was based on a new legal opinion that Barry had actually signed a valid contract for future services with the NBA team a few seasons earlier, when he had expressed dissatisfaction with the league's shifting of his Oakland ballclub. This blow to ABA drawing power was magnified by the escape of scoring champ Charlie Scott to greener pastures with the NBA Phoenix Suns. The dual loss of Barry and Scott was partially softened by the arrival of NBA star Billy Cunningham with the Carolina Cougars. And it was somewhat further mollified by the emergence of Julius Erving as the league's new dominant player and scoring star.

If the early years of the ABA history had been marred by constant moving—of franchises and of players—the most important move in league annals would not take place until season seven. In the fall of 1973, Dr. J would fill the void left by Barry in New York by taking his "magic medicine show" from the Virginia Squires back to his original hometown in the Big Apple. The league now had some hope for survival with its best player and best team located in the nation's media capital and its acknowledged basketball capital as well. Erving quickly led the Nets straight to the top as they captured both regular-season and post-season honors. The playoff victory came over the Utah Stars in a one-sided five-game affair that found Erving scoring 47 points in the opening game and then matching his league-best 27 ppg. average throughout post-season play. Erving was the league scoring champ for the second time as he outdistanced McGinnis, Issel, Gervin, and all the rest of the competition. And it was an honor he would hold in three of the league's final four seasons.

Two other moves—less spectacular but only slightly less important— also marked the 1973–74 ABA season. Wilt Chamberlain left the NBA Los Angeles Lakers to join the San Diego Conquistadors as a player coach. In still another of the endless legal chess matches carried out between the rival leagues, the Lakers were able to obtain court assistance to block Wilt from suiting up for game action until his Laker option year had fully expired. But basketball's biggest draw of all-time was now a part of the still surviving rebel league. And in another development, the shifting of the Dallas Chaparrals into San Antonio was a true boon to ABA chances for survival. Rechristened as the Spurs, the San Antonio club was a gate hit overnight and thus established itself as one of the healthiest franchises in the circuit.

Modest successes in New York and San Antonio were only the exceptions that proved the rule, however. Constant rumors of the league's imminent collapse surrounded the ABA's eighth season of ongoing struggle for survival. Such rumors had their most devastating negative impact on the efforts to sign up the best collegiate talent in the player wars with the healthier NBA. Len Elmore (University of Maryland, Indiana Pacers), Bobby Jones (North Carolina, Denver Nuggets), and Billy Knight (University of Pittsburgh, Indiana Pacers) were among those rookies who did join the circuit. Larry Brown had now taken over as head coach in Denver and the renamed Nuggets ran away with regular-season honors. The post-season, however, saw two old rivals—Indiana and Kentucky—emerge as the final survivors. The Pacers were led by scoring champ George McGinnis, but had now lost Roger Brown, Mel Daniels, and Freddie Lewis, and looked very little like the championship outfits of a few short seasons back. Thus in the end Kentucky had too much balance for the Pacers and reigned as the sixth ABA champion in eight years.

The ABA had a new man at the top as it entered what would soon prove to be its final season. After a single campaign as general manager of the New York Nets, former NBA star Dave Debusschere was named as third league commissioner. But the now weakly-bound fabric of the league had already begun to hopelessly unravel. Failure to achieve a national television contract kept the ABA playing in obscurity and one of the league's brightest stars—George McGinnis—had already opted to bail out for the heftier exposure of NBA play. But there were more ominous signs of disintegration as well. The Denver Nuggets and New York Nets in September applied for formal admission to the NBA, and it was now apparent that the healthier ballclubs were just as disenchanted as the more marketable ballplayers. The weaker clubs, by contrast, were scraping for survival. The Baltimore Claws traded their star Dan Issel to Denver for a song and then folded up operations altogether. Attendance waned even further at such signs of instability, and by November the San Diego Sails folded up camp as well. Down to just seven clubs, the league scrapped its divisional format and limped through a final season as a seven-team league.

The league remained entertaining on the court during its final season, even if fewer fans in fewer cities were there to appreciate the action. Denver again dominated regular-season play under the leadership of Larry Brown and chugged to its second 60–plus wins in a row. With McGinnis gone from Indiana, Julius Erving re-emerged as the league's most prolific scorer as well as its main gate attraction and best entertainment feature. Erving also led the Nets to their second league title—the final in league history.

In the end it was timing as much as anything that killed off the colorful ABA. America was not yet ready for two big-time pro basketball circuits. The hoop sport was now struggling in the face of booming football popularity during the late sixties, a re-emergence of baseball interest in the early '70s, and perhaps also a widely perceived lack of competitiveness at the pro level in the wake of the Boston Celtics' domination of the NBA throughout almost all of the 1960s. The NBA itself was scrambling to regain the popularity it had seemed to acquire at the outset of the '60s in the heyday of Wilt Chamberlain, Bill Russell, Oscar Robertson and Elgin Baylor. Basketball needed an upgrade in image—as well as a fat television deal—before two pro circuits could hope to share the diminishing lime-light. It is the ironic final chapter of the ABA saga, of course, that in its very demise the ABA would leave the lasting legacy—three-point buckets, slam dunk excitement, and Julius Erving—that would offer the salvation of the pro game just a few short seasons down the road.

Suggested Readings on American Basketball Association

Klein, Dave. **Playoff! Twenty-Four Seconds to Glory—A Chronicle of NBA and ABA Title Series**. New York: Stadia Sports Publishing, 1973.

Neft, David S. and Richard M. Cohen, Editors. **The Sports Encyclopedia: Pro Basketball**. Fourth Edition. New York: St. Martin's Press, 1991.

O'Brien, Jim. **ABA All-Stars**. New York: Lancer Books, 1972.

Pluto, Terry. **Loose Balls—The Short, Wild Life of the American Basketball Association as Told by the Players, Coaches, and Movers and Shakers Who Made It Happen**. New York and London: Simon and Schuster, 1990.

Season-by-Season ABA League Summary

Year	Best Regular-Season Record (Coach)	Playoff Champion (Runner-Up)	Scoring Leader (PPG) (Team)
1967–1968	Pittsburgh Pipers (54–24) (Vince Cazetta)	**Pittsburgh Pipers** (New Orleans Bucs)	Connie Hawkins (26.8) (Pittsburgh Pipers)
1968–1969	Oakland Oaks (60–18) (Alex Hannum)	**Oakland Oaks** (Indiana Pacers)	Rick Barry (34.0) (Oakland Oaks)
1969–1970	Indiana Pacers (59–25) (Bob "Slick" Leonard)	**Indiana Pacers** (Los Angeles Stars)	Spencer Haywood (30.0) (Denver Rockets)
1970–1971	Indiana Pacers (58–26) (Bob "Slick" Leonard)	**Utah Stars** (Kentucky Colonels)	Dan Issel (29.8) (Kentucky Colonels)
1971–1972	Kentucky Colonels (68–16) (Joe Mullaney)	**Indiana Pacers** (New York Nets)	Charlie Scott (34.6) (Virginia Squires)
1972–1973	Carolina Cougars (57–27) (Larry Brown)	**Indiana Pacers** (Kentucky Colonels)	Julius Erving (31.9) (Virginia Squires)
1973–1974	New York Nets (55–29) (Kevin Loughery)	**New York Nets** (Utah Stars)	Julius Erving (27.4) (New York Nets)
1974–1975	Denver Nuggets (65–19) (Larry Brown)	**Kentucky Colonels** (Indiana Pacers)	George McGinnis (29.8) (Indiana Pacers)
1975–1976	Denver Nuggets (60–24) (Larry Brown)	**New York Nets** (Denver Nuggets)	Julius Erving (29.3) (New York Nets)

ABA All-Time Individual Career/Season/Single Game Records

Points Scored (Career)	13,726	Louie Dampier (Kentucky, 1967–76)
Points Scored (Season)	2,538	Dan Issel (Kentucky, 1971–72)
Points Scored (Game)	67	Larry Miller (Carolina, 3–18–72 vs. Memphis)
Scoring Average (Career)	27.8 ppg.	Julius Erving (Virginia, New York, 1971–76)
Games Played (Career)	728	Louie Dampier (Kentucky, 1967–76)
Minutes Played (Career)	27,770	Louie Dampier (Kentucky, 1967–76)
Field Goals (Career)	5,290	Louie Dampier (Kentucky,1967–76)
Field Goals (Season)	986	Spencer Haywood (Denver, 1969–70)
Field Goal Pct. (Career)	.557	Artis Gilmore (Kentucky, 1971–76)
Field Goal Pct. (Season)	.604	Bobby Jones (Denver, 1974–75)
3-Pt. Field Goals (Career)	794	Louie Dampier (Kentucky, 1967–76)
3-Pt. Field Goals (Season)	199	Louie Dampier (Kentucky, 1968–69)
Free Throws Made (Career)	3,554	Mack Calvin (Los Angeles, Miami, Carolina, Denver, Virginia, 1969–76)
Free Throws Made (Season)	696	Mack Calvin (Floridians, 1970–71)
Free Throw Pct. (Career)	.866	Mack Calvin (Los Angeles, Miami, Carolina, Denver, Virginia, 1969–76)
Free Throw Pct. (Season)	.896	Mack Calvin (Denver, 1974–75)
Rebounds (Season)	1,637	Spencer Haywood (Denver, 1969–70)
Rebounds (Game)	40	Artis Gilmore (Kentucky, 2–3–74 at New York)
Assists (Career)	4,084	Louie Dampier (Kentucky, 1967–76)
Assists (Season)	689	Don Buse (Indiana, 1975–76)
Assists (Game)	23	Larry Brown (Denver, 2–20–72 vs. Pittsburgh)
Steals (Career)	658	Don Buse (Indiana, 1973–76)
Steals (Season)	346	Don Buse (Indiana, 1975–76)
Steals (Game)	12	Ted McClain (Carolina, 12–26–73 vs. New York)
Blocked Shots (Career)	750	Artis Gilmore (Kentucky, 1973–76)
Blocked Shots (Season)	287	Artis Gilmore (Kentucky, 1973–74)
Blocked Shots (Game)	12	Julius Keye (Denver, 12–14–72 vs. Virginia)
	12	Caldwell Jones (San Diego, 1–6–74 vs. Carolina)
Personal Fouls (Season)	382	Gene Moore (Kentucky, 1969–70)

Summary of ABA Individual Team Season-by-Season Records

Indiana Pacers, 1967–1976
427–317, .574 Pct. (9 seasons)
Championships (3): 1969–70, 1971–72, 1972–73

Season	Record	Finish	Coach(es)	Scoring Leader(s)	Playoffs (W-L Record)
Key: # = League Scoring Leader					
1967–68	38–40	3rd	L. Staverman	Freddie Lewis (20.6)	Lost in 1st Round (0–3)
1968–69	44–34	1st	L. Staverman	Mel Daniels (24.0)	Lost in 3rd Round (9–8)
			Bob Leonard		
1969–70	59–25	1st	Bob Leonard	Roger Brown (23.0)	**ABA Champion** (12–3)
1970–71	58–26	1st	Bob Leonard	Mel Daniels (21.0)	Lost in 2nd Round (7–4)
1971–72	47–37	2nd	Bob Leonard	Mel Daniels (19.1)	**ABA Champion** (12–8)
1972–73	51–33	2nd	Bob Leonard	George McGinnis (27.6)	**ABA Champion** (12–6)
1973–74	46–38	2nd	Bob Leonard	George McGinnis (25.9)	Lost in 2nd Round (7–7)
1974–75	45–39	3rd	Bob Leonard	George McGinnis (29.8)#	Lost in 3rd Round (9–9)
1975–76	39–45	5th	Bob Leonard	Billy Knight (28.1)	Lost in 1st Round (1–2)

Greatest Franchise Player: Mel Daniels (9,364 Points, 19.5 ppg., 1968–1974)
All-Time Leading Scorer: Mel Daniels (9,364 Points, 19.5 ppg., 1968–1974)
Most Successful Coach: Bob "Slick" Leonard (387–270, .589 Pct., 1969–1976)

New York Nets (New Jersey Americans), 1967–1976
374–370, .503 Pct. (9 seasons)
Championships (2): 1973–74, 1975–76

Season	Record	Finish	Coach(es)	Scoring Leader(s)	Playoffs (W-L Record)
Key: * = Tied for Position; # = League Scoring Leader					
New Jersey Americans					
1967–68	36–42	4th*	Max Zaslofsky	Tony Jackson (19.4)	Did Not Qualify
New York Nets					
1968–69	17–61	5th	Max Zaslofsky	Walt Simon (21.1)	Did Not Qualify
1969–70	39–45	4th	York Larese	Levern Tart (24.1)	Lost in 1st Round (3–4)
1970–71	40–44	3rd	Lou Carnesecca	Rick Barry (29.4)	Lost in 1st Round (2–4)
1971–72	44–40	3rd	Lou Carnesecca	Rick Barry (31.5)	Lost in ABA Finals (10–9)
1972–73	30–54	4th	Lou Carnesecca	George Carver (19.0)	Lost in 1st Round (1–4)
1973–74	55–29	1st	Kevin Loughery	Julius Erving (27.4)#	**ABA Champion** (12–2)
1974–75	58–26	1st*	Kevin Loughery	Julius Erving (27.9)	Lost in 1st Round (1–4)
1975–76	55–29	2nd	Kevin Loughery	Julius Erving (29.3)#	**ABA Champion** (8–5)

Greatest Franchise Player: Julius Erving (7,104 Points, 28.2 ppg., 1973–1976)
All-Time Leading Scorer: Julius Erving (7,104 Points, 28.2 ppg., 1973–1976)
Most Successful Coach: Kevin Loughery (168–84, .667 Pct., 1973–1976)

Kentucky Colonels, 1967–1976
448–296, .602 Pct. (9 seasons)
Championships (1): 1974–75

Season	Record	Finish	Coach(es)	Scoring Leader(s)	Playoffs (W-L Record)
Key: * = Tied for Position; # = League Scoring Leader					
1967–68	36–42	4th*	John Givens Gene Rhodes	Darel Carrier (22.9)	Lost in 1st Round (2–3)
1968–69	42–36	3rd	Gene Rhodes	Louie Dampier (24.8)	Lost in 1st Round (2–4)
1969–70	45–39	2nd	Gene Rhodes	Louie Dampier (26.0)	Lost in 2nd Round (5–7)
1970–71	44–40	2nd	Gene Rhodes Alex Groza Frank Ramsey	Dan Issel (29.9)#	Lost in ABA Finals (11–8)
1971–72	68–16	1st	Joe Mullaney	Dan Issel (30.6)	Lost in 1st Round (2–4)
1972–73	56–28	2nd	Joe Mullaney	Dan Issel (27.3)	Lost in ABA Finals (11–8)
1973–74	53–31	2nd	Babe McCarthy	Dan Issel (25.5)	Lost in 2nd Round (4–4)
1974–75	58–26	1st	Hubie Brown	Artis Gilmore (23.6)	**ABA Champion** (12–3)
1975–76	46–38	4th	Hubie Brown	Artis Gilmore (24.6)	Lost in 2nd Round (5–5)

Greatest Franchise Player: Dan Issel (10,893 Points, 26.2 ppg., 1970–1975)
All-Time Leading Scorer: Louis Dampier (13,726 Points, 18.9 ppg., 1967–1976)
Most Successful Coach: Joe Mullaney (124–44, .738 Pct., 1971–1973)

Utah Stars (Los Angeles Stars), 1967–1975
366–310, .541 Pct. (8 seasons)
Championships (1): 1970–71

Season	Record	Finish	Coach(es)	Scoring Leader(s)	Playoffs (W-L Record)
Anaheim Amigos					
1967–68	25–53	5th	Al Brightman Harry Dinnel	Steve Chubin (18.2)	Did Not Qualify
Los Angeles Stars					
1968–69	33–45	5th	Bill Sharman	George Lehmann (18.9)	Did Not Qualify
1969–70	43–41	4th	Bill Sharman	Wayne Hightower (19.1)	Lost in ABA Finals (10–7)
Utah Stars					
1970–71	57–27	2nd	Bill Sharman	Donnie Freeman (23.6)	**ABA Champion** (12–6)
1971–72	60–24	1st	LaDell Andersen	Zelmo Beaty (23.6)	Lost in 2nd Round (7–4)
1972–73	55–29	1st	LaDell Andersen	Willie Wise (22.0)	Lost in 2nd Round (6–4)
1973–74	51–33	1st	Joe Mullaney	Willie Wise (22.3)	Lost in ABA Finals (9–9)
1974–75	38–46	4th	B. Buckwalter Tom Nissalke	Ron Boone (25.2)	Lost in 1st Round (2–4)
1975–76	4–12	—	Tom Nissalke	Disbanded on December 2, 1975	

Greatest Franchise Player: Ron Boone (7,358 Points, 18.6 ppg., 1971–1975)
All-Time Leading Scorer: Willie Wise (8,147 Points, 19.7 ppg., 1969–1974)
Most Successful Coach: LaDell Andersen (115–53, .685 Pct., 1971–1973)

Virginia Squires (Oakland Oaks), 1967–1976
326–417, .439 Pct. (9 seasons)
Championships (1): 1968–69

Season	Record	Finish	Coach(es)	Scoring Leader(s)	Playoffs (W-L Record)

Key: # = League Scoring Leader

Oakland Oaks

Season	Record	Finish	Coach(es)	Scoring Leader(s)	Playoffs (W-L Record)
1967–68	22–56	6th	Bruce Hale	Levern Tart (26.9)	Did Not Qualify
1968–69	60–18	1st	Alex Hannum	Rick Barry (34.0)#	**ABA Champion** (12–4)

Washington Capitols

Season	Record	Finish	Coach(es)	Scoring Leader(s)	Playoffs (W-L Record)
1969–70	44–40	3rd	Al Bianchi	Rick Barry (27.7)	Lost in 1st Round (3–4)

Virginia Squires

Season	Record	Finish	Coach(es)	Scoring Leader(s)	Playoffs (W-L Record)
1970–71	55–29	1st	Al Bianchi	Charlie Scott (27.1)	Lost in 2nd Round (6–6)
1971–72	45–39	2nd	Al Bianchi	Charlie Scott (34.6)#	Lost in 2nd Round 97–4)
1972–73	42–42	3rd	Al Bianchi	Julius Erving (31.9)#	Lost in 1st Round (1–4)
1973–74	28–56	4th	Al Bianchi	George Gervin (25.4)	Lost in 1st Round (1–4)
1974–75	15–69	5th	Al Bianchi	Willie Wise (20.9)	Did Not Qualify
1975–76	15–68	7th	Al Bianchi	Ticky Burden (19.9)	Did Not Qualify
			Bill Musselman		
			Zelmo Beaty		

Greatest Franchise Player: Julius Erving (4,558 Points, 29.4 ppg., 1971–1973)
All-Time Leading Scorer: Charlie Scott (4,800 Points, 30.6 ppg., 1970–1972)
Most Successful Coach: Alex Hannum (60–18, .769 Pct., 1968–1969)

Pittsburgh Pipers (Minnesota Pipers), 1967–1972
180–228, .441 Pct. (5 seasons)
Championships (1): 1967–68

Season	Record	Finish	Coach(es)	Scoring Leader(s)	Playoffs (W-L Record)

Key: # = League Scoring Leader

Pittsburgh Pipers

Season	Record	Finish	Coach(es)	Scoring Leader(s)	Playoffs (W-L Record)
1967–68	54–24	1st	Vince Cazetta	Connie Hawkins (26.8)#	**ABA Champion** (11–4)

Minnesota Pipers

Season	Record	Finish	Coach(es)	Scoring Leader(s)	Playoffs (W-L Record)
1968–69	36–42	4th	Jim Harding	Connie Hawkins (30.2)	Lost in 1st Round (3–4)
			Vern Mikkelsen		
			Gus Young		

Pittsburgh Pipers

Season	Record	Finish	Coach(es)	Scoring Leader(s)	Playoffs (W-L Record)
1969–70	29–55	5th	John Clark	John Brisker (21.0)	Did Not Qualify
			Buddy Jeannette		

Pittsburgh Condors

Season	Record	Finish	Coach(es)	Scoring Leader(s)	Playoffs (W-L Record)
1970–71	36–48	5th	Jack McMahon	John Brisker (29.3)	Did Not Qualify
1971–72	25–59	6th	Jack McMahon	John Brisker (28.9)	Did Not Qualify
			Mark Binstein		

Greatest Franchise Player: Connie Hawkins (3,295 Points, 28.2 ppg., 1967–1969)
All-Time Leading Scorer: John Brisker (5,349 Points, 26.1 ppg., 1969–1972)
Most Successful Coach: Vince Cazetta (54–24, .692 Pct., 1967–1968)

Denver Rockets (Denver Nuggets), 1967–1976
413–331, .555 Pct. (9 seasons)
Championships: None

Season	Record	Finish	Coach(es)	Scoring Leader(s)	Playoffs (W-L Record)

Key: * = Tied for Position; # = League Scoring Leader

Denver Rockets

Season	Record	Finish	Coach(es)	Scoring Leader(s)	Playoffs (W-L Record)
1967–68	45–33	3rd	Bob Bass	Larry Jones (22.9)	Lost in 1st Round (2–3)
1968–69	44–34	3rd	Bob Bass	Larry Jones (28.4)	Lost in 1st Round (3–4)
1969–70	51–33	1st	John McClendon Joe Belmont	Spencer Haywood (30.0)#	Lost in 2nd Round (5–7)
1970–71	30–54	4th*	Joe Belmont Stan Albeck	Larry Cannon (26.6)	Did Not qualify
1971–72	34–50	4th	Alex Hannum	Ralph Simpson (27.4)	Lost in 1st Round (3–4)
1972–73	47–37	3rd	Alex Hannum	Ralph Simpson (23.3)	Lost in 1st Round (1–4)
1973–74	37–47	4th	Alex Hannum	Ralph Simpson (18.7)	Did Not Qualify

Denver Nuggets

Season	Record	Finish	Coach(es)	Scoring Leader(s)	Playoffs (W-L Record)
1974–75	65–19	1st	Larry Brown	Ralph Simpson (20.6)	Lost in 2nd Round (7–6)
1975–76	60–24	1st	Larry Brown	David Thompson (26.0)	Lost in Finals (6–7)

Greatest Franchise Player: Spencer Haywood (2,519 Points, 30.0 ppg., 1969–1970)
All-Time Leading Scorer: Ralph Simpson (9,953 Points, 20.4 ppg., 1970–1976)
Most Successful Coach: Larry Brown (125–43, .744 Pct., 1974–1976)

San Antonio Spurs (Dallas Chaparrals), 1967–1976
378–366, .508 Pct. (9 seasons)
Championships: None

Season	Record	Finish	Coach(es)	Scoring Leader(s)	Playoffs (W-L Record)

Key: * = Tied for Position; ** = Player Coach

Dallas Chaparrals

Season	Record	Finish	Coach(es)	Scoring Leader(s)	Playoffs (W-L Record)
1967–68	46–32	2nd	Cliff Hagan**	John Beasley (19.7)	Lost in 2nd Round (4–4)
1968–69	41–37	4th	Cliff Hagan **	Cincy Powell (19.4)	Lost in 1st Round (3–4)
1969–70	45–39	2nd	Cliff Hagan** Max Williams	Glen Combs (22.2)	Lost in 1st Round (2–4)

Texas Chaparrals

Season	Record	Finish	Coach(es)	Scoring Leader(s)	Playoffs (W-L Record)
1970–71	30–54	4th*	Max Williams Bill Blakely	Donnie Freeman (23.6)	Lost in 1st Round (0–4)

Dallas Chaparrals

Season	Record	Finish	Coach(es)	Scoring Leader(s)	Playoffs (W-L Record)
1971–72	42–42	3rd	Tom Nissalke	Donnie Freeman (24.1)	Lost in 1st Round (0–4)
1972–73	28–56	5th	Babe McCarthy Dave Brown	Rich Jones (22.3)	Did Not Qualify

San Antonio Spurs

Season	Record	Finish	Coach(es)	Scoring Leader(s)	Playoffs (W-L Record)
1973–74	45–39	3rd	Tom Nissalke	George Gervin (19.4)	Lost in 1st Round (3–4)
1974–75	51–33	2nd	Tom Nissalke Bob Bass	George Gervin (23.4)	Lost in 1st Round (2–4)
1975–76	50–34	3rd	Bob Bass	James Silas (23.8)	Lost in 1st Round (3–4)

Greatest Franchise Player: George Gervin (4,219 Points, 22.2 ppg., 1974–1976)
All-Time Leading Scorer: James Silas (4,907 Points, 19.6 ppg., 1972–1977)
Most Successful Coach: Bob Bass (83–57, .593 Pct., 1974–1976)

Carolina Cougars (Spirits of St. Louis), 1967–1976
334–410, .449 Pct. (9 seasons)
Championships: None

Season	Record	Finish	Coach(es)	Scoring Leader(s)	Playoffs (W-L Record)
Houston Mavericks					
1967–68	29–49	4th	Slater Martin	Willie Somerset (21.7)	Lost in 1st Round (0–3)
1968–69	23–55	6th	Slater Martin Jim Weaver	Bob Verga (24.7)	Did Not Qualify
Carolina Cougars					
1969–70	42–42	3rd	Bones McKinney	Bob Verga (27.5)	Lost in 1st Round (0–4)
1970–71	34–50	6th	Bones McKinney Jerry Steele	Joe Caldwell (23.3)	Did Not Qualify
1971–72	35–49	5th	Tom Meschery	Jim McDaniels (26.8)	Did Not Qualify
1972–73	57–27	1st	Larry Brown	Billy Cunningham (24.1)	Lost in 2nd Round (7–5)
1973–74	47–37	3rd	Larry Brown	Billy Cunningham (20.5)	Lost in 1st Round (0–4)
Spirits of S. Louis					
1974–75	32–52	3rd	Bob MacKinnon	Marvin Barnes (24.0)	Lost in 2nd Round (5–5)
1975–76	35–49	6th	Rod Thorn Joe Mullaney	Marvin Barnes (24.1)	Did Not Qualify

Greatest Franchise Player: Billy Cunningham (2,684 Points, 23.1 ppg., 1972–1974)
All-Time Leading Scorer: Bob Verga (4,543 Points, 22.9 ppg., 1969–1971)
Most Successful Coach: Larry Brown (104–64, .619 Pct., 1971–1974)

Memphis Tams (New Orleans Buccaneers), 1967–1975
251–385, .395 Pct. (8 seasons)
Championships: None

Season	Record	Finish	Coach(es)	Scoring Leader(s)	Playoffs (W-L Record)
New Orleans Buccaneers					
1967–68	48–30	1st	Babe McCarthy	Doug Moe (24.2)	Lost in ABA Finals (10–7)
1968–69	46–32	2nd	Babe McCarthy	Jimmy Jones (26.0)	Lost in 2nd Round (4–7)
1969–70	42–42	5th	Babe McCarthy	Steve Jones (21.5)	Did Not Qualify
Memphis Pros					
1970–71	41–43	3rd	Babe McCarthy	Steve Jones (22.1)	Lost in 1st Round (0–4)
1971–72	26–58	5th	Babe McCarthy	Johnny Neumann (18.3)	Did Not Qualify
Memphis Tams					
1972–73	24–60	5th	Bob Bass	George Thompson (21.6)	Did Not Qualify
1973–74	21–63	5th	Van Breda Kolff	George Thompson (19.2)	Did Not Qualify
Memphis Sounds					
1974–75	27–57	4th	Joe Mullaney	George Carter (18.4)	Lost in 1st Round (1–4)
Baltimore Claws					
1975–76	——	—	Disbanded before opening of season		

Greatest Franchise Player: Steve Jones (5,193 Points, 21.2 ppg., 1968–1971)
All-Time Leading Scorer: Steve Jones (5,193 Points, 21.2 ppg., 1968–1971)
Most Successful Coach: Babe McCarthy (204–205, .499 Pct., 1967–1972)

Miami Floridians (Minnesota Muskies), 1967–1972
189–219, .463 Pct. (5 seasons)
Championships: None

Season	Record	Finish	Coach(es)	Scoring Leader(s)	Playoffs (W-L Record)
Minnesota Muskies					
1967–68	50–28	2nd	Jim Pollard	Mel Daniels (22.2)	Lost in 2nd Round (4–6)
Miami Floridians					
1968–69	43–35	2nd	Jim Pollard	Donnie Freeman (22.1)	Lost in 2nd Round (5–7)
1969–70	23–61	5th	Jim Pollard	Donnie Freeman (27.4)	Did Not Qualify
			Hal Blitman		
Floridians					
1970–71	37–47	4th	Hal Blitman	Mack Calvin (27.2)	Lost in 1st Round (2–4)
			Bob Bass		
1971–72	36–48	4th	Bob Bass	Mack Calvin (21.0)	Lost in 1st Round (0–4)

Greatest Franchise Player: Donnie Freeman (3,887 Points, 24.8 ppg., 1968–1970)
All-Time Leading Scorer: Mack Calvin (3,927 Points, 24.1 ppg., 1970–1972)
Most Successful Coach: Jim Pollard (98–78, .557 Pct., 1967–1969)

San Diego Conquistadors (San Diego Sails), 1972–1975
101–162, .384 Pct. (3 seasons)
Championships: None

Season	Record	Finish	Coach(es)	Scoring Leader(s)	Playoffs (W-L Record)
Key: * = Tied for Position					
San Diego Conquistadors					
1972–73	30–54	4th	K.C. Jones	Stew Johnson (22.1)	Lost in 1st Round (0–4)
1973–74	37–47	4th*	W. Chamberlain	Bo Lamar (20.4)	Lost in 1st Round (2–4)
1974–75	31–53	5th	Alex Groza	Travis Grant (25.2)	Did Not Qualify
			Beryl Shipley		
San Diego Sails					
1975–76	3–8	—	Bill Musselman	Disbanded on November 12, 1975	

Greatest Franchise Player: Travis Grant (2,191 Points, 20.1 ppg., 1973–1975)
All-Time Leading Scorer: Stew Johnson (3,707 Points, 19.2 ppg., 1972–1975)
Most Successful Coach: Wilt Chamberlain (37–47, .440 Pct., 1973–1974)

Chapter 29

NATIONAL BASKETBALL LEAGUE (1946–1949)

Just Where is Sheybogan, Anyway?

Professional basketball began long before the coming of giant George Mikan and the post-World War II popularity boom of the roundball sport. Barnstorming teams crisscrossed the nation (especially the eastern and midwestern sectors) for makeshift exhibition contests almost from the turn of the century. Three such teams—the Original Celtics of New York, the Chicago-based Harlem Globetrotters, and the New York-based Harlem Rens—developed a widespread national following and thus considerable notoriety. The Harlem Globetrotters of Abe Saperstein (actually formed in Chicago, but hoping to identify with the popularity of the Gotham-based Celtics and Rens) in particular pushed upward the popularity of the round-ball sport with their adroit mixture of clowning showmanship and expert serious play.

But organized leagues were another matter. There had been a few experiments which met with only partial success—the National Basketball League formed in the Philadelphia area in 1898 and lasting only until 1903; the Philadelphia League; the New England League; the Central League and Tri-State League, both operating out of Pennsylvania; the Hudson Valley League; Eastern League; New York State League; and the Inter-State League. All were regional in character, makeshift in nature, and short-lived at best. Ex-collegiate players filled most rosters and were hired on a game-by-game basis; better players often appeared with several teams in several leagues simultaneously. The travel was rough, the play was rougher, and fame was indeed fleeting. The reputation of most quality teams rarely spread beyond the region in which they played, and media coverage was sparse or nonexistent. In general, organized basketball was chaotic beyond the level of college competition. What did enjoy some success, however, were the midwestern industrial leagues and also the first attempt at a big-time pro circuit, which was known as the American Basketball League,

455

and which showcased the New York Celtics and enjoyed its heyday in the late '20s and early '30s.

The National Basketball League—with roots stretching back to the late '30s—was the most successful of the play-for-pay circuits. It came into existence in 1937 when three large midwestern corporations—Firestone and Goodyear of Akron, Ohio, and General Electric of Fort Wayne, Indiana—decided that there were public relations and recreational benefits to entering the fledgling professional basketball arena. The companies had all fielded strong amateur teams in the Midwest Basketball Conference for several years, and now joined their clubs with ten independent professional clubs around the region to inaugurate the N.B.L. As regional entertainment, the NBL of the late '30s enjoyed moderate popularity, but it was not to enjoy any real prosperity (or status as true big-time sport) until the close of the Second World War brought a new affluence, and consequently a new desperate search for sporting entertainment which suddenly swept the entire the nation.

As World War II came to an end and a new euphoria swept across the United States, the word best describing the American scene was "explosion"—it was the American era of the "boom" phenomena. The nation enjoyed a general economic boom, a housing boom, a television boom, certainly a baby boom, and on the sporting scene, eventually even a basketball boom. Relieved of the relentless pressures of war and personal and economic sacrifice, a nation now turned with an unrestrained hunger to recreation. And it turned first and foremost to making new families. No boom was greater than the baby boom. And when it came to the realm of new sporting entertainment, it was also the baby of the American sports scene—professional basketball—that was now positioned for a youthful growth spurt.

There were already signs, at the very end of the war, that the Midwest-based NBL was now headed for prosperous times. A record throng of better than 23,000, for example, crammed Chicago's Soldiers Field in November 1945 to watch the NBL Fort Wayne Pistons tackle a roster of collegians in the annual College All-Star Game. Feeling prosperity and increased ticket sales around the corner, the NBL had hired well-known Purdue University coach Ward "Piggy" Lambert as its new commissioner and added the Rochester Royals and Indianapolis Kautskys as its seventh and eight members. Collegiate stars like Bob Davies of Seton Hall, Red Holzman of C.C.N.Y. and Northwestern's Otto Graham (of later football fame) were signed on by the league. But the first true signs of legitimacy and impending widespread popularity for the circuit came the following fall when the NBL added five new teams in one fell swoop and inked the most prestigious collegiate recruit of all, rookie center George Mikan of DePaul, who would now play for the Chicago American Gears club. Mikan was the most famous college star since set-shooting Hank Luisetti had pioneered high-scoring basketball for Stanford in the late '30s. With Mikan in tow, it seemed like the NBL had finally grabbed a permanent niche on the now exploding American pro sports scene.

The three years of the NBL during the post-war boom period would represent one of the two clay feet on which the soon-to-be NBA would eventually struggle to an upright posture. While never quite as glamorous as the rival BAA, the NBL began the first great surge of mid-century basketball interest with two things definitely in its favor. While the rival BAA, which was born in 1946, had the deeper financial resources of eastern pro hockey owners, as well as the larger arenas located in larger eastern population centers, the NBL had longstanding tradition and a few showcase players on its side. It would quickly lose both, however.

The NBL moved out of its industrial league phase and into its more established "professional" phase during the 1946–'47 season. It did so with the addition of its five new teams—Toledo, Syracuse, Tri-Cities, Anderson, Detroit—and one new headline star player. It was George Mikan on whom the league hoped to build its rock-solid foundation. But the initial ride was a most turbulent one. Mikan seemed to have it all when it came to court skills that were bound to revolutionize the game. With his unmatched strength and nearly unmatched 6'10" frame, he could score seemingly at will with arching hooks and soft tap-ins. He was also an exceptional passer from the pivot; he rebounded with authority, and his defense was rugged and tireless. Mikan had already joined the Gears in time for the year-end world tournament in 1946, but would now launch his first full season. But when fall rolled around that much-anticipated season almost never got off the ground.

The new season wasn't a month old when Mikan returned to the sidelines as a holdout, claiming the Gears were attempting to cut his salary below a promised $12,000. It took six weeks for his lawyers to work out a satisfactory agreement with the Chicago ballclub and in the interim the Gears sagged in the standings and went hungry at the gate. Once Mikan was back in the fold, the Chicago team suddenly turned things around by also acquiring talented Fort Wayne player-coach Bobby McDermott. Mikan and McDermott provided a potent inside-outside punch and the Gears were overnight a title contender once more. But Mikan's contract dispute with the Chicago American Gears had almost ruined the season for Chicago and had also almost sunk the entire league in its wake.

The regular season in 1946–'47 saw the Rochester Royals—an old standby in the league—dominate all rivals in the early going. But the playoffs were a different matter, as the red-hot Chicago American Gears had now polished their act with the return of towering George Mikan, and the revamping of lineup and playing style under McDermott. In the end, Mikan would be just too much for Rochester to handle in the crunch time of post-season. Chicago's 17–6 finish down the stretch had bumped Anderson out of a final playoff spot. Neither Arnie Risen (at 6'9") with the Indianapolis Kautskys nor Leroy "Cowboy" Edwards (at 6'4") of the Oshkosh All-Stars could slow down the taller and more physical Mikan in the first two playoff rounds. Thus the championship round would be a classic matchup of Mikan's inside power game against the outside bombing and ballhandling of Bob Davies, Red Holzman and Al Cervi with Rochester. It wasn't much of a contest as Mikan topped the 20-point barrier twice and paced the stronger Gears to a three-games-to-one sweep of the series, and an expected league title.

If Mikan had almost left the league in a lurch with his absence for part of the previous season, his entire team nearly pulled the rug out from under the circuit a mere season later. Buoyed by his successes in the NBL, president Maurice White of the American Gear Company now attempted to build an entire league around the play of Mikan and his successful teammates. The new circuit would be called the Professional Basketball League of America, and would operate as a loose confederation of 24 ballclubs. White's dream was admirable but overambitious and undercapitalized and the entire scheme came crashing down only two weeks after the new league's start-up date. Relieved NBL officials quickly scrambled in the wake of this PBLA fiasco to redistribute the better players back onto NBL clubs. The luckiest beneficiary of this makeshift lottery (outside of the league itself) was the new Minneapolis team which had just been moved up from Detroit and had also undergone a name change from Gems to Lakers. While Mikan was assigned to a delirious Minneapolis management some other Chicago Gears also found new homes: aging star guard Bobby McDermott wound up in Sheboygan, Tri-Cities received Dick Triptow, and George Ratkovicz joined Rochester.

With the marriage of Mikan and the sports-crazy city of Minneapolis, a true basketball dynasty was being born right before the eyes of 1947–'48 NBL fans. But Mikan was not the only weapon in the arsenal of the newly reconstituted Minneapolis Lakers team. There was also Jim Pollard, the Kangaroo Kid, a supremely talented 6'4" forward who had been playing AAU basketball since his collegiate career with Stanford ended in 1942. Pollard was one of the new breed of jump shooters who could pop bombs from the corner or drill missiles from the top of the key. Minneapolis had also picked up ballhandling whiz Herman Schaefer from Indianapolis, who could now make a living feeding the ball upcourt to the stallions inside. With Mikan (21.3) and Pollard (12.9) combining for better than 34 points per game the Lakers (43–17) were able to walk away from their Western Division rivals during the regular season.

The Eastern Division of the NBL was more balanced, however, and three teams played up to the level of the Lakers. Rochester (44–16) for the second consecutive year had the league's best overall record and also its most balanced lineup, with Bob Davies in the forecourt, Arnie Risen (acquired mid-season from Indianapolis) at center, and Cervi and Holzman in the guard slots. Anderson (42–18) and Fort Wayne (40–20) also showed strength, even if they lacked big-name star ballplayers. But in the playoffs Mikan would again prove he was too much of a force to be contained in any short series when there was a trophy hanging in the balance. And again Rochester's Royals would once more see their season's-best record come to naught in the face of Mikan's post-season onslaughts.

The best odds at beating Minneapolis seemed to rest with the Tri-Cities Blackhawks who could at least pressure the Lakers' giant center with one of their own—seven-footer Don Otten. When Otten didn't prove up to the task, however, Minneapolis was paired off in the finals with a hard-luck Rochester team which had already lost their best weapons against the Lakers' overpowering front line. Rochester center Arnie Risen had suffered a season-ending fractured jaw in the last semifinal matchup with the Anderson Packers, and guards Holzman and Cervi were also both hobbled by nagging knee injuries. The result was hardly surprising, with Mikan pouring in 26, 25, 32 and 27 points as Minneapolis wrapped up the series with three victories in four games. Minneapolis now owned an NBL championship after only one year in the league, but Mikan already could boast of two championship rings.

Mikan's second and final season in the NBL had been one of record-breaking proportions. While the numbers which Mikan posted no longer seem impressive by today's standards, nonetheless they were awesome for the day in which he played. The bulky center had poured in points at a 16.5 ppg. rate a year earlier, but was not considered a legitimate league scoring champion having played in only 25 contests after his early-season holdout. His second campaign, however, brought a 21.3 average across 56 games that outdistanced the league's next best point maker (Arnie Risen at 14.5) by better than 30 per cent. A total 1,195 points by the Lakers star also nearly doubled the previous league scoring record of 632 points by Rochester's Al Cervi a season earlier. George Mikan was already singlehandedly changing the game of basketball.

Whereas Mikan's two defections from the NBL in 1946 and 1947 were temporary blows which were quickly nullified with his eventual return, the huge star's final defection in the fall of 1948 was a true death knell for the midwest-based circuit. And to make matters worse, Mikan didn't depart alone. Four top teams defected from the circuit during the summer preceding the 1948–'49 campaign, seeking to hitch their fortunes to the more prosperous BAA in the east. The four departing teams were Mikan's Lakers, the Fort Wayne Pistons, the Indianapolis Kautskys, and the always strong Rochester Royals. These four had been the league's healthiest franchises—both oncourt and off—and their joint loss was now as costly as that of George Mikan himself. It was only the final proverbial straw that these four teams also took with them such top-flight stars as Jim Pollard, Bob Davies, Red Holzman, Bobby Wanzer and Arnie Risen.

The handwriting was now on the wall for the crippled NBL when the Mikan-less season eventually began. The league had pulled together under a new commissioner, Doxie Moore. Five remaining clubs (Anderson, Syracuse, Tri-Cities, Sheboygan, and Oshkosh) were joined by four new ones in Hammond, Detroit, Waterloo (Iowa), and Denver. The enthusiastic fanbase of these small but basketball-crazy midwestern towns was barely enough to sustain one final season. And it was a rather exciting season of pioneering basketball at that.

With their more powerful rivals in Rochester, Minneapolis and Fort Wayne now out of the way, it was the turn of the Anderson Duffy Packers to secure some first-place glory. The Packers posted the best regular-season record in league history (49–15) and outdistanced Syracuse by eight and a half games in the east. They then also won an exciting final playoff series from Western Division leader Oshkosh. The series was a one-sided sweep with the Packers winning by counts of 74–70, 72–70 and 88–64. But it was also a series full of Anderson's fast-breaking action-style of race-horse play. For the past few seasons Anderson's quickness had been neutralized by the pounding play of taller insider men like Mikan or Arnie Risen, who could bully the Packers' shorter but quicker 6'6" Howie Schultz. But the towering Mikan and rugged Risen had departed the NBL, leaving Schultz and guard Frankie Brian free to pioneer a fast-breaking type offense. A new basketball era was indeed dawning.

One interesting historical footnote to the final NBL season was the last-minute appearance in league play of the famed all-Black New York Rens. A hold-over from basketball's earlier barnstorming days, the Rens team was a mid-season addition to the circuit necessitated by the folding in December of the Detroit Vagabond Kings franchise. Delays in completing a planned Detroit Forum had left the Vagabond Kings without a suitable home site and the club folded altogether 19 games into the fall season. Commissioner Doxie Moore was able to lure a much-weakened edition of Robert Douglas's famous Rens team that had won 2,078 barnstorming contests over the previous quarter-century, and still featured legendary player-coach ''Pop'' Gates. The Rens would be called the Dayton Rens but would play a majority of their games on the road and thus would represented the Ohio City largely in name only.

The Rens would bring into the league a lineup too old and too short to compete very successfully in the drastically upgraded professional game. Dayton's only truly standout performer would be future major league base-baller George Crowe, a first-ever Indiana high school ''Mr. Basketball'' back in 1939 who, at 6'6" and a svelt 210 pounds, played at both the forward and center positions. But the team was nonetheless unique as the only all-black franchise in the history of American major league sports. While the NBA (brought into ''official'' being with the merger of the NBL and BAA a season later) would not admit black players on integrated teams until Earl Lloyd (the first NBA black to actually play in a league game), Chuck Cooper (the first black draftee) and Sweetwater Clifton (the first black inked to a league contract) jointly broke the color line at the outset of the 1950–'51 season, black players had thus quietly entered the NBL two seasons earlier. Crowe (10.9). Gates (11.2) and Hank DeZonie (12.4 in a injury-shortened 18-game stint) all averaged double figures for the Rens who limped home with a barely respectable 14–26 season's tally.

When the NBL closed up shop forever, at the end of 1949 campaign, there were still a few valuable pieces left over. The forming of the new NBA alignment through merger of the healthier BAA and the Midwest-based NBL kept a small part of NBL tradition alive. Six NBL clubs had managed to keep their heads above water and joined the new NBA circuit—Syracuse, Anderson, Tri-Cities, Waterloo, Sheybogan and Denver. Of these only Syracuse and Tri-Cities would survive very far down the road. The Syracuse team would remain an NBA fixture for several seasons to come and then relocate to an eastern Pennsylvania metropolis where it would take on a new identity as the Philadelphia 76ers. And the Tri-Cities club would eventually resurrect itself as the Milwaukee Hawks, who later became the potent St. Louis Hawks. Tri-Cities would also contribute a solid player to the new circuit in the person of seven-footer Don Otten.

One other piece of the wreckage from NBL days was destined to have an even larger impact on the new BAA. During its final NBL season Syracuse had showcased a hardnosed new rookie bursting with enthusiasm and loaded with unmatched overall basketball talent. This top 1948 draft choice out of NYU was named Dolph Schayes and he was so versatile and skilled that for most of the coming decade he would rank in the league's top ten annually in four different categories—points, rebounds, assists, and free-throw percentage. The 6'8" forward was a scoring machine by the standards of his day (he would end up with over 18,000 points) but was also such a tenacious scrapper that he would soon be out-rebounding George Mikan himself. Schayes, in fact, would claim the NBA rebound title (with 16.4 rpg. in 1951) the very first year official statistics were recognized in that category. The slow plodding big-man's game introduced by Mikan would soon be neutralized in the new NBA by a bushel load of highscoring and mobile forwards. And none would be any better in a few short seasons than Dolph Schayes of the Syracuse Nationals.

Suggested Readings on National Basketball League

Bjarkman, Peter C. **The History of the NBA**. New York and Avenel, New Jersey: Crescent Books (Outlet Books, Random House), 1992.

Neft, David S. and Richard M. Cohen, Editors. **The Sports Encyclopedia: Pro Basketball**. Fourth Edition. New York: St. Martin's Press, 1991.

Peterson, Robert W. **Cages to Jump Shots—Pro Basketball's Early Years**. New York: Oxford University Press, 1990.

Season-by-Season NBL League Summary (1946–1949)

	1946–47	1947–48	1948–49
Playoff Champion	Chicago American Gears	Minneapolis Lakers	Anderson Duffy Packers
Championship Coach	Bobby McDermott	Johnny Kundla	Murray Mendenhall
Playoff Runner-Up	Rochester Royals	Rochester Royals	Oshkosh All-Stars
Regular Season Leader	Rochester Royals (31–13)	Rochester Royals (44–16)	Anderson Duffy Packers (49–15)
Best-Record Coach	Eddie Malanowicz	Eddie Malanowicz	Murray Mendenhall
Leading Scorer (PPG)	George Mikan (16.5)	George Mikan (21.3)	Don Otten (14.0)
Leading Scorer (Points)	Al Cervi (632)	George Mikan (1195)	Don Otten (899)

Year-by-Year NBL Regular Season Champions (1937–1949)

1937–38	Akron Firestones
1938–39	Akron Firestones
1939–40	Oshkosh All-Stars
1940–41	Oshkosh All-Stars
1941–42	Oshkosh All-Stars
1942–43	Fort Wayne Pistons
1943–44	Fort Wayne Pistons
1944–45	Fort Wayne Pistons
1945–46	Rochester Royals
1946–47	Rochester Royals
1947–48	Rochester Royals
1948–49	Anderson Duffy Packers

NBL Individual Scoring Champions (1937–1949)

Year	Player	G	FG	FT	Points	Average
1937–38	Leroy Edwards (Oshkosh)	13	82	45	209	16.1
1938–39	Leroy Edwards (Oshkosh)	28	124	86	334	11.9
1939–40	Leroy Edwards (Oshkosh)	28	111	140	362	12.9
1940–41	Ben Stephens (Goodyear)	24	98	67	253	10.9
1941–42	Chuck Chuckovits (Toledo)	22	143	120	406	18.4
1942–43	Bob McDermott (Fort Wayne)	23	130	54	314	13.6
1943–44	Mel Riebe (Cleveland)	18	113	98	324	18.0
1944–45	Mel Riebe (Cleveland)	30	224	143	606	20.2
1945–46	Bob Carpenter (Oshkosh)	34	186	101	473	13.9
1946–47	Al Cervi (Rochester)	44	228	176	632	14.4
1947–48	George Mikan (Minneapolis)	56	406	383	1195	21.3
1948–49	Don Otten (Tri-Cities)	64	301	297	899	14.0

NBL All-Time Individual Season and Game Records

Scoring Average (Season)	21.3	George Mikan (Minneapolis, 1947–48)
Points Scored (Season)	1,195	George Mikan (Minneapolis, 1947–48)
Points Scored (Game)	42	George Mikan (Minneapolis, 1948)
Field Goals (Season)	406	George Mikan (Minneapolis, 1947-48)
Field Goals (Game)	17	George Mikan (Minneapolis, 1948)
Free Throws (Season)	383	George Mikan (Minneapolis, 1947–48)
Free Throws (Game)	20	George Clamack (Indianapolis, 1948)
Personal Fouls (Season)	219	Harry Boycoff (Toledo, 1947–48)

Summary of Major NBL Individual Team Year-by-Year Records

Rochester Royals, 1946–1948
75–29, .721 Pct. (2 seasons)
Championships: None

Season	Record	Finish	Coach(es)	Scoring Leader(s)	Playoffs (W-L Record)
Key: # = League Leading Scorer					
1946–47	31–13	1st	Ed Malanowicz	Al Cervi (14.4)#	Lost in NBL Finals (6–5)
1947–48	44–16	1st	Ed Malanowicz	Arnie Risen (14.5)$	Lost in NBL Finals (6–5)
			Les Harrison		

$ Acquired from Indianapolis during season
Greatest Franchise Player: Arnie Risen (1947–48; Center, 6'9")

Anderson Duffy Packers, 1946–1949
115–53, .685 Pct. (3 seasons)
Championships (1): 1948–49

Season	Record	Finish	Coach(es)	Scoring Leader(s)	Playoffs (W-L Record)
1946–47	24–20	5th	M. Mendenhall	Howie Schultz (11.1)	Did Not Qualify
1947–48	42–18	2nd	M. Mendenhall	John Hargis (10.9)	Lost in 2nd Round (4–2)
1948–49	49–15	1st	M. Mendenhall	Frankie Brian (9.9)	**NBL Champion** (6–1)

Greatest Franchise Player: Howie Schultz (1946–47; Center, 6'7")

Minneapolis Lakers, 1947–1948
43–17, .717 Pct. (1 season)
Championships (1): 1947–48

Season	Record	Finish	Coach(es)	Scoring Leader(s)	Playoffs (W-L Record)
Key: # = League Scoring Leader					
1947–48	43–17	1st	John Kundla	George Mikan (21.3)#	**NBL Champion** (8–2)

Greatest Franchise Player: George Mikan (1947–48; Center, 6'10")

Chicago American Gears, 1946–1947
26–18, .591 Pct. (1 season)
Championships (1): 1946–47

Season	Record	Finish	Coach(es)	Scoring Leader(s)	Playoffs (W-L Record)

Key: * = Tied for Position; ** = Playing Coach

Season	Record	Finish	Coach(es)	Scoring Leader(s)	Playoffs (W-L Record)
1946–47	26–18	3rd*	Harry Foote	George Mikan (16.5)	**NBL Champion** (8–3)
			Bob McDermott**		

Greatest Franchise Player: George Mikan (1946–47; Center, 6'10")

Oshkosh All-Stars, 1946–1949
94–74, .560 Pct. (3 seasons)
Championships: None

Season	Record	Finish	Coach(es)	Scoring Leader(s)	Playoffs (W-L Record)
1946–47	28–16	1st	Lon Darling	Bob Carpenter (11.7)	Lost in 2nd Round (3–4)
1947–48	29–31	3rd	Lon Darling	Gene Englund (12.7)	Lost in 1st Round (1–3)
1948–49	37–27	1st	Lon Darling	Gene Englund (13.5)	Lost in NBL Finals (3–4)

Greatest Franchise Player: Gene Englund (1946–47; Forward-Center, 6'5")

Syracuse Nationals (Nats), 1946–1949
85–82, .509 Pct. (3 seasons)
Championships: None

Season	Record	Finish	Coach(es)	Scoring Leader(s)	Playoffs (W-L Record)

Key: ** = Playing Coach

Season	Record	Finish	Coach(es)	Scoring Leader(s)	Playoffs (W-L Record)
1946–47	21–23	4th	Benny Borgmann	Mike Novak (11.2)	Lost in 1st Round (1–3)
			Jerry Rizzo		
1947–48	24–36	4th	Benny Borgmann	Jim Homer (12.5)	Lost in 1st Round (0–3)
			Dan Biasone		
1948–49	40–23	2nd	Al Cervi**	Dolph Schayes (12.8)	Lost in 2nd Round (3–3)

Greatest Franchise Player: Dolph Schayes (1948–49; Forward-Center, 6'7")

Tri-Cities Blackhawks, 1946–1949
85–83, .506 Pct. (3 seasons)
Championships: None

Season	Record	Finish	Coach(es)	Scoring Leader(s)	Playoffs (W-L Record)

Key: ** = Playing Coach; # = League Scoring Leader

Season	Record	Finish	Coach(es)	Scoring Leader(s)	Playoffs (W-L Record)
1946–47*	19–25	5th	Nat Hickey	Don Otten (12.9)	Did Not Qualify
1947–48	30–30	2nd	Nat Hickey	Don Otten (13.7)	Lost in 2nd Round (3–3)
			Bob McDermott**		

Season	Record	Finish	Coach(es)	Scoring Leader(s)	Playoffs (W-L Record)
1948–49	36–28	2nd	Roger Potter Bob McDermott**	Don Otten (14.0)#	Lost in 2nd Round (3–3)

* Began season as Buffalo Braves
Greatest Franchise Player: Don Otten (1946–49; Center, 7'0")

Sheboygan Redskins, 1946–1949
84–84, .500 Pct. (3 seasons)
Championships: None

Season	Record	Finish	Coach(es)	Scoring Leader(s)	Playoffs (W-L Record)
Key: * = Tied for Position; ** = Playing Coach					
1946–47	26–18	3rd*	Doxie Moore	Fred Lewis (13.3)	Lost in 1st Round (2–3)
1947–48	23–37	5th	Doxie Moore Bob McDermott**	Mike Todorovich (13.0)	Did Not Qualify
1948–49	35–29	3rd	Kenny Suesens	Mike Todorovich (10.8)	Lost in 1st Round (0–2)

Greatest Franchise Player: Mike Todorovich (1947–49; Forward, 6'5")

Fort Wayne Zollner Pistons, 1946–1948
65–39, .625 Pct. (2 seasons)
Championships: None

Season	Record	Finish	Coach(es)	Scoring Leader(s)	Playoffs (W-L Record)
Key: ** = Player Coach					
1946–47	25–19	2nd	Carl Bennett Bob McDermott**	Bob McDermott (11.4)	Lost in 2nd Round (4–4)
1947–48	40–20	3rd	Carl Bennett	Jack Pelkington (9.3)	Lost in 1st Round (1–3)

Greatest Franchise Player: Bobby McDermott (1946–47; Guard, 6'0")

Indianapolis Kautskys, 1946–1948
51–52, .495 Pct. (2 seasons)
Championships: None

Season	Record	Finish	Coach(es)	Scoring Leader(s)	Playoffs (W-L Record)
Key: ** = Playing Coach					
1946–47	27–17	2nd	Ernie Andres	Arnie Risen (13.2)	Lost in 1st Round (2–3)
1947–48	24–35	4th	Glenn Curtis Bruce Hale**	Arnie Risen (12.1)$	Lost in 1st Round (1–3)

\$ Traded to Rochester during season
Greatest Franchise Player: Arnie Risen (1946–48; Center, 6'9")

Chapter 30

BASKETBALL ASSOCIATION OF AMERICA (1946–1949)

A Good Idea Whose Time Had Definitely Come

One largely lost fact of basketball history remains the deeply planted Canadian roots of the most native among North American national games. Dr. James Naismith was, of course, a Canadian by birth—born and raised in rural Ontario, educated at Montreal's McGill University, and relocated to the United States only in 1891, in the very year of his fortuitous invention. And when pro basketball showed signs of coming finally to life with the birth of the new Basketball Association of America in the fall of 1946, the first game would be played not in New York or Philadelphia or anywhere along the eastern seaboard of the USA, but rather in Toronto, Canada. The deepest Canadian roots off all, however, had to do with pro basketball's inescapable hockey connections. Basketball's deepest Canadian flavor thus had to do with the motives and prime movers which stood firmly behind the birth of a league that would, in three short years, develop into the fledgling National Basketball Association.

While the time had perhaps come for pro basketball to stand firmly on its own with the ending of World War II and the return of a booming peace time economy, the men who founded the most successful pro circuit of all time saw the game they were creating at the moment as being a mere adjunct to their primary business interest, which was the hockey business. For men like Ned Irish, owner of the New York Rangers and of Madison Square Garden, and Walter Brown, who controlled the Boston Garden and the Boston Bruins, it made good business sense to exploit the new popularity of basketball with a confederation of pro clubs that could fill up dormant arenas on some of the nights local hockey teams would inevitably be out of town.

Teams which first made up the new circuit were located in New York, Toronto, Boston, Providence, Philadelphia, Washington, Pittsburgh, Cleveland, Detroit, Chicago and St. Louis. The owners of each of these new franchises were already linked to each other through membership in the

Arena Management Association and through ownership of teams in either the National Hockey League or the American Hockey League. This existing partnership was underscored with the naming of AHL president Maurice Podoloff (who knew next to nothing about basketball, it turned out) as the first BAA executive officer. There was, of course, an immediate advantage built into this entire operation—that of playing in large arenas in the nation's leading population centers. Fans would more likely accept as "major league" and legitimate teams playing in venues like New York and Chicago and dismiss as bush league those bearing names like Oshkosh, Tri-Cities, and Anderson. Indeed, as far as the BAA was concerned, there would be no embarrassing questions in the press like "where the heck is Sheybogan anyway?"

Thus it was that one of the most legendary hockey venues of all time played host to the birth of modern pro basketball—at least the strand of pro basketball that would soon be able to boast a direct lineage to the modern-day National Basketball Association of the Knicks, Celtics, Warriors and Lakers. The first scheduled game of the fledgling BAA was pencilled in for Friday night, November 1, 1946; it matched the Toronto Huskies of player-coach Ed Sadowski and the New York Knickerbockers under coach Neil Cohalan, and would be played in Toronto's Maple Leaf Gardens. A curious crowd of 7,090 paid admissions ranging from 75 cents to $2.50 that night to watch not only a rare basketball game but also an advertised program of opening ceremonies, warm-ups, a basketball clinic, and demonstrations by players of both teams. New York, featuring the 6'5" Bud Palmer, and Toronto, led in scoring that first season by Leo Mogus, put on an entertaining show spoiled for the local fandom only by the Knicks' tight 68–66 victory. The evening's prime moment came only seconds after the opening tipoff. New York's Leo Gottlieb would recover the opening tap, dribble upcourt, and then feed a driving Ossie Schectman for a layup basket and the NBA's first historic points. The league's first tip-off, its opening baskets, its first victory and defeat—none were fated to transpire on US soil.

While Toronto would play a major role in the opening of the new league, the city would not be part of the pro basketball scene for very long. Lagging press coverage and dismal attendance in Toronto, Cleveland, Detroit, and Pittsburgh, would bring down all four franchises by the end of the league's first season. And if attendance didn't meet expectations, another disappointment was the failure to lure into the circuit the three top collegiate stars who had just graduated in spring, 1946. George Mikan opted to carry his bulky body and considerable talent over to the Chicago Gears NBL franchise. Don Otten, a 7-foot giant joined the NBL as well by casting his lot with the Tri-Cities Blackhawks. And the biggest potential star of all—another seven-foot giant named Bob Kurland out of Oklahoma A&M—decided on the more secure future of a plush desk job with Phillips Petroleum and an adjunct playing career in AAU industrial league basketball.

And if the BAA lost the collegiate recruiting war with its older rival, it also didn't fair well at all in attracting NBL players to jump leagues and sign on with the new eastern pro ballclubs. Yet despite these recruiting setbacks the BAA got off to a rousing start in the first campaign of 1946–'47. Washington, under a 29-year-old ex-high school coach named Red Auerbach, quickly proved to be the cream of the league. An experienced lineup in Washington featured guard Bob Feerick, the one NBL star who *had* jumped, as well as another fine shooting backcourt player, Freddie Scolari. Washington's strongest performer, however, was a 27-year-old, 6'6" sharpshooter who had just completed a stellar war-interrupted college career at North Carolina. Horace "Bones" McKinney had an unforgettable nickname and an unforgettable scoring touch which accounted for a 12 ppg. scoring average that was equivalent to about 30 ppg. in any later era. The Caps ran off a 17-game winning streak early in the season that would remain a pro record for several seasons to come. Bob Feerick anchored an experienced backcourt with a 16.3 scoring average that was third best in the league. The Washington team thus coasted through the regular season with the best won-loss record (49–11) of the BAA's three-year history.

There were other teams in the league that first season that could also boast considerable individual talent. Eddie Gottlieb's Philadelphia Warriors, for one, had high-scoring Joe Fulks who poured in points at an unheard-of rate for the immediate post-war era. Fulks had starred at Murray State before the war and had developed such a deadly and rapid-fire jump shooing technique that defenses were helpless to stop him. His 23.2 ppg. scoring mark that first season would be almost matched a year later by Mikan's totals over in the NBL. But Mikan was not yet reaching some of the lofty numbers posted by Fulks, which included a 41-point game against Toronto on January 14. In the west the Chicago Stags featured Max Zaslofsky who could also shoot with deadly accuracy and a fast-breaking offense that averaged a team-high 77.0 ppg. The Cleveland Rebels had two fine guards in Kenny Sailors and baseballer Frank Baumholtz, who doubled as a hard-hitting outfielder for the Chicago Cubs.

One flaw of the new circuit was a not-very-well-thought-through format for post-season play. The playoff tournament paired first place, second place and third place teams from the two divisions against each other, assuring that one of the division winners would immediately be eliminated by the other during the opening round. Thus when the Chicago Stags were able to wear out the high-flying Washington Caps, the door was suddenly wide open to a surprise champion in the BAA's first post-season derby. And Gottlieb's Warriors stepped right up to the task. In a one-sided final series that took only five games "Jumpin Joe" Fulks and the Warriors took home the first-ever BAA crown. Fulks would fire home 37 points in a Warriors 84–71 opening-game victory. Then with the Philadelphia club holding a commanding 3–1 lead in the series Fulks would answer with 34 more and Howie Dallmar would score the winning bucket of an 82–80 championship clincher. Since the pioneering BAA is today considered in most quarters as the direct parent of the NBA, most historians now credit the Philadelphia Warriors coached by Eddie Gottlieb as the first true NBA champion.

The BAA entered its second season on somewhat wobbly legs, still shaking from the collapse of four franchises in major midwestern and northeastern cities. Commissioner Podoloff was able to apply some patchwork repairs, however, by talking the Baltimore Bullets into jumping over to the BAA from the American Basketball League. This defection would start a trend which would pick up full steam a year later with wholesale raiding of the NBL franchises by Podoloff as well. Nonetheless the league for 1947 had been pared from eleven teams to eight and the schedule trimmed from 60 games to 48. Neither were encouraging signs of league stability. The biggest improvement in year two, however, came with the influx of fresh playing talent. Players from the disbanded clubs strengthened the remaining ones. Kenny Sailors (Cleveland), for example, wound up with Providence while Ed Sadowski (Cleveland) found a home in Boston and all-league center Stan Miasek (Detroit) went to Chicago. And several rookies—especially Carl Braun, Red Rocha and Andy Phillip—also freshened the scene. The BAA already seemed to have the upper hand over the NBL. Despite the fact that the older circuit still had Mikan, the BAA with is bigger arenas was rapidly becoming the league of choice among the growing population of hardwood fans.

League health in year two was also propped up by torrid first-place races in both divisions. All four teams in the western division fought down to the wire, and three (Baltimore, Chicago and Washington) tied for second. Philadelphia, the defending champion, battled it out with New York in the east with the Warriors prevailing by a single game in the standings. Joe Fulks was again the league's showcase player in Philadelphia although his 22.1 scoring average (949 points) barely retained the scoring crown against a vastly improved Max Zaslofsky (21.0, with 1,007 points). But New York, with the biggest potential fan market, also displayed a quartet of talented young players in Carl Braun, Bud Palmer, Dick Holub and Sid Tannenbaum. The rookie Braun, out of Colgate, utilized an old-style one-handed set shot to post a league-record 47 points in one December 6 game versus Providence.

The same askew playoff system again allowed one of the league's strongest clubs to tumble in the first playoff round of 1948. This time it was the St. Louis Bombers, winners of a league-best 29 games, who fell immediately to Gottlieb's defending champions. The winner of the first-place face-off now awaited the semi-final round between the second and third place winners, Baltimore and Chicago. When the Bullets prevailed, a title matchup was set between the heavily favored Warriors with Fulks, and the colorless Bullets with no marquee players at all. Philadelphia seemed to relax after an opening easy 71–60 homecourt victory in game one. After that the surprising Bullets took command of the title series by sweeping to victory in games two, three, four and six.

BAA supporters and officials could not have felt very good about post-season results in 1948. The champion Baltimore team—a dull club to watch without a single big scorer or flashy ball handler—could hardly be compared seriously to the NBL champion Lakers and George Mikan when it came to debating pro basketball's superior team. But in an ingenious move during the off-season, Commissioner Podoloff was again able to solve the potential image problem with a stunning backroom move. This time Podoloff—who had only recently smuggled the champion Bullets into the league—convinced the Lakers to leave the NBL and cast their lot with his own rapidly improving circuit. And not only the Lakers, but the Fort Wayne, Rochester, and Indianapolis franchises as well, would now make the jump. While the league's future was not by any means assured by these off-season transfers, the BAA had now taken several giant steps forward. And the biggest step was the overnight welcome of basketball's biggest hero, George Mikan, into the surging league.

The Lakers and Rochester Royals had battled tooth and nail throughout the previous NBL regular season and post-season as well. Now that rivalry was to be renewed within the BAA. The Lakers with Mikan and Jim Pollard were now the biggest drawing card on the east coast as well as in the midwest. Joe Fulks was even pushed from the limelight once Mikan was on the scene. "Jumpin Joe" would ironically now post his highest scoring mark during the new season (26.0 ppg., 1,560 points) and it would not even be good enough to win him another scoring title. The story everywhere around the league was now seemingly Mikan and Mikan alone. At long last this "legend" that east coast fans had hungered to see was coming to town in New York, Boston, Philadelphia, Providence and Washington. At one point early in the season the huge marquee on the front of Madison Square Garden best indicated the impact of the league's new big man. "Tonight, Mikan Versus Knicks" was all the sign read. Michael Jordan was not the first player to become the league's solo showcase marketing piece.

On the court, if not on the marquees, there was, of course, more than just Mikan performing in the league. Rochester was every bit as potent as Minneapolis and even posted a better record (45–15) over the course of the long season, if only by a single game in the end. A post-season showdown between Rochester and Mikan was what seemed inevitable almost from opening night, however. This time there would be a revised playoff format that would increase the likelihood of the league's best teams facing off in the finals. Teams played only within their divisions (a model taken from baseball) until the final east-west showdown of the championship match.

Mikan had his shootout with the Royals in the semi-final round and won handily, if not convincingly, in a two-game set. In the previous year's face-off of these same two clubs for an NBL title, injuries had so riddled the Rochester lineup that any true comparison of the ballclubs was difficult. This time around Rochester put up a gamer battle against Mikan, falling by a single point at home and then leading 52–49 at the end of three quarters in game two at St. Paul. The Minneapolis triumph now set up a Finals between the newly arrived Lakers and the Washington Capitols, one of the BAA's strongest three-year franchises.

The 1949 championship series was indeed a thrilling matchup. The Lakers charged ahead behind Mikan for three quick victories. The huge center was neutralized in game two by Washington's Bones McKinney and Kleggie Hermson and scored only 10 in a 72–62 victory; but Mikan owned the first and third contests as he camped under the basket and flipped in first 42 and then 35 in 88–84 and 94–74 triumphs. Then the giant broke his wrist in game four and the Lakers slumped to back-to-back losses against the revived Washington team. But even a crippled Mikan was too much once again in game six—broken wrist, cumbersome plaster cast and all—and Minneapolis cruised on the home floor in St. Paul to clinch yet another banner. The Lakers had now won their third straight playoff title, each in a different league.

While the BAA survived the 1948–'49 season with flying colors, the NBL did not. The loss of not only the Lakers and Royals, but the Fort Wayne and Indianapolis franchises as well, was more of a blow to gate receipts than the league could reasonably hope to absorb. Commissioner Doxie Moore now seemed to be holding the elder circuit together with a very loose shoe string indeed. But the NBL did have one final ace to play in its bag of tricks, and that trump card occurred shortly after the 1949 season. Commissioner Moore assured at least some leverage for his league when he was able to convince the graduating starters from the glorious University of Kentucky NCAA champion team to sign on as a unit and form a new team, to be known most appropriately as the Indianapolis Olympians.

Alex Groza, Ralph Beard, Wah Wah (Wallace) Jones, Joe Holland, Mal McMullen and Cliff Barker as a unit had been the cream of the college crop and had comprised the 1948 Olympic squad which had breezed to a gold medal victory as well. This was enough to convince BAA officials that a merger would now be in the vested interests of both leagues. The NBL needed an established circuit with healthy clubs and large arenas in order to meet travel and payroll expenses and, hopefully, even turn a profit. The BAA could use a few extra teams, especially the one now slated to debut in Indianapolis, where it would play head-to-head with the BAA's own Indianapolis Jets. It was at the time an unseen irony, of course, that two of the former Kentucky stars, Beard and Groza, about to take the court in Indianapolis would soon be implicated in a breaking college game-fixing scandal and thus quickly banned from the sport for life.

The amalgamated league that would open play in the fall would henceforth be known as the National Basketball Association; it might better have been known as the far-flung hodgepodge confederation of independent basketball satellites. For this new loose-knit union of teams would be an unruly conglomerate at first, spread out around the country in an era before regular air travel and demanding an unbalanced schedule between eastern and western clubs. Teams from the BAA would include New York, Boston, Washington, Philadelphia, Baltimore, Rochester, Minneapolis, Chicago, St. Louis and Fort Wayne. From the NBL came Syracuse, Anderson (Indiana), Tri-Cities (Moline, Illinois), Waterloo (Iowa), Sheybogan (Wisconsin), and Denver. Only five teams were left by the wayside by the merger: Providence (BAA), Indianapolis (BAA), Hammond (NBL), Oshkosh (NBL), and Dayton (NBL). There were tremendous scheduling problems (Eastern and Central teams, for example, played 68 games while Western teams played 62) but the new circuit began with a healthy dose of optimism and just enough success to survive. But that success also had to do with the foundation already laid over the course of the previous three seasons, especially by the large-city eastern teams boasting large arenas located in major urban centers. For NBA basketball had already been born and mildly aged during the first three seasons of the league known as the BAA.

Suggested Readings on Basketball Association of America

Bjarkman, Peter C. **The History of the NBA**. New York and Avenel, New Jersey: Crescent Books (Outlet Books, Random House), 1992.
Neft, David S. and Richard M. Cohen, Editors. **The Sports Encyclopedia: Pro Basketball**. Fourth Edition. New York: St. Martin's Press, 1991.
Peterson, Robert W. **Cages to Jump Shots—Pro Basketball's Early Years**. New York: Oxford University Press, 1990.

Season-by-Season BAA League Summary (1946–1949)

	1946–47	1947–48	1948–49
Playoff Champion	Philadelphia Warriors	Baltimore Bullets	Minneapolis Lakers
Championship Coach	Eddie Gottlieb	Buddy Jeannette	Johnny Kundla
Playoff Runner-Up	Chicago Stags	Philadelphia Warriors	Washington Capitols
Regular Season Leader	Washington Capitols (19–11)	St. Louis Bombers (29–19)	Rochester Royals (45–15)
Best-Record Coach	Red Auerbach	Ken Loeffler	Les Harrison
Leading Scorer (PPG)	Joe Fulks (23.2)	Joe Fulks (22.1)	George Mikan (28.3)
Leading Scorer (Points)	Joe Fulks (1389)	Max Zaslofsky (1007)	George Mikan (1698)

BAA All-Time Individual Season and Career Records

Scoring Average (Career)	23.9*	Joe Fulks (Philadelphia, 1946–49)
Scoring Average (Season)	28.3	George Mikan (Minneapolis, 1948–49)
Points Scored (Career)	3,898	Joe Fulks (Philadelphia, 1946–49)
Points Scored (Season)	1,698	George Mikan (Minneapolis, 1948–49)
Field Goals (Season)	583	George Mikan (Minneapolis, 1948–49)
Field Goal Pct. (Season)	.423	Arnie Risen (Rochester, 1948–49)
Free Throws (Season)	532	George Mikan (Minneapolis, 1948–49)
Free Throw Pct. (Season)	.859	Bob Feerick (Washington, 1948–49)
Assists (Career)	572	Ernie Caverly (Providence, 1946–49)
Assists (Season)	321	Bob Davies (Rochester, 1948–49)
Personal Fouls (Season)	273	Ed Sadowski (Philadelphia, 1948–49)

*Two seasons or more

Summary of BAA Individual Team Year-by-Year Records

Philadelphia Warriors, 1946–1949
94–78, .547 Pct. (3 seasons)
Championships (1): 1946–47

Season	Record	Finish	Coach(es)	Scoring Leader(s)	Playoffs (W-L Record)
Key: # = League Leading Scorer					
1946–47	39–25	2nd	Eddie Gottlieb	Joe Fulks (23.2)#	**BAA Champion** (8–2)
1947–48	27–21	1st	Eddie Gottlieb	Joe Fulks (22.1)#	Lost in BAA Finals (6–7)
1948–49	28–32	4th	Eddie Gottlieb	Joe Fulks (26.0)	Lost in 1st Round (0–2)
Best Player: "Jumpin' Joe" Fulks (Forward, 6'5")					

Baltimore Bullets, 1947–1949
57–51, .528 Pct. (2 seasons)
Championships (1): 1947–48

Season	Record	Finish	Coach(es)	Scoring Leader(s)	Playoffs (W-L Record)
Key: * = Tied for Position					
1947–48	28–20	2nd*	Buddy Jeannette	Kleggie Hermsen (12.0)	**BAA Champion** (9–3)
1948–49	29–31	3rd	Buddy Jeannette	Connie Simmons (13.0)	Lost in 1st Round (1–2)
Best Player: Connie Simmons (Center, 6'8")					

Minneapolis Lakers, 1948–1949
44–16, .733 Pct. (1 season)
Championships (1): 1948–49

Season	Record	Finish	Coach(es)	Scoring Leader(s)	Playoffs (W-L Record)

Key: # = League Leading Scorer

Season	Record	Finish	Coach(es)	Scoring Leader(s)	Playoffs (W-L Record)
1948–49	44–16	2nd	Johnny Kundla	George Mikan (28.3)#	**BAA Champion** (8–2)

Best Player: George Mikan (Center, 6'10")

Washington Capitols, 1946–1949
115–53, .685 Pct. (3 seasons)
Championships: None

Key: * = Tied for Position

Season	Record	Finish	Coach(es)	Scoring Leader(s)	Playoffs (W-L Record)
1946–47	49–11	1st	Red Auerbach	Bob Feerick (16.8)	Lost in 1st Round (2–4)
1947–48	28–20	2nd*	Red Auerbach	Bob Feerick (16.1)	Lost in Tie Breaker (0–1)
1948–49	38–22	1st	Red Auerbach	Bob Feerick (13.0)	Lost in BAA Finals (6–5)

Best Player: Bob Feerick (Forward-Guard, 6'3")

Chicago Stags, 1946–1949
105–64, .621 Pct. (3 seasons)
Championships: None

Key: * = Tied for Position

Season	Record	Finish	Coach(es)	Scoring Leader(s)	Playoffs (W-L Record)
1946–47	39–22	1st	Ole Olsen	Max Zaslofsky (14.4)	Lost in BAA Finals (5–6)
1947–48	28–20	2nd*	Ole Olsen / Jim Seminoff	Max Zaslofsky (21.])	Lost in 2nd Round (2–3)
1948–49	38–22	3rd	Ole Olsen	Max Zaslofsky (20.6)	Lost in 1st Round (0–2)

Best Player: Max Zaslofsky (Guard-Forward, 6'2")

St. Louis Bombers, 1946–1949
96–73, .568 Pct. (3 seasons)
Championships: None

Season	Record	Finish	Coach(es)	Scoring Leader(s)	Playoffs (W-L Record)
1946–47	38–23	2nd	Ken Loeffler	Johnny Logan (12–6)	Lost in 1st Round (1–2)
1947–48	29–19	1st	Ken Loeffler	Johnny Logan (13.4)	Lost in 1st Round (3–4)
1948–49	29–31	4th	Grady Lewis	Belus Smawley (15.5)	Lost in 1st Round (0–2)

Best Player: Johnny Logan (Guard-Forward, 6'2")

New York Knickerbockers, 1946–1949
91–77, .542 Pct. (3 seasons)
Championships: None

Season	Record	Finish	Coach(es)	Scoring Leader(s)	Playoffs (W-L Record)
1946–47	33–27	3rd	Neil Cohalan	Bud Palmer (9.5)	Lost in 2nd Round (2–3)
1947–48	26–22	2nd	Joe Lapchick	Carl Braun (14.3)	Lost in 1st Round (1–2)
1948–49	32–28	2nd	Joe Lapchick	Carl Braun (14.2)	Lost in 2nd Round (3–3)

Best Player: Carl Braun (Forward-Guard, 6'5")

Boston Celtics, 1946–1949
67–101, .399 Pct. (3 seasons)
Championships: None

Season	Record	Finish	Coach(es)	Scoring Leader(s)	Playoffs (W-L Record)
Key: * = Tied for Position					
1946–47	22–38	5th*	John Russell	Connie Simmons (10.3)	Did Not Qualify
1947–48	20–28	3rd	John Russell	Ed Sadowski (19.4)	Lost in 1st Round (1–2)
1948–49	25–35	5th	Alvin Julian	George Kaftan (14.5)	Did Not Qualify

Best Player: Ed Sadowski (Center, 6'5")

Providence Steamrollers, 1946–1949
46–122, .274 Pct. (3 seasons)
Championships: None

Season	Record	Finish	Coach(es)	Scoring Leader(s)	Playoffs (W-L Record)
1946–47	28–32	4th	Bob Morris	Ernie Calverly (14.3)	Did Not Qualify
1947–48	6–42	4th	Hank Soar	Ernie Caverly (11.9)	Did Not Qualify
			Nat Hickey	Kenny Sailors (11.9)	
1948–49	12–48	6th	Ken Loeffler	Kenny Sailors (15.8)	Did Not Qualify

Best Player: Ernie Caverly (Guard, 5'10")

Rochester Royals, 1948–1949
45–15, .750 Pct. (1 season)
Championships: None

Season	Record	Finish	Coach(es)	Scoring Leader(s)	Playoffs (W-L Record)
1948–49	45–15	1st	Les Harrison	Arnie Risen (16.6)	Lost in 2nd Round (2–2)

Best Player: Arnie Risen (Center, 6'9")

Cleveland Rebels, 1946–1947
30–30, .500 Pct. (1 season)
Championships: None

Season	Record	Finish	Coach(es)	Scoring Leader(s)	Playoffs (W-L Record)
1946–47	30–30	3rd	Dutch Dehnert Roy Clifford	Ed Sadowski (16.5)	Lost in 1st Round (1–2)

Best Player: Ed Sadowski (Center, 6'5")

Fort Wayne (Zollner) Pistons, 1948–1949
22–38, .367 Pct. (1 season)
Championships: None

Season	Record	Finish	Coach(es)	Scoring Leader(s)	Playoffs (W-L Record)
1948–49	22–38	5th	Carl Bennett Curly Armstrong	Bruce Hale (10.5)	Did Not Qualify

Best Player: Bruce Hale (Guard-Forward, 6'1")

Toronto Huskies, 1946–1947
22–38, .367 Pct. (1 season)
Championships: None

Season	Record	Finish	Coach(es)	Scoring Leader(s)	Playoffs (W-L Record)
1946–47	22–38	5th	Red Rolfe	Leo Mogus (13.0)	Did Not Qualify

Best Player: Leo Mogus (Forward, 6'4")

Detroit Falcons, 1946–1947
20–40, .333 Pct. (1 season)
Championships: None

Season	Record	Finish	Coach(es)	Scoring Leader(s)	Playoffs (W-L Record)
1946–47	20–40	4th	Glenn Curtis Cincy Sachs	Stan Miasek (14.9)	Did Not Qualify

Best Player: Stan Miasek (Center-Forward, 6'5")

Indianapolis Jets, 1948–1949
18–42, .300 Pct. (1 season)
Championships: None

Season	Record	Finish	Coach(es)	Scoring Leader(s)	Playoffs (W-L Record)
1948–49	18–42	6th	Bruce Hale Burl Friddle	Blackie Towery (10.0)	Did Not Qualify

Best Player: Leo Mogus (Center-Forward, 6'4")

Pittsburgh Ironmen, 1946–1947
15–45, .250 Pct. (1 season)
Championships: None

Season	Record	Finish	Coach(es)	Scoring Leader(s)	Playoffs (W-L Record)
1946–47	15–45	5th	Paul Birch	Colby Gunther (14.1)	Did Not Qualify

Best Player: Colby Gunther (Forward, 6'4")

Epilogue

Basketball's Dozen Greatest Heroes

Baseball's myths are the very essence of the diamond game and of its wonderous and sustaining history. Baseball fans cling to such cherished beliefs as the story of Abner Doubleday's invention of the sport in Cooperstown, the heroics of Babe Ruth's called home run "shot" in the 1932 World Series; the inspired tales of Jackie Robinson's role as the first black man ever to play major league baseball; and dozens more such staples of the game. Little matter that all are myths and all are more or less false accounts of the game's actual on-field history. Such cheerful distortions of the record are, after all, the ingrained fabric of baseball lore. They are the necessary fanciful tales of a sport built on the back of folklore, tales passed from generation to generation as a living legacy of a game which is more stories, records and empheria than spell-binding action itself.

Basketball—with its less visible historic overtones—has only one such myth and it is a fabrication of rather recent origins. It is the myth that Michael Jordan was the greatest all-around player ever to lace a pair of sneakers and to shoot at the modern versions of Dr. Naismith's peach baskets. This myth suggests that no one is even close to Jordan when it comes to selecting the most accomplished player the sport has ever produced. And it is just as much bunk as a Babe Ruth "called shot."

The myth of Jordan's unquestioned superiority among the legends of the game is one that will simply not hold up as time passes, however, and as historical perspective returns to the hoop sport. As more clear-minded historians flock to basketball as their subject matter, and as the din of the world's greatest marketing and promotion blitz eventually subsides around the remnants of Jordan's career, a balance will inevitably be struck. It will be realized at some point that the slam dunk soaring moves which are almost the sole gradification for today's fans are not the only standard for

481

judging great play—in fact they attach to an extremely small dimension of basketball skill. And as more fans look at the statistical records compiled by earlier generations of players, it will remain obvious that Jordan is barely in the same league of measured performance with a handful of basketball's lost avatars. He does not match up as a scorer to the beheamoth Chamberlain, who once scored 100 points in a game and averaged 50 for a full season. He never dominanted a game or an entire post-season as did the imposing Russell, who controlled the sport without any scoring at all. And most certainly, he does not rank in versatility with the incomparable Oscar Robertson who came within a narrow margin of averaging a triple-double (double figures in scoring, rebounding and assists) for an entire decade-and-half NBA career (and did do so for five full NBA seasons).

The greatest injustice of basketball's relative obscurity in the 1950s and 1960s is that the half-dozen greatest performers of the sport's history have inevitably been largely lost on the shortsighted American sporting public. But the records of this fabuolus handful of true superstars are enough— once revived—to speak loudly for themselves. Today it is point scoring and the hallmark of versatility—the triple-double—that are everywhere touted as the true milestones of individual hoop performance. The triple-double holds special favor with today's media as a measure of all-around skill; whenever a player reaches such totals in a single game, it can not fail to be mentioned as a rare mark of achievement. But Oscar Robertson— great shooting, passing and rebounding guard for the '60s Cincinnati Royals—posted triple-double numbers with such regularity that the real story was those occasional nights when opponents somehow happened to hold Oscar under ten rebounds or ten assists.

Fans also goggle when Jordan scores 60 in a game (something he has done on five occasions). But the fabulous Chamberlain accomplished this same feat 31 times. And Bill Russell, for his part, was the only player in history to pile up championships in record numbers and dominate ballgames for more than a decade—night in and night out—without ever needing to score a point. When Russell ever did make baskets (he averaged 15.1 ppg. for his career) it was almost totally irrelevant. George Mikan, to take another example, was so dominant that the league's front-office types had to drastically alter the long-standing rules under which the game was being played. And Elgin Baylor invented high-flying "moves" that were so good that writer Alexander Wolff described him as "a pioneer of the game's third dimension, the uncharted fastness that makes wannabes of fans everywhere." Finally, Jerry West was such a frequent and deadly outside shooter that, had a three-point goal existed in his day, the Lakers guard would likely have outstripped Jordan in annual scoring titles (as well as outdistancing him by 10,000 or more career points); as it is West scored 25,192 points in 14 seasons, to Jordan's 21,541 in nine campaigns.

In its modern era the game of pro basketball was first reinvented and redefined by high-flying Julius Erving and the invention of "hangtime" moves and acrobatic above-the-rim styles of play. Julius Erving indeed made Michael Jordan possible, but he also enjoyed his halcyon days in the forgotten and ignored ABA; when Erving transfered his game to the NBA arenas in the late '70s, he did so at a time when the sport was withering under lack of national television exposure and the absence of broad-based fan enthusiasm. Pro basketball in the wake of Dr. J was soon rescued from growing obscurity by the twin arrival of Magic Johnson and Larry Bird—the glamor heroes of the '80s. Bird was perhaps the greatest all-around forward, and Magic the most talented and athletic playmaker the game had ever known. And fortuitously for the Bird-Magic duals, the television networks found the game at exactly the same time. Finally, in the wake of Bird and Magic and on the crest of the game's new televised popularity, rode Michael Jordan, the most celebrated ballplayer ever, and one who was (for the first time in the NBA) as much a product of Wall Street advertising and pop culture promotion as he was of on-floor basketball feats. Of course Jordan's game-time feats were themselves spectacular, and Air Jordan and the NBA have rode hand and hand into a rosy present which is the zenith of the sport's history.

From Mikan and Cousy and Pettit, who were the forgotten heroes of the '50s, to Wilt Chamberlain, who was perhaps too awesome a phenomenon to appreciate fully in his own era or to assess adequately from the vantage point of later eras, on to the undervalued superstars of basketball's lost "Golden Age" of the '60s—Oscar Robertson, Elgin Baylor and Jerry West, through the "savior" roles of Julius Erving in the '70s and Bird and Magic in the '80s, and finally down to Air Jordan, who was perhaps somewhat overrated and certainly overhyped, but was nonetheless just the spectacular showpiece needed by the new masses tuned in and turned on to basketball's television age of the '90s. Across a full half century, the National Basketball Association has provided a pantheon of heroes equal to those in any other American sport. Until recent times they have not been as visible or as fashionable as their baseball or football counterparts. But now, seemingly, their time has finally come.

Here, then, is one basketball historian's choice for the game's all-time greatest heroes of both past and present eras. The list begins with the two most superior all-around players ever to lace up sneakers—Oscar Robertson and Magic Johnson—as well as with the most outstanding offensive and defensive immortals—Wilt Chamberlain (who would often score 50 or 60 points in a losing effort) and Bill Russell (who could fail to score in double figures, yet still lead his time to championship victories). Michael Jordan receives a slight (but ever so slight) edge over Julius Erving and Larry Bird to round out the starting five. This is basketball's true "Dream Team," and truly a team made for all ages.

The "dozen greatest" list is followed up with the thirteen "honorable mention" players who also belong in any complete discussion of hoop immortals. This, then, is the true "Dream Team II"—all-stars whose status is based on a full career of legendary play. The twenty-five players featured

in this chapter are judged for their ground-breaking achievements as well
as their status during their own playing age. It would be absurd to leave
a George Yardley or Paul Arizin or Dolph Schayes off such a list simply
because he did not slam dunk like Dominique Wilkins or Spud Webb or
almost any modern-day player. Yardley and Arizin and Schayes towered
above the players of their own epoch, even if they rarely left the floor or
flashed playground moves that are today's stylish invention of a "showtime" television age.

Oscar "Big O" Robertson—Greatest All-Around Player on the Planet

Few fans who have come to the sport alongside Magic, Bird and Jordan
will be easily convinced, but Oscar Robertson was far and away the greatest basketball player ever to take to the hardwood floor. The evidence is
so convincing as to be almost redundant.

For starters, there is the 1962 season in which Oscar's prime statistics
(30.8 ppg., 12.5 rebounds, 11.4 assists) stand as the most balanced overall
performance in basketball history. No one else has reached double figures
for a full year in all three primary hallmarks of performance. While leading
the circuit regularly in assists (six times, with two second-place finishes)
he also reached the top ten in rebounds (as a guard!), and posted two
second-place finishes and five third-place finishes in the individual scoring
race during his first seven seasons. Jordan scored slightly more (but didn't
match up in assists or rebounds); Magic Johnson is the only player to top
Oscar's career assists per-game average (but can't compare as a scorer);
and no guard ever rebounded better. The case is already closed.

The true measure for selecting the "greatest player" is the degree to
which he rates at or near the top in all the game's major categories of
performance. And the three standard statistical measures of such individual
greatness have been, from the earliest days, a player's totals in scoring,
rebounding, and feeding the ball (assists) to teammates in scoring positions.
While triple-doubles in a single game are today's hallmark of greatness,
in Oscar's case such milestones were a matter of normalcy. He regularly
approached triple-double seasonal numbers in four of his first five NBA
campaigns: 1961 (**30.5** ppg., **10.1** rpg., 9.7 apg.), 1962 (**30.8** ppg., **12.5**
rpg., **11.4** apg.), 1963 (**28.3** ppg., **10.4** rpg., 9.5 apg.), 1964 (**31.4** ppg.,
9.9 rpg., **11.0** apg.), 1965 (**30.4** ppg., 9.0 rpg., **11.5** apg.). The **five-year**
totals?—**30.3** ppg., **10.4** rpg., **10.6** apg.! If occasional triple-doubles are
any standard for superstar sanction, then Oscar Robertson played on a
separate planet.

Oscar didn't dominate the league by ranking first as a scorer, simply
because he fell into an age which had too many competitors named Chamberlain, Baylor, West, Bellamy and Barry—immortals not for a moment

to be confused with the Wilkinses, David Robinsons, Karl Malones and Alex Englishes that Jordan battled annually for scoring dominance. And Oscar also didn't dominate the highlight films (when there were any) by courting the fancy dunks or dipsy-doodle moves seemingly required for appeal in today's "showtime" market. What Oscar Robertson *did do* was perform at a higher level (and for a extremely long period) in more vital areas than any other player before or since. His only weakness—the one area besides pure flashiness where Jordan was clearly superior—was in the area of defense. Oscar never ranked among the best defenders in the league. But then he didn't have to. He was a solid enough defender, and that was what was demanded of him in his time on an NBA floor. Oscar's best defensive weapons were rebounding and keeping his opponents so off-balance when *he* had that ball that their own stamina and offense suffered drastically. Oscar may not have blocked shots or logged many steals, but he did absolutely everything else—and did it all better than anyone before or since.

Oscar Robertson's Career Statistics and Achievements

NBA Teams: Cincinnati Royals, Milwaukee Bucks (1960–1974)

Points (PPG.)	26,710 (25.7)
Games	1040
Seasons	14
Assists (APG.)	9,887 (9.5)
Rebounds (RPG.)	7,804 (7.5)
Field Goals (Pct.)	9,508 (.485)
Free Throws (Pct.)	7,694 (.838)
NBA MVP Seasons	1 (1964)
All-Star Game MVP	3 (1961, 1964, 1969)
Scoring Titles	NONE
NBA Championships	1 (1971)
Rookie-of-the-Year	1961

Wilt "The Stilt" Chamberlain—Best Offensive Player By A City Mile

It is almost impossible in today's age of heavily hyped flyers like Michael Jordan and Charles Barkley to come close to appreciating the one-time stature of the giant Wilt Chamberlain. All excuses aside for Chamberlain's lack of hustle, and for the uneven talent of the age he played in, it is axiomatic that Wilt's stature as the game's greatest force can never be challenged. Here, simply put, was the greatest big man basketball has ever known. And even more simply put (and equally provable by the numbers alone), here was the greatest scorer that ever lit up the nets of college and pro arenas everywhere he played. Wilt's scoring totals are his ultimate legacy, and like the man himself they are simply huge.

One season alone is sufficient to put Chamberlain in an unmatchable class by himself. That year was his third in the league and it was also the year that sent basketball's individual scoring milestones into the strato-sphere. It was a year of aberrant performances, quite like Ruth's or Maris's 60-homer seasons, and yet in the end there is no true comparison. For Wilt outdistanced all his rivals (past and future) like no one has ever done on a baseball diamond. Ruth would have had to hit nearly 100 homers to enjoy the same cushion. And Wilt did it in the very season when Baylor also averaged 38.3 ppg. (a total that no one except Chamberlain has ever man-aged), the season when a rookie named Walt Bellamy also conquered the 30-point level, and a guard in Cincinnati averaged a triple-double as well.

The numbers Wilt posted now simply stand out of reach of any mere mortal—he played every minute of the season (itself truly phenomenal in the NBA), netted 100 in a single game, posted his 50.4 scoring average, registered 45 games of 50 points or more, scored 50 in seven consecutive games (also in five straight and six straight on two other occasions), topped 4,000 points for the only time in history, and registered 63 games of 40-plus points. Double the totals of Jordan's very best year and you have an equal contest!

Forget about the endless claims that "The Big Dipper" could always be counted on to "wilt" in the heat of post-season; that Chamberlain had the soft attitude of a loser and was easily intimidated by a more ferocious Russell; that Chamberlain could seemingly do everything on a basketball court except what he was paid for—to win championships. Most of these complaints are meanspirited naysaying. The list of Wilt's statistical accom-plishments reads like the pages of a science fiction novel entitled "Giant From Plant Zenon Conquers Basketball"—there are two distinct ages of scoring and rebounding statistics in NBA history, one is the epoch before and after Wilt, and the other is the "Age of Chamberlain" from 1960 to 1967. And for those who think that Chamberlain was nothing more than a one-dimensional dunker who only went out after scoring titles, it is also instructive to recall the "New Wilt" of the late '60s and early '70s. Chamberlain underwent a career transformation in mid-stream that is un-paralleled within the hoop sport. Convinced by Sixers' coach Alex Han-num that he could prove more effective to a championship unit by rebounding, playing defense a lá Russell, and dishing to unguarded team-mates, Wilt became a consumate team player. Six years after burning up the NBA with his 50.4 scoring average, the same player was leading the cir-cuit in assists with 702. Teamed with Goodrich and West in Los Angeles four seasons later, Wilt earned another NBA title by setting up the hot-shoot-ing Lakers outside game with his total domination of the inside boards.

In the end, it was the true test of Wilt Chamberlain's rare basketball skills that in the latter phases of his career he was so able to do a complete about-face and become another kind of player altogether. Here was sufficient evidence in itself that Wilt Chamberlain could do absolutely anything he wanted to on a basketball court.

Wilt Chamberlain's Career Statistics and Achievements

NBA Teams: Philadelphia Warriors, Golden State Warriors, Philadelphia 76ers, Los Angeles Lakers (1959–1973)

Points (PPG.)	31,419 (30.1)
Games	1045
Seasons	14
Assists (APG.)	4,643 (4.4)
Rebounds (RPG.)	23,924 (22.9) (NBA Record)
Field Goals (Pct.)	12,681 (.540)
Free Throws (Pct.)	6,075 (.511)
NBA MVP Seasons	4 (1960, 1966–1968)
All-Star Game MVP	1 (1960)
Scoring Titles	7 (1960, 1961, 1962, 1963, 1964, 1965, 1966) (NBA Record)
NBA Championships	2 (1967, 1972)
Rookie-of-the-Year	1960

Earvin "Magic" Johnson—Basketball's Greatest Champion Playmaker

Few rookies have held a starring role on an NBA championship team; fewer still have been the dominant factor in bringing a league title to their brand new team. The list of such "rookie winners" contains exactly two names—Bill Russell and Earvin "Magic" Johnson. And the list grows shorter still when we talk of rookies who have claimed NBA playoff MVP status—Magic Johnson. Averaging 41 minutes, 18.3 points, 10 rebounds, 10 assists and three steals—and subbing at the center slot for an injured Kareem Jabbar (posting 42 points and 15 rebounds in the process) in the game-six clincher—Magic simply stole center stage of the 1980 NBA season's finale. And that was only the first act of one of the most brilliant all-around careers in NBA history.

Only one player truly comes close to Oscar Robertson in the race for "all-time" greatest player—at least if one is to judge by the numbers alone—and that player is Earvin Johnson. There can be little argument that Magic saved the NBA in 1980 with his inspired play and infectious personality at the very time when NBA hoops needed a large image up-grade for the coming video era. Magic (with Bird and Jordan) is as respon-sible as anyone for the current revivial of the league and its takeover of the American sporting scene at the outset of the '90s. And a strong argu-ment can be made as well that Johnson is indeed the finest ''total-package player'' of the past decade and a half. Bird was a better offensive show; Jordan did more to turn on the crowds with his rim-rattling moves. But no one did more to win basketball games.

Magic Johnson's numbers indeed compare most favorably to those of Oscar Robertson, especially when it comes to assessing balanced overall performance. Here was the game's second greatest career-long triple-dou-ble man. While a slide in late-career totals left Oscar a tad short of triple-double numbers in the rebounding and assists departments, Magic in the end missed out only in a single category—rebounds. Johnson owns the only career double-figure average in the assists category (John Stockton's playing days are far from over and his numbers may or may not stand the test of time); and Magic posted rebound numbers from the guard slot that miss Oscar's by only a mere fraction (7.3 to 7.5).

But in the end the real legacy of Magic Johnson—like that of Russell and Cousy—comes down to the matter of winning coveted NBA champi-onships. Jordan's Bulls may flaunt their three-peat, but Magic's Lakers remained in the league's upper echelons for a full decade, and not just a three-season tidal wave. Magic thus surpasses Michael by two world titles and Larry Bird by three. Only Bill Russell seems to have done more to win more championships over the course of his career. Cousy and Tom Heinsohn own more championship rings, but both have Russell to thank for that. Magic Johnson rode to five world titles on nobody's coattails but his own.

Magic Johnson's Career Statistics and Achievements

NBA Teams: Los Angeles Lakers (1979–1991)

Points (PPG.)	17,239 (19.7)
Games	874
Seasons	11
Assists (APG.)	9,921 (11.4) (NBA Record for Total Assists)
Rebounds (RPG.)	6,376 (7.3)
Field Goals (Pct.)	6,074 (.521)
Free Throws (Pct.)	4,788 (.848)
NBA MVP Seasons	3 (1987, 1989, 1990)
All-Star Game MVP	2 (1990, 1992)
Scoring Titles	NONE
NBA Championships	5 (1980, 1982, 1985, 1987, 1988)
Rookie-of-the-Year	NO

Bill Russell—The Greatest Defensive Player Ever Invented

When Bill Russell played in the NBA, blocked shots were neither counted as an "official statistic" nor kept in the sport's record books. This is about the same as not counting home runs when Babe Ruth played or not tracking batting averages for Ted Williams and Tony Gwynn. Or perhaps ignoring steals as an official category in the age of Ty Cobb or the era of Rickey Henderson. But while there are no official numbers on Bill Russell's blocked shots, there are indeed plenty of eye-witness accounts from fans, writers and the players themselves. And all agree that Bill Russell used the blocked shot to totally dominate games and even change the sport as no one had ever done before him.

Much of the credit for creating Bill Russell can be laid at the doorstep of Red Auerbach. Perhaps no other coach would have made the gangly shot-blocker a top draft pick, traded away his star player and top prospect to obtain such a one-dimensional star, and then build a complete team around him. More likely, other NBA coaches inheriting Bill's physical talents would have labored to turn him into a scorer, and in the process would have lost much of his unique contributions to the game. Auerbach saw from the beginning that here was a special and rare player who didn't have to score points to be effective. Nor was his defensive prowess the run-of-the-mill sort of stuff. Russell didn't block shots simply to intimidate and make personal statements based on ego like today's defenders. His game was controlled and oriented entirely to fit into Auerbach's scheme for fashioning an invincible champion. Russell used his defense to launch the Boston offense. He would defend the goal in order to open up the inevitable fast brake that would be ignited after each enemy missed shot. Russ would never knock an opponents shot into the third row of courtside seats; instead he would guide the ball (either a shot he blocked or a rebound he corralled) to a fast-breaking guard (usually Cousy) who would propel it ahead to a streaking Heinsohn or Frank Ramsey for an instant score. Russell was thus the ultimate defensive weapon. And as such he dominated games, seasons, a whole decade, without having to score a basket at all.

There were other unique facets of Bill Russell the basketball player. He was laconic and efficient on the floor, yet burned with a competitive fire perhaps never matched in any other player—certainly not another post-player of his size and his awesome talent. Here was the ultimate advantage that Russell always owned over Wilt. And Russell was also one of the smartest men ever to play the game—a student of defensive positioning and of angles and movements and nearly invisible elements of the game. He was also his own man and thus not always popular with the press nor with Boston fans. He shunned signing autographs (maintaining a strong distaste for hero worship), spoke out on civil rights and racial intolerance, openly criticized the city of Boston for its treatment of black athletes, bypassed his own induction ceremony at the Naismith Hall of Fame, and attended the retirement ceremony for his number 6 in Boston only on condition that it be held before the Boston Garden gates were opened to the public. Grace and composure on the playing court were an effective mask for inner turmoil and seething hidden anger; Russell usually vomited in the locker room before any important game, a surefire signal to his teammates that Big Bill was more than ready for the heat of battle.

The true legacy of Bill Russell, of course, is not found when one looks at his statistical line in the *Basketball Encyclopedia*. But it is found in the record books nonetheless—over on the page devoted to yearly NBA champions. No other player in hoop history owns 11 world titles and perhaps none ever will; no one even comes close. Teammate Cousy was around for the raising of six of those banners; Tom Heinsohn survived long enough to share eight of those rings. Auerbach's Celtics (when the Redhead was coach and then later GM) won 11 titles in but 13 seasons in what still stands without challenge as the greatest winning legacy in all of American professional sports. And they didn't win a single one of those titles without their big man, Bill Russell. In fact it seems quite clear that they won every one of those titles only because of Bill Russell.

Bill Russell's Career Statistics and Achievements

NBA Teams: Boston Celtics (1956–1969)

Points (PPG.)	14,522 (15.1)
Games	963
Seasons	13
Assists (APG.)	4,096 (4.3)
Rebounds (RPG.)	21,721 (22.6)
Field Goals (Pct.)	5,687 (.440)
Free Throws (Pct.)	3,148 (.561)
NBA MVP Seasons	5 (1958, 1961, 1962, 1963, 1965)
All-Star Game MVP	1 (1963)
Scoring Titles	NONE
NBA Championships	11 (1957, 1959, 1960, 1961, 1962, 1963, 1964, 1965, 1966, 1968, 1969)
Rookie-of-the-Year	NO

Michael "Air" Jordan—The Most Popular Player on Madison Avenue

Let's put the issue to rest immediately—Michael Jordan is not the greatest player of all time. He is undoubtedly the most celebrated athlete ever to walk the face of the earth. None has earned more television time, pitched more products, banked more dollars, thrilled more groupies, or enjoyed more instant recognition worldwide. The man known simply as "Michael" was also arguably the most flashy showman ever to grace the NBA (though some may still contend that Erving is the reigning champion in this quarter). In an age that worships style and showmanship and confuses celebrity and fame with raw talent or polished performance, it is little wonder that Jordan has been so widely hyped as "the greatest" in the game's history. But the greatest showman is not automatically the greatest player.

The case can be put succinctly. Julius Erving was a more powerful, and even a more dramatic dunker than Michael was. Bill Russell remained a more dominant individual force since he was able to lead his club single-handedly to championship after championship, and do so by playing at only one end of the court—the end where the Celtics didn't even have the ball! Wilt Chamberlain was a more intimidating athlete and the greatest offensive machine the planet has ever witnessed. Michael never scored 100 in a game, averaged 50 points for a season, averaged nearly 30 rebounds nightly for a season, scored 50 points in a playoff game as a rookie (Wilt did it twice); scored better than 40 points over 270 times (Jordan reached the mark slightly more than 100 times), tallied 45 50-point games in a single season. Jordan's numbers simply don't challenge Wilt's by any angle of comparison. And for overall play, Jordan's exceptional versatility still does not match that of Oscar Robertson, the efficient and workmanlike guard who average a triple-double for an entire NBA campaign.

Why then do so many still believe Jordan to be the greatest. Three elements contribute most strongly to Jordan's recent deification by press and public. For one thing, the great multitudes of today's hoop fans have only discovered the game a decade or so back. There lamentably has been no tradition in basketball where a previous generation of fans has handed down the legends of Robertson and Chamberlain and Baylor and West, the way that baseball fans for decades have kept alive the sparkling legends of Ruth, Cobb, Mantle, Mays and Jackie Robinson. Secondly, today's standards now elevate "showtime" moves above all-around basketball skills. It is the TV highlight film that we employ as the main measure of professional skill. Dazzling dunks and end-to-end solos outstrip subtler points of efficient ballhandling and the engineering of team offense.

And then there is the issue of a print and video media which has constructed a full-fledged industry around hyping Michael Jordan. The league itself has largely done the same, basing its recent popularity on the image of Jordan as the greatest sportsworld showman of all time. Michael has sold countless books, floods of newspapers and television time, a tidal wave of video tapes, and also millions of NBA game tickets. But even more telling in this final regard is the seemingly ceaseless propaganda blitz mounted by a Nike Shoe Company campaign designed to generation billions of dollars in corporate sales. Michael's rank as the greatest basketball player, the greatest pure athlete, the greatest everything imaginable, was all a necessary element in the corporate success of Nike and the several dozen other high-profile companies that rode precariously on the coattails of Air Jordan's legend. In short, Michael Jordan has been a pure marketing sensation.

This is not to say that Jordan was not a spectacular basketball player. If only as the highest-scoring pro basketballer in history on a per-game basis, he demands legendary status. He played the major role in winning three consecutive NBA championships, although these came in years when the league was at its competitive weakest in perhaps two decades. He did post seven straight scoring titles, although again in an era when for much of the time there was a paucity of other great scorers. And he was a great offensive showman who ranks right alongside Erving, Elgin Baylor, and perhaps Connie Hawkins, as the best sure-fire generators of instant crowd thrills.

And then there was the 1988 season, in which Jordan was MVP, All-Star Game MVP, and league scoring champ, racked up 40 points in the All-Star Game, registered 10 steals in one game and 59 points in another, and was even the league's defensive player of the year. Only Wilt, in 1961-'62, had a better year. Only Erving had a more flamboyant style. Only "The Big O" possessed a fuller and more balanced arsenal of talents. But neither Wilt not Dr. J nor Oscar had Nike or the age of the ubiquitous television image.

Michael Jordan's Career Statistics and Achievements

NBA Teams: Chicago Bulls (1984–1993)

Points (PPG.)	21,541 (32.3) (NBA Record for PPG)
Games	667
Seasons	9
Assists (APG.)	3,925 (5.9)
Rebounds (RPG.)	4,228 (6.3)
Field Goals (Pct.)	8,079 (.516)
Free Throws (Pct.)	5,096 (.846)
NBA MVP Seasons	3 (1988, 1991, 1992)
All-Star Game MVP	1 (1988)
Scoring Titles	7 (1987, 1988, 1989, 1990, 1991, 1992, 1993) (NBA Record)
NBA Championships	3 (1991, 1992, 1993)
Rookie-of-the-Year	1985

Julius "Dr. J" Erving—The Inventor of "Hangtime"

Few events have impacted on NBA history like Dr. J's arrival in the league way back in 1976, at the crucial moment of the NBA-ABA merger. Perhaps only the coming of Wilt Chamberlain had quite the same earth-shaking significance. Wilt took the NBA into the new era of spectacular offense, just as Babe Ruth had done for baseball with his home run blasts back in the '20s. Now Julius Erving would similarly save the run-and-shoot game from boring predictability with his "hangtime" dunking style and his almost unimaginable playground "moves." Facing the onslaught of football popularity in the '70s, baseball needed to introduce its designated hitter rule to generate scoring and thus provide upscale excitement. The NBA needed only the fabulous Dr. J to accomplish the very same effect.

Veteran NBA/ABA coach Kevin Loughery (Erving's mentor with the New York Nets) has put Dr. J's ABA days into helpful perspective: "He had the biggest and best hands in basketball. It was like he was playing with a grapefruit. I honestly believe that Doc did more for pro basketball than anybody, on or off the court. He wasn't just 'the franchise' with the Nets—he was the league."

Julius Erving made Michael "Air" Jordan and all other such airborne, slamdunking, "in-your-face" intimidators entirely possible. He sent the game moving in a direction that culminated with Jordan, and with other current skywalkers like Drexler, and Pippen, and Shawn Kemp. He certainly changed the level of expectations about what basketball could potentially be like. And he introduced "flamboyant style," and with it thrills that had turned on playground afficionados for years, but had not yet impacted on the more conservative professional game. And with his new, made-for-television brand of soaring from the key to the rim, he set the expectations for the next generation of basketball fans. Thus Erving's position in the game is now legendary. Dr. J is the world of slam dunk personified, a personality so unique that it was not even excessive hype for Sixers GM Pat Williams to crow in 1976 that "we just got the Babe Ruth of basketball."

Erving has left a statistical legacy as well as a indelible image of soaring flight. His combined ABA-NBA scoring totals rank him with the top handful of scoring stars. He is, in fact, one of only three 30,000-point men, and the only one who was not seven feet tall. And those 30,000 points were—almost unbelievably—even more notable for the flair and grace with which they were delivered. One can only imagine what today's advertisers would have done with a showman and an athlete like Julius Erving in his prime. Madison Avenue could not have held him any more effectively than did the measured dimensions of the NBA courts on which he once played.

Julius Erving's Career Statistics and Achievements

ABA-NBA Teams: Virginia Squires, New York Nets, Philadelphia
Sixers (1971–1987)

Points (PPG.)	30,026 (24.2)
Games	1242
Seasons	16
Assists (APG.)	5,176 (4.2)
Rebounds (RPG.)	10,525 (8.5)
Field Goals (Pct.)	11,818 (.506)
Free Throws (Pct.)	6,256 (.777)
NBA MVP Seasons	1 (1981)
All-Star Game MVP	2 (1977, 1983)
Scoring Titles (ABA)	3 (1973, 1974, 1976)
NBA Championships	1 (1983)
Rookie-of-the-Year	NO

Larry Bird—Basketball's Best All-Time Forward

Bird and Magic will be forever linked throughout basketball history. Their mano-a-mano duel in the NCAA finals at the end of the '70s was the highlight of a college basketball decade that had also included the zenith of the John Wooden UCLA dynasty. And together they fully resurrected the NBA at the beginning of the '80s. And then they carried out their continued personal warfare in three of the most exciting NBA Finals matchups of all-time. But if Bird and Magic are always to be linked by fate, they were also two of the most different ballplaying heroes in NBA annals. Johnson was a stylish black player who was the epitome of pure grace personified. He was also the new prototype for perfection at the guard position. Bird was a small-town white star who didn't look quite so cool (he lacked foot speed and seemingly couldn't jump) yet possessed enough hidden proficiency to make him the greatest forward ever to play the game.

Bird's statistical legacy alone makes him the game's greatest forward. While he never won an individual scoring title (no Celtics player ever has), yet he scored with deadly proficiency throughout the full decade of the '80s. His 30.3 collegiate average at Indiana State remains one of the loftiest in history; he once topped 60 in a single NBA game and averaged better than 25 ppg. on four different occasions; his nearly 22,000 career points rank second in Boston history. But he did other things even better. Bird was the best passing forward ever to play basketball; his full-court heaves on the fast break rival those of Russell and his over-the-shoulder blind feeds are the equal of Cousy's. He shot the ball from the outside like no corner man before him, ranking in the career top ten in 3-point goals and free-throw percentage, and barely missing out on that distinction in career scoring average when his lifetime mark dipped below 25.0 ppg. during his final season. And Bird specialized in three-pointers as Erving had specialized in dunks. He controlled games like a guard and had an unmatched intelligence and unmatched set of physical reflexes that made him one of the most dangerous all-around offensive performers ever to step on a court.

And above all else, Larry Bird was a proven winner. With his pinpoint blind passes delivered softly to the open man, and his amazing sense of every movement on the court surrounding him, Bird ran the Boston offense from his forward slot like a true point guard; and like most great players, he always made his teammates better as well. Perhaps the most deadly outside shooter of all-time (save perhaps Jerry West), Bird always wanted the ball when the game was on the line. It was for this reason alone that the greatest of all basketball talent judges, Red Auerbach, pronounced Bird as the one player he would choose above all others if he were building a franchise from scratch. "If I had to start a team, the one guy in all of history I would take would be Larry Bird," pronounces Auerbach; "This is the greatest ballplayer who ever played the game."

Auerbach may have grown slightly nostalgic and effusive in his old age. Bird, above Robertson or Chamberlain or Jordan, is perhaps a stretch; and it was Auerbach himself who built a far greater team on Russell's shoulders than on Bird's. But it is a strong endorsement nonetheless. There is a long line of superstars in the annals of the Boston Celtics. But only Russell today remains a brighter star in the Celtics' firmament than Larry Bird.

Larry Bird's Career Statistics and Achievements

NBA Teams: Boston Celtics (1979–1992)

Points (PPG.)	21,791 (24.3)
Games	897
Seasons	13
Assists (APG.)	5,695 (6.4)
Rebounds (RPG.)	8,974 (10.0)
Field Goals (Pct.)	8,591 (.496)
Free Throws (Pct.)	3,960 (.886)
NBA MVP Seasons	3 (1984, 1985, 1986)
All-Star Game MVP	1 (1982)
Scoring Titles	NONE
NBA Championships	3 (1981, 1984, 1986)
Rookie-of-the-Year	1980

Jerry West—Hoopdom's Greatest Pure Shooter Ever

Jerry West could flat out shoot the basketball. From all distances and under all imaginable conditions he pumped in shots with unflappable grace and relentless regularity. He poured in tons of points across a 14-year NBA career, enough in fact to stand eighth on the all-time scoring list (counting NBA points alone) and remain the leading franchise scorer for a Lakers ballclub that has also had such superstars as Baylor, Chamberlain, Jabbar and Magic Johnson. Jerry West today owns the fourth highest point-per-game average in pro basketball history; only Jordan, Chamberlain and Baylor outdistance the shooting wizard known fondly in playing days as "The Hick from Cabin Creek" (a reference to his small-town West Virginia origins).

West was Mr. Outside to Elgin Baylor's Mr. Inside. And so many of his bombs were from such long range that had there been a three-point shot at the time when West played, his scoring totals would likely have been as much as 30% higher. In other worlds, playing by today's standards, he would likely have soared even above Jordan's totals and have owned the distinction as the sports highest scorer—in total career points, total number of league scoring championships, and career scoring average as well.

As it was, West won but a single scoring title when he rippled the nets for 31.2 ppg. in 1969–'70. But that was because like everyone else in the '60s, he had the bad timing to play in the era of Wilt Chamberlain. And he also had to share the ball with Baylor, and later Chamberlain and Gail Goodrich, who demanded plenty of shooting opportunities of their own. Put him in any other decade (even without a three-point rule) or on any other team, and he would likely have won individual honors almost every season running. And West's scoring was easily as spectacular as it was proficient. His 55-foot game-tying bomb against the Knicks in game three of the '70 Finals is the most famous clutch shot in basketball history. In fact "Mr. Clutch" was his very nickname, for no one ever shot better when important games were on the line. When it came to post-season playoff time, Jerry was among the greatest scorers in the game's history. Twice he averaged better than 40 ppg. for a playoff series, and his 46.5 in the 1965 Baltimore series is an all-time mark; his 29.1 ppg. playoff average trails only Jordan's, and his 4,500 post-season points are second only to Jabbar.

Jerry West's career was no joyride, however, despite his brilliant scoring onslaughts and milestones. Of course there was the frustration of always playing second or third fiddle to Wilt and Oscar and Elgin Baylor in the individual scoring races. There was the physical abuse that he regularly took as a player of unmatch hustle and drive. Nine times West had his nose painfully broken in league action. And above all there was the frustration of playing on a team that was always itself second best. For West not only played in the epoch of Wilt, but also in the era of the unbeatable Auerbach Celtics. The Lakers always seemed to get straight to the bridal altar and then be deeply disappointed bridesmaids. Seven incredible times in West's first eleven NBA seasons his Los Angeles team was loser of an NBA Final.

Even when the Celtics collapsed, there were several more seasons of frustration for West and the snake-bit Lakers. And this was destined to be the case no matter how hard and how well West played in post-season—in 1970 he poured in 31.2 ppg. in a losing Finals series with the Knicks, a year earlier his 30.9 average paced all playoff scorers, but couldn't stave off another seven-game loss to Boston. Then finally—after seven uninterrupted defeats in the NBA Finals—the Lakers eventually broke through with a title in 1972, with West this time leading all post-season performers in assists. The long-sought championship sadly came one year too late for Elgin Baylor, who had been forced into retirement by injury. But fortuitously it didn't come too late for Jerry West, who now finally had a championship ring to go with all his other unmatched credentials.

Jerry West's Career Statistics and Achievements

NBA Teams: Los Angeles Lakers (1960–1974)

Points (PPG.)	25,192 (27.0)
Games	932
Seasons	14
Assists (APG.)	6,238 (6.7)
Rebounds (RPG.)	5,376 (5.8)
Field Goals (Pct.)	9,016 (.474)
Free Throws (Pct.)	7,160 (.814)
NBA MVP Seasons	NONE
All-Star Game MVP	1 (1972)
Scoring Titles	1 (1970)
NBA Championships	1 (1972)
Rookie-of-the-Year	NO

Bob Cousy—Boston's Houdini of the Hardwoods

Bob Cousy was basketball's first great wizard of ballhandling. He was also one of the most intense and focussed athletes of American sports history. Cousy was driven by an almost maniacal will to succeed and to win. And once he had shot-swatting Bill Russell at his side, he would win time and again with the greatest offensive weapon pro basketball has ever known. That weapon was the Boston Celtics fast-breaking attack—conceived on the chalkboard by Red Auerbach, unleashed by Russell's shot-blocking and rebounding exploits, and directed down the floor by Cousy's ballhandling and dribbling skills.

Few fans today remember exactly what Cousy's original razzle-dazzle showmanship looked like. Today a behind-the-back dribble or blind pass is almost commonplace; before Cousy these maneveurs were simply unheard of and even unthinkable. As an All-American at Holy Cross, Cousy had fine-tuned his skills and already earned a reputation as "The Houdini of the Hardwood." But despite this status as local legend at the Massachusetts college the new Celtics coach, Red Auerbach, did not see any value in a 6'1" pro player, no matter what his collegiate scoring exploits might be. Auerbach stirred controversy by ignoring the popular Cousy in the draft, refusing to take the local star under the Celtics' territorial draft option. "Am I supposed to please the local yokels or win ballgames?" Auerbach groused when pressed about slighting Cousy. But fate immediately conspired to put Cousy in Boston anyway; his original NBA team in Chicago folded without playing a game and the star of the 1947 Holy Cross NCAA champions—behind-the-back passes and between-the-legs dribbles and all—went straight to Boston via a dispersal-draft coin flip. Bob Cousy—despite the best-laid plans of Red Auerbach himself—backed into his ready-made role as a key ingredient in Auerbach's new style of running and winning basketball.

Cousy could do more than dribble and pass and amaze with his bag of ballhandling tricks. He was an effective scorer as well, and often ranked at the top of his team and near the top of the league before the superscorers (Wilt, Oscar, Baylor, Jerry West) came along at the end of the '50s and outset of the '60s. For four straight seasons, between 1951 and 1955, he paced the Boston offense, twice averaging a hair over 20 and twice a fraction under; in 1954 he was second in the league behind Neil Johnston; he once rang up 50 in a playoff game; and his point total reached 17,000 before his 14-year career had closed. But his true badge was delivering the ball, even before Russell was available to reconstitute Auerbach's fast-breaking offense; eight times he was the NBA assists champ, and he still ranks seventh in that lifetime category, three full decades after his retirement. Cousy was also an intelligent student of the game, who became a long-time coach after playing days ended and was truly a "coach on the floor" while he ran the versatile Boston offense.

But Boston's immortal number 14 was also a ruthless perfectionist who could endure nothing less than 100% effort, total victory, and perfect execution—from himself and all others as well—and in the end excessive intensity sabotaged Cousy's coaching effectiveness with the Boston College team, as well as with the NBA's Cincinnati Royals. As a player, however, Cousy's burning intensity (along with a giant assist from Auerbach and Russell) made him a tireless winner as well as one of the game's greatest innovators. None ever delivered a pass better or with more crowd pleasing finesse and invention—not Magic Johnson or John Stockton, or even Joe Montana or Joe Namath. Cousy was to passing a basketball what Jordan was to dunking it, or Rick Barry was to shooting it. He was the Picasso, Rembrandt and Dali of the ballhandling art.

Bob Cousy's Career Statistics and Achievements

NBA Teams: Boston Celtics, Cincinnati Royals (1950–1963, 1969–70)

Points (PPG.)	16,960 (18.4)
Games	924
Seasons	14
Assists (APG.)	6,959 (7.5)
Rebounds (RPG.)	4,794 (5.2)
Field Goals (Pct.)	6,168 (.375)
Free Throws (Pct.)	4,624 (.803)
NBA MVP Seasons	1 (1957)
All-Star Game MVP	2 (1954, 1957)
Scoring Titles	NONE
NBA Championships	6 (1957, 1959, 1960, 1961, 1962, 1963)
Rookie-of-the-Year	NO AWARD GIVEN

Kareem Abdul-Jabbar (a.k.a. Lew Alcindor)— Basketball's True Ironman

There are three unsquelchable memories of Kareem Abdul-Jabbar. One is the famed "Sky Hook" which was perhaps the most devastating offensive weapon of all basketball history. A second is the almost other-worldly appearance of this giant with the shaved head and the spaceage gloggles. And the final, and most lasting memory is that of the ironman paragon of durability and dedication who lasted season after weary season and set records for endurance that almost defy imagination. Jabbar's twenty-year string of NBA seasons, in a sport as demanding as basketball, ranks right alongside Cal Ripken's consecutive-game string in baseball and actor George Burns's near century-long tenure on this planet. All three are products of pure luck, of a disciplined lifestyle beyond the capacity of most mortals, and of a monomanical dedication to one's craft. And all such seemingly endless strings are unmatched tributes to the indomitable "human spirit" as well.

It is also a wonderful irony that Kareem Abdul-Jabbar is always the first player listed in the *National Basketball Association Register* and, by coincidence, the game's all-time leader in games played and points scored as well. Jabbar's scoring records are, of course, like Pete Rose's baseball mark for most career hits. Rose caught Cobb's seemingly invincible standard simply by outlasting all other challengers. He played longer than anyone else had ever been willing to play, and he maintained the ability to stay competitive, which itself is a rare feat indeed. Jabbar did the same in the pursuit of Wilt's 30,000 point mark. No one would claim that Jabbar, for all his talent and athletic grace, was the game's greatest pure scorer. After his first several seasons in Milwaukee, he never again won another scoring title. Most of his yearly totals are not overly impressive— except that they continued on, and on, and on. Jabbar won out by attrition over all the game's other great point producers, just as Rose outstretched all other hitters.

Kareem's career was so long that it was actually three NBA careers rolled into one. First came the phenomenal rookie named Lew Alcindor, who may have been the greatest impact player ever to hit the pro hoops circuit. In three short seasons Alcindor not only took over as the game's greatest offensive machine—winning two scoring titles and averaging 30 ppg. against the best the NBA could offer. But he also took a raw expansion team straight to a world championship faster than any expansion club had ever gotten there before. Then came the sudden change of identity to Kareem Abdul-Jabbar, and the transfer of ballclubs to the fabulous west coast Lakers. For the middle phase of his career Jabbar was the Lakers's franchise player—one they had actually traded away almost a whole franchise just to get.

Finally came phase three, most of which stretched past a time when almost any other player would have retired. This was the period in the '80s spent as senior leader on a powerhouse ballclub lead by a young buck named Magic Johnson. Just as the young Alcindor had needed a veteran, Oscar Robertson, backing him up in order to win the league title a decade earlier in Milwaukee, now Jabbar himself played the roll as assistant to Magic. Kareem did have more than one great championship performance of his own, however, earning a post-season MVP in 1985, then pouring home 32 points during the 1987 finale against Boston. But most of those proud Los Angeles years in the '80s were played out in the shadow of Magic Johnson. Thanks to Magic, Kareem was able to spend his final decade piling up championships as well as piling up a ton of new personal scoring milestones.

Kareem Abdul-Jabbar's Career Statistics and Achievements

NBA Teams: Milwaukee Bucks, Los Angeles Lakers (1969–1989)

Points (PPG.)	38,387 (24.6) (NBA Record for Total Points)
Games	1560 (NBA Record)
Seasons	20 (NBA Record)

Assists (APG.)	5,660 (3.6)
Rebounds (RPG.)	17,440 (11.2)
Field Goals (Pct.)	15,837 (.559)
Free Throws (Pct.)	6,712 (.721)
NBA MVP Seasons	6 (1971, 1972, 1974, 1976, 1977, 1980)
All-Star Game MVP	NONE
Scoring Titles	2 (1971, 1972)
NBA Championships	6 (1971, 1980, 1982, 1985, 1987, 1988)
Rookie-of-the-Year	1970

Elgin Baylor—Basketball's Most Underrated Performer

Elgin Baylor was basketball's greatest hardluck victim. He was also perhaps the sport's greatest survivor—toppling scoring records, setting eye-popping milestones, and leaving an image as the most spectacular one-on-one player ever seen, despite every injury, setback and bad break that might beset him. Baylor was certainly the first great exponent of "show-time moves" and "hangtime" exploits. In fact, when Elgin Baylor first arrived on the NBA scene, the league's fans and its players had never quite witnessed his likes: "Either he's got three hands or two basketballs," mused New York Knicks guard Richie Guerin, "Guarding Baylor is like guarding a flood!"

But for a series of bad breaks, and Baylor's talent might have been enough to establish a string of personal scoring records and team championships that would have placed him alone on a pedestal as the all-time best. As it is, Baylor ranks near the very top as a scorer: first he toppled Joe Fulk's unthinkable record of 63 in a single NBA game; then he was the first to score 70, lighting up the Knicks for 71 points in 1960; his career average of 27.4 ppg. trails only the marks of Chamberlain (30.1) and Jordan (32.3). Only Wilt surpassed Baylor's 38.3 average for one abbreviated season of 48 games (which came in the same spectacular year when Wilt averaged 50.4 and Oscar Robertson averaged a year-long triple-double). Baylor had been forced into military service that fall, and was restricted by this fate to commuting only to weekend games. His point totals, in spite of several such missed or shortened seasons, eventually positioned him as the 14th best scorer of all-time, yet he stood behind only Wilt and Oscar at the time of his 1971 retirement. When it came to explosive single games, only Wilt and Jordan have soared above Elgin Baylor's level, although Jordan never did reach the 70-point plateau which is shared by Chamberlain (four times), Baylor (the only forward) and Denver's David Thompson alone. And Baylor was more than just a scorer. His soaring athletic ability and amazing body control made him an unparalleled rebounder as well, and his career total of 11,463 is still the second best ever among forwards, trailing only the 12,851 boards compiled by Bob Pettit (who actually played center a good part of his career).

Elgin Baylor's injury-riddled career in the end reminds one of the fate of Ted Williams in baseball. Had not injury and wartime military service intervened, "Teddy Ballgame" would likely have smashed 700 homers and won a half-dozen more batting titles. Baylor also lost a prime season to the military in the very year that he was at his uncanny best as a scorer (and the year when scoring records where falling like flies everywhere around the league). And then injuries wiped out several more stretches: knee troubles reduced his effectiveness on almost a nightly basis after 1963, worsening knees limited him to 54 games in '69–'70, and then wiped out the following campaign altogether, and at one point he played a full month with a steel plate on a finger of his shooting hand, yet still averaged 30 ppg.

But it was not only injuries (especially tattered knee muscles) that victimized Baylor. For one thing, his poor academic standing in high school had prevented a more glorious collegiate career at one of the country's prime basketball powers. Elgin's only ticket to athletic fame was, at first, a football scholarship to tiny College of Idaho, where a perceptive coach noticed his basketball talents in a pickup game and engineered a fortuitous switch in sports. Eventually transferring to small-time Seattle University, Baylor made the best of his chances by averaging 31 ppg. as a senior, pacing the nation in rebounding, and leading the unheralded Seattle Chieftains to an NCAA title matchup with Kentucky. Baylor overnight had put himself and the school on the basketball map. Here was simply too much spectacular athletic talent to get lost in any shuffle imaginable—no matter how many bad breaks.

Once reaching the pros with the Lakers, Elgin was victim of other misfortunes as well. He came to a glorious team (winner of four titles in the first nine NBA seasons) at the very time when they had fallen on hard times. Elgin's first several seasons—including a spectacular 1959 Rookie-of-the-Year performance which led a sub-.500 Lakers club all the way into the playoff finals against Boston—were wasted on a losing outfit that he alone single-handedly made competitive with his offensive fireworks. And then, when the Lakers team moved westward and Baylor got a running mate appropriately also named West, things got only slightly better. Baylor, like West and like Wilt, saw his title dreams postponed time and again by an invincible Boston Celtics juggernaut and by the defensive exploits of Bill Russell. There were some near misses, however, and several of those misses were a direct result of Baylor's own lingering injuries. The Lakers lost seventh-game matchups in the title round in both 1969 and 1970, both times with an injured Elgin Baylor either hobbled, or sitting on the sidelines. And then, when Wilt was added and the Lakers eventually broke through, Baylor was a victim yet one more time. Nagging injuries had finally forced him to retire (still a relatively young man, even by athletic standards) only a single season earlier.

Elgin Baylor's Career Statistics and Achievements

NBA Teams: Minneapolis Lakers, Los Angeles Lakers (1958–1972)

Points (PPG.)	23,149 (27.4)
Games	846
Seasons	14
Assists (APG.)	3,650 (4.3)
Rebounds (RPG.)	11,463 (13.6)
Field Goals (Pct.)	8,693 (.431)
Free Throws (Pct.)	5,763 (.780)
NBA MVP Seasons	NONE
All-Star Game MVP	1 (1959)
Scoring Titles	NONE
NBA Championships	NONE
Rookie-of-the-Year	1959

George "Mr. Basketball" Mikan—The Big Man Who Changed the Game

First Julius Erving, and later, Michael Jordan revolutionized the public perception of how basketball was supposed to be played. From a game of shooting and passing and organized team flow these two masters of "hang-time" turned the sport into one-on-one displays of high-flying acrobatics. More than any others "Dr. J" and "MJ" made the slam dunk the glamor piece of basketball's high-speed spectacle, just as the home run stands supreme in baseball and the long touchdown pass rules in football. And others also had major impacts on the sport that were truly revolutionary in scope. Bob Cousy seemingly invented fancy dribbling, Houdini-like ballhandling and magical passing. Bill Russell first established defense as the game's most unbeatable weapon.

But no one ever had quite the same degree of impact on basketball by his very presence on the floor alone as did the game's first recognized superstar, George Mikan. For it was Mikan who once caused the entire strategy of play to shift in drastic ways. Elaborate defensive schemes (some pushing the limits of legality) were first designed to stop him. And when all these failed to keep down Mikan's relentless scoring, the men controlling the game's management were next forced to change the rules.

Because the bulky and bespectacled 6'11" Mikan would set up under the basket and simply make layups that were unguardable in an age of smaller players, teams first fouled ruthlessly, then took to holding the ball and stalling the clock, hoping to win on a last-second basket after first neutralizing the big man for much of the game. The result was first a widening of the foul lines in '51–'52, from six to twelve feet. Then came the 24-second shot clock at the start of the 1954–'55 season. It was as if today's rules makers should have to raise the basket to 14 feet to stop Shaquille O'Neal's dunks. Or if they changed the regulations on traveling (perhaps ruling that each player was allowed but one step and one dribble) in order to eliminate Michael Jordan's drives toward the bucket. That's what the rules makers did to George Mikan when they stretched out the lanes and forced teams to speed up offense with the ever-ticking shot clock.

History still records Mikan's impact on the rules. But what often gets forgotten after so many years of drastic change and evolution in the game is exactly how good a player George Mikan actually was during his own heyday. And also how big a star he was for the new sport and the three new leagues he helped put squarely on the sporting map. Mikan was pro basketball's one showcase talent in an era when he alone was the sure-bet gate attraction—although perhaps as much for his freakish size as for his predictable scoring. The original Mr. Basketball was indeed a truly dominating scorer, outdistancing all competitors in pointmaking his two seasons in the NBL, outscoring the phenomenal jump shooter Joe Fulks during his one BAA campaign, and then earning the first two scoring titles in the history of the newly-constituted NBA.

Mikan's moves were primitive, and perhaps would be easily defensible today—he simply camped within four feet of the hoop, waited patiently for a lob pass (which his mates could take forever delivering in the pre-shot-clock-era), elbowed defenders aside and dropped in an easy layup or short hook. No one dunked in those days—there didn't seem to be any point to such extra expenditures of showy energy. But in his own era Mikan was more unstoppable than almost any scorer before, or since. And with Mikan in the lineup, the Lakers were unstoppable also. Mikan would lead his team to six championships in seven seasons. And in three different leagues as well, as the vagabond Minneapolis club first jumped from the National Basketball League (1948 champs) over to the Basketball Association of America (1949 champs), which then reconstituted itself into the renamed National Basketball Association (1950, 1952, 1953, and 1954 champions). Only Bill Russell surpasses such a winning legacy as this one.

The winning of team championships and individual scoring titles at an unprecedented rate, the unparalleled impact on the game's reshaped appearance and rules, the magnetism of basketball's first one-man spectacle, all conspired to write a lasting legend. When the ballots were counted in 1950, George Mikan was named "The Greatest Basketball Player of the First Half Century" in a landslide.

George Mikan's Career Statistics and Achievements

NBL-BAA-NBA Teams: Chicago American Gears, Minneapolis Lakers (1946–1956)

Points (PPG.)	11,764 (22.6)
Games	520
Seasons	9
Assists (APG.)	1,245 (2.8)*
Rebounds (RPG.)	4,167 (9.5)*
Field Goals (Pct.)	4,097 (.404)
Free Throws (Pct.)	3,570 (.777)
NBA MVP Seasons	NO AWARDS GIVEN
All-Star Game MVP	1 (1953)
Scoring Titles	5 (1947, 1948, 1949, 1950, 1951)
NBA Championships	4 (1950, 1951, 1952, 1953)
NBL Championships	2 (1947, 1948)
BAA Championships	1 (1949)
Rookie-of-the-Year	NO AWARD GIVEN

*=NBA Records only (no assists records or rebounds records kept for NBL)

Honorable Mention: A Second (Baker's) Dozen Among Basketball's All-Time Greatest Stars

Bob Pettit (1954–1965; Milwaukee Hawks and St. Louis Hawks; 20,880 points, 26.4 ppg., and 12,851 rebounds; NBA Scoring Champion in 1955–'56 and 1958–'59). Pettit replaced Mikan as the game's greatest offensive center and retired in 1965 at the top of the career list in scoring, although Wilt was already close on his heels in both categories. Although a dozen players have now passed Pettit's career rebound totals, his legacy remains in tact as the first ever to score 20,000 NBA points. And in the first ten of his eleven league seasons this rugged clutch player never finished lower than fifth among the league leaders in rebounding or scoring, a claim no other NBA player can make to this day.

Rick Barry (1965–1980; San Francisco Warriors, Oakland Oaks (ABA), Washington Caps (ABA), New York Nets (ABA), Golden State Warriors, Houston Rockets; 25,279 points; ABA Scoring Champion in 1968–'69; NBA Scoring Champion in 1966–'67). Some contend that Rick Barry still edges out Larry Bird as the greatest forward ever; certainly he was among the half-dozen greatest pure scorers, and right at the top of the list among efficient free-throw shooters. Losing parts of some of his earliest and best ABA and NBA seasons to nagging injuries and contract holdouts, Barry still stands eleventh on the all-time ABA-NBA scoring list with over 25,000 points (18,395 in ten NBA seasons).

Elvin Hayes (1968–1984; San Diego Rockets, Houston Rockets, Washington (Capital) Bullets; 27,313 points; NBA Scoring Champion in 1968–'69). One of only three rookies (along with Chamberlain and Joe Fulks) ever to pace the NBA (BAA) in scoring, Hayes closed out a glorious 16-year career second in all-time minutes played (50,000), third in total games (1,303), fourth in total rebounds (16,279) and fifth in career scoring (27,313)—third if only NBA points are counted. With an unstoppable turn-around jumper, both along the baseline and outside the paint, Hayes was the finest shooting big man in all basketball history.

Dominique (Nique) Wilkins (1982–1994 (still active); Atlanta Hawks, Los Angeles Clippers, Boston Celtics; 24,019 points and 26.5 ppg.; NBA Scoring Champion in 1985–'86). Basketball's "Human Highlight Film" has evolved from the NBA's greatest acrobatic sideshow into one of the premier offense players in history. Overcoming a severe Achilles Tendon injury which nearly ended his career in 1992, Wilkins has stormed back in spectacular fashion. His scoring totals now place him fifth all-time in career average and twelfth in total points, and with several more productive seasons, a 30,000-point career is now not impossible.

Moses Malone (1976–1994 (still active); Buffalo Braves, Houston Rockets, Philadelphia Sixers, Washington Bullets, Atlanta Hawks, Milwaukee Bucks; 27,360 points and 15,940 rebounds). Basketball's most durable big man, behind Kareem Abdul-Jabbar, Malone passed Elvin Hayes in 1994 to move into fifth place on the all-time combined ABA-NBA career scoring list. He is now also the NBA career record holder for offensive rebounds, and overtook Hayes and Havlicek for third on the all-time games-played list (1,312) as well.

John (Hondo) Havlicek (1962–1978, Boston Celtics, 26,395 points and 6,114 assists). There was never a better sixth man or team-oriented player, a more effective clutch scorer and defender, a more versatile athlete at any spot on the floor, or a more dedicated "winner" than Hondo Havlicek of Auerbach's Boston Celtics. Havlicek is the only man in the game's history to combine a career of "role playing" and "backup status" with front-line stats that rank among those of the all-time greats. Hondo is fourth all-time in games played (1,270), fourth as well in career minutes (46,471), ninth in points scored (26,395), and sixth in field goals made (10,513).

Paul Arizin (1950–1962, Philadelphia Warriors, 22.8 ppg., NBA Scoring Champion in 1951–'52 and 1956–'57). "Pitchin' Paul" huffed and puffed up and down the court (he was asthmatic) and pumped in an endless array of undefendable jumpers that made him a two-time league scoring champ. If his teammate Joe Fulks introduced the jumper as an offensive weapon in the NBA, then Arizin perfected it. At Villanova he was the nation's scoring leader, and once pumped home 85 points in a college contest. In the NBA he reached the 10,000-point scoring plateau faster than any man before him and became the most effective 6'4" forward ever to mix it up inside with the game's front-wall giants.

Dolph Schayes (1948–1964, Syracuse Nats (NBL and NBA) and Phila-delphia 76ers, 19,247 points). Never a scoring champion, yet a true scoring machine of the NBA's first decade, Schayes was a slashing driver and adept free-throw shooter who specialized in breaking to the basket for a bucket and an inevitable "fouled in the act of shooting" charity toss. He was thus the game's first "three-point" specialist when three points were still earned the hard way.

Walt (Clyde) Frazier (1967–1980; New York Knicks and Cleveland Cavaliers; 15,581 points and 5,040 assists). No one—except maybe Air Jordan—played as well on both ends of the court; as an offensive force Frazier was a deadly shooter from the guard slot with any game on the line, and as a defender he had no parallel among backcourt men of any era. Walt Frazier was heart-and-soul for the early '70s New York Knicks championship teams and a regular member of the NBA All-Defensive first team for seven straight seasons.

George (Ice Man) Gervin (1972–1986; Virginia Squires (ABA), San Antonio Spurs (ABA and NBA), Chicago Bulls; 26.2 ppg. and 20,708 points; NBA Scoring Champion in 1977–'78, 1978–'79, 1979–'80 and 1981–'82). A modern-day version of the '50s George Yardley—skinny, stork-like, offensive-minded, and a deadly scorer. Gervin's combined ABA-NBA scoring totals place him seventh all-time (as of 1993) on the points-per-game list, and eighth in total points scored. He is one of only six NBA shooting stars to win scoring titles in three consecutive seasons (joining Mikan, Neil Johnston, Chamberlain, Bob McAdoo and Jordan for that honor). And Gervin possessed a range of different shots—inside stuffs, outside jumpers, finger-rolls, scooping layups, hooks with either hand—as varied as any of the game's greatest pointmakers.

Hal Greer (1958–1973, Syracuse Nats and Philadelphia 76ers, 21,586 points and 4,540 assists). A deadly shooter who specialized in 15-foot jumpers, this durable guard topped the 20,000 career point mark, scored 20 or better seven straight years, and fed enough assists to Wilt Chamberlain to account for nearly another couple thousand points. Upon retirement after 15 seasons, Greer held the NBA career mark for games played (since broken) and appeared in at least 70 games every season save his first and last campaigns.

George (The Bird) Yardley (1953–1960; Fort Wayne (Detroit) Pistons, Syracuse Nats; 19.2 ppg.; NBA Scoring Champion in 1957–'58). A balding and awkward-looking 6'5" cornerman who ran the floor like a crazed flamingo, Yardley was not at all graceful, but he was a truly pioneering scorer and record-breaking shooter nonetheless. "The Bird" was the first to cross the 2,000 point barrier for a single season, and reigned as the game's most potent offensive weapon between the era of Paul Arizin and Bob Pettit, and the era of Wilt Chamberlain.

Joe (Jumpin' Joe) Fulks (1946–1954, Philadelphia Warriors (BAA and NBA), 16.4 ppg., BAA Scoring Champion in 1946–'47 and 1947–'48). This skinny 6'5" cornerman popularized the jump shot (called his "ear shot" because that's where he released the ball) which revolutionized the pro game. He also tossed in an incredible 63 points in a single BAA game in February, 1949, a full decade before Wilt's arrival and during an era when 20 points was a truly high-scoring evening. Here was basketball's first great pure shooter.

Suggested Readings on Basketball's Greatest Superstars

Abdul-Jabbar, Kareem (with Mignon McCarthy). **Kareem**. New York: Random House, 1990.

Bell, Marty. **The Legend of Dr. J.** New York: Coward, McCann & Geoghegan, 1975.

Berkow, Ira. **Oscar Robertson: The Golden Year, 1964**. New York: McFadden-Bartell, 1971.

Bjarkman, Peter C. **The History of the NBA**. New York and Avenel, New Jersey: Crescent Books (Random House Publishers), 1992.

Devaney, John. **Bob Cousy, A Biography**. New York: G. P. Putnam's Sons, 1965.

Garber, Greg. **Basketball Legends**. New York: Friedman-Fairfax Publishers, 1993.

Gutman, Bill. **Magic: More Than a Legend, A Biography**. New York: HarperCollins, 1992.

Hoffman, Anne Byrne. **Echoes from the Schoolyards: Informal Portraits of NBA Greats**. New York: Hawthorn Books, 1977. (**Elgin Baylor** on pp. 92–101; plus **George Mikan** on pp. 20–25; **Bob Cousy** on pp. 40–49; **Oscar Robertson** on pp. 64–71; **Jerry West** on pp. 72–83; **Kareem Abdul-Jabbar** on pp. 162–167; **Julius Erving** on pp. 192–203)

Krugel, Mitchell. **Michael Jordan**. New York: St. Martin's Press, 1992.

Levine, Lee Daniel. **Bird: The Making of an American Sports Legend**. New York: McGraw-Hill, 1988.

Mikan, George (as told to Bill Carlson). **Mr. Basketball: George Mikan's Own Story**. New York: Greenberg Publishers, 1951.

Russell, Bill (as told to William McSweeny). **Go Up For Glory**. New York: Coward-McCann, 1966.

Sullivan, George. **Wilt Chamberlain**. New York: Grosset & Dunlap, 1966.

West, Jerry (with Bill Libby). **Mr. Clutch: The Jerry West Story**. New York: Grosset & Dunlap, 1969.

Wolff, Alexander. **100 Years of Hoops—A Fond Look Back at the Sport of Basketball**. New York: Oxmoor House (in cooperation with **Sports Illustrated**), 1991.

Bibliography

One Hundred Essential Pro Basketball Books For Adult and Juvenile Readers

Key: ** = General History of the NBA;
* = Juvenile History or Biography

*Aaseng, Nathan. **Basketball's Power Players**. Minneapolis: Lerner Publications, 1985.

*Aaseng, Nathan. **Basketball's High Flyers**. Minneapolis: Lerner Publications, 1980.

*Aaseng, Nathan. **Sports Great Michael Jordan**. Hillside, New Jersey: Enslow Publishers, 1992.

Abdul-Jabbar, Kareem and Peter Knobler. **Giant Steps—The Autobiography of Kareem Abdul-Jabbar**. New York: Bantam Books, 1983.

Abdul-Jabbar, Kareem (with Mignon McCarthy). **Kareem**. New York: Warner Books (Random House), 1990 (New York: Times Warner, 1990).

Anderson, Dave ("Forward" by Julius Erving). **The Story of Basketball**. New York: William Morrow and Company, 1988.

Auerbach, Arnold "Red" (with Paul Sann). **Red Auerbach: Winning the Hard Way**. Boston: Little, Brown and Company, 1966.

Auerbach, Arnold "Red" and Joe Fitzgerald. **On and Off the Court**. New York: Macmillan Publishers, 1985.

Auerbach, Arnold "Red" (with Joe Fitzgerald). **Red Auerbach: An Autobiography**. New York: G. P. Putnam's Sons, 1977.

Axthelm, Pete. **The City Game: Basketball from the Garden to the Playgrounds**. New York: Harper's Magazine Press, 1970 (New York: Penguin Books, 1982).

Barkley, Charles (with Roy S. Johnson). **Outrageous! The Fine Life and Flagrant Good Times of Basketball's Irresistable Force**. New York: Simon and Schuster, 1992.

Barry, Rick (with Bill Libby). **Confessions of a Basketball Gypsy: The**

Rick Barry Story. Englewood Cliffs, New Jersey: Prentice-Hall Publishers, 1972.

Bell, Marty. **The Legend of Dr. J**. New York: Coward, McCann & Geoghegan Publishers, 1975.

Berger, Phil. **Miracle on 33rd Street: The New York Knickerbockers' Championship Season**. New York: Simon and Schuster, 1970.

Berkow, Ira. **Oscar Robertson—The Golden Year, 1964**. New York: MacFadden-Bartell Books, 1972.

*Bjarkman, Peter C. **Sports Great Scottie Pippen**. Hillside, New Jersey: Enslow Publishers, 1996 (to appear).

*Bjarkman, Peter C. **Sports Great Dominique Wilkins**. Hillside, New Jersey: Enslow Publishers, 1996 (to appear).

Bjarkman, Peter C. **Slam Dunk Superstars**. New York: Crescent Books (Random House, Outlet Books), 1994.

Bjarkman, Peter C. **Shaq: The Making of a Legend**. New York: Smithmark (W.H. Smith), 1994.

Bjarkman, Peter C. **The History of the NBA. New York and Avenel, New Jersey: Crescent Books (Outlet Books, Random House), 1992.

Bukata, Jim. **One on One—The Great Matchups, Highlighting Over Fifty Great NBA and ABA Cage Stars**. New York: Stadia Sports Publishing, 1973.

Carr, M.L. **Don't Be Denied: My Story**. Boston: Quinlan Press, 1987.

Castello, Bob and Matt Marsom. **Meet Shaquille O'Neal: An Unauthorized Biography**. Lincolnwood, Illinois: Publications Unlimited International, 1993.

Chamberlain, Wilt and David Shaw. **Wilt—Just Like Any Other 7-Foot Black Millionaire Who Lives Next Door**. New York: Collier-Macmillan, 1973.

Chamberlain, Wilt. **A View From Above**. New York: Villard Books, 1991 (New York: New American Library, 1992).

Clary, Jack. **Michael Jordan**. New York: Smithmark (W.H. Smith), 1993.

Clary, Jack. **Basketball's Great Dynasties: The Celtics**. New York: Smithmark (W.H. Smith), 1992.

Clary, Jack. **Basketball's Great Dynasties: The Lakers**. New York: Smithmark (W.H. Smith), 1992.

Clary, Jack. **The NBA: Today's Stars, Tomorrow's Legends**. Rocky Hill, Connecticut: Great Pond Publishing, 1992.

Clary, Jack. **Basketball's Great Moments**. New York: McGraw-Hill Book Company, 1988.

*Cohen, Joel. **Big A: The Story of Lew Alcindor**. New York: Scholastic Book Services, 1971.

Cole, Lewis. **A Loose Game: The Sport and Business of Basketball**. Indianapolis: The Bobbs-Merrill Company, 1978.

Cole, Lewis. **Dream Team: The Candid Story of the Champion 1969–1970 Knicks—Their Collective Triumphs and Individual Fates**. New York: William Morrow and Company, 1981.

Cousy, Bob (and Bob Ryan). **Cousy on the Celtic Mystique**. New York: McGraw-Hill Publishers, 1988.

Cousy, Bob (with John Devaney). **The Killer Instinct**. New York: Random House, 1975.

Cousy, Bob (with Ed Linn). **The Last Load Roar**. Englewood Cliffs, New Jersey: Prentice-Hall Publishers, 1964.

Cousy, Bob (as told to Al Hirshberg). **Basketball is My Life**. Englewood Cliffs, New Jersey: Prentice-Hall Publishers, 1957.

DeBusschere, Dave (Edited by Paul D. Zimmerman and Dick Schaap). **The Open Man: The Diary of the New York Knicks' Championship Year**. New York: Grove Press, 1970.

Devaney, John. **The Story of Basketball**. New York: Random House, 1976.

*Devaney, John. **Bob Cousy**. New York: G.P. Putnam's Sons, 1965.

Garber, Gene (Angus). **Basketball Legends**. New York: Friedman and Fairfax Publishers, 1993.

George, Nelson. **Elevating the Game—Black Men and Basketball**. New York: Harper Collins Publishers, 1992.

Goldaper, Sam. **Great Moments in Pro Basketball**. New York: Grosset and Dunlap (Tempo Books), 1977.

Greenfield, Jeff. **The World's Greatest Team—A Portrait of the Boston Celtics, 1957–69**. New York: Random House, 1976.

Gutman, Bill. **Magic, More Than a Legend: A Biography**. New York: Harper Collins Publishers, 1992.

Gutman, Bill. **Shaquille O'Neal: A Biography**. New York and London: Archway Paperbacks (Pocket Books), 1993.

Gutman, Bill. **Pistol Pete Maravich—The Making of a Basketball Superstar**. New York: Grosset and Dunlap (Tempo Books), 1972.

Harris, Merv (Editor). **On Court With the Superstars of the NBA**. New York: Viking Press, 1973.

Harris, Merv. **The Fabulous Lakers**. New York: Lancer Books (Associated Features), 1972.

Havlicek, John (and Bob Ryan). **Hondo: Celtic Man in Motion**. Englewood Cliffs, New Jersey: Prentice-Hall Publishers, 1977.

Higdon, Hal. **Find the Key Man**. New York: G.P. Putnam's Sons, 1974.

*Hill, Raymond. **Unsung Heroes of Pro Basketball**. New York: Random House, 1973.

*Hirshberg, Al. **Bill Russell of the Boston Celtics**. New York: Julian Messner, 1963.

Hunter, Bruce. **Shaq Impaq—The Unauthorized and Untold Story Behind the NBA's Newest Superstar, Shaquille O'Neal**. Chicago: Bonus Books, 1993.

Jares, Joe. **Basketball: The American Game**. Chicago: Follett Publishing Company (Rutledge Books), 1971.

Johnson, Blaine. **What's Happenin'? A Revealing Journey Through** the World of Professional Basketball. Englewood Cliffs, New Jersey: Prentice-Hall, 1978.

Johnson, Earvin "Magic" and Richard Levin. Magic. New York: Signet Books (Penguin), 1991.

Johnson, Earvin "Magic" and Roy S. Johnson. Magic's Touch. Reading, Massachusetts: Addison-Wesley Publishers, 1989 (New York: Addison-Wesley Publishers, 1992).

Jones, K.C. (with Jack Warner). Rebound. Boston: Quinlan Press, 1986.

*Klein, Dave. Playoff! Twenty-Four Seconds to Glory—A Chronicle of NBA and ABA Title Series. New York: Stadia Sports Publishing, 1973.

**Koppett, Leonard. 24 Seconds to Shoot: An Informal History of the National Basketball Association. Silver Anniversary Special Revised Edition (1945–1970). New York: Macmillan Publishers, 1970.

Krugel, Mitchell. Michael Jordan. New York: St. Martin's Press, 1988.

**Lazenby, Roland. The NBA Finals: The Official Illustrated History. Dallas, Texas: Taylor Publishing Company, 1990.

Levine, Lee Daniel. Bird: The Making of an American Sports Legend. New York: McGraw-Hill Publishers, 1988.

Logan, Bob. The Bulls and Chicago: a Stormy Affair. Chicago: Follett Publishing Company, 1975.

Love, Stan and Ron Rapoport. Love in the NBA: A Player's Uninhibited Diary. New York: E.P. Dutton and Company (Saturday Review Press), 1975.

May, Peter. The Big Three: The Best Frontcourt in the History of Basketball. New York and London: Simon and Schuster, 1994.

McCallum, Jack. Unfinished Business—On and Off the Court with the 1990–91 Boston Celtics. New York: Summit Books (Simon and Schuster), 1992.

*Mikan, George (as told to Bill Carlson). Mr. Basketball: George Mikan's Own Story. New York: Greenberg Publishers, 1951.

Montville, Leigh. Manute—The Center of Two Worlds. New York and London: Simon and Schuster, 1993.

Mullooly, Patrick. The Signet Ultimate Basketball Quiz Book. New York: Signet Penguin Books, 1993.

Nadel, Eric. The Night Wilt Scored One Hundred—Tales from Basketball's Past. Dallas: Taylor Publishing Company, 1990.

Naughton, Jim. Taking to the Air—The Rise of Michael Jordan. New York: Warner Books, 1992.

*O'Brien, Jim. ABA All-Stars. New York: Lancer Books, 1972.

O'Neal, Shaquille (with Jack McCallum). Shaq Attaq! New York: Hyperion Books, 1993.

Pepe, Phil. The Incredible Knicks. New York: Popular Library, 1970.

Peterson, Robert W. Cages to Jump Shots—Pro Basketball's Early Years. New York: Oxford University Press, 1990.

Pluto, Terry. Loose Balls—The Short, Wild Life of the American Basketball Association as Told by the Players, Coaches, and Movers and Shakers Who Made It Happen. New York: Simon and Schuster (Fireside Books), 1990.

Pluto, Terry. **Tall Tales—The Glory Years of the NBA, in the Words of the Men Who Played, Coached, and Built Pro Basketball**. New York: Simon and Schuster, 1992.

Powers, John. **The Short Season—A Boston Celtics Diary, 1977–1978**. New York: Harper and Row, 1979.

Powers, Richie (with Mark Mulvoy). **Overtime! An Uninhibited Account of a Referee's Life in the NBA**. New York: David McKay Company, 1975.

Riley, Pat. **Show Time—The Lakers' Breakthrough Season**. New York: Warner Books, 1988.

Russell, Bill (as told to William McSweeny). **Go Up for Glory**. New York: Coward-McCann Publishers, 1966.

Russell, Bill and Branch Taylor. **Second Wind: The Memoirs of an Opinionated Man**. New York: Random House, 1979.

Ryan, Bob. **The Boston Celtics—The History, Legends, and Images of America's Most Celebrated Team**. Reading, Massachusetts: Addison-Wesley Publishers, 1989.

Ryan, Bob and Terry Pluto. **Forty-Eight Minutes: A Night in the Life of the NBA**. New York: Collier-Macmillan, 1987.

*Sabin, Lou and Dave Sendler. **Stars of Pro Basketball**. New York: Random House, 1970.

*Sabin, Lou. **Great Teams of Pro Basketball**. New York: Random House, 1971.

Salzberg, Charles. **From Set Shot to Slam Dunk: The Glory Days of Basketball in the Words of Those Who Played It**. New York: E.P. Dutton, 1987 (New York: Bantam Doubleday, 1990).

Scott, Jack. **Bill Walton—On the Road with the Portland Trail Blazers**. New York: Thomas Y. Crowell, 1978.

Shaughnessy, Dan. **Ever Green, The Boston Celtics—A History in the Words of Their Players, Coaches, Fans and Foes, from 1946 to the Present**. New York: St. Martin's Press, 1990.

Smith, Sam. **The Jordan Rules—The Inside Story of a Turbulent Season with Michael Jordan and the Chicago Bulls**. New York: Simon and Schuster, 1992.

Stauth, Cameron. **The Franchise: Building a Winner with the World Champion Detroit Pistons, Basketball's Bad Boys**. New York: William Morrow and Company, 1990.

Strom, Earl (with Blaine Johnson). **Calling the Shots—My Five Decades in the NBA**. New York: Simon and Schuster (Fireside Books), 1990.

Sullivan, George. **Wilt Chamberlain**. New York: Grosset and Dunlap Publishers, 1966.

Taragano, Martin. **Pro Basketball Statistics—Top Players and Teams by Game, Season and Career**. Jefferson, North Carolina and London: McFarland and Company Publishers, 1993.

Taragano, Martin. **Basketball Biographies—434 U.S. Players, Coaches and Contributors to the Game, 1891–1990**. Jefferson, North Carolina and London: McFarland and Company Publishers, 1991.

Thornley, Stew. **Basketball's Original Dynasty: The History of the Lakers**. Minneapolis: Nodin Press, 1989.

*Vescey, George. **Pro Basketball Champions**. New York: Scholastic Book Services, 1970.

West, Jerry (with Bill Libby). **Mr. Clutch: The Jerry West Story**. New York: Grosset and Dunlap (Tempo Books), 1969.

Wolf, David. **Foul! Connie Hawkins, Schoolyard Star to NBA Superstar**. New York: Holt, Rinehart and Winston, 1972.

*Wolf, Dave and Bill Bruns. **Great Moments in Pro Basketball**. New York: Random House, 1968.

Wolff, Alexander. **100 Years of Hoops—A Fond Look Back at the Sport of Basketball.** New York: Oxmoor House, 1991.

NBA Statistical Appendix

NBA Year-By-Year Playoff Champions and Coaches (1946–1994)

Year	Playoff Champion	Winning Team Coach	Opponent in Finals	Results
		* = Playing Coach		
National Basketball League (NBL)				
1946–1947	Chicago American Gears	Harry Foot/Bruce Hale*	Rochester Royals	3–1
1947–1948	Minneapolis Lakers	John Kundla	Rochester Royals	3–1
1948–1949	Anderson Duffey Packers	Murray Mendenhall	Oshkosh All-Stars	3–0
Basketball Association of American (BAA)				
1946–1947	Philadelphia Warriors	Eddie Gottlieb	Chicago Stags	4–1
1947–1948	Baltimore Bullets	Buddy Jeannette*	Philadelphia Warriors	4–2
1948–1949	Minneapolis Lakers	John Kundla	Washington Capitols	4–2
National Basketball Association (NBA)				
1949–1950	Minneapolis Lakers	John Kundla	Syracuse Nationals	4–2
1950–1951	Rochester Royals	Les Harrison	New York Knicks	4–3
1951–1952	Minneapolis Lakers	John Kundla	New York Knicks	4–3
1952–1953	Minneapolis Lakers	John Kundla	New York Knicks	4–1
1953–1954	Minneapolis Lakers	John Kundla	Syracuse Nationals	4–3
1954–1955	Syracuse Nationals	Al Cervi	Ft. Wayne Pistons	4–3
1955–1956	Philadelphia Warriors	George Senesky	Ft. Wayne Pistons	4–1
1956–1957	Boston Celtics	Red Auerbach	St. Louis Hawks	4–3
1957–1958	St. Louis Hawks	Alex Hannum	Boston Celtics	4–2
1958–1959	Boston Celtics	Red Auerbach	Minneapolis Lakers	4–0
1959–1960	Boston Celtics	Red Auerbach	St. Louis Hawks	4–3
1960–1961	Boston Celtics	Red Auerbach	St. Louis Hawks	4–1
1961–1962	Boston Celtics	Red Auerbach	Los Angeles Lakers	4–3
1962–1963	Boston Celtics	Red Auerbach	Los Angeles Lakers	4–2
1963–1964	Boston Celtics	Red Auerbach	San Francisco Warriors	4–1
1964–1965	Boston Celtics	Red Auerbach	Los Angeles Lakers	4–1
1965–1966	Boston Celtics	Red Auerbach	Los Angeles Lakers	4–3
1966–1967	Philadelphia 76ers	Alex Hannum	San Francisco Warriors	4–2
1967–1968	Boston Celtics	Bill Russell*	Los Angeles Lakers	4–2
1968–1969	Boston Celtics	Bill Russell*	Los Angeles Lakers	4–3
1969–1970	New York Knicks	Red Holzman	Los Angeles Lakers	4–3
1970–1971	Milwaukee Bucks	Larry Costello	Baltimore Bullets	4–0
1971–1972	Los Angeles Lakers	Bill Sharman	New York Knicks	4–1
1972–1973	New York Knicks	Red Holzman	Los Angeles Lakers	4–1
1973–1974	Boston Celtics	Tom Heinsohn	Milwaukee Bucks	4–3
1974–1975	Golden State Warriors	Al Attles	Washington Bullets	4–0
1975–1976	Boston Celtics	Tom Heinsohn	Phoenix Suns	4–2
1976–1977	Portland Trail Blazers	Jack Ramsay	Philadelphia 76ers	4–2
1977–1978	Washington Bullets	Dick Motta	Seattle SuperSonics	4–3
1978–1979	Seattle SuperSonics	Lenny Wilkens	Washington Bullets	4–1
1979–1980	Los Angeles Lakers	Paul Westhead	Philadelphia 76ers	4–2
1980–1981	Boston Celtics	Bill Fitch	Houston Rockets	4–2
1981–9182	Los Angeles Lakers	Pat Riley	Philadelphia 76ers	4–2
1982–1983	Philadelphia 76ers	Billy Cunningham	Los Angeles Lakers	4–0
1983–1984	Boston Celtics	K.C. Jones	Los Angeles Lakers	4–3
1984–1985	Los Angeles Lakers	Pat Riley	Boston Celtics	4–2
1985–1986	Boston Celtics	K.C. Jones	Houston Rockets	4–2

Year	Playoff Champion	Winning Team Coach	Opponent in Finals	Results
1986–1987	Los Angeles Lakers	Pat Riley	Boston Celtics	4–2
1987–1988	Los Angeles Lakers	Pat Riley	Detroit Pistons	4–3
1988–1989	Detroit Pistons	Chuck Daly	Los Angeles Lakers	4–0
1989–1990	Detroit Pistons	Chuck Daly	Portland Trail Blazers	4–1
1990–1991	Chicago Bulls	Phil Jackson	Los Angeles Lakers	4–1
1991–1992	Chicago Bulls	Phil Jackson	Portland Trail Blazers	4–2
1992–1993	Chicago Bulls	Phil Jackson	Phoenix Suns	4–2
1993–1994	Houston Rockets	Rudy Tomjanovich	New York Knicks	4–3

NBA Year-By-Year Playoff Scoring Leaders and All-Star Results

Year	Top Playoff Scorer	All-Star Game Score	All-Star Game MVP
		# = Overtime Game	
National Basketball League (NBL)			
1946–1947	George Mikan (19.7)	No Game Played	No Game Played
1947–1948	George Mikan (24.4)	No Game Played	No Game Played
1948–1949	Don Otten (15.2)	No Game Played	No Game Played
Basketball Association of America (BAA)			
1946–1947	Ed Sadowski (23.7)	No Game Played	No Game Played
1947–1948	Joe Fulks (21.7)	No Game Played	No Game Played
1948–1949	George Mikan (30.3)	No Game Played	No Game Played
National Basketball Association (NBA)			
1949–1950	George Mikan (31.3)	No Game Played	No Game Played
1950–1951	Alex Groza (32.2)	East 111, West 94 (Boston)	Ed Macauley
1951–1952	Bob Cousy (31.0)	East 108, West 91 (Boston)	Paul Arizin
1952–1953	Bob Cousy (25.5)	West 79, East 75 (Ft. Wayne)	George Mikan
1953–1954	Bob Cousy (21.0)	East 98, West 93# (New York)	Bob Cousy
1954–1955	Bob Cousy (21.7)	East 100, West 91 (New York)	Bill Sharman
1955–1956	Paul Arizin (28.9)	West 108, East 94 (Rochester)	Bob Pettit
1956–1957	Bob Pettit (29.8)	East 109, West 97 (Boston)	Bob Cousy
1957–1958	Cliff Hagan (27.7)	East 130, West 118 (St. Louis)	Bob Pettit
1958–1959	Cliff Hagan (28.5)	West 124, East 108 (Detroit)	Elgin Baylor
1959–1960	Elgin Baylor (33.4)	East 125, West 115 (Philadelphia)	Wilt Chamberlain
1960–1961	Elgin Baylor (38.1)	West 153, East 131 (Syracuse)	Oscar Robertson
1961–1962	Elgin Baylor (38.6)	West 150, East 130 (St. Louis)	Bob Pettit
1962–1963	Elgin Baylor (32.6)	East 115, West 108 (Los Angeles)	Bill Russell
1963–1964	Wilt Chamberlain (34.7)	East 111, West 107 (Boston)	Oscar Robertson
1964–1965	Jerry West (40.6)	East 124, West 123 (St. Louis)	Jerry Lucas
1965–1966	Jerry West (34.2)	East 137, West 94 (Cincinnati)	Adrian Smith
1966–1967	Rick Barry (34.7)	West 135, East 120 (S. Francisco)	Rick Barry
1967–1968	Jerry West (30.8)	East 144, West 124 (New York)	Hal Greer
1968–1969	Jerry West (30.9)	East 123, West 112 (Baltimore)	Oscar Robertson
1969–1970	Lew Alcindor (35.2)	East 142, West 135 (Philadelphia)	Willis Reed
1970–1971	Bob Love (26.7)	West 108, East 107 (San Diego)	Lenny Wilkens
1971–1972	Kareem Abdul-Jabbar (28.7)	West 112, East 110 (Los Angeles)	Jerry West
1972–1973	Lou Hudson (29.7)	East 104, West 84 (Chicago)	Dave Cowens
1973–1974	Kareem Abdul-Jabbar (32.2)	West 134, East 123 (Seattle)	Bob Lanier
1974–1975	Bob McAdoo (37.4)	East 108, West 102 (Phoenix)	Walt Frazier

Year	Top Playoff Scorer	All-Star Game Score	All-Star Game MVP
1975–1976	Fred Brown (28.5)	East 123, West 109 (Philadelphia)	Dave Bing
1976–1977	Kareem Abdul-Jabbar (34.6)	West 125, East 124 (Milwaukee)	Julius Erving
1977–1978	George Gervin (33.2)	East 133, West 125 (Atlanta)	Randy Smith
1978–1979	George Gervin (28.6)	West 134, East 129 (Detroit)	David Thompson
1979–1980	Kareem Abdul-Jabbar (31.9)	East 144, West 135# (Landover)	George Gervin
1980–1981	George Gervin (27.1)	East 123, West 120 (Cleveland)	Nate Archibald
1981–1982	George Gervin (29.4)	East 120, West 118 (New Jersey)	Larry Bird
1982–1983	Kareem Abdul-Jabbar (27.1)	East 132, West 123 (Los Angeles)	Julius Erving
1983–1984	Adrian Dantley (32.2)	East 154, West 145# (Denver)	Isiah Thomas
1984–1985	Alex English (30.2)	West 140, East 129 (Indianapolis)	Ralph Sampson
1985–1986	Dominique Wilkins (28.6)	East 139, West 132 (Dallas)	Isiah Thomas
1986–1987	Hakeem Olajuwon (29.2)	West 154, East 149# (Seattle)	Tom Chambers
1987–1988	Michael Jordan (36.3)	East 138, West 133 (Chicago)	Michael Jordan
1988–1989	Michael Jordan (34.8)	West 143, East 134 (Houston)	Karl Malone
1989–1990	Michael Jordan (36.7)	East 130, West 113 (Miami)	Magic Johnson
1990–1991	Michael Jordan (31.1)	East 116, West 114 (Charlotte)	Charles Barkley
1991–1992	Michael Jordan (34.5)	West 153, East 113 (Orlando)	Magic Johnson
1992–1993	Michael Jordan (35.1)	West 135, East 132# (Utah)	Karl Malone/John Stockton
1993–1994	Hakeem Olajuwon (27.4)	East 127, West 118 (Minneapolis)	Scottie Pippen

NBA Year-By-Year Regular Season Review (1946–1994)

Year	Best Regular-Season Record	Championship Coach	Leading Scorer (PPG)
		* = Playing Coach	
National Basketball League (NBL)			
1946–1947	Rochester Royals (31–13)	Ed Malanowicz	George Mikan (16.5)
1947–1948	Rochester Royals (44–16)	Ed Malanowicz	George Mikan (21.3)
1948–1949	Anderson Duffey Packers (49–15)	Murray Mendenhall	Don Otten (14.0)
Basketball Association of America (BAA)			
1946–1947	Washington Capitols (49–11)	Red Auerbach	Joe Fulks (23.2)
1947–1948	Baltimore Bullets (28–20)	Buddy Jeannette*	Joe Fulks (22.1)
1948–1949	Rochester Royals (45–15)	Ed Malanowicz	George Mikan (28.3)
National Basketball Association (NBA)			
1949–1950	Syracuse Nationals (51–13)	Al Cervi	George Mikan (27.4)
1950–1951	Minneapolis Lakers (44–24)	John Kundla	George Mikan (28.4)
1951–1952	Rochester Royals (41–25)	Les Harrison	Paul Arizin (25.4)
1952–1953	Minneapolis Lakers (48–22)	John Kundla	Neil Johnston (22.3)
1953–1954	Minneapolis Lakers (46–26)	John Kundla	Neil Johnston (24.4)
1954–1955	Syracuse Nationals (43–29)	Al Cervi	Neil Johnston (22.7)
1955–1956	Philadelphia Warriors (45–27)	George Senesky	Bob Pettit (25.7)
1956–1957	Boston Celtics (44–28)	Red Auerbach	Paul Arizin (25.6)
1957–1958	Boston Celtics (49–23)	Red Auerbach	George Yardley (27.8)
1958–1959	Boston Celtics (52–20)	Red Auerbach	Bob Pettit (29.2)
1959–1960	Boston Celtics (59–16)	Red Auerbach	Wilt Chamberlain (37.6)
1960–1961	Boston Celtics (57–22)	Red Auerbach	Wilt Chamberlain (38.4)
1961–1962	Boston Celtics (60–20)	Red Auerbach	Wilt Chamberlain (50.4)
1962–1963	Boston Celtics (58–22)	Red Auerbach	Wilt Chamberlain (44.8)

Year	Best Regular-Season Record	Championship Coach	Leading Scorer (PPG)
1963–1964	Boston Celtics (59–21)	Red Auerbach	Wilt Chamberlain (36.9)
1964–1965	Boston Celtics (62–18)	Red Auerbach	Wilt Chamberlain (34.7)
1965–1966	Philadelphia 76ers (55–22)	Dolph Schayes	Wilt Chamberlain (33.5)
1966–1967	Philadelphia 76ers (68–13)	Alex Hannum	Rick Barry (35.6)
1967–1968	Philadelphia 76ers (62–20)	Alex Hannum	Dave Bing (27.1)
1968–1969	Baltimore Bullets (57–25)	Gene Shue	Elvin Hayes (28.4)
1969–1970	New York Knicks (60–22)	Red Holzman	Jerry West (31.2)
1970–1971	Milwaukee Bucks (66–16)	Larry Costello	Lew Alcindor (31.7)
1971–1972	Los Angeles Lakers (69–13)	Bill Sharman	K. Abdul-Jabbar (34.8)
1972–1973	Boston Celtics (68–14)	Tom Heinsohn	Nate Archibald (34.0)
1973–1974	Milwaukee Bucks (59–23)	Larry Costello	Bob McAdoo (30.6)
1974–1975	Boston Celtics (60–22)	Tom Heinsohn	Bob McAdoo (34.5)
1975–1976	Golden State Warriors (59–23)	Al Attles	Bob McAdoo (31.1)
1976–1977	Los Angeles Lakers (53–29)	Jerry West	Pete Maravich (31.1)
1977–1978	Portland Trail Blazers (58–24)	Jack Ramsay	George Gervin (27.2)
1978–1979	Washington Bullets (54–28)	Dick Motta	George Gervin (29.6)
1979–1980	Boston Celtics (61–21)	Bill Fitch	George Gervin (33.1)
1980–1981	Boston Celtics (62–20)	Bill Fitch	Adrian Dantley (30.7)
1981–1982	Boston Celtics (63–19)	Bill Fitch	George Gervin (32.3)
1982–1983	Philadelphia 76ers (65–17)	Bill Cunningham	Alex English (28.4)
1983–1984	Boston Celtics (62–20)	K.C. Jones	Adrian Dantley (30.6)
1984–1985	Boston Celtics (63–19)	K.C. Jones	Bernard King (32.9)
1985–1986	Boston Celtics (67–15)	K.C. Jones	Dominique Wilkins (30.3)
1986–1987	Los Angeles Lakers (65–17)	Pat Riley	Michael Jordan (37.1)
1987–1988	Los Angeles Lakers (62–20)	Pat Riley	Michael Jordan (35.0)
1988–1989	Detroit Pistons (63–19)	Chuck Daly	Michael Jordan (32.5)
1989–1990	Los Angeles Lakers (63–19)	Pat Riley	Michael Jordan (33.6)
1990–1991	Chicago Bulls (61–21)	Phil Jackson	Michael Jordan (31.5)
1991–1992	Chicago Bulls (67–15)	Phil Jackson	Michael Jordan (30.1)
1992–1993	Phoenix Suns (62–20)	Paul Westphal	Michael Jordan (32.6)
1993–1994	Seattle SuperSonics (63–19)	George Karl	David Robinson (29.8)

NBA Year-By-Year Regular Season MVPs, Top Coaches & Rookies

Year	League MVP	Coach of the Year	Rookie of the Year
National Basketball League (NBL)			
1946–1947	No Award Given	No Award Given	No Award Given
1947–1948	No Award Given	No Award Given	No Award Given
1948–1949	No Award Given	No Award Given	No Award Given
Basketball Association of America (BAA)			
1946–1947	No Award Given	No Award Given	No Award Given
1947–1948	No Award Given	No Award Given	No Award Given
1948–1949	No Award Given	No Award Given	No Award Given
National Basketball Association (NBA)			
1949–1950	No Award Given	No Award Given	No Award Given
1950–1951	No Award Given	No Award Given	No Award Given
1951–1952	No Award Given	No Award Given	No Award Given

Year	League MVP	Coach of the Year	Rookie of the Year
1952–1953	No Award Given	No Award Given	Don Meineke (Ft. Wayne)
1953–1954	No Award Given	No Award Given	Ray Felix (Baltimore)
1954–1955	No Award Given	No Award Given	Bob Pettit (Milwaukee)
1955–1956	Bob Pettit	No Award Given	Maurice Stokes (Rochester)
1956–1957	Bob Cousy	No Award Given	Tom Heinsohn (Boston)
1957–1958	Bill Russell	No Award Given	Woody Sauldsberry (Philadelphia)
1958–1959	Bob Pettit	No Award Given	Elgin Baylor (Minneapolis)
1959–1960	Wilt Chamberlain	No Award Given	Wilt Chamberlain (Philadelphia)
1960–1961	Bill Russell	No Award Given	Oscar Robertson (Cincinnati)
1961–1962	Bill Russell	No Award Given	Walt Bellamy (Chicago)
1962–1963	Bill Russell	Harry Gallatin	Terry Dischinger (Chicago)
1963–1964	Oscar Robertson	Alex Hannum	Jerry Lucas (Cincinnati)
1964–1965	Bill Russell	Red Auerbach	Willis Reed (New York)
1965–1966	Wilt Chamberlain	Dolph Schayes	Rick Barry (San Francisco)
1966–1967	Wilt Chamberlain	Johnny Kerr	Dave Bing (Detroit)
1967–1968	Wilt Chamberlain	Richie Guerin	Earl Monroe (Baltimore)
1968–1969	Wes Unseld	Gene Shue	Wes Unseld (Baltimore)
1969–1970	Willis Reed	Red Holzman	Lew Alcindor (Milwaukee)
1970–1971	Lew Alcindor	Dick Motta	Dave Cowens and Geoff Petrie (tie)
1971–1972	Kareem Abdul-Jabbar	Bill Sharman	Sidney Wicks (Portland)
1972–1973	Dave Cowens	Tom Heinsohn	Bob McAdoo (Buffalo)
1973–1974	Kareem Abdul-Jabbar	Ray Scott	Ernie DeGregorio (Buffalo)
1974–1975	Bob McAdoo	Phil Johnson	Keith Wilkes (Golden State)
1975–1976	Kareem Abdul-Jabbar	Bill Fitch	Alvan Adams (Phoenix)
1976–1977	Kareem Abdul-Jabbar	Tom Nissalke	Adrian Dantley (Buffalo)
1977–1978	Bill Walton	Hubie Brown	Walter Davis (Phoenix)
1978–1979	Moses Malone	Cotton Fitzsimmons	Phil Ford (Kansas City)
1979–1980	Kareem Abdul-Jabbar	Bill Fitch	Larry Bird (Boston)
1980–1981	Julius Erving	Jack McKinney	Darrell Griffith (Utah)
1981–1982	Moses Malone	Gene Shue	Buck Williams (New Jersey)
1982–1983	Moses Malone	Don Nelson	Terry Cummings (San Diego)
1983–1984	Larry Bird	Frank Layden	Ralph Sampson (Houston)
1984–1985	Larry Bird	Don Nelson	Michael Jordan (Chicago)
1985–1986	Larry Bird	Mike Fratello	Patrick Ewing (New York)
1986–1987	Magic Johnson	Mike Schuler	Chuck Person (Indiana)
1987–1988	Michael Jordan	Doug Moe	Mark Jackson (New York)
1988–1989	Magic Johnson	Cotton Fitzsimmons	Mitch Richmond (Golden State)
1989–1990	Magic Johnson	Pat Riley	David Robinson (San Antonio)
1990–1991	Michael Jordan	Phil Jackson	Derrick Coleman (New Jersey)
1991–1992	Michael Jordan	Don Nelson	Larry Johnson (Charlotte)
1992–1993	Charles Barkley	Pat Riley	Shaquille O'Neal (Orlando)
1993–1994	Hakeem Olajuwon	Lenny Wilkens	Chris Webber (Golden State)

All-Time NBA Individual Career Records (1946–1994)

Scoring Records

Most Points Scored	—Kareem Abdul-Jabbar	38,387 (1970–89)
	—Wilt Chamberlain	31,419 (1960–73)
Highest Scoring Average	—Michael Jordan	32.3 (21,541 points)
	—Wilt Chamberlain	30.1 (31,419 points)

Peter C. Bjarkman

Seasons Leading League Scoring	—Wilt Chamberlain	7
	—Michael Jordan	7
Most Seasons 2,000 or more Points	—Kareem Abdul-Jabbar	9
Most Seasons 1,000 or more Points	—Kareem Abdul-Jabbar	19
Most Games 50 or more Points	—Wilt Chamberlain	118
Most Consecutive Games 50 points	—Wilt Chamberlain	7 (1961–62)
Most Consecutive Games 40 Points	—Wilt Chamberlain	14 (1961–62)
Most Consecutive Games 30 points	—Wilt Chamberlain	65 (1961–62)
Most Field Goals Attempted	—Kareem Abdul-Jabbar	28,307
Most Field Goals Made	—Kareem Abdul-Jabbar	15,837
Most Seasons, Field Goal Leader	—Wilt Chamberlain	7
Highest Field Goal Percentage	—Artis Gilmore	.599 (9,570 attempts)
Highest 3-Pt. Field Goal Percentage	—Steve Kerr	.445 (1988–94)
Most 3-Pt. Field Goals Attempted	—Michael Adams	2,816
Most 3-Pt. Field Goals Made	—Dale Ellis	1,013
Consecutive Games, 3-Pt. Goals	—Michael Adams	79
Most Free Throws Attempted	—Wilt Chamberlain	11,862
	—Moses Malone	11,058 (1976–94)
Most Free Throws Made	—Moses Malone	8,509
Most Seasons, FTs Made Leader	—Adrian Dantley	5
Most Seasons, FT Attempts Leader	—Bill Sharman	7
Highest Free Throw Percentage	—Mark Price	.906 (1986–94)

Non-Scoring Records

Most Rebounds	—Wilt Chamberlain	23,924
	—Bill Russell	21,620
Most Seasons, Rebound Leader	—Wilt Chamberlain	11
Rebounding Average per Game	—Wilt Chamberlain	22.9
Most Defensive Rebounds	—Kareem Abdul-Jabbar	9,394
Most Offensive Rebounds	—Moses Malone	6,605
Most Blocked Shots	—Kareem Abdul-Jabbar	3,189
Blocked Shots per Game Average	—Mark Eaton	3.50 (1982–93)
Most Assists	—Magic Johnson	9,921
	—Oscar Robertson	9,887
Assists Average per Game	—Magic Johnson	11.2 (1979–91)
Most Seasons, Assists Leader	—Bob Cousy	8
Most Steals	—Maurice Cheeks	2,066
Steals per Game Average	—Michael Ray Richardson	2.63 (1978–86)

Dubious Distinction Records

Most Turnovers	—Moses Malone	3,205
Most Personal Fouls	—Kareem Abdul-Jabbar	4,657
Most Disqualifications	—Vern Mikkelsen	127
Most Games Played	—Kareem Abdul-Jabbar	1,560 (1970–89)
	—Robert Parish	1,413 (1976–94)
Most Minutes Played	—Kareem Abdul-Jabbar	57,446
Season Leader, Minutes Played	—Wilt Chamberlain	8
Most Consecutive Games Played	—Randy Smith	906
Most Seasons Played	—Kareem Abdul-Jabbar	20 (1969–89)

All-Time NBA Individual Single-Season Records (1946–1994)

Scoring Records

Most Points Scored	—Wilt Chamberlain	4,029 (1961–62)
Highest Scoring Average	—Wilt Chamberlain	50.4 (1961–62)
	—Wilt Chamberlain	44.8 (1962–63)
Most Points Scored, Rookie	—Wilt Chamberlain	2,707 (1959–60)
Highest Scoring Average, Rookie	—Wilt Chamberlain	37.6 (1959–60)
Most Games 50 or more Points	—Wilt Chamberlain	45 (1961–62)
Most Consecutive Games 50 Points	—Wilt Chamberlain	7 (1961–62)
Most Consecutive Games 40 Points	—Wilt Chamberlain	14 (1961–62)
Most Consecutive Games 30 Points	—Wilt Chamberlain	65 (1961–62)
Most Field Goals Made	—Wilt Chamberlain	1,597 (1961–62)
Consecutive Field Goals, no misses	—Wilt Chamberlain	35 (1966–67)
Most Field Goals Attempted	—Wilt Chamberlain	3,159 (1961–62)
Highest Field Goal Percentage	—Wilt Chamberlain	.727 (1972–73)
Most 3-Pt. Field Goals Made	—Dan Majerle	192 (1993–94)
Most 3-Pt. Field Goals Attempted	—Michael Adams	529 (1990–91)
Highest 3-Pt. Field Goal Percentage	—Jon Sundvold	.522 (1988–89)
	—Steve Kerr	.507 (1989–90)
Most Consecutive 3-Pt. Field Goals	—Scott Wedman	11 (1984–85)
Consecutive Games, 3-Pt Goals	—Michael Adams	43 (1987–88)
Most Free Throws Made	—Jerry West	840 (1965–66)
Free Throws Attempted	—Wilt Chamberlain	1,363 (1961–62)
Highest Free Throw Percentage	—Calvin Murphy	.958 (1980–81)
	—M. Abdul-Rauf (C. Jackson)	.956 (1993–94)
Consecutive Free Throws	—Micheal Williams	84 (1992–93)

Non-Scoring Records

Most Rebounds	—Wilt Chamberlain	2,149 (1960–61)
Most Rebounds, Rookie Season	—Wilt Chamberlain	1,941 (1959–60)
Seasons 1000 or more Rebounds	—Wilt Chamberlain	13
Average Rebounds per Game	—Wilt Chamberlain	27.2 (1960–61)
Most Defensive Rebounds	—Kareem Abdul-Jabbar	1,111 (1975–76)
Most Offensive Rebounds	—Moses Malone	587 (1978–79)
Most Blocked Shots	—Mark Eaton	456 (1984–85)
Blocked Shots, Rookie	—Manute Bol	397 (1985–86)
Blocked Shots per Game Average	—Mark Eaton	5.56 (1984–85)
Most Assists	—John Stockton	1,164 (1990–91)
Most Assists, Rookie	—Marc Jackson	868 (1987–88)
Assists per Game Average	—Isiah Thomas	13.9 (1984–85)
Most Steals	—Alvin Robertson	301 (1985–86)
Steals per Game Average	—Alvin Robertson	3.67 (1985–86)
Most Steals, Rookie	—Dudley Bradley	211 (1979–80)

Dubious Distinction Records

Most Turnovers	—Artis Gilmore	366 (1977–78)
Most Personal Fouls	—Darryl Dawkins	386 (1983–84)
Most Disqualifications	—Don Meineke	26 (1952–53)
Most Complete Games Played	—Wilt Chamberlain	79 (1961–62)
Highest Average Minutes per Game	—Wilt Chamberlain	48.5 (1961–62)

All-Time NBA Individual Single-Game Records (1946–1994)

Scoring Records

Most Points Scored	—Wilt Chamberlain	100 (3-2-1962)
Most Points Scored, Rookie	—Wilt Chamberlain	58 (1-25-1960)
Most Points One Half	—Wilt Chamberlain	59 (3-2-1962)
Most Points One Quarter	—George Gervin	33 (4-9-1978)
Most Points Overtime Period	—Butch Carter	14 (3-20-1984)
Most Field Goals Made	—Wilt Chamberlain	36 (3-2-1962)
Most Field Goals, One Half	—Wilt Chamberlain	22 (3-2-1962)
Most Field Goals, One Quarter	—David Thompson	13 (4-9-1978)
Most Field Goals Attempted	—Wilt Chamberlain	63 (3-2-1962)
Most Field Goals Attempted, Half	—Wilt Chamberlain	37 (3-2-1962)
Field Goals Attempted, Quarter	—Wilt Chamberlain	21 (3-2-1962)
Most Consecutive Field Goals Made	—Wilt Chamberlain	18 (11-27-1963)
	—Wilt Chamberlain	18 (2-24-1967)
Most 3-Pt. Field Goals	—Dale Ellis	9 (4-20-1990)
	—Michael Adams	9 (4-13-1991)
Most 3-Pt. Field Goals Attempted	—Michael Adams	15 (3-14-1988)
Most Free Throws Made	—Wilt Chamberlain	28 (3-2-1962)
	—Adrian Dantley	28 (1-4-1984)
Most Free Throws Attempted	—Wilt Chamberlain	34 (2-22-1962)
Free Throws Made, One Half	—Oscar Robertson	19 (12-27-1964)
Free Throws Made, One Quarter	—Rick Barry	14 (12-6-1966)
	—Pete Maravich	14 (11-28-1973)
	—Adrian Dantley	14 (12-10-1986)
Consecutive Free Throws Made	—Bob Pettit	19 (11-22-1961)
	—Bill Cartwright	19 (11-17-1981)
	—Adrian Dantley	19 (12-15-1987)

Non-Scoring Records

Most Rebounds	—Wilt Chamberlain	55 (11-24-1960)
Most Rebounds Rookie Game	—Wilt Chamberlain	45 (2-6-1960)
Most Rebounds, One Half	—Bill Russell	32 (11-16-1957)
Most Rebounds, One Quarter	—Nate Thurmond	18 (2-28-1965)
Most Defensive Rebounds	—Kareem Abdul-Jabbar	29 (12-14-1975)
Most Offensive Rebounds	—Moses Malone	21 (2-11-1982)
Most Blocked Shots	—Elmore Smith	17 (10-28-1973)
Most Steals	—Larry Kenon	11 (12-26-1976)
Most Assists	—Scott Skiles	30 (12-30-1990)
Most Assists, Rookie	—Ernie DeGregorio	25 (1-1-1974)
	—Nate McMillan	25 (2-23-1987)
Most Assists, One Half	—Bob Cousy	19 (2-27-1959)
Most Assists, One Quarter	—John Lucas	14 (4-15-1984)

Dubious Distinction Records

Most Turnovers	—John Drew	14 (3-1-1978)
Most Minutes, no turnovers	—Marques Johnson	51 (4-8-1980)
Most Free Throws Missed	—Wilt Chamberlain	22 (12-1-1967)
Most Personal Fouls	—Don Otten	8 (11-24-1949)
Fewest Minutes, Disqualification	—Bob Lochmueller	7 (3-19-1953)
Most Minutes, no personal fouls	—Randy Wittman	54 (4-25-1986)

NBA Post-Season Statistic Sheet and Playoff Summary (1947–94)

NBA Championships by Franchise

Team	Number	Last	Coach
Boston Celtics	16	1985–86	K.C. Jones
Los Angeles Lakers (Minneapolis)	11	1987–88	Pat Riley
Chicago Bulls	3	1992–93	Phil Jackson
Golden State Warriors (Philadelphia)	3	1974–75	Al Attles
Philadelphia 76ers (Syracuse Nats)	3	1982–83	Billy Cunningham
Detroit Pistons	2	1989–90	Chuck Daly
New York Knickerbockers (Knicks)	2	1972–73	Red Holzman
Baltimore Bullets*	1	1947–48	Buddy Jeannette
Milwaukee Bucks	1	1970–71	Larry Costello
Portland Trail Blazers	1	1976–77	Jack Ramsay
Sacramento Kings (Rochester Royals)	1	1950–51	Lester Harrison
Atlanta Hawks (St. Louis)	1	1957–58	Alex Hannum
Seattle SuperSonics	1	1978–79	Lenny Wilkens
Washington Bullets (Baltimore)	1	1977–78	Dick Motta
Houston Rockets	1	1993–94	Rudy Tomjanovich

* Defunct Franchise

NBA Finals Most Valuable Player (Jeep/Eagle Award)

1969—Jerry West, Los Angeles
1970—Willis Reed, New York
1971—Kareem Abdul-Jabbar, Milwaukee
1972—Wilt Chamberlain, Los Angeles
1973—Willis Reed, New York
1974—John Havlicek, Boston
1975—Rick Barry, Golden State
1976—JoJo White, Boston
1977—Bill Walton, Portland
1978—Wes Unseld, Washington
1979—Dennis Johnson, Seattle
1980—Magic Johnson, Los Angeles
1981—Cedric Maxwell, Boston

1982—Magic Johnson, Los Angeles
1983—Moses Malone, Philadelphia
1984—Larry Bird, Boston
1985—Kareem Abdul-Jabbar, Los Angeles
1986—Larry Bird, Boston
1987—Magic Johnson, Los Angeles
1988—James Worthy, Los Angeles
1989—Joe Dumars, Detroit
1990—Isiah Thomas, Detroit
1991—Michael Jordan, Chicago
1992—Michael Jordan, Chicago
1993—Michael Jordan, Chicago
1994—Hakeem Olajuwon, Houston

NBA Finals, Series and Overall Franchise-by-Franchise Records

Team	Series Won-Lost Totals	Game Won-Lost Totals
Chicago Bulls	3–0 (1.000 Pct.)	12–5 (.706 Pct.)
Baltimore Bullets*	1–0 (1.000 Pct.)	4–2 (.667 Pct.)
Sacramento Kings (Rochester Royals)	1–0 (1.000 Pct.)	4–3 (.571 Pct.)
Boston Celtics	16–3 (.842 Pct.)	70–46 (.603 Pct.)
Golden State Warriors (San Francisco)	3–3 (.500 Pct.)	17–14 (.548 Pct.)
Milwaukee Bucks	1–1 (.500 Pct.)	7–4 (.636 Pct.)
Seattle SuperSonics	1–1 (.500 Pct.)	7–5 (.583 Pct.)
Los Angeles Lakers	11–13 (.458 Pct.)	66–75 (.468 Pct.
Detroit Pistons (Fort Wayne)	2–3 (.400 Pct.)	15–13 (.536 Pct.)
Philadelphia 76ers (Syracuse Nats)	3–5 (.375 Pct.)	23–25 (.479 Pct.)
Houston Rockets	1–2 (.333 Pct.)	8–11 (.421 Pct.)

Team	Series Won-Lost Totals	Game Won-Lost Totals
Portland Trail Blazers	1–2 (.333 Pct.)	7–10 (.412 Pct.)
New York Knickerbockers (Knicks)	2–5 (.286 Pct.)	19–24 (.442 Pct.)
Atlanta Hawks (St. Louis)	1–3 (.250 Pct.)	11–14 (.440 Pct.)
Washington Bullets (Baltimore)	1–3 (.250 Pct.)	5–15 (.250 Pct.)
Chicago Stags*	0–1 (.000 Pct.)	1–4 (.200 Pct.)
Washington Capitols*	0–1 (.000 Pct.)	2–4 (.333 Pct.)
Phoenix Suns	0–2 (.000 Pct.)	4–8 (.333 Pct.)

* Defunct Franchise

Five Greatest Players in Pro Basketball History (by position)

Center	—Wilt Chamberlain—Philadelphia (Golden State) Warriors, Los Angeles Lakers
Guard	—Oscar Robertson—Cincinnati Royals, Milwaukee Bucks
Guard	—Magic Johnson—Los Angeles Lakers
Forward	—Elgin Baylor—Minneapolis (Los Angeles) Lakers
Forward	—Julius Erving—Philadelphia 76ers

Decade-by-Decade Honorable Mention Dream Teams

1940s	Star of the Decade—George Mikan, Minneapolis Lakers
Center	—George Mikan, Minneapolis Lakers
Guard	—Max Zaslofsky, Chicago Stags
Guard	—Bob Davies, Rochester Royals
Forward	—Joe Fulks, Philadelphia Warriors
Forward	—Jim Pollard, Minneapolis Lakers

1950s	Star of the Decade—Bob Cousy, Boston Celtics
Center	—Neil Johnston, Philadelphia Warriors
Guard	—Bob Cousy, Boston Celtics
Guard	—Slater Martin, St. Louis Hawks
Forward	—Bob Pettit, St. Louis Hawks
Forward	—Dolph Schayes, Syracuse Nationals

1960s	Star of the Decade—Wilt Chamberlain, Philadelphia Warriors
Center	—Bill Russell, Boston Celtics and Wilt Chamberlain, Philadelphia Warriors
Guard	—Sam Jones, Boston Celtics
Guard	—Hal Greer, Philadelphia Warriors
Forward	—John Havlicek, Boston Celtics
Forward	—Tom Heinsohn, Boston Celtics

1970s	Star of the Decade—Kareem Abdul-Jabbar, Los Angeles Lakers
Center	—Kareem Abdul-Jabbar, Los Angeles Lakers
Guard	—Dave Bing, Detroit Pistons
Guard	—Walt Frazier, New York Knicks
Forward	—Dave Cowens, Boston Celtics
Forward	—Elvin Hayes, San Diego Rockets, Washington Bullets

1980s	Stars of the Decade—Magic Johnson, Los Angeles and Larry Bird, Boston Celtics
Center	—Moses Malone, Houston Rockets, Philadelphia Sixers, Washington Bullets
Guard	—Magic Johnson, Los Angeles Lakers
Guard	—Isiah Thomas, Detroit Pistons
Forward	—Larry Bird, Boston Celtics
Forward	—George Gervin, San Antonio Spurs, Chicago Bulls

1990s	Star of the Decade—Michael Jordan, Chicago Bulls
Center	—David Robinson, San Antonio Spurs and Hakeem Olajuwon, Houston Rockets
Guard	—Michael Jordan, Chicago Bulls
Guard	—Scottie Pippin, Chicago Bulls
Forward	—Patrick Ewing, New York Knicks
Forward	—Dominique Wilkins, Atlanta Hawks

NBA ALL-TIME TOP TEN LEADERS LISTS

Highest Scoring Average (1946–1993) (Minimum 10,000 Points)

Michael Jordan	32.3 (21,541 Points)
Wilt Chamberlain	30.1 (31,419)
Elgin Baylor	27.4 (23,149)
Jerry West	27.0 (25,192)
Dominique Wilkins	26.5 (22,096)
Bob Pettit	26.4 (20,880)
George Gervin	26.2 (20,708)
Karl Malone	26.1 (16,987)
Oscar Robertson	25.7 (26,710)
Kareem Abdul-Jabbar	24.6 (38,387)

Most Games Played (1946–1993)

Kareem Abdul-Jabbar	1,560
Robert Parish	1,339
Elvin Hayes	1,303
John Havlicek	1,270
Moses Malone	1,257
Paul Silas	1,254
Alex English	1,193
Hal Greer	1,122
Jack Sikma	1,107
Maurice Cheeks	1,101

Most Minutes Played (1946–1993)

Kareem Abdul-Jabbar	57,446
Elvin Hayes	50,000
Wilt Chamberlain	47,859
John Havlicek	46,471
Moses Malone	44,304
Oscar Robertson	43,886
Robert Parish	40,873

Bill Russell	40,726
Hal Greer	39,788
Walt Bellamy	38,940

Most Total Rebounds (1946–1993)

Wilt Chamberlain	23,924
Bill Russell	21,620
Kareem Abdul-Jabbar	17,440
Elvin Hayes	16,279
Moses Malone	15,940
Nate Thurmond	14,464
Walt Bellamy	14,241
Wes Unseld	13,769
Robert Parish	13,431
Jerry Lucas	12,942

Most Points Scored (1946–1993)

Kareem Abdul-Jabbar	38,387
Wilt Chamberlain	31,419
Julius Erving	**30,026* NBA-ABA Combined**
Dan Issel	**27,482* NBA-ABA Combined**
Elvin Hayes	27,313
Moses Malone	27,066
Oscar Robertson	26,710
George Gervin	**26,595* NBA-ABA Combined**
John Havlicek	26,395
Alex English	25,613
Jerry West	25,192
Adrian Dantley	23,177
Elgin Baylor	23,149

Most Total Assists (1946–1993)

Earvin "Magic" Johnson	9,921
Oscar Robertson	9,887
Isiah Thomas	8,662
John Stockton	8,352
Maurice Cheeks	7,392
Lenny Wilkens	7,211
Bob Cousy	6,955
Guy Rodgers	6,917
Nate Archibald	6,476
John Lucas	6,454

Most 3-Point Field Goals Made (through 1993)

Dale Ellis	882
Michael Adams	851
Danny Ainge	844
Reggie Miller	717

Larry Bird	649
Terry Porter	619
Derek Harper	608
Chuck Person	584
Mark Price	581
Trent Tucker	575

Most Personal Fouls (1946–1993)

Kareem Abdul-Jabbar	4,657
Elvin Hayes	4,193
Robert Parish	4,001
Jack Sikma	3,879
Hal Greer	3,855
James Edwards	3,847
Dolph Schayes	3,664
Bill Laimbeer	3,603
Walt Bellamy	3,536
Caldwell Jones	3,527

Most Steals (1946–1993)

Maurice Cheeks	2,310
Alvin Robertson	1,946
John Stockton	1,832
Michael Jordan	1,815
Isiah Thomas	1,793
Earvin "Magic" Johnson	1,698
Gus Williams	1,638
Clyde Drexler	1,623
Larry Bird	1,556
Julius Erving	1,508

Most Blocked Shots (through 1993)

Kareem Abdul-Jabbar	3,189
Mark Eaton	3,064
Wayne "Tree" Rollins	2,471
Hakeem Olajuwon	2,444
Robert Parish	2,156
George T. Johnson	2,082
Manute Bol	2,061
Larry Nance	1,972
Elvin Hayes	1,771
Patrick Ewing	1,767

Highest Field Goal Percentage (1946–1993) (Minimum of 2,000 Field Goals Made)

Artis Gilmore	.599 (5,732 FGM)
Darryl Dawkins	.572 (3,477)
Steve Johnson	.572 (2,841)
James Donaldson	.570 (3,061)

Charles Barkley	.569 (5,741)
Jeff Ruland	.564 (2,105)
Kareem Abdul-Jabbar	.559 (15,837)
Kevin McHale	.554 (6,830)
Buck Williams	.554 (5,362)
Otis Thorpe	.554 (4,449)

Highest Free Throw Percentage (1946–1993) (Minimum of 1,200 Free Throws Made)

Mark Price	.908 (1,497 FTM)
Rick Barry	.900 (3,818)
Calvin Murphy	.892 (3,445)
Larry Bird	.886 (3,960)
Bill Sharman	.883 (3,143)
Ricky Pierce	.876 (2,751)
Jeff Malone	.874 (2,662)
Kiki Vandeweghe	.872 (3,484)
Reggie Miller	.872 (2,400)
Mike Newlin	.870 (3,005)

Highest 3-Point Field Goal Percentage (through 1993) (minimum of 100 3-Point Field Goals Made)

Steve Kerr	.455 (147 3-FGM)
B.J. Armsrong	.443 (116)
Drazen Petrovic	.437 (255)
Mark Price	.412 (581)
Trent Tucker	.408 (575)
Dana Barros	.407 (274)
Hersey Hawkins	.406 (476)
Mike Iuzzolino	.404 (113)
Dale Ellis	.403 (882)
Jim Les	.403 (183)

Most Foul Disqualifications (1946–1993)

Vern Mikkelsen	127
Walter Dukes	121
Charlie Share	105
Paul Arizin	101
Darryl Dawkins	100
James Edwards	95
Tom Gola	94
Tom Sanders	94
Steve Johnson	93
Wayne "Tree" Rollins	91

Most Field Goals Made (1946–1993)

Kareem Abdul-Jabbar	15,837
Wilt Chamberlain	12,681
Julius Erving	**11,818* NBA-ABA Combined**
Elvin Hayes	10,976

Alex English	10,659
John Havlicek	10,513
Dan Issel	**10,431* NBA-ABA Combined**
Oscar Robertson	9,508
Moses Malone	9,320
Jerry West	9,016
Robert Parish	8,909
Elgin Baylor	8,693

Most Free Throws Made (1946–1993)

Moses Malone	8,419
Oscar Robertson	7,694
Jerry West	7,160
Dolph Schayes	6,979
Adrian Dantley	6,832
Kareem Abdul-Jabbar	6,712
Bob Pettit	6,182
Wilt Chamberlain	6,057
Elgin Baylor	5,763
Lenny Wilkens	5,394